WordPress®
ALL-IN-ONE
FOR DUMMIES
A Wiley Brand
2nd Edition

by Lisa Sabin-Wilson
author of *WordPress For Dummies* and
WordPress Web Design For Dummies

WordPress® All-in-One For Dummies®, 2nd Edition

Published by
John Wiley & Sons, Inc.
111 River Street
Hoboken, NJ 07030-5774

www.wiley.com

About the Author

Lisa Sabin-Wilson (*WordPress For Dummies*, *WordPress Web Design For Dummies*) has 10 years experience working with the WordPress platform, having adopted it early in its first year of release in 2003. Lisa is the owner of a successful design studio, E.Webscapes (`http://ewebscapes.com`), and is a regular speaker on topics related to design and WordPress at several national conferences. Additionally, she hosts WordPress workshops around the country, teaching people how to use the WordPress platform to publish their own sites on the World Wide Web. You can find Lisa online at her personal blog (`http://lisasabin-wilson.com`) and Twitter (@LisaSabinWilson).

Dedication

To WordPress . . . and all that entails from the developers, designers, forum helpers, bug testers, educators, consultants, plugin makers, and theme bakers.

Author's Acknowledgments

Every person involved in the WordPress community plays a vital role in making this whole thing work, and work well. Kudos to all of you! Also, big thanks to my wonderful husband, Chris Wilson, for his incredible support, backbone, and ability to put up with my crazy days of writing — I could *not* have done it without you!

Special thanks to the co-authors of the 1st Edition of this book who helped form the framework of the publication and ensured its initial success: Cory Miller, Kevin Palmer, Andrea Rennick, and Michael Torbert. Additional thanks and gratitude to individuals who have contributed content to this edition: Dre Armeda and Tony Perez for Chapter 5 in Book II and Chris Jean for Book VII.

Publisher's Acknowledgments

We're proud of this book; please send us your comments at http://dummies.custhelp.com. For other comments, please contact our Customer Care Department within the U.S. at 877-762-2974, outside the U.S. at 317-572-3993, or fax 317-572-4002.

Some of the people who helped bring this book to market include the following:

Acquisitions and Editorial

Project Editor: Rebecca Senninger

    (Previous Edition: Christopher Morris)

Acquisitions Editor: Amy Fandrei

Copy Editor: Virginia Sanders

Technical Editor: Mitch Canter

Editorial Manager: Leah Michael

Editorial Assistant: Anne Sullivan

Sr. Editorial Assistant: Cherie Case

Cover Photo: Background © FotoMak / iStockphoto; W © mohamed sadath / iStockphoto

Composition Services

Project Coordinator: Katherine Crocker

Layout and Graphics: Jennifer Creasey, Joyce Haughey

Proofreaders: Melissa Cossell, The Well-Chosen Word

Indexer: Infodex Indexing Services, Inc.

Publishing and Editorial for Technology Dummies

    Richard Swadley, Vice President and Executive Group Publisher

    Andy Cummings, Vice President and Publisher

    Mary Bednarek, Executive Acquisitions Director

    Mary C. Corder, Editorial Director

Publishing for Consumer Dummies

    Kathleen Nebenhaus, Vice President and Executive Publisher

Composition Services

    Debbie Stailey, Director of Composition Services

Contents at a Glance

Table of Contents

Book II: Setting Up the WordPress Software.................. *61*

Introduction

WordPress is the most popular blogging software on the planet. Between the hosted service at WordPress.com and the self-hosted software available at WordPress.org, millions of bloggers use WordPress today! That's impressive. And with WordPress, you can truly tailor a blog to your own tastes and needs.

With no cost for using the benefits of the WordPress platform to publish content on the web, WordPress is as priceless as it is free. WordPress makes writing, editing, and publishing content on the Internet a delightful, fun, and relatively painless experience whether you're a publisher, designer, developer — or just blogging as a hobby.

About This Book

WordPress being free and accessible to all, however, doesn't make it inherently easy for everyone. For some, the technologies, terminology, and coding practices can be a little intimidating or downright daunting. *WordPress All-in-One For Dummies* eliminates any intimidation about using WordPress. With a little research, knowledge, and time, you'll soon have a blog that suits your needs and gives your readers an exciting experience that keeps them coming back for more.

WordPress All-in-One For Dummies — a complete guide to WordPress — covers the basics: installation and configuration, the Dashboard, publishing content, creating themes, and developing plugins. Additionally, this book provides advanced information about security, the WordPress tools, using the multisite features, and optimizing your blog for search engines.

Foolish Assumptions

I make some inescapable assumptions about you and your knowledge, including the following:

✦ You're comfortable using a computer, mouse, and keyboard.

✦ You have a good understanding of how to access the Internet, use e-mail, and use a web browser to access web pages.

✦ You have a basic understanding of what a blog is; perhaps you already maintain your own blog.

✦ You want to use WordPress for your online publishing or use the various WordPress features to improve your online publishing.

If you consider yourself an advanced user of WordPress, or if your friends refer to you as an all-knowing WordPress guru, chances are good that you'll find some of the information in this book elementary. However, this book is for the beginner, intermediate, and advanced user — there is something for everyone.

Conventions Used in This Book

Throughout the book, I apply the following typography conventions to guide you through some of the information I present:

✦ When I ask you to type something, the text you're supposed to type is **bold.**

✦ I also use **bold** in step list instructions.

✦ When I suggest a keyword that you may want to enter in a search engine, the term appears in *italics.*

✦ I apply *italics* to terms you may not be familiar with to let you know that I'm defining them.

✦ When the text that you see onscreen may be different from what I write in the book, depending on your settings and preferences, I apply *italics* to that text to indicate that it's a placeholder.

✦ Text that appears in this `special font` is certain to be a URL (web address), an e-mail address, a filename, a folder name, or code.

✦ In some instances, I provide blocks of code to use on your WordPress website. Code looks like this:

```
<html>
<head>
<title>This is my website</title>
</head>
```

Icons Used in This Book

The little pictures in the margins of the book emphasize a point to remember, a danger to be aware of, or information that you may find helpful. This book uses the following icons:

Tips are little bits of information that you may find useful — procedures that aren't necessarily obvious to the casual user or beginner.

When your mother warned you, "Don't touch that pan — it's hot!" but you touched it anyway, you discovered the meaning of "Ouch!" I use this icon for situations like that. Out of curiosity, you may very well touch the hot pan, but you can't say that I didn't warn you!

All geeky stuff goes here. I use this icon when talking about technical information. You can skip it, but I think you'll find some great nuggets of information next to these icons. You may even surprise yourself and find you enjoy them. Be careful — you may turn into a geek overnight!

When you see this icon, brand the text next to it into your brain so that you remember whatever it was I thought you should remember.

Beyond the Book

I have a lot of extra content that you're not going to find in this book. Go online to find:

✦ **Bonus content:** Here you can find additional information about WordPress at

www.dummies.com/extras/wordpressaio

✦ **The cheat sheet for this book at**

www.dummies.com/cheatsheet/wordpressaio

✦ **Any updates to this book at**

www.dummies.com/go/wordpressaiofdupdates

Where to Go from Here

From here, you can go anywhere you please! *WordPress All-in-One For Dummies* is designed so that you can read either one or all of the minibooks between the front and back cover, depending on what topics interest you.

Book I is a great place to get a good introduction into the world of WordPress if you've never used it before and would like to find out more. Book II is also extremely helpful in giving you insight into the programming techniques and terminology involved with running a WordPress website — and that information is extremely helpful when you move forward to the other minibooks.

Above all else, have fun with the information contained within these pages! Read the books on topics you think you already know about — you might just come across something new! Then dig into the books that contain topics that you really want to discover more about.

Book I
WordPress Basics

getting started
with
WordPress

web
extras

Visit www.dummies.com for great *For Dummies* content online.

Contents at a Glance

Chapter 1: Exploring Basic WordPress Concepts

In This Chapter

✔ **Discovering blogging**

✔ **Publishing and archiving content**

✔ **Interacting through comments**

✔ **Syndicating through RSS**

✔ **Using WordPress as a content management tool to create different types of sites**

By providing regular, nontechnical Internet users the ability to publish content on the World Wide Web quickly and easily, blogging has taken the world by storm. These days, blogging is considered mainstream. Regular Internet users are blogging, but so are major corporations, news organizations, and educational institutions. Over the past decade, the question went from "What the heck is a blog?" to "What do you mean you don't have a blog?" Blogs have become a part of everyday life.

Nowadays, you can choose from several software platforms. For many bloggers, WordPress has the best combination of options. WordPress is unique in that it offers a variety of ways to run your website — WordPress is not only a blogging platform, but also a full-featured content management system (CMS) that includes all the tools and features you need to publish a blog or a complete website on your own, without a whole lot of technical expertise or understanding.

In this chapter, I introduce you to such blogging basics as publishing and archiving content, interacting with readers through comments, and providing ways for readers to have access to your content through syndication, or RSS technologies. This chapter also helps you sort the differences between a blog and a website, and introduces how WordPress, as a CMS, can help you build an entire website. Finally, I show you some websites that you can build with the WordPress platform.

Discovering the World of Blogging

A blog is a fabulous tool for publishing your diary of thoughts and ideas; however, blogs also serve as excellent tools for business, editorial journalism, news, and entertainment. Here are some ways that people use blogs:

✦ **Personal:** You're considered a personal blogger if you use your blog mainly to discuss topics related to you or your life — your family, your cats, your children, or your interests (for example, technology, politics, sports, art, or photography). My blog, which you find at `http://lisa sabin-wilson.com`, is an example of a personal blog.

✦ **Business:** Blogs are very effective tools for promotion and marketing, and business blogs usually offer helpful information to readers and consumers, such as sales events and product reviews. Business blogs also let readers provide feedback and ideas, which can help a company improve its services. A good example of a business blog is ServerBeach, which you can find on the hosted WordPress.com service at `http://serverbeach.wordpress.com`.

✦ **Media/journalism:** Popular news outlets, such as Fox News, MSNBC, and CNN, are using blogs on their websites to provide information on current events, politics, and news on regional, national, and international levels. These news organizations often have editorial bloggers, too. CNN's Anderson Cooper, for example, maintains a blog on CNN's website at `http://ac360.blogs.cnn.com`, with news and commentary from the *Anderson Cooper 360°* television show. Readers are invited to join in, too, by leaving comments about the news stories.

✦ **Government:** Governments use blogs to post news and updates to the web quickly and to integrate social media tools as a means to interact with their citizens and representatives. Number 10 (`www.number10.gov.uk`) is the official site of the British Prime Minister from his headquarters at 10 Downing Street in London. (See Figure 1-1.) The Prime Minister and his staff provide content by way of blog posts, photos, and videos, and they integrate feeds from their Twitter and Facebook accounts.

✦ **Citizen journalism:** Citizens are using blogs with the intention of keeping the media and politicians in check by fact-checking news stories and exposing inconsistencies. Major cable news programs interview many of these bloggers because the mainstream media recognize the importance of the citizen voice that's emerging via blogs. An example of citizen journalism is Power Line at `www.powerlineblog.com`.

✦ **Professional:** Check out Darren Rowse's ProBlogger blog at `www.problogger.net`. Darren is considered the grandfather of all professional bloggers.

Figure 1-1:
Number 10, the official blog of the British Prime Minister, is powered by WordPress.

The websites and blogs I provide in this list run on the WordPress platform. A wide variety of organizations and individuals choose WordPress to run their blogs and websites.

Understanding Blogging Technologies

The WordPress software is a personal publishing system that uses a PHP-and-MySQL platform, which provides you everything you need to create your blog and publish your content dynamically without having to program the pages yourself. In short, with this platform, all your content is stored in a MySQL database in your hosting account.

PHP (which stands for *PHP Hypertext Preprocessor*) is a server-side scripting language for creating dynamic web pages. When a visitor opens a page built in PHP, the server processes the PHP commands and then sends the results to the visitor's browser. MySQL is an open source relational database management system (RDBMS) that uses Structured Query Language (SQL), the most popular language for adding, accessing, and processing data in a database. If that all sounds like Greek to you, think of MySQL as a big filing cabinet where all the content on your blog is stored.

Keep in mind that PHP and MySQL are the technologies that the WordPress software is built on, but that doesn't mean you need experience in these languages to use it. Anyone from any level of experience can easily use WordPress without knowing anything about PHP or MySQL.

Every time a visitor goes to your blog to read your content, he makes a request that's sent to your server. The PHP programming language receives that request, obtains the requested information from the MySQL database, and then presents the requested information to your visitor through his web browser.

Book II, Chapter 1 gives you more in-depth information about the PHP and MySQL requirements you need to run WordPress. Book II, Chapter 3 introduces you to the basics of PHP and MySQL and provides information about how they work together with WordPress to create your blog or website.

Archiving your publishing history

Content, as it applies to the data that's stored in the MySQL database, refers to your blog posts, comments, and options that you set up on the WordPress Dashboard, or the control/administration panel of the WordPress software where you manage your site settings and content (Book III, Chapter 1).

WordPress maintains chronological and categorized archives of your publishing history automatically. This archiving process happens with every post you publish to your blog. WordPress uses PHP and MySQL technology to organize what you publish so that you and your readers can access the information by date, category, author, tag, and so on. When you publish to your WordPress blog, you can file that post under any category you specify — a nifty archiving system in which you and your readers can then find posts in specific categories. The archives page on my blog (http://lisasabin-wilson.com/archives) contains a Posts by Category section, where you find a list of categories I've created for my blog posts. Clicking the Blog Design link below the Posts by Category heading takes you to a listing of posts on that topic. (See Figure 1-2.)

Figure 1-2:
A page with
posts in the
Blog Design
category.

WordPress lets you create as many categories as you want for filing your blog posts. Some blogs have just one category and others have up to 1,800 categories. When it comes to organizing your content, WordPress is all about personal preference. On the other hand, using WordPress categories is your choice. You don't have to use the category feature if you'd rather not.

When you look for a hosting service, keep an eye out for hosts that provide daily backups of your site so that your content will not be lost if a hard drive fails or someone makes a foolish mistake. Web hosting providers that offer daily backups as part of their services can save the day by restoring your site to a previous form.

The theme (design) you choose for your blog (whether it's the default theme, one you create, or one that you have custom designed) isn't part of the content. Those files are part of the file system and aren't stored in the database. Therefore, it's a good idea to create a backup of any theme files you're using. See Book VI for further information on WordPress theme management.

Interacting with your readers through comments

An exciting aspect of blogging with WordPress is receiving feedback from your readers after you post to your blog. Receiving feedback, or *blog comments,* is akin to having a guestbook on your blog. People can leave notes for you that publish to your site, and you can respond and engage your readers in conversation. (See Figure 1-3.) These notes can expand the thoughts and ideas you present in your blog post by giving your readers the opportunity to add their two cents' worth.

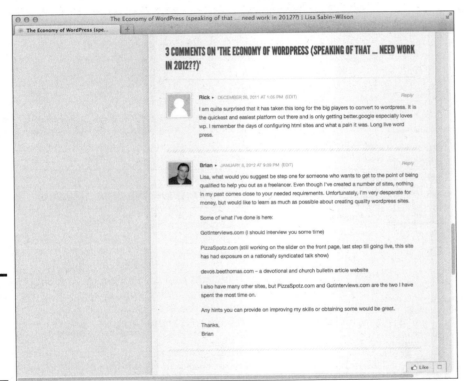

Figure 1-3:
Blog
comments
and
responses
on a blog.

On the WordPress Dashboard, you have full administrative control over who can leave comments. Additionally, if someone leaves a comment with questionable content, you can edit the comment or delete it. You're also free to not allow comments on your blog.

The blogging community says that a blog without comments isn't a blog at all because exchanging views with visitors is part of what makes blogging popular. Allowing comments on your blog invites your audience members to involve themselves in your discussion. However, publishing a blog without comments lets your readers partake of your published words passively, and sometimes that's okay. You can choose to disallow comments for just one or all blog posts on your site. For example, if your content on a controversial topic may attract visitor insults, it would be reasonable to publish a post without enabling the comment feature. Mostly, readers find commenting to be a satisfying experience when they visit blogs because comments make them part of the discussion. Still, it's up to you.

Feeding your readers

RSS stands for *Really Simple Syndication.* An *RSS feed* is a standard feature that blog readers have come to expect. So what is RSS, really?

RSS is written to the web server in XML (Extensible Markup Language) as a small, compact file that can be read by RSS readers (as I outline in Table 1-1). Think of an RSS feed as a syndicated, or distributable, auto-updating list of "What's New" for your website.

By using tools called *feed readers,* readers can download your feed automatically — that is, they can set their feed readers to automatically discover new content (such as posts and comments) from your blog and download that content for their consumption. Table 1-1 lists some of the most popular feed readers.

Table 1-1	Popular RSS Feed Readers	
Reader	*Source*	*Description*
Bloglines	www.bloglines.com	Bloglines is a free online service for searching, subscribing to, and sharing RSS feeds. You have no software to download or install; Bloglines is all web-based. You need to sign up for an account to use this service.
Google Reader	http://google. com/reader	This free online service is provided by Internet search giant Google. With Google Reader, you can keep up with your favorite blogs and websites that have syndicated (RSS) content. You have no software to download or install, but you need to sign up for an account with Google.
FeedDemon	http://feed demon.com	This free service requires that you download the RSS reader application to your computer.

For blog readers to stay up-to-date with the latest and greatest content you post, they need to subscribe to your RSS feed. WordPress allows RSS feeds to be *autodiscovered* by the various feed readers. The reader needs only to enter your site's URL, and the program automatically finds your RSS feed.

Most web browsers alert visitors to the RSS feed on your site by displaying the universally recognized orange RSS feed icon, shown in the margin.

WordPress has RSS feeds in several formats. Because the feeds are built into the software platform, you don't need to do anything to provide your readers an RSS feed of your content.

Tracking back

The best way to understand *trackbacks* is to think of them as comments, except for one thing: Trackbacks are comments left on your blog by other blogs, not people. Sounds perfectly reasonable, doesn't it? After all, why wouldn't inanimate objects want to participate in your discussion?

Actually, maybe it's not so crazy after all. A trackback happens when you make a post on your blog, and within that post, you provide a link to a post made by another blogger on a different blog. When you publish that post, your blog sends a sort of electronic memo to the blog you linked to. That blog receives the memo and posts an acknowledgment of receipt in the form of a comment to the post that you linked to on their site. The information that is contained within the trackback includes a link back to the post on your site that contains the link to theirs — along with the date and time, as well as a short excerpt of your post. Trackbacks are displayed within the comments section of the individual posts.

The memo is sent via a *network ping* (a tool used to test, or verify, whether a link is reachable across the Internet) from your site to the site you link to. This process works as long as both blogs support trackback protocol. Almost all major blogging platforms support the trackback protocol.

Sending a trackback to a blog is a nice way of telling the blogger that you like the information she presented in her blog post. Every blogger appreciates trackbacks to their posts from other bloggers.

Dealing with comment and trackback spam

Ugh. The absolute bane of every blogger's existence is comment and trackback spam. When blogging became the "It" thing on the Internet, spammers saw an opportunity. If you've ever received spam in your e-mail program, you know what I mean. For bloggers, the concept is similar and just as frustrating.

Before blogs, you often saw spammers filling Internet guestbooks with their links but not relevant comments. The reason is simple: Websites receive higher rankings in the major search engines if they have multiple links coming in from other sites. Enter blog software with comment and trackback technologies, and blogs become prime breeding ground for millions of spammers.

Because comments and trackbacks are published to your site publicly — and usually with a link to the commenter's website — spammers got their site links posted on millions of blogs by creating programs that automatically seek websites with commenting systems and then hammer those systems with tons of comments that contain links back to their sites.

No blogger likes spam. Therefore, blogging services, such as WordPress, spend untold hours in the name of stopping these spammers in their tracks, and for the most part, they're successful. Occasionally, however, spammers sneak through. Many spammers are offensive, and all of them are frustrating because they don't contribute to the conversations that occur in blogs.

All WordPress systems have one important thing in common: Akismet, which kills spam dead. Akismet is a WordPress plugin brought to you by Automattic, the maker of WordPress.com. I cover the Akismet plugin, and comment spam in general, in Book III, Chapter 4.

Using WordPress as a Content Management System

You hear it a lot if you browse different websites that publish posts about WordPress: "WordPress is more than a blogging platform; it's a full content management system." What does that mean?

A *content management system* (CMS) is a platform that lets you run a full website on your domain. This means that WordPress, in addition to a blog, allows you to create pages and build additional features into your website that have nothing to do with the content on your blog.

A website and a blog are two different things. Although a website can contain a blog, a blog cannot contain a full website. That probably sounds confusing, but after you read this section and explore the differences between the two, you'll have a better understanding.

A *blog* is a chronological display of content — most often, written by the blog author. The posts are published and, usually, categorized into topics and archived by date. Blog posts can have comments activated so readers can leave their feedback and the author can respond, creating a dialogue about the blog post.

A *website* is a collection of published pages and different sections that offer the visitor a different experience. A website can incorporate a blog but usually contains other sections and features. These other features include

✦ **Photo galleries:** Albums of photos uploaded and collected in a specific area so that visitors can browse through and comment on them.

✦ **E-commerce stores:** Fully integrated shopping area into which you can upload products for sale and from which your visitors can purchase them.

✦ **Discussion forums:** Where visitors can join, create discussion threads, and respond to one another in specific threads of conversation.

✦ **Social communities:** Where visitors can become members, create pro- files, become friends with other members, create groups, and aggregate community activity.

✦ **Portfolios:** Photographers, artists, or web designers can devote sections of their sites to displaying their work.

✦ **Feedback forms:** Contact forms that your visitors fill out with information that then gets e-mailed to you directly.

✦ **Static pages (such as a Bio, FAQ, or Services page):** Pages that don't change as often as a blog page. Blog pages change each time you publish a new post.

The preceding list isn't exhaustive; it's just a listing of some of the most often seen website sections.

For example, Figure 1-4 shows what the front page of my blog at `http://lisasabin-wilson.com` looked like at the time of this writing. Notice that the site displays a chronological listing of my most recent blog posts. Primarily, my blog uses WordPress as a blogging tool.

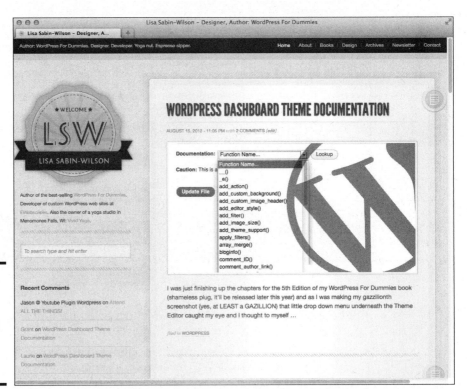

Figure 1-4: My blog uses WordPress as a blogging tool.

Comparatively, my business website at `http://ewebscapes.com` uses WordPress as a CMS to publish a full website. This full site includes a static front page of information that acts as a portal to the rest of the site, on which you can find a blog, a portfolio of work, a contact form, an order form, and various other static pages, including Services, FAQ (Frequently Asked Questions), Terms of Service, Privacy Policy, and more. Check out Figure 1-5 for a look at my website; it's quite different from my personal blog site.

Using WordPress as a CMS means that you're creating more than just a blog; you're creating an entire website full of sections and features that offer a different experience for your visitors.

Book I
Chapter 1

Exploring Basic
WordPress
Concepts

Figure 1-5: A business website that uses WordPress as a content management system.

Chapter 2: Exploring the World of Open Source Software

In This Chapter

✔ Exploring open source concepts

✔ Discovering examples of open source projects

✔ Understanding WordPress licensing

✔ Applying WordPress licensing

*O*pen source software is a movement that started in the software industry in the 1980s. Its origins are up for debate, but most believe that the concept came about in 1983 when a company called Netscape released its Navigator web browser source code to the public, making it freely available to anyone who wanted to dig through it, modify it, or redistribute it.

WordPress software users need a basic understanding of the open source concept and the licensing upon which WordPress is built because WordPress's open source policies affect you as a user — and greatly affect you if you plan to develop plugins or themes for the WordPress platforms. A basic understanding helps you conduct your practices in accordance with the license at the heart of the WordPress platform.

This chapter introduces you to open source, the Open Source Initiative (OSI), and the GPL (General Public License), which is the specific license that WordPress is built upon (GPLv2, to be exact). You also discover how the GPL applies to any projects you may release (if you are a developer of plugins or themes) that depend on the WordPress software and how you can avoid potential problems by abiding by the GPL as it applies to WordPress.

IANAL — *I Am Not a Lawyer* — is an acronym you find in articles about WordPress and the GPL. I use it here because I am not a lawyer, and the information found in this chapter shouldn't be construed as legal advice. Rather, you should consider the chapter an introduction to the concepts of open source and the GPL. The information presented here is meant to inform and introduce you to the concepts as they relate to the WordPress platform.

Defining Open Source

Open source software is software whose source code is freely available to the public and can be modified and redistributed by anyone without restraint or consequence. This is a very simple, watered-down version of the definition of open source. An official organization called the Open Source Initiative (`http://opensource.org`), founded in 1998 to organize the open source software movement in an official capacity, has provided a very clear and easy-to-understand definition of open source. During the course of writing this book, I obtained permission from the OSI Board to include it here.

Open source doesn't just mean access to the source code. The distribution terms of open source software must comply with the following criteria:

1. **Free Redistribution**

   The license shall not restrict any party from selling or giving away the software as a component of an aggregate software distribution containing programs from several different sources. The license shall not require a royalty or other fee for such sale.

2. **Source Code**

   The program must include source code, and must allow distribution in source code as well as compiled form. Where some form of a product is not distributed with source code, there must be a well-publicized means of obtaining the source code for no more than a reasonable reproduction cost preferably, downloading via the Internet without charge. The source code must be the preferred form in which a programmer would modify the program. Deliberately obfuscated source code is not allowed. Intermediate forms such as the output of a preprocessor or translator are not allowed.

3. **Derived Works**

   The license must allow modifications and derived works, and must allow them to be distributed under the same terms as the license of the original software.

4. **Integrity of the Author's Source Code**

   The license may restrict source-code from being distributed in modified form only if the license allows the distribution of "patch files" with the source code for the purpose of modifying the program at build time. The license must explicitly permit distribution of software built from modified source code. The license may require derived works to carry a different name or version number from the original software.

5. **No Discrimination Against Persons or Groups**

   The license must not discriminate against any person or group of persons.

6. **No Discrimination Against Fields of Endeavor**

   The license must not restrict anyone from making use of the program in a specific field of endeavor. For example, it may not restrict the program from being used in a business, or from being used for genetic research.

7. **Distribution of License**

   The rights attached to the program must apply to all to whom the program is redistributed without the need for execution of an additional license by those parties.

8. **License Must Not Be Specific to a Product**

   The rights attached to the program must not depend on the program's being part of a particular software distribution. If the program is extracted from that distribution and used or distributed within the terms of the program's license, all parties to whom the program is redistributed should have the same rights as those that are granted in conjunction with the original software distribution.

9. **License Must Not Restrict Other Software**

   The license must not place restrictions on other software that is distributed along with the licensed software. For example, the license must not insist that all other programs distributed on the same medium must be open-source software.

10. **License Must Be Technology-Neutral**

    No provision of the license may be predicated on any individual technology or style of interface.

The preceding items comprise the definition of open source, as provided by the Open Source Initiative; the definition is found at `http://opensource.org/docs/osd` and shown in Figure 2-1.

Open source software source code must be freely available, and any licensing of the open source software must abide by this definition. Based on the OSI definition, WordPress is an open source software project. Its source code is accessible and publicly available for anyone to view, build on, and distribute at no cost anywhere, at anytime, or for any reason.

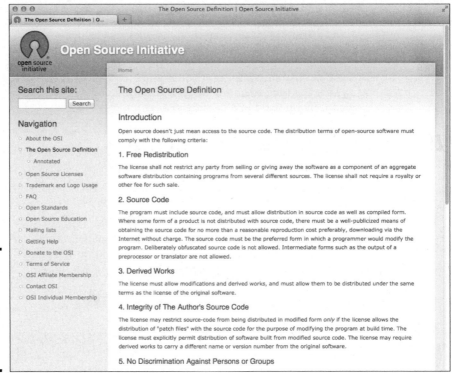

Figure 2-1:
Definition
of open
source from
the Open
Source
Initiative.

Several examples of high profile software enterprises, such as the ones
in the following list, are also open source. You'll recognize some of these
names:

✦ **Mozilla (**www.mozilla.org**):** Projects include the popular Firefox
Internet browser and Thunderbird, a popular e-mail client. All projects
are open source and considered public resource.

✦ **PHP (**http://php.net**):** An HTML-embedded scripting language that
stands for PHP Hypertext Preprocessor, PHP is a popular software that
runs on most web servers today. Actually, WordPress requires the presence of PHP on your web server for you to run the WordPress platform
successfully on your site.

✦ **MySQL (**www.mysql.com**):** The world's most popular open source
database. Used by your web server to store all the data from your
WordPress installation, including your posts, pages, comments, links,
plugin options, theme option, widgets, and more.

✦ **Linux (**www.linux.org**):** A free and open source operating system used
by web hosting providers, among other organizations.

As open source software, WordPress is in some fine company. Open source itself is not a *license* — I cover licenses in the next section. Rather, open source is a movement — some consider it a philosophy — created and promoted as a way to provide software as a public resource open to community collaboration and peer review. WordPress development is clearly community driven and focused. You can read about the WordPress community in Book I, Chapter 4.

Understanding WordPress Licensing

Most software projects are licensed, meaning they have legal terms governing the usage or distribution of the software. Different kinds of software licenses are out there, ranging from very restrictive to least restrictive. WordPress is licensed by the GPL (General Public License), one of the least restrictive software licenses available.

If you are bored, read the GPL text at `www.gnu.org/licenses/gpl-2.0.html`. Licensing language on any topic can be a difficult thing to navigate and understand. Mostly, have just a basic understanding of the concept of GPL and let the lawyers, if necessary, sort out the rest.

A complete copy of the GPL is included in every copy of the WordPress download package in the `license.txt` file. The directory listing of the WordPress software files shown in Figure 2-2 lists the `license.txt` file.

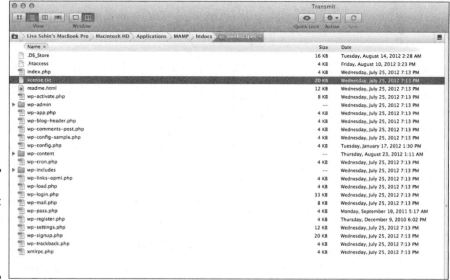

Figure 2-2:
The GPL text is included in every copy of WordPress.

Simply put, any iteration of a piece of software developed and released under the GPL must be released under the very same license in the future. Check out the nearby "The origins of WordPress" sidebar that tells the story of how the WordPress platform came into existence. Essentially, it was *forked* — meaning, the original software (in this case, a blogging platform called b2) was abandoned by its original developer, and the founders of WordPress took the b2 platform, called it WordPress, and began a new project with a new plan, outlook, and group of developers.

Because the b2 platform was originally developed and released under the GPL, the WordPress software (all current and future iterations of the platform) must also abide by the GPL, by law. Because of the nature of the GPL, you, your next-door neighbor, or I could do the very same thing with the WordPress platform. There is nothing stopping you, or anyone, from taking WordPress, giving it a different name and re-releasing it as a completely different project. Typically, open source projects are forked when the original project development stalls or is abandoned (as was the case with b2) or (in rare cases) when the majority of the development community is at odds with the leadership of the open source project. I'm not suggesting you do that, though, because WordPress has one of the most active development communities of any open source project I've come across.

The origins of WordPress

Once upon a time, there was a simple PHP-based blogging platform called b2. This software, developed in 2001, slowly gained a bit of popularity among geek types as a way to publish content on the Internet. Its developer, Michel Valdrighi, kept development active until early 2003, when users of the software noticed that Valdrighi seemed to have disappeared. They became a little concerned about b2's future.

Somewhere deep in the heart of Texas, one young man in particular was very concerned, because b2 was his software of choice for publishing his own content on the World Wide Web. He didn't want to see his favorite publishing tool become obsolete. You can view the original post to his own blog in which he wondered what to do (http://ma.tt/2003/01/the-blogging-software-dilemma).

In that post, he talked briefly about some of the other software that was available at the time, and he tossed around the idea of using the b2 software to "to create a fork, integrating all the cool stuff that Michel would be working on right now if only he was around."

Create a fork he did. In the absence of b2's developer, this young man developed from the original b2 codebase a new blogging application called WordPress.

That blog post was made on January 24, 2003, and the young man's name was (and is) Matt Mullenweg. On December 26, 2003, with the assistance of a few other developers, Mullenweg announced the arrival of the first official version of the WordPress software. The rest, as they say, is history. The history of this particular piece of software surely is one for the books, as it is the most popular blogging platform available today.

Applying WordPress Licensing to Your Projects

Regular users of WordPress software need never concern themselves with the GPL of the WordPress project at all. You don't have to do anything special to abide by the GPL. You don't have to pay to use the WordPress software, and you aren't required to acknowledge that you're using the WordPress software on your site. (That said, providing on your site at least one link back to the WordPress website is common courtesy and a great way of saying thanks.)

Most people aren't even aware of the software licensing because it doesn't affect the day-to-day business of blogging and publishing sites with the platform. However, it's not a bad idea to educate yourself on the basics of the GPL and try to be certain that any plugins and themes you use with your WordPress installation abide by the GPL so that you have peace of mind that all applications and software you're using are in compliance.

However, your knowledge of the GPL must increase dramatically if you develop plugins or themes for the WordPress platform. I cover WordPress themes in Book VI, and WordPress plugins in Book VII.

The public licensing that pertains to WordPress plugins and themes wasn't decided in a court of law. The current opinion of the best (legal) practices is just that, opinion. The opinion of the WordPress core development team, as well as the opinion of the Software Freedom Law Center (`http://en.wikipedia.org/wiki/Software_Freedom_Law_Center`), is that WordPress plugins and themes are derivative works of WordPress and, therefore, must abide by the GPL by releasing the development works under the same license that WordPress has.

A *derivative work,* as it relates to WordPress, is a work that contains programming whose functionality depends on the core WordPress files. Because plugins and themes contain PHP programming that call WordPress core functions, they rely on the core WordPress framework to work properly and, therefore, are extensions of the software.

The text of the opinion from James Vasile from the Software Freedom Law Center is available at `http://wordpress.org/news/2009/07/themes-are-gpl-too`.

To maintain compliance with the GPL, plugin or theme developers cannot release development work under any (restrictive) license other than the GPL. Nonetheless, many plugin and theme developers have tried to release material under other licenses, and some have been successful (from a moneymaking standpoint). However, the WordPress community generally doesn't support these developers and their plugins and themes.

Additionally, the core WordPress development team considers such works noncompliant with the license, and therefore, the law.

WordPress has made it publicly clear that it will not support or promote any theme or plugins not in 100 percent compliance with the GPL. If you are not 100 percent compliant with the GPL, then you cannot include your plugin or theme in the WordPress Plugin Directory hosted at `http://wordpress.org`. If you develop plugins and themes for WordPress, or are considering dipping your toe into that pool, do it in accordance with the GPL so that your works are in compliance and your good standing in the WordPress community is protected. Table 2-1 gives you a quick review of what you can (and cannot) do as a WordPress plugin and theme developer.

Table 2-1   Development Practices Compliant with GPL

Development/Release Practice	GPL Compliant?
Distribute to the public for free with GPL	Yes
Distribute to the public for a cost with GPL	Yes
Restrict the number of users of one download with GPL	No
Split portions of your work between different licenses (PHP files are GPL; JavaScript or CSS files are licensed with the Creative Commons license)	Yes (however, WordPress.org will not promote works that are not 100 percent GPL across all files)
Released under a different license, such as the PHP License	No

The one and only way to make sure that your plugin or theme is 100 percent compliant with the GPL is to take the following few steps before you release your development work to the world:

✦ Include a statement in your work that indicates the work is released under the GPLv2 license in the `license.txt` file, which WordPress does. (Refer to Figure 2-2.) Alternatively, you can include this statement in the header of your plugin file:

```php
<?php

    This program is free software; you can redistribute it and/or modify
    it under the terms of the GNU General Public License, version 2, as
    published by the Free Software Foundation.
```

```
This program is distributed in the hope that it will be useful,
but WITHOUT ANY WARRANTY; without even the implied warranty of
MERCHANTABILITY or FITNESS FOR A PARTICULAR PURPOSE.  See the
GNU General Public License for more details.

You should have received a copy of the GNU General Public License
along with this program; if not, write to the Free Software
Foundation, Inc., 51 Franklin St, Fifth Floor, Boston, MA 02110-1301
USA
*/
?>
```

✦ Do not restrict the use of your works by the number of users per download.

✦ If you charge for your work, which is compliant with the GPL, the licensing doesn't change, and users still have the freedom to modify your work and rerelease it under a different name.

✦ Do not split the license of other files included in your work, such as CSS or graphics. Although this practice complies with the GPL, it won't be approved for inclusion in the WordPress Plugin Directory.

Chapter 3: Understanding Development and Release Cycles

In This Chapter

✔ Delving into WordPress release cycles

✔ Exploring betas, release candidates, and final release versions

✔ Navigating WordPress release archives

✔ Tracking WordPress development

✔ Using bleeding-edge builds

*I*f you're planning to dip your toe into the WordPress waters (or you've already dived in and gotten completely wet), the WordPress platform's development cycle is really good to know about and understand because it affects every WordPress user on a regular basis.

WordPress and its features form the foundation of your website. WordPress is a low-maintenance way to publish content on the web, and the software is free in terms of monetary cost. However, WordPress isn't 100 percent *maintenance* free, and part of maintenance is ensuring that your WordPress software is up-to-date to keep your website secure and safe.

This chapter explains the development cycle for the WordPress platform and shows you how you can stay up-to-date and informed about what's going on. This chapter also gives you information on WordPress release cycles and shows you how you can track ongoing WordPress development on your own.

Discovering WordPress Release Cycles

Book I, Chapter 2 introduces you to the concept of open source software and discusses how the WordPress development community is primarily volunteer developers who donate their time and talents to the WordPress platform. The development of new WordPress releases is a collaborative effort, sometimes requiring contributions from more than 300 developers.

The public schedule for WordPress updates is, roughly, one new release every 120 days. As a user, you can expect a new release of the WordPress software about three times per year. The WordPress development team sticks to that schedule closely, with exceptions only here and there. When they make exceptions to the 120-day rule, they usually make a public announcement about it so that you know what to expect and when to expect it.

Mostly, interruptions to the 120-day schedule occur because the development of WordPress is primarily on a volunteer basis. A few developers — employees of Automattic, the company behind WordPress.com — are paid to develop for WordPress, but most developers are volunteers. Therefore, the progress of WordPress development depends on the developers' schedules.

I'm confident in telling you that you can expect to update your WordPress installation at least three, if not four, times per year.

Upgrading your WordPress experience

Don't be discouraged or frustrated by the number of times you'll upgrade your WordPress installation. The WordPress development team is constantly striving to improve the user experience and bring exciting and fun new features to the WordPress platform. Each upgrade improves security and adds new features to enhance your (and your visitors') experience on your website. WordPress also makes the upgrades easy to perform, which I discuss in Book II, Chapter 6.

The following list gives you some good reasons why you should upgrade your WordPress software each time a new version becomes available:

✦ **Security:** When WordPress versions come and go, outdated versions are no longer supported and are vulnerable to malicious attacks and hacker attempts. Most WordPress security failures occur when you're running an outdated version of WordPress on your website. To make sure that you're running the most up-to-date and secure version, upgrade to the latest release as soon as you can.

✦ **New features:** Major WordPress releases (I discuss the difference between major versus minor, or point, releases later in the chapter), offer great new features that are fun to use, improve your experience, and boost your efficiency and productivity. Upgrading your WordPress installation ensures that you always have access to the latest and greatest tools and features that WordPress has to offer.

✦ **Plugins and themes:** Most plugin and theme developers work hard to make sure that their product is up-to-date with the latest version of WordPress. Generally, plugin and theme developers don't worry about backwards compatibility, and they tend to ignore out-of-date versions of WordPress. To be sure that the plugins and themes you've chosen are current and not breaking your site, make sure that you're using the latest version of WordPress and the latest versions of your plugins and themes. (See Book VI for information about themes, and Book VII for details about plugins.)

Understanding the cycles of a release

By the time the latest WordPress installation becomes available, that version has gone through several iterations, or *versions*. This section helps you understand what it takes to get the latest version to your website, and explains some of the WordPress development terminology.

The steps and terminology involved in the release of a new version of WordPress include

✦ **Alpha:** This is the first developmental phase of a new version. This is typically the "idea" phase in which developers gather ideas, including ideas from users and community members. During the alpha phase, developers determine which features to include in the new release and then develop an outline and a project plan. After features are decided, developers start developing, and testers start testing until they reach a "Feature Freeze" point in the development cycle where all new features are considered complete. The development moves on to perfecting new features through user testing and bug fixes.

✦ **Beta:** This phase is to fix bugs and clear any problems that testers report. Beta cycles can last up to four to six weeks, if not more. WordPress often releases several different beta versions with such names as WordPress version 3.2 Beta, WordPress version 3.2 Beta 1, and so on. The beta process continues until the development team decides that the software is ready to move into the next phase in the development cycle.

✦ **Release candidate:** A version becomes a release candidate (RC) when the bugs from the beta versions are fixed and the version is nearly ready for final release. You sometimes see several release candidate iterations, referred to as RC-1, RC-2, and so on.

✦ **Final release:** After a version has gone through full testing in several (hopefully all) types of environments, use cases, and user experiences, any bugs from the alpha, beta, and RC phases have been squashed, and no major bugs are being reported, the development team releases the final version of the WordPress software.

After the WordPress development team issues a final release version, they start again in the alpha phase, gearing up and preparing to go through the development cycle for the next major version.

Typically, a development cycle lasts 120 days. However, this is an approximation because any number of things can happen (from developmental problems to difficult bugs) to delay the process.

Finding WordPress release archives

WordPress keeps a historical archive of all versions it has ever released at `http://wordpress.org/download/release-archive`, as shown in Figure 3-1. On that page, you find releases dating back to version 0.17 from 2003.

None of the releases found on the WordPress website is safe for you to use except for the latest release in the 3.0.x series. Using an older version leaves your website open to hackers. WordPress just likes to have a recorded history of every release for posterity's sake.

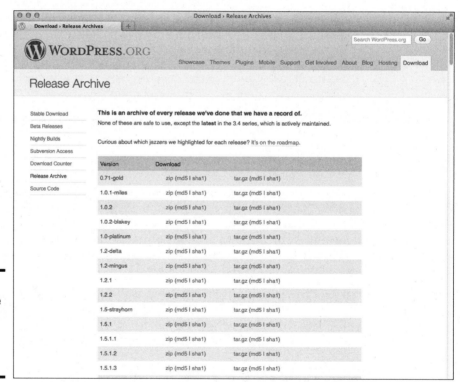

Figure 3-1: The archive of every WordPress release on record.

Major versus point releases

You may have noticed that WordPress versions are numbered. These numbers show the progress of the development of the software, but the numbers also serve a purpose and tell you something else about the version you are using. *Software versioning* is a method of assigning unique numbers to each version release. Generally, the two types of versioning are

✔ **Point release:** Point releases usually only increase the numbered version by a decimal point or two, indicating a relatively minor release. Such releases include insignificant updates or minor bug fixes. For example, when the version number jumps from 3.4 to 3.4.1, you can be certain that the new version was released to fix existing minor bugs or to clean up the source code rather than to add new features.

✔ **Major release:** A major release most often contains new features and jumps by a more seriously incremented version number. For example, WordPress going from 2.9.2 to 3.0 (release 2.9 versioned into 2.9.1 and 2.9.2 before jumping to 3.0) was considered a major release because it jumped a whole number, rather than incrementally going up another decimal point. A large jump is a sign to users that new features are included in this version, rather than just bug fixes or clean up of code. The bigger the jump in version number, the more major the release. For example, a release jumping from 3.0 to 3.5 is an indication of some major new features.

Keeping Track of WordPress Development

If you know where to look, keeping track of the WordPress development cycle is easy, especially because the WordPress development team tries to make the development process as transparent as possible. You can track updates by reading about them in various spots on the Internet and by listening to conversations between developers. If you're so inclined, you can jump in and lend the developers a hand, too.

You have several ways to stay up-to-date on what's going on in the world of WordPress development, including blog posts, live chats, development meetings, tracking tickets, and bug reports, just to name a few. The following list gives you a solid start on where you can go to stay informed:

✦ **WordPress Development Updates (**`http://make.wordpress.org/core`**):** The WordPress development team's blog is where you can follow and keep track of the progress of the WordPress software project while it happens. (See Figure 3-2.) You find agendas, schedules, meeting minutes, and discussions surrounding the development cycles.

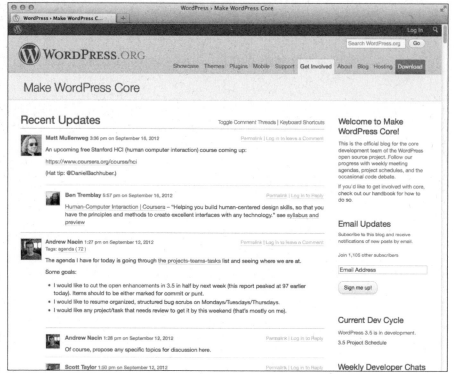

Figure 3-2:
The
WordPress
development
blog.

✦ **WordPress developers' chats (**`irc.freenode.net in #wordpress-dev`**):** Using an Internet chat program called IRC (Internet Relay Chat), WordPress developers gather weekly to discuss a predetermined agenda of items that need to be addressed during the development cycle. You're invited to join the IRC chat room to listen in or participate if you want to. (You can download a free IRC program called mIRC from `www.mirc.com` for PC users or a program called Ircle from `www.ircle.com` for Mac users. Follow the program's user manual for instructions on how to use IRC to chat via the Internet.)

✦ **WordPress Trac (**`http://core.trac.wordpress.org`**):** Here are ways to stay informed about the changes in WordPress development:

   • Follow the timeline: `http://core.trac.wordpress.org/timeline`

   • View the road map: `http://core.trac.wordpress.org/roadmap`

   • Read reports: `http://core.trac.wordpress.org/report`

   • Perform a search: `http://core.trac.wordpress.org/search`

✦ **WordPress mailing lists (**`http://codex.wordpress.org/Mailing_Lists`**):** Join mailing lists focused on different aspects of WordPress development, such as bug testing, documentation, and hacking WordPress. (Specifics about mailing lists are in Book II, Chapter 4.)

Downloading Nightly Builds

WordPress development moves pretty fast. Often, changes in the WordPress software's development cycle occur daily. While the developers are working on alpha and beta versions and release candidates, they will commit the latest core changes to the repository and make those changes available to the public to download, install, and test on individual sites. The changes are released in a full WordPress software package called a *nightly build* — which contains the latest core changes submitted to the project, changes that have not yet released as a full and final version.

Using nightly builds is not a safe practice for a live site. I strongly recommend creating a test environment to test the nightly builds. Many times, especially during alpha and beta phases, the core code may break and cause problems with your existing installation, so use nightly builds in a test environment only and leave your live site intact until the final release is available.

Hundreds of members of the WordPress community help in the development phases, even though they aren't developers or programmers. They help by downloading the nightly builds, testing them in various server environments, and reporting to the WordPress development team by way of Trac tickets (shown in Figure 3-3; check out `http://core.trac.wordpress.org/report`) any bugs and problems they find with that version of the software.

Figure 3-3:
WordPress
Trac tickets.

You can download the latest nightly build from the WordPress repository at `http://wordpress.org/download/nightly`. For information about installing WordPress, see Book II, Chapter 4.

WordPress Beta Tester (`http://wordpress.org/extend/plugins/wordpress-beta-tester`) is a super plugin that allows you to use the automatic upgrade tool in your WordPress Dashboard to download the latest nightly build. For information about installing and using WordPress plugins, check out Book VII, Chapter 1.

Running the latest nightly build on your website is referred to as using *bleeding-edge* software because it's an untested version requiring you to take risks just to run it on your website.

Chapter 4: Meeting the WordPress Community

In This Chapter

↳ Finding WordPress users

↳ Locating users on social networks

↳ Noticing members helping members in support forums

↳ Participating in testing and bug squashing

↳ Discovering professional consultants and services

↳ Attending and organizing local WordCamps

Allow me to introduce you to the fiercely loyal folks who make up the WordPress user base, better known as the WordPress community. These merry ladies and gentlemen come from all around the globe, from California to Cairo, Florida to Florence, and all points in between.

In March 2005, Matt Mullenweg of WordPress proudly proclaimed that the number of WordPress downloads had reached 900,000 — an amazing landmark in the history of the software. By August 2006, WordPress had logged more than 1 million downloads, and by 2007, more than 3 million. The number of downloads of WordPress continues to grow with each passing day. 2010 was a landmark year for WordPress when Microsoft announced that it would be transferring their 30-million+ users of its Windows Live service to WordPress. In 2011, a popular technology blog, TechCrunch, announced that WordPress powers 22 percent of all newly active websites in the United States (`http://techcrunch.com/2011/08/19/wordpress-now-powers-22-percent-of-new-active-websites-in-the-us`). This popularity makes for a large community of users, to say the least.

This chapter introduces you to the WordPress community and the benefits of membership within that community, such as where to find support, how to locate other WordPress users on various social networks, getting support and assistance from other users, how you can participate in WordPress development, and hooking up with WordPress users face to face at WordPress events, such as WordCamp.

Finding Other WordPress Users

Don't let the sheer volume of users intimidate you: WordPress has bragging rights to the most helpful blogging community on the web today. Thousands of websites exist that spotlight everything, including WordPress news, resources, updates, tutorials, training — the list is endless. Do a quick Google search for *WordPress* and you'll get about 1.9 billion results.

My point is that WordPress users are all over the Internet, from websites to discussion forums and social networks to podcasts, and more. For many people, the appeal of the WordPress platform lies not only in the platform itself, but in its passionate community of users.

Finding WordPress news and tips on community websites

WordPress-related websites cover an array of topics related to the platform, including everything from tutorials to news, and even a little gossip, if that's your flavor. The Internet has no shortage of websites related to the popular WordPress platform; here are a few that stand out:

✦ **WP Candy** (`http://wpcandy.com`)**:** Covers everything from soup to nuts: news, resources, tools, tutorials, and interviews with standout WordPress personalities. You can pretty much count on WP Candy to be on top of what's new and going on in the WordPress community. WP Candy also hosts a popular weekly WordPress podcast called WP Late Night.

✦ **Smashing Magazine** (`http://wp.smashingmagazine.com`)**:** This very popular and established online design magazine and resource has dedicated a special section of its website just to WordPress news, resources, tips, and tools written by various members of the WordPress community.

✦ **Code Poet** (`http://build.codepoet.com`)**:** A resource website the team at Automattic created to help anyone who builds websites with WordPress. It includes e-books, articles, and interviews with WordPress community members who are doing great things with the software.

✦ **Make WordPress.org** (`http://make.wordpress.org`)**:** A website that aggregates content from all of the "Make WordPress" websites built and maintained by the Wordpress.org community. It includes resources for everything from contributing to WordPress core, making plugins and themes, planning WordPress events, supporting WordPress, and more.

Locating users on social networks

In addition to WordPress, many bloggers use different microblogging tools, such as Twitter (`http://twitter.com`), and/or social-media networks, such as Facebook (`www.facebook.com`), to augment their online presence and market their blog, services, and products. Within these different networks, you can find WordPress users, resources, and links, including the following:

✦ **WordPress Twitter Lists:** Twitter allows users to create lists of people and their tweets who have the same interests, such as WordPress. You can find a few of these lists here:

- Wefollow WordPress: `http://wefollow.com/twitter/wordpress`

- Listorious WordPress People and Lists: `http://listorious.com/tags/wordpress`

✦ **Facebook Pages on WordPress:** Facebook users create pages and groups around their favorite topics of interest, such as WordPress. You can find some interesting WordPress pages and groups here:

- WordPress.org Fan Page: `www.facebook.com/WordPress`

- WordPress For Dummies Fan Page: `www.facebook.com/pages/WordPress-For-Dummies/47542644546`

- Matt Mullenweg on Facebook (Founder of WordPress): `www.facebook.com/matt.mullenweg`

You can also include Twitter Lists on your site by using the handy Twitter Lists for WordPress plugin at `http://wordpress.org/extend/plugins/twitter-lists-for-wordpress`.

Users Helping Users

Don't worry if you're not a member of the WordPress community. Joining is easy: Simply start your own blog by using the WordPress platform. If you're already blogging on a different platform, such as Blogger or Movable Type, WordPress makes migrating your data from that platform to a new WordPress setup simple. (See Book II, Chapter 7 for information on migrating to WordPress from a different platform.)

WordPress support forums

The WordPress Forums page (shown in Figure 4-1) can be found at `http://wordpress.org/support`. This is where you find users helping other users in their quest to use and understand the platform.

The support forums are hosted on the WordPress.org website; however, don't expect to find any official form of support from the WordPress developers. Instead, you find a large community of people from all walks of life seeking answers and providing solutions.

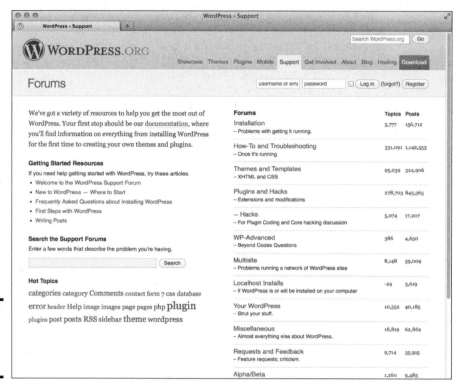

Figure 4-1:
WordPress
Forums
page.

Users from beginner and novice level to the most advanced level browse the forums, providing support for one another. Each user has their own experiences, troubles, and knowledge level with WordPress, and the support forums are where they share those experiences and seek out the experiences of other users.

It is important to remember that the people you find and interact with on these official forums are offering their knowledge on a volunteer basis only — so, as always, common courtesy rules apply. Using "please" and "thank you" go a long, long way in the forums.

If you find solutions and assistance in the WordPress support forums, consider browsing through the forum entries to see whether you can help someone else by answering a question or two.

WordPress user manual

You can also find users contributing to the very helpful WordPress Codex (a collection of how-to documents) at http://codex.wordpress.org. *Codex,* by the way, is Latin for *book*.

The WordPress Codex is a collaborative effort to document the use of the WordPress software. All contributors to the Codex are WordPress users who donate their time as a way of giving back to the free, open source project that has given them a dynamic piece of software for publishing freely on the web.

WordPress mailing lists

You can subscribe to various mailing lists, too. These lists offer you the opportunity to become involved in various aspects of the WordPress community as well as future development of the software. All the available WordPress mailing lists are on the Automattic website at `http://lists.automattic.com/mailman/listinfo`. The most popular ones include

✦ **wp-hackers** (`http://lists.automattic.com/mailman/listinfo/wp-hackers`)**:** Subscribe to this mailing list to interact and talk to other WordPress users about *hacking* WordPress — otherwise known as altering WordPress code to make it do what you want it to do.

✦ **wp-testers** (`http://lists.automattic.com/mailman/listinfo/wp-testers`)**:** This mailing list is filled with people who are testing new releases (as well as beta versions) of WordPress and reporting any bugs or problems that they find.

✦ **wp-edu** (`http://lists.automattic.com/pipermail/wp-edu`)**:** This is a mailing list dedicated to people in the education field who use WordPress, such as teachers and professors.

Discovering Professional WordPress Consultants and Services

You have big plans for your blog, and your time is valuable. Hiring a professional to handle the back-end design and maintenance of your blog enables you to spend your time creating the content and building your readership on the front end.

Many bloggers who decide to go the custom route by hiring a design professional do it for another reason: They want the designs/themes of their blogs to be unique. Free themes are nice, but you run the risk that your blog will look like hundreds of other blogs out there.

A *brand,* a term often used in advertising and marketing, refers to the recognizable identity of a product — in this case, your blog. Having a unique brand or design for your site sets yours apart from the rest. If your blog has a custom look, people will associate that look with you. You can accomplish branding with a single logo or an entire layout and color scheme of your choosing.

Many consultants and design professionals put themselves up for hire. Who are these people? I get to that topic in just a second. First, you want to understand what services they offer, which can help you decide whether hiring a professional is the solution for you.

Here are some of the many services available:

✦ Custom graphic design and CSS styling for your blog

✦ Custom templates

✦ WordPress plugin installation and integration

✦ Custom WordPress plugins

✦ WordPress software installation on your web server

✦ Upgrades of the WordPress software

✦ Web hosting and domain registration services

✦ Search engine optimization and site marketing

Some bloggers take advantage of the full array of services provided, whereas others use only a handful. The important thing to remember is that you aren't alone. Help is available for you and your blog.

Table 4-1 pairs the three types of blog experts — designers, developers, and consultants — with the services they typically offer.

Many of these folks are freelancers with self-imposed titles, but I've matched titles to typical duties. Keep in mind that some of these professionals wear all these hats; others specialize in only one area.

Table 4-1	Types of WordPress Professionals
Title	*Services*
Designers	These folks excel in graphic design, CSS, and the development of custom WordPress themes.
Developers	These guys and gals are code monkeys. Some of them don't know a stitch about design; however, they can provide you custom code to make your blog do things you never thought possible. Usually, you'll find these people releasing plugins in their spare time for the WordPress community to use free.
Consultants	If you're blogging for a business, these folks can provide you a marketing plan for your blog or a plan for using your blog to reach clients and colleagues in your field. Many of these consultants also provide search engine optimization to help your domain reach high ranks in search engines.

I wish I could tell you what you could expect to pay for any of these services, but the truth is the levels of expertise — and expense — vary wildly. Services can range from $5 per hour to $300 or more per hour. As with any purchase, do your research and make an informed decision before you buy.

Listing all the professionals who provide WordPress services is impossible, but Tables 4-2 through 4-4 list some of the more popular ones. I tried to cover a diverse level of services so that you have the knowledge to make an informed decision about which professional to choose.

WordPress designers

WordPress designers can take a simple blog and turn it into something dynamic, beautiful, and exciting. These people are experts in the graphic design, CSS styling, and template tagging needed to create a unique theme for your website. Often, WordPress designers are skilled in installing and upgrading WordPress software and plugins; sometimes, they're even skilled in creating custom PHP or plugins. These folks are the ones you want to contact when you're looking for someone to create a unique design for your website that is an individual, visual extension of you or your company, such as my own premium WordPress theme business shown in Figure 4-2.

Figure 4-2:
The design of E.Webscapes premium WordPress themes site.

Some blog designers post their rates on their websites because they offer design *packages,* whereas other designers quote projects on a case-by-case basis because every project is unique. When you're searching for a designer, if the prices aren't displayed on the site, just drop the designer an e-mail and ask for an estimate. Armed with this information, you can do a little comparison shopping while you search for just the right designer.

The designers and design studios listed in Table 4-2 represent a range of styles, pricing, services, and experience. All of them excel in creating custom WordPress blogs and websites. This list is by no means exhaustive, but it's a nice starting point.

Table 4-2	Established WordPress Designers
Who They Are	*Where You Can Find Them*
WebDevStudios	`http://webdevstudios.com`
10up	`http://10up.com`
Range	`http://ran.ge`

Developers

The WordPress motto sits at the bottom of the WordPress home page:

> Code is poetry.

No one knows this better than the extremely talented blog developers in the core WordPress development team. A developer can take some of the underlying code, make a little magic happen between PHP and the MySQL database that stores the content of your blog, and create a dynamic display of that content for you. Most likely, you'll contact a developer when you want to do something with your blog that's a little out of the ordinary and you can't find a plugin that does the trick.

If you've gone through all the available WordPress plugins and still can't find the exact function that you want your WordPress blog to perform, contact one of these folks. Explain what you need. The developer can tell you whether it can be done, whether she is available to do it, and how much it will cost. (Don't forget that last part!) You may recognize some of the names in Table 4-3 as developers/authors of some popular WordPress plugins.

Table 4-3	Established WordPress Developers
Who They Are	*Where You Can Find Them*
Crowd Favorite	`http://crowdfavorite.net/wordpress`
eHermits, Inc.	`http://ehermitsinc.com`
Covered Web Services — Mark Jaquith	`http://coveredwebservices.com`
Voce Communications	`http://vocecommunications.com`

Consultants

Blog consultants may not be able to design or code for you, but they're probably connected to people who can. Consultants can help you achieve your goals for your blog in terms of online visibility, marketing plans, and search engine optimization. Most of these folks can help you find out how to make money with your blog and connect you with various advertising programs. Quite honestly, you can do what blog consultants do by investing just a little time and research in these areas. As with design and coding, however, figuring everything out and then implementing it takes time. Sometimes it's easier — and more cost effective — to hire a professional rather than do it yourself.

Who hires blog consultants? Typically, a business that wants to incorporate a blog into its existing website or a business that already has a blog but wants help taking it to the next level. Table 4-4 lists some people and organizations that offer this kind of consulting.

Table 4-4	Established Blog Consultants	
Who They Are	*Where You Can Find Them*	*Type of Consulting*
Copyblogger Media	`www.copyblogger.com`	SEO, Marketing
Convertiv — Kevin Palmer	`http://convertiv.com`	WordPress Design and Development; Social Media Consulting
WebDesign.com	`http://webdesign.com`	WordPress Training

Contributing to WordPress

Contributing code to the core WordPress software is only one way of participating in the WordPress project. You do not need to be a coder or developer to contribute to WordPress — and it's easier than you might think. Here are several ways you can contribute to the project, including, but not limited to, code:

✦ **Code:** One of the more obvious ways you can contribute to WordPress is by providing code to be used in the core files. The WordPress project has several hundred developers who contribute code at one time or another. You submit code through the WordPress Trac at `http://core.trac.wordpress.org`. Within the Trac, you can follow current development and track changes. To contribute, you can use the Trac to download and test a code patch or look at reported bugs to see whether you can offer a fix or submit a patch. Required skills include, at the very least, PHP programming, WordPress experience, and MySQL database administration. (That isn't an exhaustive list, mind you.)

✦ **Testing:** You can join the wp-testers mailing list to test beta versions of WordPress and report your own user experience. WordPress developers monitor this mailing list and try to fix any true bugs or problems.

✦ **Documentation:** Anyone can submit documentation to the Codex (the user documentation for WordPress); all you need to do is visit `http://codex.wordpress.org`, create an account, and dig in! Be sure to check out the article in the Codex titled "Codex: Contributing" (`http://codex.wordpress.org/Codex:Contributing`), which provides good tips on how to get started, including guidelines for documentation contributions.

✦ **Tutorials:** Do you feel like you have a few tips and tricks you want to share with other WordPress users? Take it to your blog! What better way to contribute to WordPress than sharing your knowledge with the rest of the world? Write up your how-to tutorial and publish it on your website — then promote your tutorial on Twitter and Facebook.

✦ **Support Forums:** Volunteer your time and knowledge on the WordPress support forums at `http://wordpress.org/support`. The involvement of WordPress users donating their time and talents in the support forum is an essential part of the WordPress experience.

✦ **Presentations:** In the next section of this chapter, I discuss live WordPress events where users meet face to face. Consider offering to speak at one of those events to share your knowledge and experience with other users — or host one in your local area.

Participating in Live WordPress Events

Not only can you find out about WordPress and contribute to the project online via the Internet, but you can get involved in WordPress offline, too.

Live WordPress events, called WordPress Meetups and WordCamps, are where users and fans get together to discuss, learn, and share about their favorite platform. The two events are somewhat different:

✦ **WordPress Meetups:** Generally, these local WordPress events occur in small groups of people from the same geographical location. Typically, speakers, organizers, and attendees are from the same area and enjoy gathering on a monthly or bimonthly basis.

You can find a WordPress Meetup near your community by visiting the Meetup website at www.meetup.com or by performing a search, using the keyword *WordPress* and your city or zip code.

✦ **WordCamps:** These annual WordPress events are usually much larger than Meetups and are attended by people from all over the country. WordCamps are hosted in almost every major city in the United States and abroad. Usually, WordCamps cost a small amount to attend, and speakers at WordCamps are well-known personalities from the WordPress community.

You can find a WordCamp event close to you by visiting the WordCamp website at http://central.wordcamp.org and browsing through the upcoming WordCamps.

If there is not a Meetup or WordCamp near your area, consider getting involved and organizing one! Some great tips and information about organizing WordCamps can be found at http://central.wordcamp.org.

Chapter 5: Discovering Different Versions of WordPress

In This Chapter

✔ **Getting hosted with WordPress.com**

✔ **Self-hosting with WordPress.org**

✔ **Running a network of blogs with the multisite feature**

✔ **Exploring enterprise options and VIP services**

Bloggers have a wealth of software platforms to choose from. You want to be sure that the platform you choose has all the options you're looking for. WordPress is unique in that it offers two versions of its software. Each version is designed to meet the various needs of bloggers.

One version is a hosted platform available at WordPress.com that meets your needs if you do not want to worry about installing or dealing with software; the other is the self-hosted version of the WordPress software available at `http://wordpress.org`, which offers you a bit more freedom and flexibility, as described throughout this chapter.

This chapter introduces you to both versions of the WordPress platform so you can choose which version suits your particular needs the best.

Comparing the Two Versions of WordPress

The two versions of WordPress are

+ The hosted version at WordPress.com

+ The self-installed and self-hosted version available at WordPress.org

Certain features are available to you in every WordPress blog setup, whether you're using the self-hosted software from WordPress.org or the hosted version at WordPress.com. These features include (but aren't limited to)

+ Quick-and-easy installation and setup

+ Full-featured blogging capability, letting you publish content to the web through an easy-to-use web-based interface

+ Topical archiving of your posts, using categories

✦ Monthly archiving of your posts, with the ability to provide a listing of those archives for easy navigation through your site

✦ Comment and trackback tools

✦ Automatic spam protection through Akismet

✦ Built-in gallery integration for photos and images

✦ Media Manager for video and audio files

✦ Great community support

✦ Unlimited number of static pages, letting you step out of the blog box and into the sphere of running a fully functional website

✦ RSS capability with RSS 2.0, RSS 1.0, and Atom support

✦ Tools for importing content from different blogging systems (such as Blogger, Movable Type, and LiveJournal)

Table 5-1 compares the two WordPress versions.

Table 5-1	Exploring the Differences between the Two Versions of WordPress	
Feature	*WordPress.org*	*WordPress.com*
Cost	Free	Free
Software download	Yes	No
Software installation	Yes	No
Web hosting required	Yes	No
Custom CSS control	Yes	$30/year
Template access	Yes	No
Sidebar widgets	Yes	Yes
RSS syndication	Yes	Yes
Access to core code	Yes	No
Ability to install plugins	Yes	No
WP themes installation	Yes	No
Multi-author support	Yes	Yes
Unlimited number of blog setups with one account (multisite)	Yes*	Yes
Community-based support forums	Yes	Yes

* With the multisite feature enabled only

Choosing the hosted version from WordPress.com

WordPress.com (see Figure 5-1) is a free service. If downloading, installing, and using software on a web server sound like Greek to you and are chores you'd rather avoid, the WordPress folks provide a solution for you at WordPress.com.

WordPress.com is a *hosted solution,* which means it has no software requirement, no downloads, and no installation or server configurations. Everything's done for you on the back end, behind the scenes. You don't even have to worry about how the process happens; it happens quickly, and before you know it, you're making your first blog post.

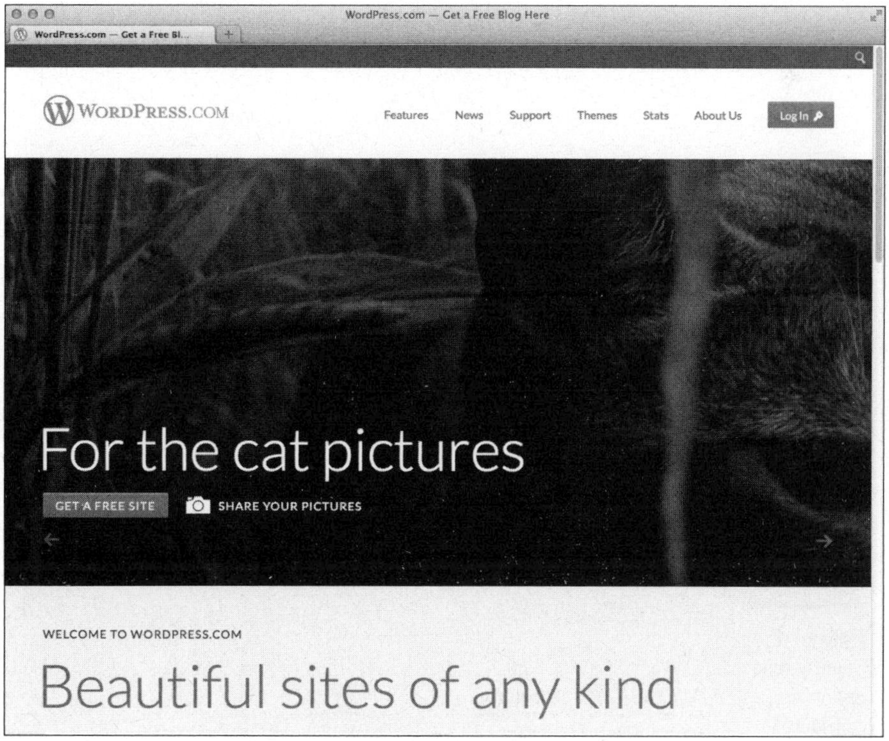

Figure 5-1:
The
WordPress.
com
website.

WordPress.com offers several upgrades (see Figure 5-2) to help make your blogging life easier. Here's a list of upgrades you can purchase to enhance your WordPress.com account, with prices reflecting the annual cost:

✦ **Add a Domain:** This upgrade allows you to add your own domain name to your WordPress.com account; see Book II, Chapter 1. This service costs $5.00 for the domain registration and $13.00 for the domain mapping.

✦ **VideoPress:** This upgrade equips you with the ability to upload, store, and share your videos from your WordPress.com account. This service covers the storage space that your video files take up on the WordPress.com servers. The service costs $60.00 per year.

✦ **Custom Design:** This upgrade lets you customize the fonts used on your site, change the color scheme, and customize the Cascading Style Sheet (CSS) for the theme you're using in the WordPress.com system. It's recommended for users who understand CSS. The cost is $30.00 per year.

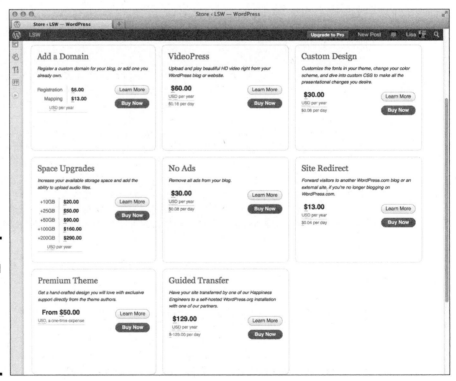

Figure 5-2: Several paid upgrades available on the WordPress.com free service.

+ **Space Upgrades:** With the free WordPress.com blog, you have 5GB of hard drive space in your upload directory. The various space upgrades add more, letting you upload more files (images, videos, audio files, and so on). You can add 10GB for $20.00 per year, 25GB for $50.00 per year, 50GB for $90.00 per year, 100GB for $160.00 per year, and 200GB for $290.00 per year.

+ **No Ads:** For $30.00 per year, you can ensure that your WordPress.com blog is ad free. Occasionally, WordPress.com does serve ads on your blog pages to defray the costs of running a popular service. If you'd rather not have those ads appearing on your blog, pay for the No Ads upgrade and you'll be ad free!

+ **Site Redirect:** Allows you to forward your WordPress.com URL to an off-site domain; this is helpful if you choose to move away from WordPress.com to your own domain with the WordPress.org software — you can forward the traffic that you have built for $13 per year.

+ **Premium Theme:** Use a special handcrafted theme built exclusively for WordPress by community theme authors for $50.00 per theme.

+ **Guided Transfer:** Have the folks at WordPress.com complete a transfer of your WordPress.com hosted website to a WordPress.org self-hosted installation on one of their hosting partner's services (`http://get.wp.com/hosting`).

WordPress.com has some limitations; you cannot install plugins or custom themes, for example, and you cannot customize the base code files, nor are you able to sell advertising or monetize your blog on WordPress.com. But even with its limitations, WordPress.com is an excellent starting point if you're brand new to blogging and a little intimidated by the configuration requirements of the self-installed WordPress.org software.

The good news is that if you outgrow your WordPress.com-hosted blog and want to move to the self-hosted WordPress.org software, you can. You can even take all the content from your WordPress.com-hosted blog with you and easily import it into your new setup with the WordPress.org software.

Therefore, in the grand scheme of things, your options aren't really that limited.

Self-hosting with WordPress.org

The self-installed version from WordPress.org is the primary focus of *WordPress All-in-One For Dummies*. Using WordPress.org requires you to download the software from the WordPress website at `http://wordpress.org` (shown in Figure 5-3), and then you need to install it on a server from which your blog or website operates.

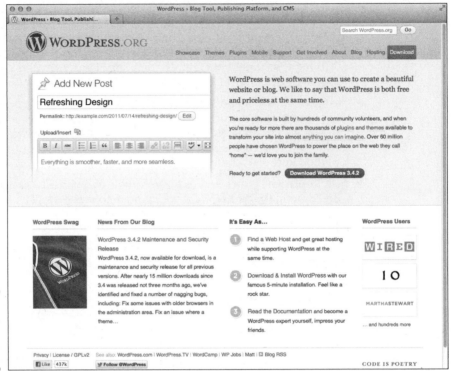

Figure 5-3:
The
WordPress.
org website.

The WordPress.org website is an excellent repository of tools and resources for you throughout the lifespan of your WordPress-powered blog, so be sure to bookmark it for future reference! Here's a list of helpful things that you can find on the website:

✦ **Plugins** (http://wordpress.org/extend/plugins): The Plugin page of the WordPress.org website houses a full directory of plugins available for WordPress. You can search for and find the plugins you need for SEO enhancement, comment management, and social media integration, among many others.

✦ **Themes** (http://wordpress.org/extend/themes): The Free Themes Directory page, shown in Figure 5-4, is a repository of WordPress themes free for the taking. In this section of the WordPress.org website, you can browse more than 1,500 themes to use on your site to dress up your content.

✦ **Docs** (http://codex.wordpress.org): Almost every piece of software released comes with documentation and user manuals. The Docs section of the WordPress.org website contains the WordPress Codex, which tries to help you answer questions about the use of WordPress and its various features and functions.

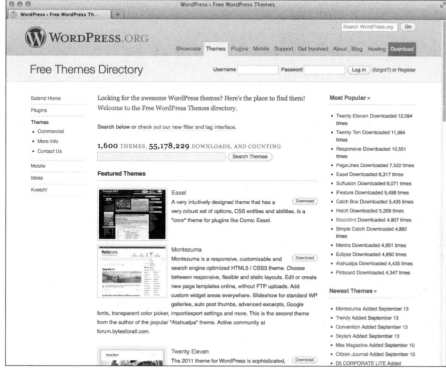

Figure 5-4:
The Free
Themes
Directory on
WordPress.
org.

✦ **Forums (**`http://wordpress.org/support`**):** The support forums at
  WordPress.org consist of WordPress users from all over with one goal —
  learning how to use WordPress to suit their particular needs. The
  support forums are very much a community of users (from beginners
  to advanced) helping other users, and you can generally obtain a
  solution to your WordPress needs here from other users of the
  software.

✦ **Roadmap (**`http://wordpress.org/about/roadmap`**):** This section
  of the WordPress.org website doesn't contain support information or
  tools that you can download; it offers an at-a-glance peek at what's new
  and upcoming for WordPress. The Roadmap page gives you a pretty
  accurate idea of when WordPress will release the next version of its
  software; see Chapter 3 of this minibook for information about versions and release cycles. (Hint: Click the version number to visit the
  WordPress Trac and see what features developers are working on and
  adding.)

WordPress.org is the self-installed, self-hosted software version of WordPress
you install on a web server that you have set up on a domain you have

registered. Unless you own your own web server, you need to lease one. Leasing space on a web server is *web hosting,* and unless you know someone who knows someone, hosting generally isn't free.

That said, web hosting doesn't cost a whole lot, either. You can usually obtain a good, basic web hosting service for anywhere from $10 to $15 per month. (Book II, Chapters 1 and 2 give you some great information on web hosting accounts and tools.) However, you need to make sure that any web host you choose to work with has the required software installed on the web server. The recommended minimum software requirements for WordPress include

✦ PHP version 5.2.4 or greater

✦ MySQL version 5.0 or greater

After you have WordPress installed on your web server (see the installation instructions in Book II, Chapter 4), you can start using it to blog to your heart's content. With the WordPress software, you can install several plugins that extend the functionality of the blogging system, which I describe in Book VII. You also have full control of the core files and code that WordPress is built on. If you have a knack for PHP and knowledge of MySQL, you can work within the code to make changes that you think would be good for you and your blog.

You don't need design or coding ability to make your blog look great. Members of the WordPress community have created more than 1,600 WordPress themes (designs), and you can download them free and install them on your WordPress blog (Book VI, Chapter 2). Additionally, if you're creatively inclined, like to create designs on your own, and know Cascading Style Sheets (CSS), you have full access to the template system within WordPress and can create your own custom themes. (See Book VI, Chapters 3 through 7.)

Hosting Multiple Sites with One WordPress Installation

The self-hosted WordPress.org software also lets you run an unlimited number of blogs on one installation of its software platform, on one domain. When you configure the options within WordPress to enable a multisite interface, you become administrator of a network of blogs. All the options remain the same, but with the multisite options configured, you can add more blogs and domains and allow registered users of your website to host their own blog within your network. More information about the multisite feature in WordPress is found in Book VIII.

The following types of sites use the Network options within WordPress:

+ **Blog networks,** which can have more than 150 blogs. The popular electronics retail store, Best Buy, uses WordPress to power 1,050 local store blogs (example: `http://stores.bestbuy.com/577`).

+ **Newspapers and magazines,** such as *The New York Times,* and universities, such as Harvard Law School, use WordPress to manage the blog sections of their websites.

+ **Niche-specific blog networks,** such as Edublogs.org, use WordPress to manage their full networks of free blogs for teachers, educators, lecturers, librarians, and other education professionals.

Extensive information on running a network of sites by using the multisite feature in WordPress is found in Book VIII. The chapters there take you through everything: setting it up, maintaining it, and using it to run a network of sites with one WordPress installation.

Anyone using a WordPress platform prior to version 3.0 may recognize *WordPress MU,* the separate piece of software you needed in order to run multiple sites with WordPress. The multisite feature that replaced WordPress MU was introduced into WordPress version 3.0. All you old dogs out there need to forget WordPress MU and embrace the multisite feature in version 3.0+ because WordPress MU no longer exists.

With the multisite features enabled, users of your network can run their own sites within your installation of WordPress. They also have access to their own Dashboard with the same options and features you read about in Book III. Heck, it would probably be a great idea to buy a copy of this book for every member within your network so everyone can become familiar with the WordPress Dashboard and features, too. At least have a copy on hand so people can borrow yours!

If you plan to run just a few of your own sites with the WordPress multisite feature, your current hosting situation is probably well suited. (See Book II, Chapter 1 for information on web hosting services.) However, if you plan to host a large network with hundreds of blogs and multiple users, you should consider contacting your host and increasing your bandwidth and the disk space limitations on your account.

The best example of a large blog network with hundreds of blogs and users (actually, more like millions) would be the hosted service at WordPress. com (which I discuss earlier in this chapter). At WordPress.com, people are invited to sign up for an account and start a blog by using the multisite feature within the WordPress platform on the WordPress server. When you enable this feature on your own domain and enable the user registration feature (covered later in this chapter), you invite users to:

✦ Create an account

✦ Create a blog on your WordPress installation (on your domain)

✦ Create content by publishing blog posts

✦ Upload media files, such as photos, audio, and video

✦ Invite their friends to view their blog or sign up for their own account

In addition to the necessary security measures, time, and administrative tasks that go into running a community of blogs, you have a few things to worry about. Creating a community increases the resource use, bandwidth, and disk space on your web server. In many cases, if you go over the allotted limits given to you by your web host, you will incur great cost. Make sure that you anticipate your bandwidth and disk space needs before running a large network on your website! (Don't say you weren't warned.)

Many WordPress network communities start with grand dreams of being a large and active community — be realistic on how your community will operate in order to make the right hosting choice for yourself and your community.

Small blogging communities are handled easily with a shared-server solution; larger, more active communities should really consider a dedicated server solution for operation. The difference between the two lies in their names:

✦ **Shared-server solution:** You have one account on one server that has several other accounts on it. Think of this as apartment living. One building has several apartments under one roof.

✦ **Dedicated server:** You have one account on one server. The server is dedicated to your account, and your account is dedicated to the server. Think of this as owning a home where you don't share your living space with anyone else.

A dedicated-server solution is a more expensive investment for your blog community; a shared-server solution is the most economical. Base your decision regarding which solution to go with for your WordPress network on how big and how active you estimate your community will be. You can move from a shared-server solution to a dedicated-server solution if your community becomes larger than you expect; however, starting with the right solution for your community from day one is best. More information on hosting WordPress is found in Book II, Chapter 1.

Discovering WordPress VIP Services

The company behind the Automattic WordPress.com service is owned and operated by the WordPress cofounder, Matt Mullenweg. Although Automattic doesn't own the WordPress.org software (as an open source platform, WordPress.org is owned by the community and hundreds of developers that contribute to the core code), Automattic is a driving force behind all things WordPress.

Have a look at the Automattic website at `http://automattic.com` (shown in Figure 5-5). The folks behind WordPress own and operate a number of different properties and services that can extend the features of your WordPress site, including

✦ **WordPress.com** (`http://wordpress.com`): A hosted WordPress blogging service, discussed previously in this chapter.

✦ **Jetpack** (`http://jetpack.me`): A suite of plugins that can be installed on a WordPress.org self-hosted site.

✦ **VaultPress** (`http://vaultpress.com`): Premium backup and restore service for your blog.

✦ **Akismet** (`http://akismet.com`): Spam protection for your blog. This service comes with every WordPress.org install, but there are different levels of service, as discussed in Book III, Chapter 4.

✦ **Polldaddy** (`http://polldaddy.com`): A polling and survey software that easily plugs into the WordPress platform.

✦ **VideoPress** (`http://videopress.com`): Video hosting and sharing application for WordPress.

✦ **Gravatar** (`http://gravatar.com`): Photos or graphical icons for comment authors (discussed in Book III, Chapter 2).

✦ **IntenseDebate** (`http://intensedebate.com`): An integrated commenting system for your WordPress blog.

✦ **After the Deadline** (`http://afterthedeadline.com`): A fancy and useful spelling and grammar checker for WordPress with such features as contextual spell checking, advanced style checking, and intelligent grammar checking.

✦ **Plinky** (`http://plinky.com`): Even great authors get writer's block from time to time; Plinky provides a daily source of inspiration.

✦ **Code Poet** (`http://codepoet.com`): A WordPress community resource website.

✦ **WordPress.com VIP** (`http://vip.wordpress.com`): Enterprise level web hosting and WordPress support starting at $15,000 per year (usually reserved for heavy hitters, such as CNN, BBC, and *Time*, for example).

✦ **P2** (`http://p2theme.com`): A unique, free WordPress theme with such features as in-line comments, real-time updates, and a posting form right on the home page so users don't ever touch the Dashboard.

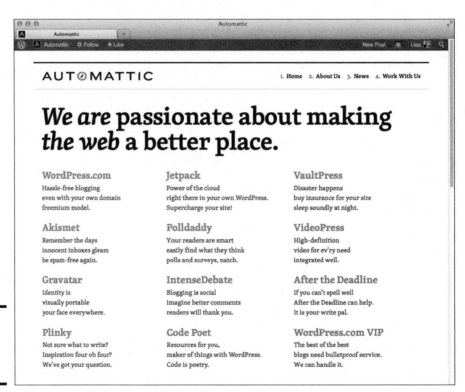

Figure 5-5:
The
Automattic
website.

Book II

Setting Up the WordPress Software

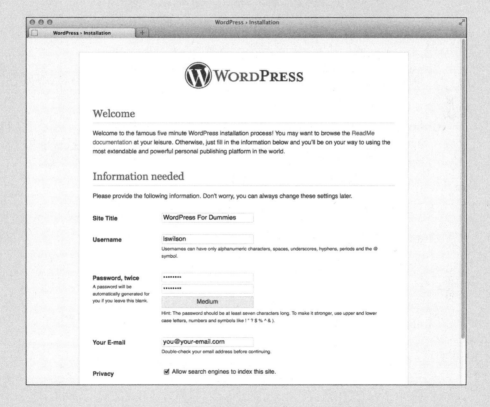

Visit www.dummies.com/extras/wordpressaio to find more WordPress security resources.

Contents at a Glance

Chapter 1: Understanding the System Requirements

In This Chapter

- ✔ **Registering a domain name**
- ✔ **Exploring web hosting environments**
- ✔ **Knowing the basic requirements for PHP and MySQL**
- ✔ **Getting web hosting recommendations for WordPress**
- ✔ **Understanding bandwidth and disk space needs**

*B*efore you can start blogging with WordPress, you have to set up your foundation. Doing so involves more than simply downloading and installing the WordPress software. You also need to establish your *domain* (your blog address) and your *web hosting service* (the place that houses your blog). Although you initially download your WordPress software onto your hard drive, you install it on a web hosting server.

Obtaining a web server and installing software on it is something you may already have done on your site; in which case, you can move on to the next chapter. If you haven't installed WordPress, you must first consider many factors, as well as cope with a learning curve, because setting up your blog through a hosting service involves using some technologies that you may not feel comfortable with. This chapter takes you through the basics of those technologies, and by the last page of this chapter, you'll have WordPress successfully installed on a web server with your own domain name.

Establishing Your Domain

You've read all the hype. You've heard all the rumors. You've seen the flashy blogs on the web powered by WordPress. But where do you start?

The first steps toward installing and setting up a WordPress blog are making a decision about a domain name and then purchasing the registration of that name through a domain registrar. A *domain name* is the *unique* web address that you type in a web browser's address bar to visit a website. Some examples of domain names are WordPress.org and Google.com.

Domain names: Do you own or rent?

When you "buy" a domain name, you don't really own it. Rather, you're purchasing the right to use that domain name for the time specified in your order. You can register a domain name for one year or up to ten years. Be aware, however, if you don't renew the domain name when your registration period ends, you lose it — and most often, you lose it right away to someone who preys on abandoned or expired domain names. Some people keep a close watch on expiring domain names, and as soon as the buying window opens, they snap the names up and start using them for their own websites, in the hope of taking full advantage of the popularity that the previous owners worked so hard to attain for those domains.

I emphasize *unique* because no two domain names can be the same. If someone else has registered the domain name you want, you can't have it. With that in mind, it sometimes takes a bit of time to find a domain that isn't already in use.

Understanding domain name extensions

When registering a domain name, be aware of the *extension* that you want. The .com, .net, .org, .info, or .biz extension that you see tagged on to the end of any domain name is the *top-level domain extension*. When you register your domain name, you're asked to choose the extension you want for your domain (as long as it's available, that is).

A word to the wise here: Just because you registered your domain as a .com doesn't mean that someone else doesn't, or can't, own the very same domain name with a .net. Therefore, if you register MyDogHasFleas.com, and the site becomes hugely popular among readers with dogs that have fleas, someone else can come along, register MyDogHasFleas.net, and run a similar site to yours in the hope of riding the coattails of your website's popularity and readership.

If you want to avert this problem, you can register your domain name with all available extensions. My business website, for example, has the domain name EWebscapes.com; however, I also own EWebscapes.net, EWebscapes.biz, and EWebscapes.info.

Considering the cost of a domain name

Registering a domain costs you anywhere from $3 to $30 per year, depending on what service you use for a registrar and what options (such as privacy options and search engine submission services) you apply to your domain name during the registration process.

When you pay the domain registration fee today, you need to pay another registration fee when the renewal date comes up again in a year, or two, or five — however many years you chose to register your domain name for. (See the nearby "Domain names: Do you own or rent?" sidebar.) Most registrars give you the option of signing up for a service called Auto Renew to automatically renew your domain name and bill the charges to the credit card you set up on that account. The registrar sends you a reminder a few months in advance, telling you it's time to renew. If you don't have Auto Renew set up, you need to log in to your registrar account before it expires and manually renew your domain name.

When choosing a domain name for your website, you may find that the domain name you want isn't available. You know if it's available when you search for it at the domain registrar's website (listed in the next section). Have some backup domain names prepared just in case the one you want isn't available. For example, if your chosen domain name is `cutepuppies.com`, but it's not available, you could have some variations of the domain ready to use, such as `cute-puppies.com` (notice the dash) or `mycutepuppies.com`, or `reallycutepuppies.com`.

Registering your domain name

Domain registrars are certified and approved by the Internet Corporation for Assigned Names and Numbers (ICANN). Although hundreds of domain registrars exist, the ones in the following list are popular because of their longevity in the industry, competitive pricing, and the variety of services they offer in addition to domain name registration (such as web hosting and website traffic builders):

✦ **Go Daddy:** `www.godaddy.com`

✦ **Register.com:** `www.register.com`

✦ **Network Solutions:** `www.networksolutions.com`

✦ **NamesDirect:** `http://namesdirect.com`

No matter where you choose to register your domain name, here are the steps you can take to accomplish this task:

1. **Decide on a domain name.**

A little planning and forethought are necessary here. Many people think of a domain name as a *brand* — a way of identifying their websites or blogs. Think of potential names for your site and then proceed with your plan.

2. **Verify the domain name's availability.**

In your web browser, enter the URL of the domain registrar of your choice. Look for the section on the registrar's website that lets you enter the domain name (typically, a short text field) to see whether it's available. If the domain name isn't available as a `.com`, try `.net` or `.info`.

3. **Purchase the domain name.**

   Follow the domain registrar's steps to purchase the name, using your credit card. After you complete the checkout process, you receive an e-mail confirming your purchase, so be sure to use a valid e-mail address during the registration process.

The next step is obtaining a hosting account, which the next section covers.

Some of the domain registrars have hosting services that you can sign up for, but you don't have to use those services. Often, you can find hosting services for a lower cost than most domain registrars offer. It just takes a little research.

Finding a Home for Your Blog

After you register your domain, you need to find a place for it to live — a web host. Web hosting is the second piece of the puzzle that you need to complete before you begin working with WordPress.org.

A *web host* is a business, a group, or an individual that provides web server space and bandwidth for file transfer to website owners who don't have it. Usually, web hosting services charge a monthly or an annual fee — unless you're fortunate enough to know someone who's willing to give you server space and bandwidth free. The cost varies from host to host, but you can obtain quality web hosting services for $3 to $10 per month to start.

When discussing web hosting considerations, it is important to understand where your hosting account ends and WordPress begins. Support for the WordPress software may or may not be included in your hosting package.

Some web hosts consider WordPress to be a *third-party application*. This means that the host typically won't provide technical support on the use of WordPress (or any other software application) because software support generally isn't included in your hosting package. The web host supports your hosting account but, typically, doesn't support the software you choose to install.

On the other hand, if your web host supports the software on your account, it comes at a cost: You have to pay for that extra support. To find whether your chosen host supports WordPress, ask first. If your host doesn't offer software support, you can still find WordPress support in the support forums at `http://wordpress.org/support`, as shown in Figure 1-1.

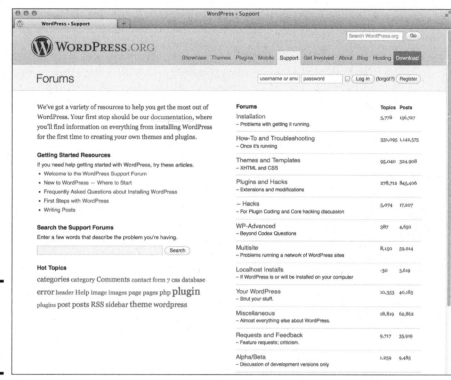

**Book II
Chapter 1**

**Understanding
the System
Requirements**

Figure 1-1:
The
WordPress
support
forums.

Several web hosting providers also have WordPress-related services available for additional fees. These services can include technical support, plugin installation and configuration, and theme design.

Generally, hosting services provide (at least) these services with your account:

✦ Hard drive space

✦ Bandwidth (transfer)

✦ Domain e-mail with web mail access

✦ File Transfer Protocol (FTP) access

✦ Comprehensive website statistics

✦ MySQL database(s)

✦ PHP

Because you intend to run WordPress on your web server, you need to look for a host that provides the *minimum* requirements needed to run the software on your hosting account, which are

✦ PHP version 5.2.4 (or greater)

✦ MySQL version 5.0 (or greater)

You also want a host that provides daily backups of your site so that your content won't be lost in case something happens. Web hosting providers who offer daily backups as part of their services can save the day by restoring your site to its original form.

The easiest way to find whether a host meets the minimum requirement is to check the FAQ (Frequently Asked Questions) section of the host's website, if it has one. If not, find the contact information for the hosting company and fire off an e-mail requesting information on exactly what it supports. Any web host worth dealing with will answer your e-mail within a reasonable amount of time. (A response within 12–24 hours is a good barometer.)

If the technojargon confuses you — specifically, all that talk about PHP, MySQL, and FTP in this section — don't worry! Chapter 2 of this minibook gives you an in-depth look into what FTP is and how you will use it on your web server; Book II, Chapter 3 introduces you to the basics of PHP and MySQL. Become more comfortable with these topics because they're important when using WordPress.

Getting help with hosting WordPress

The popularity of WordPress has given birth to web services — including designers, consultants, and (yes) web hosts — that specialize in using WordPress.

Many web hosts offer a full array of WordPress features, such as an automatic WordPress installation included with your account, a library of WordPress themes, and a staff of support technicians who are very experienced in using WordPress.

Here is a list of some of those providers:

✦ **Pagely:** `http://page.ly`

✦ **WP Engine:** `http://wpengine.com` (shown in Figure 1-2)

✦ **ZippyKid:** `www.zippykid.com`

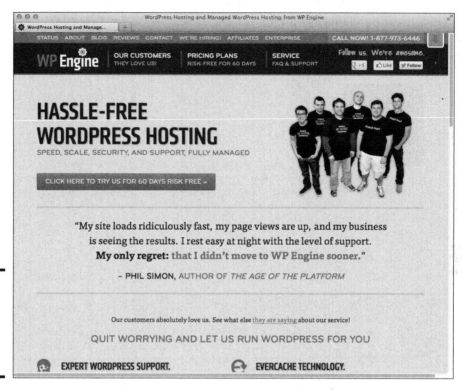

Figure 1-2:
The WP
Engine
WordPress
hosting
provider.

A few web hosting providers offer free domain name registration when you sign up for hosting services. Research this topic and read their terms of service because that free domain name may come with conditions. Many clients have gone this route, only to find out a few months later that the web hosting provider has full control of the domain name, and the client can't move that domain off the host's servers, either for a set period (usually, a year or two) or for infinity. You need control in *your* hands, not someone else's, so stick with an independent domain registrar, such as Network Solutions.

Dealing with disk space and bandwidth

Web hosting services provide two very important things with your account:

✦ **Disk space:** The amount of space you can access on the web servers' hard drive; generally measured in megabytes (MB) or gigabytes (GB).

✦ **Bandwidth transfer:** The amount of transfer your site can do per month; typically, traffic is measured in gigabytes (GB).

Think of your web host as a garage that you rent to park your car in. The garage gives you the place to store your car (disk space). It even gives you the driveway so that you, and others, can get to and from your car (bandwidth). It won't, however, fix your rockin' stereo system (WordPress or any other third-party software application) that you've installed — unless you're willing to pay a few extra bucks for that service.

 Most web hosting providers give you access to a hosting account manager that allows you to log in to your web hosting account to manage services. cPanel is perhaps the most popular management interface, but Plesk and NetAdmin are still widely used. These management interfaces give you access to your server logs, where you can view such things as bandwidth and hard disk usage. Get into a habit of checking those things occasionally to make sure that you stay informed about how much usage your site is using. Typically, I check monthly.

Managing disk space

Disk space is nothing more complicated than the hard drive on your own computer. Each hard drive has the capacity, or space, for a certain amount of files. An 80GB (gigabyte) hard drive can hold 80GB of data — no more. Your hosting account provides you a limited amount of disk space, and the same concept applies. If your web host provides you 10GB of disk space, that's the absolute limit you have. If you want more disk space, you need to upgrade your space limitations. Most web hosts have a mechanism in place for you to upgrade your allotment.

Starting with a self-hosted WordPress blog doesn't take much disk space at all. A good starting point for disk space is 3–5GB of storage space. If you find that you need additional space, contact your hosting provider for an upgrade.

Choosing the size of your bandwidth pipe

Bandwidth refers to the amount of data that is carried from point A to point B within a specific period (usually, only a second or two). I live out in the country — pretty much the middle of nowhere. The water that comes to my house is provided by a private well that lies buried in the backyard somewhere. Between my house and the well are pipes that bring the water to my house. The pipes provide a free flow of water to our home so that everyone else can enjoy long, hot showers while I labor over dishes and laundry, all at the same time. Lucky me!

The very same concept applies to the bandwidth available with your hosting account. Every web hosting provider offers a variety of bandwidth limits on the accounts it offers. When I want to view your website in my browser window, the bandwidth is essentially the pipe that lets your data flow from your "well" to my computer. The bandwidth limit is similar to the pipe connected to my well: It can hold only a certain amount of water before it reaches maximum capacity and won't bring the water from the well any longer. Your bandwidth pipe size is determined by how much bandwidth your web host allows for your account — the larger the number, the bigger the pipe. A 50MB bandwidth limit makes for a smaller pipe than a 100MB limit.

Web hosts are pretty generous with the amount of bandwidth they provide in their packages. Like disk space, bandwidth is measured in gigabytes (GB). Bandwidth provision of 10–50GB is generally a respectable amount to run a website with a blog.

In my experience, I've found that if your website exceeds its allowed bandwidth, the web host won't turn off your website or limit traffic; they'll continue to allow inbound web traffic to your site, but they'll bill you at the end of month for any bandwidth overages. Those charges can get pretty expensive, so if you find your website is consistently exceeding the bandwidth amount every month, contact your web host to find out if you can get an upgrade to allow for increased bandwidth.

Websites that run large files — such as video, audio, or photo files — generally benefit from higher disk space compared with sites that don't involve large files. Keep this point in mind when you're signing up for your hosting account. Planning now will save you a few headaches down the road.

Be wary of hosting providers that offer things like unlimited bandwidth, domains, and disk space. That is a great selling point, but what they don't tell you outright (you may have to look into the fine print of their agreement) is that although they may not put those kinds of limits on you, they will limit your site's CPU usage.

CPU stands for *central processing unit* and is the part of a computer (or web server in this case) that handles all the data-processing requests sent to your web servers whenever anyone visits your site. Although you may have unlimited bandwidth to handle a large amount of traffic, if a high spike in traffic increases your site's CPU usage, your host will throttle your site because it limits the CPU use.

What do I mean by *throttle*? I mean the host shuts down your site, turns it off. Not permanently, though; maybe for only a few minutes to an hour. The host does this to kill any connections to your web server causing the spike in CPU use. Your host eventually turns your site back on — but the inconvenience happens regularly with many clients across various hosting environments.

When looking into different web hosting providers, ask about their policies on CPU use and what they do to manage a spike in processing. It's better to know about it upfront than to find out about it after your site's been throttled.

Chapter 2: Using File Transfer Protocol

In This Chapter

✓ Discovering FTP

✓ Understanding file transfer

✓ Exploring easy-to-use FTP clients

✓ Making sense of FTP terminology

✓ Editing files by using FTP

✓ Changing file permissions

Throughout this entire book, you run into the term FTP. FTP (File Transfer Protocol) is a network protocol used to copy files from one host to another over the Internet. With FTP, you can perform various tasks, including uploading and downloading WordPress files, editing files, and changing permissions on files.

Read this chapter to familiarize yourself with FTP, understand what it is and how to use it, and discover some free, easy-to-use FTP clients or programs that make your life as a WordPress website owner much easier. If you run across sections in this book that ask you to perform certain tasks by using FTP, you can refer to this chapter to refresh your memory on how to do it, if needed.

Understanding FTP Concepts

This section introduces you to the basic elements of File Transfer Protocol (FTP). The ability to use FTP with your hosting account is a given for almost every web host on the market today. FTP offers ways of moving files from one place to another:

✦ **Uploading:** Transferring files from your local computer to your web server

✦ **Downloading:** Transferring files from your web server to your local computer

You can do several other things with FTP, including the following, which I discuss later in this chapter:

✦ **View files:** After you log in via FTP, you can see all the files that are located on your web server.

✦ **View Date Modified:** You can see the date a file was last modified, which can sometimes be helpful when trying to troubleshoot problems.

✦ **View file size:** You can see the size of each file on your web server, which is helpful if you need to manage the disk space on your account.

✦ **Edit files:** Almost all FTP clients allow you to open and edit files through the client interface, which is a convenient way to get the job done.

✦ **Change permissions:** Commonly referred to as CHMOD, the command that controls what type of read/write/execute permissions the files on your web server have.

FTP is a convenient utility that gives you access to the files located on your web server, which makes managing your WordPress website a bit easier.

SFTP (Secret File Transfer Protocol) is also a method of FTP. SFTP provides an additional layer of security as it uses SSH (Secure Shell) and encrypts sensitive information, data, and passwords from being clearly transferred within the hosting network. Encrypting the data ensures that anyone monitoring the network is not able to read the data freely — and therefore, cannot obtain information that should be secured, such as passwords and user-names. I highly recommend using SFTP over FTP if it is available with your hosting provider.

Setting Up FTP on Your Hosting Account

Many web hosts today offer FTP as part of their hosting packages, so just confirm that your hosting provider makes FTP available to you for your account. In Book II, Chapter 1, I mention the hosting account management interface called cPanel. cPanel is by far the most popular hosting account management software used by hosts on the web, eclipsing other popular tools, such as Plesk and NetAdmin. It's cPanel, or your hosting account management interface, that allows you to set up an FTP account for your website.

In this chapter, I use cPanel as the example. If your hosting provider gives you a different interface to work with, the concepts are still the same, but you'll need to refer to your hosting provider for the specifics to adapt these directions to your specific environment.

Mostly, the FTP for your hosting account is set up automatically. Figure 2-1 shows you the FTP Accounts page in cPanel — follow these steps to get to this page and set up your FTP account:

1. **Log in to the cPanel for your hosting account.**

Typically, you'll browse to `http://yourdomain.com/cpanel` to bring up the login screen for your cPanel. Enter your specific hosting account username and password in the login fields and click OK.

2. **Browse to the FTP Accounts page.**

Click the FTP Accounts link or icon in your cPanel to open the FTP Accounts page shown in Figure 2-1.

3. **View the existing FTP account.**

If your hosting provider automatically sets you up with an FTP account, you will see it listed in the Account Management section. Ninety-nine percent of the time, the default FTP account uses the same username and password combination as your hosting account or the login information you used to log in to your cPanel in Step 1.

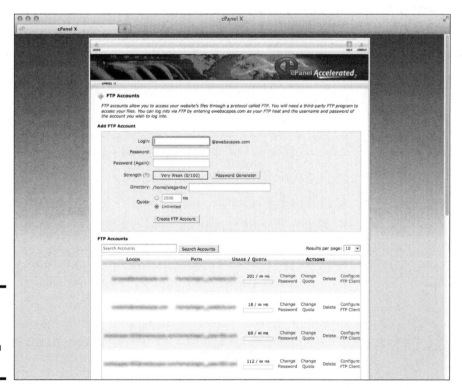

Figure 2-1: The FTP Accounts page within cPanel.

If the FTP Accounts page doesn't display a default FTP user in the Account Management section, you can create one easily in the Add FTP Account section:

1. **Type your desired username in the Login field.**

   This creates the username of *username@yourdomain*.com (where *username* is the desired username you typed and *yourdomain*.com is your specific domain name).

2. **Type your desired password in the Password field.**

   You can choose to type in your own password or click the Password Generator button to have the server generate a secure password for you. Retype the password in the Password (Again) field to validate it.

3. **Check the Strength indicator.**

   The server tells you if your password is Very Weak, Weak, Good, Strong, or Very Strong. (Refer to Figure 2-1.) You want to have a very strong password for your FTP account that's very hard for hackers and malicious Internet users to guess and crack.

4. **(Optional) Type the directory access for this FTP user.**

   Leaving this field blank gives this new FTP user access to the root level of your hosting account, which, as the site owner, you want. So leave this field blank. (In the future, if you set up FTP accounts for other users, you can lock down their access to your hosting directory by indicating which directory the FTP user has access to.)

5. **Indicate the space limitations in the Quota field.**

   Because you're the site owner, leave the radio button selection set to Unlimited. (In the future, if you add a new FTP user, you can limit the amount of space, in megabytes [MB], by selecting the radio button to the left of the text field and typing the numeric amount in the text box; for example, 50MB.)

6. **Click the Create FTP Account button.**

   A new screen with a message that the account was created successfully appears. Additionally, the settings for this new FTP account appear, which you should copy and paste into a blank text editor window (such as Notepad for PC, or TextMate for Mac users). The settings for the FTP account are the connection details you need to connect to your web server via FTP.

7. **Save the following settings:**

   FTP Username, Password, and FTP Server are specific to your domain and the information you entered in the preceding steps.

- FTP Username: *username@yourdomain*.com
- Password: *yourpassword*
- FTP Server: ftp.*yourdomain*.com
- FTP Server Port: 21
- Quota: Unlimited MB

Ninety-nine point nine percent of the time, the FTP Server Port will be 21. Be sure to double-check your FTP settings to make sure that this is the case.

At any time, you can revisit the FTP Accounts page to delete the FTP accounts you've created, change the quota, change the password, and find the connection details specific to that account.

Finding and Using Free and Easy FTP Programs

FTP programs are referred to as FTP *clients* or FTP *client software*. Whatever you decide to call it, an FTP client is software that you use to connect to your web server to view, open, edit, and transfer files to and from your web server.

Using FTP to transfer files requires an FTP client. Many FTP clients are available for download. Here are some good (and free) ones:

✦ **SmartFTP (PC):** www.smartftp.com/download

✦ **FileZilla (PC or Mac):** http://sourceforge.net/projects/filezilla

✦ **Cyberduck (PC or Mac):** http://cyberduck.ch

✦ **FTP Explorer (PC):** www.ftpx.com

In Book II, Chapter 1, you discover how to obtain a hosting account, and in the previous section of this chapter, you discover how to create an FTP account on your web server. By following the steps in the previous section, you also have the FTP username, password, server, and port information you need to connect your FTP client to your web server so you can begin transferring files. In the next section, you discover how to connect to your web hosting account via FTP.

Connecting to the web server via FTP

For the purposes of this chapter, I use the FileZilla FTP client (http://sourceforge.net/projects/filezilla) because it's very easy to use, and the cost is free ninety-nine (that's open source geek-speak for free!).

Figure 2-2 shows a FileZilla client that's not connected to a server. By default, the left side of the window displays a directory of files and folders on the local computer.

The right side of the window displays content when the FileZilla client is connected to a web server; specifically, it shows directories of the web server's folders and files.

If you use a different FTP client software than FileZilla, the steps and look of the software will differ, and you will need to adapt your steps and practice for the specific FTP client software you're using.

Connecting to a web server is an easy process. Remember the FTP settings you saved from Step 7 in the previous section? As a reminder, here they are again (these are also the same settings you'll see in your cPanel FTP Settings page if your FTP was set up automatically for you):

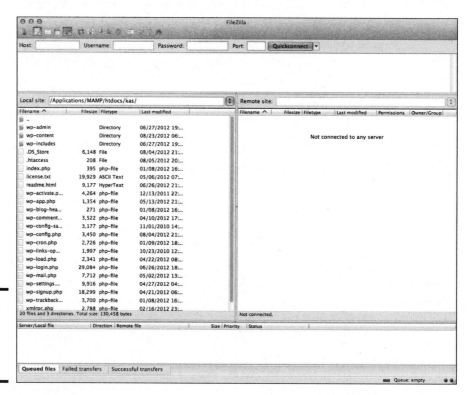

Figure 2-2:
Mozilla
FileZilla
FTP client
software.

FTP Username: *username@yourdomain*.com

Password: *yourpassword*

FTP Server: ftp.*yourdomain*.com

FTP Server Port: 21

Quota: Unlimited MB

This is where you need that information. To connect to your web server via the FileZilla FTP client, follow these few steps:

1. **Open the FTP client software on your local computer.**

Locate the program on your computer and click (or double-click) the program icon to launch the program.

2. **Choose File⇨Site Manager to open the Site Manager utility.**

The Site Manger utility appears, as shown in Figure 2-3.

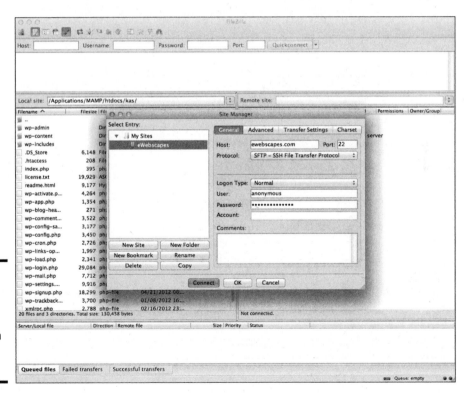

Figure 2-3:
The Site Manager utility in the FileZilla FTP client software.

3. **Click the New Site button.**

4. **Type a name for your site that helps you identify the site.**

   This site name can be anything you want it to be because it isn't part of the connection data you add in the next steps. (In Figure 2-4, you see My Site — original, I know.)

5. **Enter the FTP server in the Host field.**

   Host is the same as the FTP server information provided to you when you set up the FTP account on your web server. In the example, the FTP server is ftp.*yourdomain*.com, so that's entered in the Host field, as shown in Figure 2-4.

6. **Enter the FTP port in the Port field.**

   Typically, in most hosting environments, FTP uses port 21, and this never changes. However, double-check your port number and enter it in the Port field, as shown in Figure 2-4.

7. **Select the server type.**

   FileZilla asks you to select a server type (as do most FTP clients). Choose FTP - File Transfer Protocol from the Protocol drop-down menu, as shown in Figure 2-4.

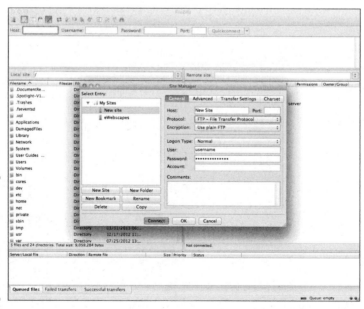

Figure 2-4:
FileZilla Site Manager utility with FTP account information filled in.

8. **Select the logon type.**

   FileZilla gives you several different logon types to choose from (as do most FTP clients). Choose Normal from the Logon Type drop-down menu.

9. **Enter your username in the Username field.**

   This is the username given to you in the FTP settings.

10. **Type your password in the Password field.**

    This is the password given to you in the FTP settings.

11. **Click the Connect button.**

    This step connects your computer to your web server. The directory of folders and files from your local computer display on the left side of the FileZilla FTP client window, and the directory of folders and files on your web server display on the right side, as shown in Figure 2-5.

    Now you can take advantage of all the tools and features FTP has to offer you!

Transferring files from point A to point B

Now that your local computer is connected to your web server, transferring files between the two couldn't be easier. Within the FTP client software, you can browse the directories and folders on your local computer on the left side and browse the directories and folders on your web server on the right side.

**Book II
Chapter 2**

Using File Transfer Protocol

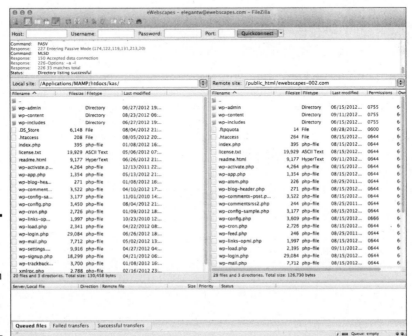

Figure 2-5: FileZilla displays local files on the left and server files on the right.

FTP clients make it easy to transfer files from your computer to your hosting account by using a drag-and-drop method. Two methods of transferring files are

✦ **Uploading:** Generally, transferring files from your local computer to your web server. To upload a file from your computer to your web server, click the file you want to transfer from your local computer and drag and drop it onto the right side (the web server side).

✦ **Downloading:** Transferring files from your web server to your local computer. To download a file from your web server to your local computer, click the file you want to transfer from your web server and drag and drop it onto to the left side (the local computer side).

Downloading files from your web server is a very efficient, easy, and smart way of backing up files to your local computer. It's always a good idea to keep your files safe, especially things like theme files and plugins, which Books VI and VII cover.

Editing files by using FTP

You will run into situations where you need to edit certain files that live on your web server. You can use the methods described in the preceding section to download a file, open it, edit it, save it, and then upload it back to your web server. That is one way to do it. Another way is to use the built-in edit feature that exists in most FTP client software, by following these steps:

1. **Connect the FTP client to your web server.**

2. **Locate the file you want to edit.**

3. **Open the file by using the internal FTP editor.**

Right-click the file with your mouse and choose View/Edit. (Remember I'm using FileZilla; your FTP client may use different labels, such as Open or Edit.) FileZilla, like most FTP clients, uses a program (such as Notepad for a PC or TextMate for Mac) designated for text editing that already exists on your computer. In some rare cases, your FTP client software may have its own internal text editor.

4. **Edit the file to your liking.**

5. **Save the changes you made to the file.**

Click the Save icon or choose File➪Save.

6. **Upload the file to your web server.**

After you save the file, FileZilla alerts you that the file has changed and asks whether you want to upload the file to the server. Click the Yes button; the newly edited file replaces the old one.

That's all there is to it. Use the FTP edit feature to edit, save, and upload files as you need to.

When you edit files by using the FTP edit feature, you're editing files in a "live" environment, meaning that when you save the changes and upload the file, the changes take effect immediately and affect your live website. For this reason, I strongly recommend downloading a copy of the original file to your local computer before making changes. That way, if you happen to make a typo on the saved file and your website goes haywire, you have a copy of the original to upload to restore it to its original state.

Changing file permissions

Every file and folder on your web server has a set of assigned attributions, called *permissions,* that tells the web server three things about the folder or file. On a very simplistic level, these permissions include:

✦ **Read:** This setting determines whether the file/folder is readable by the web server.

✦ **Write:** This setting determines whether the file/folder is writable by the web server.

✦ **Execute:** This setting determines whether the file/folder is executable by the web server.

Each set of permissions has a numeric code assigned to it, identifying what type of permissions are assigned to that file or folder. There are a lot of them, so here are the most common ones that you run into when running a WordPress website:

✦ **644:** Files with permissions set to 644 are readable by everyone and writable only by the file/folder owner.

✦ **755:** Files with permissions set to 755 are readable and executable by everyone, but they're writable only by the file/folder owner.

✦ **777:** Files with permissions set to 777 are readable, writable, and executable by everyone. For security reasons, you should not use this set of permissions on your web server unless absolutely necessary.

Typically, folders and files within your web server are assigned permissions of either 644 or 755. Usually, you'll see PHP files, or files that end with the .php extension, with permissions set to 644 if the web server is configured to use PHP Safe Mode.

This is a very basic look at file permissions because, usually, you will not need to mess with file permissions on your web server. In case you do need to dig further, you can find a great reference on file permissions from Elated. com at www.elated.com/articles/understanding-permissions.

You may run across a situation where you're asked to edit and change the file permissions on a particular file on your web server. With WordPress sites, this usually happens when dealing with plugins or theme files that require files or folders to be writable by the web server. This practice is referred to as *CHMOD*, an acronym for Change Mode. When someone says, "You need to CHMOD that file to 755," you'll know what they are talking about.

Here are some easy steps for using your FTP program to CHMOD a file, or edit its permissions on your web server:

1. **Connect the FTP client to your web server.**

2. **Locate the file you want to CHMOD.**

3. **Open the file attributes for the file.**

   Right-click the file on your web server and choose File Permissions. (Your FTP client, if not FileZilla, may use different terminology.)

   The Change File Attributes window appears, as shown in Figure 2-6.

4. **Type the correct file permissions number in the Numeric Value field.**

   This is the number assigned to the permissions you want to give the file. Most often, the plugin or theme developer tells you which permissions number to assign to the file or folder; typically, it will be either 644 or 755. (The permissions in Figure 2-6 are assigned the value of 644.)

5. **Click OK to save the file.**

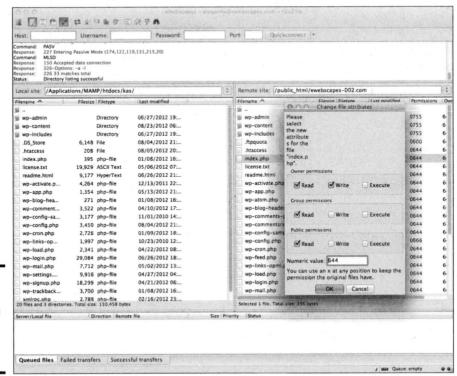

Figure 2-6:
The
Change File
Attributes
window in
FileZilla.

Chapter 3: Getting to Know PHP and MySQL

*I*n Book VI, you dig into the code necessary to create functions and features on your website. Many, if not all, of these functions and features use PHP Hypertext Preprocessor (PHP) tags. When combined with the WordPress code, these tags make things happen (such as displaying post content, categories, archives, links, and more) on your website.

One of the reasons WordPress is the most popular content management system (CMS) is that you don't need to know PHP code to use it. That's to say, you can use WordPress easily without ever looking at any of the code or template files contained within it. However, if you want to tweak the settings of your WordPress theme (flip to Book VI) or the code of a particular plugin (see Book VII), you need to understand some basics of how PHP works. But don't worry; you don't need to be a PHP programmer.

This chapter introduces you to the very basics of PHP and *MySQL,* which is the database system that stores your WordPress data. After you read this chapter, you'll understand how PHP and MySQL work together with the WordPress platform to serve up your website in visitors' browsers.

This book doesn't turn you into a PHP programmer or MySQL database administrator, but it gives you a glimpse of how PHP and MySQL work together to help WordPress build your website. If you're interested in finding out how to program PHP or become a MySQL database administrator, check out *PHP & MySQL For Dummies* by Janet Valade.

Understanding How PHP and MySQL Work Together

WordPress uses a PHP/MySQL platform, which provides everything you need to create your own blog and publish your own content dynamically, without knowing how to program those pages. In short, all your content is stored in a MySQL database in your hosting account.

PHP is a server-side scripting language for creating dynamic web pages. When a visitor opens a page built in PHP, the server processes the PHP commands and then sends the results to the visitor's browser. *MySQL* is an open source relational database management system (RDBMS) that uses *Structured Query Language* (SQL), the most popular language for adding, accessing, and processing data in a database. If that all sounds like Greek to you, just think of MySQL as a big file cabinet where all the content on your blog is stored.

Every time a visitor goes to your blog to read your content, he makes a request that's sent to a host server. The PHP programming language receives that request, makes a call to the MySQL database, obtains the requested information from the database, and then presents the requested information to your visitor through his web browser.

Here *content* refers to the data stored in the MySQL database; that is, your blog posts, pages, comments, links, and options that you set up on the WordPress Dashboard. However, the *theme* (or design) you choose to use for your blog — whether it's the default theme, one you create, or one you have custom designed — isn't part of the content in this case. Theme files are part of the file system and aren't stored in the database. Therefore, it's a good idea to create and keep a backup of any theme files that you're currently using. See Book VI for further information on WordPress theme management.

Make sure your web host backs up your site daily so that your content (data) won't be lost in case something happens. Web hosting providers who offer daily backups as part of their services can save the day by restoring your site to its original form. Additionally, Book II, Chapter 5 covers important information about backing up your website.

Exploring PHP Basics

WordPress requires PHP in order to work; therefore, your web hosting provider must have PHP enabled on your web server. If you already have WordPress up and running on your website, you know PHP is running and working just fine. Currently, the PHP version required for WordPress is version 5.2.4 or later.

Before you play around with template tags (covered in Book VI) in your WordPress templates or plugin functions, you need to understand what makes up a template tag and why, as well as the correct syntax, or function, for a template tag as it relates to PHP. Additionally, have a look at the WordPress files contained within the download files. Many of the files end with the .php file extension — an extension required for PHP files, which separates them from other file types, such as JavaScript (.js) or CSS (.css).

As I state earlier, WordPress is based in *PHP* (a scripting language for creating web pages) and uses PHP commands to pull information from the MySQL database. Every tag begins with the function to start PHP and ends with a function to stop it. In the middle of those two commands lives the request to the database that tells WordPress to grab the data and display it.

A typical template tag, or function, looks like this:

```
<?php get_info(); ?>
```

This example tells WordPress to do three things:

+ **Start PHP:** <?php
+ **Use PHP to get information from the MySQL database and deliver it to your blog:** get_info();
+ **Stop PHP:** ?>

In this case, get_info() represents the tag function, which grabs information from the database to deliver it to your blog. The information retrieved depends on what tag function appears between the two PHP commands.

Every PHP command you start requires a stop command. For every <?php, you must include the closing ?> command somewhere later in the code. PHP commands structured improperly cause ugly errors on your site, and they've been known to send programmers, developers, and hosting providers into loud screaming fits. You find a lot of starting and stopping of PHP throughout the WordPress templates and functions. The process seems as though it would be resource intensive, if not exhaustive, but it really isn't.

Always, always make sure that the PHP start and stop commands are separated from the function with a single space. You must have a space after <?php and a space before ?> — if not, the PHP function code doesn't work. So make sure that the code looks like this: <?php get_info(); ?> — not like this: <?phpget_info();?>

Trying Out a Little PHP

To test some PHP code, follow these steps to create a simple HTML web page with an embedded PHP function:

1. **Open a new, blank file in your default text editor — Notepad (Windows) or TextMate (Mac) — type** <html>, **and then press Enter.**

The <html> tag tells the web browser that this is an HTML document and should be read as a web page.

2. **Type** <head> **and then press Enter.**

The <head> HTML tag contains elements that tell the web browser about the document; this information is read by the browser but hidden from the web page visitor.

3. **Type** <title>This is a Simple PHP Page</title> **and then press Enter.**

The <title> HTML tag tells the browser to display the text between two tags as the title of the document in the browser title bar. (*Note:* All HTML tags need to be opened and then closed, just like PHP tags that I describe in the preceding section. In this case the <title> tag opens the command, and the </title> tag closes it and tells the web browser that you're finished dealing with the title.)

4. **Type** </head> **to close the** <head> **tag from Step 2 and then press Enter.**

5. **Type** <body> **to define the body of the web page and then press Enter.**

Anything that appears after this tag displays in the web browser window.

6. **Type** <?php **to tell the web browser to start a PHP function and then press the spacebar.**

See the preceding section on starting and stopping PHP functions.

7. **Type** echo '<p>Testing my new PHP function</p>'; **and then press the spacebar.**

This is the function that you want PHP to execute on your web page. This particular function echoes the text "Testing my new PHP function" and displays it on your website.

8. **Type** ?> **to tell the web browser to end the PHP function and then press Enter.**

9. **Type** </body> **to close the** <body> **HTML tag from Step 5 and then press Enter.**

This tells the web browser that you're done with the body of the web page.

10. **Type** </html> **to close the** <html> **tag from Step 1 and then press Enter.**

This tells the web browser that you're at the end of the HTML document.

When you're done with Steps 1–10, double-check that the code in your text editor looks like this:

```
<html>
<head>
<title>This is a Simple PHP Page</title>
    </head>
    <body>
    <?php echo '<p>Testing my new PHP function</p>'; ?>
    </body>
    </html>
```

After you write your code, follow these steps to save and upload your file:

1. **Save the file to your local computer as `testing.php`.**

2. **Upload the `testing.php` file.**

Via File Transfer Protocol, upload `testing.php` to the root directory of your web server. If you need a review on how to use FTP to transfer files to your web server, look through the information presented in Book II, Chapter 2.

3. **Open a web browser and type the address (**http://*yourdomain*.com/testing.php**) in the web browser's address bar (where *yourdomain* is your actual domain name).**

A single line of text displays: `Testing my new PHP function`, as shown in Figure 3-1.

If the `testing.php` file displays correctly in your browser, congratulations! You programmed PHP to work in a web browser!

If the `testing.php` file doesn't display correctly in your browser, a PHP error message gives you an indication of the errors in your code. (Usually included with the error message is the line number where the error exists in the file.)

Figure 3-1:
A basic PHP page in a browser window.

Managing Your MySQL Database

Many new WordPress users are intimidated by the MySQL database, perhaps because it seems to be way above their technical skills or abilities. Truth be told, regular users of WordPress — those who just use it to publish content — don't really ever have to dig into the database unless they want to. You need to explore the database only if you're dealing with theme or plugin development, or if you're contributing code to the WordPress project. This section gives you a basic overview of the WordPress database stored in MySQL so that you have an understanding of the structure and know where items are stored.

Currently, WordPress requires MySQL version 5.0 (or greater) in order to work correctly. If your web hosting provider doesn't have 5.0 (or greater) installed on your web server, kindly ask to upgrade.

After WordPress is installed on your server (which I discuss in Chapter 4 of this minibook), the database gets populated with 11 tables that exist to store different types of data from your WordPress blog. Figure 3-2 displays the structure of the tables, as follows:

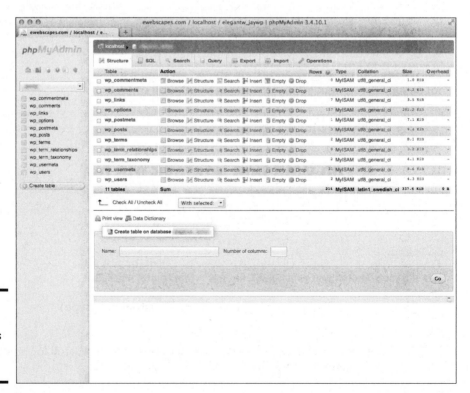

Figure 3-2:
The WordPress database structure.

✦ wp_commentmeta: This table stores every comment published to your site and contains information, or *metadata,* that includes

- A unique comment ID number

- A comment meta key, meta value, and meta ID (unique numerical identifiers assigned to each comment left by you, or visitors, on your site)

✦ wp_comments: This table stores the body of the comments published to your site, including

- A post ID that specifies which post the comment belongs to

- The comment content

- The comment author's name, URL, IP address, and e-mail address

- The comment date (day, month, year, and time)

- The comment status (approved, unapproved, or spam)

✦ wp_links: This stores the name, URL, and description of all links you create by using the WordPress Link Manager. It also stores all the advanced options for the links you created, if any.

✦ wp_options: This stores all the option settings that you set for WordPress after you install it, including all theme and plugin option settings.

✦ wp_postmeta: This includes all posts or pages published to your site and contains metadata that includes

- The unique post ID number. (Each blog post has a unique ID number to set it apart from the others.)

- The post meta key, meta value (unique numerical identifiers for each post created on your site), and any custom fields you've created for the post.

✦ wp_posts: This table features the body of any post or page you've published to your blog, including autosaved revisions and post option settings, such as

- The post author, date, and time

- The post title, content, and excerpt

- The post status (published, draft, or private)

- The post comment status (open or closed)

- The post type (page, post, or custom post type)

- The post comment count

✦ wp_terms: This stores the categories you've created for posts and links as well as tags that have been created for your posts.

✦ `wp_term_relationships`: This stores the relationships among the posts as well as the categories and tags that have been assigned to them.

✦ `wp_term_taxonomies`: WordPress has three types of taxonomies by default: category, link, and tag. This table stores the taxonomy associated for the terms stored in the `wp_terms` table.

✦ `wp_usermeta`: This table features metadata from every user with an account on your WordPress website. This metadata includes

- A unique user ID

- A user meta key, meta value, and meta ID, which are unique identifiers for users on your site

✦ `wp_users`: The list of users with an account on your WordPress website is maintained within this table and includes

- The username, first name, last name, and nickname

- The user login

- The user password

- The user e-mail

- The registration date

- The user status and role (subscriber, contributor, author, editor, or administrator)

Most web hosting providers give you a *utility,* or an interface, to view your MySQL database, and the most common one is phpMyAdmin (as shown in Figure 3-2). If you're unsure how you can view your database on your hosting account, get in touch with your hosting provider to find out.

When the multisite feature in WordPress is activated (check out Book VIII for information about the multisite feature), WordPress adds six additional tables in the database:

✦ `wp_blogs`: This table stores information about each blog created in your network, including

- A unique blog numerical ID

- A unique site ID number (determines the ID of the site the blog belongs to)

- The blog domain

- The blog server path

- The date the blog was registered

- The date the blog was updated

- The blog status (public, private, archived, spam; see Book VIII for more information on blog status)

✦ `wp_blog_versions`: This table stores general information about each network blog ID, database version, and date of last update.

✦ `wp_registration_log`: This table stores information about registered users, including

- Unique user numerical ID

- User e-mail address

- User IP address

- User Blog ID

- The date the user registered

✦ `wp_signups`: This table stores information about user sign-ups, including all the information from the `wp_registration_log` table, the date the user account was activated, and the unique activation key the user accessed during the sign-up process.

✦ `wp_site`: This table stores information about your main installation site, including the site ID, domain, and server path.

✦ `wp_sitemeta`: This table stores all the information about the multisite configurations set after you install the multisite feature. See Book VIII.

Chapter 4: Installing WordPress on Your Web Server

In This Chapter

✔ **Installing WordPress via Fantastico**

✔ **Manually installing WordPress**

✔ **Running installation scripts**

This chapter takes you through two installation methods for WordPress — an automatic, one-click installation with the Fantastico script installer, which is available from your web hosting provider, and a manual installation.

I also show you how to set up a MySQL database by using the cPanel web hosting management interface. By the time you're done reading this chapter, you'll be logged in to and looking at your brand-spanking-new WordPress Dashboard, ready to start publishing content right away. (If you already have WordPress installed, go ahead and skip to Chapter 5 in this minibook, which contains great information about configuring WordPress for optimum performance and security.)

Before you can install WordPress, you need to complete the following tasks:

✦ Purchase the domain name registration for your account (Chapter 1 of this minibook).

✦ Obtain a hosting service on a web server for your blog (Chapter 1 of this minibook).

✦ Establish your hosting account username, password, and File Transfer Protocol (FTP) address (Chapters 1 and 2 of this minibook).

✦ Acquire an FTP client for transferring files to your hosting account (Chapter 2 of this minibook).

If you omitted any of the preceding items, flip to the chapter listed to complete the step.

Installing WordPress with Fantastico

Fantastico is a very popular script installer that several web hosting providers make available to their clients. Fantastico contains different types of scripts and programs that you can install on your hosting account, notably, the WordPress software.

You can use Fantastico if your web host meets these two requirements:

✦ Your hosting provider has Fantastico available for your use.

✦ Your hosting account has the cPanel account management interface.

 If your hosting provider doesn't give you access to an installation script, such as Fantastico, skip to the next section in this chapter for the steps to install WordPress manually, via FTP.

Follow these steps to install WordPress with Fantastico:

1. **Log in to the cPanel for your hosting account:**

   a. *Browse to* http://yourdomain.com/cpanel *(where* yourdomain. com *is your actual domain name) to bring up the cPanel login screen.*

   b. *Enter your specific hosting account username and password in the login fields and then click OK. The page refreshes and displays the cPanel for your account.*

2. **Click the Fantastico icon.**

   The Fantastico page loads in your browser window and displays a list of available scripts on the left side of the page, as shown in Figure 4-1.

3. **Click the WordPress link in the Blogs heading.**

   The WordPress page loads, displaying a short description of WordPress and the version that's available with Fantastico. (See Figure 4-2.)

 Fantastico is a third-party script that exists as an add-on to cPanel. Web hosts subscribe to Fantastico and add it to your cPanel as an extra service for you to take advantage of; however, web hosting providers are completely dependent upon the makers of Fantastico as to what scripts and script versions are available. Fantastico is usually about a month or so behind the game when updating the programs in its script installer.

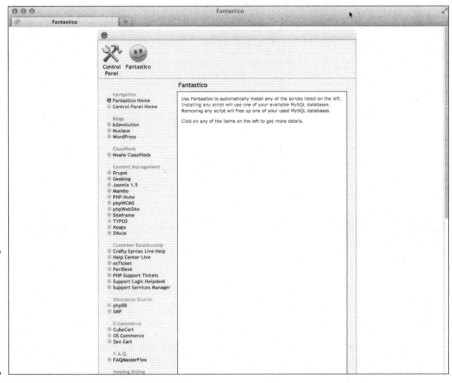

Book II
Chapter 4

Installing
WordPress on Your
Web Server

Figure 4-1:
The
Fantastico
script
installer
page within
cPanel.

4. **Click the New Installation link.**

   The Install WordPress (1/3) page, shown in Figure 4-3, appears.

5. **Select the WordPress installation location by selecting the domain you want to install WordPress on from the Install on Domain drop-down list.**

6. **Type the directory name for installation in the Install in Directory text field.**

   Leave this text field empty to install WordPress in the root directory (`http://yourdomain.com`), or enter the name of the directory you want to install WordPress into, such as `http://yourdomain.com/wordpress`. If you type in this text field, the directory should *not* exist on your web server; if it does, Fantastico tells you that WordPress can't be installed.

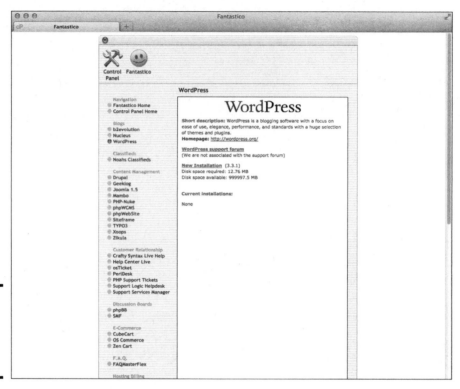

Figure 4-2:
The
WordPress
page in
Fantastico.

7. **Provide the Admin Access Data info by typing the desired username in the Administrator Username text field and then typing your desired password in the Password text field.**

   These two items are the username and password for the WordPress administrator, and you use them to log in to the WordPress Dashboard after it's installed. (See Book III, Chapter 1.)

8. **Provide the Base Configuration info for WordPress.**

   The information you enter in this section can be changed later in the general settings of the WordPress Dashboard (after it's installed and you've logged in). Enter the info as follows:

   a. *Type your desired nickname in the Admin Nickname text field.*

      This name displays on your website after you start publishing to your WordPress blog.

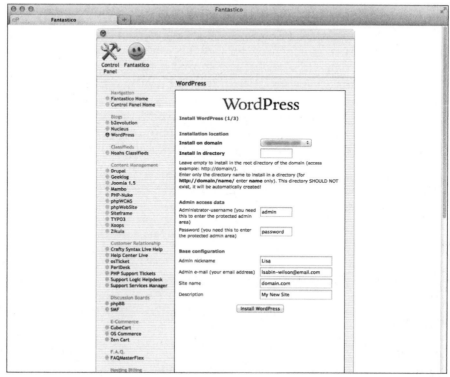

Book II
Chapter 4

Installing
WordPress on Your
Web Server

Figure 4-3:
WordPress
access and
administrator
data in
Fantastico.

   b. *Type your e-mail address in the Admin E-Mail text field.*

     This e-mail address is used for your administrator user account in
     WordPress after it's installed on your web server in Step 9.

   c. *Type your site name in the Site Name text field.*

     The site name displays on your site and can be changed later, if you
     want.

   d. *Type a short description of your site in the Description text field.*

     The description displays on your site and can be changed later, if
     you want.

9. **Click the Install WordPress button.**

The Install WordPress (2/3) page displays with several messages. The
Fantastico script installer creates the MySQL database for you and displays the name of the database. This page also displays a confirmation
message about the domain and directory that WordPress is installed into.

10. **Click the Finish Installation button.**

    The page refreshes in your browser and Fantastico displays a message confirming the success of the WordPress installation and displays the login URL, username, and password.

    If you enter your own e-mail address in the Email the Details of This Installation To text field and then click the Send E-mail button, the URL, username, and password are sent to your inbox for safe storage. (This is an optional feature, but I strongly recommend doing this in case your browser crashes and you lose the information.)

Your WordPress installation via Fantastico is complete, and you're ready to start using WordPress on your web server. If you installed WordPress by using the Fantastico method and don't want to review the steps to install WordPress manually, flip to Chapter 5 in this minibook to optimize your WordPress installation for performance and security.

Installing WordPress Manually

If you install WordPress manually, here's where the rubber meets the road — that is, you're putting WordPress's famous five-minute installation to the test. Set your watch and see whether you can meet that deadline.

The famous five-minute installation includes only the time it takes to install the software. This doesn't include the time to register a domain name; the time to obtain and set up your web hosting service; or the time to download, install, configure, and figure out how to use the FTP software.

Setting up the MySQL database

The WordPress software is a personal publishing system that uses a PHP/MySQL platform, which provides everything you need to create your own blog and publish your own content dynamically without knowing how to program those pages. In short, all your content (options, posts, comments, and other pertinent data) is stored in a MySQL database in your hosting account.

Every time visitors go to your blog to read your content, they make a request that's sent to your server. The PHP programming language receives that request, obtains the requested information from the MySQL database, and then presents the requested information to your visitors through their web browsers.

Every web host is different in how it gives you access to set up and manage your MySQL database(s) for your account. In this section, I use cPanel, the popular hosting interface. If your host provides a different interface, the same basic steps apply; however, the setup in the interface that your web host provides may be different.

To set up the MySQL database for your WordPress site with cPanel, follow these steps:

1. **Log in to the cPanel for your hosting account:**

    a. *Browse to* `http://yourdomain.com/cpanel` *(where* yourdomain. com *is your actual domain name) to bring up the login screen for your cPanel.*

    b. *Enter your specific hosting account username and password in the login fields, and then click OK.*

    The page refreshes and displays the cPanel for your account.

2. **Locate the MySQL Databases icon.**

    Click the MySQL Databases icon to load the MySQL Databases page in your cPanel.

3. **Enter a name for your database in the Name text box.**

    Be sure to make note of the database name because you need it to install WordPress.

4. **Click the Create Database button.**

    A message appears, confirming that the database was created.

5. **Click the Go Back link or the Back button on your browser toolbar.**

    The MySQL Databases page displays in your browser window.

6. **Locate MySQL Users on the MySQL Databases page.**

    Scroll to the approximate middle of the page to locate this section.

7. **Choose a username and password for your database, enter them in the Username and Password text boxes, and then click the Create User button.**

    A confirmation message appears stating that the username was created with the password you specified.

    For security reasons, make sure that your password isn't something that sneaky hackers can easily guess. Give your database a name that you'll remember later. This practice is especially helpful if you run more than one MySQL database in your account. For instance, if you name a database *WordPress* or *wpblog,* you can be reasonably certain a year from now when you want to access your database to make some configuration changes that you know exactly which credentials to use.

Make sure that you note the database name, username, and password that you set up during this process. You need them in the section "Running the installation script" later in this chapter before officially installing WordPress on your web server. Jot them down on a piece of paper, or copy and paste them into a text editor window; either way, make sure that you have them handy.

8. **Click the Go Back link or the Back button on your browser toolbar.**

   The MySQL Databases page displays in your browser window.

9. **In the Add Users to Database section of the MySQL Databases page, select the user you just set up from the User drop-down list and then select the new database from the Database drop-down list.**

   The MySQL Account Maintenance, Manage User Privileges page appears in cPanel.

10. **Assign user privileges by selecting the All Privileges check box.**

    Because you're the *administrator* (or owner) of this database, you need to make sure that you assign all privileges to the new user you just created.

11. **Click the Make Changes button.**

    A page opens with a confirmation message that you've added your selected user to the selected database.

12. **Click the Go Back link or the Back button on your browser toolbar.**

    You return to the MySQL Databases page.

The MySQL database for your WordPress website is complete and you're ready to proceed to the final step of installing the software on your web server.

Downloading the WordPress software

Without further ado, get the latest version of the WordPress software at `http://wordpress.org/download`.

WordPress gives you two compression formats for the software: `.zip` and `.tar.gz`. Use the Zip file because it's the most common format for compressed files and because both Windows and Mac operating systems can use the format. Generally, the `.tar.gz` file format is used for Unix operating systems.

Download the WordPress software to your computer and then *decompress* (unpack or unzip) it to a folder on your computer's hard drive. These steps begin the installation process for WordPress. Having the program on your own computer isn't enough, however. You also need to *upload* (or transfer) it to your web server account (the one you obtained in Chapter 1 of this minibook).

Before you install WordPress on your web server, you need to make sure that you have the MySQL database set up and ready to accept the WordPress installation. Be sure that you've followed the preceding steps to set up your MySQL database before you proceed.

Uploading the WordPress files via FTP

To upload the WordPress files to your host, return to the /wordpress folder (shown in Figure 4-4) on your computer where you unpacked the WordPress software that you downloaded earlier. If you need a review on using FTP (File Transfer Protocol) to transfer files from your computer to your web server, see Chapter 2 in this minibook.

Using your FTP client, connect to your web server and upload all these files to the root directory of your hosting account.

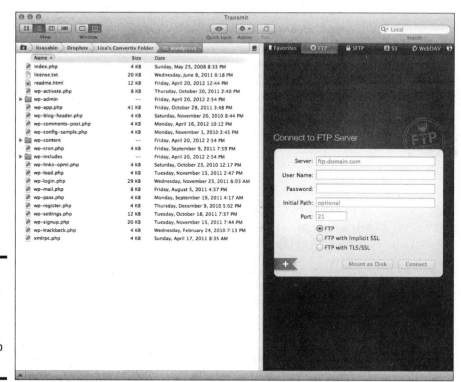

Figure 4-4: WordPress installation files to be uploaded to your web server.

Book II
Chapter 4

Installing
WordPress on Your
Web Server

If you don't know what your root directory is, contact your hosting provider and ask, "What is my root directory for my account?" Every hosting provider's setup is different. The root directory is most likely the `public_html` folder, but you may find an `httpdocs` folder. The answer depends on what type of setup your hosting provider has. When in doubt, ask!

Here are a few things to keep in mind when you upload your files:

✦ **Upload the *contents* of the /wordpress folder to your web server — not the folder itself.** Most FTP client software lets you select all the files and drag and drop them to your web server. Other programs have you highlight the files and click a Transfer button.

✦ **Choose the correct transfer mode.** File transfers via FTP have two forms: ASCII and binary. Most FTP clients are configured to autodetect the transfer mode. Understanding the difference as it pertains to this WordPress installation is important so that you can troubleshoot any problems you have later:

   • *Binary transfer mode* is how images (such as JPG, GIF, BMP, and PNG files) are transferred via FTP.

   • *ASCII transfer mode* is for everything else (text files, PHP files, JavaScript, and so on).

   For the most part, it's a safe bet to make sure that the transfer mode of your FTP client is set to autodetect. But if you experience issues with how those files load on your site, retransfer the files by using the appropriate transfer mode.

✦ **You can choose a different folder from the root.** You aren't required to transfer the files to the root directory of your web server. You can choose to run WordPress on a subdomain or in a different folder on your account. If you want your blog address to be `http://your domain.com/blog`, you transfer the WordPress files into a `/blog` folder (where *yourdomain* is your domain name).

✦ **Choose the right file permissions.** *File permissions* tell the web server how these files can be handled on your server — whether they're files that can be written to. Generally, PHP files need to have a permission (CHMOD is explained in Chapter 2 of this minibook) of 666, whereas file folders need a permission of 755. Almost all FTP clients let you check and change the permissions on the files, if you need to. Typically, you can find the option to change file permissions within the menu options of your FTP client.

Some hosting providers run their PHP software in a more secure format — *safe mode*. If this is the case with your host, you need to set the PHP files to 644. If you're unsure, ask your hosting provider what permissions you need to set for PHP files.

Running the installation script

The final step in the installation procedure for WordPress is connecting the WordPress software you uploaded to the MySQL database. Follow these steps:

1. **Type the URL of your website into the address bar in your web browser.**

   If you chose to install WordPress in a different folder from the root directory of your account, make sure you indicate that in the URL for the install script. For example, if you transferred the WordPress software files to the `/blog` folder, you would point your browser to the following URL to run the installation: `http://`*`yourdomain`*`.com/blog/wp-admin/install.php`. If WordPress is in the root directory, use the following URL to run the installation: `http://`*`yourdomain`*`.com/wp-admin/install.php` (where *yourdomain* is your domain name).

   Assuming that you did everything correctly (see Table 4-1 for help with common installation problems), you see the message shown in Figure 4-5.

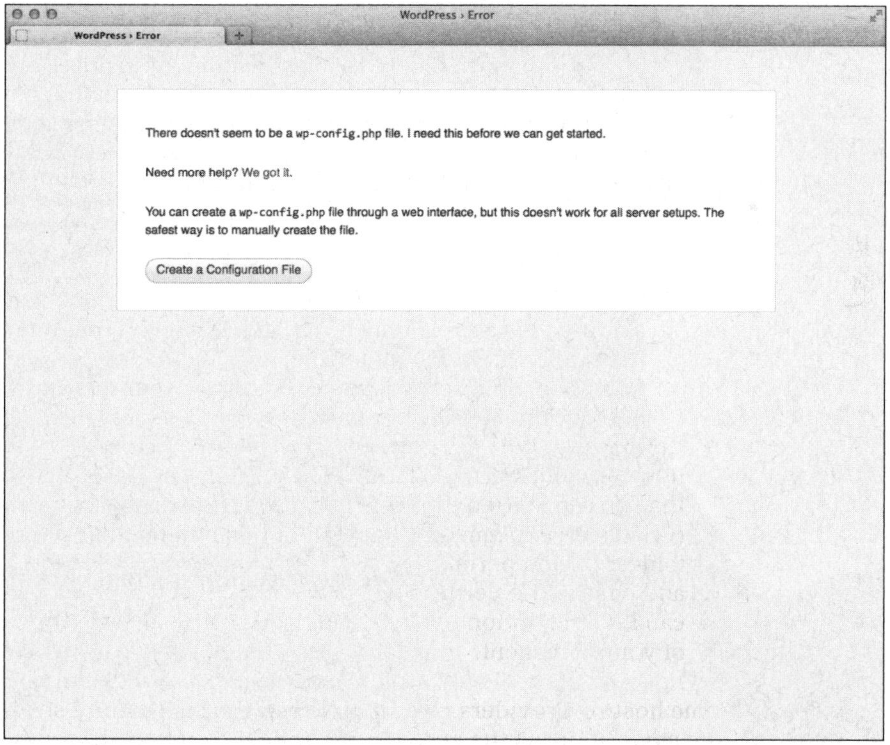
WordPress › Error
WordPress › Error
There doesn't seem to be a wp-config.php file. I need this before we can get started.
Need more help? We got it.
You can create a wp-config.php file through a web interface, but this doesn't work for all server setups. The safest way is to manually create the file.
Create a Configuration File

Figure 4-5: The first time you run the installation script for WordPress, you see this message.

2. Click the Create a Configuration File button.

The Welcome to WordPress page appears, giving you the information you need to proceed with the installation.

3. Click the Let's Go button at the bottom of that page.

4. Dig out the database name, username, and password that you saved in the earlier section "Setting up the MySQL database" and use that information to fill in the following fields, as shown in Figure 4-6:

- *Database Name:* Type the database name you used when you created the MySQL database before this installation. Because hosts differ in configurations, you need to enter the database name by itself or a combination of your username and the database name, separated by an underscore mark (_).

  If you named your database *wordpress,* for example, you enter that in this text box. If your host requires you to append the database name with your hosting account username, you enter ***username_ wordpress***, substituting your hosting username for *username.* For example, my username is *lisasabin,* so I enter lisasabin_wordpress.

- *User Name:* Type the username you used when you created the MySQL database before this installation. Depending on what your host requires, you may need to enter a combination of your hosting account username and the database username separated by an underscore mark (_).

- *Password:* Type the password you used when you set up the MySQL database. You don't need to append the password to your hosting account username here.

- *Database Host:* Ninety-nine percent of the time, you leave this field set to localhost. Some hosts, depending on their configurations, have different hosts set for the MySQL database server. If local host doesn't work, you need to contact your hosting provider to find out the MySQL database host.

- *Table Prefix:* Leave this field set to wp_.

  You can change the table prefix to create an environment secure from outside access. See Chapter 5 in this minibook for more information.

5. After you fill in the MySQL database information, click the Submit button.

You see a message that says, "All right, sparky! You've made it through this part of the installation. WordPress can now communicate with your database. If you're ready, time to run the install!"

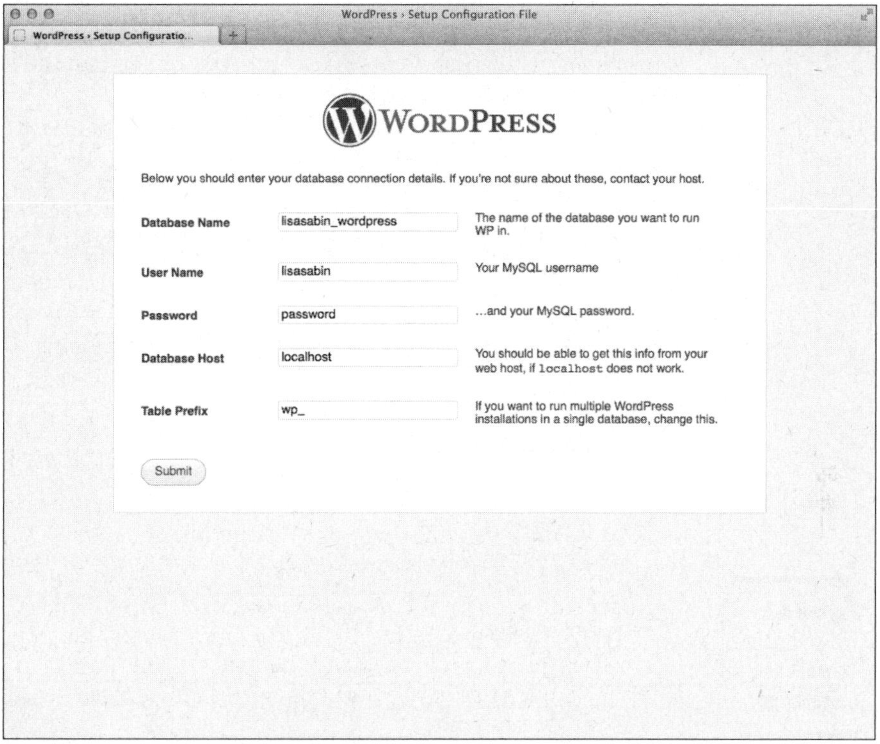

Book II
Chapter 4

Installing
WordPress on Your
Web Server

Figure 4-6:
Entering the database name, username, and password.

6. Click the Run the Install button.

Another page appears with a message welcoming you to the famous five-minute WordPress installation process, as shown in Figure 4-7.

7. Enter the following information:

- *Site Title:* Enter the title you want to give your site. The title you enter isn't written in stone; you can change it later, if you like. The site title also displays on your site.

- *Username:* This is the name you use to log in to WordPress. By default, the username is *admin,* and you can leave it that way. However, for security reasons, I recommend you change your username to something unique to you. This username is different from the one you set for the MySQL database in previous steps. You use this username when you log in to WordPress to access the Dashboard (which is covered in Book III), so be sure to make it something you'll remember.

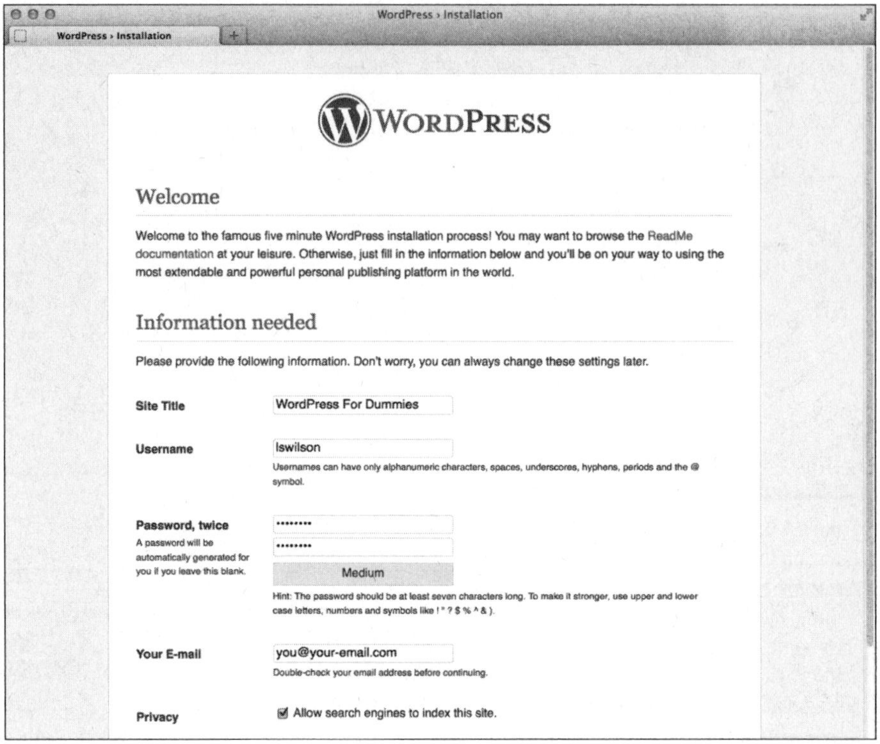

Figure 4-7:
Finishing the WordPress installation.

- *Password, Twice:* Type your desired password in the first text box and then type it again in the second to confirm that you've typed it correctly. If the two versions of your password don't match, WordPress alerts you with an error message. If you don't enter a password, one is generated automatically for you. For security reasons, it's a good thing to set a different password here than the one you set for your MySQL database in the previous steps — just don't get them confused.

For security reasons (and so other people can't make a lucky guess), passwords should be at least seven characters long and use as many different characters in as many combinations as possible. Use a mixture of uppercase and lowercase letters, numbers, and symbols (such as ! " ? $ % ^ &).

- *Your E-Mail:* Enter the e-mail address you want to use to be notified of administrative information about your blog. You can change this address later, too.

- *Allow Search Engines to Index This Site:* By default, this check box is selected, which lets the search engines index the content of your blog and include your blog in search results. To keep your blog out of the search engines, deselect this check box. (See Book V for information on search engine optimization.)

8. Click the Install WordPress button.

The WordPress installation machine works its magic and creates all the tables within the database that contain the default data for your blog. WordPress displays the login information you need to access the WordPress Dashboard. Make note of this username and password before you leave this page. Scribble them on a piece of paper or copy them into a text editor, such as Notepad.

After you click the Install WordPress button, you're sent an e-mail with the login information and login URL. This information is handy if you're called away during this part of the installation process. So go ahead and let the dog out, answer the phone, brew a cup of coffee, or take a 15-minute power nap. If you somehow get distracted away from this page, the e-mail sent to you contains the information you need to log in to your WordPress blog.

9. Click the Log In button to log in to WordPress.

If you happen to lose this page before clicking the Log In button, you can always find your way to the login page by entering your domain followed by the call to the login file (for example, `http://`*yourdomain*`.com/ wp-login.php` — where *yourdomain* is your domain name).

You know that you're finished with the installation process when you see the login page, as shown in Figure 4-8. Check out Table 4-1 if you experience any problems during this installation process; it covers some of the common problems users run into.

So do tell — how much time does your watch show for the installation? Was it five minutes? Stop by my blog sometime at `http://lisasabin-wilson. com` and let me know whether WordPress stood up to its famous five-minute installation reputation.

The good news is — you're done! Were you expecting a marching band? WordPress isn't that fancy . . . yet. Give it time, though. If anyone can produce it, the folks at WordPress can.

Table 4-1	Common WordPress Installation Problems	
Error Message	*Common Cause*	*Solution*
`Error Connecting to the Database`	The database name, username, password, or host was entered incorrectly.	Revisit your MySQL database to obtain the database name, username, and password and then reenter that information.
`Headers Already Sent Error Messages`	A syntax error occurred in the `wp-config.php` file.	Open the `wp-config.php` file in a text editor. The first line needs to contain only this line: `<?php`. The last line needs to contain only this line: `?>`. Make sure that those lines contain nothing else — not even white space. Save the file changes.
`500: Internal Server Error`	Permissions on PHP files are set incorrectly.	Try setting the permissions (CHMOD) on the PHP files to 666. If that change doesn't work, set them to 644. Each web server has different settings for how it lets PHP execute on its servers.
`404: Page Not Found`	The URL for the login page is incorrect.	Double-check that the URL you're using to get to the login page is the same as the location of your WordPress installation (such as `http://yourdomain.com/wp-login.php`).
`403: Forbidden Access`	An `index.html` or `index.htm` file exists in the WordPress installation directory.	WordPress is a PHP application, so the default home page is `index.php`. Look in the WordPress installation folder on your web server. If an `index.html` or `index.htm` file is there, delete it.

Let me be the first to congratulate you on your newly installed WordPress blog! When you're ready, log in and familiarize yourself with the Dashboard, which I describe in Book III.

Figure 4-8:
You know
you've run a
successful
WordPress
installation
when you
see the
login page.

Chapter 5: Configuring WordPress for Optimum Security

In This Chapter

✓ **Introducing web security**

✓ **Understanding today's web threats**

✓ **Reducing the risk of attack**

✓ **Using sources you can trust**

✓ **Cleaning up to avoid a soup kitchen server**

✓ **Hardening WordPress**

*I*n this chapter, you deal with web security and how it pertains to WordPress. There are a lot of scary threats on the Internet, but with this chapter — and WordPress, of course — you'll have no problem keeping your website safe and secure.

Always have a reliable backup system in place so if something goes wrong with your website you can reset it back to the last version you know worked. Chapter 7 in this minibook shows you how to back up your website.

Understanding the Basics of Web Security

Information security is the act of protecting information and information systems from unwanted or unauthorized use, access, modification, and disruption. Information security is built on principles of protecting confidentiality, integrity, and availability of information. The ultimate goal is managing your risk.

There is no silver bullet that can ensure you are never compromised. Consider your desktop: The idea of running an operating system (whether it be Windows or Mac OS X) without antivirus software is highly impractical. The same principle applies to your website. You can never reduce the percentage of risk to zero, but you can implement controls to minimize impact and to take a proactive approach to threat preparedness.

The beginning of the Information Security industry

An entire industry has arisen out of web security. The Information Security (InfoSec) industry goes back to as early as 2005/2006. Similar to their close cousins, the desktop viruses, some of the early infections were often reflected in what is known today as *defacement* (modifying the appearance of a website). The ability to compromise a website and replace its content showed technical prowess by the attacker.

With the introduction of client-side interactive and dynamic content through applications built on technologies (such as JavaScript, Active X, Flash, and even PHP and ASP) to supplement static HTML websites and other similar, browser-based products, attacks on websites became much more serious for the website owner and hosting provider. These applications enrich the experience and overall usability on all today's modern websites, but can also provide a point of entry for a hacker to perform malicious attacks.

You need to be familiar with six distinct types of risk (or threats):

✦ **Defacements:** The motivation behind most defacements is to change the appearance of a website. Defacements are often very basic and make some kind of social stance, such as supporting a cause or bringing attention to your poor security posture. If you visit your website and it doesn't look anything like you expect it to, contact your host to find out if it has been defaced and, if so, ask for assistance in restoring it.

✦ **SEO spam:** This kind of attack sets out to ruin your search engine results — search engines can warn viewers away from your website. The most popular one is the Pharma hack. It injects code into your website and search engine links to redirect your traffic to pharmaceutical companies and their products. If you find that your website listing disappears from major search engines, such as Google, you should be concerned that your website has been a victim to SEO spam and contact your hosting provider for assistance.

✦ **Malicious redirects:** Malicious redirect attacks direct your traffic somewhere else, most likely another website. For example, if your domain is `http://domain.com`, a malicious redirect might redirect it to a `http://adifferentdomain.com`. Malicious redirects are often integrated with a number of other attacks (SEO spam being one). If you visit your website and discover that your domain redirects to a different domain that you don't recognize, your website has been a victim of a malicious redirect attach, and you should contact your hosting provider for assistance.

✦ **iFrame injections:** This kind of attack embeds a hidden iFrame in your website that loads another website onto your visitor's browser (like a pop-up ad). These embedded websites or ads can lead to malicious websites that carry a multitude of infections.

✦ **Phishing scams:** Phishing scams used to belong only to the world of e-mail: You get an e-mail from your bank asking you to confirm your login information, but if you follow the instructions, your information actually goes to the attacker's servers rather than the legitimate site.

WordPress websites are now used for the distribution of these attacks. Attackers develop malicious files and code that look like plugins and themes and then exploit credentials to a server or WordPress site, or the attackers use a known vulnerability to infect the plugins and themes. They then use the bait-and-hook approach through ads or e-mails to redirect traffic to these fake pages stored on legitimate websites. Keep an eye out for abnormal behavior on your website, such as the display of ads that you didn't insert yourself, or the redirect to other domains you're not familiar with. If at any time you suspect your website, and underlying files, have been tampered with by anyone, contact your web hosting provider for assistance.

✦ **Backdoor shells:** With a backdoor shell, an attacker uploads a piece of PHP code to your website, which allows him to take control of it and download your files and upload his own. This kind of attack is more difficult to discover because it doesn't always change the appearance or your experience with your site. You typically will discover this kind of attack by noticing new files in your file system or notice a marked increase in your bandwidth usage.

**Book II
Chapter 5**

Configuring
WordPress for
Optimum Security

The rest of this chapter shows you how you can prevent any of these nasty attacks happening to your WordPress website, so you can keep you and your visitors safe.

Part of being a website owner is keeping your website and subscribers safe from hackers.

Preventing Attacks

You can't ever be 100 percent secure. But with a WordPress website, you're in good hands because the WordPress developers understand the importance of security, and they built a highly effective system to address any vulnerabilities you'll run across.

Updating WordPress

The first way to prevent hackers is to keep your WordPress website up-to-date. The quick-and-easy way to do so is through the automatic update feature. The next chapter in this minibook takes you through the process of updating WordPress step by step.

The beauty of applying updates is that they often introduce new streamlined features, improve overall usability, and work to patch and close identified or known vulnerabilities.

As technology and concepts evolve, so do attackers and their methods for finding new vulnerabilities. The further behind you get, the harder it will be to update later and the higher your risk increases, which in turn impacts how vulnerable you are to attacks.

Installing patches

All WordPress updates are not created equally; but there are a few that you should pay special attention to when it comes to the WordPress core software.

There are major releases, which contain feature additions, UI changes, and bug fixes and security updates. You can always tell what major release you're on by the first two numbers in the version number (as in 3.4). See Book I, Chapter 3 for more information about the difference between major and minor releases.

Then you have *point releases*, which are minor releases that can be identified by the third number in the version number (as in 3.4.2). These releases contain bug fixes and security patches but do not introduce new features.

When you see a point release, apply it. Point releases rarely cause issues with your site, and they help close off vulnerabilities in a lot of cases.

Using a firewall

A firewall builds a wall between your website and the much larger Internet; a good firewall thwarts a lot of attacks.

Your web server should also have a good firewall protecting it. Every day there are countless visits, good and bad, to every website — some are from real visitors, but many from automated bots. A Web Application Firewall (WAF) helps protect your WordPress installation from those bad visitors.

Web application firewalls don't offer 100 percent protection, but they are good deterrents for everyday attacks.

If you plan to manage and administer your own server, install and configure a tool such as ModSecurity (www.modsecurity.org) — an open source WAF-like solution that lives at the web server level as a module to Apache.

If you're using a managed hosting solution, you're probably in luck because most offer WAF-like solutions built into their services.

However, as a user, you can also install a plugin for WordPress called CloudFlare, which can be found in the official WordPress Plugin Directory at http://wordpress.org/extend/plugins/cloudflare. CloudFlare (see Figure 5-1) provides the best available WAF-like features for your WordPress website on a managed hosting solution. If you would like to use the CloudFlare plugin on your WordPress website, you do need to have a

CloudFlare account at `http://cloudflare.com`. There is a free account option, but also upgrades to paid accounts that include more features. After you've installed the plugin on your website, follow the instructions on the CloudFlare configuration page to connect your WordPress blog to your CloudFlare account.

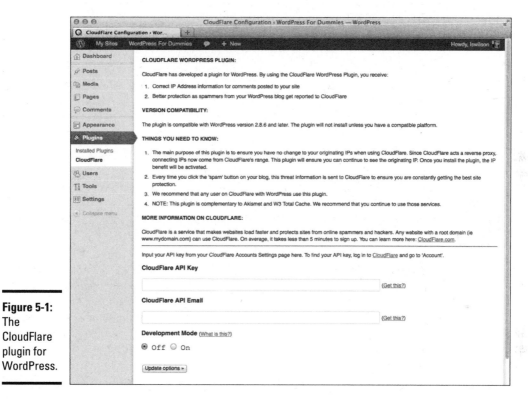

Figure 5-1:
The
CloudFlare
plugin for
WordPress.

Using Trusted Sources

One of the simplest things you can do to keep your website secure is to vet all the people who work on your website. This includes website administrators, website designers, developers, and web hosts, as well as trusted plugins, themes, and applications. If you're running a self-hosted WordPress website, this could be quite a few people.

If you're using themes or plugins, use the WordPress.org theme and plugin repository (`http://wordpress.org/extend/themes` and `http://wordpress.org/extend/plugins`, respectively). Each plugin and theme you find there has gone through a documented review process, which reduces the risk of downloading dangerous code.

Engage the WordPress user community. The WordPress forums (http://wordpress.org/support) are a great place to start. Ask for community references and identify the support mechanisms in place to support the theme or plugin long-term.

Managing Users

The concept of *Least Privilege* has been in practice for ages: Give someone the required privileges for as long as they need it to perform their job or a task. If a task is completed then reduce the privileges at the completion of the task.

Apply these safeguards not just to your WordPress Dashboard, but also to your website host control panels and server transfer protocols. (See Chapter 2 in this minibook for information on file transfer protocol.)

Generating passwords

Password management is perhaps the simplest of tasks, yet it's the Achilles heel of all applications, including both desktop and web-based apps. You can keep your files and data on your web server safe and secure through these simple password-management techniques:

✦ **Length:** Create passwords that are more than 15 characters — this makes it more difficult for harmful users to guess your password.

✦ **Uniqueness:** Don't use the same passwords across all services. If someone does discover the password for one of your applications or services, he won't be able to use it to log in to another application or service that you manage.

✦ **Complexity:** A strong password contains a minimum of 8 characters and is made up of upper- and lowercase letters, numbers, and symbols, which makes any password hard to guess.

Use password managers and generators. Two of the more popular products right now are LastPass (https://lastpass.com) and 1Password (https://agilebits.com/onepassword).

Limiting built-in user roles

Not all users of your website need administrator privileges. WordPress gives you five user roles to choose from, and those roles provide sufficient flexibility for your websites.

You can find detailed information on each of the roles in Book III, Chapter 3. You can also discover more information on users and roles in the WordPress.org codex: http://codex.wordpress.org/Roles_and_Capabilities.

Create a separate account with a lower role (such as Author) and use that account for everyday posting. Reserve the Administrator account purely for administration of your website.

Establishing user accountability

The use of generic accounts should be the last thing you ever consider because the more generic accounts you have, the greater your risk of being compromised. If a compromise does happen, you want to have full account-ability for all users and be able to quickly answer questions like these:

✦ Who was logged in?

✦ Who made what changes?

✦ What did the users do while logged in?

Generic accounts preclude you from doing appropriate incident handling in the event of a compromise. In Book III, Chapter 3, you find all the information and step-by-step details on how to create new users in your WordPress Dashboard — keep the principles of Least Privilege and User Accountability in mind as you're creating users.

Staying Clear of Soup Kitchen Servers

One of the regular issues plaguing website owners is *soup kitchen servers.* A soup kitchen server is one that has never been maintained properly and has a combination of websites, old software, archives, unneeded files, folders, e-mail, and so on, all living on the hard drive of the web server.

The real problem comes into play with the "out of sight, out of mind" phe-nomena. A server owner can forget about software installations on a server that may be outdated or insecure. Over time this forgetfulness introduces new vulnerabilities to the environment:

✦ Disabled installs or websites that live on the server are as accessible and susceptible to external attacks as live sites.

✦ When a forgotten install or website is infected, it leads to *cross-site con-tamination* — a worm-like effect where the infection can jump and repli-cate itself across the server.

✦ In many instances, these forgotten installs or websites house the backdoor and engine of the infection. This means that as you try to rigorously clean your live website, you continuously get re-infected.

Figure 5-2 demonstrates what a soup kitchen server looks like. `$wp_version` indicates the version of WordPress that is currently installed in the directory listed. With a lot of listings for `$wp_version = 2.9` — considering the most recent version of WordPress, at the time of this writing, is 3.5 — you can see how many out of date installations of WordPress this particular soup kitchen server has.

If you have more than one installation of WordPress on your current hosting account, try the following to help reduce your risk of running a soup kitchen server:

✦ Isolate each installation with its own user — this action minimizes internal attacks that come from cross-site contamination.

✦ Keep your installs up-to-date and remove them when you no longer need them — this action lessens the risk of attacks that result from outdated software on your server.

```
Warning: Found outdated WordPress install inside: /../httpdocs - Version: $wp_version = '2.9.1';
Warning: Found outdated WordPress install inside: /../httpdocs - Version: $wp_version = '2.9.2';
Warning: Found outdated WordPress install inside: /../httpdocs - Version: $wp_version = '3.2.1';
Warning: Found outdated WordPress install inside: /../httpdocs - Version: $wp_version = '3.3';
Warning: Found outdated WordPress install inside: /../httpdocs - Version: $wp_version = '3.0.1';
Warning: Found outdated WordPress install inside: /../httpdocs - Version: $wp_version = '2.8.6';
Warning: Found outdated WordPress install inside: /../httpdocs - Version: $wp_version = '2.8.4';
Warning: Found outdated WordPress install inside: /../httpdocs/.. - Version: $wp_version = '3.3';
Warning: Found outdated WordPress install inside: /../httpdocs - Version: $wp_version = '3.0.1';
Warning: Found outdated WordPress install inside: /../httpdocs/blog - Version: $wp_version = '2.5';
Warning: Found outdated timthumb.php version at /../httpdocs/wp-content/plugins/WordPress-popular-posts/scripts/timthumb.php (bellow 2.0). Please update asap!
Warning: Found outdated WordPress install inside: /../httpdocs - Version: $wp_version = '3.0.4';
Warning: Found outdated timthumb.php version at /../subdomains/fcdoc/httpdocs/wp-content/plugins/WordPress-gallery-plugin/timthumb.php (bellow 2.8.2). Update recommended.
Warning: Found outdated WordPress install inside: /../subdomains/fcdoc/httpdocs - Version: $wp_version = '3.2';
Warning: Found vulnerable plugin inside /../subdomains/staging/httpdocs/../wp-content/plugins/wp-spamfree. Details: http://www.exploit-db.com/exploits/17970/
Warning: Found outdated WordPress install inside: /../subdomains/staging/httpdocs/.. - Version: $wp_version = '2.5.1';
Warning: Found outdated WordPress install inside: /../subdomains/../httpdocs - Version: $wp_version = '2.8.4';
Warning: Found outdated WordPress install inside: /../subdomains/../httpdocs - Version: $wp_version = '2.9.1';
Warning: Found outdated WordPress install inside: /../subdomains/../httpdocs - Version: $wp_version = '3.0.1';
Warning: Found vulnerable plugin inside /../httpdocs/../wp-content/plugins/wp-spamfree. Details: http://www.exploit-db.com/exploits/17970/
Warning: Found outdated WordPress install inside: /../httpdocs/.. - Version: $wp_version = '2.5.1';
Warning: Found outdated WordPress install inside: /../web_users/../../.. - Version: $wp_version = '3.3';
Warning: Found outdated timthumb.php version at /../httpdocs-2-17-11/wp-content/plugins/meenews/inc/classes/timthumb.php (bellow 2.0). Please update asap!
Warning: Found outdated WordPress install inside: /../httpdocs-2-17-11 - Version: $wp_version = '3.0.4';
Warning: Found outdated timthumb.php version at /../httpdocs/wp-content/plugins/meenews/inc/classes/timthumb.php (bellow 2.0). Please update asap!
Warning: Found outdated WordPress install inside: /../httpdocs - Version: $wp_version = '3.1.4';
```

Figure 5-2:
A fileserver listing from a typical soup kitchen server.

Hardening WordPress

When you *harden* (that is, take the steps taken to secure your system) your WordPress installation, you can the necessary steps to reduce your risk of being hacked by malicious attackers.

Hardening your website involves following these five steps:

1. Enabling multi-factor authentication.

2. Limiting login attempts.

3. Disabling Theme and Plugin Editors

4. Filtering by Internet Protocol.

5. Killing PHP execution.

I cover each of these steps in the following sections.

Website hardening resources

I recommend a few website resources to follow for your WordPress hardening and security needs:

✔ **WordPress.org | Hardening,** `http://codex.wordpress.org/Hardening_WordPress`

✔ **Perishable Press | Security,** `http://perishablepress.com/category/web-design/security`

✔ **Sucuri,** `http://blog.sucuri.net`

✔ **WPsecure.net,** `http://wpsecure.net`

Book II
Chapter 5

Configuring
WordPress for
Optimum Security

Hardening your website doesn't guarantee your protection, but it definitely reduces your risk.

Multi-factor authentication

Authentication, in this case, refers to the act of confirming the identity of the person who is attempting to log in and obtain access to your WordPress installation — just like when you log in to your WordPress website by using a username and password. The idea for multi-factor authentication stems from the idea that one password alone is not enough to secure access to any environment. *Multi-factor authentication* is also called *strong authentication* and, when in use, it requires more than one user-authentication method. WordPress, by default, requires only one: a username with password. Multi-factor authentication adds layers of authentication measures for extra security for user logins.

To use multi-factor authentication, you can use a free plugin called Google Authenticator. It provides two-factor user authentication through the use of an application on your mobile or tablet device (iPhone, iPad, Droid, and so on). For this plugin to work, you need the following:

✦ **Google Authentication app:** Find it at the Apple App Store for iOS devices or the Google Play Store for Android devices.

✦ **Google Authenticator plugin:** You can find this in the Plugin Directory. See Book VII, Chapters 1 and 2 to find, install, and activate this plugin.

When you have both of those tasks accomplished, you can configure the plugin for use on your website. Follow these steps to configure the plugin for each individual user on your site:

1. **Click the All Users link on the Users menu on your Dashboard.**

The Users page opens.

2. **Select the users profile you'd like edit by clicking the Edit link underneath their name in the Users list.**

   The Edit Users page opens.

3. **Select the Active check box in the Google Authentication Settings section, as shown in Figure 5-3.**

4. **Type a description in the Description text box.**

   This is the description you can see in the Google Authenticator application on your mobile device. In Figure 5-3, I gave it the description of *WPBlog*.

   If you're using an iPhone or iPad as your authentication device, the description field must not have any spaces. At the time of this writing, a bug in the Apple application prevents it from working if there are any spaces in the description; this is why my example description of *WPBlog* is all one word, with no spaces.

5. **Click the Show/Hide QR code button.**

   This displays the QR code on the page, as shown in Figure 5-3. A QR code is a scannable bar code which is readable by a mobile or tablet device using the camera.

6. **Open the Google Authenticator application on your mobile or tablet device.**

7. **On the Dashboard of your WordPress site, click the Create New Secret button.**

   This refreshes the secret key and QR code needed to connect your mobile or tablet device.

Google Authenticator Settings

Active	☑
Relaxed mode	☐ *Relaxed mode allows for more time drifting on your phone clock (±4 min).*
Description	WPBlog *Description that you'll see in the Google Authenticator app on your phone.*
Secret	LWIH3YDBBFKZGXJF [Create new secret] [Show/Hide QR code]

Scan this with the Google Authenticator app.

Enable App password	☑ *Enabling an App password will decrease your overall login security.*
	XXXX XXXX XXXX XXXX [Create new password]

Figure 5-3:
The Google
Authenticator
Settings.

8. **In the Google Authenticator application on your mobile or tablet device, click the Scan Barcode button.**

   The camera on your device starts.

9. **Scan the bar code displayed on the Google Authenticator page on your WordPress Dashboard by taking a photo of it with your device.**

   Point your device camera at your computer screen and line up the QR code within the camera brackets of your mobile device. The application automatically reads the QR code as soon as it is aligned correctly and displays a 6-digit code identifying your blog. The 6-digit code will refresh on a time-based interval. After the QR code is scanned, the user receives a message on her mobile device that contains a unique, numeric code.

10. **Click the Update Profile button at the bottom of the Edit Users screen in your Dashboard.**

    This refreshes the Edit Users page with a message at the top stating that the Google Authenticator settings have been successfully saved.

Now, with the Google Authenticator plugin in place, whenever anyone tries to log in to your WordPress Dashboard, she has to fill in her username and password, like usual; however, with multi-factor authentication in place, the user also needs to enter the authentication code that was sent to her mobile device in Step 9 in. Without this unique code, the user can't log in to the WordPress Dashboard.

With the previous steps completed, you have enabled a form of multi-factor authentication, to your WordPress Dashboard.

The Google Authenticator application verification code is time based, which is why it is very important that your mobile phone and your WordPress blog are set to the same time zone. If you get the message that the Google Authentication verification code you're using is either invalid or expired, you need to delete the plugin and then go into your WordPress Dashboard settings and make sure the time zone is set to the same time zone as your mobile or tablet device. See Book III, Chapter 1 for information on time settings for your WordPress site.

The following steps show you how the multi-factor authentication is now implemented on your blog:

1. **Log out of your WordPress Dashboard.**

   This step logs you out completely and displays the login page, shown in Figure 5-4.

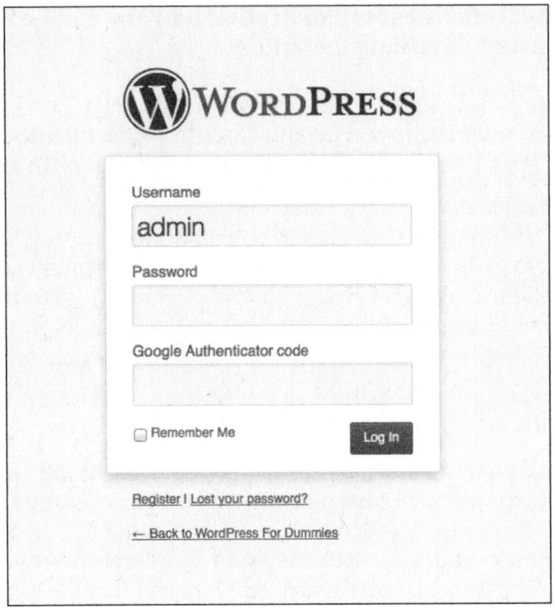

Figure 5-4:
The
WordPress
login form
with Google
Authen-
tication.

2. **Type your username in the Username field.**

3. **Type your password in the Password field.**

   Do *not* click the Log In button yet. (If you're like me, you probably have an urge to click that button a split second after typing your password. For these steps, you have to resist that urge.)

4. **Open the Google Authenticator application on your mobile or tablet device and locate the 6-digit number code assigned to your blog.**

   This 6-digit number code refreshes every 60 seconds. If you have more than one blog using the application, find the code that corresponds to the description you assigned to the site from Step 4 in the previous list.

5. **Type the 6-digit number verification code in the Google Authenticator code field.**

6. **Click the Log In button.**

   You are now successfully logged into your WordPress Dashboard using a two-factor authentication method.

The biggest shortcoming with this plugin is the inability to force all users to configure by default. This is why it's important the principle of least privilege is employed on your site — give access only to the users who absolutely require it. In an ideal world, however, every single one of your user accounts will require a two-factor authentication in order to log in to their accounts on your site.

If you do not have access to a mobile device, WordPress does have a couple of plugins you can use, including these two:

✦ **Perfect Paper Passwords:** `http://wordpress.org/extend/plugins/perfect-paper-passwords`

✦ **Yubikey Plugin:** `http://wordpress.org/extend/plugins/yubikey-plugin`

Limiting login attempts

Limiting the number of times a user can attempt to log in to your WordPress site helps reduce the risk of brute force attack. A *brute force* attack happens when an attacker tries to gain access by guessing your username and password through the process of cycling through combinations.

To help protect against brute force attacks, you want to limit the number of times any user can try to log in to your website. You can accomplish this in WordPress easily enough through the use of the Limit Login Attempts plugin. You can find this plugin in the WordPress Plugin Directory. See Book VII, Chapters 1 and 2 to find, install, and activate it.

When you have the Limit Login Attempts plugin installed, follow these steps to configure the settings:

1. **Click the Limit Login Attempts link in the Settings menu on your Dashboard.**

The Limit Login Attempts Settings page opens in your Dashboard, as shown in Figure 5-5.

2. **Select a configuration.**

Under the Options heading, you see these four configurations:

• *4 allowed retries:* This is the maximum number of times users are allowed to retry failed logins.

• *20 minutes lockout:* This is the amount of time a user is prevented from retrying a login after he has reached the maximum allowed number.

• *4 lockouts increase lockout time to 24 hours:* If a user is locked out 4 times after numerous failed login attempts, he then gets locked out for 24 hours.

• *12 hours until retries are reset:* This is the amount of time before login retries are completely reset.

Figure 5-5:
Limit Login
Attempts
Settings.

3. Select the Direct Connection option in the Site Connection section.

This option limits site connection to a single Internet Protocol. Alternatively, you can select this plugin to limit site connection from behind a proxy, if your users are using proxy IP's to connect to the site.

4. Select Yes in the Handle Cookie Login section.

This option tells WordPress to set a cookie in the users browser for further identification. Alternatively, you can set this to No if you're not worried about it — however, having Cookie Login Handling is a good extra security measure to have in place.

5. Select the Log IP option in the Notify on Lockout section.

This will notify the site administrator via email every time a user gets locked out. Alternatively, you can select the number of lockouts that will happen for a single user before it notifies the administrator via email.

6. Click the Change Options button at the bottom of the Limit Login Attempts Settings page.

This Limit Login Attempts Setting page refreshes with a message telling you that the plugin settings have been successfully saved.

If you are managing your own server, monitor your log in attempts to see if a malicious attacker is attempting repeated attempts to obtain passwords and usernames. Keep track of those IPs and if they repeatedly attempt to log in, add them to your server firewall to prevent them from burdening your server access points.

Disabling theme and plugin editors

By default, when you log in to the WordPress Dashboard, you have the ability to edit any theme and plugin file using the Theme Editor (found by clicking the Appearance link on the Editor menu) and the Plugin Editor (found by clicking the Plugins link on the Editor menu). The idea makes a lot of sense; it gives you the ability to do everything within your Admin panel without having to worry about logging into your server via FTP to edit files.

Unfortunately, having the theme and plugin editors available also provides any attacker that gains access to the Dashboard full rights to modify any theme or plugin file, which is very dangerous because even just one embedded within any file can grant an attacker remote access to your environment without ever having to touch your Dashboard.

You can completely avoid this by disabling the Theme Editor and Plugin Editor by adding a WordPress constant (or rule) to the WordPress configuration file (`wp-config.php`) found in the installation folder on your web server. Download the `wp-config.php` via FTP (see Book II, Chapter 2) and open the file in a text editor, such as Notepad (PC) or TextMate (Mac). Look for the following line of code:

```
define('DB_COLLATE', '');
```

Add the following constant (rule) on the line directly beneath the previous line:

```
define('DISALLOW_FILE_EDIT',true);
```

Although the addition of this constant won't prevent an attack, it will help you when it comes to reducing the impact of a compromise. You can find more information on other constants you can add in the `wp-config.php` file on the WordPress.org website at `http://codex.wordpress.org/Editing_wp-config.php`.

You can also disable the automatic updates in WordPress (the system by which you are allowed to automatically update WordPress core and WordPress plugins), to include the administrator. This means you'd have to do everything, manually, via FTP. To do this you would use the following constant in your `wp-config.php` file:

```
define('DISALLOW_FILE_MODS',true);
```

Book II
Chapter 5

Configuring
WordPress for
Optimum Security

Filtering by Internet Protocol (IP) address

Another option you have is to limit access to the Dashboard to specific Internet Protocols only. You also hear this method referred to as *whitelisting* (allowing) access, which compliments your *blacklisting* (disallowing) solutions you have put in place.

Everything that touches the Internet, such as your computer, a website, or a server network, has what is known as an Internet Protocol (IP) address. An IP on your computer is like your home address; it uniquely identifies you so the Internet knows where your computer is located, physically. An example of what an IP looks like is 12.345.67.89 — it's a series of numbers that uniquely identifies the physical location of a computer or network.

You can edit the `.htaccess` file on your web server so that only IPs that you approve can access your Admin Dashboard, which blocks everyone else from having Dashboard access.

The lines of code that define the access rules get added to the `.htaccess` file located in on your web server where WordPress is installed, in a folder called `/wp-admin`. Download that file to your computer via FTP and open it using a text editor, such as Notepad (PC) or TextMate (Mac), and add the following lines to it:

```
order allow,deny
deny from all
allow from 12.345.67.89
```

In this example, the order defines what comes first. An IP that follows the `allow` rules is given access; any IP that doesn't follow the `allow` rules is denied access. In this example, only the IP 12.345.67.89 can access the Admin Dashboard; all other IPs are denied.

If the `/wp-admin` folder in your WordPress installation doesn't contain a file called `.htaccess`, you can easily create one using your FTP program by opening the `/wp-admin` folder and then right click with your mouse and select New File. Give that new file the name: `.htaccess` and make sure the new rules from the previous section are added.

Limiting access via IP does involve the following potential negatives:

✦ **This technique works only with static Internet Protocols.** A dynamic Internet Protocol constantly changes. There are ways to make this work with dynamic IP's but that would beyond this chapter.

✦ **The ability to use `.htaccess` is highly dependent on a web server that is running Apache.** It won't do you any good if your web server is Windows based or IIS, or if you're using the latest NGINX web server.

✦ **Your Apache web server needs to be configured to allow directives to be defined by `.htaccess` files.** Ask your web host about configuration.

Killing PHP execution

For most backdoor intrusion attempts to function, a PHP file has to be executed. The term *backdoor* describes ways of obtaining access to a web server through means that bypass regular authentication methods, such as file injections through programming languages such as PHP or JavaScript. Disabling PHP execution prevents an attack or compromise from taking place because PHP cannot be executed at all.

To disable PHP execution, you add 4 lines of code to the .htaccess file on your web server. Those lines look like this:

```
<Files *.php>
Order allow,deny
Deny from all
</Files>
```

By default, you have an .htaccess file in the WordPress directory on your web server. But you can also create an .htaccess file in other folders; — particularly the folders in which you would like to disable PHP execution.

To disable PHP execution for maximum security, create an .htaccess file with those four lines of code in the following folders in your WordPress installation:

+ /wp-includes

+ /wp-content/uploads

+ /wp-content

This WordPress installation directory is important because it is the only directory that has to be writeable for WordPress to work. This means if an image is uploaded with a modified header, or if a PHP file is uploaded and PHP execution is allowed, an attacker would be able exploit this weakness to create havoc in your environment. With PHP execution disabled, the attacker is unable to create any havoc.

To further your knowledge, and find additional information on web application security, consider checking out *The Web Application Hacker's Handbook: Finding and Exploiting Security Flaws,* 2nd Edition, by Dafydd Stuttard and Marcus Pinto (Wiley).

Chapter 6: Upgrading WordPress

In This Chapter

✔ **Finding upgrades notifications**

✔ **Backing up your database before upgrading**

✔ **Deactivating plugins**

✔ **Upgrading from the dashboard**

✔ **Upgrading manually**

In Book I, Chapter 3, the schedule of WordPress development and release cycles shows you that WordPress releases a new version (upgrade) of its platform roughly once every 120 days (or every 4 months). That chapter also explains why you need to keep your WordPress software up-to-date by using the most recent version for security purposes, mostly, but also to make sure you're taking advantage of all the latest features the WordPress developers pack within every major new release.

In this chapter, you discover the WordPress upgrade notification system and find out what to do when WordPress notifies you that a new version is available. This chapter also covers the best practices to upgrade the WordPress platform on your site to ensure the best possible outcome (that is, how not to break your website after a WordPress upgrade).

The upgrade process occurs on a regular basis, at least three or four times per year. For some users, this is a frustrating reality of using WordPress. However, this active development environment is part of what makes WordPress the most popular platform available. Because WordPress is always adding great new features and functions to the platform, upgrading always ensures that you're on top of the game and using the latest tools and features.

Getting Notified of an Available Upgrade

After you install WordPress and log in for the first time, you can see the version number on the WordPress Dashboard, as shown in Figure 6-1. (Note that I've scrolled down in the figure.) Therefore, if anyone asks what version you're using, you know exactly where to look to find out.

Find what version you're using.

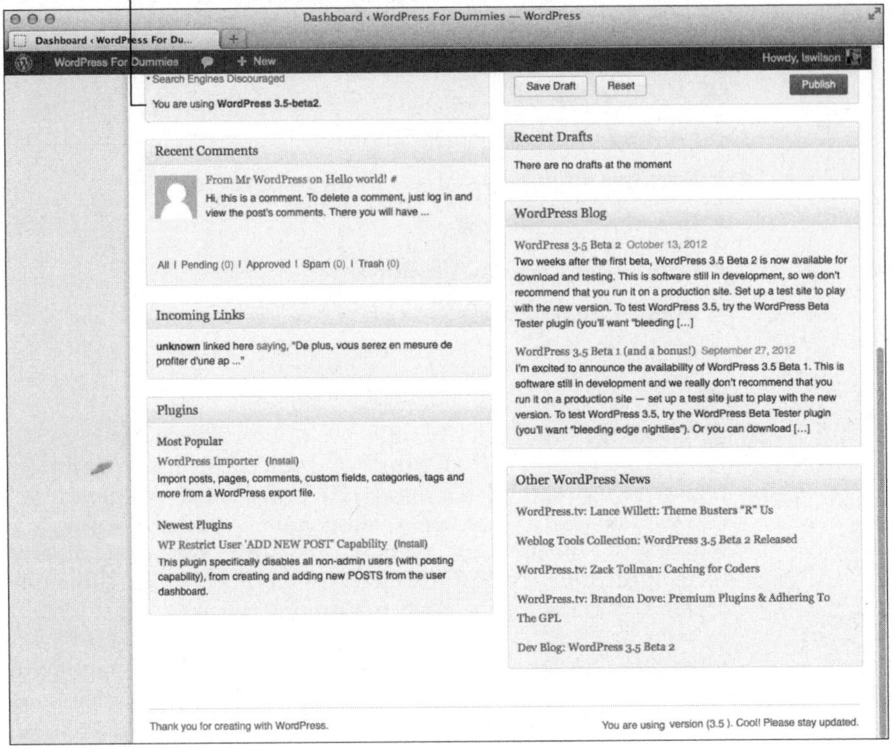

Figure 6-1:
The
WordPress
version
displayed
in the
Dashboard.

Say you have WordPress installed and you've been happily publishing content to your website with it for several weeks, maybe even months, and then one day you log in to your Dashboard and see a message at the top of your screen you've never seen before that reads, "WordPress X.X.X is available! Please update now." (Figure 6-2 shows the message and a small black circle, or *notification bubble,* on the left side of the page.)

Both the message at the top of the page and the notification bubble on the Dashboard menu are visual indicators that you're using an outdated version of WordPress and that you can (and need to) upgrade the software.

New version available

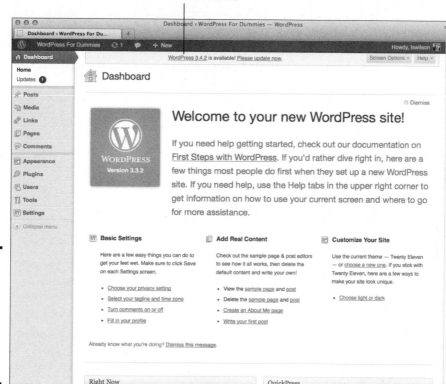

**Book II
Chapter 6**

Upgrading
WordPress

Figure 6-2:
A Dash-
board
notification
of an
available
WordPress
upgrade.

The message at the top of your Dashboard includes two links that you can click
for more information. (See Figure 6-2.) The first is a link called WordPress 3.x.
Clicking this link takes you to the WordPress Codex page titled Version 3.x,
which is filled with information about the version upgrade, including

+ Installation/upgrade information

+ Summary of the development cycle for this version

+ List of files that have been revised

The second link, Please Update Now, takes you to another page in the WordPress
Dashboard — the WordPress Updates page, as shown in Figure 6-3.

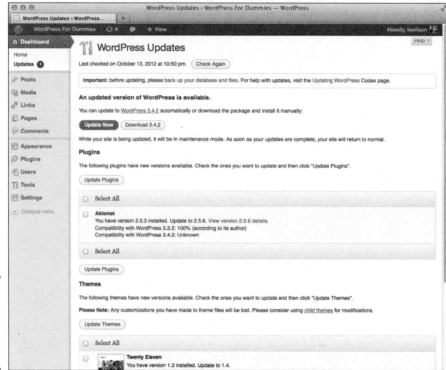

Figure 6-3:
The
WordPress
Updates
page.

At the very top of the WordPress Updates page is another important message for you:

```
Important: before updating, please backup your database and
    files. For help with updates, visit the Updating WordPress
    Codex page.
```

Both links in the message take you to pages in the WordPress Codex that contain helpful information on creating backups and updating WordPress.

Book II, Chapter 7 has extensive information on how to back up your WordPress website, content, and files.

The WordPress Updates page tells you that an updated version of WordPress is available. You can update two ways:

✦ Automatically, by using the built-in WordPress updater

✦ Manually, by downloading the files and installing them on your server

These ways to update are discussed later in the chapter.

Backing Up Your Database

Before upgrading your WordPress software installation, make sure you back up your database. This step isn't required, of course, but it's a smart step to take to safeguard your website and ensure you have a complete copy of your website data in the event that your upgrade goes wrong.

The best way to back up your database is to use the MySQL administration interface provided to you by your web hosting provider. (Book II, Chapter 4 takes you through the steps of creating a new database by using the phpMyAdmin interface.)

 cPanel is a web hosting interface provided by many web hosts as a web hosting account management tool that contains phpMyAdmin as the preferred tool to use to manage and administer databases. Not all web hosts use cPanel or phpMyAdmin, however, so if yours doesn't, you need to consult the user documentation for the tools that your web host provides. The instructions in this chapter use cPanel and phpMyAdmin.

Book II
Chapter 6

Upgrading
WordPress

The following takes you through the steps of creating a database backup, using the phpMyAdmin interface:

1. **Log in to the cPanel for your hosting account.**

   Typically, browse to `http://yourdomain.com/cpanel` to bring up the login screen for your cPanel. Enter your specific hosting account username and password in the login fields and click OK to log in.

2. **Click the phpMyAdmin icon.**

   The phpMyAdmin interface opens and displays your database.

3. **Click the name of the database that you want to back up.**

   If you have more than one database in your account, the left-side menu in phpMyAdmin displays the names of all of them. Click the one you want to back up; the database loads in the main interface window.

4. **Click the Export tab at the top of the screen.**

   The page refreshes and displays the backup utility page.

5. **Select the Save as File check box.**

6. **Select the option labeled *zipped*.**

   This compiles the database backup file in a `.zip` file and prepares it for download.

7. **Click the Go button.**

   A pop-up window appears, allowing you to select a location on your computer to store the database backup file.

8. **Click the Save button to download it and save it to your computer.**

Book II, Chapter 7 contains in-depth information on making a complete backup of your website, including all your files, plugins, themes, and images. For the purposes of upgrading, a database backup is sufficient, but be sure to check out that chapter for valuable information on extensive backups, including how to restore a database backup in case you ever need to go through that process.

Upgrading WordPress Automatically

WordPress provides you with an easy, quick, and reliable method to update the core software from within your Dashboard. I recommend using this option whenever possible to make sure you are accurately updating the WordPress software. To update WordPress automatically, follow these steps:

1. **Back up your WordPress website.**

Backing up your website before updating is an important step in case something goes wrong with the upgrade. Give yourself some peace of mind knowing that you have a full copy of your website that can be restored, if needed. My advice is not to skip this step under any circumstances. If you're not sure how to back up, back up (pun intended!) to the previous section.

2. **Deactivate all plugins.**

This step prevents any plugin conflicts caused by the upgraded version of WordPress from affecting the upgrade process, and it ensures that your website won't break after the upgrade is completed. More information on working with and managing plugins can be found in Book VII; for the purposes of this step, you can deactivate plugins by following these steps:

a. *On the Dashboard, hover your pointer over Plugins on the navigation menu and click the Installed Plugins link.*

   The Plugins page appears.

b. *Select all plugins by selecting the check box to the left of the plugin names listed on that page. (See Figure 6-4.)*

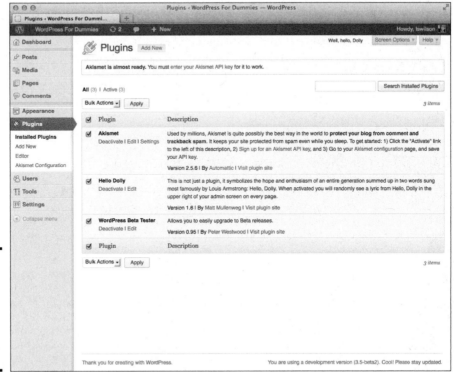

Book II
Chapter 6

Upgrading
WordPress

Figure 6-4:
The Plugins
page with
all plugins
selected,
ready to
deactivate.

    c. In the drop-down list at the top, select Deactivate.

    d. Click the Apply button.

3. **Choose Dashboard⇨Updates.**

   The WordPress Updates page appears.

4. **Click the Update Automatically button.**

   The Update WordPress page appears with a series of messages (as shown in Figure 6-5).

5. **Click the Go to Dashboard link.**

   The Dashboard page appears in your web browser. Notice that both the update alert message at the top of the site and the notification bubble on the Dashboard menu are no longer visible. Your WordPress installation is now using the latest version of WordPress.

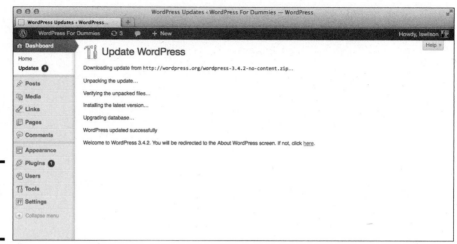

Figure 6-5:
WordPress
update
messages.

After you complete the WordPress software upgrade, you can revisit the Plugins page and reactivate the plugins you deactivated in Step 2 (Figure 6-4) in the above list.

Upgrading WordPress Manually

The second and least used method of upgrading WordPress is the manual method. The method is least used mainly because the automatic method, discussed in the preceding section, is so quick and easy to accomplish. However, certain circumstances — probably related to the inability of your hosting environment to accommodate the automatic method — exist where you have to manually upgrade WordPress.

To upgrade WordPress manually, take these steps:

1. **Back up your WordPress website and deactivate all plugins.**

Refer to Steps 1 and 2 in the preceding "Upgrading WordPress Automatically" section.

2. **Navigate to the WordPress Updates page by clicking the Please Update Now link.**

3. **Click the Download button.**

A dialog box opens that allows you to save the .zip file of the latest WordPress download package to your local computer, as shown in Figure 6-6.

Book II
Chapter 6

Upgrading
WordPress

Figure 6-6:
Downloading
the
WordPress
files to your
local
computer.

4. **Select a location to store the download package and click Save.**

   The `.zip` file downloads to your selected location on your computer.

5. **Browse to the `.zip` file on your computer.**

6. **Unzip the file.**

   Use a program like WinZip (`www.winzip.com`).

7. **Connect to your web server via FTP.**

   See Book II, Chapter 2 for a refresher on how to use FTP.

8. **Delete all the files and folders in your existing WordPress installation directory *except* the following:**

   • `/wp-content` folder

   • `.htaccess`

   • `wp-config.php`

9. **Upload the contents of the `/wordpress` folder to your web server — not the folder itself.**

   Most FTP client software lets you select all the files to drag and drop them to your web server. Other programs have you highlight the files and click a Transfer button.

10. **Navigate to the following URL on your website: `http://yourdomain.com/wp-admin`.**

    Don't panic — your database still needs to be upgraded to the latest version; so instead of seeing your website on your domain, you see a message telling you that a database upgrade is required, as shown in Figure 6-7.

11. **Click the Upgrade WordPress Database button.**

    WordPress initiates the upgrade of the MySQL database associated with your website. When the database upgrade is complete, the page refreshes and displays a message that the process has finished.

12. **Click the Continue button.**

    Your browser loads the WordPress login page. The upgrade is complete, and you can continue using WordPress with the newly upgraded features.

 If you're uncomfortable with performing administrative tasks, such as upgrading and creating database backups, you can hire someone to perform these tasks for you — either a member of your company (if you are a business) or a WordPress consultant skilled in the practice of performing these tasks. Book I, Chapter 4 includes a listing of experienced consultants who can lend a hand.

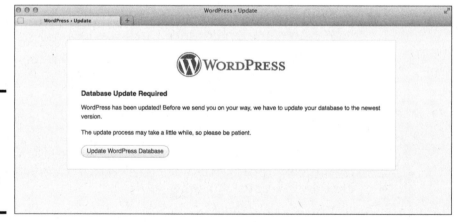

Figure 6-7:
Click the
button to
upgrade
your
WordPress
database.

Chapter 7: Backing Up, Packing Up, and Moving to a New Host

In This Chapter

- ✔ Moving to WordPress from a different platform
- ✔ Handling the database backup management
- ✔ Backing up plugins and themes
- ✔ Storing images and media files
- ✔ Exporting data from WordPress
- ✔ Using plugins to make backups and moving easier

A s a WordPress website owner, you may need to move your site to a different home on the web; either to a new web host or into a different account on your current hosting account. Or maybe you're an owner who needs to move your site right now.

This chapter covers the best way to migrate a blog that exists within a different blogging platform (such as Movable Type or TypePad) to WordPress. This chapter also takes you through how to back up your WordPress files, data, and content and move them to a new hosting provider or a different domain.

Migrating Your Existing Blog to WordPress

So you have a blog on a different blogging system and want to move your blog to WordPress? This chapter helps you accomplish just that. WordPress makes it relatively easy to pack up your data and archives from one blog platform and move to a new WordPress blog.

WordPress lets you move your blog from such platforms as Blogspot (also called Blogger), TypePad, and Movable Type. It also gives you a nifty way to migrate from any blogging platform via RSS feeds, as long as the platform you're importing from has an RSS feed available. Some platforms, such as Myspace, have some limitations on RSS feed availability, so be sure to check with your platform provider. In this chapter, you discover how to prepare your blog for migration and how to move from the specific platforms for which WordPress provides importer plugins.

For each blogging platform, the WordPress.org platform provides you with a quick and easy way to install plugins that allows you to import and use your content right away. The importers are packaged in a plugin format because most people use an importer just once, and some people don't use the importer tools at all. The plugins are there for you to use if you need them. WordPress.com, on the other hand, has the importers built into the software. Note the differences for the version you are using.

Movin' on up

Bloggers have a variety of reasons to migrate from one system to WordPress:

✦ **Curiosity:** There is a *lot* of buzz around the use of WordPress and the whole community of WordPress users. People are naturally curious to check out something that all the cool kids are doing.

✦ **More control of your blog:** This reason applies particularly to those who have a blog on Blogspot, TypePad, or any other hosted service. Hosted programs limit what you can do, create, and mess with. When it comes to plugins, add-ons, and theme creation, hosting a WordPress blog on your own web server wins hands down. Additionally, you have complete control of your data, archives, and backup capability when you host your blog on your own server.

✦ **Ease of use:** Many people find the WordPress interface easier to use, more understandable, and a great deal more user-friendly than many of the other blogging platforms available today.

The hosted version of WordPress.com and the self-hosted version of WordPress.org allow you to migrate your blog to their platforms; however, WordPress.com does not provide as many options for import as WordPress.org does. The following is a list of blogging platforms that have built-in importers, or import plugins, for migration to WordPress:

✦ Blogger

✦ LiveJournal

✦ Movable Type

✦ TypePad

✦ RSS Feeds

✦ Tumblr

✦ WordPress.com

In the WordPress.org software (self-hosted), the importers are added to the installation as plugins. The importer plugins included in the preceding list are plugins packaged within the WordPress.org software or found by searching in the Plugin Directory at `http://wordpress.org/extend/plugins/tags/importer`. You can import content from several other platforms by installing other plugins from the WordPress Plugin Directory, but you may have to search a bit on Google to find them.

Preparing for the big move

Depending on the size of your blog (that is, how many posts and comments you have), the migration process can take anywhere from 5 to 30 minutes. As with any major change or update you make, no matter where your blog is hosted, the very first thing you need to do is create a backup of your blog. You should back up the following:

✦ **Archives:** Posts, comments, and trackbacks

✦ **Template:** Template files and image files

✦ **Links:** Any links, banners, badges, and elements you have in your current blog

✦ **Images:** Any images you use in your blog

Book II
Chapter 7

Backing Up,
Packing Up,
and Moving to
a New Host

Table 7-1 gives you a few tips on creating the export data for your blog in a few major blogging platforms. *Note:* You need to be logged in to your blog software.

Table 7-1	Backing Up Your Blog Data on Major Platforms
Blogging Platform	*Backup Information*
Movable Type	Click the Import/Export button in the menu of your Movable Type Dashboard and then click the Export Entries From link. When the page stops loading, save it on your computer as a `.txt` file.
TypePad	Click the name of the blog you want to export and then click the Import/Export link on the Overview menu. Click the Export link at the bottom of the Import/Export page. When the page stops loading, save it on your computer as a `.txt` file.
Blogspot	Back up your template by copying the text of your template to a text editor, such as Notepad. Save it on your computer as a `.txt` file.
LiveJournal	Browse to `http://livejournal.com/export.bml` and enter your information; choose XML as the format. Save this file on your computer.
Tumblr	Browse to `http://www.tumblr.com/oauth/apps` and follow the directions there to create a Tumblr app. When done, copy the OAuth Consumer Key and Secret Key and paste them in a text file on your computer. Use these keys to connect your WordPress blog to your Tumblr account.

(continued)

Table 7-1 *(continued)*

Blogging Platform	Backup Information
WordPress	Choose Tools➪Export on the Dashboard; choose your options on the Export page and then click the Download Export File button. Save this file on your computer.
RSS feed	Point your browser to the URL of the RSS feed you want to import. Wait until it loads fully. (You may need to set your feed to display all posts.) View the source code of the page, copy and paste that source code into a .txt file, and save the file on your computer.

This import script allows for a maximum file size of 128MB. If you get an "out of memory" error, try dividing the import file into pieces and uploading them separately. The import script is smart enough to ignore duplicate entries, so if you need to run the script a few times to get it to take everything, you can do so without worrying about duplicating your content. (You could also attempt to, temporarily, increase your PHP memory limit by making a quick edit of the wp-config.php file; more information on this is found in Book II, Chapters 3 and 4.)

Converting templates

Every blogging program has a unique way of delivering content and data to your blog. Template tags vary from program to program; no two are the same, and each template file requires conversion if you want to use *your* template with your new WordPress blog. In such a case, you have two options:

✦ **Convert the template yourself.** To accomplish this task, you need to know WordPress template tags and HTML. If you have a template that you're using on another blogging platform and want to convert it for use with WordPress, you need to swap the original platform tags for WordPress tags. The information provided in Book VI gives you the rundown on working with themes, as well as basic WordPress template tags; you may find that information useful if you plan to attempt a template conversion yourself.

✦ **Hire an experienced WordPress consultant to do the conversion for you.** See Book I, Chapter 4 for a list of WordPress consultants.

To use your own template, make sure that you saved *all* the template files, the images, and the stylesheet from your previous blog setup. You need them to convert the template(s) for use in WordPress.

Hundreds of free templates are available for use with WordPress, so it may be a lot easier to abandon the template you're currently working with and find a free WordPress template that you like. If you paid to have a custom design done for your blog, contact the designer of your theme and hire him to perform the template conversion for you. Alternatively, you can hire several WordPress consultants to perform the conversion for you — including yours truly.

Moving your blog to WordPress

You've packed all your stuff, and you have your new place prepared. Moving day has arrived!

This section takes you through the steps for moving your blog from one blog platform to WordPress. This section assumes that you already have the WordPress software installed and configured on your own domain.

Find the import function that you need by following these steps:

1. **On the Dashboard, choose Tools⇨Import.**

   The Import page appears, listing blogging platforms such as Blogger and Movable Type, from which you can import content. (See Figure 7-1.)

2. **Click the link for the blogging platform you're working with.**

3. **Click the Install Now button to install the importer plugin and begin using it.**

The following sections provide some import directions for a few of the most popular blogging platforms (other than WordPress, that is). Each platform has its own content export methods, so be sure to check the documentation for the blogging platform that you are using.

Book II
Chapter 7

Backing Up,
Packing Up,
and Moving to
a New Host

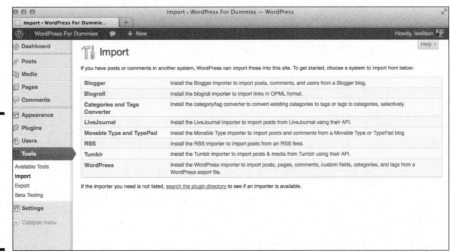

Figure 7-1: The Import feature of the (self-hosted) WordPress.org Dashboard.

Importing from Blogspot, er, Blogger

I call it Blogspot; you call it Blogger — a rose by any other name would smell as sweet. The blogging application owned by Google is referenced either way. In the end, we're talking about the same application.

To begin the import process, first complete the steps in the "Moving your blog to WordPress" section, earlier in this chapter. Then follow these steps:

1. **Click the Blogger link on the Import page and install the plugin for importing from Blogger.**

2. **Click the Activate Plugin & Install Importer link.**

   The Import Blogger page loads with instructions to import your file, as shown in Figure 7-2.

3. **Click the Authorize button to tell WordPress to access your account.**

   A page from Google opens with a message that says your WordPress blog is trying to access your Google account.

4. **Enter the e-mail address and password you use for Google; then click the Sign In button.**

   The Access Request page in your Google Account opens. When you have successfully logged in, you receive a message from Google stating that your blog at WordPress is requesting access to your Blogger account so that it can post entries on your behalf.

Figure 7-2: Import Blogger page on the WordPress Dashboard.

5. **Give your permission by clicking the Grant Access button on the Access Request page.**

   If you have many posts and comments in your Blogger blog, the import can take 30 minutes or more.

   After the import script has performed its magic, you're redirected to your WordPress Dashboard, where the name of your Blogger blog is listed.

6. **To finish importing the data from Blogger, click the Import button (below the Magic Button header).**

   The text on the button changes to *Importing . . .* while the import takes place. When the import is complete, the text on the button changes to *Set Authors* (no wonder it's called the Magic Button!).

7. **Click the Set Authors button to assign the authors to the posts.**

   The Blogger username appears on the left side of the page; a drop-down menu on the right side of the page displays the WordPress login name.

8. **Assign authors by using the drop-down menu.**

   If you have just one author on each blog, the process is especially easy: Use the drop-down menu on the right to assign the WordPress login to your Blogger username. If you have multiple authors on both blogs, each Blogger username is listed on the left side with a drop-down menu to the right of each username. Select a WordPress login for each Blogger username to make the author assignments.

9. **Click Save Changes.**

   You're done!

Importing from LiveJournal

Both WordPress.com and WordPress.org offer an import script for LiveJournal users, and the process of importing from LiveJournal to WordPress is the same for each platform.

From the Import page on your WordPress Dashboard, follow these steps:

1. **Click the LiveJournal link and install the plugin for installing from LiveJournal.**

2. **Click the Activate Plugin & Install Importer link.**

   The Import LiveJournal page loads with instructions to import your file, as shown in Figure 7-3.

3. **In the LiveJournal Username field, type the username for your LiveJournal account.**

4. **In the LiveJournal Password field, type the password for your LiveJournal account.**

**Book II
Chapter 7**

Backing Up,
Packing Up,
and Moving to
a New Host

Figure 7-3:
Import
LiveJournal
page on the
WordPress
Dashboard.

5. **In the Protected Post Password field, enter the password you want to use for all protected entries in your LiveJournal account.**

   If you don't complete this step, every entry you import into WordPress will be viewable by anyone. Be sure to complete this step if any of your entries in your LiveJournal account are password protected (or private).

6. **Click the Connect to LiveJournal and Import button.**

   This connects your WordPress site to your LiveJournal account and automatically imports all entries from your LiveJournal into your WordPress installation. If your LiveJournal site has a lot of entries, this could take a long time — so be patient.

Importing from Movable Type and TypePad

Six Apart created both Movable Type and TypePad. These two blogging platforms run on essentially the same code base, so the import/export procedure is the same for both. Refer to Table 7-1, earlier in this chapter, for details on how to run the export process in both Movable Type and TypePad. This import script moves all your blog posts, comments, and trackbacks to your WordPress blog.

Go to the Import page on your WordPress Dashboard by following Steps 1 and 2 in the "Moving your blog to WordPress" section, earlier in this chapter. Then follow these steps:

1. **Click the Movable Type and TypePad link and install the plugin for importing from Movable Type and TypePad.**

2. **Click the Activate Plugin & Install Importer link.**

   The Import Movable Type or TypePad page loads with instructions to import your file, as shown in Figure 7-4.

3. **Click the Browse button.**

   A window opens, listing your files.

4. **Double-click the name of the export file you saved from your Movable Type or TypePad blog.**

5. **Click the Upload File and Import button.**

   Sit back and let the import script do its magic. When the script finishes, it reloads the page with a confirmation message that the process is complete.

6. **When the import script finishes, assign users to the posts, matching the Movable Type or TypePad usernames with WordPress usernames.**

   If you have just one author on each blog, this process is easy; you simply assign your WordPress login to the Movable Type or TypePad username by using the drop-down menu. If you have multiple authors on both blogs, match the Movable Type or TypePad usernames with the correct WordPress login names.

7. **Click Save Changes.**

Book II
Chapter 7

Backing Up,
Packing Up,
and Moving to
a New Host

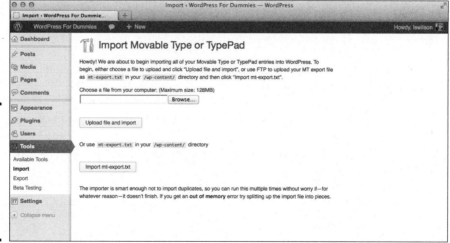

Figure 7-4: Import Movable Type or TypePad page on the WordPress Dashboard.

Importing from Tumblr

With the Tumblr import script for WordPress, it's easy to import the content from your Tumblr account to your WordPress blog. To complete the import, follow these steps:

1. **Go to** www.tumblr.com/oauth/apps.

   The Tumblr login page appears.

2. **Enter your e-mail and password to log in to your Tumblr account.**

   The Register Your Application page appears.

3. **Complete the Register Your Application form by filling in the following fields:**

   - *Application Name:* Type the name of your WordPress website in the text box.

   - *Application Website:* Type the URL of your WordPress website in the text box.

   - *Default Callback URL:* Type the URL of your WordPress website in the text box.

   Seven text fields are in this form, but you only have to fill in these fields; you can leave the rest blank.

4. **Click the Register button.**

   The Applications page refreshes and displays your registered app information at the top.

5. **Copy the OAuth Consumer Key and paste it into a text file on your computer.**

6. **Copy the Secret Key and paste it into the same text file you placed the OAuth Consumer Key in Step 5.**

7. **From your Dashboard, choose Tools⇨Import and click the Tumblr link.**

   The Import Tumblr page on your Dashboard opens.

8. **Insert the OAuth Consumer Key in the indicated text box.**

   Use the OAuth Consumer Key you saved to a text file in Step 5.

9. **Insert the Secret Key in the indicated text box.**

   Use the Secret Key you saved to a text file in Step 6.

10. **Click the Connect to Tumblr button.**

    The Import Tumblr page appears with a message instructing you to authorize Tumblr.

11. **Click the Authorize the Application link.**

    The Authorization page on the Tumblr website asks you to authorize your WordPress site access to your Tumblr account.

12. **Click the Allow button.**

    The Import Tumblr page opens in your WordPress Dashboard and displays a list of your sites from Tumblr.

13. **Click the Import This Blog button in the Action/Status section.**

The content from your Tumblr account is imported into WordPress. Depending on how much content you have on your Tumblr site, this may take several minutes to complete. The Import Tumblr page then refreshes with a message telling you that the import is complete.

Importing from WordPress

With the WordPress import script, you can import one WordPress blog into another; this is true for both the hosted and self-hosted versions of WordPress. WordPress imports all your posts, comments, custom fields, and categories into your blog. Refer to Table 7-1, earlier in this chapter, to find out how to use the export feature to obtain your blog data.

When you complete the export, follow these steps:

1. **Click the WordPress link on the Import page and install the plugin to import from WordPress.**

2. **Click the Activate Plugin & Install Importer link.**

The Import WordPress page loads with instructions to import your file, as shown in Figure 7-5.

3. **Click the Browse button.**

A window opens, listing the files on your computer.

4. **Double-click the export file you saved earlier from your WordPress blog.**

Book II
Chapter 7

Backing Up,
Packing Up,
and Moving to
a New Host

Figure 7-5:
Import
WordPress
page on the
WordPress
Dashboard.

5. **Click the Upload File and Import button.**

   The import script gets to work, and when it finishes, it reloads the page with a confirmation message that the process is complete.

Importing from an RSS feed

If all else fails, or if WordPress doesn't provide an import script that you need for your current blog platform, you can import your blog data via the RSS feed for the blog you want to import. With the RSS import method, you can import posts only; you can't use this method to import comments, trackbacks, categories, or users.

WordPress.com currently doesn't let you import blog data via an RSS feed; this function works only with the self-hosted WordPress.org platform.

Refer to Table 7-1, earlier in this chapter, for the steps to create the file you need to import via RSS. Then follow these steps:

1. **On the Import page of the WordPress Dashboard, click the RSS link and install the plugin to import from an RSS feed.**

2. **Click the Activate & Install link.**

   The Import RSS page loads with instructions to import your RSS file, as shown in Figure 7-6.

3. **Click the Browse button on the Import RSS page.**

   A window opens, listing the files on your computer.

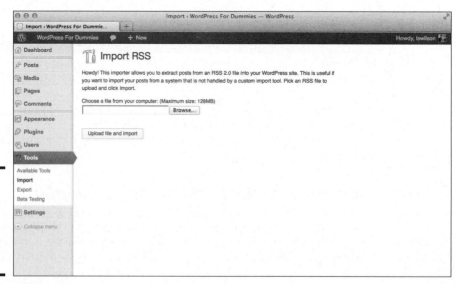

Figure 7-6:
The Import RSS page of the WordPress Dashboard.

4. **Double-click the export file you saved earlier from your RSS feed.**

5. **Click the Upload File and Import button.**

   The import script does its magic and then reloads the page with a confirmation message that the process is complete.

Finding other import resources

The WordPress Codex has a long list of other available scripts, plugins, workarounds, and outright hacks for importing from other blog platforms. You can find that information at `http://codex.wordpress.org/Importing_Content`.

Note, however, that volunteers run the WordPress Codex. When you refer to the Codex, be aware that not everything listed in it is necessarily up-to-date or accurate, including import information (or any other information about running your WordPress blog).

Moving Your Website to a Different Host

There may come a time that you decide you need to switch from your current hosting provider to a new one. There are reasons why you'd have to do this — either you're unhappy with your current provider and want to move to a new one, or your current provider is going out of business and you're forced to move. And transferring an existing website, with all of its content, files, and data, from one host to another can seem a very daunting task. This section of the chapter should make it easier for you.

You can go about it two ways:

✦ Manually through backing up your database and downloading essential files

✦ Using a plugin to automate as much of the process as possible

Obviously, using a tool to automate the process for you to make it easier is the more desirable way to go, but just in case you need to do it manually, in the next section of this chapter, I provide you with the instructions for doing it both ways.

Creating a backup and moving manually

Book II, Chapter 6 provides you with step-by-step instructions on how to take a backup of your database by using phpMyAdmin. Follow the steps available in that chapter and you'll have a backup of your database with all the recent content you've published to your blog — *content* being what you've (or someone else has) written or typed into your blog via the WordPress Dashboard, including

✦ Blog posts, pages, and custom post types

✦ Links, categories, and tags

✦ Post and page options, such as excerpts, time and date, custom fields, post categories, post tags, and passwords

✦ WordPress settings you configured under the Settings menu on the Dashboard

✦ All widgets that you created and configured

✦ All plugin options that you configured for the plugins you installed

Other elements of your website aren't stored in the database, which you need to download, via FTP, from your web server. The following is a list of those elements, including instructions on where to find them and how to download them to your local computer:

✦ **Media files:** The files you uploaded by using the WordPress media upload feature, including images, videos, audio files and documents. Media files are located in the `/wp-content/uploads` folder. Connect to your web server via FTP and download that folder to your local computer.

✦ **Plugin files:** Although all the plugin settings are stored in the database, the actual plugin *files* are not. The plugin files are located in the `/wp-content/plugins` folder. Connect to your web server via FTP and download that folder to your local computer.

✦ **Theme files:** Widgets and options you've set for your current theme are stored in the database; however, the physical theme template files, images, and stylesheets are not. They're stored in the `/wp-content/themes` folder. Connect to your web server via FTP and download that folder to your local computer.

Now you have your database and WordPress files stored safely on your local computer; moving them to a new host just involves reversing the process:

1. **Create a new database on your new hosting account.**

The steps for creating a database are found in Book II, Chapter 4.

2. **Import your database backup into the new database you just created:**

a. Log in to the cPanel for your hosting account.

b. Click the phpMyAdmin icon and click the name of your new database in the left menu.

c. Click the Import tab at the top.

    d. Click the Browse button and select the database backup from your local computer.

    e. Click the Go button; the old database imports into the new.

3. Install WordPress on your new hosting account.

The steps for installing WordPress are found in Book II, Chapter 4.

4. Edit the `wp-config.php` file to include your new database name, username, password, and host.

Information on editing the information in the `wp-config.php` file is found in Book II, Chapter 3 and Chapter 4.

5. Upload all that you downloaded from the `/wp-content` folder to your new hosting account.

6. Browse to your domain in your web browser.

Your website should work, and you can log in to the WordPress Dashboard by using the same username and password as before because that information is stored in the database you imported.

Book II
Chapter 7

Backing Up,
Packing Up,
and Moving to
a New Host

Using a plugin to back up and move to a new host

BackupBuddy is a plugin that moves a WordPress website from one hosting environment to another. This plugin is not free or available in the WordPress Plugin Directory, but it's worth every penny because it takes the entire backup and migration process and makes mincemeat out of it — meaning, it makes moving the site easy to accomplish and can be done in minutes rather than hours. Follow these steps to use this plugin to move your site to a new hosting server:

1. Purchase and download the BackupBuddy plugin from `http://ithemes.com/purchase/backupbuddy/`.

At this time, the cost for the plugin starts at $45.

2. Install the plugin on your current WordPress website.

By *current,* I mean the old one, not the new hosting account yet.

3. Activate the plugin on your WordPress Dashboard.

Choose Plugins in the navigation menu and then click the Activate link under the BackupBuddy plugin name.

4. Navigate to the Backups section on the BackupBuddy options page.

Click the Backups link in the BackupBuddy menu.

5. Click the Full Backup button.

This initiates a full backup of your database, files, and content and wraps it neatly into one `.zip` file for you to store on your local computer.

6. **Download the `importbuddy.php` file.**

   Click the `importbuddy.php` file on the Backups page and download it to your local computer, preferably in the same directory as the backup file you downloaded in Step 5.

7. **Connect to your new web server via FTP.**

8. **Upload the `backup.zip` file and the `importbuddy.php` file.**

   These files should be uploaded in the root, or top level, directory on your web server. (On some web servers, this is the `/public_html` folder; on others it might be the `/httpdocs` folder. If you're unsure what your root directory is, your hosting provider should be able to tell you.)

9. **Create a new database on your new hosting account.**

   The steps for creating a database are found in Book II, Chapter 4.

10. **Navigate to the `importbuddy.php` file in your web browser.**

    The URL for this looks similar to `http://yourdomain.com/import buddy.php`.

    The BackupBuddy page loads in your web browser.

11. **Follow the steps to import the backup file and install WordPress, including the database information needed: database username, name, password, and host.**

    This entire process takes about five to ten minutes, maybe more depending on the size of your website.

12. **Load your website in your web browser.**

    After BackupBuddy does its thing, your website is ready to use like always.

Book III

Exploring the WordPress Dashboard

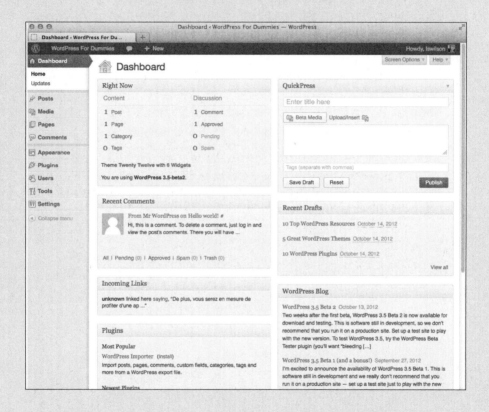

Visit www.dummies.com/extras/wordpressaio to discover GPL commercial themes and plugins..

Contents at a Glance

Chapter 1: Logging In and Taking a Look Around

*W*ith WordPress successfully installed, you can explore your new blogging software. This chapter guides you through the preliminary setup of your new WordPress blog by using the Dashboard. When you blog with WordPress, you spend a lot of time on the Dashboard, which is where you make all the exciting behind-the-scenes stuff happen. In this panel, you can find all the settings and options that enable you to set up your blog just the way you want it. (If you still need to install and configure WordPress, check out Book II, Chapter 4.)

Feeling comfortable with the Dashboard sets you up for successful entrance into the WordPress blogging world. You'll tweak your WordPress settings several times throughout the life of your blog. In this chapter, while you go through the various sections, settings, options, and configurations available to you, understand that nothing is set in stone. You can set options today and change them at any time.

Logging In to the Dashboard

I find that the direct approach (also known as *jumping in*) works best when I want to get familiar with a new software tool. To that end, follow these steps to log in to WordPress and take a look at the guts of the Dashboard:

1. **Open your web browser and type the WordPress login-page address (or URL) in the address box.**

   The login-page address looks something like this (exchange that .com for a .org or a .net as needed):

   ```
   http://www.yourdomain.com/wp-login.php
   ```

   If you installed WordPress in its own folder, include that folder name in the login URL. If you installed WordPress in a folder ingeniously named wordpress, the login URL becomes

   ```
   http://www.yourdomain.com/wordpress/wp-login.php
   ```

2. **Type your username in the Username text box and your password in the Password text box.**

In case you forget your password, WordPress has you covered. Click the Lost Your Password link (located near the bottom of the page), enter your username and e-mail address, and then click the Submit button. WordPress resets your password and e-mails the new password to you.

After you request a password, you receive two e-mails from your WordPress blog. The first e-mail contains a link that you click to verify that you requested the password. After you verify your intentions, you receive a second e-mail containing your new password.

3. **Select the Remember Me check box if you want WordPress to place a cookie in your browser.**

The cookie tells WordPress to remember your login credentials the next time you show up. The cookie set by WordPress is harmless and stores your WordPress login on your computer. Because of the cookie, WordPress remembers you the next time you visit. Because this option tells the browser to remember your login, don't select Remember Me when you're using your work computer, other devices such as a tablet or mobile phone, or a computer at an Internet café.

Note: Before you set this option, make sure that your browser is configured to allow cookies. (If you aren't sure how to do this, check the help documentation of the Internet browser you're using.)

4. **Click the Log In button.**

After you log in to WordPress, you see the Dashboard page.

Navigating the Dashboard

You can consider the Dashboard to be a Control Panel of sorts because it offers several quick links and areas that provide information about your blog, starting with the actual Dashboard page shown in Figure 1-1. When you view your Dashboard for the very first time, all the modules appear in the expanded (open) position by default.

You can change how the WordPress Dashboard looks by modifying the order in which the modules (for example, Right Now and Recent Comments) appear on it. You can expand (open) and collapse (close) the individual modules by clicking your mouse anywhere within the gray title bar of the module. This feature is really nice because you can use the Dashboard for just those modules that you use regularly. The concept is easy: Keep the modules you use all the time open and close the ones that you use only occasionally — open those modules only when you really need them. You save screen space by customizing your Dashboard to suit your needs.

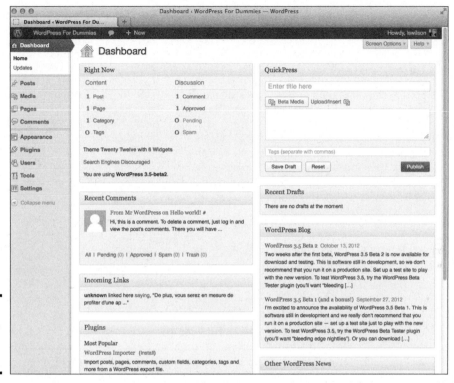

Book III
Chapter 1

Logging In and
Taking a Look
Around

Figure 1-1:
Log in to the
WordPress
Dashboard.

The navigation menu on the WordPress Dashboard appears on the left side of your browser window. When you need to get back to the main Dashboard page, click the Dashboard link at the top of the navigation menu found on any of the pages within your WordPress Dashboard.

In the following sections, I cover the Dashboard page as it appears when you log in to your WordPress Dashboard for the very first time; later in this chapter, in the section "Arranging the Dashboard to Your Tastes," I show you how to configure the appearance of your Dashboard so that it best suits how you use the available modules.

Right Now

The Right Now module in the Dashboard shows what's going on in your blog right now — right this very second! Figure 1-2 shows the expanded Right Now module in a brand-spanking-new WordPress blog.

Discovering the admin bar

The admin bar is the menu you see at the top of the Dashboard (refer to Figure 1-1). The admin bar appears at the top of every page on your site, by default, and across the top of every page of the Dashboard if you set it to do so in your profile settings (as explained in Chapter 3 of this minibook). The nice thing is that the only person who can see the admin bar is you because it displays only for the user who is logged in. The admin bar contains shortcuts that take you to the most frequently viewed areas of your WordPress Dashboard, from left to right:

✔ **The name of your website:** Go to the front page of your website.

✔ **Comments page:** The next link is a comment balloon icon; click that and visit the Comments page on your Dashboard.

✔ **New:** Hover your mouse and you find links to Post and Page, which you click to go to either the Add New Post page or the Add New Page screen. You can also navigate to the Media Library or the Users page on the Dashboard.

✔ **Your photo and name display:** Hover your mouse pointer over this to open a drop-down menu that provides you with links to two areas on your Dashboard: Edit Your Profile, and Log Out.

Again, the admin bar is seen only by you at the top of your site, no matter what page you're on, as long as you are logged in to your WordPress site.

Website name   New Post or Page

Comments page   Your photo and name

Figure 1-2:
The Right
Now module
in the
Dashboard,
expanded
so that you
can see the
available
features.

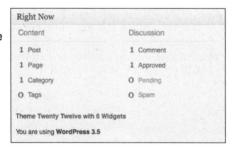

The Right Now module shows the following default information below the Content and Discussion headers:

✦ **The number of posts you have:** This number reflects the total number of posts you currently have in your WordPress blog; the blog in Figure 1-2 has one post. The number is blue, which means it's a clickable link. When you click the link, you go to the Edit Posts page, where you can edit the posts on your blog. Book IV, Chapter 1 covers editing posts.

✦ **The number of pages:** The number of pages on your blog, which changes when you add or delete pages. (*Pages,* in this context, refer to the static pages you create in your blog.) Figure 1-2 shows that the blog has one page.

Clicking this link takes you to the Edit Pages page, where you can view, edit, and delete your current pages. (Find the difference between WordPress posts and pages in Book IV, Chapter 2.)

✦ **The number of categories:** The number of categories on your blog, which changes when you add and delete categories. Figure 1-2 shows that this blog has one category.

Clicking this link takes you to the Categories page, where you can view, edit, and delete your current categories or add brand-new ones. (For details about the management and creation of categories, see Book III, Chapter 5.)

✦ **The number of tags:** The number of tags in your blog, which changes when you add and delete categories. The blog shown in Figure 1-2 has zero tags because it's brand-new and I haven't added any tags yet.

Clicking this link takes you to the Tags page, where you can add new tags and view, edit, and delete your current tags. (You can find more information about tags in Book III, Chapter 5.)

✦ **The number of comments:** The number of comments on your blog. Figure 1-2 shows that this blog has 1 comment, 1 approved comment, 0 (zero) pending comments, and 0 (zero) comments marked as spam.

Clicking any of these four links takes you to the Edit Comments page, where you can manage the comments on your blog. Book III, Chapter 4 covers comments.

The last section of the Dashboard's Right Now module shows the following information:

✦ **Which WordPress theme you're using:** Figure 1-2 shows that the blog is using the theme called Twenty Twelve. The theme name is a link that, when clicked, takes you to the Manage Themes page, where you can view and activate themes on your blog.

✦ **How many widgets you've added to your blog:** The number of WordPress widgets you're using in your blog. Figure 1-2 shows that this blog has 6 widgets. The number 6 is a link that, when clicked, takes

**Book III
Chapter 1**

Logging In and
Taking a Look
Around

you to the Widgets page, where you can change your widget options by editing them, moving them, or removing them. (Widgets are covered in detail in Book VI, Chapter 1.)

✦ **The version of WordPress you're using:** The last statement in the Right Now section. Figure 1-2 shows that this blog is using WordPress version 3.5. This version announcement changes if you're using an earlier version of WordPress. When WordPress software is upgraded, this statement tells you that you're using an outdated version of WordPress and encourages you to upgrade to the latest version.

Recent Comments

The module below the Right Now module is the Recent Comments module, as shown in Figure 1-3. Within this module, you find

✦ **Most recent comments published to your blog:** WordPress displays a maximum of five comments in this area.

✦ **The author of each comment:** The name of the person who left the comment appears below it. This section also displays the author's picture (or avatar), if she has one.

✦ **A link to the post the comment was left on:** The post title appears to the right of the commenter's name. Click the link to go to that post on the Dashboard.

✦ **An excerpt of the comment:** This is a snippet of the comment this person left on your blog.

✦ **Comment management links:** When you hover your mouse pointer over the comment, five links appear underneath the comment. These links give you the opportunity to manage those comments right from your Dashboard: The first link is Unapprove, which appears only if you have comment moderation turned on. (Find out more about moderating comments in Chapter 4 of this minibook.) The other four links are Reply, Edit, Spam, and Trash.

✦ **View links:** These links appear at the bottom of the Recent Comments module, where you can click All, Pending, Approved, Spam, and Trash.

Figure 1-3:
The Recent Comments module in the Dashboard.

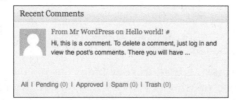

Recent Comments

From Mr WordPress on Hello world! #
Hi, this is a comment. To delete a comment, just log in and view the post's comments. There you will have ...

All | Pending (0) | Approved | Spam (0) | Trash (0)

You can find even more information on managing your comments in Book III, Chapter 4.

Incoming Links

The next module visible on the Dashboard is Incoming Links. It lists all the blog-savvy people who wrote a blog post that links to your blog. When your blog is brand-new, you won't see any incoming links listed in this section. Don't despair, however; as time goes on, you will see this listing of links fill up as more and more people discover you and your inspired writings!

In the meantime, the Incoming Links module shows the following message: This dashboard widget queries Google Blog Search so that when another blog links to your site it will show up here. It has found no incoming links ... yet. It's okay — there is no rush. The phrase *Google Blog Search* is a link; when you click it, you go to the Google Blog Search directory, which is a search engine for blogs only.

You're not restricted to using the Google Blog Search engine (http:// google.com/blogsearch) to provide your Incoming Links information. The following steps show you how to edit the Incoming Links module, including which site to provide links:

1. **Hover your mouse pointer over the title of the Incoming Links module, and a new link labeled *Configure* appears directly to the right of the title. Click that link.**

   Now you can change the settings of the Incoming Links module. See Figure 1-4.

2. **Add a URL in the Enter the RSS Feed URL Here text box.**

   You can enter the URL of any RSS feed you want to display incoming links to your site. Examples of feeds you can use include the following:

   - Technorati (http://technorati.com)
   - Yahoo! Search (http://search.yahoo.com)
   - Social Mention (www.socialmention.com)

**Book III
Chapter 1**

**Logging In and
Taking a Look
Around**

Figure 1-4:
Changing the settings of the Incoming Links module by clicking the Configure link.

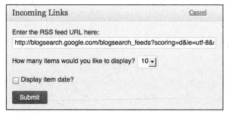

3. **Specify how many items you want to display.**

The default number is 5, but making a different choice from the How Many Items Would You Like to Display drop-down menu lets you display up to 20 items (incoming links).

4. **Specify whether to display the item date.**

Select the Display Item Date check box if you want each incoming link to display the date the link was created. If you don't want the date to display, leave that box deselected.

5. **Click the Submit button to save all your preferences.**

Clicking Submit resets the Incoming Links module with your new settings saved.

Plugins

I cover the management and use of WordPress plugins in detail in Book VII; however, for the purposes of this section, I discuss the functions of the Plugins module on the Dashboard so that you know what to do with it now!

The Plugins module includes three titles of WordPress plugins linked to its page within the WordPress Plugin Directory. The Plugins module pulls information via RSS feed from the official WordPress Plugin Directory at `http://wordpress.org/extend/plugins`. This module displays a plugin from two different plugin categories in the official WordPress Plugin Directory: Most Popular and Newest Plugins. (See Figure 1-5.)

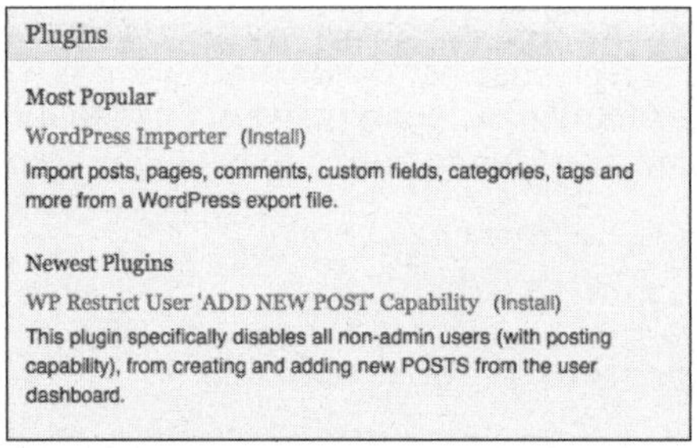

Figure 1-5: The Plugins module in the Dashboard.

The Plugins module doesn't have an Edit link, so you can't customize the information that it displays. Use this box to discover new plugins that can help you do fun and exciting things with your blog.

The Plugins module does have a very exciting feature that you can use to install, activate, and manage plugins on your blog. Just follow these steps to make it happen:

1. **Click the Install link next to the title of a plugin you're interested in.**

The Plugin Information window opens. It displays the various bits of information about the plugin you've chosen, such as title, description, version, author, date last updated, and the number of times the plugin was downloaded.

2. **Click the Install Now button.**

This button is at the top right of the Plugin Information page.

The Plugin Information window closes, and the Install Plugins page on your WordPress Dashboard opens. You see a confirmation message that the plugin has been downloaded, unpacked, and successfully installed.

3. **Specify whether to install the plugin or proceed to the Plugins page.**

Two links are shown under the confirmation message:

- *Activate Plugin:* Click this link to activate the plugin you just installed on your blog.

- *Return to Plugins Page:* Click this link to go to the Manage Plugins page.

I cover the installation and activation of WordPress plugins in further depth in Book VII.

4. **Click the Dashboard link to return to the Dashboard.**

The Dashboard link is located at the top of the left-side navigation menu on every page of your WordPress Dashboard.

QuickPress

The QuickPress module, shown in Figure 1-6, is a handy form that allows you to write, save, and publish a blog post right from your WordPress Dashboard. The options are similar to the ones I cover in Book IV, Chapter 1.

**Book III
Chapter 1**

Logging In and
Taking a Look
Around

Figure 1-6:
The
QuickPress
module
in the
Dashboard.

Recent Drafts

If you're using a brand-new WordPress blog and this is a new installation, the Recent Drafts module displays the message There Are No Drafts at the Moment because you haven't written any drafts. As time goes on, however, and you write a few posts in your blog, you may save some of those posts as drafts to be edited and published later. Those drafts show up in the Recent Drafts module.

The Recent Drafts module displays up to five drafts, showing for each the title of the post, the date it was last saved, and a short excerpt. A View All link also appears; click that link to go the Manage Posts page, where you can view, edit, and manage your blog posts. (Check out Book IV, Chapter 2 for more information.) Figure 1-7 displays the Recent Drafts module, with three posts in draft status, awaiting publication.

Figure 1-7:
The Recent
Drafts
module
in the
Dashboard.

Recent Drafts

10 Top WordPress Resources October 14, 2012

5 Great WordPress Themes October 14, 2012

10 WordPress Plugins October 14, 2012

View all

WordPress Blog

When you first install WordPress, the WordPress Blog module is by default populated with the two most recent updates from the official WordPress blog at http://wordpress.org/news. You see the title of the last post, the date it was published, and a short excerpt of the post. Click a title and you go directly to that post on the WordPress blog.

Following the updates of the WordPress Blog is very useful, and I highly recommend it because every single time you log in to your WordPress Dashboard, a glance at this section informs you about any news, updates, or alerts from the makers of WordPress. You can find out about any new versions of the software, security patches, or other important news regarding the software you're using to power your blog.

Although I recommend that you keep the WordPress Blog updates in this module, the WordPress platform lets you change this module to display posts from another blog of your choosing. You can accomplish this change by following these steps:

1. **Hover your mouse pointer over the WordPress Blog module title. Click the Configure link shown to the right of the WordPress Blog title.**

The module changes to display several options to change the information contained in the box. See Figure 1-8.

2. **Type your preferred RSS feed in the Enter the RSS Feed URL Here text box.**

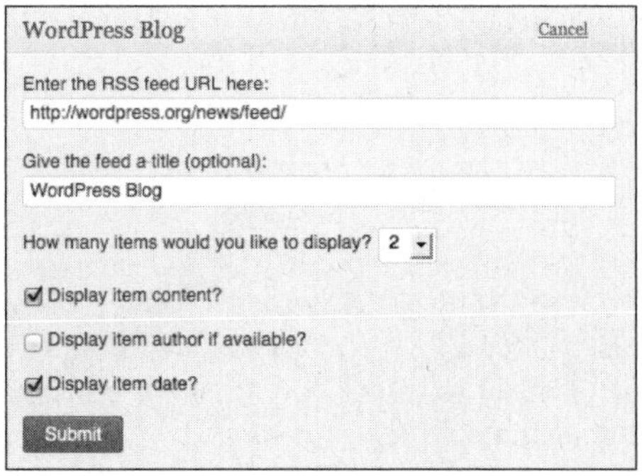

Figure 1-8:
Options
to change
the feed
title and
URL of the
WordPress
Blog
module.

WordPress Blog   Cancel

Enter the RSS feed URL here:
http://wordpress.org/news/feed/

Give the feed a title (optional):
WordPress Blog

How many items would you like to display? 2 ▾

☑ Display item content?

☐ Display item author if available?

☑ Display item date?

[Submit]

3. **Type your preferred title in the Give the Feed a Title (Optional) text box.**

4. **Specify the number of items you want to display.**

   The default number is 2, but you can display up to 20 by making a different choice from the How Many Items Would You Like to Display drop-down menu.

5. **Specify whether you want to display the item's content.**

   Item content refers to the text content of the post. If you don't select the Display Item Content check box, WordPress doesn't display an excerpt of the post — only the post title.

6. **Specify whether you want to display the name of the person who wrote the post.**

   Leave the Display Item Author If Available check box deselected if you don't want the author's name displayed.

7. **Specify whether you want to display the date.**

   Leave the Display Item Date check box deselected if you don't want the date displayed.

8. **Click the Submit button to save your changes.**

   The Dashboard page refreshes with your new changes. Click the title of the box to collapse it.

If you change your mind, click the Cancel link shown to the right of the WordPress Blog title. Clicking Cancel discards any changes you made and keeps the original settings intact.

The title of the WordPress Blog module changes to the title you chose in Step 3. Figure 1-9 shows that I changed the title to Lisas Blog.

**Book III
Chapter 1**

Logging In and
Taking a Look
Around

Figure 1-9:
The
WordPress
Blog module
changes
based on
the options
you set.

Lisas Blog

WordPress Dashboard Theme Documentation August 16, 2012
I was just finishing up the chapters for the 5th Edition of my WordPress
For Dummies book (shameless plug, it'll be released later this year) and
as I was making my gazzilionth screenshot (yes, at LEAST a
GAZILLION) that little drop down menu underneath the Theme Editor
caught my eye and I thought to myself ... [...]

Attend ALL THE THINGS! August 13, 2012
The time between now and November has me traveling a great deal for
WordCamps and other events. If you are attending any of these events,
I hope you find me there and say HI! WordCamp Grand Rapids – August
18-19th: Because who doesn't want to travel to Grand Rapids,
Michigan?? It's always been a dream ... [...]

Other WordPress News

The Other WordPress News module of the Dashboard pulls in posts from a site called WordPress Planet (http://planet.wordpress.org). By keeping the default setting in this area, you stay in touch with several posts made by folks who are involved in WordPress development, design, and troubleshooting. You can find lots of interesting and useful tidbits if you keep this area intact. Quite often, I find great information about new plugins or themes, problem areas and support, troubleshooting, and new ideas, so I tend to stick with the default setting.

WordPress is all about user experience, however, so you can change the options to specify what displays in this area. You can change the items in this module the same way that you change the options for the WordPress Blog module, as described in the preceding section.

Arranging the Dashboard to Your Tastes

One of the features I'm really quite fond of in WordPress is the ability to create my own workspace within the Dashboard. In the following sections, you can find out how to customize your WordPress Dashboard to fit your individual needs, including modifying the layout of the Dashboard, changing links and RSS feed information, and even rearranging the modules on the different pages of the Dashboard. Armed with this information, you can open up your Dashboard and create your very own workspace.

Changing the order of modules

You can arrange the order of the modules in your Dashboard to suit your tastes. WordPress places a great deal of emphasis on user experience, and a big part of that effort results in your ability to create a Dashboard that you find most useful. You can very easily change the modules to display and the order in which they display.

Follow these steps to move the Right Now module so that it appears on the right side of your Dashboard page:

1. **Hover your mouse cursor on the title bar of the Right Now module.**

When hovering over the title, your mouse cursor changes to the Move cursor (a cross with arrows on a PC or the hand cursor on a Mac).

2. **Click and hold your mouse button and drag the Right Now module to the right side of the screen.**

While you drag the module, a light-gray box with a dotted border appears on the right side of your screen. That gray box is a guide that shows you where you can drop the module. See Figure 1-10.

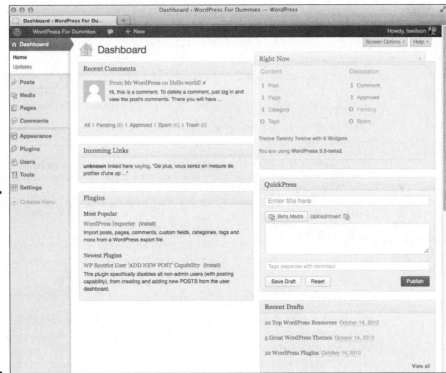

Figure 1-10:
A light gray box appears as a guide when you drag and drop modules in the WordPress Dashboard.

3. **Release the mouse button when you have the Right Now module in place.**

The Right Now module is positioned on the right side of your Dashboard page.

The other modules on the right side of the Dashboard have shifted down, and the Recent Comments Module is the module in the top left of the Dashboard page.

4. **(Optional) Click the title bar of the Right Now module.**

   The module collapses. Click the title bar again to expand the module. You can keep that module open or closed based on your own preference.

Repeat these steps with each module that you want to move on the Dashboard by dragging and dropping them so that they appear in the order you prefer.

When you navigate away from the Dashboard, WordPress remembers the changes you made. When you return, you still see your customized Dashboard, and you don't need to redo these changes in the future.

Removing Dashboard modules

If you find that your Dashboard contains a few modules that you just never use, you can get rid of them altogether by following these steps:

1. **Click the Screen Options button at the top of the Dashboard.**

   The Screen Options pop-up menu opens, displaying the title of each module with a check box to the left of each title.

2. **Deselect the check box for the module you want to hide on your Dashboard.**

   The check mark disappears from the box, and the module disappears from your Dashboard.

If you want a module that you hid to reappear, you can simply enable that module by selecting the module's check box on the Screen Options menu.

Changing the Dashboard layout

Everyone works differently, which means everyone likes a different sort of workspace layout. Personally, when it comes to the Dashboard, I like to have one long column of items so that I can scroll through and focus on one area, in particular, without other things appearing to the right and left.

In the same Screen Options area where you can remove modules (as discussed in the preceding section), you can also change the format of your Dashboard by choosing to have one, two, three, or four columns displayed on your Dashboard — just follow these few steps:

1. **Click the Screen Options button at the top of the Dashboard.**

   The Screen Options pop-up menu opens.

2. In the Screen Layout Options section of the menu, choose the number of columns you want displayed.

You have the choice of one, two, three, or four columns — select the radio button to the left of the number you want, and your Dashboard display changes immediately.

3. Click the Screen Options button again to close the Screen Options menu.

You can see that I like all my stuff in one long column, which my blog's Dashboard shows in Figure 1-11, where I chose to display my Dashboard in a one-column layout. In Figure 1-11, almost all of my Dashboard modules are closed — you can open and close them when you need to, based on what you need to see and do within your Dashboard at any given time.

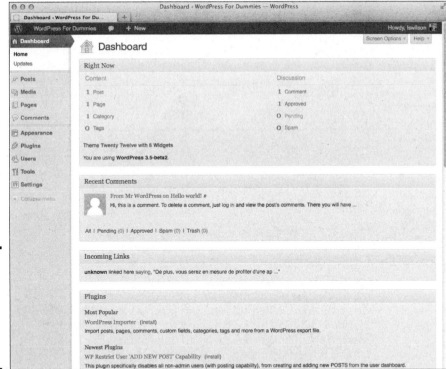

Figure 1-11: My WordPress Dashboard displays a one-column layout.

Finding Inline Documentation and Help

The developers of the WordPress software really put in time and effort to provide tons of inline documentation that gives you several tips and hints right inside the Dashboard. You can generally find inline documentation for nearly every WordPress feature you'll use.

Inline documentation refers to those small sentences or phrases that you see alongside or below a feature in WordPress that give a short, but very helpful, explanation about what the feature is. Figure 1-12 shows the General Settings page, where a lot of inline documentation and guiding tips correspond with each feature. These tips can clue you into what the features are, how to use them, and some basic recommended settings.

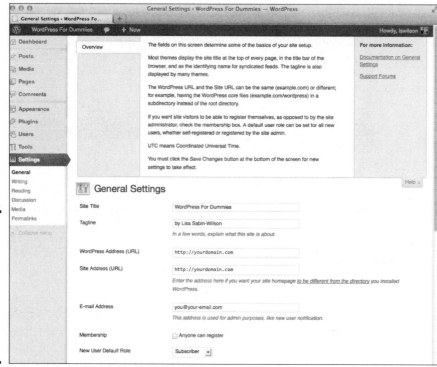

Figure 1-12: Inline document-ation on the General Settings page in the WordPress Dashboard.

In addition to the inline documentation that you find scattered throughout the Dashboard, a helpful Help tab is located in the upper-right corner of your Dashboard. Click this tab to open a panel that contains help text that is relevant to the page you're currently viewing in your Dashboard. For example, if you're viewing the General Settings page, the Help tab displays documentation relevant to the General Settings page. Likewise, if you're viewing the Add New Post page, the Help tab displays documentation with topics relevant to the settings and features you find on the Add New Post page within your Dashboard.

The inline documentation and the topics and text you find in the Help tab both exist to assist you while you work with the WordPress platform, helping make the experience as easy to understand as possible. Other places on the web that you can visit to find help and useful support for WordPress include the WordPress Support Forums at `http://wordpress.org/support`.

Chapter 2: Exploring Tools and Settings

In This Chapter

✓ Configuring your WordPress general settings

✓ Putting together your personal profile

✓ Formatting your blog

As exciting as it is to dig right in and start blogging right away, you should attend to a few housekeeping items first, including adjusting the settings that allow you to personalize your website or blog. I cover these settings first in this chapter because they create your readers' experience with your website.

In this chapter, you can completely explore the Settings menu on the WordPress Dashboard and discover how to configure items such as date and time settings, site titles, and e-mail notification settings. This chapter also covers important aspects of your website configuration, such as permalinks, discussion options, and privacy settings.

Some of the menu items, such as creating and publishing new posts, are covered in detail in other chapters, but they're well worth a mention here, as well.

Configuring the Settings

At the very bottom of the navigation menu, you can find the Settings option. Click Settings, and a menu opens that contains the following links, which I discuss in the sections that follow:

✦ General

✦ Writing

✦ Reading

✦ Discussion

✦ Media

✦ Permalinks

General

After you install the WordPress software and log in, you can put a personal stamp on your blog by giving it a title and description, setting your contact e-mail address, and identifying yourself as the author of the blog. You take care of these and other settings on the General Settings page.

To begin personalizing your blog, start with your general settings by following these steps:

1. **Click General link on the Settings menu.**

The General Settings page appears, as shown in Figure 2-1.

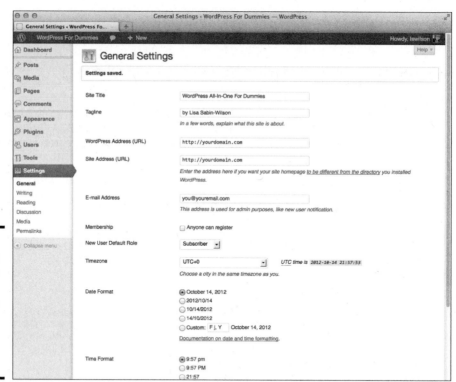

Figure 2-1:
Personalize the settings of your WordPress blog on the General Settings page.

2. **Enter the name of your blog in the Site Title text box.**

The title you enter here is the one that you gave your blog to identify it as your own. In Figure 2-1, I gave the new blog the title *WordPress All-In-One For Dummies,* which appears on the blog, as well as in the title bar of the viewer's web browser.

Give your blog an interesting and identifiable name. You can use *Fried Green Tomatoes,* for example, if you're blogging about the topic, the book, or the movie, or even anything remotely related to the lovely Southern dish.

3. **In the Tagline text box, enter a five- to ten-word phrase that describes your blog.**

Figure 2-1 shows that the tagline is *by Lisa Sabin-Wilson.* Therefore, this blog displays the blog title, followed by the tagline: *WordPress All-in-One For Dummies by Lisa Sabin-Wilson.*

The general Internet-surfing public can view your blog title and tagline, which various search engines (such as Google, Yahoo!, and Bing) grab for indexing, so choose your words with this fact in mind. (You can find more information about search engine optimization, or SEO, in Book V.)

4. **In the WordPress Address (URL) text box, enter the location where you installed your WordPress blog software.**

Be sure to include the `http://` portion of the URL and the entire path to your WordPress installation — for example, `http://yourdomain.com`. If you installed WordPress in a folder in your directory — in a folder called `wordpress`, for example — you need to make sure to include it here. If you installed WordPress in a folder called `wordpress`, the WordPress address would be `http://yourdomain.com/wordpress` (where *yourdomain.com* is your domain name).

5. **In the Site Address (URL) text box, enter the web address where people can find your blog by using their web browsers.**

Typically, what you enter here is the same as your domain name (`http://yourdomain.com`). If you install WordPress in a subdirectory of your site, the WordPress installation URL is different from the blog URL. If you install WordPress at `http://yourdomain.com/wordpress/` (WordPress URL), you need to tell WordPress that you want the blog to appear at `http://yourdomain.com` (the blog URL).

6. **Enter your e-mail address in the E-Mail Address text box.**

WordPress sends messages about the details of your blog to this e-mail address. When a new user registers for your blog, for example, WordPress sends you an e-mail alert.

7. **Select a Membership option.**

Select the Anyone Can Register check box if you want to keep registration on your blog open to anyone. Leave the check box deselected if you'd rather not have open registration on your blog.

8. **From the New User Default Role drop-down list, select the role that you want new users to have when they register for user accounts in your blog.**

Book III Chapter 2

Exploring Tools and Settings

You need to understand the differences among the user roles because each user role is assigned a different level of access to your blog, as follows:

- *Subscriber:* The default role. You may want to maintain this role as the one assigned to new users, particularly if you don't know who's registering. Subscribers have access to the Dashboard page, and they can view and change the options in their profiles on the Your Profile and Personal Options page. (They don't have access to your account settings, however — only to their own.) Each user can change his username, e-mail address, password, bio, and other descriptors in his user profile. Subscribers' profile information is stored in the WordPress database, and your blog remembers them each time they visit, so they don't have to complete the profile information each time they leave comments on your blog.

- *Contributor:* In addition to the access subscribers have, contributors can upload files and write, edit, and manage their own posts. Contributors can write posts, but they can't publish the posts; the administrator reviews all contributor posts and decides whether to publish them. This setting is a nice way to moderate content written by new authors.

- *Author:* In addition to the access contributors have, authors can publish and edit their own posts.

- *Editor:* In addition to the access authors have, editors can moderate comments, manage categories, manage links, edit pages, and edit other authors' posts.

- *Administrator:* Administrators can edit all the options and settings in the WordPress blog.

9. **From the Timezone drop-down list, select your UTC time.**

This setting refers to the number of hours that your local time differs from Coordinated Universal Time (UTC). This setting ensures that all the blog posts and comments left on your blog are time-stamped with the correct time. If you're lucky enough, like I am, to live on the frozen tundra of Wisconsin, which is in the Central Standard Time (CST) Zone, you choose **–6** from the drop-down list because that time zone is 6 hours off UTC.

If you're unsure what your UTC time is, you can find it at the Greenwich Mean Time (`http://wwp.greenwichmeantime.com`) website. GMT is essentially the same thing as UTC. WordPress also lists some major cities in the Timezone drop-down list so that you can more easily choose your time zone if you don't know it.

10. **For the Date Format option, select the format in which you want the date to appear in your blog.**

This setting determines the style of the date display. The default format displays time like this: January 1, 2013.

Select a different format by clicking the radio button to the left of the option you want. You can also customize the date display by selecting the Custom option and entering your preferred format in the text box provided. If you're feeling adventurous, you can find out how to customize the date format at `http://codex.wordpress.org/Formatting_Date_and_Time`.

11. **For the Time Format option, select the format for how you want time to display in your blog.**

This setting is the style of the time display. The default format displays time like this: 12:00 a.m.

Select a different format by clicking the radio button to the left of the option you want. You can also customize the date display by selecting the Custom option and entering your preferred format in the text box provided; find out how at `http://codex.wordpress.org/Formatting_Date_and_Time`.

You can format the time and date in several ways. Go to `http://us3.php.net/date` to find potential formats at the PHP website.

12. **From the Week Starts On drop-down list (not shown in Figure 2-1; you need to scroll down to access it), select the day on which the week starts in your calendar.**

Displaying the calendar in the sidebar of your blog is optional. If you choose to display the calendar, you can select the day of the week on which you want your calendar to start.

Click the Save Changes button at the bottom of any page where you set new options. If you don't click Save Changes, your settings aren't saved, and WordPress reverts to the preceding options. Each time you click the Save Changes button, WordPress reloads the current page, displaying the new options that you just set.

Writing

Click Writing in the Settings menu list; the Writing Settings page opens. (See Figure 2-2.)

This page lets you set some basic options for writing your posts. Table 2-1 gives you some information on choosing how your posts look and how WordPress handles some specific conditions.

After you set your options, be sure to click the Save Changes button; otherwise, the changes won't take effect.

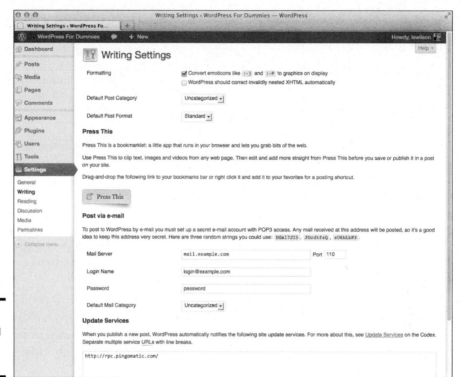

Figure 2-2:
The Writing
Settings
page.

Table 2-1	Writing Settings Options	
Option	*Function*	*Default*
Formatting	Determines whether WordPress converts emoticons to graphics and whether WordPress corrects invalidly nested XHTML automatically. In general, always select this option. (You can find more information about valid XHTML code at `http://validator.w3.org/docs/#docs_all`.)	Converts emoticons — such as :-) and :-P — to graphics.
Default Post Category	Select the category that WordPress defaults to any time you forget to choose a category when you publish a post.	Uncategorized

Option	Function	Default
Default Post Format	Select the format that WordPress defaults to any time you create a post and do not assign a post format. (This is theme specific; not all themes support post formats. See Book VI, Chapter 6.)	Standard
Press This	Drag and drop the Press This link to the bookmark toolbar of your web browser and then use it to easily publish content that you find around the Internet directly to your blog.	N/A
Post via E-Mail	Publish blog posts from your e-mail account by entering the e-mail and server information for the account you'll be using to send posts to your WordPress blog.	N/A
Update Services *Note:* This option is available only if you make your blog public.	Indicate which ping service you want to use to notify the world that you've made updates, or new posts, to your blog. The default, XML-RPC (`http://rpc.pingomatic.com`), updates all the popular services simultaneously.	`http://rpc.pingomatic.com`

Book III Chapter 2

Exploring Tools and Settings

Go to `http://codex.wordpress.org/Update_Services` for comprehensive information on update services.

Reading

The third item in the Settings drop-down list is Reading. Click the Reading link to open the Reading Settings page. (See Figure 2-3.)

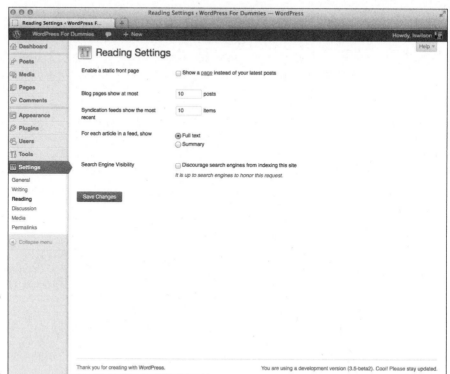

Figure 2-3:
The Reading
Settings
page.

You can set the following options on the Reading Settings page:

✦ **Enable a Static Front Page:** Select the check box to show a page instead
of your latest posts on the front page of your site. You can find detailed
information about using a static page for your front page in Book IV,
Chapter 2, including information on how to set it up by using the fields
in this section that appear after you select the check box.

✦ **Blog Pages Show at Most:** In the text box, enter the maximum number of
posts you want to appear on each blog page.

✦ **Syndication Feeds Show the Most Recent:** In the text box, enter the
maximum number of posts that you want to appear in your RSS feed
at any time.

✦ **For Each Article in a Feed, Show:** Select the radio button for either Full
Text or Summary. Full Text publishes the entire post to your RSS feed,
whereas Summary publishes only an excerpt. (Check out Book I, Chapter 1
for more information on WordPress RSS feeds.)

✦ **Search Engine Visibility:** By default, your website is visible to all search
engines such as Google and Yahoo!. If you don't want your site to be
visible to search engines, select the check box labeled Discourage
Search Engines from Indexing This Site.

Generally, you want search engines to be able to find your blog. However, if you have special circumstances, you may want to enforce privacy on your site. For example, a friend of mine has a family blog and she blocks search engine access to it because she doesn't want search engines to find it. When you have privacy enabled, search engines and other content bots can't find your website.

Be sure to click the Save Changes button after you set all your options on the Reading Settings page to make the changes take effect.

Discussion

Discussion is the fourth item on the Settings menu list; click it to open the Discussion Settings page. (See Figure 2-4.) The sections on this tab let you set options for handling comments and publishing posts to your blog.

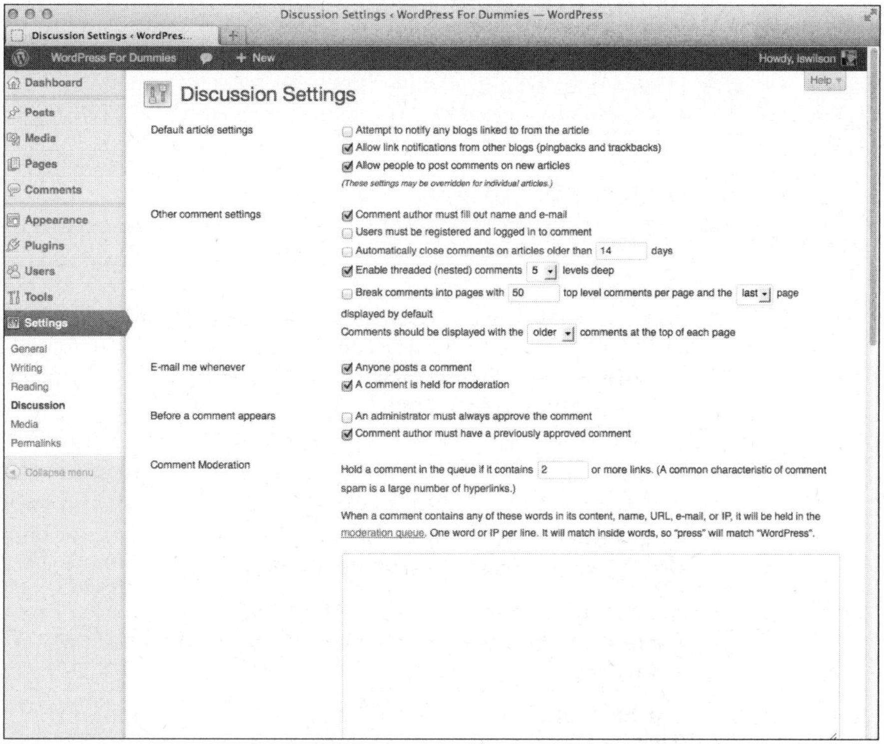

Book III
Chapter 2

Exploring Tools and Settings

Figure 2-4:
The
Discussion
Settings
page.

The following sections cover the options available to you on the Discussion Settings page, which deals mainly with how comments and trackbacks are handled in your blog.

Default Article Settings

With the Default Article Settings options, you can tell WordPress how to handle post notifications. Here are your options:

✦ **Attempt to Notify Any Blogs Linked to from the Article:** If you select this check box, your blog sends a notification (or *ping*) to any site you've linked to in your blog posts. This notification is also commonly referred to as a *trackback*. (Find out more about trackbacks in Book III, Chapter 4.) Deselect this check box if you don't want these notifications sent.

✦ **Allow Link Notifications from Other Blogs (Pingbacks and Trackbacks):** By default, this check box is selected, and your blog accepts notifications via pings or trackbacks from other blogs that have linked to yours. Any trackbacks or pings sent to your blog appear on your site in the Comments section of the blog post. If you deselect this check box, your blog doesn't accept pingbacks or trackbacks from other blogs.

✦ **Allow People to Post Comments on New Articles:** By default, this check box is selected, and people can leave comments on your blog posts. If you deselect this check box, no one can leave comments on your blog. (You can override these settings for individual articles — you can find more information about this process in Book IV, Chapter 1.)

Other Comment Settings

The Other Comment Settings section tells WordPress how to handle comments:

✦ **Comment Author Must Fill Out Their Name and E-Mail:** Enabled by default, this option requires all commenters on your blog to fill in the Name and E-Mail fields when leaving comments. This option can really help you combat comment spam. (See Book III, Chapter 4 for information on comment spam.) Deselect this check box to disable this option.

✦ **Users Must Be Registered and Logged in to Comment:** Not enabled by default, this option allows you to accept comments on your blog from only people who are registered and logged in as a user on your blog. If the user isn't logged in, she sees a message that reads, "You Must Be Logged in in Order to Leave a Comment."

✦ **Automatically Close Comments on Articles Older Than X Days:** Select the check box next to this option to tell WordPress you want comments on older articles to be automatically closed. Fill in the text box provided with the number of days you want to wait before WordPress closes comments on articles.

Many bloggers use this very effective antispam technique to keep the comment and trackback spam on their blog down.

✦ **Enable Threaded (Nested) Comments *X* Levels Deep:** From the drop-down list, you can select the level of threaded comments you want to have on your blog. The default is one; you can choose up to ten levels. Instead of all comments being displayed on your blog in chronological order (as they are by default), nesting them allows you and your readers to reply to comments within the comment itself.

✦ **Break Comments into Pages with *X* Comments Per Page and the last/ first page displayed by default:** Fill in the text box with the number of comments you want to appear on one page. This setting can really help blogs that receive a large number of comments. It provides you with the ability to break the long string of comments into several pages, which makes them easier to read and helps speed up the load time of your site because the page isn't loading such a large number of comments at once. Also select if you want the last (most recent) or first page of comments to display by selecting either Last or First in the drop-down menu.

✦ **Comments Should Be Displayed with the Older/Newer Comments at the Top of Each Page:** From the drop-down list, select Older or Newer. Selecting Older displays the comments on your blog in the order of oldest to newest. Selecting Newer does the opposite: It displays the comments on your blog in the order of newest to oldest.

E-Mail Me Whenever

The two options in the E-Mail Me Whenever section are enabled by default:

✦ **Anyone Posts a Comment:** Enabling this option means that you receive an e-mail notification whenever anyone leaves a comment on your blog. Deselect the check box if you don't want to be notified by e-mail about every new comment.

✦ **A Comment Is Held for Moderation:** This option lets you receive an e-mail notification whenever a comment is awaiting your approval in the comment moderation queue. (See Book III, Chapter 4 for more information about the comment moderation queue.) You need to deselect this option if you don't want to receive this notification.

Before a Comment Appears

The two options in the Before a Comment Appears section tell WordPress how you want WordPress to handle comments before they appear in your blog:

✦ **An Administrator Must Always Approve the Comment:** Disabled by default, this option keeps every single comment left on your blog in the moderation queue until you, the administrator, log in and approve it. Select this check box to enable this option.

◆ **Comment Author Must Have a Previously Approved Comment:**
Enabled by default, this option requires comments posted by all first-time commenters to be sent to the comment moderation queue for approval by the administrator of the blog. After comment authors have been approved for the first time, they remain approved for every comment thereafter (and this cannot be changed). WordPress stores their e-mail addresses in the database, and any future comments that match any stored e-mails are approved automatically. This feature is another measure that WordPress has built in to combat comment spam.

Comment Moderation

In the Comment Moderation section, you can set options to specify what types of comments are held in the moderation queue to await your approval.

To prevent spammers from spamming your blog with a *ton* of links, enter a number in the Hold a Comment in the Queue If It Contains X or More Links text box. The default number of links allowed is two. Try that setting, and if you find that you're getting a lot of spam comments that contain links, consider dropping that number down to 1, or even 0, to prevent those comments from being published on your blog. Sometimes, legitimate commenters will include a link or two in the body of their comment; after a commenter is marked as approved, she is no longer affected by this method of spam protection.

The large text box in the Comment Moderation section lets you type keywords, URLs, e-mail addresses, and IP addresses so that if they appear in comments, you want to hold those comments in the moderation queue for your approval.

What are avatars, and how do they relate to WordPress?

An *avatar* is an online graphical representation of an individual. It's a small graphic icon that people use to visually represent themselves on the web in areas they participate in conversations, such as discussion forums and blog comments. *Gravatars* are globally recognized avatars; they are avatars that you can take with you wherever you go. They appear alongside blog comments, blog posts, and discussion forums as long as the site you're interacting with is Gravatar-enabled. In October 2007, Automattic, the core group behind the WordPress platform, purchased the Gravatar service and integrated it into WordPress so that all could enjoy and benefit from the service. Gravatars are not automatic; you need to sign up for an account with Gravatar so that you can receive an avatar, via your e-mail address. Find out more about Gravatar by visiting http://gravatar.com.

Comment Blacklist

In this section, type a list of words, URLs, e-mail addresses, and/or IP addresses that you want to flat-out ban from your blog. Items placed here don't even make it into your comment moderation queue; the WordPress system filters them as spam. I'd give examples of blacklist words, but the words I have in my blacklist aren't family-friendly and have no place in a nice book like this one.

Avatars

The final section of the Discussion Settings page is Avatars. (See the nearby sidebar, "What are avatars, and how do they relate to WordPress?," for information about avatars.) In this section, you can select different settings for the use and display of avatars on your site:

1. **For the Avatar Display option (see Figure 2-5), decide how to display avatars on your site.**

   Select the Show Avatars check box to have your blog display avatars.

Book III
Chapter 2

Exploring Tools and Settings

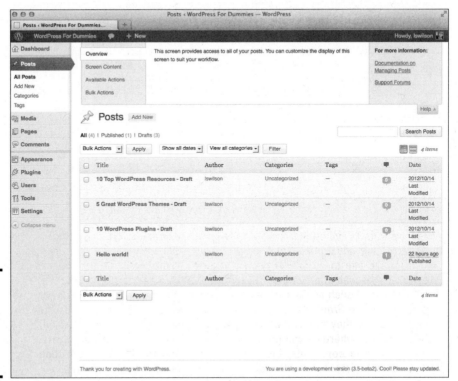

Figure 2-5:
Default avatars that you can display in your blog.

2. **Next to the Maximum Rating option, select the radio button for the maximum avatar rating you want to allow for the avatars that do appear on your site.**

   This feature works much like the American movie-rating system. You can select G, PG, R, and X ratings for the avatars that appear on your site, as shown in Figure 2-5. If your site is family-friendly, you probably don't want it to display R- or X-rated avatars, so select G or PG.

3. **Select the radio button for a default avatar next to the Default Avatar option. (See Figure 2-5.)**

Avatars appear in a couple of places:

✦ **The Comments page on the Dashboard:** In Figure 2-6, the first two comments display either the commenter's avatar or the default avatar if the commenter hasn't created his or her own.

✦ **The comments on individual blog posts in your blog:** Comments displayed on your website show the users' avatars. If a user doesn't have an avatar assigned from `http://en.gravatar.com`, the default avatar appears.

To enable the display of avatars in comments on your blog, the Comments template (`comments.php`) in your active theme has to contain the code to display them. Hop on over to Book VI to find information about themes and templates, including template tags that allow you to display avatars in your comment list.

Figure 2-6:
Authors'
avatars
appear
in the
Comments
page in the
WordPress
Dashboard.

Click the Save Changes button after you set all your options on the Discussion Settings page to make the changes take effect.

Media

The next menu item in the Settings menu list is Media; click the Media link to make the Media Settings page open. (See Figure 2-7.)

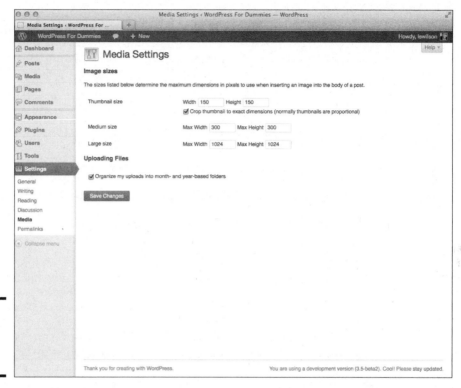

Figure 2-7:
The Media
Settings
page.

On the Media Settings page, you can configure the options for how your image files (graphics and photos) are resized for use in your blog.

The first set of options on the Media Settings page deals with images. WordPress automatically resizes your images for you in three different sizes. The dimensions are referenced in pixels by width, and then height. (For example, 150 x 150 means 150 pixels in width by 150 pixels in height.)

✦ **Thumbnail Size:** The default is 150 x 150; enter the width and height of your choice. Select the Crop Thumbnail to Exact Dimensions check box to resize the thumbnail exactly to the width and height you specify. Deselect this check box to make WordPress resize the image proportionally.

✦ **Medium Size:** The default is 300 x 300; enter the width and height numbers of your choice.

✦ **Large Size:** The default is 1024 x 1024; enter the width and height numbers of your choice.

Book VI goes into detail about WordPress themes and templates, including how you can add image sizes other than just these three. You can use these additional image sizes in and around your website, as well as a feature called Featured Image for your posts and articles.

The last set of options on the Media Settings page is the Uploading Files section. Here, you can tell WordPress where to store your uploaded media files. Select the Organize My Files into Month and Year-Based Folders check box to have WordPress organize your uploaded files in folders by month and by year. Files you upload in February 2013, for example, would be in the following folder: `/wp-content/uploads/2013/02/`. Likewise, files you upload in January 2013, would be in `/wp-content/uploads/2013/01/`.

This check box is selected by default; deselect it if you don't want WordPress to organize your files by month and year.

Be sure to click the Save Changes button to save your configurations!

Book IV, Chapter 3 details how to insert images in your WordPress posts and pages.

Permalinks

The next link on the Settings menu list is Permalinks; click the Permalinks link to view the Permalink Settings page, as shown in Figure 2-8.

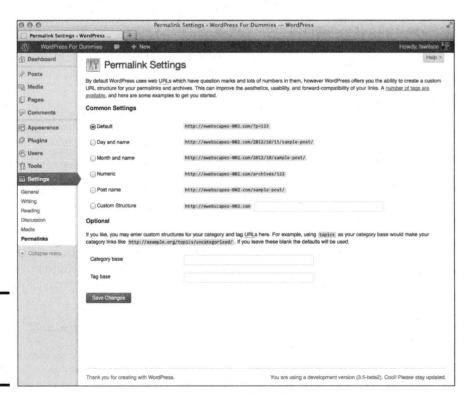

Figure 2-8:
The
Permalink
Settings
page.

Each WordPress blog post is assigned its own web page, and the address (or URL) of that page is called a *permalink*. Posts that you see in WordPress blogs usually have the post permalink in four typical areas:

✦ The title of the blog post

✦ The Comments link below the post

✦ A Permalink link that appears (in most themes) below the post

✦ The titles of posts appearing in a Recent Posts sidebar

Permalinks are meant to be permanent links to your blog posts (which is where the *perma* part of that word comes from, in case you're wondering). Other bloggers can use a post permalink to refer to that particular blog post. Ideally, the permalink of a post never changes. WordPress creates the permalink automatically when you publish a new post.

By default, a blog post permalink in WordPress looks like this:

`http://yourdomain.com/?p=100/`

The p stands for *post,* and 100 is the ID assigned to the individual post. You can leave the permalinks in this format if you don't mind letting WordPress associate each post with an ID number.

Book III
Chapter 2

Exploring Tools
and Settings

WordPress, however, lets you take your permalinks to the beauty salon for a bit of makeover so that you can create pretty permalinks. You probably didn't know that permalinks could be pretty, did you?

Changing the structure of your permalinks in the future affects the permalinks for all the posts on your blog . . . new and old. Keep this fact in mind if you ever decide to change the permalink structure. An especially important reason: Search engines (such as Google and Yahoo!) index the posts on your site by their permalinks, so changing the permalink structure makes all those indexed links obsolete.

Making your post links pretty

Pretty permalinks are links that are more pleasing to the eye than standard links and, ultimately, more pleasing to search-engine spiders. (See Book V for an explanation of why search engines like pretty permalinks.) Pretty permalinks look something like this:

`http://yourdomain.com/2011/01/01/pretty-permalinks`

Break down that URL, and you see the date when the post was made, in year/month/day format. You also see the topic of the post.

To choose how your permalinks look, click Permalinks in the Settings drop-down list. The Permalink Settings page opens. (Refer to Figure 2-8.)

On this page, you can find several options for creating permalinks:

✦ **Default** (ugly permalinks): WordPress assigns an ID number to each blog post and creates the URL in this format: `http://yourdomain.com/?p=100`.

✦ **Day and Name** (pretty permalinks): For each post, WordPress generates a permalink URL that includes the year, month, day, and post slug/title: `http://yourdomain.com/2013/10/31/sample-post/`.

✦ **Month and Name** (also pretty permalinks): For each post, WordPress generates a permalink URL that includes the year, month, and post slug/title: `http://yourdomain.com/2013/10/sample-post/`.

✦ **Numeric** (not so pretty): WordPress assigns a numerical value to the permalink. The URL is created in this format: `http://yourdomain.com/archives/123`.

✦ **Post Name (my preferred):** WordPress takes the title of your post or page and generates the permalink URL from those words. For example, the name of the page that contains my bibliography of books is called simply *Books;* therefore, with this permalink structure, WordPress creates the permalink URL: `http://lisasabin-wilson.com/books`. Likewise, a post titled *WordPress Is Awesome* gets a permalink URL like this: `http://lisasabin-wilson.com/wordpress-is-awesome`.

✦ **Custom Structure:** WordPress creates permalinks in the format you choose. You can create a custom permalink structure by using tags or variables, as I discuss in the next section.

To create the pretty-permalink structure, select the Day and Name radio button; then click the Save Changes button at the bottom of the page.

Customizing your permalinks

A *custom permalink structure* is one that lets you define which variables you want to see in your permalinks by using the tags in Table 2-2.

Table 2-2	Custom Permalinks
Permalink Tag	**Results**
`%year%`	Four-digit year (such as `2013`)
`%monthnum%`	Two-digit month (such as `02` for February)
`%day%`	Two-digit day (such as `30`)
`%hour%`	Two-digit hour of the day (such as `15` for 3 pm)

Permalink Tag	Results
`%minute%`	Two-digit minute (such as `45`)
`%second%`	Two-digit second (such as `10`)
`%postname%`	Text — usually, the post name — separated by hyphens (such as `making-pretty-permalinks`)
`%post_id%`	The unique numerical ID of the post (such as `344`)
`%category%`	The text of the category name in which you filed the post (such as `books-i-read`)
`%author%`	The text of the post author's name (such as `lisa-sabin-wilson`)

If you want your permalink to show the year, month, day, category, and post name, select the Custom Structure radio button in the Customize Permalink Structure page and type the following tags in the Custom Structure text box:

`/%year%/%monthnum%/%day%/%category%/%postname%/`

By using this permalink format, the link for a post made on February 1, 2013, called WordPress All-in-One For Dummies and filed in the Books I Read category, would look like this:

```
http://yourdomain.com/2013/02/01/books-i-read/wordpress-all-
    in-one-for-dummies/
```

Be sure to include the slashes before tags, between tags, and at the very end of the string of tags. This format ensures that WordPress creates correct, working permalinks by using the correct rewrite rules located in the `.htaccess` file for your site. (See the following section for more information on rewrite rules and `.htaccess` files.)

Don't forget to click the Save Changes button at the bottom of the Customize Permalink Structure page; otherwise, your permalink changes aren't saved!

Making sure that your permalinks work with your server

After you set the format for the permalinks for your site by using any options other than the default, WordPress writes specific rules, or directives, to the `.htaccess` file on your web server. The `.htaccess` file in turn communicates to your web server how it should serve up the permalinks, according to the permalink structure you chose to use.

To use an `.htaccess` file, you need to know the answers to two questions:

✦ Does your web server configuration use and give you access to the `.htaccess` file?

✦ Does your web server run Apache with the `mod_rewrite` module?

If you don't know the answers, contact your hosting provider to find out.

If the answer to both questions is yes, proceed to the following section. If the answer is no, check out the "Working with servers that don't use Apache mod_rewrite" sidebar in this chapter.

Creating .htaccess files

You and WordPress work together in glorious harmony to create the .htaccess file that lets you use a pretty permalink structure in your blog.

To create the .htaccess file, you need to be comfortable uploading files to FTP and changing permissions. Turn to Book II, Chapter 2 if you're unfamiliar with either of those tasks.

If .htaccess already exists, you can find it in the root of your directory on your web server — that is, the same directory where you find your wp-config.php file. If you don't see it in the root directory, try changing the options of your FTP client to show hidden files. (Because the .htaccess file starts with a period [.], it may not be visible until you configure your FTP client to show hidden files.)

Working with servers that don't use Apache mod_rewrite

Using permalink structures requires that your web hosting provider has a specific Apache module option called mod_rewrite activated on its servers. If your web hosting provider doesn't have this item activated on its servers, or if you're hosting your site on a Windows server, the custom permalinks work only if you type **index.php** in front of any custom permalink tags.

For example, create the custom permalink tags like this:

/index.php/%year%/%month%/%date%/%postname%/

This format creates a permalink like this:

http://yourdomain.com/index.php/2013/02/01/wordpress-all-in-one-for-dummies

You don't need an .htaccess file to use this permalink structure.

If you do not already have an .htaccess file on your web server, follow these steps to create an .htaccess file on your web server and create a new permalink structure:

1. **Using a plain-text editor (such as Notepad for Windows or TextEdit for a Mac), create a blank file; name it htaccess.txt and upload it to your web server via FTP.**

2. **After the file is uploaded to your web server, rename the file .htaccess (notice the period at the beginning) and make sure that it is writable by the server by changing permissions to either 755 or 777.**

3. **Create the permalink structure in the Customize Permalink Structure page in your WordPress Dashboard.**

4. **Click the Save Changes button at the bottom of the Customize Permalink Structure page.**

   WordPress inserts into the .htaccess file the specific rules necessary for making the permalink structure functional in your blog.

If you follow the preceding steps correctly, you have an .htaccess file on your web server that has the correct permissions set so that WordPress can write the correct rules to it. Your pretty permalink structure works flawlessly. Kudos!

If you open the .htaccess file and look at it now, you see that it's no longer blank. It should have a set of code in it called *rewrite rules,* which looks something like this:

```
# BEGIN WordPress
<IfModule mod_rewrite.c>
RewriteEngine On
RewriteBase /
RewriteCond %{REQUEST_FILENAME} !-f
RewriteCond %{REQUEST_FILENAME} !-d
RewriteRule . /index.php [L]
</IfModule>

# END WordPress
```

I could delve deeply into .htaccess and all the things you can do with this file, but I'm restricting this chapter to how it applies to WordPress permalink structures. If you want to unlock more mysteries about .htaccess, check out "Comprehensive Guide to .htaccess" at http://javascriptkit.com/howto/htaccess.shtml.

Creating Your Personal Profile

To personalize your blog, visit your Profile page on your WordPress Dashboard.

To access your Profile page, click the down arrow to the right of Users to open the Users menu list and then click the Your Profile link. The Profile page appears, as shown in Figure 2-9.

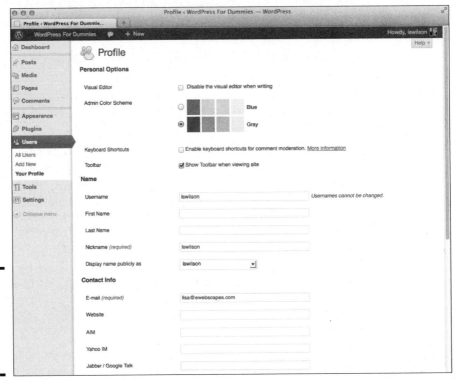

Figure 2-9: Establish your profile details on the Profile page.

Here are the settings on this page:

✦ **Personal Options:** In the Personal Options section, you can set these preferences for your blog:

- *Visual Editor:* Select this check box to indicate that you want to use the Visual Editor when writing your posts. The Visual Editor refers to the formatting options you find in the Write Post page (discussed in detail in Book IV, Chapter 1). By default, the check box is selected, which means that the Visual Editor is on. To turn it off, deselect the check box.

- *Admin Color Scheme:* These options set the colors in your Dashboard. The default is the Gray color scheme. If you've been using WordPress since before March 2007, the Blue color scheme will be familiar to you because previous versions of the Dashboard used those colors.

- *Keyboard Shortcuts:* Enables you to use keyboard shortcuts for comment moderation. To find out more about keyboard shortcuts, click the More Information link; you're taken to the Keyboard Shortcuts page (`http://codex.wordpress.org/Keyboard_Shortcuts`) in the WordPress Codex, which offers some helpful information.

- *Toolbar:* Allows you to control where the admin bar (see Book III, Chapter 1) is shown on your site. By default, the admin bar displays on the top of every page of your site when you're viewing it in your browser. You can also set it to display on the top of every Dashboard page by selecting the In Dashboard check box. You can completely disable the admin bar by removing the checks in the check boxes.

✦ **Name:** Input personal information, such as your first name, last name, and nickname, and specify how you want your name to appear publicly. Fill in the text boxes with the requested information.

✦ **Contact Info:** Provide your e-mail address and other contact information to tell your visitors who you are and where they can contact you. Aside from e-mail, you can provide your username for various Internet chat programs such as Yahoo! IM, AIM (AOL Instant Messenger), Jabber/ Google Talk, and Google+.

Your e-mail address is the only required entry in this section. This address is the one WordPress uses to notify you when you have new comments or new user registrations on your blog. Make sure to use a real e-mail address so that you get these notifications.

✦ **About Yourself:** Provide a little bio for yourself and change the password for your blog, if you want:

- *Biographical Info:* Type a short bio in the Biographical Info text box. This information can appear publicly if you're using a theme that displays your bio, so be creative!

When your profile is published to your website, not only can anyone view it, but also search engines, such as Google and Yahoo!, can pick it up. Always be careful with the information in your profile. Think hard about the information you want to share with the rest of the world!

- *New Password:* When you want to change the password for your blog, type your new password in the first text box in the New Password section. To confirm your new password, type it again in the second text box.

Directly below the two New Password text boxes is a password helper. WordPress helps you create a secure password. It alerts you if the password you chose is too short or not secure enough by telling you that it's Bad. When creating a new password, use a combination of letters, numbers, and symbols to make it hard for anyone to guess (for example, aty89!#4j). When you create a password that WordPress thinks is a good one, it lets you know by saying that the password is Strong.

Change your password frequently. Some people on the Internet make it their business to attempt to hijack blogs for their own malicious purposes. If you change your password monthly, you lower your risk by keeping hackers guessing.

When you finish setting all the options on the Profile page, don't forget to click the Update Profile button to save your changes.

Setting Your Blog's Format

In addition to setting your personal settings in the Dashboard, you can manage the day-to-day maintenance of your blog. The following sections take you through the links to these pages in the Dashboard navigation menus.

Posts

Click the down arrow to the right of Posts on the navigation menu to open a drop-down list with four links: Posts, Add New, Tags, and Categories. Each link gives you the tools you need to publish content to your blog:

✦ **Posts:** Opens the Posts page, where a listing appears of all the saved posts you've written on your blog. On this page, you can search for posts by date, category, or keyword. You can view all posts, only posts that have been published, or just posts that you've saved but haven't published *(drafts)*. You can also edit and delete posts from this page. Check out Book IV, Chapter 1 for more information on editing posts on your blog.

✦ **Add New:** Opens the Add New Post page, where you can compose your blog posts, set the options for each post (such as assigning a post to a category, or making it a private or public post), and publish the post to your blog. You can find more information on posts, post options, and publishing in Book IV, Chapter 1.

You can also get to the Add New Post page by clicking the Add New button on the Posts page, or by clicking the +New link on the admin bar and selecting Post.

✦ **Categories:** Opens the Categories page, where you can view, edit, add, and delete categories on your blog. Find more information on creating categories in Book III, Chapter 5.

✦ **Tags:** Opens the Tags page in your WordPress Dashboard, where you can view, add, edit, and delete tags on your blog. Book III, Chapter 5 provides you with more information about tags and using them on your blog.

Media

Click Media to expand the drop-down list of links for this section:

✦ **Library:** Opens the Media Library page. On this page, you can view, search, and manage all the media files you've ever uploaded to your WordPress blog.

✦ **Add New:** Opens the Upload New Media page, where you can use the built-in uploader to transfer media files from your computer to the media directory in WordPress. Book IV, Chapters 3 and 4 take you through the details of how to upload images, videos, and audio files by using the WordPress upload feature.

You can also get to the Upload New Media page by clicking Add New button on the Media Library page, or by clicking the +New link on the admin bar and selecting Media.

Pages

People use this feature to create pages on their sites such as an About Me or Contact Me page. Flip to Book IV, Chapter 2 for more information on pages. Click Pages to reveal the drop-down list:

✦ **Pages:** Opens the Pages page, where you can search, view, edit, and delete pages in your WordPress blog.

✦ **Add New:** Opens the Add New Page page, where you can compose, save, and publish a new page on your blog. Book IV, Chapter 2 describes the difference between a post and a page. The difference is subtle, but posts and pages are very different from one another!

You can also get to the Add New Page page by clicking the Add New button on the Pages page, or by clicking the +New link on the admin bar and selecting Page.

Comments

Comments in the navigation menu don't have a drop-down list of links. You simply click Comments to open the Comments page, where WordPress gives you the options to view the following:

✦ **All:** Shows all comments that currently exist on your blog, including approved, pending, and spam comments

✦ **Pending:** Shows comments that you haven't yet approved but are pending in the moderation queue

✦ **Approved:** Shows all comments that you previously approved

✦ **Spam:** Shows all the comments that are marked as spam

✦ **Trash:** Shows comments that you marked as Trash but haven't deleted permanently from your blog

Book III, Chapter 4 gives you details on how to use the Comments section of your WordPress Dashboard.

Appearance

When you click Appearance on the navigation menu, a drop-down list opens, displaying the following links:

✦ **Themes:** Opens the Manage Themes page, where you can manage the themes available on your blog. Check out Book VI, Chapter 2 to find out about using themes on your WordPress blog and managing themes on this page.

✦ **Widgets:** Opens the Widgets page, where you can add, delete, edit, and manage the widgets that you use on your blog.

✦ **Menus:** Opens the Menus page, where you can build navigation menus that will appear on your site. Book VI, Chapter 1 provides information on creating menus by using this feature.

✦ **Header:** Opens the Your Header Image page, where you can upload an image to use in the *header* (or top) of your WordPress blog; however, this menu item and page exist only if you are using a theme that has activated the Custom Header feature (covered in Book VI). The Twenty Twelve theme is activated by default on all new WordPress blogs, which is why I include this menu item in this list. Not all WordPress themes use the Custom Header feature, so you don't see this menu item if your theme doesn't take advantage of that feature.

✦ **Background:** Opens the Custom Background page, where you can upload an image to use as the background of your WordPress blog design. Like the Custom Header option, the Custom Background option exists in the Appearances menu only if you have a theme that has activated the custom background feature (covered in Book VI).

✦ **Editor:** Opens the Theme Editor page, where you can edit your theme templates. Book VI has extensive information on themes and templates.

Uploading custom header and background images helps you individualize the visual design of your blog or website. You can find more information on tweaking and customizing your WordPress theme in Book VI, as well as a great deal of information about how to use WordPress themes (including where to find, install, and activate them in your WordPress blog) and detailed information about using WordPress widgets to display the content you want.

Book VI provides information about WordPress themes and templates. You can dig deep into WordPress template tags and tweak an existing WordPress theme by using Cascading Style Sheets (CSS) to customize your theme a bit more to your liking.

Plugins

The next item in the navigation menu is Plugins. Click Plugins to expand the drop-down list:

✦ **Plugins:** Opens the Plugins page, where you can view all the plugins currently installed on your blog. On this page, you also have the ability to activate, deactivate, and delete plugins on your blog. (Book VII is all about plugins.)

✦ **Add New:** Opens the Install Plugins page, where you can search for plugins from the official WordPress Plugin Directory by keyword, author, or tag. You can also install plugins directly to your blog from the WordPress Plugin Directory — you can find out all about this exciting feature in Book VII, Chapter 2.

✦ **Editor:** Opens the Edit Plugins page, where you can edit the plugin files in a text editor. Don't plan to edit plugin files unless you know what you're doing (meaning that you're familiar with PHP and WordPress functions). Head over to Book VII, Chapter 4 to read more information on editing plugin files.

Users

The Users drop-down list has three links:

✦ **All Users:** Go to the Users page, where you can view, edit, and delete users on your WordPress blog. Each user has a unique login name and password, as well as an e-mail address assigned to his account. You can view and edit a user's information on the Users page.

✦ **Add New:** Opens the Add New User page, where you can add new users to your WordPress blog. Simply type the user's username, first name, last name, e-mail (required), website, and a password in the fields provided and click the Add User button. You can also select whether you want WordPress to send login information to the new user by e-mail. If you want, you can also assign a new role for the new user. Turn to the section "Configuring the Settings," earlier in this chapter, for more info about user roles.

✦ **Your Profile:** Turn to the "Creating Your Personal Profile" section, earlier in this chapter, for more information about creating a profile page.

Tools

The last item on the navigation menu (and subsequently in this chapter!) is Tools. Click Tools to open a drop-down list of links that includes

✦ **Available Tools:** Opens the Tools page on your Dashboard. WordPress comes packaged with two extra features that you can use on your blog, if needed. The features are Press This and Category/Tag Conversion.

✦ **Import:** Clicking this link opens the Import page on your Dashboard. WordPress gives you the ability to import from a different blog platform. This feature is covered in depth in Book II, Chapter 7.

✦ **Export:** Clicking this menu item opens the Export page on your Dashboard. WordPress allows you to export your content from WordPress so that you can import it into a different platform or to another WordPress blog.

Chapter 3: Managing Users and Multiple Authors

In This Chapter

✓ Deciding what roles to assign users

✓ Allowing new users to register

✓ Adding a new user

✓ Making changes to user profiles

✓ Using tools to manage multi-author sites

Multi-author blogging means inviting others to coauthor, or contribute articles, posts, pages, or other content to your blog. You can expand the offerings on your website or blog by using multi-author blogging because you can have several different people writing on different topics or offering different perspectives on the same topic. Many people use it to create a collaborative writing space on the web, and WordPress doesn't limit you in the number of authors you can add to your blog.

Additionally, you can invite other people to register as *subscribers,* who don't contribute content but are registered members of the blog, which can have benefits, too. (For example, you could make some content available to registered users only.)

This chapter takes you through the steps of adding users to your blog, takes the mystery out of the different user roles and capabilities, and gives you some tools for managing a multi-author website.

Understanding User Roles and Capabilities

Before you start adding new users to your site, you need to understand the differences among the user roles because each user role is assigned a different level of access and grouping of capabilities to your blog, as follows:

✦ **Subscriber:** The default role. Maintain this role as the one assigned to new users, particularly if you don't know who's registering. Subscribers get access to the Dashboard page, and they can view and change the options in their profiles on the Your Profile and Personal Options page. (They don't have access to your account settings, however — only to their own.) Each user can change her username, e-mail address, password, bio, and other descriptors in her user profile. The WordPress database stores subscribers' profile information, and your blog remembers them each time they visit, so they don't have to complete the profile information each time they leave comments on your blog.

✦ **Contributor:** In addition to the access subscribers have, contributors can upload files and write, edit, and manage their own posts. Contributors can write posts, but they can't publish the posts; the administrator reviews all contributor posts and decides whether to publish them. This setting is a nice way to moderate content written by new authors.

✦ **Author:** In addition to the access contributors have, authors can publish and edit their own posts.

✦ **Editor:** In addition to the access authors have, editors can moderate comments, manage categories, manage links, edit pages, and edit other authors' posts.

✦ **Administrator:** Administrators can edit all the options and settings in the WordPress blog.

✦ **Super Admin:** This role exists only when you have the multisite feature activated in WordPress — see Book VIII for more about the multisite feature.

Table 3-1 gives you an at-a-glance reference for the basic differences in roles and capabilities for WordPress users.

Table 3-1   **WordPress User Roles and Capabilities**

	Super Admin	Administrator	Editor	Author	Contributor	Subscriber
Manage multisite features	Yes	No	No	No	No	No
Add/edit users	Yes	Yes	No	No	No	No
Add/edit/install plugins	Yes	Yes	No	No	No	No
Add/edit/install themes	Yes	Yes	No	No	No	No
Manage comments	Yes	Yes	Yes	No	No	No
Manage categories, tags, and links	Yes	Yes	Yes	No	No	No
Publish posts	Yes	Yes	Yes	Yes	No (moderated)	No
Edit published posts	Yes	Yes	Yes	No	No	No
Edit others' posts	Yes	Yes	Yes	No	No	No
Edit own posts	Yes	Yes	Yes	Yes	Yes	No
Publish pages	Yes	Yes	Yes	No	No	No
Read	Yes	Yes	Yes	Yes	Yes	Yes

Table 3-1 doesn't offer exhaustive information, by any means. However, it covers the basic user roles and capabilities for WordPress, or the most common capabilities for each user role. For a full listing of user roles and capabilities, check out the WordPress Codex at `http://codex.wordpress. org/Roles_and_Capabilities`.

Allowing New User Registration

As you can see in Table 3-1, each user level has a different set of capabilities. Book III, Chapter 2 discusses the General Settings in the WordPress Dashboard, in which you set the default role for users who register on your website. Keep the default role set to Subscriber because when you open registration to the public, you don't always know who's registering until after they register — and you don't want to arbitrarily hand out higher levels of access to the settings of your website unless you know and trust the user.

When users register on your website, you, as the Administrator, get an e-mail notification (sent to the e-mail address you set on the General Settings page), so you always know when new users register, and you can then go into your Dashboard and edit the user to set his role any way you see fit.

New users can register on your site only after you enable the Anyone Can Register option on the General Settings page within your Dashboard (Book III, Chapter 2). If you don't have it enabled, users see a message on the Registration page that tells them registration isn't allowed, as shown in Figure 3-1.

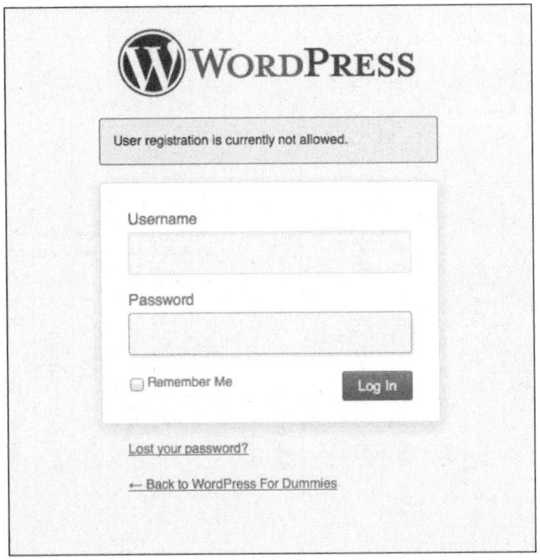

Figure 3-1: The message to users that registration isn't allowed.

(W) WORDPRESS

User registration is currently not allowed.

Username

Password

☐ Remember Me   Log In

Lost your password?

← Back to WordPress For Dummies

By the way, the direct URL for registration on a blog that has registration enabled is http://*yourdomain*.com/wp-register.php. With registration enabled (in the General Settings), a user sees a form inviting her to input her desired username and e-mail address. After she does, she gets a confirmation notice in her inbox that includes an authorization link that she must click in order to authenticate her registration.

After a user has registered, you, as the site Administrator, can manage her user account and assign a user role. (Refer to Table 3-1.)

Adding New Users Manually

Allowing new users to register by using the WordPress registration interface is only one way to add users to your site. As the site Administrator, you have the ability to add new users manually by following these steps:

1. **Log in to your WordPress Dashboard by inputting your username and password in the form at http://*yourdomain*.com/wp-admin.**

2. **Click the Add New link on the Users menu on the Dashboard.**

The Add New User page, shown in Figure 3-2, loads.

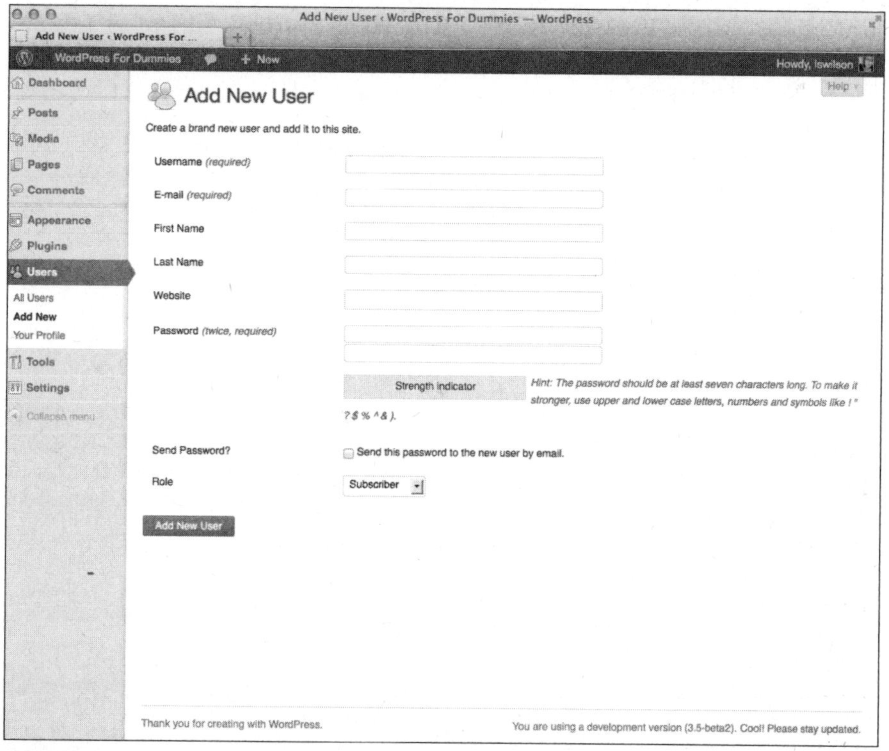

Figure 3-2:
The Add New User page in the WordPress Dashboard.

3. **Enter the username in the Username text box.**

   You can't skip this text box. The new user types in this username when he's prompted to log in to your site.

4. **Enter the user's e-mail address in the E-Mail text box.**

   You can't skip this text box, either. The user receives notifications from you and your site at this e-mail address.

5. **Enter the user's first name in the First Name text box.**

6. **Enter the user's last name in the Last Name text box.**

7. **Enter the URL for the user's website in the Website text box.**

8. **Enter the desired password in the Password text box.**

   WordPress asks you to type the password twice as a way of *authenticating* the password (making sure that you typed it correctly the first time). WordPress provides a strength indicator that gives you an idea of how *strong*, or secure, your chosen password is. You want secure passwords so that no one can easily guess them, so make the password at least seven characters long and use a combination of letters, numbers, and symbols (such as @, #, $, and ^).

9. **If you want the user to receive his password by e-mail, select the Send This Password to the New User by Email check box.**

10. **Select Subscriber, Contributor, Author, Editor, or Administrator from the Role drop-down list.**

11. **Click the Add New User button.**

    The Add New User page loads and the e-mail notification is sent to the user you just added. When the page loads, all the fields are cleared, allowing you to add another new user, if you want.

Editing User Details

After users register and settle into their accounts on your site, you, as the site Administrator, have the ability to edit their accounts. You may never have to edit user accounts at all; however, you have the option if you need it. Most often, users can access the details of their own accounts and change e-mail addresses, names, passwords, and so on; however, circumstances under which you may need to edit user accounts would be to do things such as

✦ **Edit user roles.** When a user registers, you may want to increase her role, or level of access, on your site; promote an existing user to Administrator; or conversely, demote an existing Administrator or Editor down a notch or two.

✦ **Edit user e-mails.** If a user loses access to the e-mail account that she registered with, she may ask you to change her account e-mail address so that she can access her account notifications again.

✦ **Edit user passwords.** If a user loses access to the e-mail account with which she registered, she can't use WordPress's Lost Password feature, which allows users to gain access to their account password through e-mail recovery. In that case, a user may ask you to reset her password for her so that she can log in and access her account again.

In any of these circumstances, you can make the necessary changes by clicking the Users link on the Users menu on your WordPress Dashboard, which loads the Users page shown in Figure 3-3.

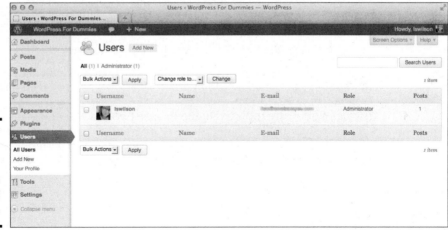

Figure 3-3:
The Users page lets you manage all the users on your site.

Figure 3-3 shows you the Users page on a site that has multiple users who have different levels of access, or roles. (The e-mail address is blurred in Figure 3-3 to protect the user's privacy.)

When you hover your mouse pointer over the name of the user, an Edit link appears below the user listing. Click that Edit link to access the Edit User page, where you can edit different pieces of information for that user, including

✦ **Personal Options:** These options include Visual Editor and Color Scheme preferences.

✦ **Name:** Specify a user's role, first and last name, and nickname.

✦ **Contact Info:** Includes users' e-mail addresses; websites; and AIM, Yahoo! IM, and Google Talk IDs.

✦ **Biographical Info:** A few lines of biographical info for the user (optional, but some WordPress themes display authors' biographies).

✦ **New Password:** Change the password for the user.

The Edit User page looks the same, and has the very same features, as the Profile page that you deal with in Book III, Chapter 2 — feel free to visit that chapter to get the lowdown on the different options and settings on this page.

Managing a Multi-Author Site

You may love running a multi-author site, but it has its challenges. The minute you become the owner of a multi-author site, you immediately assume the role of manager for the authors you invited into your space. At times, those authors look to you for support and guidance, not only on their content management, but also for tips and advice about how to use the WordPress interface — it's a good thing you have this book at the ready so that you can offer up the gems of information you're finding within these pages!

You can find many tools available to assist you in managing a multi-author site, as well as making your site more interactive by adding some features, which can make it a more rewarding and satisfying experience not only for you and your readers, but for your authors, as well.

The tools listed in the following sections come by way of plugins, which are add-ons that extend the scope of WordPress by adding different functionality and features. You can find information on the use and installation of plugins in Book VII.

Tools that help authors communicate

When you're running a multi-author site, communication is crucial for sharing information, giving and receiving inspiration, and making certain that no two authors are writing the same (or a similar) article on your site. Use the following tools to help you manage the flow of communication between everyone involved:

✦ **WP Status Notifier:** In the section "Understanding User Roles and Capabilities," earlier in this chapter, I mention that the role of Contributor can write and save posts to your site, but those posts don't get published to the site until an Administrator approves them. This plugin notifies the Contributor author, via e-mail, when his post is published to (or rejected by) your site.

`http://wordpress.org/extend/plugins/wp-status-notifier`

✦ **Editorial Calendar:** This plugin gives you an overview of scheduled posts, post authors, and the dates when you scheduled the posts to publish to your blog. This plugin can help you prevent multiple author posts from publishing too close together or, in some cases, right on top of one another — you simply reschedule posts by using a drag-and-drop interface.

`http://wordpress.org/extend/plugins/editorial-calendar`

✦ **Email Users:** This plugin allows you to send e-mails out to all registered users of your blog, and users can send e-mails back and forth to one another by using the plugin interface on the Dashboard. This tool provides the authors and users on your multi-author blog the ability to keep in touch and communicate with one another.

`http://wordpress.org/extend/plugins/email-users`

✦ **Subscribe to Authors Post Feed:** This plugin adds an RSS feed to each author's post archives, which allows you, other users, and site visitors to subscribe to that author's RSS feed so that you receive immediate notification through your RSS feed reader when the author publishes new content.

`http://wordpress.org/extend/plugins/subscribe-to-author-posts-feed`

✦ **Dashboard Notepad:** This plugin gives you a widget that appears on your main Dashboard page and allows you and other users (depending on the user role that you set in the plugin options) to leave notes for each other. You can use this plugin to ask and answer questions and to create to-do lists for your authors.

`http://wordpress.org/extend/plugins/dashboard-notepad`

Tools to promote author profiles

One way to operate a successful multi-author blog involves taking every opportunity to promote your authors and their information as much as possible. Authors often get involved in posting content on other websites, in addition to yours, for exposure, and the plugins in this list give you tools to promote authors bios, links, social network feeds, and more:

✦ **Author Information Widget:** This plugin gives you a widget that you can place in the sidebar of a single post page, displaying the post author's name, biography (from the About Me section of the Author Profile page in the Dashboard), Avatar (author's photo) and Social Network and Contact links.

```
http://wordpress.org/tags/author-info-widget
```

✦ **List Authors:** This plugin provides a widget that displays a list of the authors on your site, where the author's name is a link to her post archive. Figure 3-4 displays the List Authors widget with the different options that you can set for it.

```
http://wordpress.org/extend/plugins/list-authors
```

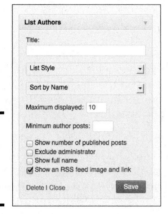

Figure 3-4:
The List
Authors
widget
options.

✦ **Profile Pic:** This plugin gives your authors the ability to add their own photos to their profiles on your site, and it provides you with a widget that can display each author's photo, as well as his name and a link to his post archive.

```
http://wordpress.org/extend/plugins/profile-pic
```

✦ **Author Spotlight:** This plugin provides a widget that you can place in your sidebar, displaying the profile of the author of the post being viewed. The author information automatically appears on only a single post page and displays the profile of the author of the post.

```
http://wordpress.org/extend/plugins/author-profile
```

✦ **Author Based Twitter:** This plugin gives your authors the ability to show their own Twitter feeds in the sidebar by using a handy widget. The author's Twitter feed information appears on her post page only — so authors can promote their own Twitter accounts on your website.

```
http://wordpress.org/extend/plugins/author-based-
twitter-widget
```

Tools to manage multi-author blog posts

The plugins listed in this section can help you, the site Administrator, manage your group of authors and registered users by giving you some tools to track users' activity, list their posts, and stay up-to-date and notified when your authors publish new content:

✦ **Co-Authors Plus:** This plugin allows you to assign multiple authors to one post, which you may find especially helpful when you have more than one author collaborating on one article, allowing the authors to share the byline and credit.

```
http://wordpress.org/extend/plugins/co-authors-plus/faq
```

✦ **Author Complete Post List:** This plugin provides a very easy way to show a complete list of an author's posts, enabling you to display an archive page per author.

```
http://wordpress.org/extend/plugins/author-complete-
post-list
```

✦ **Custom Author Byline:** This plugin adds a custom author byline module below the Post Editor on the Add New Posts page, which enables you to include the name of an author who isn't a registered member of your site (helpful when you need to give credit to collaborators).

```
http://wordpress.org/extend/plugins/custom-author-
byline
```

✦ **Pending Post Notifier:** This plugin sends an e-mail to the site Administrator whenever posts are ready for review. For example, when a user who has the role of Contributor writes and saves a post, an e-mail is sent to the Administrator, telling him that new posts are awaiting his review.

```
http://wordpress.org/tags/wp-pending-post-notifier
```

✦ **Audit Trail:** This plugin records the actions of the registered users on your site, such as when they log in or log out, when they publish posts and pages, and when they visit pages within your site. As the site Administrator, you can keep track of the actions your authors and users take on your website.

```
http://wordpress.org/extend/plugins/audit-trail
```

Chapter 4: Dealing with Comments and Spam

In This Chapter

✓ Making the decision to allow comments

✓ Working with comments and trackbacks

✓ Using Akismet to help combat spam

One of the most exciting aspects of blogging with WordPress is getting feedback from your readers on articles your publish to your blog. Feedback, also known as *blog comments,* is akin to having a guestbook on your blog.

People leave notes for you that are published to your site, and through these notes, you can respond and engage your readers in conversation about the topic. Having this function on your blog allows you to expand the thoughts and ideas you present in your blog posts by giving readers the opportunity to add their two cents' worth.

In this chapter, you can decide whether to allow comments on your site, figure out how to manage those comments, use trackbacks, and discover the negative aspects of allowing comments (such as spam).

Deciding to Allow Comments on Your Site

Some blog users say that a blog without comments isn't a blog at all because the point of having a blog, in some minds, is to foster communication and interaction between the site authors and the readers. This belief is common in the blogging community because experiencing visitor feedback via comments is part of what's made blogging so popular. However, allowing comments is a personal choice, and you don't have to do it if you don't want to.

Positive aspects of allowing comments

Allowing comments on your blog lets audience members actively involve themselves in your blog by creating a discussion and dialogue about your content. Mostly, readers find commenting a satisfying experience when they visit blogs because comments make them part of the discussion.

Depending on the topic you write about on your blog, allowing comments sends the message that you, as the author/owner of the site, are open to the views and opinions of your readers. Having a comment form on your site that readers can use to leave their feedback on your articles (such as the one shown in Figure 4-1) is like having a great big Welcome to My Home sign on your site — it invites users in to share thoughts and participate in discussions.

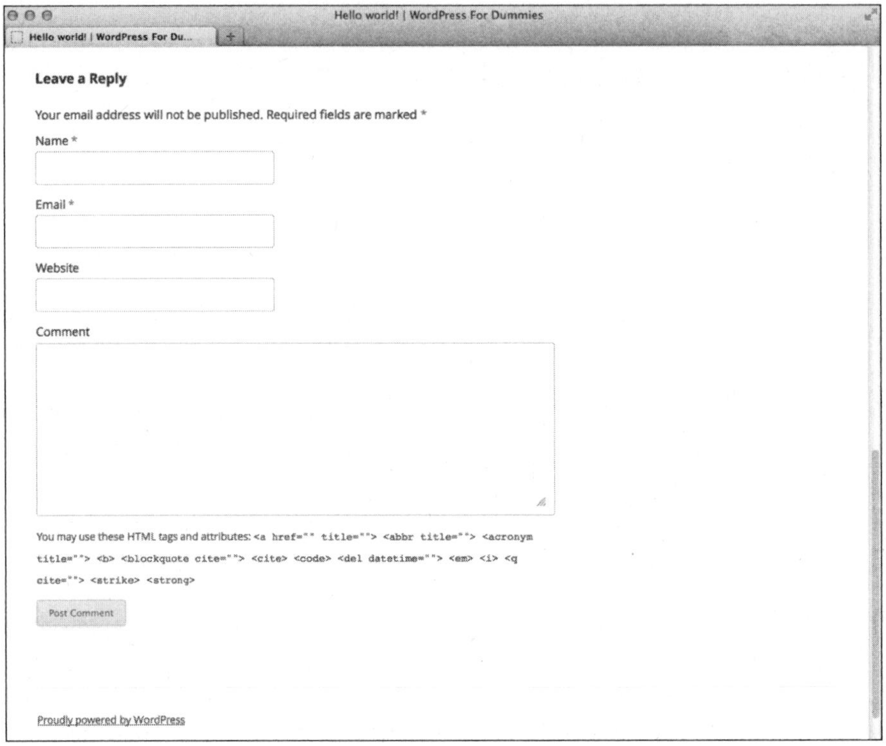

Figure 4-1: Readers use the Leave a Reply form to share their comments.

If you want to build a community of people who come back to your site frequently, respond to as many comments that your readers leave on your blog as possible. When people take the time to leave you a comment on your content, they like to know that you're reading it and they appreciate hearing your feedback to them. Plus, it keeps discussions lively and active on your site. Figure 4-2 illustrates what comments look like after they're published to your site. (*Note:* The actual design and layout of the comments on sites varies from theme to theme; you can find information on theme design in Book VI.)

Figure 4-2:
Blog
readers
comment
on a blog.

Exploring reasons to disallow comments

Under certain circumstances, you may not want to allow readers to leave comments freely on your site. For example, if you wrote a blog post on a topic that is considered very controversial, you may not want to invite comments because the topic may incite flame wars or comments that are insulting to you or your readers. If you're not interested in the point of view or feedback of readers on your site, or if your content doesn't really lend itself to reader feedback, you may decide to disallow comments entirely.

In making the decision to have comments, you have to be prepared for the fact that not everyone is going to agree with what you write; especially if you're writing on a topic that invites a wide array of opinions, such as politics, religion, or op-ed pieces. As a site owner, you make the decision, ahead of time, whether you want readers dropping in and leaving their own views, or even disagreeing with you on yours (sometimes vehemently!).

If you're on the fence about whether to allow comments, the WordPress platform allows you to toggle that decision on a per-post basis. Therefore, each time you publish a post or article on your website, you can indicate in the Post Options (on the Add New Post page of your Dashboard) whether this particular post should allow discussion. You may choose to disallow comments entirely on your site, which you can configure in the Discussion Settings on the Dashboard, or disallow them on only certain posts, which you can configure on the Dashboard on the Edit Post page, which I talk about in Book IV, Chapter 1.

Interacting with Readers through Comments

People can leave notes for you that are published to your site, and you can respond and engage your readers in conversation about the topic at hand. (Refer to Figure 4-1 and Figure 4-2.) Having this function on your blog creates the opportunity to expand the thoughts and ideas that you present in your blog post by giving your readers the opportunity to share their own thoughts.

On the WordPress Dashboard, you have full administrative control over who can and can't leave comments. In addition, if someone leaves a comment that has questionable content, you can edit the comment or delete it. You're also free to disallow comments on your blog. The Discussion Settings page on your Dashboard contains all the settings for allowing, or disallowing, comments on your site; flip back to Book III, Chapter 2 to dig into those settings, what they mean, and how you can use them to configure the exact interactive environment that you want for your site.

Tracking back

The best way to understand trackbacks is to think of them as comments, except for one thing: *Trackbacks* are comments left on your blog by other blogs, not by actual people. Although this process may sound mysterious, it's actually perfectly reasonable.

A trackback happens when you make a post on your blog and, within that post, you provide a link to a post made by another blogger in a different blog. When you publish that post, your blog sends a sort of electronic memo to the blog you linked to. That blog receives the memo and posts an acknowledgment of receipt in a comment within the post that you linked to on their site. Trackbacks work between most blogging platforms; for example, between WordPress and Blogger or WordPress and Typepad.

That memo is sent via a *network ping* (a tool used to test, or verify, whether a link is reachable across the Internet) from your site to the site you link to. This process works as long as both blogs support trackback protocol. Trackbacks can also come to your site by way of a *pingback* — which, really, is the same thing as a trackback, but the terminology varies from blog platform to blog platform.

Sending a trackback to a blog is a nice way of telling the blogger that you like the information she presented in her blog post. Every blogger appreciates the receipt of trackbacks to their posts from other bloggers. Figure 4-3 shows one trackback link.

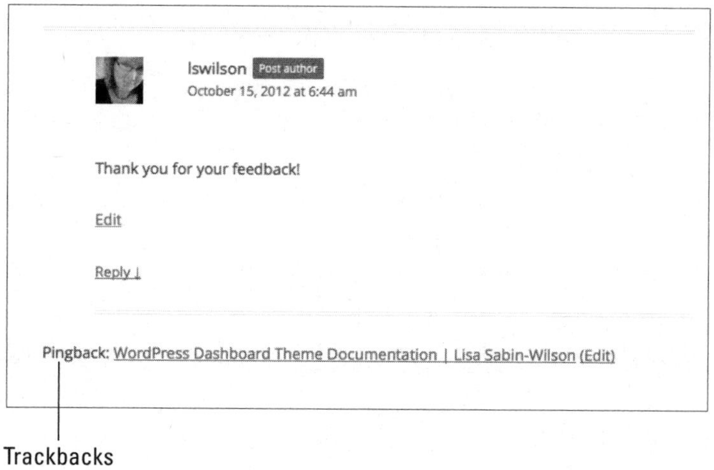

Figure 4-3:
Trackback
links on a
blog.

Trackbacks

Comment and trackback display

Almost every single WordPress theme displays comments at the bottom of each post published in WordPress. You can do custom styling of the comments so that they match the design of your site by using several items:

✦ **WordPress template tags:** Tags related to the display of comments and trackbacks. For more on these tags, see Book VI, Chapter 3.

✦ **Basic HTML:** Using HTML markup helps you provide unique styles to display content. For information about the use of basic HTML, check out Book VI.

✦ **CSS:** Every WordPress theme has a Cascading Style Sheet (CSS) template called `style.css`. Within this CSS template, you define the styles and CSS markup that creates a custom look and feel for the comment and trackback display on your site. You can find more information about using CSS in Book VI.

✦ **Graphics:** Using graphics to enhance and define your branding, style, and visual design is an integral part of web design. Because a single chapter isn't sufficient to fully cover graphic design, you may want to check out *WordPress Web Design For Dummies,* which I wrote, for great information on graphic and website design with WordPress.

✦ **WordPress widgets:** WordPress has a built-in widget to display the most recent comments published to your site by your visitors. You also can find several plugins that display comments in different ways, including top comments, most popular posts based on the number of comments, comments that display the author's photo, and more. For information about widgets and plugins for these purposes, flip to Book VI, Chapter 1 and Book VII, Chapters 1 and 2, respectively.

Managing Comments and Trackbacks

When you invite readers to comment on your site, you, as the site administrator, have full access to manage and edit those comments through the Comments page, which you can access on your WordPress Dashboard.

To find your comments, click the Comments link on the Comments menu; the Comments page opens. (See Figure 4-4.)

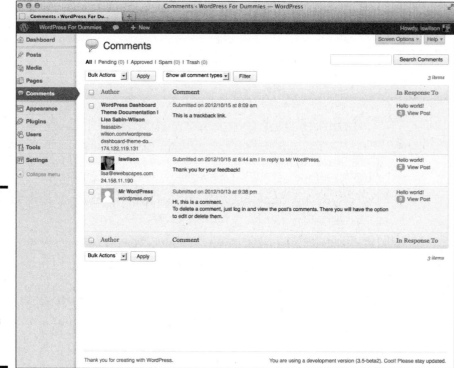

Figure 4-4: The Comments page contains all the comments and trackbacks on your blog.

When you hover your mouse pointer over a comment, several links appear that give you the opportunity to manage the comment:

✦ **Unapprove:** This link appears only if you have comment moderation turned on. Also, it appears only on approved comments. The comment is placed in the moderation queue, which you can get to by clicking the Pending link that appears below the Comments page header. The moderation queue is kind of a holding area for comments that haven't yet been published to your blog.

✦ **Reply:** Makes a text box drop down. In the text box, you can type and submit your reply to this person. This feature eliminates the need to load your live site in order to reply to a comment.

✦ **Quick Edit:** Opens the comment options inline without ever leaving the Comments page. You can configure options such as name, e-mail address, URL, and comment content. Click the Save button to save your changes.

✦ **Edit:** Opens the Edit Comment page, where you can edit the different fields, such as name, e-mail address, URL, and comment content. (See Figure 4-5.)

✦ **Spam:** Marks the comment as spam and marks it as spam in the data-base, where it will never be heard from again! (Actually, it's stored in the database as spam; you just don't see it in your comments list unless you click the Spam link at the top of the Comments page.)

✦ **Trash:** This link does exactly what it says; it sends the comment to the trash and deletes it from your blog. You can access comments that have been sent to the trash to permanently delete them from your blog or to restore them.

Figure 4-5:
Edit a user's
comment
on the Edit
Comment
page.

If you have a lot of comments listed on the Comments page and want to edit them in bulk, select the check boxes to the left of all the comments you want to manage; then select one of the following from the Bulk Actions drop-down list at the bottom left of the page: Approve, Mark as Spam, Unapprove, or Delete.

If you have your options set so that comments aren't published to your blog until you approve them, you can approve comments from the Comments page, as well. Just click the Pending link to list the comments that are pending moderation. If you have comments and/or trackbacks awaiting moderation, they appear on this page, and you can approve them, mark them as spam, or delete them.

WordPress immediately notifies you of any comments sitting in the moderation queue, awaiting your action. This notification, which appears on every single page, is a small circle, or bubble, on the left navigation menu, to the right of Comments. Figure 4-6 shows that I have 30 comments pending moderation. I had better get busy and deal with those comments!

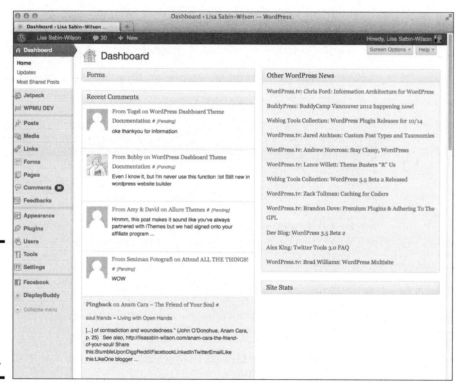

Figure 4-6:
A small circle tells me that I have 30 comments pending moderation.

Tackling Spam with Akismet

No blogger likes spam. In fact, blogging services such as WordPress have spent untold hours in the name of stopping spammers in their tracks, and for the most part, the services have been successful. Occasionally, however, spammers sneak through. Many spammers are offensive, and all of them are frustrating because they don't contribute to the ongoing conversations that occur in blogs. (A spammer's only goal is to generate traffic to his website.)

All WordPress installations have one significant thing in common: Akismet, a WordPress plugin. It's my humble opinion that Akismet is the mother of all plugins and that no WordPress blog is complete without a fully activated version of Akismet running in it.

Apparently, WordPress agrees because the plugin is packaged in every WordPress software release beginning with version 2.0. Akismet was created by the folks at Automattic, the same folks who brought you the WordPress. com-hosted version.

Akismet is the answer to combating comment and trackback spam. Matt Mullenweg of Automattic says Akismet is a "collaborative effort to make comment and trackback spam a non-issue and restore innocence to blogging, so you never have to worry about spam again" (from the Akismet website at `http://akismet.com`).

I started blogging in 2002 with the Movable Type blogging platform and moved to WordPress in 2003. As blogging became more and more popular, comment and trackback spam became more and more of a nuisance. One morning in 2004, I found that 2,300 pieces of disgusting comment spam had been published to my blog. Something had to be done! The folks at Automattic did a fine thing with Akismet. Since the emergence of Akismet, I barely had to think about comment or trackback spam except for the few times a month I check my Akismet spam queue.

I cover the use of plugins in Book VII. However, this chapter wouldn't be complete if I didn't show you how to activate and use the Akismet plugin on your site. Book VII covers the use, installation, and management of other plugins for your WordPress site.

Akismet is already included in every WordPress installation, so you don't have to worry about downloading and installing it, because it's already there. Follow these steps to activate and begin using Akismet:

1. **Click the Plugins link on the left navigation menu of the Dashboard to load the Plugins page.**

2. **Click the Activate link below the Akismet plugin name and description.**

   A yellow box appears at the top of the page, saying `Akismet is almost ready. You must enter your Akismet API key for it to work.` (See Figure 4-7.) An *API key* is a string of numbers and letters that functions like a unique password given to you by Akismet; it's the key that allows your WordPress.org application to communicate with your Akismet account.

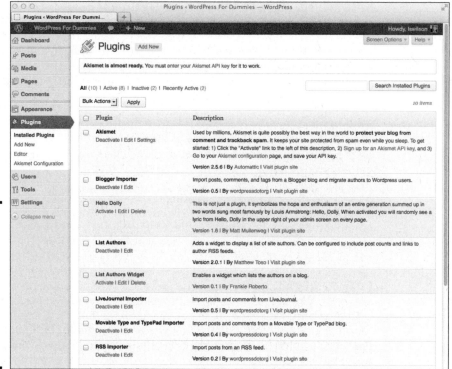

Figure 4-7:
After you
activate
Akismet,
WordPress
tells you
that the
plugin isn't
quite ready
to use.

3. **Click the link in the yellow box to navigate to the Akismet Configuration page.**

4. **If you have an API key, enter it in the Akismet API Key text field and then click the Update Options button to save your changes.**

   You can stop here if you already have a key, but if you do not have an Akismet key, keep following the steps in this section.

5. **Click the Akismet.com link on the Akismet Configuration page.**

   The Akismet website opens at http://akismet.com/wordpress.

6. **Click the Get an Akismet API Key button.**

   The signup page on the Akismet website (http://akismet.com/signup) opens, where you can choose from several different options for obtaining an Akismet key:

   • *Enterprise:* $50/month for people who own multiple WordPress-powered websites and want to use Akismet on all of them.

   • *Pro:* $5/month for people who own one small, nonpersonal (or business) WordPress-powered site.

- *Personal:* $0–$120/year for people who own one small, personal, WordPress-powered blog. You can choose to pay nothing ($0), or if you'd like to contribute a little cash toward the cause of combating spam, you can opt to spend up to $120 per year for your Akismet key subscription.

7. Select and pay for (if needed) your Akismet key.

After you've gone through the signup process, Akismet provides you with an API key. Copy that key by selecting it with your mouse pointer, right-clicking, and choosing Copy.

8. When you have your API key, go to the Akismet Configuration page by clicking the Akismet Configuration link on the Plugins menu on your WordPress Dashboard.

9. Enter the API key in the Akismet API Key text box (see Figure 4-8) and click the Update Options button to fully activate the Akismet plugin.

On the Akismet Configuration Page, after you've entered and saved your key, you also have two options that you can select to further manage your spam protection:

**Book III
Chapter 4**

Dealing with Comments and Spam

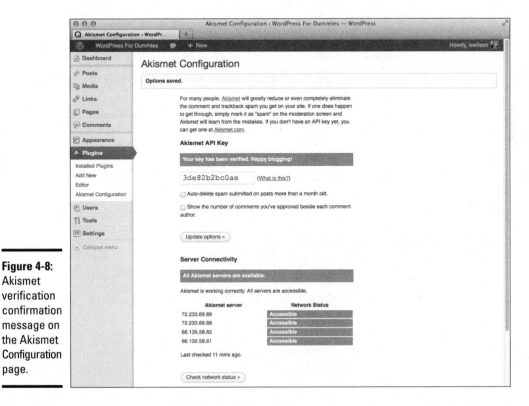

Figure 4-8:
Akismet verification confirmation message on the Akismet Configuration page.

✦ **Auto-delete Spam Submitted on Posts More Than a Month Old:** Enable this option by selecting the check box next to it to tell Akismet to automatically delete spam comments on posts that are more than a month old.

✦ **Show The Number of Comments You've Approved Beside Each Comment Author:** Enable this option by selecting the check box next to it to tell Akismet to display the number of approved comments each comment author on your blog has.

Akismet catches spam and throws it into a queue, holding the spam for 15 days and then deleting it from your database. It's probably worth your while to check the Akismet Spam page once a week to make sure that the plugin hasn't captured any legitimate comments or trackbacks.

You can rescue those non-spam captured comments and trackbacks by following these steps (after you log in to your WordPress Dashboard):

1. **Click Comments on the left navigation menu.**

   The Comments page appears, displaying a list of the most recent comments on your blog.

2. **Click the Spam link.**

   The Comments page now displays all spam comments that the plugin caught.

3. **Browse through the list of spam comments, looking for any comments or trackbacks that are legitimate.**

4. **If you locate a comment or trackback that's legitimate, click the Approve link directly below the entry.**

   The comment is marked as legitimate. In other words, WordPress recognizes that you don't consider this comment to be spam. WordPress then approves the comment and publishes it on your blog.

Check your spam filter often. I just found four legitimate comments caught in my spam filter; I was able to de-spam them, releasing them from the binds of Akismet and unleashing them upon the world.

Chapter 5: Creating Categories and Tags

In This Chapter

✔ Exploring content archive options in WordPress

✔ Creating and editing categories

✔ Creating tags and editing them

WordPress provides you with many different ways to organize, categorize, and archive content on your website or blog. Packaged within the WordPress software is the capability to automatically maintain chronological, categorized archives of your publishing history, which provides your website visitors with different ways to find your content. WordPress uses PHP and MySQL technology to sort and organize everything you publish in an order that you and your readers can access by date and category. This archiving process occurs automatically with every post you publish to your blog.

In this chapter, you can find out all about WordPress archiving, from categories to tags and more. You also can discover how to take advantage of the category description feature to improve your search engine optimization, how to distinguish between categories and tags, and how to use categories and tags to create topical archives of your site content.

Archiving Content with WordPress

When you create a post on your WordPress blog, you can file that post under a category that you specify. This feature makes for a nifty archiving system in which you and your readers can find articles/posts that you've placed within a specific category. Articles you post are also sorted and organized by date (day/month/year) so that you can easily locate articles that you posted at a certain time. The archives page on my website (see it at `http://ewebscapes.com/sitemap`) contains a Chronological Archive section, which has a list of months followed by the content I published in that particular month and year. If you click a date on that page, a listing of articles from that month drops down, and each article title is linked to that article. (See Figure 5-1.)

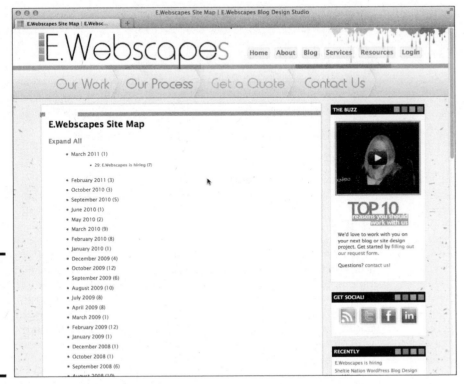

Figure 5-1:
An archive listing of posts by month and year on my website.

 You can easily create an archive listing like the one on my Sitemap page (shown in Figure 5-1) by using a WordPress plugin called Clean Archives Reloaded, which you can find in the WordPress Plugin Directory at `http://wordpress.org/extend/plugins/clean-archives-reloaded`. This plugin is easy to install, and to use it, you just need to create a page and add a short code segment (`[cleanarchivesreloaded]`) to the page content; that code automatically builds a Chronological Archives page that links to all the content you've published on your site. Easy archives!

WordPress archives and organizes your content for you in more ways than by date and category. In this section, I give you an overview of the several other ways; later in this chapter, I show you how you can leverage those archive types to create a dynamic website that's easy to navigate for your readers. The different types of archives and content include

✦ **Categories:** Create categories of topics in which you can file your articles so that you can easily archive relevant topics. Many websites display content by category — typically referred to as a *magazine theme,* in which all content is displayed by topic, rather than in a simple chronological listing. Figure 5-2 shows an example of a magazine theme.

You can find out how to create one of your own by customizing your site (see Book VI); also be sure to check out Book VI, Chapter 6 to discover how to use template tags and category templates to display category-specific content — exciting stuff!

✦ **Tags:** Tagging your posts with microkeywords, called *tags,* further defines related content within your site, which can improve your site for SEO purposes by assisting the search engines in finding related and relevant content, as well as provide additional navigation to help your readers find relevant content on your site.

✦ **Date Based:** Your content is automatically archived by date based on the day, month, year, and time of day you publish it.

✦ **Author:** Content is automatically archived by author based on the author of the post and/or page — you can create an author archive if your site has multiple content contributors.

✦ **Keyword (or Search):** WordPress has a built-in search function that allows you and your readers to search for keywords, which presents an archive listing of content that's relevant to your chosen keywords.

Figure 5-2:
A magazine theme created with WordPress (Syndicate News Theme by iThemes.com).

✦ **Custom Post Types:** You can build custom post types based on the kind of content your site offers. You can find detailed information on custom post types and how to create them in Book VI, Chapter 7.

✦ **Attachments:** WordPress has a built-in media library where you can upload different media files such as photos, images, documents, videos, and audio files (to name a few). You can build an archive of those files to create things such as photo galleries, eBook archives (PDFs), or video galleries.

Building categories

In WordPress, a *category* is what you determine to be the main topic of a blog post. By using categories, you can file your blog posts into topics by subject. To improve your readers' experiences in navigating through your blog, WordPress organizes posts by the categories you assign to them. Visitors can click the categories they're interested in to see the blog posts you've written on those particular topics. You can display the list of categories you set up on your blog in a few different places, including the following:

✦ **Body of the post:** In most WordPress themes, you see the title followed by a statement, such as Filed In: *Category 1, Category 2.* The reader can click the category name to go to a page that lists all the posts you've made in that particular category. You can assign a single post to more than one category.

✦ **Sidebar of your blog theme:** You can place a full list of category titles in the sidebar by using the Categories widget included in your WordPress installation. A reader can click any category to open a page on your site that lists the posts you made within that particular category.

Subcategories (also known as *category children*) can further refine the main category topic by listing specific topics related to the main *(parent)* category. In your WordPress Dashboard, on the Manage Categories page, subcategories appear directly below the main category. Here's an example:

Books I Enjoy (main category)

> Fiction (subcategory)

> Nonfiction (subcategory)

> Trashy romance (subcategory)

> Biographies (subcategory)

> *For Dummies* (subcategory)

You can create as many levels of categories as you like. For example, Biographies and *For Dummies* could be subcategories of Nonfiction, which is a subcategory of the Books category. You aren't limited to the number of category levels you can create.

Changing the name of a category

When you install WordPress, it gives you one default category called Uncategorized. (See the Categories page shown in Figure 5-3.) This category name is pretty generic, so you definitely want to change it to one that applies to you and your blog. (On my blog, I changed it to Life in General. Although that name's still a bit on the generic side, it doesn't sound quite so . . . well, uncategorized.)

REMEMBER

The default category also serves as kind of a fail-safe. If you publish a post to your blog and don't assign that post to a category, the post is assigned to the default category automatically, no matter what you name the category.

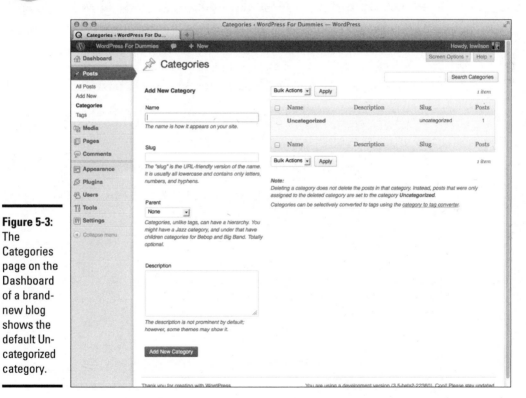

Figure 5-3:
The Categories page on the Dashboard of a brand-new blog shows the default Uncategorized category.

Book III
Chapter 5

Creating Categories and Tags

So, how do you change the name of that default category? When you're logged in to your WordPress Dashboard, just follow these steps:

1. Select Categories from the Posts drop-down list.

The Categories page opens, containing all the tools you need to set up and edit category titles for your blog.

2. **Click the title of the category that you want to edit.**

   If you want to change the Uncategorized category, click the word Uncategorized to open the Edit Category page. (See Figure 5-4.)

3. **Type the new name for the category in the Name text box.**

4. **Type the new slug in the Slug text box.**

   The term *slug* refers to the word(s) used in the web address for the specific category. For example, the category of Books has a web address of `http://yourdomain.com/category/books`; if you change the Category Slug to Books I Like, the web address is `http://your domain.com/category/books-i-like` (WordPress automatically inserts a dash between the slug words in the web address).

5. **Select a parent category from the Parent drop-down list.**

   If you want this category to be a main category, not a subcategory, select None.

6. **(Optional) Type a description of the category in the Description text box.**

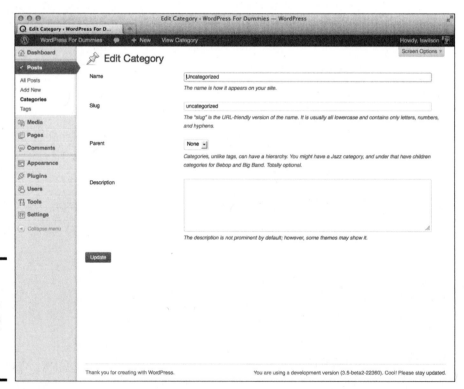

Figure 5-4:
Editing a category in WordPress on the Edit Category page.

Use this description to remind yourself what your category is about. Some WordPress themes display the category description right on your site, too, which your visitors may find helpful. (See Book VI for more about themes.) You know that your theme is coded in this way if your site displays the category description on the category page(s).

7. Click the Update button.

The information you just edited is saved, and the Categories page reloads, showing your new category name.

Creating new categories

Today, tomorrow, next month, next year — while your blog grows in size and age, continuing to add new categories further defines and archives the history of your blog posts. You aren't limited in the number of categories and subcategories you can create for your blog.

Creating a new category is as easy as following these steps:

1. Click the Categories link on the Posts menu of your Dashboard.

The Categories page opens. The left side of the Categories page displays the Add New Category section. (See Figure 5-5.)

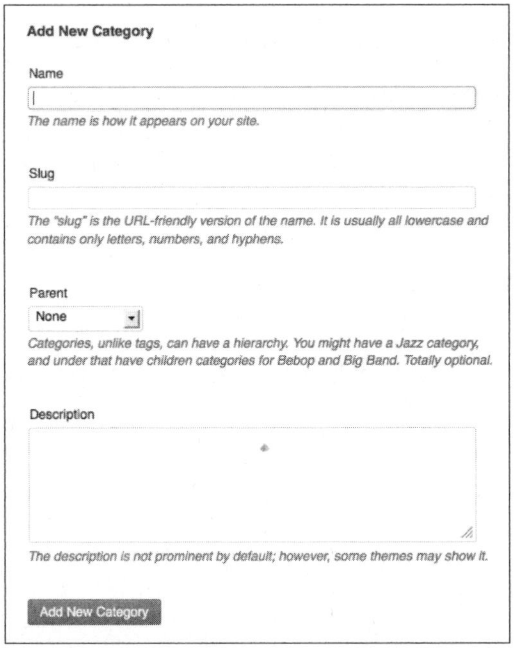

Add New Category

Name

The name is how it appears on your site.

Slug

The "slug" is the URL-friendly version of the name. It is usually all lowercase and contains only letters, numbers, and hyphens.

Parent

None ▾

Categories, unlike tags, can have a hierarchy. You might have a Jazz category, and under that have children categories for Bebop and Big Band. Totally optional.

Description

The description is not prominent by default; however, some themes may show it.

Add New Category

Figure 5-5: Create a new category on your blog.

2. **Type the name of your new category in the Name text box.**

   Suppose that you want to create a category in which you file all your posts about the books you read. In the Name text box, type something like **Books I Enjoy**.

3. **Type a name in the Slug text box.**

   The slug creates the link to the category page that lists all the posts you made in this category. If you leave this field blank, WordPress automatically creates a slug based on the category name. If the category is Books I Enjoy, WordPress automatically creates a category slug like `http://yourdomain.com/category/books-i-enjoy`. If you want to shorten it, however, you can! Type **books** in the Category Slug text box, and the link to the category becomes `http://yourdomain.com/category/books`.

4. **Select the category's parent from the Parent drop-down list.**

   Select None if you want this new category to be a parent (or top-level) category. If you want to make this category a subcategory of another category, select the category that you want to be the parent of this one.

5. **(Optional) Type a description of the category in the Description text box.**

   Some WordPress templates are set up to actually display the category description directly beneath the category name. (See Book VI.) Providing a description further defines the category intent for your readers. The description can be as short or as long as you want.

6. **Click the Add New Category button.**

   That's it! You've added a new category to your blog. Armed with this information, you can add an unlimited number of categories to your blog.

You can delete a category on your blog by hovering your mouse pointer on the title of the category you want to delete and then clicking the Delete link that appears below the category title.

Deleting a category doesn't delete the posts and links in that category. Instead, posts in the deleted category are reassigned to the Uncategorized category (or whatever you've named the default category).

If you have an established WordPress blog that has categories already created, you can convert some or all of your categories to tags. To do so, look for the Category to Tag Converter link on the right side of the Category page in your WordPress Dashboard. Click it to convert your categories to tags. (See the nearby sidebar, "What are tags, and how/why do I use them?," for more information on tags.)

What are tags, and how/why do I use them?

Don't confuse tags with categories (a lot of people do). *Tags* are clickable, comma-separated keywords that help you micro-categorize a post by defining the topics in it. Unlike WordPress categories, tags don't have a hierarchy; you don't assign parent tags and child tags. If you write a post about your dog, for example, you can put that post in the Pets category — but you can also add some specific tags that let you get a whole lot more specific, such as *poodle* or *small dogs*. If someone clicks your *poodle* tag, he finds all the posts you ever made that contain the *poodle* tag.

Besides defining your post topics for easy reference, you have another reason to use tags: Search-engine spiders harvest tags when they crawl your site, so tags help other people find your site when they search for specific words.

You can manage your tags in the WordPress Administration panel by selecting Tags from the Pages drop-down list. The Tags page, where you can view, edit, delete, and add new tags, opens.

Book VI, Chapter 6 takes you through the steps of really taking advantage of categories in WordPress to build a dynamic theme that displays your content in a way that highlights the different topics available on your site. Book VI describes how to use WordPress template tags to manipulate category archives for display and distribution on your website.

**Book III
Chapter 5**

Creating Categories
and Tags

Creating and Editing Tags

In Book IV, Chapter 1, you can find out all about publishing your posts in WordPress and how you can assign different tags to your content. This section takes you through the steps of managing tags, which is similar to the way you manage categories. To create a new tag, follow these steps:

1. **Click the Tags link on the Posts menu on your Dashboard.**

   The Tags page opens, as shown in Figure 5-6.

   Unlike categories and links, WordPress doesn't create a default tag for you, so when you visit the Tags page for the first time, no tags are listed on the right side of the page.

   The left side of the Tags page displays the Add New Tag section (shown in Figure 5-6).

2. **Type the name of your new tag in the Name text box.**

   Suppose that you want to create a tag in which you file all your posts about the books you read. In the Name text box, type something like **Fictional Books**.

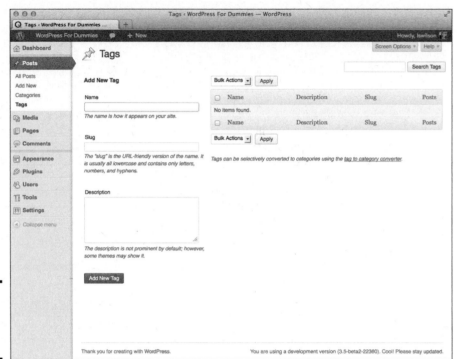

Figure 5-6:
The Tags
page on the
Dashboard.

3. **Type a name in the Slug text box.**

   The *slug* is the permalink of the tag and can help identify tag archives on your site by giving them their own URL, such as `http://yourdomain.com/tag/fictional-books`. By default, the tag slug adopts the words from the tag name.

4. **(Optional) Type a description of the tag in the Description text box.**

   Some WordPress templates are set up to actually display the tag description directly beneath the tag name. Providing a description further defines the category intent for your readers. The description can be as short or as long as you want.

5. **Click the Add New Tag button.**

   That's it! You've added a new tag to your blog. The Add New Tag page refreshes in your browser window with blank fields, ready for you to add another tag to your site.

6. **Repeat Steps 1 through 5 to add an unlimited number of tags to your blog.**

You use the Tags and the Categories pages on your Dashboard to manage, edit, and create new tags and categories to which you assign your posts when you publish them. Book IV, Chapter 1 contains a lot of information about how to go about assigning tags and categories to your posts, as well as a few good tips on how you can create new categories and tags right on the Edit Posts page itself.

Many WordPress websites use a cool feature called a *tag cloud,* which is a unique way to display a list of tags used on your site to give your readers navigation options to view your content. Figure 5-7 shows the tag cloud displayed on the sidebar of my design blog.

At the top of the right sidebar in Figure 5-7, the tag cloud gives you an at-a-glance peek at the topics I write about. You can tell the topic I write about most often because that tag appears in the largest text; likewise, the topics displayed in small text aren't written about quite as often. My tag cloud shows that I am quite a fan of WordPress.

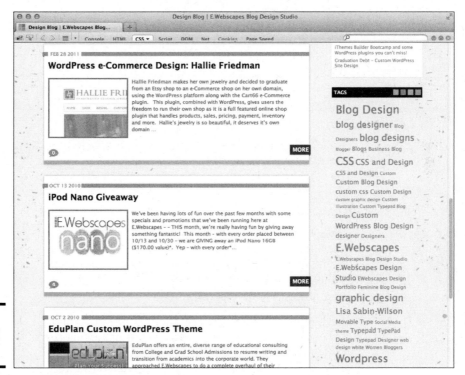

Figure 5-7:
A tag cloud
on a blog.

Book IV
Publishing Your Site with WordPress

Visit www.dummies.com/extras/wordpressaio to find out how to create link lists and blogrolls with WordPress.

Contents at a Glance

Chapter 1: Writing Your First Post

In This Chapter

✔ **Navigating the Add New Post page**

✔ **Writing and publishing your posts**

✔ **Creating a unique work space for writing**

*I*t's time to write your first post in your new WordPress blog! The topic you choose to write about and the writing techniques you use to get your message across are all up to you; I have my hands full writing this book! I *can* tell you, however, all about the techniques you'll use to write the wonderful passages that can bring you blog fame. Ready?

This chapter covers everything you need to know about the basics of publishing a blog post on your site, from writing a post to formatting, categorizing, tagging, and publishing it to your site.

Composing Your Blog Post

Composing a blog post is a lot like typing an e-mail: You give it a title, you write the message, and you click a button to send your words into the world. This section covers the steps you take to compose and publish a blog post on your site. By using the different options that WordPress provides — discussion options, categories, and tags, for example — you can configure each post however you like.

You can collapse or reposition all the modules on the Add New Post page to suit your needs. The only part of the Add New Post page that can't be collapsed and repositioned is the actual Title and Post text boxes (where you write your blog post).

Follow these steps to write a basic blog post:

1. **Click the Add New link on the Posts menu on the Dashboard.**

The Add New Post page opens, as shown in Figure 1-1.

2. **Type the title of your post in the Enter Title Here text field at the top of the Add New Post page.**

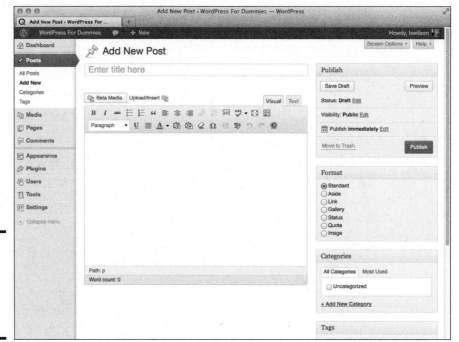

Figure 1-1:
Give your
blog post
a title and
write your
post body.

3. **Type the content of your post in the large text box below the Enter Title Here text box.**

   You can use the Visual Text Editor to format the text in your post. I explain the Visual Text Editor, and the buttons and options, later in this section.

4. **Click the Save Draft button in the Publish module, located at the top right of the Add New Post page.**

   The page refreshes with your post title and content saved but not yet published to your blog. At this point, you can skip to the "Publishing your post" section of this chapter for information on publishing your post to your blog, or you can continue with the following sections to discover how to refine the options for your post.

By default, the area in which you write your post is in Visual Editing mode, as indicated by the Visual tab that appears above the text. Visual Editing mode provides WYSIWYG (What You See Is What You Get) options for formatting. Rather than having to embed HTML code in your post, you can simply type your post, highlight the text you want to format, and click the buttons (shown in Figure 1-1) that appear above the text box in which you type your post.

If you've ever used a word processing program, such as Microsoft Word, you'll recognize many of these buttons:

✦ **Bold:** Embeds the `<strong> </strong>` HTML tag to emphasize the text in bold. Example: **Bold Text.**

✦ **Italic:** Embeds the `<em> </em>` HTML tag to emphasize the text in italics. Example: *Italic Text.*

✦ **Strikethrough:** Embeds the `<strike> </strike>` HTML tag that puts a line through your text. Example: `Strikethrough Text.`

✦ **Unordered List:** Embeds the `<ul><li> </li></ul>` HTML tags that create an *unordered* (bulleted) list.

✦ **Ordered List:** Embeds the `<ol><li> </li></ol>` HTML tags that create an *ordered* (numbered) list.

✦ **Blockquote:** Inserts the `<blockquote> </blockquote>` HTML tag that indents the paragraph or section of text you've selected.

✦ **Align Left:** Inserts the `<p align="left"> </p>` HTML tag that lines up the selected text against the left margin.

✦ **Align Center:** Inserts the `<p align="center"> </p>` HTML tag that positions the selected text in the center of the page.

✦ **Align Right:** Inserts the `<p align="right"> </p>` HTML tag that lines up the selected text against the right margin.

✦ **Insert/Edit Link:** Inserts the `<a href=" "> </a>` HTML tag around the text you've selected to create a hyperlink.

✦ **Unlink:** Removes the hyperlink from the selected text, if it was previously linked.

✦ **Insert More Tag:** Inserts the `<!--more-->` tag, which lets you split the display on your blog page. It publishes the text written above this tag with a Read More link, which takes the user to a page with the full post. This feature is good for really long posts.

✦ **Toggle Spellchecker:** Perfect for typo enthusiasts! Checking your spelling before you post is always a good idea.

✦ **Toggle Full Screen Mode:** Lets you focus purely on writing, without the distraction of all the other options on the page. Click this button, and the Post text box expands to fill the full height and width of your browser screen and displays only the barest essentials for writing your post. To bring the Post text box back to its normal state, click the Exit Full Screen link. Voilà — it's back to normal!

But wait, there's more! To the right of the Toggle Full Screen More button is the Show/Hide Kitchen Sink button. I saw this button and thought, "Wow! WordPress does my dishes, too!" Unfortunately, the button's name is a metaphor that describes the advanced formatting options available with the Visual Text Editor. Click this button to make a new formatting list drop down, providing options for underlining, font color, custom characters, undo and redo, and so on — a veritable kitchen sink full of options:

✦ **Format:** This drop-down list allows you to select the different text formatting available:

- *Paragraph:* Inserts the `<p>` `</p>` HTML tags around the text to indicate paragraph breaks.

- *Address:* Inserts the `<address>` `</address>` HTML tags around the text to indicate the author or owner of a document.

- *Preformatted:* Inserts the `<pre>` `</pre>` HTML tags around the text to indicate preformatted text and preserves both spaces and line breaks.

- *Headings 1, 2, 3, 4, 5, 6:* Inserts header HTML tags such as `<H1>` `</H1>` around text to indicate HTML headings. (H1 defines the largest, H6 defines the smallest; heading formats are usually defined in the CSS [see Book VI, Chapter 4] with font size and/or colors.)

✦ **Underline:** Inserts the `<u>` `</u>` HTML tags around the text to display it as underlined.

✦ **Text Color:** Displays the text in the color chosen.

✦ **Paste as Plain Text:** Useful if you copy text from another source, this option removes all formatting and special/hidden characters from the text and adds it to your post as unformatted text.

✦ **Paste from Word:** Useful if you're copying text from a Microsoft Word document because Word inserts a lot of hidden HTML and characters that could make your post text look funny on your website. Use the Paste from Word feature to transfer posts from Word to WordPress to preserve formatting without the hidden mess.

✦ **Remove Formatting:** Removes all formatting inside the post.

✦ **Insert Custom Character:** If you click this option, a pop-up window appears (see Figure 1-2), offering different characters such as $, %, &, and ©. In the pop-up window, click the symbol that you want to add to your post.

✦ **Outdent:** Moves text to the left one preset level with each click.

✦ **Indent:** Moves text to the right one preset level with each click.

✦ **Undo:** Click to undo your last formatting action.

✦ **Redo:** Click to redo the last formatting action that you undid.

✦ **Help:** Pops open a window with helpful information about using the text editor, including timesaving keyboard shortcuts, shown in Figure 1-3.

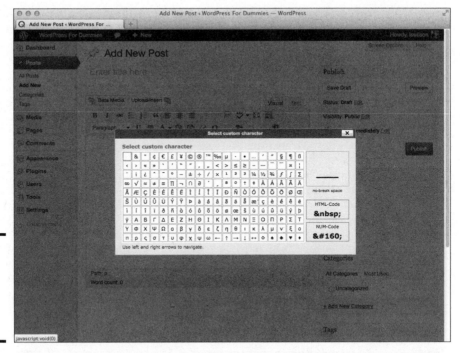

Figure 1-2:
Insert custom characters into your post.

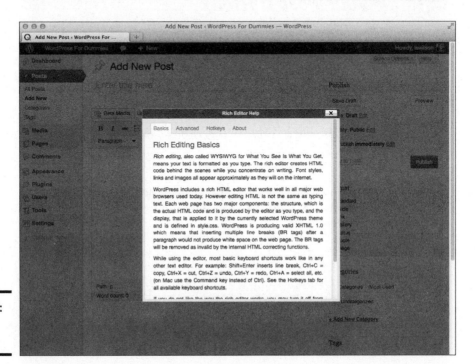

Figure 1-3:
Keyboard shortcuts.

You can turn off the Visual Text Editor by clicking the Your Profile link on the Users menu. Deselect the Use the Visual Editor When Writing box to turn off this editor if you'd rather insert the HTML code yourself in your posts.

If you'd rather embed your own HTML code and skip the Visual Text Editor, click the HTML tab that appears to the right of the Visual tab. If you're planning to type HTML code in your post — for a table or video files, for example — you have to click the HTML tab before you insert that code. If you don't, the Visual Text Editor formats your code, and it most likely will look nothing like you intended it to.

WordPress has a nifty, built-in autosave feature that saves your work while you're typing and editing a new post. If your browser crashes or you accidentally close your browser window before you've saved your post, it will be there for you when you get back. Those WordPress folks are so thoughtful!

Directly above the Visual Text Editor row of buttons, you see the Add Media button. Click this button if you want to insert images/photos, photo galleries, videos, and audio files into your posts. WordPress has an entire Media Library capability, which you can find out about in great detail in Chapters 2 and 3 of this minibook.

Refining Your Post Options

After you write the post, you can choose a few extra options before you publish it for the entire world to see. These settings apply to the post you're currently working on — not to any future or past posts. You can find these options below and to the right of the Post text box. (See Figure 1-4.) Click the title of each option to make the settings for that specific option expand.

You can reposition the various post option modules on the Add New Post page to fit the way you use this page by using the drag-and-drop method.

Here are the options that appear below the Post text box:

✦ **Excerpt:** Excerpts are short summaries of your posts. Many bloggers use snippets to show teasers of their blog posts on their website, thereby encouraging the reader to click the Read More links to read the posts in their entirety. Type your short summary in the Excerpt box. Excerpts can be any length in terms of words; however, the point is to keep it short and sweet and to tease your readers into clicking the Read More link. Figure 1-5 shows a blog post published to my site; however, it displays only an excerpt of the post on the front page, requiring the reader to click the title link to view the post in its entirety. (Some blog themes include a "Read More" link for readers to click in order to read the rest of the post.)

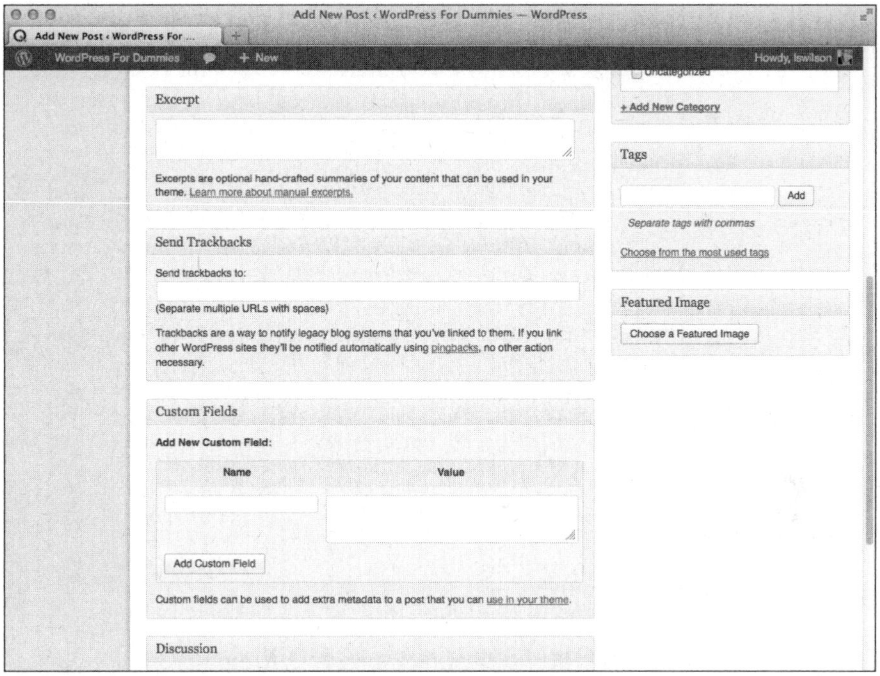

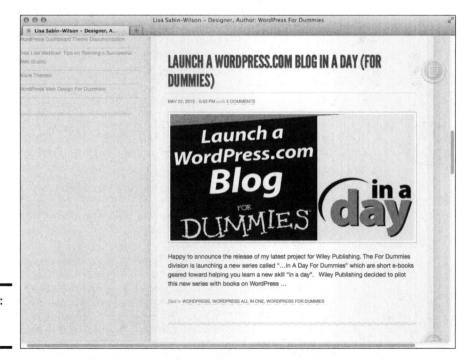

Figure 1-4:
Several options are available for your blog post.

Figure 1-5:
A post excerpt.

✦ **Send Trackbacks:** If you want to send a trackback to another blog, enter the blog's trackback URL in the Send Trackbacks To text box. You can send trackbacks to more than one blog; just be sure to separate track-back URLs with a space between each URL. For more on trackbacks, refer to Book III, Chapter 4.

✦ **Custom Fields:** Custom fields add extra data to your posts, and you can fully configure them. You can read more about the Custom Fields feature in WordPress in Book IV, Chapter 5.

✦ **Discussion:** Decide whether to let readers submit comments through the comment system by selecting the Allow Comments on this Post check box. By default, the box is selected; deselect it to disallow comments on this post.

✦ **Author:** If you're running a multi-author blog, you can select the name of the author who wrote this post. By default, your own author name appears selected in the Author drop-down list.

Here are the options that appear to the right of the Post text box:

✦ **Publish:** Publishing and privacy options for your post, which I cover in more detail in the following section of this chapter.

✦ **Format:** This module appears only when the theme that you're using on your site supports a WordPress feature called Post Formats (which I cover in detail in Book VI, Chapter 6). In the Format module, you can select the type of format you want to use for the post you're publishing.

✦ **Categories:** You can file your posts in different categories to organize them by subject. (See more about organizing your posts by category in Book III, Chapter 5.) Select the check box to the left of the category you want to use. You can toggle between listing all categories or seeing just the categories that you use the most by clicking the All Categories or Most Used links, respectively.

Don't see the category you need? Click the Add New Category link, and you can add a category right there on the Add New Post page.

✦ **Post Tags:** Type your desired tags in the Add New Tag text box. Be sure to separate each tag with a comma so that WordPress knows where each tag begins and ends. `Cats, Kittens, Feline` represents three different tags, for example, but without the commas WordPress would consider those three words to be one tag. You can also click the Choose from the Most Used Tags link to see a listing of tags that you use most often in your content — click any of the tags displayed, and WordPress adds it to the post you are editing. See Book III, Chapter 5 for more information on tags and how to use them.

✦ **Featured Image:** Some WordPress themes are configured to use an image (photo) to represent each post that you have on your blog. The image can appear on the home/front page, blog page, archives, or anywhere within the content display on your website. If you're using a theme that has this option, you can easily define the post thumbnail by clicking Set Featured Image below the Featured Image module on the Add New Post page. You can find more information about using Featured Images in Book VI, Chapter 6.

When you finish setting the options for your post, don't navigate away from this page; you haven't yet fully saved your options. The following section on publishing your post covers all the options you need for saving your post settings!

Publishing Your Post

You've given your new post a title and written the content of the post. Maybe you've even added an image or other type of media file to the post (see Chapters 3 and 4 of this minibook), and you've definitely configured the tags, categories, and other options. Now the question is: To publish? Or not to publish (yet)?

WordPress gives you three options for saving or publishing your post when you're done writing it. The Publish module is located on the right side of the Add New (or Edit) Post page. Just click the title of the Publish module to expand the settings you need. Figure 1-6 shows the available options in the Publish module.

Figure 1-6: The publish status for your blog posts.

The Publish module has several options:

✦ **Save Draft:** Click this button to save your post as a draft. The Add New Post page reloads with all your post contents and options saved; you can continue editing it now, tomorrow, the next day, or next year — the post is saved as a draft until you decide to publish it or delete it. To access your draft posts, click the Posts link on the Posts menu.

✦ **Preview:** Click the Preview button to view your post in a new window, as it would appear on your live blog if you'd published it. Previewing the post doesn't publish it to your site yet. It gives you the opportunity to view it on your site and check it for any formatting or content changes you want to make.

✦ **Status:** Click the Edit link to open the settings for this option. A drop-down list appears, from which you can select one of two options:

  • *Draft:* Save the post in draft form but don't publish it to your blog.

  • *Pending Review:* The post shows up in your list of drafts next to a Pending Review header. This option lets the administrator of the blog know that contributors have entered posts that are waiting for administrator review and approval (helpful for blogs that have multiple authors). Generally, only contributors use the Pending Review option.

Click the OK button to save your Status setting.

✦ **Visibility:** Click the Edit link to open the settings for this option:

  • *Public:* Select this option to make the post viewable to everyone who visits your site. Select the *Stick This Post to the Front Page* check box to have WordPress publish the post to your blog and keep it at the very top of all blog posts until you change this setting for the post.

    This option is otherwise known as a *sticky post*. Typically, posts are displayed in chronological order on your blog, displaying the most recent post on top. If you make a post sticky, it remains at the very top, no matter how many other posts you make after it. When you want to unstick the post, deselect the Stick This Post to the Front Page check box.

  • *Password Protected:* By assigning a password to a post, you can publish a post to your blog that only you can see. You can also share the post password with a friend, who can see the content of the post after he or she enters the password. But why would anyone want to password-protect a post? Imagine that you just ate dinner at your mother-in-law's house and she made the *worst* pot roast you've ever eaten. You can write all about it! Protect it with a password and give the password to your trusted friends so that they can read about it without offending your mother-in-law. Figure 1-7 shows a published post that's private; visitors see that a post exists, but they need to enter a password in the text box and then click Submit in order to view it.

Figure 1-7:
A password-protected post.

• *Private:* Publish this post to your blog so that only you can see it — no one else will be able to see it, ever. You may want to protect personal and private posts that you write only to yourself (if you're keeping a personal diary, for example).

✦ **Publish Immediately:** Click the Edit link to make the publish date options appear, where you can set the timestamp for your post. If you want the post to have the current time and date, ignore this setting altogether.

If you want to future-publish this post, you can set the time and date for anytime in the future. For example, when you have a vacation planned and you don't want your blog to go without updates while you're gone, you can write a few posts and set the date for a time in the future. Those posts are published to your blog while you're somewhere tropical, diving with the fishes.

✦ **Publish:** This button wastes no time! It bypasses all the previous draft, pending review, and sticky settings and publishes the post to your blog immediately.

After you select an option from the Publish drop-down list, click the Update button. The Write Post page saves your publishing-status option.

If you click Publish and for some reason don't see the post appear on the front page of your blog, you probably left the Status drop-down list set to Draft. Your new post appears in the draft posts, which you can find on the Dashboard's Posts page — just click the Posts link on the navigation menu.

Being Your Own Editor

While I write this book, I have editors looking over my shoulder, making recommendations, correcting typos and grammatical errors, and telling me when I get too long winded. You, on the other hand, are not so lucky! You're your own editor and have full control of what you write, when you write it, and how you write it. You can always go back and edit previous posts to correct typos, grammatical errors, and other mistakes by following these steps:

1. **Find the post that you want to edit by clicking the All Posts link on the Posts menu on the Dashboard.**

   The Posts page opens and lists the 20 most recent posts you've made to your blog.

   To filter that listing of posts by date, select a date from the Show All Dates drop-down list at the top of the Posts page (Dashboard➪Posts). For example, if you select February 2013, the Posts page reloads, displaying only those posts that were published in the month of February in 2013.

   You can also filter the post listing by category. Select your desired category from the View All Categories drop-down list.

2. **When you find the post you need, click its title.**

   Alternatively, you can click the Edit link that appears below the post title.

   The Edit Post window opens. In this window, you can edit the post and/or any of its options.

   If you need to edit only the post options, click the Quick Edit link. A drop-down Quick Edit menu appears, displaying the post options that you can configure, such as the title, status, password, categories, tags, comments, and timestamp. Click the Save button to save your changes.

3. **Edit your post; then click the Update Post button.**

   The Edit Post window refreshes with all your changes saved.

Creating Your Own Workspace for Writing

In Book III, Chapter 1, you can discover how to organize the Dashboard to create your own customized workspace by rearranging modules and screen options. The Add New Post page, where you write, edit, and publish your post, has the same options available, allowing you to fully control the workspace arrangement to create your own custom, unique space that suits your writing needs.

To start customizing your workspace, open the Add New Post page by clicking the Add New link on the Posts menu on the Dashboard.

You can make the Post text box (where you write the content of your post) bigger. Click your mouse in the bottom corner of the box, hold down your mouse button, drag it until the box is the length you want, and then release your mouse button. (Conversely, you can make the box smaller by dragging it up rather than down.) Figure 1-8 shows a large Post text box on my Add New Post page.

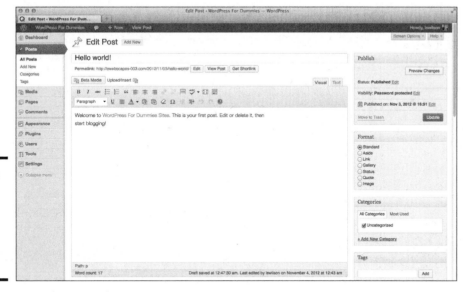

Figure 1-8:
Adjust the size of the Post text box on the Add New Post page.

Adjusting screen options

Several items appear on the Add New Post page, as described in the section "Publishing Your Post," earlier in this chapter. You may not use all these items; in fact, you may find that simply removing them from the Add New Post page (and the Edit Post page) makes writing your posts easier and more efficient. To remove an item, follow these steps:

1. **Click the Screen Options tab at the top of the screen.**

The Screen Options panel drops down, as shown in Figure 1-9.

2. **Select or deselect items below the Show on Screen heading.**

Select an item by placing a check mark in the check box to the left of its name; deselect it by removing the check mark. Selected items appear on the page, and deselected items are removed from the page.

If you deselect an item that you want to include again on the Add New Post page, it's not gone forever! Revisit the Screen Options panel and reselect its check box to make that item appear on the page once again.

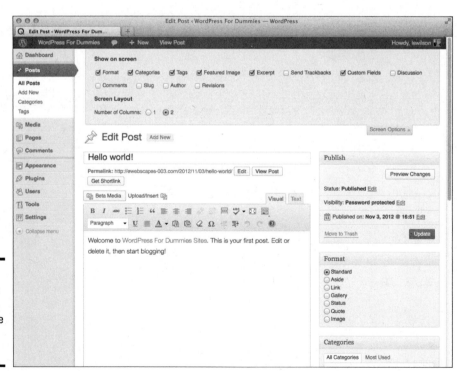

Figure 1-9:
The Screen Options panel on the Add New Post page.

3. **Select your preferred Screen Layout.**

   You can choose whether your Dashboard appears in one column or two columns (the default option).

4. **Click the Screen Options tab when you're done.**

   The Screen Options panel closes, and the options you've chosen are saved and remembered by WordPress.

Arranging post modules

Aside from being able to make the Post text box bigger (or smaller), you can't edit the Post text box module. You can configure all other modules on the Add New Post page (and the Edit Post page) — you can remove them (in the Screen Options panel, as I discuss in the preceding section), expand and collapse them, and drag them around to place them in a different spot on your screen.

Collapse (that is, close) any of the modules by hovering your mouse pointer over the module title and then clicking the down arrow that appears to the right of the module name, as shown in Figure 1-10 for the Categories module. Likewise, you can *expand* (or open) a module by doing the same when it's collapsed.

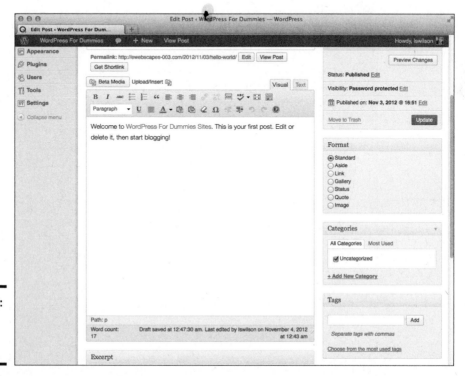

Figure 1-10:
Expand or collapse modules.

Book IV
Chapter 1

Writing Your
First Post

You can also drag and drop a module on the Add New Post screen to position it wherever you want. Just click a module and, while holding down the mouse button, drag it to different area on the screen. WordPress displays a dashed border around the area when you have the module hovering over a spot where you can drop it. Because I use the Categories module on every post I publish, I've dragged that module to the top right of my writing space, as shown in Figure 1-11.

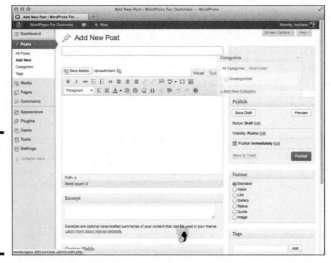

Figure 1-11:
Drag
and drop
modules
on the Add
New Post
page.

On the Post page within your Dashboard, you can really configure your own custom workspace that suits your style, work habits, and needs. WordPress remembers all the changes you make to this page, including the screen options and modules, so you have to set up this page only once. You can drag and drop modules on any Dashboard page in the same way you do on the main Dashboard page, as covered in Book III, Chapter 1.

Chapter 2: Creating a Static Page

*I*n Book III, Chapter 5, I discuss the different ways that content gets archived by WordPress, and in Book III, Chapter 1, I give you a very brief introduction to the concept of pages and where to find them on the WordPress Dashboard.

This chapter takes you through the full concept of pages in WordPress, including how to write and publish them. This chapter also fully explains the difference between posts and pages in WordPress so that you know which to publish for different situations.

Understanding the Difference between Posts and Pages

Pages, in WordPress, are different from posts because they don't get archived the way your blog posts do: They aren't categorized or tagged, don't appear in your listing of recent blog posts or date archives, and aren't syndicated in the RSS feeds available on your site — because content within pages generally doesn't change. (Book III, Chapter 5 gives you all the details on how the WordPress archives work.)

Use pages for static or standalone content that exists separately from the archived post content on your site.

With the page feature, you can create an unlimited amount of static pages separate from your blog posts. People commonly use this feature to create About Me or Contact Me pages, among other things. Table 2-1 illustrates the differences between posts and pages by showing you the different ways the WordPress platform handles them.

Table 2-1	Differences between a Post and a Page	
WordPress Options	*Page*	*Post*
Appears in blog post listings	No	Yes
Appears as a static page	Yes	No
Appears in category archives	No	Yes
Appears in monthly archives	No	Yes
Appears in Recent Posts listings	No	Yes
Appears in site RSS feed	No	Yes
Appears in search results	Yes	Yes
Uses tags and/or categories	No	Yes

Creating the Front Page of Your Website

For the most part, when you visit a blog powered by WordPress, the blog appears on the main page. My personal blog at `http://lisasabin-wilson.com`, powered by WordPress (of course), shows my latest blog posts on the front page, along with links to the post archives (by month or by category) in the sidebar. This setup is typical of a site run by WordPress. (See Figure 2-1.)

But the front page of my business site at `http://ewebscapes.com`, also powered by WordPress, contains no blog and displays no blog posts. (See Figure 2-2.) Instead, it displays the contents of a static page that I created in the WordPress Dashboard. This static page serves as a portal to my design blog, my portfolio, and other sections of my business site. The site includes a blog but also serves as a full-blown business website with all the sections I need to provide my clients the information they want.

Both of my sites are powered by the self-hosted version of WordPress.org, so how can they differ so much in what they display on the front page? The answer lies in the templates in the WordPress Dashboard.

You use static pages in WordPress to create content that you don't want to appear as part of your blog but do want to appear as part of your overall site (such as a bio page, a page of services, and so on).

Figure 2-1:
My personal
blog, set
up like a
typical site
powered by
WordPress.

Figure 2-2:
My business
site, set
up as a
business
website,
rather than
a blog.

Creating a front page is a three-step process:

1. Create a static page.

2. Designate that static page as the front page of your site.

3. Tweak the page to look like a website rather than a blog.

By using this method, you can create unlimited numbers of static pages to build an entire website. You don't even need to have a blog on this site unless you want one.

Creating the static page

To have a static page appear on the front page of your site, you need to create that page. Follow these steps:

1. **Click the Add New link on the Pages menu on the Dashboard.**

   The Add New Page page opens, where you can write a new page for your WordPress site, as shown in Figure 2-3.

2. **In the Title text box, type a title for the page.**

3. **Type the content of your page in the large text box.**

4. **Set the options for this page.**

   I explain the options on this page in the following section.

5. **Click the Publish button.**

   The page is saved to your database and published to your WordPress site with its individual URL (or *permalink*). The URL for the static page consists of your blog URL and the title of the page. For example, if you titled your page About Me, the URL of the page is `http://your domain.com/about-me`. (See Book III, Chapter 2 for more information about permalinks.)

The Page Template option is set to Default Template. This setting tells WordPress that you want to use the default page template (`page.php` in your theme template files) to format the page you're creating. The default page template is the default setting for all pages you create; you can assign a different page template to pages you create, if your theme has made different page templates available for use. In Book VI, Chapter 6, you can find extensive information on advanced WordPress themes, including information on page templates and how to create and use them on your site.

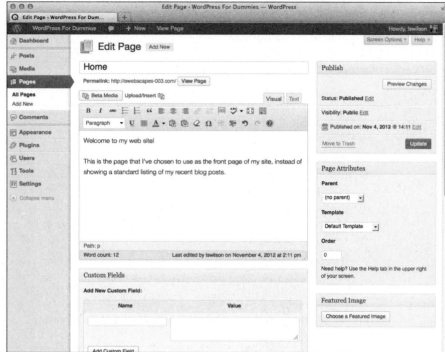

Figure 2-3:
Create the
static page
that you
want to use
as your front
page.

Setting page options

Before you publish a new page to your site, you can change options to use
different features available in WordPress. These features are similar to the
ones available for publishing posts, which you can read about in Book IV,
Chapter 1:

✦ **Custom Fields:** Custom fields add extra data to your page, and you can
fully configure them. You can read more about the Custom Fields feature
in Book IV, Chapter 5.

✦ **Discussion:** Decide whether to let readers submit comments through the
comment system by selecting or deselecting the Allow Comments text
box. By default, the box is selected; deselect it to disallow comments on
this page.

Typically, you don't see a lot of static pages that have the Comments
feature enabled because pages offer static content that doesn't generally
lend itself to a great deal of discussion. There are exceptions, however,
such as a Contact page, which might use the Comments feature as a way
for readers to get in touch with you through that specific page. Of course,
the choice is yours to make based on the specific needs of your website.

✦ **Author:** If you're running a multi-author site, you can select the name of the author you want to be attributed to this page. By default, your own author name appears selected here.

✦ **Publish:** The publishing and privacy options for your post, which I cover in Book IV, Chapter 1.

✦ **Parent:** Select a parent for the page you're publishing. Book III, Chapter 5 covers the different archiving options, including the ability to have a hierarchical structure for pages that create a navigation of main pages and subpages (called parent and child pages).

✦ **Template:** You can assign the page template if you're using a template other than the default one. (Book VI, Chapter 7 contains more information about themes and templates, including using page templates on your site.)

✦ **Order:** By default, this option is set to 0 (zero). You can enter a number, however, if you want this page to appear in a certain spot on the page menu of your site.

If you're using the built-in menu feature in WordPress, you can use this option; but you don't have to use it, because you can define the order of pages and how they appear on your menu by assigning a number to the page order — for example, a page with the page order of 1 appears first on your navigation menu, a page with the page order of 2 appears second, and so on. Book VI, Chapter 1 covers the Menu feature in greater detail.

✦ **Featured Image:** Some WordPress themes are configured to use an image (photo) to represent each post that you have on your blog. The image can appear on the home/front page, blog page, archives, or anywhere within the content display on your website. If you're using a theme that has this option, you can easily define a post's thumbnail by clicking the Set Featured Image link below the Featured Image module on the Add New Post page. Then you can assign an image that you've uploaded to your site as the featured image for a particular post.

Assigning a static page as the front page

After you create the page you want to use for the front page of your website, tell WordPress that you want the static page to serve as the front page of your site. Follow these steps:

1. **Click the Reading link on the Settings menu on the Dashboard to display the Reading Settings page.**

2. **Select the Static Page check box in the Enable a Static Front Page section.**

3. **Select the page you want used for the front page of your site from the drop-down list. (See Figure 2-4.)**

4. **Click the Save Changes button at the bottom of the Reading Settings page.**

   WordPress displays the page you selected in Step 3 as the front page of your site. Figure 2-5 shows my site displaying a static page.

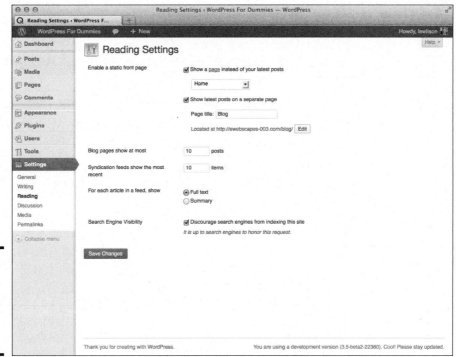

Figure 2-4:
Choosing
which page
to display
as the front
page.

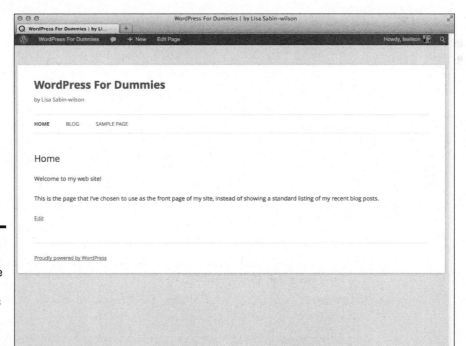

Figure 2-5:
WordPress
displays the
page you
selected as
your front
page.

Adding a Blog to Your Website

If you want a blog on your site but don't want to display the blog on the front page, you can add one from the WordPress Dashboard. To create the blog for your site, first follow these steps:

1. **Click the Add New link on the Pages menu on the Dashboard.**

    The page where you can write a new page to your WordPress site opens.

2. **Type** Blog **in the Title text box.**

    The page slug is automatically set to /blog. (Read more about slugs in Book III, Chapter 5.)

3. **Leave the Page Content text box blank.**

4. **Click the Publish button.**

    The page is saved to your database and published to your WordPress site.

    Now, you have a blank page that redirects to http://*yourdomain.com*/blog. Next, you need to assign the page you just created as your blog page.

5. **Click the Reading link on the Settings menu on the Dashboard.**

    The Reading Settings page opens.

6. **Select your page under Posts Page in the Front Page Displays option.**

7. **Click the Save Changes button.**

    The options you just set are saved, and your blog is now at http://*yourdomain.com*/blog (where *yourdomain.com* is the actual domain name of your site).

When you navigate to http://*yourdomain.com*/blog, your blog appears.

This method of using the /blog page slug works only if you're using custom permalinks with your WordPress installation. (See Book III, Chapter 2 if you want more information about permalinks.) If you're using the default permalinks, the URL for your blog page is different; it looks something like http://*yourdomain.com*/?p=4 (where 4 is the ID of the page you created for your blog).

Chapter 3: Uploading and Displaying Photos and Galleries

In This Chapter

✔ Using the built-in image-upload feature

✔ Inserting a photo in your post

✔ Creating photo galleries in WordPress

Adding images and photos to your posts can really dress up the content. By using images and photos, you give your content a dimension that you can't express in plain text. Through visual imagery, you can call attention to your post and add depth to it. With WordPress, you can insert single images or photographs, or you can use a few nifty plugins to turn some of the pages in your site into a full-fledged photo gallery.

In this chapter, you discover how to add some special touches to your blog posts by adding images and photo galleries, all by using the built-in image-upload feature and image editor in WordPress.

Inserting Images into Your Blog Posts

You can add images to a post pretty easily by using the WordPress image uploader. Jump right in and give it a go: From the Dashboard, click the Add New link on the Posts menu and then, on the Add New Post page, click the Add Media button. The Insert Media window that appears lets you choose images from your hard drive or from a location on the web. (See Figure 3-1.)

Adding an image from your computer

To add an image from your own hard drive, follow these steps:

1. **Click the Add Media button on the Add New Post page.**

   The Insert Media window appears. (Refer to Figure 3-1.)

2. **Click the Upload Files tab at the top and then click the Select Files button.**

   A dialog box, from which you can select an image (or multiple images) from your hard drive, opens.

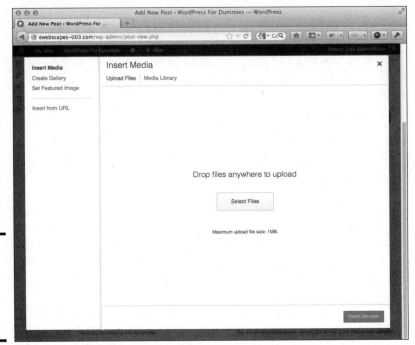

Figure 3-1:
The
WordPress
Insert
Media
window.

3. **Select your image(s) and then click Open.**

   The image is uploaded from your computer to your web server, and the Insert Media window displays your uploaded image selected and ready for editing.

4. **Edit the details for the image(s) under the Attachment Details section of the Insert Media window. (See Figure 3-2.)**

   The Attachment Details section provides you with several image options:

   - *Title:* Type a title for the image.

   - *Caption:* Type a caption for the image (such as **This is a flower from my garden**).

   - *Alternate Text:* Type the alternative text for the image. More information on alternative text is found in Chapter 6 of this minibook.

   - *Description:* Type a description of the image.

   - *Alignment:* Select None, Left, Center, or Right. (See Table 3-1, later in this chapter, for styling information regarding image alignment.)

   - *Link URL:* If you want the image linked to a URL, type that URL in this text box. Alternatively, select the appropriate option button to determine where your readers go when they click the image you uploaded: Selecting None means the image isn't clickable, File URL directs readers through to the image itself, and Post URL directs readers through to the post in which the image appears.

- *Size:* Select Thumbnail, Medium, Large, or Full Size.

WordPress automatically creates small- and medium-sized versions of the original images you upload through the built-in image uploader. A thumbnail is a smaller version of the original file. You can edit the size of the thumbnail by clicking the Settings link and then clicking the Media menu link. In the Image Sizes section of the Media Settings page, designate your desired height and width of the small and medium thumbnail images generated by WordPress.

If you're uploading more than one image, skip to the "Inserting a Photo Gallery" section, later in this chapter.

5. **Click the Edit Image link (shown in Figure 3-2) to edit the appearance of the image.**

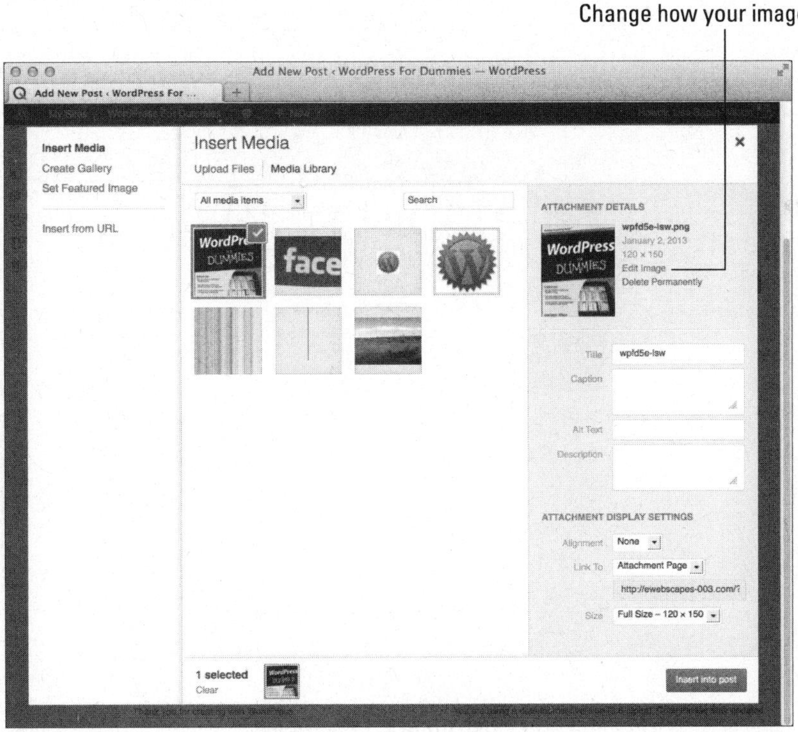

Change how your image looks.

Figure 3-2: You can set several options for your images after you upload them.

Book IV Chapter 3

Uploading and Displaying Photos and Galleries

The Edit Media page opens (see Figure 3-3) and options are represented by icons shown above the image and include

- *Crop:* Cut the image down to a smaller size.

- *Rotate Counter-Clockwise:* Rotate the image to the left.

- *Rotate Clockwise:* Rotate the image to the right.

- *Flip Vertically:* Flip the image upside down and back again.

- *Flip Horizontally:* Flip the image from right to left and back again.

- *Undo:* Undo any changes you made.

- *Redo:* Redo images edits that you've undone.

- *Scale Image:* The option drop-down list appears, giving you the ability to set a specific width and height for the image.

6. **Click the Update button on the Edit Media page when you're done editing the image.**

7. **Return to the post you would like to insert the image into by clicking the All Posts link on the Posts menu and then clicking the title of the post you need.**

8. **Click the Add Media button.**

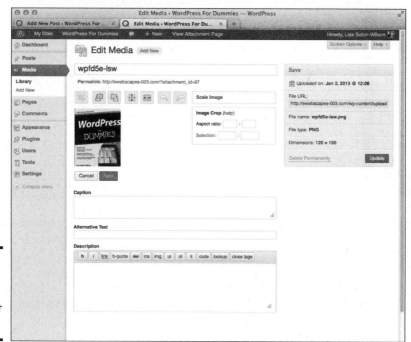

Figure 3-3:
The
WordPress
image editor
options.

9. **Click the Media Library tab in the Insert Media Window.**

    This loads all the images you've ever uploaded to your site.

10. **Select the image you would like to use by clicking it once.**

11. **Click the Insert into Post button.**

    The Add an Image window closes, and the Add New Post page (or the Add New Page page, if you're writing a page) reappears. WordPress has inserted the HTML to display the image in your post, as shown in Figure 3-4; you can continue editing your post, save it, or publish it.

To see the actual image, and not the code, click the Visual tab just above the Post text box.

Aligning your images through the stylesheet

When you upload your image, you can set its alignment as None, Left, Center, or Right. The WordPress theme you're using, however, may not have these alignment styles accounted for in its stylesheet. If you set the alignment to Left, for example, but the image on your blog doesn't appear to be aligned at all, you may need to add a few styles to your theme's stylesheet.

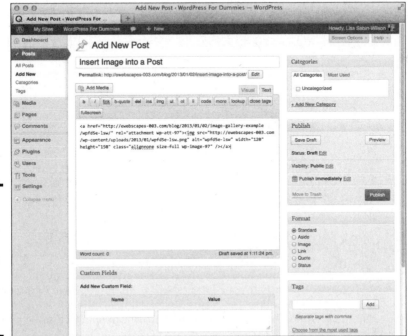

Figure 3-4: WordPress inserts the correct HTML code for your uploaded image into your post.

Themes and templates are discussed in greater detail in Book VI; however, for purposes of making sure that you have the correct image alignment for your newly uploaded images, follow these steps for a quick-and-dirty method:

1. **Select Editor from the Appearance drop-down list.**

   The Edit Themes page opens. All the template files for your active theme are listed on the right side of the page.

2. **Click the Stylesheet template.**

   The Stylesheet (`style.css`) template opens in the text box on the left side of the page.

3. **Add your desired styles to the stylesheet.**

Table 3-1 shows the styles you can add to your stylesheet to make sure that image-alignment styling is present and accounted for in your theme.

Table 3-1	Styling Techniques for Image Alignment
Image Alignment	*Add This to Your Stylesheet* (`style.css`)
None	`img.alignnone {float:none; margin: 5px 0 5px 0;}`
Left	`img.alignleft {float:left; margin: 5px 10px 5px 0;}`
Center	`img.aligncenter {display:block; float:none; margin: 5px auto;}`
Right	`img.alignright {float:right; margin: 5px 0 5px 10px;}`

These styles are just examples of what you can do. Get creative with your own styling. You can find more information about using CSS (Cascading Style Sheets) to add style to your theme(s) in Book VI, Chapter 4.

Inserting a Photo Gallery

You can also use the Insert Media window to insert a full photo gallery into your posts. Upload all your images and then, instead of clicking the Insert into Post button, click the Create Gallery link on the left side of the Insert Media window. The Create Gallery window opens and displays all the images you've uploaded to your site.

Follow these steps to insert a photo gallery into a blog post:

1. **In the Create Gallery window, select the images you want to use in your gallery.**

Click each image once in order to select it for use in the gallery. A selected image displays a small checkmark in its upper-right corner. (See Figure 3-5.)

2. **Click the Create New Gallery button.**

The Edit Gallery page opens.

3. **(Optional) Add a caption for each image by clicking in the Caption This Image area and typing a caption or short description for the image.**

4. **(Optional) Set the order the images appear in the gallery by using the drag-and-drop option on the Edit Gallery page.**

Click and then drag and drop images to change the order.

Figure 3-5:
The Create Gallery window.

5. **(Optional) Specify the following options under the Gallery Settings section on the right side of the Edit Gallery Page:**

   - *Link To:* Media File or Attachment Page.

   - *Random Order:* Select to randomize the order in which the images are displayed in the gallery.

   - *Gallery Columns:* Select how many columns of images you want to appear in your gallery.

6. **Click the Insert Gallery button.**

   WordPress inserts into your post a piece of shortcode that looks like this: [gallery ids"1,2,3"].

7. **(Optional) Change the order of appearance of the images in the gallery, as well as the markup (HTML tags or CSS selectors).**

   Use the WordPress gallery shortcode (see Table 3-2) to change different aspects of the display of the gallery in your post:

   - *captiontag:* Change the markup that surrounds the image caption by altering the gallery shortcode. For instance, [gallery captiontag="div"] places <div></div> tags around the image caption. (The <div> tag is considered a block-level element and creates a separate container for the content — see more about <div> tags and CSS in Book VI, Chapter 4.) If you want to have the gallery appear on a line of its own, the [gallery captiontag="p"] code places <p class="gallery-caption"></p> tags around the image caption. The default markup for the captiontag option is dd.

   - *icontag:* Defines the HTML markup around each individual thumbnail image in your gallery. Change the markup around the icontag (thumbnail icon) of the image by altering the gallery shortcode to something like [gallery icontag="p"], which places <p class="gallery-icon"></p> tags around each thumbnail icon. The default markup for icontag is dt.

   - *itemtag:* Defines the HTML markup around each item in your gallery. Change the markup around the itemtag (each item) in the gallery by altering the gallery shortcode to something like [gallery itemtag="span"], which places <span class="gallery-item"></span> tags around each item in the gallery. The default markup for the itemtag is dl.

   - *orderby:* Defines the order in which the images are displayed within your gallery. Change the order used to display the thumbnails in the gallery by altering the gallery shortcode to something like [gallery orderby="menu_order ASC"], which displays the thumbnails in ascending menu order. Another parameter you can use is ID_order ASC, which displays the thumbnails in ascending order according to their IDs.

Table 3-2	Gallery Short Code Examples
Gallery Short Code	*Output*
`[gallery columns="4" size="medium"]`	A four-column gallery containing medium-sized images
`[gallery columns= "10" id="215" size="thumbnail"]`	A ten-column gallery containing thumbnail images pulled from the blog post with the ID 215
`[gallery captiontag="p" icontag="span"]`	A three-column (default) gallery in which each image is surrounded by `<span>` `</span>` tags and the image caption is surrounded by `<p></p>` tags

8. **Define the style of the `<span>` tags in your CSS stylesheet.**

   The `<span>` tags create an inline element. An element contained within a `<span>` tag stays on the same line as the element before it; there's no line break. You need a little knowledge of CSS to alter the `<span>` tags. Click the Design tab in your WordPress Dashboard, and then click the Theme Editor subtab to edit the stylesheet for your theme. Here's an example of what you can add to the stylesheet (`style.css`) for your current theme:

   ```
   span.gallery-icon img {
   padding: 3px;
   background: white;
   border: 1px solid black;
   margin: 0 5px;
   }
   ```

   Placing this bit of CSS in the stylesheet (`style.css`) of your active theme automatically places a 1-pixel black border around each thumbnail, with 3 pixels of padding and a white background. The left and right margins are 5 pixels wide, creating nice spacing between images in the gallery.

9. **Click the Update File button to save changes to your Stylesheet (`style.css`) template.**

Figure 3-6 shows my post with a photo gallery displayed, using the preceding steps and CSS example in the default WordPress theme: Twenty Twelve. I used the gallery shortcode for the gallery shown in Figure 3-6 — `[gallery icontag="span" size="thumbnail"]`.

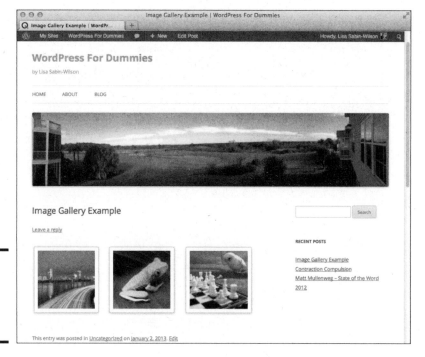

Figure 3-6:
A photo
gallery
displayed
in a post.

Matt Mullenweg, cofounder of the WordPress platform, created a very extensive photo gallery by using the built-in gallery options in WordPress. Check out the fabulous photo gallery at `http://ma.tt/category/gallery`, as shown in Figure 3-7.

WordPress gallery plugins

Here are a handful of great gallery plugins:

✔ **NextGEN Gallery by Photocrati** (`http://wordpress.org/extend/plugins/nextgen-gallery`): Creates sortable photo galleries and more.

✔ **Random Image widget by Marcel Proulx** (`http://wordpress.org/extend/plugins/random-image-widget`): Displays images at random from your image-upload folder.

✔ **Mini-Slides by Roland Rust** (`http://wordpress.org/extend/plugins/mini-slides`): Creates inline slide shows.

Figure 3-7:
A photo
gallery
created with
WordPress
by founder
Matt
Mullenweg.

Chapter 4: Exploring Podcasting and Video Blogging

In This Chapter

✔ Uploading and embedding videos in posts

✔ Adding audio files to posts

✔ Exploring podcasting and vlogging

✔ Using the Media Library

Many website owners want to go beyond just offering written content for the consumption of their visitors by offering different types of media, including audio and video files. WordPress makes it pretty easy to include these different types of media files in your posts and pages by using the built-in file-upload feature.

The audio files you add to your site can include music or voice in formats such as `.mp3`, `.midi`, or `.wav` (to name just a few). Some website owners produce their own audio files in regular episodes, called *podcasts,* to create an Internet radio show. Often you can find these audio files available for syndication through RSS and can subscribe to them in a variety of audio programs, such as iTunes.

You can include videos in blog posts or pages by embedding code offered by popular third-party video providers such as YouTube (`www.youtube.com`) or Vimeo (`www.vimeo.com`). Website owners can also produce and upload their own video shows, an activity known as vlogging (video blogging).

This chapter takes you through the steps to upload and embed audio and video files within your content, and it provides you with some tools that can help you more easily embed those files without having to use elaborate coding techniques.

When dealing with video and audio files on your site, remember to upload and use only media that you own or have permission to use. Copyright violation is a very serious offense, especially on the Internet, and using media that you do not have permission to use can have serious consequences, such as having your website taken down, facing heavy fines, and even going to jail. I would really hate to see that happen to you — so play it safe and use only those media files that you have permission to use.

Inserting Video Files into Your Blog Posts

Whether you're producing your own videos for publication or embedding other people's videos, placing a video file in a blog post has never been easier with WordPress.

Check out a good example of a video blog at `www.tmz.com/videos`. TMZ is a popular celebrity news website that produces and displays videos for the web and for mobile devices.

Several video galleries on the web today allow you to add videos to blog posts — Google's YouTube service (`www.youtube.com`) is a good example of a third-party video service that allows you to share its videos.

Adding a link to a video from the web

Adding a video from the web, in these steps, adds only a hyperlink to the video. Use these steps if all you want to do is link to a page that has the video on it, rather than embedding the video in your blog post or page (covered in the Adding Video with Auto-Embed section later in this chapter).

To add a link to a video from the web, follow these steps:

1. **Click the Add Media button on the Add New Post page to open the Insert Media window.**

2. **Click the Insert from URL link on the left.**

   The Insert from URL page appears, as shown in Figure 4-1.

3. **Type the URL (Internet address) of the video in the Insert from URL text box.**

   Type the full URL, including the `http://` and www portion of the address. Video providers, such as YouTube, usually list the direct links for the video files on their sites; you can copy and paste one of those links into the Video URL text box.

4. **(Optional) Type the title of the video in the Title text box.**

   Giving a title to the video allows you to provide a bit of a description of the video. Provide a title if you can so that your readers know what the video is about.

5. **Click the Insert into Post button.**

   A link to the video is inserted into your post. WordPress doesn't embed the actual video in the post; it inserts only a link to the video. Your blog visitors click the link to load another page in which the video plays.

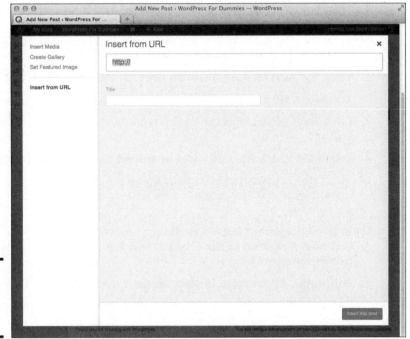

Figure 4-1:
Add a video by linking to a URL.

Adding video with Auto-Embed

The preceding steps give you the ability to insert a hyperlink that your readers can click to view the video on another website (such as YouTube). However, if you use WordPress's nifty Auto-Embed feature, WordPress will automatically embed many of these videos within your posts and pages.

With this feature, WordPress automatically detects that a URL you typed in your post is a video (from YouTube, for example) and wraps the correct HTML embed code around that URL to make sure that the video player appears in your post (in a standard, XHTML-compliant way). The Auto-Embed feature is automatically enabled on your WordPress site; all you need to do is type the video URL within the content of your post or page.

Currently, WordPress automatically embeds videos from YouTube, Vimeo, Dailymotion, Blip, Flickr, Hulu, Viddler, Qik, Revision3, Photobucket, and Google Video, as well as VideoPress-type videos from WordPress.tv.

**Book IV
Chapter 4**

Exploring
Podcasting and
Video Blogging

Adding video from your computer

To upload and post to your blog a video from your computer, follow these steps:

1. **Click the Add Media button on the Edit Post or Add New Post page.**

   The Insert Media window appears.

2. **Click the Upload Files tab at the top and then click the Select Files button.**

3. **Select the video file you want to upload and then click Open.**

   The video is uploaded from your computer to your web server, and the Insert Media window displays your uploaded video selected and ready for editing.

4. **In the Attachment Details section, type a title for the file in the Title text box, a caption in the Caption text box, and a description in the Description text box.**

5. **Still in the Attachment Details section, select the Link To option.**

   You can link to a custom URL, the attachment page, or the media file, or you can link to nothing at all.

6. **Click the Insert into Post button.**

   WordPress doesn't embed a video player in the post; it inserts only a link to the video. However, if you have the Auto-Embed feature activated, WordPress attempts to embed the video within a video player. If WordPress cannot embed a video player, it displays the link that your visitors can click to open the video in a new window.

Inserting Audio Files into Your Blog Posts

Audio files can be music files or voice recordings, such as recordings of you speaking to your readers. These files add a nice personal touch to your blog. You can easily share audio files on your blog by using the Add Media feature in WordPress. After you insert an audio file in a blog post, your readers can listen to it on their computers or download it onto an MP3 player and listen to it while driving to work, if they want.

To upload an audio file to your site, follow the same steps outlined in the preceding section for uploading a video.

WordPress doesn't automatically include an audio player interface for playing your file. Instead, WordPress inserts a link your readers can click to listen to the audio file.

Some great WordPress plugins for handling audio can enhance the functionality of the file uploader and help you manage audio files in your blog posts.

Check out Book VII for information on how to install and use WordPress plugins in your blog.

Podcasting with WordPress

When you provide regular episodes of an audio show that visitors can download to a computer and listen to on an audio player, you're podcasting. Think of podcasting as a weekly radio show that you tune into, except that it's hosted on the Internet, rather than on a radio station.

In the sidebar "WordPress video and audio plugins" in this chapter, you can find a few plugins that allow you to easily insert audio files in your WordPress posts and pages — however, a few plugins are dedicated to podcasting, and they provide features to podcasters that go beyond just embedding audio files in a website. Some of the more important of these features include

✦ **Archives:** Create an archive of your audio podcast files so that your listeners can catch up on your show by listening to past episodes.

✦ **RSS Feed:** An RSS feed of your podcast show gives visitors the opportunity to subscribe to your syndicated content so that they can be notified when you publish future episodes.

✦ **Promotion:** A podcast isn't successful without listeners, right? You can upload your podcast to iTunes (www.apple.com/itunes) so that when people search iTunes for podcasts by subject, they find your podcast.

These three plugins go beyond just audio-file management. They're dedicated to podcasting and all the features you need:

✦ **PowerPress (**http://wordpress.org/extend/plugins/power press**):** PowerPress includes full iTunes support; audio players; multiple file-format support (.mp3, .m4a, .ogg, .wma, .ra, .mp4a, .m4v, .mp4v, .mpg, .asf, .avi, .wmv, .flv, .swf, .mov, .divx, .3gp, .midi, .wav, .aa, .pdf, .torrent, .m4b, .m4r); statistics to track the popularity of your different podcast offerings; and tagging, categorizing, and archiving of podcast files.

✦ **Podcast Channels (**http://wordpress.org/extend/plugins/podcast-channels**):** WordPress provides some of the basic stuff needed for podcasting, such as media-file embedding, archiving, and RSS feed handling. The Podcast Channels plugin gives you iTunes metadata that enables you to specify channels for your podcast files and include them in the iTunes library.

✦ **Podcasting Plugin (**http://wordpress.org/extend/plugins/podcasting**):** Enhances the built-in WordPress audio-management features by adding iTunes support, compatible RSS feeds, and media players. This plugin also allows you to have multiple podcasting feeds, in case you have different podcast shows that cover a range of topics.

I discuss web hosting requirements in Book II. If you're a podcaster and intend to store audio files on your web hosting account, you may need to increase the storage and bandwidth for your account so that you don't run out of space or incur higher fees from your web hosting provider. Discuss these issues with your web hosting provider to find out upfront what you have to pay for increased disk space and bandwidth needs.

Keeping Media Files Organized

If you've been running your blog for any length of time, you can easily forget what files you've uploaded by using the WordPress uploader. The WordPress Media Library allows you to conveniently and easily discover which files are in your Uploads folder.

WordPress video and audio plugins

You can find some great WordPress plugins for audio and video handling. Check out Book VII for information on how to install and use WordPress plugins.

Here are a few great plugins for audio:

- ✔ **Audio Player by Martin Laine** (`http://wordpress.org/extend/plugins/audio-player`): Embeds a Flash MP3 player in your blog posts without any special HTML

- ✔ **1 Bit Audio Player by Mark Wheeler** (`http://wordpress.org/extend/plugins/1-bit-audio-player`): Autodetects MP3 files on your site and inserts a stylish player

- ✔ **Podcasting Plugin by TSG** (`http://wordpress.org/extend/plugins/podcasting`): Supports several media formats and automatically creates a podcast RSS feed

Here are a few great plugins for video:

- ✔ **wordTube by Alex Rabe** (`http://wordpress.org/extend/plugins/wordtube`): Creates a YouTube-like player when you insert video files within your posts without any special HTML

- ✔ **Smart YouTube by Vladimir Prelovac** (`http://wordpress.org/extend/plugins/smart-youtube`): Inserts YouTube videos into blog posts, comments, and RSS feeds

- ✔ **WP-Vidavee by Vidavee Labs** (`http://wordpress.org/extend/plugins/wp-vidavee-film-manager`): Uploads, manages, organizes, and displays video in your blog

- ✔ **Video Embedder by Kristoffer Forsgren** (`http://wordpress.org/extend/plugins/video-embedder`): Embeds video from various sources

To find an image, a video, or an audio file you've already uploaded by using the file uploader and to use that file in a new post, follow these steps:

1. **Click the Add Media icon on the Add New Post page to open the Insert Media window.**

2. **Click the Media Library tab at the top of the window.**

   All the files you've ever uploaded to your blog appear because of the File Uploader feature. (See Figure 4-2.) Files you uploaded through other methods, such as FTP, don't appear in the Media Library.

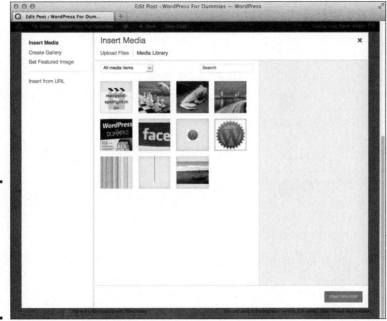

Figure 4-2:
The Media Library shows all the files you've ever uploaded to your blog.

3. **Select the file that you want to reuse.**

4. **In the settings menu that appears, set the options for that file: Title, Caption, Description, Link URL, Order, Alignment, and Size.**

5. **Click the Insert into Post button.**

   The correct HTML code is inserted into the Post text box.

If you want to view only the files you've uploaded, click the Library link on the Media menu (found on the left navigation menu of the Dashboard), which opens the Media Library page.

The Media Library page lists all the files you've ever uploaded to your WordPress blog. By default, the page displays all types of files, but you can click the Images, Audio, or Video link to specify which file type you want to see (as shown in Figure 4-3).

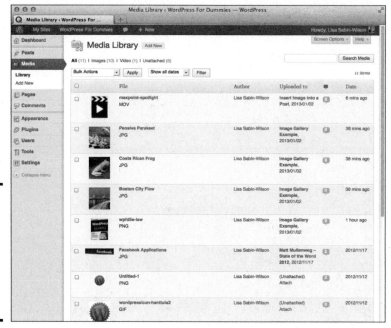

Figure 4-3:
The
WordPress
Media
Library,
displaying
only audio
files.

You can do the following tasks on the Media Library page:

✦ **Filter media files by date.** If you want to view all media files that were uploaded in July of 2010, select that date from the drop-down list and click the Filter button; the page reloads and displays only the media files uploaded in the month of July, 2010.

✦ **Search media files by using a specific keyword.** If you want to search your Media Library for all files that reference kittens, type the word **kittens** in the Search box in the upper-right corner of the Media Library page. Then click the Search Media button; the page reloads and displays only media files that contain the keyword or tag *kittens*.

✦ **Delete media files.** To delete files, click the small white box that appears to the left of the file's thumbnail on the Media Library page (on the Dashboard, hover your pointer over Media and click the Library link); then select the Delete Permanently option in the Bulk Actions drop-down list, which appears at the top left of the page, and then click the Apply button. The page reloads, and the media file you just deleted is now gone.

✦ **View media files.** On the Manage Media page, click the thumbnail of the file you want to view. The Edit Media page opens in your web browser. If you need the URL of the file, you can copy the permalink of the file from the File URL field found in the top right side of the Edit Media page.

Chapter 5: Working with Custom Fields

In This Chapter

✔ Understanding what Custom Fields can do for you

✔ Working with the Custom Fields interface

✔ Adding custom field codes to your templates

✔ Using custom fields in a variety of ways

In Book IV, Chapter 1, I discuss all the different elements you can add to your blog posts and pages when you publish them. By default, WordPress allows you to give your posts and pages titles and content, to categorize and tag posts, to select a date and time for publishing, and to control the discussion options on a per-post or per-page basis.

However, you may sometimes want to add extra items to your posts — items you may not want to add to every post, necessarily, but that you add often enough to make manually adding them each time you publish a nuisance. These items can include a multitude of things, from telling your readers your current mood to what you're currently listening to or reading — pretty much anything you can think of.

WordPress gives you the ability to create and add *metadata* (additional data that can be added to define you and your post) to your posts by using a feature called Custom Fields. In Book IV, Chapter 2, I briefly touch on the Custom Field interface on the Add New Post page on the Dashboard, and in this chapter, I go through Custom Fields in depth by explaining what they are and how to implement them, as well as offering some cool ideas for using Custom Fields on your site.

Understanding Custom Fields

A WordPress template contains static pieces of data that you can count on to appear on your site. These static items include elements such as the title, the content, the date, and so on. But what if you want more? Say you write a weekly book-review post on your site and want to include a listing of recent reviews and accompanying thumbnails of the books; you can, through the use of Custom Fields, without having to retype the list each time you do a review.

You can add literally thousands of auto-formatted pieces of data (such as book reviews or movie reviews, for example) by adding Custom Fields on your WordPress blog. Okay, so thousands of Custom Fields would be pretty difficult, if not impossible, to manage — my point here is that the Custom Fields feature doesn't limit you to the number of fields you can add to your site.

You create Custom Fields on a per-post or per-page basis, which means that you can create an unlimited amount of them and add them only to certain posts. They help you create extra data for your posts and pages by using the Custom Fields interface, which is covered in the following section.

So, what can you do with Custom Fields? Really, the only right answer is: anything you want. Your imagination is your only limit when it comes to the different types of data you can add to your posts by using Custom Fields. Custom Fields allow you the flexibility of defining certain pieces of data for each post.

To use Custom Fields, you do need a bit of knowledge about how to navigate through WordPress theme templates because you have to insert a WordPress function tag, with specific parameters, in the body of the template file. Book VI takes you through all the information you need to understand WordPress themes, templates, and template tags — so you may want to hit that minibook before you attempt to apply what I discuss in the rest of this chapter. If you're already comfortable and familiar with WordPress templates and tags, you probably won't have any trouble with this chapter at all.

Exploring the Custom Fields Interface

The Custom Fields module appears on both the Add New Post and Add New Page (see Book IV, Chapters 1 and 2) pages on the WordPress Dashboard, below the Post text box, as shown in Figure 5-1.

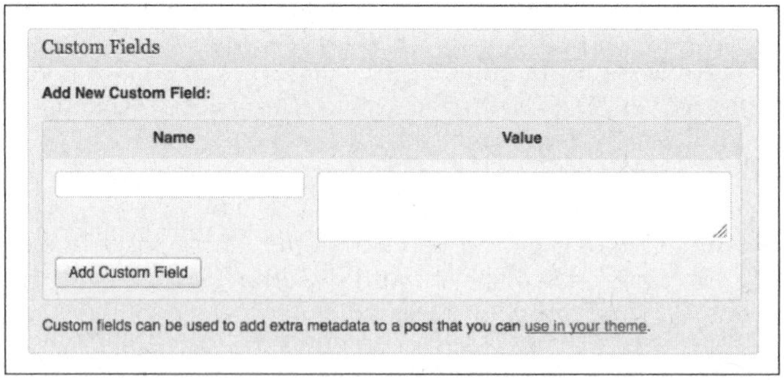

Figure 5-1:
The Custom Fields module on the Add New Post page on the Dashboard.

Custom Fields

Add New Custom Field:

Name	Value

Add Custom Field

Custom fields can be used to add extra metadata to a post that you can use in your theme.

The Custom Fields module has two different text boxes:

✦ **Name:** Also known as the Key, you give this name to the Custom Field you're planning to use. The name needs to be unique: It's used in the template tag that you can read about in the section "Adding Custom Fields to Your Template File," later in this chapter. Figure 5-2 shows a Custom Field with the name mood.

✦ **Value:** Assigned to the Custom Field name and displayed in your blog post on your site if you use the template tag that you can also read about in the section "Adding Custom Fields to Your Template File," later in this chapter. In Figure 5-2, the value assigned to the mood (the Custom Field name) is Happy.

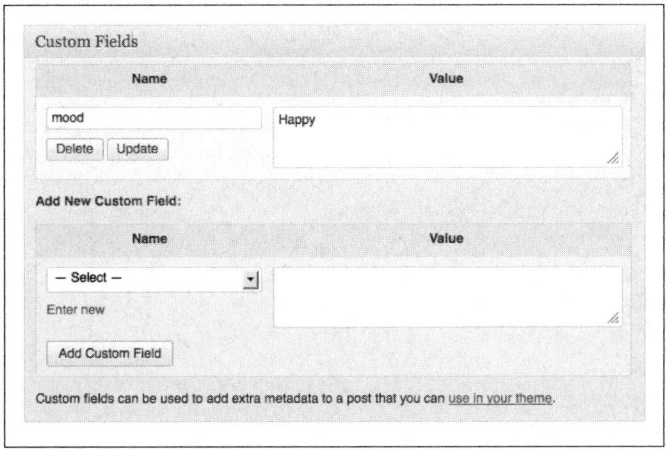

Figure 5-2:
Custom Fields that have name and value assigned.

Custom Fields

Name	Value
mood	Happy

Delete   Update

Add New Custom Field:

Name	Value
— Select — ▾	

Enter new

Add Custom Field

Custom fields can be used to add extra metadata to a post that you can use in your theme.

Simply fill out the Name and Value text boxes and then click the Add Custom Field button to add the data to your post or page. Figure 5-2 shows a Custom Field that I added to my post with the Name of mood and with the assigned value Happy. In the section "Adding Custom Fields to Your Template File," later in this chapter, I show you the template tag you need to add to your WordPress theme template in order to display this Custom Field, which appears in my post like this: My Current Mood is: Happy, shown in Figure 5-3, where the Custom Field appears at the end of my post.

You can add multiple Custom Fields to one post. To do so, simply add the name and the value of the Custom Field in the appropriate text boxes on the Add New Post page; then click the Add Custom Field button to assign the data to your post. Do this for each Custom Field you want to add to your post.

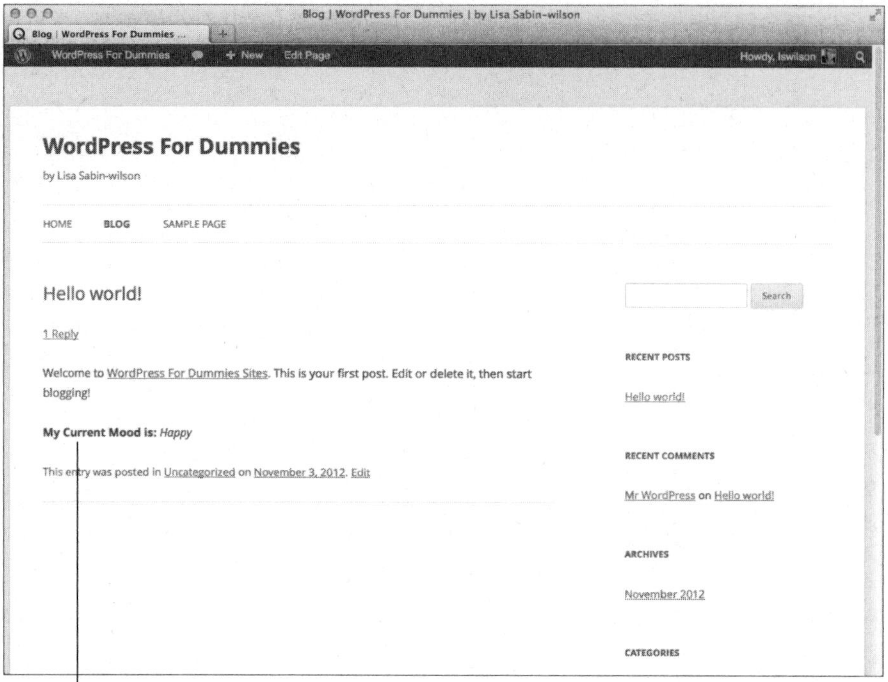

Figure 5-3:
A Custom
Field output
appears in
a published
post.

Custom field at end of post.

After you add a particular Custom Field (such as the `mood` Custom Field I added in Figure 5-2), you can always add it to future posts. So, you can make a post tomorrow and use the `mood` Custom Field but assign a different value to it. If tomorrow you assign the value `Sad`, your post displays `My Current Mood is: Sad`. You can easily use just that one Custom Field on subsequent posts.

You can access your Custom Fields from the drop-down list below the Name field, as shown in Figure 5-4. You can easily select it again and assign a new value to it in the future, because WordPress saves that Custom Field Key, assuming you may want to use it again sometime in the future.

Custom Fields are considered extra data, separate from the post content itself, for your blog posts. WordPress refers to Custom Fields as *metadata*. The Custom Field name and value get stored in the database in the `wp_postmeta` table, which keeps track of which names and values are assigned to each post. See Book II, Chapter 7 for more information about the WordPress database structure and organization of data.

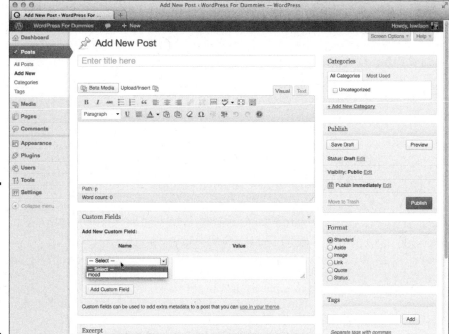

Figure 5-4:
Custom
Field
names are
saved and
displayed
in a drop-
down list for
future use.

You can find a Custom Fields module on the Add New Page page on the Dashboard, as well, so you can add Custom Fields to either your posts or pages as needed.

Adding Custom Fields to Your Template File

If you followed along in the previous sections and added the mood Custom Field to your own site, notice that the data doesn't appear on your site the way it does on mine. To get the data to display properly, you must open the template files and dig into the code a little bit. If the idea of digging into the code of your template files intimidates you, you can put this section aside and read up on WordPress themes, template files, and template tags in Book VI.

You can add Custom Fields in several ways to your templates in order to display the output of the fields you've set. The easiest way involves using the get_post_meta(); template tag function, which looks like this:

```
<?php $key="NAME"; echo get_post_meta($post->ID, $key, true); ?>
```

Here's how that function breaks down:

✦ `<?php`: Part of the functions begins PHP. (Every template tag or function needs to first start PHP with `<?php`. You can read more about basic PHP in Book II, Chapter 3.)

✦ `$key="`*NAME*`";`: Defines the name of the key that you want to appear. You define the name when you add the Custom Field to your post.

✦ `echo get_post_meta`: Grabs the Custom Field data and displays it on your site.

✦ `$post->ID,`: A parameter of the `get_post_meta` function that dynamically defines the specific ID of the post being displayed so that WordPress knows which metadata to display.

✦ `$key,`: A parameter of the `get_post_meta` function that gets the value of the Custom Field based on the name, as defined in the `$key="`*NAME*`";` setting earlier in the code string.

✦ `true);`: A parameter of the `get_post_meta` function that tells WordPress to return a single result rather than multiple results. (By default, this parameter is set to `true`; typically, don't change it unless you're using multiple definitions in the Value setting of your Custom Field.)

✦ `?>`: Ends the PHP function.

Based on the preceding code, to make the `mood` Custom Field example, you define the key name as mood (replace the *NAME* in the preceding code with the word `mood`); it looks like this:

```
<?php $key="mood"; echo get_post_meta($post->ID, $key, true); ?>
```

The part of the functions that says `$key="mood";` tells WordPress to return the value for the Custom Field with the Name field of `mood`.

Entering the code in the template file

So that you can see how to enter the code in your template file, I use the default WordPress theme Twenty Twelve in this section. If you're using a different theme (and you can find thousands of different WordPress themes available), you need to adapt these instructions to your particular theme.

Follow these steps to add the template tag, along with a little HTML code to make it look nice, to your theme (these steps assume that you've already added the `mood` Custom Field to your blog post and have assigned a value to it):

1. **Log in to your WordPress Dashboard.**

2. **Click the Editor link on the Appearances menu.**

The Edit Themes page loads in the Dashboard, as shown in Figure 5-5.

3. **Locate the template files for your theme (in this case, Twenty Twelve).**

The available templates are listed on the right side of the Edit Themes page, as shown in Figure 5-5.

4. **Click** `content.php` **in the list of templates.**

The `content.php` template opens in the text editor on the left side of the screen, where you can edit the template file.

5. **Scroll down and locate the template tag that looks like this:** `<?php the_content() ?>`.

6. **On the new line underneath the preceding one, type this:**

```
<p><strong>My Current Mood is:</strong><em>
```

`<p>` and `<strong>` open the HTML tags for paragraph and bold text, respectively; followed by the words to display in your template (`My Current Mood is:`). `<em>` opens the HTML tag for italics style text, which gets applied to the value. (The `</strong>` HTML tag closes the bold text display.)

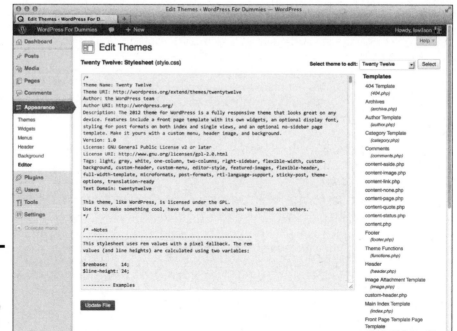

Book IV
Chapter 5

Working with
Custom Fields

Figure 5-5:
The Edit
Themes
page on the
Dashboard.

7. **Type the PHP that makes the custom field work:**

   ```
   <?php $key="mood"; echo get_post_meta($post->ID, $key, true); ?>
   ```

8. **Type** </em></p>.

   This code closes the HTML tags you opened in Step 6.

9. **Click the Update File button.**

   Located at the bottom of the Edit Themes page, this step saves the changes you made to the content.php file and reloads the page with a message that says your changes have been successfully saved.

10. **View your post on your site to see your Custom Field data displayed.**

    The data should look just like the My Current Mood is: Happy message shown earlier in Figure 5-3.

WordPress now displays your current mood at the bottom of the posts to which you've added the mood Custom Field.

The entire code, put together, should look like this in your template:

```
<p><strong>My Current Mood is:</strong> <em><?php $key="mood"; echo get_post_
    meta($post->ID, $key, true); ?></em></p>
```

The code is case sensitive, which means that the words you input for the key in your Custom Field need to match case with the $key in the code. For example, if you input mood in the Key field, then the code needs to be lowercase, as well: $key="mood". If you attempt to change the case like this: $key="Mood", the code won't work.

You have to add this code for the mood Custom Field only one time; after you add the template function code to your template for the mood Custom Field, you can define your current mood in every post you publish to your site by using the Custom Fields interface.

This example is just one type of Custom Field that you can add to your posts.

Getting WordPress to check for your Custom Field

The previous sections show you how to add the necessary code to your template file to display your Custom Field; however, what if you want to publish a post on which you don't want the mood Custom Field to appear? If you leave your template file as you set it up by following the steps in the previous sections, even if you don't add the mood Custom Field, your blog post displays My Current Mood is: without a mood because you didn't define one.

IF, ELSE

In your daily life, you probably deal with IF, ELSE situations every day, like in these examples:

✔ **IF** I have a dollar, then I'll buy coffee, or **ELSE** I won't.

✔ **IF** it's warm outside, then I'll take a walk, or **ELSE** I won't.

✔ **IF** I understand this code, then I'll be happy, or **ELSE** I won't.

But you can easily make WordPress check first to see whether the Custom Field is added. If it finds the Custom Field, WordPress displays your mood; if it doesn't find the Custom Field, WordPress doesn't display the Custom Field.

If you followed along in the previous sections, the code in your template looks like this:

```
<p><strong>My Current Mood is:<strong> <em><?php $key="mood"; echo get_post_
    meta($post->ID, $key, true); ?></em></p>
```

To make WordPress check to see whether the mood Custom Field exists, add this code to the line above your existing code:

```
<?php if ( get_post_meta($post->ID, 'mood', true) ) : ?>
```

Then add this line of code to the line below your existing code:

```
<?php endif; ?>
```

Put together, the lines of code in your template should look like this:

```
<?php if ( get_post_meta($post->ID, 'mood', true) ) : ?>
<p><strong>My Current Mood is:</strong> <em><?php $key="mood"; echo get_post_
    meta($post->ID, $key, true); ?></em></p>
<?php endif; ?>
```

The first line is an IF statement and basically asks, "Does the mood key exist for this post?" If it does, the value gets displayed. If it doesn't, WordPress skips over the code, ignoring it completely so that nothing gets displayed for the mood Custom Field. The final line of code simply puts an end to the IF question. See the nearby "IF, ELSE" sidebar to find out about some everyday situations that explain the IF question. Apply this statement to the code you just added to your template and you get this: IF the mood Custom Field exists, then WordPress will display it, or ELSE it won't.

Book IV Chapter 5

Working with Custom Fields

You can find extensive information on working with WordPress template files within your theme in Book VI.

Exploring Different Uses for Custom Fields

In this chapter, I use the example of adding your current mood to your blog posts by using Custom Fields. But you can use Custom Fields to define all sorts of data on your posts and pages; you're limited only by your imagination when it comes to what kind of data you want to include.

Obviously, I can't cover every possible use for Custom Fields, but I can give you some ideas that you may want to try on your own site. At the very least, you can implement some of these ideas to get yourself into the flow of using Custom Fields, and they may spark your imagination on what types of data you want to include on your site:

✦ **Music:** Display the music you're currently listening to. Use the same method I describe in this chapter for your current mood, except create a Custom Field named music. Use the same code template, just define the key as $key="music"; and alter the wording from *My Current Mood is:* to *I am Currently Listening to:*.

✦ **Books:** Same as the mood or music Custom Field, you can display what you're currently reading by creating a Custom Field named book, defining the key in the code as $key="book";, and then altering the wording from *My Current Mood is:* to *I Am Currently Reading:*.

✦ **Weather:** Let your readers know what the weather is like in your little corner of the world by adding your current weather conditions to your published blog posts. Create a Custom Field named weather and use the same code for the template — just define the key as $key="weather"; and alter the wording from *My Current Mood is:* to *Current Weather Conditions:*.

If you want to get really fancy with your Custom Fields, you can also define an icon for the different metadata displays. For example, using the mood Custom Field, you can add little *emoticons* (or smiley-face icons that portray mood) after your mood statement to give a visual cue of your mood, as well as a textual one. Follow these steps to add an emoticon to the mood Custom Field that you add in the previous sections in this chapter:

1. **Visit the Posts page on the Dashboard by clicking the Posts link in the left navigation menu.**

2. **Click the title of the post that you want to edit.**

3. **Add a new Custom Field by selecting Enter New from the drop-down list and entering** mood-icon **in the Name text box.**

4. **Click the Add Media button above the Post text box to open the Add Media window.**

   The Insert Media window opens, shown in Figure 5-6.

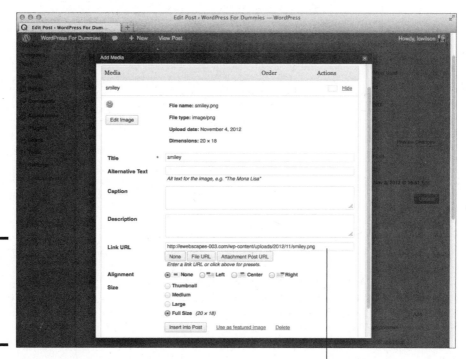

Figure 5-6:
The Link
URL in
the Insert
Media
window.

Copy the URL.

5. **Click the Select Files button and upload an image from your computer.**

   See Book IV, Chapter 3 for information on uploading images.

6. **From the Link URL text box, copy the file URL of the image you uploaded.**

7. **Click the X in the top-right corner to close the Insert Media window.**

8. **Paste the Link URL in the Value text box for the mood-icon Name. (See Figure 5-7.)**

9. **Click the Add Custom Field button.**

   The Name and Key values are saved.

**Book IV
Chapter 5**

**Working with
Custom Fields**

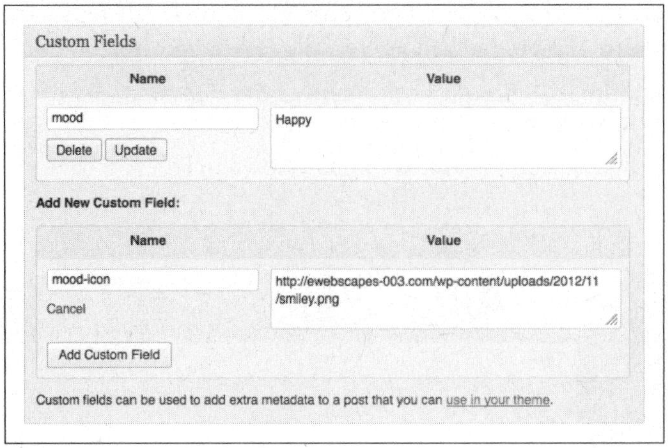

Figure 5-7:
Adding a
mood icon.

10. **Click the Update button in the Publish module.**

The changes in your post are saved and updated on your site.

11. **Update the function code in your template file to include the new mood icon.**

Follow these steps to add that code:

a. *Click the Editor link in the Appearance menu on your Dashboard.*

b. *Click the* `content.php` *file.*

The `content.php` template displays in the text box on the left side of the page.

c. *Locate the code you added for the* `mood` *Custom Field.*

d. *Before the closing* `</strong>` *HTML tag, add the following line of code:*

```
<img src="<?php $key="mood-icon"; echo get_post_meta($post->ID, $key,
    true); ?>" />
```

The `<img src="` that precedes the Custom Field code is the HTML tag used to display an image on your site. The `" />` code that appears after the Custom Field code is part of the HTML tag and it closes the `<img src="` HTML tag. I changed the `$key` to indicate that I'm calling the `mood-icon` Custom Field.

e. *Click the Update File button to save your changes.*

f. *Visit the post on your site to view your new mood icon.*

You can see my mood icon in Figure 5-8.

The entire snippet of code you add in the preceding steps should look like this when put all together (be sure to double-check your work!):

```php
<?php if ( get_post_meta($post->ID, 'mood', true) ) : ?>
<p><strong>My Current Mood is:</strong> <em><?php $key="mood"; echo
    get_post_meta($post->ID, $key, true); ?></em> <img src="<?php
    $key="mood-icon"; echo get_post_meta($post->ID, $key, true); ?>"
    /></strong></p>
<?php endif; ?>
```

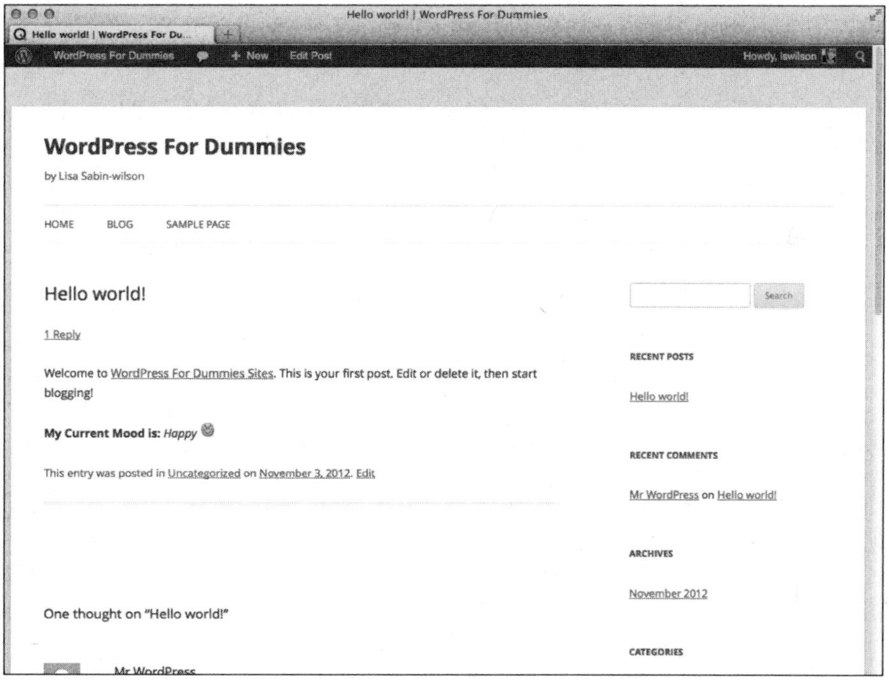

Figure 5-8:
I am displaying my current mood with a mood icon.

Chapter 6: Using WordPress as a Content Management System

In This Chapter

✔ Defining a content management system

✔ Creating a template for each static page, post category, and sidebar

✔ Custom styles for sticky posts, categories, and tags

✔ Using Custom Post Types

✔ Optimizing for search engine success

If you've avoided using WordPress as a solution for building your own website because you think it's only a blogging platform and you don't want to have a blog (not every website owner does, after all), it's time to rethink your position. WordPress is a powerful content management system that's flexible and extensible enough to run an entire website — with no blog at all, if you prefer.

A *content management system* (CMS) is a system used to create and maintain your entire site. It includes tools for publishing and editing, as well as for searching and retrieving information and content. A CMS lets you maintain your website with little or no knowledge of HTML. You can create, modify, retrieve, and update your content without ever having to touch the code required to perform those tasks.

This chapter shows you a few ways that you can use the WordPress platform to power your entire website, with or without a blog. It covers different template configurations that you can use to create separate sections of your site. This chapter also dips into a feature in WordPress called Custom Post Types, which lets you control how content is displayed on your website.

This chapter dips into working with WordPress templates and themes, a concept that is covered in depth in Book VI. If you find templates and themes intimidating, check out Book VI first.

You can do multiple things with WordPress to extend it beyond the blog. I use the default Twenty Twelve theme to show you how to use WordPress to create a fully functional website that has a CMS platform — anything from the smallest personal site to a large business site.

Creating Different Page Views Using WordPress Templates

As I explain in Book IV, Chapter 2, a *static page* contains content that doesn't appear on the blog page, but as a separate page within your site. You can have numerous static pages on your site, and each page can have a different design, based on the template you create. (Flip to Book VI to find out all about choosing and using templates on your site.) You can create several static-page templates and assign them to specific pages within your site by adding code to the top of the static-page templates.

Here's the code that appears at the top of the static-page template I use for my About Us and Our Blog Designers page at www.ewebscapes.com/about:

```
<?php
/*
Template Name: About
*/
?>
```

Using a template on a static page is a two-step process: Upload the template and then tell WordPress to use the template by tweaking the page's code.

In Book VI, you can discover information about Custom Menus, including how to create different navigation menus for your website. You can create a menu of links that includes all the pages you created on your WordPress Dashboard. You can display that menu on your website by using the Custom Menus feature.

Uploading the template

To use a page template, you have to create one. You can create this file in a text-editor program, such as Notepad. (To see how to create a template, flip over to Book VI, which gives you extensive information on WordPress templates and themes.) To create an About page, for example, you can save the template with the name about.php.

When you have your template created, follow these steps to make it part of WordPress:

1. **Upload the template file to your WordPress theme folder.**

   You can find that folder on your web server in /wp-content/themes. (See Book II, Chapter 2 for more information about FTP.)

2. **Log in to your WordPress Dashboard and click the Editor link on the Appearance menu.**

The Edit Themes page opens.

3. **Click the `about.php` template link located on the right side of the page.**

4. **Type the Template Name tag directly above the `get_header()` template tag.**

    The header tag looks like this: `<?php get_header(); ?>`.

    If you're creating an About Page, the code to create the Template Name looks like this:

    ```
    <?php
    /*
    Template Name: About
    */
    ?>
    ```

5. **Click the Update File button.**

    The file is saved, and the page refreshes. If you created an About page template, the `about.php` template is now called About Page in the template list on the right side of the page.

Figure 6-1 shows the Page template and displays the code needed to define a specific name for the template.

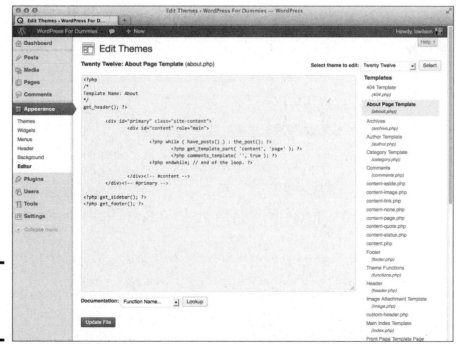

Figure 6-1:
Naming a
static-page
template.

Book IV
Chapter 6

Using WordPress
as a Content
Management
System

Assigning the template to a static page

After you create the template and name it the way you want, assign that template to a page by following these steps:

1. **Click the Add New link on the Pages menu on the Dashboard.**

   The Add New Page page opens, and you can write a new post to your WordPress blog.

2. **Type the title in the Title text box and the page content in the large text box.**

3. **Select the page template from the Template drop-down list.**

   By default, the Template drop-down list in the Page Attributes module appears on the right side of the page. You can reposition the modules on this page; see Book III, Chapter 1 for more information.

4. **Click the Publish button to save and publish the page to your site.**

Figure 6-2 shows the layout of my home page on my business site at www.ewebscapes.com and the information it contains, whereas Figure 6-3 shows the layout and information provided on the About page at www.ewebscapes.com/about. Both pages are on the same site, in the same WordPress installation, with different page templates to provide different looks, layouts, and sets of information.

Figure 6-2:
Lisa's home page at E.Web scapes.

**Book IV
Chapter 6**

Using WordPress as a Content Management System

Figure 6-3:
The About page at E.Web-scapes.

Creating a Template for Each Post Category

You don't have to limit yourself to creating a static-page template for your site. You can use specific templates for the categories you've created on your blog (which I talk about in Book III, Chapter 5) and create unique sections for your site.

Figure 6-4 shows my design portfolio. Design Portfolio is the name of a category that I created on the WordPress Dashboard. Instead of using a static page for the display of my portfolio, I'm using a category template to handle the display of all posts made to the Design Portfolio category.

You can create category templates for all categories in your blog simply by creating template files that have filenames that correspond to the category slug and then upload those templates to your WordPress `themes` directory via FTP. (See Book II, Chapter 2.) Here's the logic to creating category templates:

✦ A template that has the filename `category.php` is a catchall for the display of categories.

✦ Add a dash and the category slug to the end of the filename (shown in Table 6-1) to specify a template for an individual category.

Figure 6-4:
The Design
Portfolio
page, which
uses a
category
template.

✦ If you don't have a `category.php` or `category-slug.php` file, the category display gets defined from the Main Index template (`index.php`).

Table 6-1 shows three examples of the category template naming requirements.

Table 6-1   WordPress Category Template Naming Conventions

If the Category Slug Is . . .	The Category Template Filename Is . . .
design-portfolio	`category-design-portfolio.php`
books	`category-books.php`
music-i-like	`category-music-i-like.php`

Pulling in Content from a Single Category

WordPress makes it possible to pull in very specific types of content on your website through the use of the WP_Query class. If you include WP_Query before The Loop (see Book VI, Chapter 3), it lets you specify which category you want to pull information from. If you have a category called *WordPress* and you want to display the last three posts from that category — on your front page, in your blog sidebar, or somewhere else on your site — you can use this template tag.

 The WP_Query class accepts several parameters that let you display different types of content, such as posts in specific categories and content from specific pages/posts or dates in your blog archives. The WP_Query class lets you pass so many variables and parameters that I just can't list all the possibilities. Instead, you can visit the WordPress Codex and read about the options available with this tag: http://codex.wordpress.org/Class_Reference/WP_Query#Parameters.

Here are two parameters that you can use with WP_Query:

✦ posts_per_page=*X*: This parameter tells WordPress how many posts you want to display. If you want to display only three posts, enter **posts_per_page=3**.

✦ category_name=*slug*: This parameter tells WordPress that you want to pull posts from the category with a specific slug. If you want to display posts from the WordPress category, this would be category_name=wordpress.

Follow these steps to filter posts by category using WP_Query:

1. **Click the Editor link on the Appearance menu on the Dashboard.**

The Edit Themes page opens.

2. **Click the template in which you want to display the content.**

If you want to display content in a sidebar, for example, choose the Sidebar template: sidebar.php.

3. **Locate the ending </div> tag at the bottom of the template for the theme you're using.**

Using the Twenty Twelve theme, the ending </div> tag is the second-to-last line.

**Book IV
Chapter 6**

**Using WordPress
as a Content
Management
System**

4. **Type the following code directly above the ending `</ul>` tag:**

```
<?php $the_query = new WP_Query( posts_per_page=3&category_
   name=wordpress); ?>
<h2>Type Your Desired Title Here</h2>
<?php while ( $the_query->have_posts() ) : $the_query->the_post(); ?>
<strong><a href="<?php the_permalink() ?>" rel="bookmark"
   title="Permanent Link to <?php the_title_attribute(); ?>"><?php the_
   title(); ?></a></strong>
<?php the_excerpt(); endwhile; wp_reset_postdata(); ?>
```

In the first line, you indicate the following: `posts_per_page=3&` `category_name=wordpress`. You can change these numbers to suit your specific needs. Just change 3 to whatever number of posts you want to display (there's no limit!) and change `wordpress` to the specific category slug that you want to use.

5. **Click the Update File button.**

The changes you just made are saved to the `sidebar.php` template.

In past versions of WordPress, you used the `query_posts();` tag to pull content from a specific category, but the `WP_Query` class is more efficient. Although the `query_posts();` tag provides the same result, it increases the number of calls to the database and increases page load and server resources.

Using Sidebar Templates

You can create separate sidebar templates for different pages of your site by using a simple `include` statement. When you write an `include` statement, you're simply telling WordPress that you want it to include a specific file on a specific page.

The code that pulls the usual Sidebar template (`sidebar.php`) into all the other templates, such as the Main Index template (`index.php`), looks like this:

```
<?php get_sidebar(); ?>
```

What if you create a page and want to use a sidebar that has different information from what you have in the Sidebar template (`sidebar.php`)? Follow these steps:

1. **Create a new sidebar template in a text editor such as Notepad.**

See Book VI for information on template tags and themes.

2. **Save the file as `sidebar2.php`.**

In Notepad, choose File➪Save. When you're asked to name the file, type **sidebar2.php** and then click Save.

3. **Upload `sidebar2.php` to your Themes folder on your web server.**

See Book II, Chapter 2 for FTP information and review Book VI, Chapter 2 for information on how to locate the Themes folder.

The template is now in your list of theme files on the Edit Themes page. (Log in to your WordPress Dashboard and click the Editor link on the Appearance drop-down menu.)

4. **To include the `sidebar2.php` template in one of your page templates, replace `<?php get_sidebar(); />` with this code:**

```
<?php get_template_part('sidebar2'); ?>
```

This code calls in a template you've created within your theme.

By using that `get_template_part` function, you can include virtually any file in any of your WordPress templates. You can use this method to create footer templates for pages on your site, for example. First, create a new template that has the filename `footer2.php`. Then locate the following code in your template:

```
<?php get_footer(); ?>
```

and replace it with this code:

```
<?php get_template_part('footer2'); ?>
```

Creating Custom Styles for Sticky, Category, and Tag Posts

In Book VI, you can find the method for putting a very basic WordPress theme together, which includes a Main Index template that uses the WordPress Loop. You can use a custom tag to display custom styles for sticky posts, categories, and tags on your blog. That special tag looks like this:

```
<div <?php post_class() ?> id="post-<?php the_ID(); ?>">
```

The `post_class()` section is the coolest part of the template. This template tag tells WordPress to insert specific HTML markup in your template that allows you to use CSS to make custom styles for sticky posts, categories, and tags.

In Book IV, Chapter 1, I tell you all about how to publish new posts to your blog, including the different options you can set for your blog posts, such as categories, tags, and publishing settings. One of the settings is the Stick This Post to the Front Page setting. In this chapter, I show you how to custom-style those sticky posts. It's not as messy as it sounds!

Book IV
Chapter 6

Using WordPress
as a Content
Management
System

For example, say that you publish a post that has the following options set:

✦ Stick this post to the front page.

✦ Filed in a category called WordPress.

✦ Tagged with News.

By having the `post_class()` tag in the template, WordPress inserts HTML markup that allows you to use CSS to style sticky posts, or posts assigned to specific tags or categories, with different styling than the rest of your posts. WordPress inserts the following HTML markup for your post:

```
<div class="post sticky category-wordpress tag-news">
```

In Book VI, you can discover CSS selectors and HTML markup and how they work together to create style and format for your WordPress theme. With the `post_class()` tag in place, you can go to your CSS file and define styles for the following CSS selectors:

✦ `.post`: Use this as the generic style for all posts on your blog. The CSS for this tag is

```
.post {background: #ffffff; border: 1px solid silver; padding: 10px;}
```

A style is created for all posts that have a white background with a thin silver border and 10 pixels of padding space between the post text and the border of the post.

✦ `.sticky`: You stick a post to your front page to call attention to that post, so you may want to use different CSS styling to make it stand out from the rest of the posts on your blog:

```
.sticky {background: #ffffff; border: 4px solid red; padding: 10px;}
```

This code creates a style for all posts that have been designated as sticky in the post options on the Write Post page to appear on your site with a white background, a thick red border, and 10 pixels of padding space between the post text and border of the post.

✦ `.category-wordpress`: Because I blog a lot about WordPress, my readers may appreciate it if I gave them a visual cue as to which posts on my blog are about that topic. I can do that through CSS by telling WordPress to display a small WordPress icon on the top-right corner of all my posts in the WordPress category:

```
.category-wordpress {background: url(wordpress-icon.jpg) top right
    no-repeat; height: 100px; width: 100px;}
```

This code inserts a graphic — `wordpress-icon.jpg` — that's 100 pixels in height and 100 pixels in width at the top-right corner of every post I assign to the WordPress category on my blog.

✦ `.tag-news`: I can style all posts tagged with News the same way I style the WordPress category:

```
.tag-news {background: #f2f2f2; border: 1px solid black; padding: 10px;}
```

This CSS styles all posts tagged with News with a light gray background and a thin black border with 10 pixels of padding between the post text and border of the post.

You can easily use the `post-class()` tag, combined with CSS, to create dynamic styles for the posts on your blog!

Working with Custom Post Types

A nice feature in WordPress (as of version 3.0) is a feature called Custom Post Types. This feature allows you, the site owner, to create different content types for your WordPress site that give you more creative control over how different types of content are entered, published, and displayed on your WordPress website.

Personally, I wish WordPress had called this feature Custom Content Types so that people didn't incorrectly think that Custom Post Types pertain to posts only. Custom Post Types aren't really the posts that you know as blog posts. Custom Post Types are a way of managing your blog content by defining what type of content it is, how it is displayed on your site, and how it operates — but they're not necessarily posts.

By default, WordPress already has different post types built into the software, ready for you to use. These default post types include

✦ Blog posts

✦ Pages

✦ Navigation menus (see Book VI, Chapter 6)

✦ Attachments

✦ Revisions

Custom Post Types give you the ability to create new and useful types of content on your website, including a smart and easy way to publish those content types to your site.

You really have endless possibilities for how to use Custom Post Types, but here are a few ideas that can kick-start your imagination (they're some of the most popular and useful ideas that others have implemented on their sites):

✦ Photo gallery

✦ Podcast or video

✦ Book reviews

✦ Coupons and special offers

✦ Events calendar

Book IV
Chapter 6

Using WordPress
as a Content
Management
System

To create and use Custom Post Types on your site, you need to be sure that your WordPress theme contains the correct code and functions. In the following steps, I create a very basic Custom Post Type called Generic Content. Follow these steps to create the Generic Content basic Custom Post Type:

1. **Click the Editor link on the Appearance menu on the Dashboard to open the Theme Editor page.**

2. **Click the Theme Functions template link to open the `functions.php` file in the text editor on the left side of the page.**

3. **Add the Custom Post Types code to the bottom of the Theme Functions template file.**

   Scroll down to the bottom of the `functions.php` file and include the following code to add a Generic Content Custom Post Type to your site:

   ```
   add_action( 'init', 'create_my_post_types' );
   function create_my_post_types() {
       register_post_type( 'generic_content', array(
           'label' => __( 'Generic Content' ),
           'singular_label' => __( 'Generic Content' ),
           'description' => __( 'Description of the Generic Content type' ),
           'public' => true,
           )
       );
   }
   ```

4. **Click the Update File button to save the changes made to the `functions.php` file.**

The function `register_post_type` can accept several different arguments and parameters, which are detailed in Table 6-2. You can use a variety and combination of different arguments and parameters to create a specific post type. You can find more information on Custom Post Types and using the `register_post_type` function in the official WordPress Codex at `http://codex.wordpress.org/Function_Reference/register_post_type`.

After you complete the preceding steps to add the Generic Content Custom Post Type to your site, a new post type labeled Generic appears on the left navigation menu of the Dashboard.

You can add and publish new content by using the new Custom Post Type, just like when you write and publish blog posts. (See Book IV, Chapter 1.) The published content isn't added to the chronological listing of blog posts, but rather, it's treated like separate content from your blog (just like static pages).

View the permalink for it and you see that it adopts the post type name Generic Content and uses it as part of the permalink structure, creating a permalink that looks like `http://yourdomain.com/generic-content/new-article`.

Table 6-2	Arguments and Parameters for register_post_type();		
Parameter	*Information*	*Default*	*Example*
`label`	The name of the post type	None	`'label' => __( 'Generic Content' ),`
`singular_label`	Same as label, but singular. For example if your label is "Movies", the singular label would be "Movie"	None	`'singular_label' => __( 'Generic Content' ),`
`description`	The description of the post type; displayed in the Dashboard to represent the post type	None	`'description' => __( 'This is a description of the Generic Content type' ),`

`public`
 	
`show_ui`
 	
`publicly_queryable`
 	
`exclude_from_search`
	Sets whether the post type is public
	
	There are three other arguments:
	
	`show_ui`: whether to show admin screens
	
	`publicly_queryable`: whether to query for this post type from the front end
	
	`exclude_from_search`: whether to show post type in search results
		true or false
		
		Default is false
			`'public' => true,`
			
			`'show_ui' => true,`
			
			`'publicly_queryable' => true,`
			
			`'exclude_from_search' => false,`

`menu_position`	Sets the position of the post type menu item in the Dashboard navigation menu	Default: 20 By default, appears after the Comments menu on the Dashboard Set integer in intervals of 5 (5, 10, 15, 20, and so on)	`'menu_position' => 25,`

(continued)

Table 6-2 *(continued)*

Parameter	Information	Default	Example
menu_icon	Defines a custom icon (graphic) to the post type menu item in the Dashboard navigation menu Creates and uploads the image into the images directory of your theme folder	None	`'menu_icon' => get_stylesheet_ directory_uri() . '/images/generic- content.png',`
hierarchical	Tells WordPress whether to display the post type content list in a hierarchical manner	true or false Default is true	`'hierarchical' => true,`
query_var	Controls whether this post type can be used with a query variable such as query_posts (see the "Adding query_posts Tag" section) or WP_Query	true or false Default is false	`'query_var' => true,`
capability_ type	Defines permissions for users to edit, create, or read the Custom Post Type.	post (default) Gives the same capabilities for those users who can edit, create, and read blog posts	`'query_var' => post,`

Parameter	Information	Default	Example
supports	Defines what meta boxes, or modules, are available for this post type in the Dashboard	`title`: Text box for the post title `editor`: Text box for the post content `comments`: Check boxes to toggle comments on/off `trackbacks`: Check boxes to toggle trackbacks and pingbacks on/off `revisions`: Allows post revisions to be made `author`: Drop-down list to define post author `excerpt`: Text box for the post excerpt `thumbnail`: The featured image selection `custom-fields`: Custom fields input area `page-attributes`: The page parent and page template drop-down lists	`'supports' => array( 'title', 'editor', 'excerpt', 'custom-fields', 'thumbnail' ),`

(continued)

Book IV Chapter 6

Using WordPress as a Content Management System

Table 6-2 *(continued)*

Parameter	Information	Default	Example
rewrite	Rewrites the permalink structure for the post type	true or false Two other arguments are available: slug: Permalink slug to use for your Custom Post Types with_front: If you've set your permalink structure with a specific prefix, such as /blog	'rewrite' => array('slug' => 'my-content', 'with_front' => false),
taxonomies	Uses existing WordPress taxonomies (category and tag)	Category post_tag	'taxonomies' => array('post_tag', 'category'),

Two very helpful plugins for building Custom Post Types pretty quickly in WordPress are

✦ **Custom Post Type UI:** Written by the folks at WebDevStudios (http://wordpress.org/extend/plugins/custom-post-type-ui), this plugin gives you a clean interface within your WordPress Dashboard that can help you easily and quickly build Custom Post Types on your website. It eliminates the need to add the code to your functions.php file by giving you options and settings so that you can configure and build the Custom Post Type that you want. Figure 6-5 shows the Custom Post Type UI options page on the Dashboard.

✦ **Betta Boxes CMS:** Available in the WordPress Plugin Directory (http://wordpress.org/extend/plugins/betta-boxes-cms), this plugin provides an interface in your Dashboard that you can use to create *meta boxes,* or special Custom Fields (see Book IV, Chapter 5) for the Custom Post Types that you build. As an example, Figure 6-6 shows some custom meta boxes built by using this plugin. This website features theater productions and the Custom Post Types for those shows. On the right side of Figure 6-6, the Purchase Link box were created by using custom meta boxes and give the website owner a quick and easy field to fill out so that he or she can include information on where to purchase show tickets in every show post published.

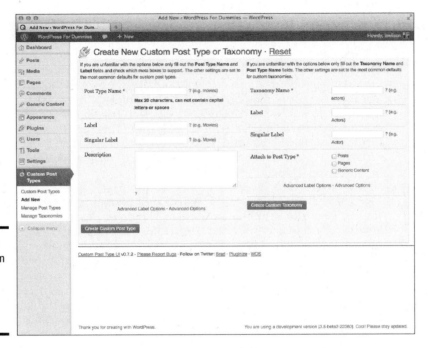

Figure 6-5:
The Custom Post Type UI plugin options page.

A custom meta box

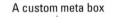

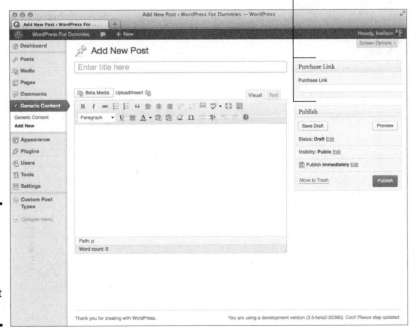

Figure 6-6:
Purchase Link meta box created for this Custom Post Type.

Optimizing Your WordPress Blog

Search engine optimization (SEO) is the practice of preparing your site to make it as easy as possible for the major search engines to crawl and cache your data in their systems so that your site appears as high as possible in the search returns. Book V contains more information on search engine optimization, as well as marketing your blog and tracking its presence in search engines and social media by using analytics. This section gives you a brief introduction to SEO practices with WordPress, and from here, you can move on to Book V to take a hard look at some of the things you can do to improve and increase traffic to your website.

If you search for the keywords **WordPress themes made to order** on Google, my business site at E.Webscapes is in the top-ten search results for those keywords. (At least, it is while I'm writing this chapter.) Those results can change from day to day, so by the time you read this book, someone else may very well have taken over that coveted position. The reality of chasing those high-ranking search engine positions is that they're here today, gone tomorrow. The goal of search engine optimization is to make sure that your site ranks as high as possible for the keywords that you think people will use to find your site. After you attain those high-ranking positions, the next goal is to keep them.

WordPress is equipped to create an environment that's friendly to search engines, giving them easy navigation through your archives, categories, and pages. WordPress provides this environment with a clean code base, content that's easily updated through the WordPress interface, and a solid navigation structure.

To extend search engine optimization even further, you can tweak five elements of your WordPress posts, pages, and templates:

✦ **Custom permalinks:** Use custom permalinks, rather than the default WordPress permalinks, to fill your post and page URLs with valuable keywords. Check out Book III, Chapter 2 for information on WordPress permalinks.

✦ **Posts and page titles:** Create descriptive titles for your blog posts and pages to provide rich keywords in your site.

✦ **Text:** Fill your blog posts and pages with keywords for search engines to find and index. Keeping your site updated with descriptive text and phrases helps the search engines find keywords to associate with your site.

✦ **Category names:** Use descriptive names for the categories you create in WordPress to place great keywords right in the URL for those category pages, if you use custom permalinks.

✦ **Images and <ALT> tags:** Place <ALT> tags in your images to further define and describe the images on your site. You can accomplish this task easily by using the description field in the WordPress image uploader.

Planting keywords in your website

If you're interested in a higher ranking for your site, use custom permalinks. By using custom permalinks, you're automatically inserting keywords into the URLs of your posts and pages, letting search engines include those posts and pages in their databases of information on those topics. If a provider that has the Apache mod_rewrite module enabled hosts your site, you can use the custom permalink structure for your WordPress-powered site.

Keywords are the first step on your journey toward great search engine results. Search engines depend on keywords, and people use keywords to look for content.

The default permalink structure in WordPress is pretty ugly. When you're looking at the default permalink for any post, you see a URL something like this:

```
http://yourdomain.com/p?=105
```

This URL contains no keywords of worth. If you change to a custom perma-link structure, your post URLs automatically include the titles of your posts to provide keywords, which search engines absolutely love. A custom per-malink may appear in this format:

```
http://yourdomain.com/2013/02/01/your-post-title
```

I explain setting up and using custom permalinks in full detail in Book III, Chapter 2.

Optimizing your post titles for search engine success

Search engine optimization doesn't completely depend on how you set up your site. It also depends on you, the site owner, and how you present your content.

You can present your content in a way that lets search engines catalog your site easily by giving your blog posts and pages titles that make sense and coordinate with the actual content being presented. If you're doing a post on a certain topic, make sure that the title of the post contains at least one or two keywords about that particular topic. This practice gives the search engines even more ammunition to list your site in searches relevant to the topic of your post.

**Book IV
Chapter 6**

**Using WordPress
as a Content
Management
System**

As your site's presence in the search engines grows, more people will find your site, and your readership will increase as a result.

A blog post with the title A Book I'm Reading doesn't tell anyone *what* book you're reading, making it difficult for people searching for information on that particular book to find the post.

If you give the post the title *WordPress All-in-One For Dummies:* My Review, you provide keywords in the title, and (if you're using custom permalinks) WordPress automatically inserts those keywords into the URL, giving the search engines a triple keyword play:

+ Keywords exist in your blog post title.

+ Keywords exist in your blog post URL.

+ Keywords exist in the content of your post.

Writing content with readers in mind

When you write your posts and pages and want to make sure that your content appears in the first page of search results so that people will find your site, you need to keep those people in mind when you're composing the content.

When search engines visit your site to crawl through your content, they don't see how nicely you've designed your site. They're looking for words to include in their databases. You, the site owner, want to make sure that your posts and pages use the words and phrases that you want to include in search engines.

If your post is about a recipe for fried green tomatoes, for example, you need to add a keyword or phrase that you think people will use when they search for the topic. If you think people would use the phrase *recipe for fried green tomatoes* as a search term, you may want to include that phrase in the content and title of your post.

A title such as A Recipe I Like isn't as effective as a title such as A Recipe for Fried Green Tomatoes. Including a clear, specific title in your post or page content gives the search engines a double-keyword whammy.

Here's another example: I once wrote a post about a rash that I developed on my finger, under my ring. I wrote that post six years ago, not really meaning to attract a bunch of people to that particular post. However, it seems that many women around the world suffer from the same rash because, six years later, that post still gets at least one comment a week. When people do a Google search by using the keywords *rash under my wedding ring,* out of a possible 128,000 results returned, my blog post appears in the top five slots.

This is how great blogs are! I was actually able to solve my problem with the rash under my finger because one woman from Australia found my blog through Google, visited my blog post, and left a comment with a solution that worked. Who says blogs aren't useful?

Creating categories that attract search engines

One little-known SEO tip for WordPress users: The names you give the categories you create for your blog provide rich keywords that attract search engines like honey attracts bees. A few services — Technorati (`http://technorati.com`) being one of the biggest — treat categories in WordPress like tags. These services use those categories to classify recent blog posts on any given topic. The names you give your categories in WordPress can serve as topic tags for Technorati and similar services.

Search engines also see your categories as keywords that are relevant to the content on your site. So, make sure that you're giving your categories names that are relevant to the content you're providing.

If you sometimes blog about your favorite recipes, you can make it easier for search engines to find your recipes if you create categories specific to the recipes you're blogging about. Instead of having one Favorite Recipes category, you can create multiple category names that correspond to the types of recipes you blog about — Casserole Recipes, Dessert Recipes, Beef Recipes, and Chicken Recipes, for example.

Creating specific category titles not only helps search engines, but it also helps your readers discover content that is related to topics they're interested in.

You can also consider having one category called Favorite Recipes and creating subcategories (also known as *child categories*) that give a few more details on the types of recipes you've written about. (See Book III, Chapter 5, for information on creating Categories and child categories.)

Categories use the custom permalink structure, just like posts do. So, links to your WordPress categories also become keyword tools within your site to help the search engines — and, ultimately, search engine users — find the content. Using custom permalinks creates category page URLs that look something like this:

```
http://yourdomain.com/category/category_name
```

**Book IV
Chapter 6**

**Using WordPress
as a Content
Management
System**

The *category_name* portion of that URL puts the keywords right into the hands of search engines.

Using the <ALT> tag for images

When you use the WordPress media uploader to include an image in your post or page, a Description text box appears, and in it you can enter a description of the image. (I cover using the WordPress image uploader in detail in Book IV, Chapter 3.) This text automatically becomes what's referred to as the <ALT> tag, or alternative text.

The <ALT> tag's real purpose is to provide a description of the image for people who, for some reason or another, can't actually see the image. In a text-based browser that doesn't display images, for example, visitors see the description, or <ALT> text, telling them what image would be there if they could see it. Also, the tag helps people who have impaired vision and rely on screen-reading technology because the screen reader reads the <ALT> text from the image. You can read more about website accessibility for people with disabilities at www.w3.org/WAI/intro/people-use-web/ Overview.html.

An extra benefit of <ALT> tags is that search engines gather data from them to further classify the content of your site. The following code inserts an image with the <ALT> tag of the code in bold to demonstrate what I'm talking about:

```
<img src="http://yourdomain.com/image.jpg" alt="This is an ALT tag within an
    image" />
```

Search engines harvest those <ALT> tags as keywords. The WordPress image uploader gives you an easy way to include those <ALT> tags without having to worry about inserting them into the image code yourself. Just fill out the Description text box before you upload and add the image to your post. Book IV, Chapter 3 covers in-depth information on adding images to your site content, including how to add descriptive text for the <ALT> tag and keywords.

Book V

Examining SEO and Social Media

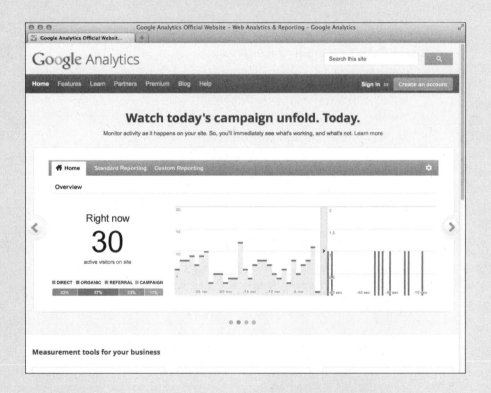

Contents at a Glance

Chapter 1: Exposing Your Content

In This Chapter

✔ **Making your content easy for readers to share**

✔ **Figuring out when to interact with readers**

✔ **Using Twitter through WordPress**

✔ **Connecting Facebook to your WordPress blog**

*A*fter you launch your blog, getting your content in front of an interested audience is one of the most important strategic decisions you make, and this chapter focuses on how to get your content in front of potential new readers. The idea that people will eventually find any content you write is a pretty big falsehood. You might have the best rock band in the world, but if you don't leave your garage and get your music in front of potential fans, you can't ever sell out arenas.

By creating good content, making it easily shareable, and then participating within groups of interested people, you can establish expertise and build a community around your content. A community is much more powerful than a bunch of empty visitors — people in a community often become advocates and cheerleaders for your blog.

You want to gain readers, not random visitors. There's a big difference between a reader and a visitor: *Readers* follow your blog on a consistent basis, and *visitors* check out your site and then move on to the next page that grabs their attention.

Understanding the Three C's of the Social Web

Before I dive into the technical how-to stuff, I should talk about general social media philosophy. Technical tips without philosophy are meaningless. If you don't have the general philosophy down, your results are going to be poor because your interactions are going to be very one-sided affairs.

You can concentrate your daily actions on the web around the Three C's: content, communication, and consistency. The next few sections go into detail about each topic. By applying the Three C's, you can avoid a lot of mistakes and have success with your website and blog.

Considering social-voting tools

A lot of online vendors recommend that you drive as many eyeballs as possible to your site by using social-voting tools (such as Facebook's Like button or Twitter's Retweet button) and other methods. Although this strategy increases your traffic numbers and may temporarily boost your confidence, it's a short-term solution. Most of your new visitors won't have a lot of interest in your content and therefore won't return to your site.

Content

The first pillar of the social web is content. Although the web has seen a growing shift away from content to community, content is still king. Communities based around common interests fall flat unless they have the content for people to gravitate around. Facebook groups, for example, dominate because of the wealth of content they offer: the posts, links, videos, and other media people create within that group. Without the content, the group wouldn't exist.

However, content for the sake of content isn't necessarily in your best interests. To ensure that you provide the best content possible, make sure that you do these things:

✦ **Focus your content.** People expect tailored content. If you write about anything, people won't know what to expect and will visit less often or stop coming to your blog altogether. People will come back to your blog for certain reasons, and they want content tailored to what they expect. The most successful bloggers have a narrow focus, and they write for a niche.

When Problogger.net author Darren Rowse (`http://problogger.net`), an authority on professional blogging, first began blogging, he tried a wide-ranging approach but discovered it didn't work:

> "My blog had four main themes and different readers resonated differently with each one. A few readers shared my diverse interests in all four areas, but most came to my blog to read about one of the (or at most a couple of) topics. A number of regular loyal readers became disillusioned with my eclectic approach to blogging and gave up coming."

Stick to two or three related topics (such as WordPress and related technology topics); you can still cover and talk about a wide variety of subjects that you excel in. People will know what they were coming to your site for and what to expect from you.

✦ **Have a voice that people want to hear.** People don't necessarily care about the mechanics of your writing as much as they care about your voice. Bloggers, especially ones who post large amounts of content, often have typos and errors in their posts. Tucker Max (`http://tuckermax.com`), one of the most popular comedy bloggers, switches between past and present tense often — a grammar no-no. He's aware of this problem and doesn't care, and neither do his readers.

Max knows that he's developing his own style:

> "I know, I know. The whole concept of tense in speech has always given me problems. In undergrad and law school, I never really took any creative writing or English courses; it was pretty much all econ, law, history, etc, so some of the basic things that most writers get right, I fail. Of course I could learn tenses, but I have never really made an effort to get it right for a reason: I want to write in my own voice, regardless of whether or not it is 'correct' grammar or not. By switching tenses, I write the way I speak, and by alternating between past and present I put the reader into the story, instead of just recounting it."

Tucker says that the only time people complain about his grammar mistakes is when users want to argue about the content of his blog. They use the grammar mistakes as a plank in their attack. However, this attempt to belittle him hasn't slowed his growth or success. His voice, after all, is what has made him successful.

Your grammar and spelling don't have to always be perfect, but you should always ensure your posts are readable. Just don't let it get in the way of your individual voice.

✦ **Present your content well.** The actual look of your presentation matters greatly. Adding images, for example, enhances your posts in a number of ways, including

- Giving posts a visual point of interest
- Grabbing attention (really making your RSS feed readers stop and read)
- Drawing people's eyes down beyond the first few lines of a post
- Illustrating examples
- Giving your blog a more personal touch
- Engaging the emotions and senses of readers
- Giving posts a professional feel, which can lead to an air of authority

Be sure the only images you use on your website are those images you have permission to use. The best-case scenario is that you use your own images that you, yourself, own the copyright to. Outside of that, be sure you've obtained permission from the owner of the image before using it on your website. Alternatively, you can purchase images for use through reputable stock photography sites such as iStockPhoto.com or GettyImages.com.

If you write long, poorly formatted postings, people most likely won't comment or interact with your content: not because of the length of those postings, per se, but because of the way that you displayed them, as long paragraphs of endless text. Pictures, highlighted words, bullet points, and other such tricks give the reader's eye a break and can make your postings more attractive and more professional looking.

✦ **Write often.** The more you write, the more people will spread the word about your writing, and you can grow your audience. Successful bloggers tended to post multiple times per week.

All these blog elements are extremely important on the social web. People want to read and view information that they find interesting, that's well presented, and that's specific to their needs. Make sure you consider all these facets of a blog when you create content for your blog.

Communication

Communication is the second pillar of the social web. The more you write, the more comments you'll get.

✦ **Respond to those comments!** The whole point of the social web is communication and people expect to engage you in a conversation. Successful bloggers engage readers in the comment section and create conversations — they use the blog post as a jumping-off point for a larger discussion.

WordPress guru Lorelle VanFossen (`http://lorelle.wordpress.com`) expresses the true value of comments and how they changed how she uses the web:

> "Comments change how you write and what you write. I suddenly wasn't writing static information. People could question what I said. They could make me think and reconsider my point of view. They could offer more information to add value to my words. And most of all, they could inspire me to write more. Comments made writing come alive."

✦ **Develop a community.** When you participate in the conversation, you'll retain more readers, who many times will revisit your page during the day to see the new comments and replies in the discussion. The evolution into community discussion can result in a drastic increase in traffic and comments on your blog. VanFossen writes of her blog,

"My site isn't about 'me' or 'my opinion' any more. It's about what I have to say and you say back and I say, and then she says, and he says, and he says to her, and she reconsiders, and I jump in with my two shekels, and then he responds with another view . . . and it keeps going on. Some of these conversations never end. I'm still having discussions on topics I wrote 11 months ago."

✦ **Don't ignore a person's comments on multiple posts.** You can offend your commenter and lose him. Reply to most comments that your blog receives, even if it's only to say thanks for the comments.

Having an approach by which you only want to take from the social web leaves you ultimately unsuccessful: No matter how great your content, you need to have a level of participation and make people feel that you're communicating with them, not just speaking at them.

Consistency

The final pillar of the social web is consistency. When you produce any type of content that you offer multiple times a week or on a daily basis, people begin to expect consistency. Many bloggers don't post consistently, and as a result, they frustrate their readers.

Although consistency applies to blogging, in general, it really matters on social networks (such as Twitter and Facebook) where the interconnectivity between the author and the audience reaches new heights. If you have large followings on Facebook and Twitter and use them as your main point of contact with your readers, be sure to post on a regular basis there, as well.

Build good blogging habits by following these consistency guidelines:

✦ **Set a schedule and stick to it.** As a blogger, you have to give people a pattern to expect so that eventually they can know when to look for your posts. This idea is like knowing when a favorite TV program is on — the viewer comes to expect it and maybe even plan around it. If you miss a day on which you usually post, you just might hear from readers wondering where your post is for that day.

If you plan to write five days a week, actually write five days a week and try not to deviate from that schedule. If you plan to post only two to three times a week, stick to the days that you usually post (unless you want to cover some important breaking news).

✦ **Don't let the increasing number of readers and comments impact your posting schedule.** The last thing you want to do is over-post. Although some bloggers would argue that you should keep momentum on a particularly popular post, you run the risk of overexposing yourself and burning yourself out — plus, your content can quickly become watered down. The quality of the content, what the people are there for, quickly begins to erode, and you can lose the audience you've built.

Commenting on other blogs

In addition to responding to comments on your blog, you should go to different blogs and take part in the discussion there. Choose blogs that are similar to yours; you can be part of the larger blogging community beyond just your blog. (Visitors of those blogs will see your witty comments and most likely follow you to your blog, thereby building your audience.)

Understanding the social aspect of the social web is vital to your blogging success. People use the social web as a major mode of communication. The communication aspect of your blog and others plays into the overall online conversation that's going on, a conversation that can get started by an article, which a blogger covers in a blog post about that topic, which a reader comments on, which prompts another person to blog a response to those comments or that blog, which gets its own set of comments. Having a grasp on this concept and seeing how it operates not only brings you better success on the social web but also makes you a better participant.

By sticking with a routine and establishing consistency in your posting, you let readers know what to expect, and your blog becomes a part of their routine. If you ingrain yourself in someone's life, he or she is going to return to your blog frequently and become an advocate for what you're doing.

✦ **Plan ahead.** You also need to account for long breaks in your posting schedule. You can prewrite posts when you have a lot to say and save them as drafts so that you could post them at times when you aren't inspired to write.

Some bloggers take a month off from writing or post very sporadically. But if you really want to build an audience, you can't suddenly decide to take a month off because you're tired of it. Taking a long stretch of time off can kill your blog's momentum and audience.

You can explore other options instead of leaving your blog dormant. If you've built an audience, you can rather easily find a guest blogger to step in for a bit.

✦ **Keep the quality consistent.** Take pains to ensure that the quality content you produce doesn't suffer for any reason. Bloggers often capitalize on a popular post, gain an audience, and then become inconsistent with the quality of their content. They either shift away from their original niche or begin to post poorly thought-out or put-together blog entries. When their blog quality suffers, those bloggers begin to lose their audience and can never recover.

+ **Expect some ups and downs.** You can't easily judge which posts are going to be successful and which aren't. You might write posts in five minutes that get more views and have a better reception than posts you take hours to craft. But readers can really tell when you're posting for the sake of posting. If you repeatedly have to force yourself to post and if that goes on for too long, the quality of your blog and your consistency can go out the window.

Making It Easy for Users to Share Your Content

When I was a child, I loved to go to a country store on a lake near where I lived. One time, my mother and I went to the store to pick up a few things, but my mother didn't have any cash (this was before ATMs were everywhere) and wanted to pay by check or credit card. The store owner told her that they accepted cash only; we put the items back on the shelves and headed to a large supermarket.

When we got into the car, my mother said to me, "I wanted to give them money, but they made it too hard for me to do it." That sentiment has stuck with me my entire life: Never put up barriers to actions that will ultimately benefit you. I'm sure that the store had reasons for not taking checks or credit cards, but it ultimately lost a sale and probably a customer.

Think of your blog as the store and your content as the products. When people want to take your content and give it to someone, you put up a barrier if you make it hard for them to pass that content along. Make it as easy as possible for people to share your content with their friends, family, and co-workers.

One of the best things about the social web is that you can share what you find with other people. Sharing is such a basic concept. It's such an easy, thoughtful, and fun thing to do. You find content that you like and share it with your friends on the web, who might find what you shared helpful or interesting and pass it on to their friends. But a lot of sites do a very poor job of allowing users to share content. While you set up your WordPress site, think about how you want readers to share your content.

Test, test, and test some more. How to best lay out your sharing options on your site takes continual testing. You can't get it right the first time — or the first five times. Sometimes, it takes months to find the right mix.

The following sections give you some simple tips to make sharing content from your website easy.

Sociable versus ShareThis

WordPress offers a multitude of plugins (see Book VII) that blend together social sharing with more traditional options, such as printing and e-mailing. The Sociable plugin by BlogPlay (`http://blogplay.com/plugin`) combines a couple of plugins to give people the ability not only to share content on social media sites but also to print posts, transfer them to PDFs, add them to their browser favorites, and e-mail them.

Other popular plugins offer similar options with some drawbacks. The ShareThis plugin (`http://sharethis.com`), for example, provides a green button that, when clicked, expands so that users can select the networks on which they want to share your content, or they can print or e-mail that content. Making users click an additional button to see their sharing options adds an extra step in the process. The Sociable plugin puts individual icons onto your posts, getting rid of the extra step that users must take to share your content through ShareThis.

Just remember, when you use the ShareThis button, a reader can easily overlook it. The individual buttons are more visible and not as easily overlooked. Test both and see which method gets more shares.

Enable the user to share content

Enabling sharing is the first thing you will want to do. If people don't have the ability to share your content, it isn't going to go anywhere.

Sharing content doesn't mean just social media sharing; your content can get spread through other methods. Include the ability to e-mail or print your posts. Although you may feel that e-mail and printing are outdated features, your users may not.

Don't overwhelm the user with choices

Sites can include too many sharing options. The reader becomes overwhelmed and probably also has trouble finding the network that he or she uses.

Pick a few sharing sites to which you want to link, test them, and cycle in new ones that people may use. Offer only a low number of sharing options at a time so that people can share your content easily. Determine which of these networks your content applies to. If you write celebrity gossip, your content might do better being distributed on sites where people can share quickly with their friends, such as Facebook (`www.facebook.com`) or Twitter (`https://twitter.com`). If you write in-depth technical resources, a social bookmarking site such as Delicious (`https://delicious.com`) might be a better place to share your content and bring your blog additional traffic. If you write about fashion and beauty, perhaps providing a sharing button to Pinterest (`www.pinterest.com`) can get you traffic from people interested in those specific topics.

Make sure that the sharing options you give visitors apply to sites where your content makes sense. Don't be afraid to try different sites and study your statistics to see where readers are discovering your content. Many of these sites allow you to search by domain, so you can check to see how often people are sharing your website and what content, specifically, they're sharing.

Present the ability to share in the right place for your audience

Where you present the sharing buttons really depends on the type of content you're posting and the audience reading it. If you post a picture and include a comment below it, this could push your sharing buttons below the fold, so make sure that your major sharing options appear next to or above the content. Some of the more popular places to display sharing buttons are the top of the post, bottom of the post, and in either the left or right margins of the website.

Below the fold refers to what doesn't appear in a user's web browser unless the user scrolls down to view it. The term is taken from newspaper printing, in which some items appear below the fold on the front page.

To get some ideas about how best to deploy your sharing buttons, check out sites that are similar to yours and see how some of the more successful bloggers have done it.

Think about the user, not yourself

Take this major lesson away from this section. Too many times, people get excited about the latest gadget or tool for their blogs. They get eager to try it out and excited to deploy it, but in the end, they aren't thinking about whether it can help the user and whether the user is going to enjoy it.

How you use the web and how you navigate a blog can be completely different than how most other people use it. Review button use and where people are sharing your blog posts and also use tools such as Google Analytics to see how people interact with your page.

By using its site-overlay feature, Google Analytics allows you to see how often someone clicks various items on your website. You can sign up for Google Analytics for free and deploy it very easily. (You just need to paste the tracking code in your WordPress footer.)

To access the site-overlay feature from your Google Analytics Dashboard, follow these steps:

1. **On the left menu, click the Content link.**

2. **Make sure that the Overview link is highlighted so that you're on the overview screen.**

3. **Click the In-Page Analytics link.**

Now, on the home page of your site, little text boxes for the various links on your home page appear, displaying percentages. (See Figure 1-1.) The percentages within these text boxes reflect how popular the various links are within your site. If you navigate through your site while using the site-overlay feature, you can see, page by page, how people are interacting with your navigation, content, sharing features, and other content.

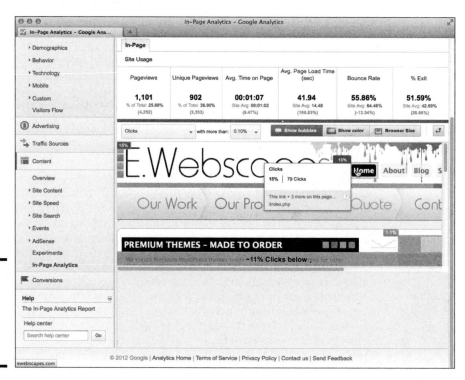

Figure 1-1: The Site Overlay feature in Google Analytics.

Determining Where You Need to Participate

Communication is such an important part of social media, and communication is a two-way street. In social media, communication isn't a bullhorn; you need to interact with people. If you want the rewards of participation, you need to listen as well as talk. This idea often gets lost when people start using social media to promote their content.

Determining who you want to interact with and where to interact with them is a large part of using social media in your marketing strategy. Finding the best communities in which you can participate and actively engage in conversations is the quickest way to build a loyal audience.

Although reaching out to audiences known for being receptive to your blog's content is a good strategy, you may find that you're following a well-trod path. Other bloggers may have already found success there. Don't be afraid to try out areas where others who have blogs similar to yours aren't participating — if you think the audience is there, go for it. Be original and trail-blaze a little.

As a blogger, you often work as the marketing person for your own blog. To gain readership, you need to participate with your potential audience members in communities where they are already participating. Additionally, you can really leverage participating in these communities if you understand the bloggers in your niche, work with them to possibly get a guest-blogging slot, or even get links from them in their blogrolls.

Taking the time to create a list of potential audiences goes a long way toward creating your own blog-marketing strategy. Your list should include social networks and message boards where you think that your content will be greeted with open arms, bloggers who work in the niche you participate in that you want to monitor, and users who have influence on other social networks (such as someone who has a large Twitter following in your niche or your particular area of interest/expertise).

Some bloggers have actually purchased lists of other bloggers in their niche from marketing firms, but this strategy isn't a good one. Although purchased lists might make for a good jumping-off point, a lot of lists are outdated or ignore important markets (such as large social networking, Twitter, or YouTube friends/followers).

The most important piece of research you can do while constructing a list is to understand the niche in which you're building a readership. Here are some items of interest that you can look for when finding out about a niche:

✦ **Who's in the niche?** Check out the link on a blogroll or in a post. Start with a major blog in your niche and see where the blogroll leads, the links to commenters' blogs, and blogs that they mention in their content to get a wide view of the niche. Knowing who associates with whom and what circles people run in can help you discover a lot about a niche. You can determine who the power players are, as well as whether the niche is competitive about news or has a collegial atmosphere. This information helps you determine how you want to approach your outreach.

✦ **Is there a niche social media site or group that acts as a connecting point for the community?** Often, in various groups, you can find one or more niche social media sites that connect blogs together. These sites can provide you with a great resource for discovering some of the top blogs, and they may help you flesh out your list of bloggers quickly. Additionally, see whether you can get your blog listed on these types of sites. Most of these kinds of sites allow free submittals, and you can find forms to fill out or an e-mail address to which you can submit your content.

The site Milblogging.com (`http://milblogging.com`) is great example of a small niche community designed around a topic; in this case, a community of members of the military. This kind of online community might be a directory with social features, a Facebook community, or a group on a large social network; whatever the case may be, you can often find large groups that have discussions within a niche. These niche sites can tell you what people in the niche you are targeting find important, what the hot topics are, and information about what other people are doing in this niche, such as pitches people have made to other bloggers.

Additionally, these sites feature the type of content that people in your niche may find interesting. Keep a Word document open to write down blogging ideas based on the conversations on these sites.

✦ **Are common discussions occurring throughout the community?** You can often discover opportunities to get your blog in front of new people or for topics to cover by looking for common threads within a niche. Maybe the bloggers are talking about how PR people are pitching them, a charity cause that they all support, or an event that they regard as important. A common theme may give you information, opportunity, or direction on how you should approach this niche.

✦ **Do they use other media to have discussions?** Find out what other social media sites people in this niche use. Maybe they use Twitter a lot, or maybe you see a high use of Facebook, LinkedIn, Pinterest, FriendFeed, or YouTube. You may find secondary ways to reach this niche where you can build a following for your blog.

It pays to determine the social media sites your niche prefers. Certain niches (such as wine bloggers) have taken to Twitter, but others have strong ties to Facebook or other social networking sites. Make the most of these sites when you pitch your blog to people. They may prefer that method of connection.

In the end, you might think you can simply buy a list, slam together a bunch of search results into a spreadsheet, and then mass e-mail everyone whom you want to contact. However, without studying how your niche operates, you can't create mutually beneficial relationships, you can't become a voice in the community, and you probably can't see a lot of success. Instead, you come off as an outsider just trying to push your message down the throats of these bloggers, and your campaign will have very poor results.

Finding Influencers

After you compile lists of bloggers you would like to target, you can begin to break the list down and determine who are the influencers in your niche, including the hidden influencers. *Hidden influencers* are people that have a large social imprint that doesn't necessarily show up on their blog. For example, some bloggers don't have a lot of commenters on their blog, but their Twitter feed is followed by tens of thousands. Here are some ways to determine whether a blogger is an influencer:

✦ **Subscriber count:** A lot of bloggers who have large audiences display their subscriber numbers on their blogs. (See Figure 1-2.)

✦ **Comment count:** An active community and commentary group on a blog usually shows that the blog has a large readership. Be wary of blogs in which the author interacts with only two or three people. When an author pays attention only to a couple commenters, she usually has a pretty narrow vision. You want to target authors that participate with more people in their audience.

✦ **Alexa/Compete:** Alexa (www.alexa.com) and Compete (www.compete.com) measure traffic to a site. They aren't 100 percent accurate, but they do a decent job of giving you a picture of the amount of traffic a site gets. Add a column to your list of bloggers where you can record either the Compete or Alexa score, and then see how the scores compare.

✦ **Klout:** Klout (www.klout.com) helps you evaluate the influence of Twitter, Facebook, and LinkedIn users. Sometimes, bloggers may have a very large reach on those social networks and are more active there than on their own blogs.

Figure 1-2:
Blog subscriber count on Problogger. net.

After you identify the influencers, you want to attract them to your blog. If influencers read your blog, they may offer you guest-blogging spots, share your content, recommend your blog to their readers, and form a relationship with you so that you can be mutually beneficial to each other.

To turn these influencers into readers, you can try multiple tactics, including the following:

✦ **Comment on their blogs.** Reading and commenting on a popular blog can help you start to build your name in your niche — if you leave quality, well-thought-out comments, of course. Most blogs allow your username to link back to a website; make sure that you use this link as a way for people to find your blog.

Not only can you get the attention of a popular blogger by engaging in conversation on his or her blog, you also get the attention of that blogger's readership. If the readers and commentators like your contribution, you can get additional traffic, new readers, and even potentially high-ranking backlinks into your website; all because you left a comment on the blog.

✦ **E-mail them.** Depending on the niche, top influencers might get slammed with e-mail, so this approach might not be the best way to reach out to someone. But it doesn't hurt to write a personal note that lets the blogger know about you and your blog, and perhaps offer to guest blog if he or she ever accepts posts from other bloggers. Make sure that the e-mail isn't all about you, which is the quickest way to turn someone off. Talk about the person's blog and show that you have knowledge about what he's writing about. Show that you have actually read his blog and demonstrate genuine interest in what he's doing.

✦ **Interact with them on their platforms of choice.** Sometimes, influencers or popular bloggers participate in areas other than their blogs. They might use a message board, a forum, Twitter, Facebook, or another type of social media site. Interacting with a blogger on his or her platform of choice can help you differentiate yourself from other bloggers.

✦ **Link to them.** Linking to bloggers in the content you create — especially if you're posting rebuttals to their posts — can really get their attention.

When you use any of the tactics in the preceding list, the three C's (content, communication, and consistency) come into effect. When you communicate with these bloggers, you need to make sure that you have consistent content on your site. Trying to reach out to another blogger when you have only three posts total doesn't present the most credibility. After you've worked at it for a few months, doing blogger outreach can provide you with a good way to grow your audience.

Leveraging Twitter for Social Media Success

Twitter has become one of the most effective ways for bloggers to build an audience. You can use Twitter to find people who have the same interests that you do, communicate with them, and steer a ton of traffic to your blog.

Building a Twitter profile into a successful tool to generate traffic is pretty straightforward. Just follow these steps on your account at `https://twitter.com`:

1. **Make sure that your profile is completely filled out, including your picture.**

2. **Follow the three C's — content, communication, and consistency — when you post to Twitter.**

By posting quality content consistently on Twitter, you *will* build an audience. Period. When you mix in the communication aspect and retweet the quality content of others, answer questions, and interact with other Twitter users, your profile will grow that much more.

3. **Find people who are interested in what you're writing about and interact with them.**

4. **Use a tool such as Followerwonk (**`http://followerwonk.com`**) to find people whose profiles contain specific keywords that you're writing about — the best part is Followerwonk is free.**

   You may want to follow and interact with these people.

Building your Twitter account by using automated tools

I hesitate to include this section because using automated tools is a fast way to get your account deleted by Twitter. Automated tools allow you to do mass additions or removals to your account. You can remove people that aren't active, that aren't following you, or allow you to target the friend's lists of other users to add them to your account. Using these mass adding-and-removal tools kind of goes against the spirit of Twitter, where you are supposed to be discovering cool content and not just mass promoting. So, I'm warning you right now, if you go down this path, you need to see losing your account as an acceptable risk. If you use the tool that I discuss in a logical and nonaggressive way, it can help you target and build an audience quickly.

I include automated tools in my discussion of building your social media accounts because a lot of people use this technique, including people who shun them. (A lot of social media experts who deride these tools have used them to get where they are.) I don't believe in giving you half the information — you need to make this choice on your own.

However, if you hyper-aggressively add people and then unfollow them on your account, Twitter will probably quickly ban you.

To target users on Twitter, here are the steps you can take:

1. **Go to Refollow (**`www.refollow.com`**).**

   Refollow.com is a great service, but it is no longer free. It used to be free, but recent changes to the Twitter platform and Refollow's need to restructure their service has led to the folks at Refollow asking for payment for their services. You can sign up for free and then click the Upgrade My Account button at the top of the site to upgrade. The prices range from $20 to $150 per month.

2. **Log in to Refollow by using your Twitter account login information.**

   This loads the Refollow Control Panel page, as shown in Figure 1-3.

3. **Select the Follow Me, And Who I Follow option under the Load People Who header.**

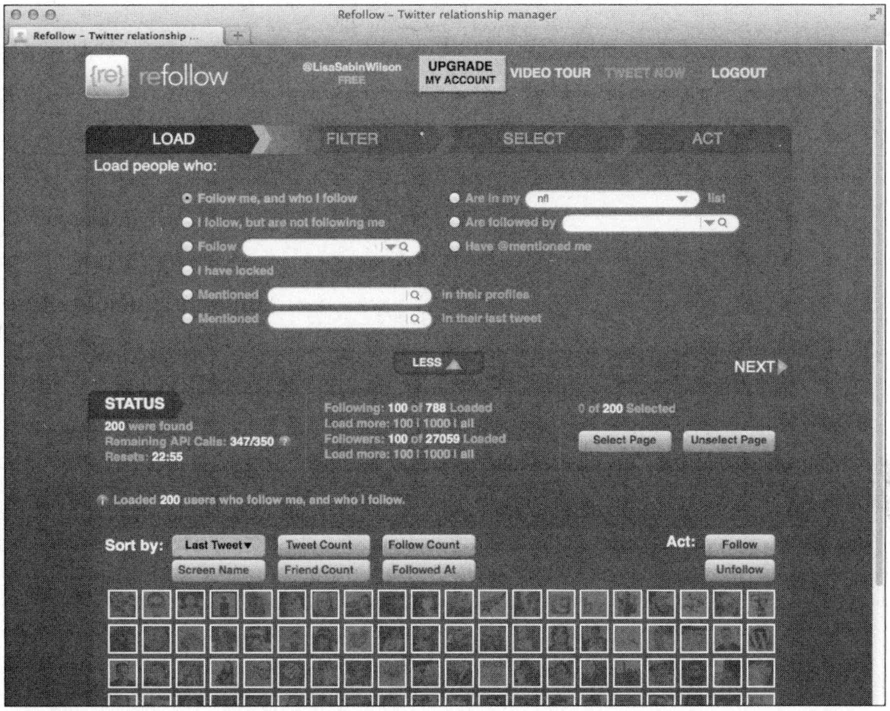

Figure 1-3:
The
Refollow
Dashboard.

4. **Click Next.**

5. **At the top of the page, select the appropriate check boxes, like:**

   - Are following me
   - Are not following me
   - I'm following
   - I'm not following
   - I've never followed
   - I have locked

6. **Select your preferred action under the Act header at the bottom right of the Refollow Dashboard.**

   You can choose to follow or unfollow the people listed after you've filtered them using the Refollow tools.

   Don't follow more than 100 to 200 people a day. This tool allows you to follow up to 500, but if you follow that many people each day, Twitter will probably ban you after a few days.

You can use Refollow to find people who are following people within your niche and add them to your Twitter account so that they may notice your content. I advise adding people in bulk only once in a 24-hour period so you don't look like you are gaming the system. Once a week, unfollow everyone who isn't following you back to keep your following ratio even. You should not be following more people than are following you.

Updating Twitter from your WordPress blog

Getting back to WordPress (that's why you bought the book, right?), you can find tons of plugins to integrate Twitter into your WordPress blog. From how the tweets show up on your sidebar to integrating tweets into your comments, the WordPress community has tons of solutions to help you show off your Twitter account on your blog.

These plugins change often, so try different ones, depending on how you want to integrate Twitter into your site. But if you want to turn your WordPress Dashboard into more of a social media command center, you can give yourself the ability to tweet right from your WordPress Dashboard.

Although tools such as TweetDeck and HootSuite are better designed for an active and strategic Twitter presence, having the ability to tweet from your WordPress Dashboard allows you to update all your social media from one spot. If you're just getting started in social media, this integration makes your social media use efficient and constantly reminds you to participate.

One of the better WordPress integration plugins for this purpose is Alex King's Twitter Tools (`http://wordpress.org/extend/plugins/twitter-tools`). This installation allows you to tweet from your WordPress Dashboard as well as create an archive page for all your tweets. And it can create a WordPress blog post of your daily tweets, among other features.

This plugin can also update your Twitter feed whenever you submit a new blog post. You can update Twitter about new blog posts by using HootSuite, FeedBurner, and other free tools, but going with the Alex King Twitter plugin allows you to use all these features through one plugin.

Engaging with Facebook

Facebook integration is another key strategy to consider when you're setting up your blog for the first time. First, integrate the Facebook-sharing feature within your blog, which can be done with the ShareThis or AddThis plugin. With over 450 million users, Facebook is a must-have sharing option for any blog.

Next, decide how you want your blog to interact with Facebook. Are you writing a very personal blog? Then you might want to use a Facebook profile as your connecting place on Facebook. Some WordPress plugins (such as the Facebook Dashboard Widget) integrate a Facebook profile so that you can update your status right from the WordPress Dashboard.

However, if you don't want your Facebook account attached to your blog, you may want to consider creating a Facebook Page. A Facebook Page doesn't have the Dashboard controls that a profile does, but it allows you to leverage your social media presence. By setting up a Facebook Fan page, you can deeply integrate the Facebook Like option, which allows users to Like your site and become a fan of your page with a couple of clicks. Integrating the Like feature allows you to get exposure for your website through each of your fans' friends on Facebook.

When you have a Facebook Page, you can display a community widget on the side of your WordPress blog, letting everyone know who your fans are on Facebook. Basically, if a Facebook user clicks the Like button on your page, he can show up in this widget. Facebook offers a lot of different badges and Like-button integration in its Developers section at `http://developers.facebook.com/plugins`.

In this Developers section, you really can dig deep into how you want to integrate Facebook into your blog. You can display the friends of a visitor who likes your site, recommendations based on what the visitor's friends have liked, and numerous other combinations.

The commercial service behind the WordPress.com hosted service, Automattic, has created a plugin for WordPress called Jetpack (`http://wordpress.org/extend/plugins/jetpack`) that bundles several handy social media tools for your WordPress blog, including Facebook and Twitter sharing and automatic posting to your favorite social networks.

Chapter 2: Creating a Social Media Listening Hub

In This Chapter

✔ Understanding why you need to monitor your brand

✔ Finding out which monitoring tools are right for you

✔ Cleaning and aggregating your monitoring data

✔ Turning your WordPress Dashboard into a listening post

This chapter focuses on the importance of listening to social media, the free monitoring services available for you to use, and how to integrate these sources into your WordPress installation so that you can turn your run-of-the-mill WordPress installation into a social media listening hub.

A *social media listening hub* is a collection of information from several sources, including mentions of your blog, keywords, or topics that you write about, and even information about competitors. You can sign up for services that monitor these topics, such as Salesforce Marketing Cloud (www.salesforcemarketingcloud.com), Sysomos (www.sysomos.com), and hundreds of others. But most of these services cost money and give you another place to log in to — and you may not use this kind of service to its full capability. For a small business or an independent blogger, the investment (both time and financial) doesn't always make sense. By leveraging the power of the WordPress platform, you can easily cut down on both the time and financial commitment of monitoring platforms.

In this chapter, I walk you through determining what sources you should pull your data from, how to determine and search for the keywords you deem important, and how to integrate your search results into your WordPress Dashboard. Additionally, I look at some other tools that can help expand your monitoring practices.

Exploring Reasons for a Social Media Listening Hub

When you begin to engage in the world of social media, one of the most important things you can do is monitor what Internet users are saying about your company, your blog, you, or your products. By investigating what Internet users are saying, you can find and participate in discussions about your blog or company and come to an understanding about the way your community views your blog (or company). With this information, you can participate by responding to comments on other blogs, Twitter, or message boards or by creating targeted content on your own blog.

The conversations happening about your area of interest or niche amount to really great intelligence. For a business, regardless of whether you participate in social media, social media users are talking about your company, so you need to be aware what they're saying. If you're blogging about a particular topic, you can evolve your content by tracking what members of your niche are discussing about it.

Eavesdropping on yourself

By monitoring your niche, you essentially can eavesdrop on thousands of conversations daily and then pick and choose the ones in which you want to participate. The social media listening hub you create allows you to follow various conversations going on through microblogging services such as Twitter, Facebook, blogs, news sites, message boards, and even comments on YouTube. If someone says something negative about you, you can respond quickly to fix the situation. You could make attempts to step in and make sure that people are informed about what you're doing.

Keeping tabs on your brand

Think about what keywords or phrases you want to monitor. Of course, you want to monitor your name, your blog/company name, and other keywords that are directly associated with you.

Monitor common misspellings and permutations of the name of your brand. The Bing Ads Intelligence tool (`http://advertise.bingads.micro soft.com/en-us/bingads-downloads/bingads-intelligence`) can help you determine all the common spellings and usages of the keywords you're monitoring. You can also find common misspellings for your brand by examining some of the terms people used to find your page with Google Analytics (`www.google.com/analytics`) or a paid tool such as Trellian Keyword Discovery Tool (`www.keyworddiscovery.com/search.html`).

For example, if Aaron Rodgers wanted to set up a monitoring service, he might use the following keywords: *Aaron Rodgers, Arron Rodgers, Aaron Rogers, Green Bay Packers Quarterback,* and perhaps even his touchdown celebration phrase: *discount double check.* If he wanted to expand this service past direct mentions of him or his team, he could also include more general terms such as *NFL Football* or even *NFC Teams.* The general term *NFL Football* may be *too* general, though, producing too many results to monitor.

Additionally, you may want to view your blog or company through the lens of your customers: What terms do they associate with your company? Looking at your blog from other points of view can provide you with good ideas for keywords, but not always. Although you don't always want your company known for these terms and may not see yourself that way, getting the perspective of other people can open your eyes on how users view your blog or website.

Don't think of this process as just pulling in keywords, either. You can pull in multiple feeds, just like you do with an RSS reader, which allows you to monitor specific sites. So, if you concentrate on an industry, and a website deals specifically with your industry and has an active news flow pushed through an RSS feed, you might want to consider adding specific websites into the mix of feeds you run through WordPress.

The setup in WordPress that I describe in this chapter gives you the convenience of having everything in one place and can help you monitor your brand, company, or blog. The limitations of the WordPress platform means that you can monitor only five different groupings, so you can't use this method as a replacement for an enterprise-monitoring tool for a large company. Additionally, if you own a restaurant, hotel, or bar and want to pick up review sites such as Yelp and Trip Advisor, these tools can't do it. Most social media monitoring tools don't count review sites as social media. Tools such as Reputation Ranger (`http://reputationranger.com`) can monitor ratings sites for a nominal monthly fee if you want to pay attention to those types of sites.

When your content changes, change what you're monitoring to match the evolution of what you're blogging about.

Exploring Different Listening Tools

You can find tons of different types of monitoring or listening tools that oversee the social media space. If you work for a large company, you can use large, paid tools such as Salesforce Marketing Cloud (`www.salesforcemarketingcloud.com`), Sysomos (`www.sysomos.com`), Alterian (`www.alterian.com`), Lithium (`www.lithium.com`), or others. Pricing for these tools runs from a few hundred dollars to the tens of thousands per month. Most individuals and small businesses can't make that investment. If you're one of the smaller guys, you can create your own monitoring service right in WordPress by importing free monitoring tools into your Dashboard to create a social media listening hub.

Some monitoring tools pick up blog coverage, Twitter remarks, and message board comments. Others pick up content created around video and pictures. Try the different monitoring services mentioned in the following sections and determine which give you the best results and which make you feel the most comfortable. Then choose the best tools to create a good monitoring mix. One solution probably can't cover everything, so experiment with different combinations of tools.

Most, but not all, of these tools use Boolean search methods, so you need to understand how to narrow down your searches. If you want to combine terms, put an AND between two items (for example, *cake AND pie*). If you use OR, you can broaden your search — for example, to track common misspellings *(MacDonalds OR McDonalds)*. Finally, if you want to exclude terms, you can use the NOT operator to exclude items from your search. Use NOT if you want to search for a term that could have an alternative meaning that's irrelevant to what you're actually looking for (for example, *Afghan NOT blanket,* if you're blogging about Afghanistan).

Although some of the monitoring tools in the following sections don't apply to every type of website, I would include these tools in most monitoring setups.

For each search that you do on a monitoring service, you need to log the feed address. To make recording these addresses easy, open a spreadsheet or a document into which you can paste the various feeds. You can collect them in one place before you begin to splice them together (which you do in the "Creating Your Own Personal Monitoring Mix" section later in this chapter). Think of it as a holding area.

Monitoring with Google Alerts

Most social media experts widely consider Google Alerts (www.google. com/alerts) a must-use monitoring source for anyone dabbling in social media. Google Alerts allows you to set up monitoring on news sites, blogs, pictures, videos, and groups. You can toggle the amount of results you see from 20 to 50; and you can choose how often they come in, either in real time, daily, or weekly. You can have Google deliver your alerts to your e-mail or via RSS.

Google Alerts isn't perfect, but it doesn't have many drawbacks. Some of the specialized searches (such as Boardreader, which targets message boards) pick up more around their areas of expertise than Google Alerts does, but in general, and compared with other tools, Google Alerts covers the widest range of content.

You can easily set up Google Alerts by following these steps:

1. **Navigate to** www.google.com/alerts **in your web browser.**

 The Alerts page loads, welcoming you to the Google Alerts website.

2. **In the Search query text box, type the keyword or phrase that you want to monitor.**

 If you enter a phrase in which the words have to go together in that particular order, put the phrase in quotes.

3. **From the Result Type drop-down list, select the type of monitoring that you want to use.**

The options send you different kinds of alerts:

- *Everything:* All types of Internet content available
- *News:* Only news sources
- *Blogs:* Blog sources
- *Video*: Video sources, such as YouTube
- *Discussions:* Discussion sources, such as social media
- *Books*: Mentions in the text of books

Select the Everything option so that you receive alerts in all areas of Internet content available on the web. This gives you wider coverage in regards to your tool.

4. **Select the frequency of updates from the How Often drop-down list.**

Because you'll receive the updates via RSS and not e-mail (which you set up in Step 6), you want the highest frequency possible. So, select the As-It-Happens option. (Other options include a daily, weekly, and monthly digest.)

5. **From the How Many drop-down list, select the amount of items you want to appear in each update.**

If you selected As-It-Happens in Step 4, you receive items in real time, so you don't need to specify the amount of items — select either Only the Best Results or All Results.

6. **Select your delivery type from the Deliver To drop-down list.**

To make the delivery source an RSS feed, as opposed to an e-mail, select Feed.

7. **Click the Create Alert button.**

Your Google Alert Management screen, where you can get the RSS feeds for all your Google Alerts, appears.

8. **To get the URL of the RSS feed, right-click the Feed hyperlink next to the orange RSS icon and choose Copy Link Location from the pop-up menu that appears.**

9. **Paste the copied link location into a document in which you list all the feeds that you plan to aggregate later.**

10. **Repeat Steps 2 through 9 for all the terms you want to monitor.**

Before you start importing the feed into your WordPress Dashboard, you might want to receive the update via e-mail for a few days to test the quality of the results you're getting; if your results aren't quite right, you can always narrow your search criteria. Doing this saves you the time of parsing all your

RSS feeds, blending them all together, and then having to go back and edit everything because it's set up wrong. Using the e-mail as a test is a massive timesaver.

Tracking conversations on Twitter with RSS

Tracking mentions on Twitter via RSS is relatively simple: You just need to know what you're looking for and how to build the RSS links so you can monitor them. You can look for several items on Twitter to monitor your brand and reputation via the Twitter social network, including the following:

+ **Username:** Monitor when your Twitter name is mentioned and by who.

+ **Hashtags:** Monitor specific Twitter hashtags (for example, #wordpress).

+ **Keywords:** Monitor Twitter for a specific word.

Twitter does not make it very easy to locate the native RSS feed URL on its website; however the feeds do exist and can be found using a URL such as this example: `http://search.twitter.com/search.atom?q=`*XXX* — where *XXX* is the keyword, hashtag, or username you'd like to monitor. The following examples can help you build various RSS links for Twitter:

+ Twitter RSS URL for a username: `http://search.twitter.com/search.atom?q=LisaSabinWilson`

+ Twitter RSS URL for a keyword: `http://search.twitter.com/search.atom?q=wordpress`

+ Twitter RSS URL for a hashtag: `http://search.twitter.com/search.atom?q=#wordpress`

Build the Twitter RSS URLs that you want to monitor and include them in the document where you're listing all the RSS Feeds you want to aggregate later.

Listening to blogs with Google Blog Search

Google Blog Search (`www.google.com/blogsearch`) is a blog search service created by Google. It often catches blogs that other services don't.

Google Blog Search monitors blogs only. It can't give you results from message boards or other social media sites.

You can set up monitoring via RSS with Google Blog Search by following these steps:

1. **Navigate to** `www.google.com/blogsearch`.

The Google Blogs website loads in your browser window.

2. **Type your search term in the Search text box.**

This text box appears in the center of the page.

3. **Click Enter.**

   After Google does the search, it takes you to a results page.

4. **Copy the RSS feed link of the blog search results page.**

   The RSS link appears at the very bottom of the blog search results page.

5. **Paste this link location into a document in which you list all the feeds that you plan to aggregate later.**

6. **Repeat Steps 2 through 5 to add as many Google Blog monitoring terms as you want.**

Searching communities with Boardreader

Boardreader (http://boardreader.com) is a must-add tool because its niche focuses on groups and message boards, where conversations have been happening much longer than on just Facebook and Twitter. Many other monitoring tools often overlook these areas when talking about monitoring the web, but you can find so many vibrant communities that are worth being a part of, in addition to monitoring what is being said about your blog or company.

To set up your Boardreader tracking, follow these steps:

1. **Navigate to** http://boardreader.com.

2. **In the text box, type the search term that you want to monitor; then click the Search button.**

3. **When the results appear, click the Show Tools link below the Search text box.**

   The RSS Feed link appears.

4. **Right-click the RSS Feed link next to the orange RSS icon and choose Copy Link Location from the pop-up menu that appears.**

5. **Paste this link location into a document in which you list all the feeds that you plan to aggregate later.**

6. **Repeat Steps 1 through 5 to search for and monitor as many different search terms as you want.**

Microblog searching with Twingly

Twingly Microblog Search (www.twingly.com/microblogsearch) deals with real-time search microblogging and traditional blog search. Their microblog service monitors conversations on Twitter only.

Compare the results you get from Twingly with Twitter Search, just to make sure that Twingly is picking up everything on Twitter.

To monitor conversations by using Twingly, follow these steps:

1. **Navigate to** www.twingly.com/microblogsearch.

2. **In the text box, type the search term that you want to monitor; then click the Microblog Search button.**

   All the relevant search results appear, as shown in Figure 2-1.

3. **On the right sidebar, right-click the Subscribe to RSS link next to the orange RSS icon and choose Copy Link Location from the pop-up menu that appears.**

4. **Paste this link location into a document in which you list all the feeds that you plan to aggregate later.**

5. **Repeat Steps 1 through 4 for all the terms you want to monitor.**

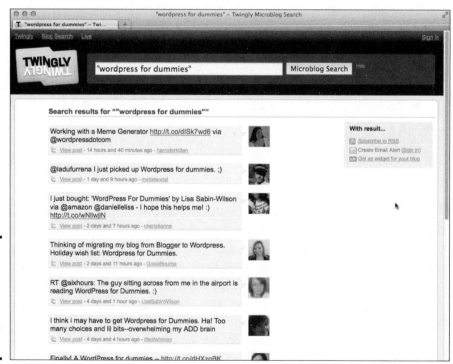

Figure 2-1:
Searching for WordPress For Dummies on Twingly.

Creating Your Own Personal Monitoring Mix

After trying out the various monitoring services, you can create a mix of services to import into your WordPress Dashboard. You import the results of these monitoring services with the help of RSS (Really Simple Syndication). You can combine different single RSS feeds into one RSS feed and create an organized setup for all the information you have to manage. For example, if you have various RSS feeds from different sources around the keyword *cookies,* you can combine them all into one RSS feed. Or if you want to combine various feeds based off sources, like all your Twitter RSS feeds, you can do that as well.

Look for the orange RSS icon that's usually found on the URL bar of your browser. Additionally, some sites offer an RSS export on the right sidebar or in the search bar for the site. Grab the address of all these feeds by clicking the feed name and copying the feed URL from the browser.

Grouping your monitoring results

After you copy the locations for all your RSS feeds in one document, you need to group those RSS feeds together. Grouping your RSS feeds keeps your monitoring system nice and tidy and allows you to more easily set up the WordPress Dashboard. After you group these feeds, you splice them together to make one master feed per grouping (see the following section). If you're tracking a variety of keywords, you may want to put your feeds into groups. For example, Wendy's Restaurants could make these keyword groupings:

✦ **Grouping 1:** Your brand, products, and other information around your company

- Wendy's (the company name)

- Frosties (a prominent product name)

- Dave Thomas (a prominent person in the company)

✦ **Grouping 2:** Competitors

- McDonald's

- Burger King

- In-N-Out

✦ **Grouping 3:** Keyword-based searches (Burgers)

- Hamburgers

- Cheeseburgers

✦ **Grouping 4:** Keyword-based searches (Fast Food)

- Fast food

- Drive thru

✦ **Grouping 5:** Keyword-based searches (Chicken)

- Chicken sandwiches

- Chicken salad

- Chicken nuggets

In each of these groups, you place your Google Alerts feed, Twingly feed, and whatever other feeds you feel will provide information about that subject area. You can blend each group of feeds together into one master feed for that group and bring them into WordPress.

WordPress limits you to five groups total. Any more than five groups slows down the Dashboard and is more than WordPress really can handle.

Grouping all your various feeds together gives you the most complete monitoring solution by covering multiple monitoring tools and blending them together. You get more coverage of your brand or blog than you would by just using Google Alerts. On the downside, you may see some duplicates because of overlaps between the different services.

If you feel overwhelmed by duplicate search results, you can blend one feed that covers only your brand, or you can simplify setting up your monitoring even more and avoid blending the feeds by keeping one feed for each item. For example:

✦ **General overview:** Google Alerts or Social Mention

✦ **Message boards:** Boardreader

✦ **Microblogging:** Twitter Search

Editing the Dashboard to Create a Listening Post

After you choose your data sources, clean up your feeds, and put them all in individual RSS feeds, you can finally bring them into WordPress and set up your social media listening hub.

You can bring these RSS feeds onto your Dashboard through the use of a plugin called Dashboard-Last-News, which you can find in the WordPress Plugin Repository at the following page:

```
http://wordpress.org/extend/plugins/dashboard-last-news
```

Follow these steps to set up the Dashboard Last News plugin and configure it to create a social-listening Dashboard in WordPress:

1. **From the Plugins menu on the left side of your WordPress installation, choose Add New.**

    This step takes you to the form where you can search for new plugins.

2. **In the Search text box, type** dashboard-last-news **and click the Search Plugins button.**

    The search results page appears.

3. **Search for the Dashboard-Last-News plugin and click the Install Now link, which installs the plugin on your site.**

4. **After the installation is complete, activate the plugin by clicking the Activate Plugin link on the Installed Plugin menu that appears below the Plugin menu.**

5. **Click the Last News link on the Settings menu on the Dashboard.**

    A new menu appears, and you can use it to select how many Dashboard widgets you want for your RSS.

6. **Select the number of Last News Dashboard widgets you want (up to five) from the drop-down list on the Dashboard-Last-News page. Then click Update.**

7. **Click the Dashboard link on the menu on the left to go back to your Dashboard.**

    A Last News section that contains the widgets you created in Step 6 appears on your Dashboard.

8. **To configure a widget, hover your pointer over the menu bar for that widget and, when the word Configure appears, click it.**

    The screen reloads, and you can now completely configure the widget.

9. **Enter a name for the widget in the Widget Title text box.**

    You may want to name it according to the subject area it covers. The example dashboard has data coming in around Social Media and Design to go along with the terms we are monitoring.

10. **(Optional) Select the Image (Y/N) check box to add an image next to the individual search results in the widget.**

    You may not want to include images, because most of the images that are automatically pulled are voting option buttons or other feed image buttons, which don't add anything by having. Also, images slow down the load time.

11. **Select a number from the Lines to Display drop-down list, which specifies how many online entries that the monitoring tools have found that you want to appear in the widget.**

    You can choose between 1 and 40.

12. **Paste the URL for your selected RSS Feed into the Fill the RSS or Atom URL Here text box and click Submit. (See Figure 2-2.)**

13. **Repeat Steps 8 through 12 for the other widgets on your Dashboard by using your other selected feeds.**

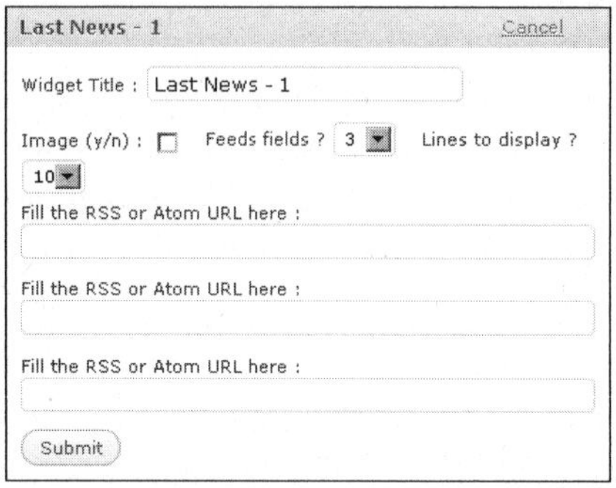

Figure 2-2: Configuring the Last News widget.

After you have your feeds set up, you can configure the appearance of your WordPress Dashboard.

14. **Drag and drop the new widget boxes where you want them on your Dashboard.**

15. **(Optional) Expand the number of columns and remove current widgets by clicking the Screen Options link in the upper-right corner of the Dashboard and then selecting or deselecting the check boxes for the widgets in the drop-down list that appears.**

Chapter 3: Understanding Analytics

In This Chapter

✓ Understanding how analytics can tell you about your blog

✓ Choosing an analytics-tracking option

✓ Deciphering analytics terminology

✓ Working with Google Analytics

*E*very business on the face of the Earth needs to figure out what works and what doesn't if it wants to succeed. Bloggers often know basic statistics about their blogs, such as the current number on their hit counters or how many people subscribe to their blogs. These stats may give you the big picture, but they don't really address why something is or isn't working.

You need to get at least a basic understanding of analytics if you want to make the most of your blog. The data provided by free programs such as Google Analytics can really help you grow as a blogger. In this chapter, you discover how to incorporate various data-measuring tools into your WordPress installation, deciphering what the data is telling you, and determining how to act on it.

Google Analytics provides you with a tremendous amount of information on your content. The goal of this chapter is to help you interpret the data, understand where your traffic is coming from, understand which of your content is the most popular among your visitors, know how to draw correlations between various data sets, and use this information to shape the content you write. This process may sound very geeky and accountant-like, but in reality, it gives you a roadmap that helps you improve your business.

Understanding the Importance of Analytics

Personally, I avoid math like my 7-year-old nephew avoids vegetables. Most people's eyes glaze over when they hear the word *analytics* followed by *stats,* any type of *percentages,* and anything that sounds like accountant-speak.

However, you should view analytics not as a bunch of numbers but as a tool set that tells a story. It can tell you how people are finding your content, what content is most popular, and where users are sharing that content. Knowing what type of content is popular, where your site is popular (in which time zones, countries, and states, for example), and even what time of day your posts get more readers is all valuable information. Understanding your audience's interest in your content, as well as preferences for when and how to read your content, is important.

At one point in my life, I had a pretty popular political blog. Through studying analytics and reactions to my content, I figured out that if I posted my blog between 9:30 a.m. and 10:00 a.m. EST, my posts garnered the most comments and got the most traffic throughout the day. When I posted after noon, my blog got about half as many comments and half as much traffic over a 24-hour period. Additionally, I saw that my site was getting shared and voted for on the social news site Reddit (www.reddit.com) more often than on Digg (www.digg.com), another social news site, so I replaced the Digg button with a Reddit button. This change increased the amount of traffic I received from Reddit because people had the visual reminder to share the post with their friends and vote for the post as a favorite of theirs.

I was able to continue to drill down from there. Not only did I have the information on where my content was being shared, but I was also able to garner more information for analytics. Posts that had a picture mixed in with the first three paragraphs often had a lower *bounce rate* (the interval of time it takes for a visitor to visit a site and then bounce away to a different site) than posts that had no picture at all. If I wrote the post while elevating my left leg and wearing a tinfoil helmet, I saw a 25 percent bump in traffic. (Okay, maybe that last one isn't true.)

Exploring the Options to Track Data

You have a lot of options when it comes to tracking data on your blog. Google Analytics is the most popular tool, but several different options are available. Analytics is popular because of its widespread use, the amount of content written on how to maximize it, and the fact that it is completely free.

Here are three popular tools:

✦ **StatCounter** (www.statcounter.com): StatCounter has both a free and a paid service. The paid service doesn't kick in until you get to 250K page views a month.

StatCounter (shown in Figure 3-1) uses the log generated by your server and gives you the ability to configure the reports to fit your needs. If you want to use a log file, you need to have a self-hosted blog and to know where your log file is stored. StatCounter requires a little more technical knowledge than your average analytics app because you have to deal with your log file instead of cutting and pasting a line of code into your site. The main advantage of StatCounter is that it is in real time, whereas Google Analytics always has a little bit of lag in its reporting.

Figure 3-1:
StatCounter
offers real-
time stats.

✦ **Jetpack** (http://wordpress.org/extend/plugins/jetpack): The Jetpack plugin provides a pretty good stat package for its hosted-blog users. Shortly after launching, WordPress.com provided a WordPress Stats plugin that self-hosted users can use. (See Figure 3-2.) If you use this package, your stats appear on the WordPress Dashboard, but to drill down deeper into them, you need to access the stats on WordPress. com. The advantages of WordPress stats are that they are pretty easy to install and present a very simplified overview of your data. On the down-side, they don't drill as deep as Google Analytics and the reporting isn't as in-depth. Nor can you customize reports.

✦ **Google Analytics** (www.google.com/analytics): Google Analytics can seem overwhelming when you sit in front of it for the first time, but it has the most robust stats features this side of Omniture. (Omniture is an enterprise-level stats package, which is overkill if you're a personal or small-business blogger.) Also, because Google has opened the analytics platform to developers, some pretty cool innovations for bloggers and social media people are on the way. This recent development gives you reason enough to try the platform.

Figure 3-2:
Try the
Jetpack
plugin.

WordPress plugins (covered in the section "Signing Up and Installing Google Analytics on Your WordPress Site," later in this chapter) bring a simplified version of Google Analytics (see Figure 3-3) to your WordPress Dashboard (much like the WordPress.com Stats plugin). If you feel overwhelmed by Google Analytics and prefer to have your stats broken down in a much more digestible fashion, this plugin is for you: It allows for a good overview of analytics information, including goals that you can set up. Although the plugin doesn't offer everything that Google Analytics brings to the table, it provides more than enough so that you can see the overall health of your website and monitor where your traffic is coming from, what posts are popular, and how people are finding your website. Besides the Dashboard Stats Overview, this plugin gives a breakdown of traffic to each post, which is a nice added bonus.

Figure 3-3:
Google
Analytics is
a powerful
tool.

Understanding Key Analytics Terminology

One of the reasons that people find analytics programs so overwhelming is their obscure terminology and jargon. Here, I've taken the time to define some of the more popular terms (I even spent the time putting them in alphabetical order for you; you can thank me later):

✦ **Bounce rate:** The percentage of single-page visits or visits in which the person leaves your site from the entrance page. This metric measures visit quality — a high bounce rate generally indicates that visitors don't find your site entrance pages relevant to them.

The more compelling your landing pages, the more visitors stay on your site and convert into purchasers, subscribers, or whatever action you want them to complete. You can minimize bounce rates by tailoring landing pages to each ad that you run (in the case of businesses) or to the audience based on the referring site (for example, if you create a special bio page for your Twitter profile). Landing pages should provide the information and services that the ad promises.

When it comes to blogging, a high bounce rate from a social media source (such as a social news site like Digg) can tell you that users didn't find the content interesting, and a high bounce rate from search engines can mean that your site isn't what users thought they were getting. In blogging, having a low bounce rate really speaks to the quality of the content on your site. If you get a lot of search and social media traffic, a bounce rate below 50 percent is a number you want to strive for.

✦ **Content:** The different pages within the site. (The Content menu of Google Analytics breaks down these pages so that they have their own statistics.)

✦ **Dashboard:** The interface with the overall summary of your analytics data. It's the first page you see when you log in to Google Analytics.

✦ **Direct traffic:** When web visitors reach your site by typing your web address directly into their browsers' address bars. (Launching a site by clicking a bookmark also falls into this category.) You can get direct-traffic visitors because of an offline promotion, repeat readers, word of mouth, or simply from your business card.

✦ **First-time unique visitor:** This metric tracks the number of visitors to your website who haven't visited prior to the time frame you're analyzing.

✦ **Hit:** Any request to the web server for any type of file, not just a post in your blog, including a page, an image (JPEG, GIF, PNG, and so on), a sound clip, or any of several other file types. An HTML page can account for several hits: the page itself, each image on the page, and any embedded sound or video clips. Therefore, the number of hits a website receives doesn't give you a valid popularity gauge, but rather it indicates server use and how many files have been loaded.

✦ **Keyword:** A database index entry that identifies a specific record or document. (That definition sounds way more fancy than a keyword actually is.) Keyword searching is the most common form of text search on the web. Most search engines do their text query and retrieval by using keywords. Unless the author of the web document specifies the keywords for his or her document (which you can do by using meta tags), the search engine has to determine them. (So you can't guarantee how Google indexes the page.) Essentially, search engines pull out and index words that it determines are significant. A search engine is more likely to deem words important if those words appear toward the beginning of a document and are repeated several times throughout the document.

✦ **Meta tag:** A special HTML tag that provides information about a web page. Unlike normal HTML tags, meta tags don't affect how the page appears in a user's browser. Instead, meta tags provide information such as who created the page, how often it's updated, a title for the page, a description of the page's content, and what keywords represent the page's content. Many search engines use this information when they build their indexes, although most major search engines rarely index the `keywords` meta tag anymore because it has been abused by people trying to fool search results.

✦ **Pageview:** A *page* is defined as any file or content delivered by a web server that would generally be considered a web document, which includes HTML pages (`.html`, `.htm`, `.shtml`), posts or pages within a WordPress installation, script-generated pages (`.cgi`, `.asp`, `.cfm`), and plain-text pages. It also includes sound files (`.wav`, `.aiff`, and so on), video files (`.mov`, `.mpeg`, and so on), and other nondocument files. Only image files (`.jpeg`, `.gif`, `.png`), JavaScript (`.js`), and Cascading Style Sheets (`.css`) are excluded from this definition. Each time a file defined as a page is served or viewed in a visitor's web browser, a *pageview* is registered by Google Analytics. The pageview statistic is more important and accurate than a hit statistic because it doesn't include images or other items that may register hits to your site.

✦ **Path:** A series of clicks that result in distinct pageviews. A path can't contain non-pages, such as image files.

✦ **Referrals:** A *referral* occurs when a user clicks any hyperlink that takes him or her to a page or file in another website; it could be text, an image, or any other type of link. When a user arrives at your site from another site, the server records the referral information in the hit log for every file requested by that user. If the user found the link by using a search engine, the server records the search engine's name and any keywords used, as well. Referrals give you an indication of what social-media site, as well as links from other websites and blogs, are directing traffic to your blog.

✦ **Referrer:** The URL of an HTML page that refers visitors to a site.

✦ **Traffic sources:** This metric tells you how visitors found your website — via direct traffic, referring sites, or search engines.

✦ **Unique visitors:** The number of unduplicated (counted only once) visitors to your website over the course of a specified time period. The server determines a unique visitor by using *cookies,* small tracking files stored in your visitors' browsers that keep track of the number of times they visit your site.

✦ **Visitor:** A stat designed to come as close as possible to defining the number of distinct people who visit a website. The website, of course, can't really determine whether any one "visitor" is really two people sharing a computer, but a good visitor-tracking system can come close to the actual number. The most accurate visitor-tracking systems generally employ cookies to maintain tallies of distinct visitors.

Signing Up and Installing Google Analytics on Your WordPress Site

In the following sections, you sign up for Google Analytics, install it on your blog, and add the WordPress plugin to your site.

Signing up for Google Analytics

To sign up for Google Analytics, follow these steps:

1. **Go to:** www.google.com/analytics **and click the Create an Account button, which is located on the top-right side of the page.**

   A page where you can sign up for a Google account or sign in via an existing Google account appears. If you don't have a Google account, follow the link to sign up for one.

2. **Sign in via your Google account by entering your e-mail address and password in the text boxes and then clicking Sign In.**

   The first of a series of walk-through pages appears.

3. **Click the Sign Up button.**

4. **On the What Would You Like to Track? page that appears (see Figure 3-4), fill in this information:**

   - The URL of your website

   - The name you want to call your account (this really doesn't matter; you can call it your website's name)

   - The country and time zone you're in

5. **Click the Get Tracking ID button.**

   The All Web Site Data page appears. (See Figure 3-5.)

   At the bottom of the page, Google Analytics provides you with your Google tracking code, as shown in Figure 3-6.

6. **Copy the tracking code by selecting it and pressing Ctrl+C.**

7. **Paste the Google tracking code into your WordPress blog.**

   If you're not sure how to complete this step, see the following section.

8. **Click the Save and Finish button.**

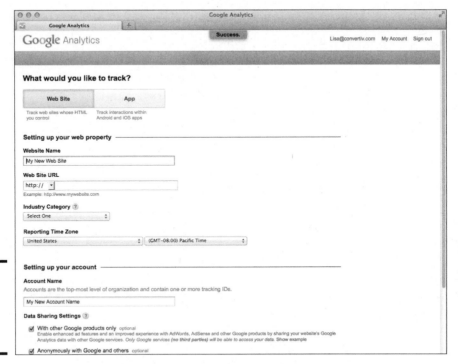

Figure 3-4:
Entering
a URL in
Google
Analytics.

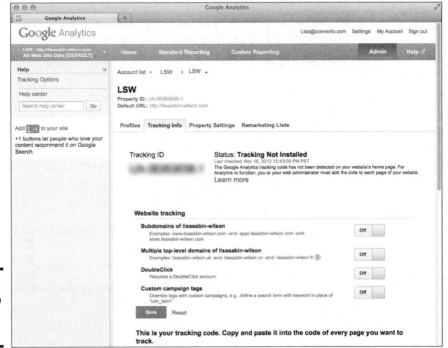

Figure 3-5:
The All Web
Site Data
page.

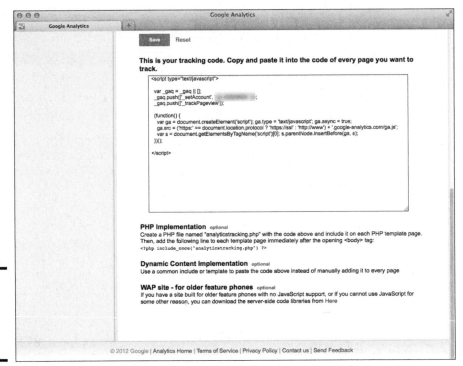

Figure 3-6:
Get your
Google
Analytics
code.

Installing the tracking code

After you set up your Google Analytics account and obtain the code to install in your WordPress site, you're ready for the installation. You can install Google Analytics by following these steps:

1. **Go to your WordPress Dashboard and log in.**

If you have a theme framework, such as Genesis or Thesis, you can paste the code in the theme's Options page, or if you're using one of the many Google for WordPress plugins, you can paste the code in the Plugin Options page. However, the simplest place you can paste the code is directly into your footer (the `footer.php` template file within your theme) because this location works for pretty much all WordPress-designed sites.

2. **Click the Appearance menu on the Dashboard and then click the Editor link.**

The Edit Themes page loads in your browser window.

3. **From the Templates menu on the right side of the Edit Themes page, click Footer (`footer.php`).**

This shows you the coding for the footer in the text box on the left side.

4. **Paste the Google Tracking code in the Footer Template file.**

Paste the code that you copied by pressing Ctrl+V. Be sure to paste the code before the closing body tag (`</body>`).

You have to put this code *before* the closing body tag, not after. If you put it after the close body tag, the code doesn't function.

5. **Click Update File.**

Figure 3-7 shows the Footer template from the Twenty Twelve theme with the Google Analytics code (from Figure 3-6) inserted above the closing `</body>` tag.

Verifying that you installed the code properly

After you install your code, check whether you installed it correctly. When you log back in to Google Analytics, your Dashboard appears. (See Figure 3-8.) The Dashboard shows the tracking data obtained from your website so far. Because your account is new, your tracking data will likely be a big fat zero, much like what you see in Figure 3-8.

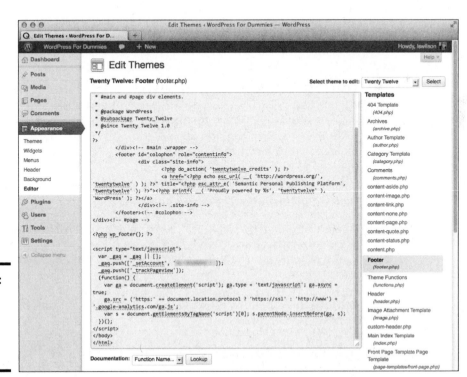

Figure 3-7:
Footer template with tracking code.

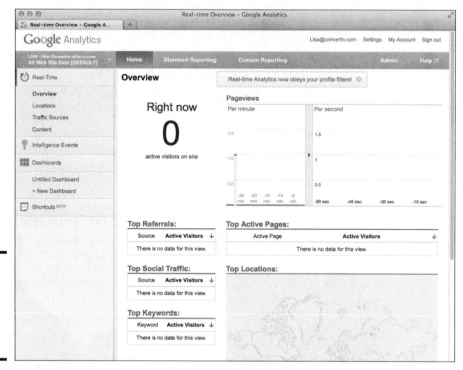

Figure 3-8:
Tracking
code in
place and
collecting
data.

Installing and configuring the Analytics plugin

After you install Google Analytics on your WordPress site and make sure that the tracking code is working properly, you can install the plugin so that you can get a basic version of your stats right on your WordPress Dashboard. Just follow these steps:

1. **Log in to your WordPress Dashboard.**

2. **On the Plugins menu, click the Add New link.**

   A search box appears so you can search for the plugin.

3. **In the Search text box, type** google analytics dashboard **and click the Install Now link.**

   This takes you to the Installing Plugin page.

4. **Activate the plugin by clicking the Activate Plugin link on the Installing Plugin page.**

5. **Click the Google Analytics Dashboard link on the Settings menu.**

   You can click the Start the Login process in the Login using the Google OAuth system, which automatically authorizes the plugin to access your Google Analytics account; alternatively, you can type your Google Analytics e-mail and password in the older authentication system section.

6. **Enter your information and click Save Options to log in.**

   A configuration page appears. (See Figure 3-9.)

7. **From the Available Accounts drop-down list, select the analytics account from which you want to pull your stats.**

8. **(Optional) Select the check boxes to remove your password and authentication information from Google.**

   You select these check boxes if you want to deactivate the plugin. If you only select to forget password or forget authentication, you will have to log back in to the menu like in Step 6.

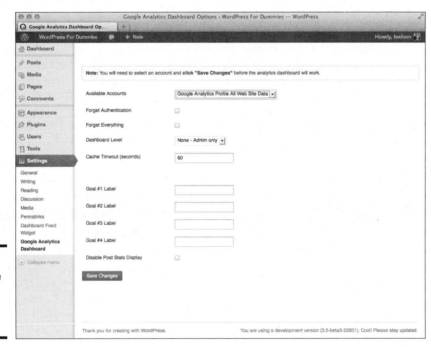

Figure 3-9:
The Google
Analytics
configura-
tion page.

9. **Specify the level (or role, such as Administrator, Contributor, and so on) of WordPress users who can see the stats by selecting an option from the Dashboard Level drop-down list.**

   This is good if your blog has multiple authors.

10. **Label your goals within analytics by entering the titles of your goals in the text boxes.**

    Goal labels can help people who are tracking specific metrics, such as sales, sign-ups, or other actions, to see whether people are converting.

11. **Click the Save Changes button.**

The plugin appears on your Dashboard.

12. **Drag and drop the plugin to the position you prefer.**

Figure 3-10 shows a WordPress Dashboard with the Google Analytics plugin.

Using the data from the plugin

After you install Google Analytics on your WordPress Dashboard, you can examine the data it provides. Your Dashboard displays two basic groups of stats:

✦ **A general overview:** The stats here include the amount of visits, pageviews, pageviews per visit, bounce rate, average time on site, and the percent of new visits. This information gives you a good overview of the base stats of your blog.

✦ **An extended stats section:** Stats here include the most popular post over the last 30 days, the top searches that found your site, and the top referrers. These stats show you the most popular content on your site, the ways people are finding your site, and the sources of your traffic. If you want get even more detailed information, go to the Posts section on WordPress (see Figure 3-11), where you can find per-page stats for each of your posts and pages. Each breakdown has a chart, number of pageviews, number of exits, and the number of unique pageviews.

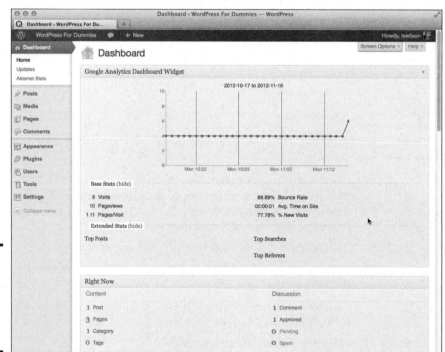

Figure 3-10:
Google Analytics on your WordPress Dashboard.

Figure 3-11:
A per-post
breakdown
by Google
Analytics for
WordPress.

By examining the two data sets, you can get a handle on the traffic that's coming to your blog. Pay attention to the following questions:

- ✦ What posts are popular?

- ✦ Do the popular posts have a unique theme or type?

- ✦ Do long posts or short posts help increase traffic?

- ✦ Do videos, lists, or any other type of specific posts give you more traffic than the rest?

The answers to these questions can help you draw various conclusions and adapt your publishing schedule, content type, and writing style to optimize the popularity of your blog.

Chapter 4: Search Engine Optimization

In This Chapter

✔ **Appreciating search engine optimization (SEO) benefits**

✔ **Improving your SEO with WordPress**

✔ **Getting your blog into good SEO shape**

✔ **Finding information about your niche**

✔ **Creating SEO-improvement strategies**

Google, Yahoo!, Bing, and other search engines have a massive impact on a website. Search engines can easily refer the largest amount of traffic to your site and, if dealt with properly, can help you grow a large audience in time. Often, bloggers don't discover the importance of search engine optimization (SEO) until their blogs have been around for a while. By taking the time to make sure that you're following SEO best practices from the get-go, you can reap the rewards of a consistent flow of search engine traffic.

If you've been blogging for a while and haven't been following the practices in this chapter, roll up your sleeves and dive back into your blog to fix some of the SEO practices that you may have overlooked (or just didn't know about) over the history of your blog. If you've been blogging for only a few months, this process doesn't take long; if you have a large backlog of content, well . . . pull up a chair — this fix is going to take a while. Either way, don't worry. You're in safe hands. This chapter helps you through the difficult task of optimizing your site for search engines.

Understanding the Importance of Search Engine Optimization

Talk about search engine optimization (SEO) usually puts most people to sleep. I'm not going to lie: Hardcore SEO is a time-consuming job that requires a strong analytical mind. Casual bloggers, or even most small-business owners, don't need to understand all the minute details that go into SEO. However, everyone with a website who desires traffic needs to get familiar with some of the basic concepts and best practices. Why, you ask?

One thousand pageviews. That's why.

Of course, you're not going to get 1,000 page views right off the bat by changing your SEO.

SEO deals with following best practices when it comes to blogging. By just following these simple guidelines and by using WordPress, you can increase search engine traffic to your blog. Period. To be honest, you probably won't rank number one in really tough categories just by following SEO best practices. But you definitely can increase your traffic significantly and improve your rank for some long-tail keywords. *Long-tail keywords* are keywords that aren't searched for often, but when you amass ranking for a lot of them over a period of time, the traffic adds up.

You want as many search results as possible on the first two pages of Google and other search engines to be from your blogs. (Most search-engine visitors don't go past the first two pages of Google.) This search-results aim is a more reasonable goal than trying to rank number one for a highly competitive keyword. If you really do want to rank number one in a competitive space, check out sites such as SEO Book (www.seobook.com) and SEOmoz (www.seomoz.org), which can help you achieve that difficult goal.

Outlining the Advantages That WordPress Presents for SEO

Using WordPress for your blogging platform or content management system comes with some advantages, including that WordPress is designed to function well with search engines. Search engines can crawl the source code of a WordPress site pretty easily, which eliminates issues that a lot of web programmers face when optimizing a site. The following list outlines some of WordPress's SEO advantages:

✦ **Permalinks:** URLs where your content is permanently housed. As your blog grows and you add more posts, the items on your front page get pushed off the front page of your blog and are replaced by recent content. Visitors can easily bookmark and share permalinks so that they can return to that specific post on your blog, so these old posts can live on. One of the technical benefits of WordPress is that it uses the Apache `mod_rewrite` module to establish the permalink system, which allows you to create and customize your permalink structure. (See Book III, Chapter 2 for more information on custom permalinks.)

✦ **Pinging:** When you post new content, WordPress has a built-in pinging system that notifies major indexes automatically so that they can come and crawl your site again. This system helps speed up the indexing process and keeps your search results current and relevant.

✦ **Plugins:** The fact that WordPress is so developer friendly allows you to use the latest SEO plugins. Do you want to submit a sitemap to Google? There's a plugin for that. Do you want to edit the metadata around a post? There's a plugin for that. Do you want to alert Google News every time you post? Guess what . . . there's a plugin for that, too. With over 10,000 plugins available at press time, you can use an advanced and eager plugin ecosystem to help power your blog. Chapter 5 of this minibook covers a few key plugins that can help you with SEO.

✦ **Theme construction:** SEO, social media, and design all go hand in hand. You can push a ton of people to your web page by using proper SEO and robust social-media profiles, but if your blog has a confusing or poorly done design, visitors aren't going to stay. Likewise, a poorly designed site prevents a lot of search engines from reading your content.

In this situation, *poorly designed* doesn't refer to aesthetics — how your site looks to the eye. Search engines ignore the style of your site and your CSS for the most part. But the structure, the coding, of your site can affect search engines that are attempting to crawl your site. WordPress is designed to accommodate search engines: It doesn't overload pages with coding so that search engines can easily access the site. Most WordPress themes have valid code (code that is up to standards based on the recommendations from www.w3c.org, The World Wide Web Consortium): Right from the start, having valid code allows search engines to access your site much more easily.

When you start changing your code or adding a lot of plugins to your site, check to see whether your code validates. Validated code means that the code on your website fits a minimum standard for browsers. Otherwise, you could be preventing search engines from easily crawling your sites.

If you want to check out whether your site validates, use the free W3C validator tool at http://validator.w3.org. (See Figure 4-1.)

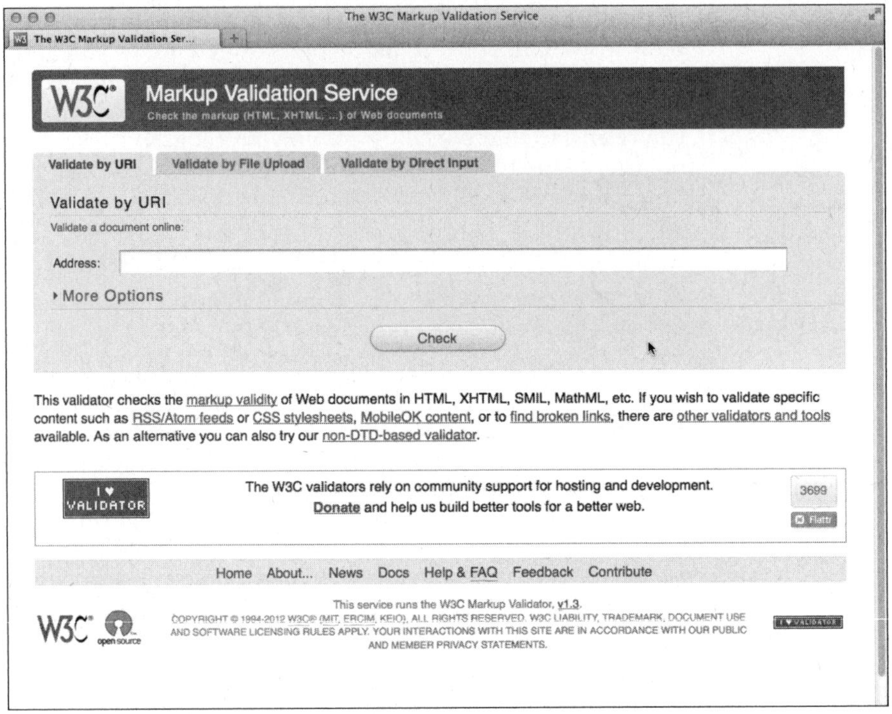

Figure 4-1:
The W3C
Markup
Validation
Service.

Understanding How Search Engines See Your Content

Search engines don't care what your site looks like because they can't see what your site looks like; their crawlers care only about the content. The crawlers care about the material in your blog, the way it's titled, the words you use, and the way you structure those words.

You need to keep this focus in mind when you create the content of your blog. Your URL structure and the keywords, post titles, and images you use in posts all have an impact on how your blog ranks. Having a basic understanding about how search engines view your content can help you write content that's more attractive to search engines. Here are a few key areas to think about when you craft your content:

✦ **Keywords in content:** Search engines take an intense look at the keywords or combination of keywords you use. Keywords are often compared to the words found within links guiding people back to the post and in the title of the post itself to see if they match. The better these keywords align, the better ranking you get from the search engine.

✦ **Post title:** Search engines analyze the title of your blog post for keyword content. If you're targeting a specific keyword in your post and that keyword is mentioned throughout the post, mention it in the post title, as well. Also, both people and search engines place a lot of value on the early words of a title.

✦ **URL structure:** One of the coolest things about WordPress is the way it allows you to edit permalinks from within a post page. (See Figure 4-2.) You can always edit the URL to be slightly different from the automated post title so that it contains relevant keywords for search terms, especially if you write a cute title for the post.

For example, say you write a post about reviewing Facebook applications and title it "So Many Facebook Applications, So Little Time." You can change the URL structure to something much more keyword based — perhaps something like `facebook-applications-review`. This reworking removes a lot of the fluff words from the URL and goes right after keywords you want to target.

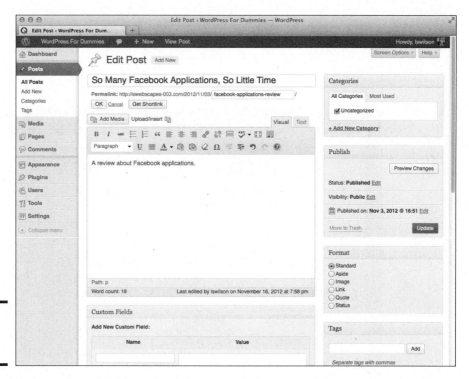

Figure 4-2:
Editing a
permalink.

✦ **Image titles and other image information:** This is probably the most-missed item when it comes to SEO. You need to fill out the image information for your posts because this is a powerful way for people to discover your content and an additional piece of content that can tie keywords to your posts. (See Figure 4-3.) This information includes the filename of your image. Saving an image file to your site as `DS-039.jpg` offers nothing for readers or search engines and thus has no value to search engines or for you because it doesn't contain a real keyword. Name a picture of a Facebook application, for example, as `Facebook-application.jpg`. Leverage the keyword title and alt tags (alternative text added to the image within the HTML markup that tell search engines what the picture is) because they provide extra content for the search engines to see and using them can help you get a little more keyword saturation within your posts.

Using links as currency

If content is king, then links are the currency that keeps the king in power. No matter how good a site you have, how great your content, and how well you optimize that content, you need links. Search engines assess the links flowing into your site for number and quality, and they evaluate your website accordingly.

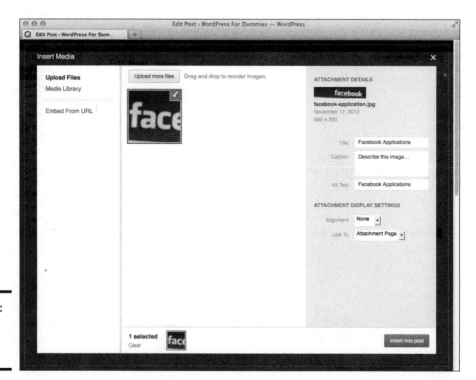

Figure 4-3:
The Insert Media window.

If a high-quality site that has a high Google Page Rank (a value from 0 to 10) features a link to your page, search engines take notice and assume that you have authority on a subject. Search engines consider these high-quality links more important than low-quality links. However, having a good amount of mid-quality links can help, as well. (This tactic, like many well-known approaches to improving site rank, is based only on trial and error. Google keeps its algorithm a secret, so no one knows for sure.)

Getting listed on a blogroll, having a pingback or trackback when a blogger mentions your content in their posts, or even leaving a comment on someone's blog can provide links back into your site. If you want to check out how many links you currently have coming into your site, go to Google and type **link:www.*yoursite*.com** into the search text box and click Google Search. You can also search for competitor's sites to see where they're listed and to what sites they're linked.

Although you do need to try and get other sites to link to your site (called outside links) because outside links factor into search engine algorithms, you can help your own ranking by adding internal links, as well. If you have an authoritative post or page on a particular subject, you should link internally to it within your site. Take ESPN.com, for example: The first time it mentions an athlete in an article, it links to the profile of that athlete on the site. It essentially tells the search engines each time they visit ESPN.com that the player profile has relevancy, and the search engine indexes it. If you repeatedly link some of your internal pages that are gaining page rank to a profile page over a period of time, that profile page is going to garner a higher search engine ranking (especially if external sites are linking to it, too).

This internal and external linking strategy uses the concept of pillar posts (authoritative or popular), in which you have a few pages of content that you consider high value and try to build external and internal links into them so that you can get these posts ranked highly on search results.

Submitting to search engines and directories

After you get some content onto your website (usually ten posts or so), submit your blog to some search engines. Plenty of sites out there charge you to submit your site to search engines, but honestly, you can submit your site easily yourself. Also, with the help of some plugins (described in Book V, Chapter 5), you can get your information to search engines even more easily than you may think.

After you submit your website or sitemap, a search engine reviews it for search engine crawling errors; if everything checks out, you're on your way to having your site crawled and indexed. This process — from the submission of your site through its first appearance in search engine results — can easily take four to six weeks. So be patient: Don't resubmit and don't freak out that search engines are never going to list your site. Give it time.

Not to be confused with search engines are website and blog directories. Directories can lead to a small amount of traffic, and some directories, such as dmoz (www.dmoz.org), actually supply information to search engines and other directories. The main benefit of getting listed in directories isn't really traffic but rather the amount of backlinks (links to your site from other websites) you can build into your site.

Although submitting your blog to directories may not be as important as submitting to search engines, you may still want to do it. Because filling out 40 or more forms is pretty monotonous, create a single document in which you prewrite all the necessary information: site title, URL, description, contact information, and your registration information. This template helps speed up the submission process to these sites.

Optimizing Your Blog under the Hood

Some optimization concepts really happen "under the hood" — you can't readily see these adjustments on your page, but they have an impact on how search engines deal with your content.

Metadata

The metadata on a website contains the information that describes to search engines what your site is about. Additionally, the information often contained in the metadata shows up as the actual search engine results in Google. The search engine pulls the page title and page description that appear in search results from the header of your blog. If you do nothing to control this information, Google and other search engines often pull their description from the page title and the first few sentences of a blog post.

Although the title and the first few sentences sound good in principle, they probably don't represent what your blog post is actually about. You probably don't sum up your post topic in the first two sentences of that post. Those first few lines likely aren't the best ad copy or the most enticing information. Thankfully, some plugins (such as the WordPress All in One SEO Pack plugin found in the WordPress plugin directory at http://wordpress.org/extend/plugins/all-in-one-seo-pack) allow you to control these details on a post and page level. Additionally, theme frameworks (see Book VI, Chapter 7) such as Genesis offer you more control over your SEO information.

Include descriptive page titles, descriptions, and targeted keywords for each post via these plugins or frameworks: This information has an impact on your results and often helps people decide to click the link to your website.

Robots.txt

When a search engine goes to your website, it first looks at your `robots.txt` file to get the information about what it should and shouldn't be looking for and where to look.

You can alter your `robots.txt` file to direct search engines to the information that they should crawl and to give specific content priority over other content. Several plugins allow you to configure your `robots.txt` file, which Book V, Chapter 5 covers.

Researching Your Niche

When you're working to improve your SEO, you can use a lot of publicly available data. This data can help you determine where you should try to get links and what type of content you may want to target. These two sites can help you get a general picture of the niche you're working in:

✦ **Google (**`www.google.com`**):** You can find what types of links are flowing into a website by typing **link:www.*yoursite.com*** into the Google search text box and clicking Google Search. (Replace *yoursite.com* with the domain you want to target.) Google gives you a list of the sites linking to your site. By doing this search for other websites in your niche, you can find out the sources of their links — industry-specific directories you may not know about, places where they've guest blogged, or other resource sites that you may be able to get listed on.

This data gives you information about what to target for a link-building campaign.

✦ **SEMRush (**`www.semrush.com`**):** SEMRush (see Figure 4-4) offers both paid and free versions, and spending a few dollars for a month's access to the light version of the product can be a good investment. (The free version lets you look up only ten results at a time.) SEMRush allows you to see the terms for which other websites rank. Use this information to judge the health of the competitor's domain, the number of terms for which it ranks in Google's top 20, and the terms themselves.

You can use this information in a lot of different ways. For example, you can see what terms you might want to work into your content. SEMRush provides not only information about what terms search engines use to rank these sites but also how competitive some of those keywords are with other websites that are similar to yours.

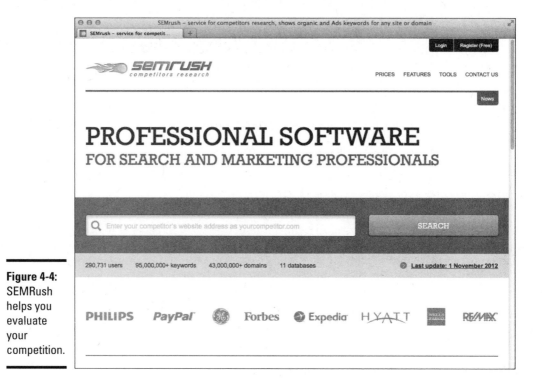

Figure 4-4:
SEMRush
helps you
evaluate
your
competition.

Creating Search Engine Strategies

You can use the techniques discussed in previous sections of this chapter when you set up your blog, write strategic content, and begin to build links into your website. The next section deals with setting up your website so that it is optimized for search engines.

Setting up your blog

When setting up your blog, you're going to want to follow some best practices to make sure that your site is optimized for search engines. Some of these best practices include

✦ **Permalinks:** First, set up your permalink structure. Log in to your WordPress account and, on your sidebar, select Permalinks in the Settings section. The Permalink Settings page appears. (See Figure 4-5.) Select the Post Name radio button.

Making this change gives you a URL that contains just your domain and the title of your blog post. If you use a really focused category structure in which you've carefully picked out keywords, you may want to add the category to the URL. In that case, you enter */%category%/%postname%/* in the text box.

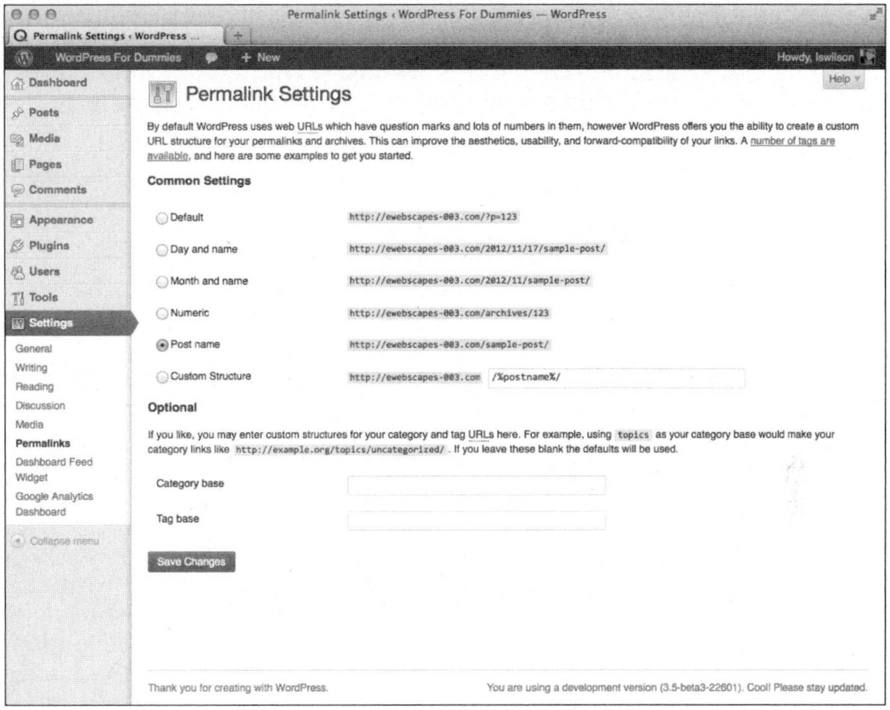

Figure 4-5:
The
WordPress
Permalinks
Settings
page.

Avoid using the default URL structure, which includes just the number of your post, and don't use dates in the URL. These numbers have no real value when doing SEO. WordPress by default numbers all your posts and pages with specific ID numbers. If you have not set up a custom permalink structure in WordPress, permalinks for your posts end up looking something like this: `http://yourdomain.com/?p=12` (where 12 is the specific post ID number). Although these numbers are used for many WordPress features, including exclusions of data and customized RSS feeds, you don't want these numbers in your URLs because they do not contain any keywords that describe what the post is about.

Also, if you already have an established blog and are just now setting up these permalinks, you must take the time to install a redirection plugin. You can find several of these plugins available in the Plugin section on WordPress.org. You must establish a redirection for your older posts so that you don't lose the links that search engines, such as Google and Yahoo!, have already indexed for your site. One good redirection plugin to use is simply called Redirection, and it can be found in the WordPress plugin directory here: `http://wordpress.org/extend/plugins/redirection`.

✦ **Privacy:** You don't want your blog to fail to be indexed because you didn't set the correct privacy settings. On the WordPress Settings menu, click the Reading Settings link. On the resulting Reading Settings page, make sure that the I Would Like My Site to Be Visible to Everyone radio button is selected.

The other radio button, *I Would Like to Block Search Engines, but Allow Normal Visitors,* if selected, blocks search engines, which kind of defeats the purpose of SEO.

Improving your blog's design

After improving your setup in the back end of your blog, you'll want to make some changes to your design so your blog works better with search engines. Some improvements you can make to your theme templates include

✦ **Breadcrumbs:** Breadcrumbs, often overlooked when creating a website, provide the valuable navigation usually seen above the title on a blog post. (See Figure 4-6.) Breadcrumbs are pretty valuable for usability and search engine navigation. They allow the average user to navigate the site easily, and they help search engines determine the structure and layout of your site. A good plugin to use to create breadcrumb navigation is called Yoast Breadcrumbs and can be found in the WordPress plugin directory here: `http://wordpress.org/extend/plugins/breadcrumbs`.

✦ **Validated code and speed:** If you're not a professional web designer, you probably don't do a lot of coding to your site. But if you make some small edits to your WordPress installation or add a lot of code through widgets, do it properly by putting it directly into your CSS rather than coding into your site. Coding these features properly helps improve the speed of your site, and how search engines crawl the site. Book VI contains a great deal of information about coding the templates in your theme; check out that book for more information about correct coding.

When it comes to improving site speed, proper code has a lot to do with the performance of your site. You can take other steps to help improve the speed of your site, such as installing caching plugins, including the W3 Total Cache plugin (`http://wordpress.org/extend/plugins/w3-total-cache`). The quality of your hosting (Book II, Chapter 1), the size of your image files (make sure that you set image-file quality to web standards), the amount of images you're using, and third-party widgets or scripts (such as installing a widget provided by Twitter or Facebook) can all impact the speed and performance of your site. If you're putting special widgets developed by sites such as blog catalog, traffic exchange sites, or banner exchange sites, these require information from other sites to load. Depending on these other sites for quick load times can often lead to slow loading times on your own site.

Figure 4-6:
Users and
search
engines
can follow
the bread-
crumbs.

Breadcrumbs

✦ **Pagination:** Another basic design feature often overlooked when setting up a site, *pagination* creates bottom navigation that allows people and search engines to navigate to other pages. (See Figure 4-7.) Pagination can really help both people and search engines navigate through your category pages.

Most themes don't have built-in pagination, so you have to add a plugin to accomplish this effect. A few of these kinds of plugins are on the market; check out Book V, Chapter 5.

✦ **Avoid sidebar bloat:** If you have a *huge* blogroll, don't include it on your sidebar throughout the site. In fact, if you want to include something that huge, create a page for all your links; having them on your sidebar throughout the site slows down the page-loading speed for your visitors, and all the outbound links bleeds page rank all over the place.

Links pass on authority. When you link to a site or a site links to you, the link is saying that your site has value for the keyword in the link. So evaluate the links that you have and think about whether you really want to link to that website.

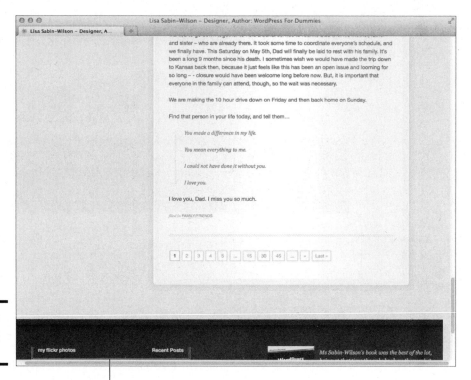

and sister – who are already there. It took some time to coordinate everyone's schedule, and we finally have. This Saturday on May 5th, Dad will finally be laid to rest with his family. It's been a long 9 months since his death. I sometimes wish we would have made the trip down to Kansas back then, because it just feels like this has been an open issue and looming for so long – - closure would have been welcome long before now. But, it is important that everyone in the family can attend, though, so the wait was necessary.

We are making the 10 hour drive down on Friday and then back home on Sunday.

Find that person in your life today, and tell them...

You made a difference in my life.

You mean everything to me.

I could not have done it without you.

I love you.

I love you, Dad. I miss you so much.

filed in FAMILY/FRIENDS

Figure 4-7:
Pagination
in action.

Pagination

Often, when bloggers start blogging, they sign up for every service under the sun, including websites that require them to place reciprocal links or banners on their sites. All those links and banners quickly turn your website into a bad NASCAR car, and your site's performance degrades because it needs to load all those external codes. Be very picky about what you put into your sidebar.

Dealing with duplicate content

WordPress does have one major problem when it comes to SEO: It creates so many places for your content to live that duplicate content can confuse search engines. Thankfully, plugins and some basic editing easily take care of these issues. Here's what to do:

✦ **Take care of your archive page on your site**. This is the page that displays archives such as category, date-based archives, and so on. You don't want your archive page to present full blog posts, only truncated versions (short excerpts) of your posts. Check your theme to see how your archive is presented. If your archive shows complete posts, see whether your theme has instructions about how to change your archive presentation. (Each theme is unique, but check out the information in Book VI; it's full of great information about tweaking and altering theme template files.)

✦ **Make sure that search engines aren't indexing all your archives by using a robots plugin.** You want robots going through only your category archive, not the author index and other archives.

Creating an editorial SEO list/calendar

Planning your posts from now until the end of time can take some of the fun out of blogging. Still, it doesn't hurt to create a list of keywords that your competitors rank for and some of the content they've discussed. Take that list and apply it to new posts, or write *evergreen content* (topics that aren't timely) centered on what you want to say. Planning out your blog can really help in figuring out what keywords you want to target when you want to write content to improve for ranking for targeted keywords.

If you feel that your blog is more news- or current-events oriented, create a reference list of keywords to incorporate into your newer posts so that you can rank for these targeted terms.

Establishing a routine for publishing posts on your site

Although you can't really call this high strategy, getting into the habit of posting content regularly on your site helps you get the basics down. Here are some things to keep in mind:

✦ **Properly title your post.** Make sure that your post includes the keyword or phrase for which you're trying to rank.

✦ **Fix your URL.** Get rid of stop words or useless words from your URL and make sure that the keywords you want to target appear in the URL of your post. *Stop words* are filler words such as *a*, *so*, *in*, *an*, and so on. For a comprehensive list of stop words, check out this list: www.link-assistant.com/seo-stop-words.html.

✦ **Choose a category.** Make sure that you have your categories set up and that you properly place your post into the category it falls under. Whatever you do, don't use the uncategorized category — it brings no SEO value to the table.

✦ **Fill out metadata.** If you're using a theme framework, the form for metadata often appears right below the post box. If you aren't using a theme framework, you can use the All in One SEO Pack plugin. (See the Chapter 5 of this minibook.) When activated, this plugin usually appears toward the bottom of your posting page. (See Figure 4-8.) Make sure that you completely fill out the title, description, keywords, and other information the plugin or theme framework asks for.

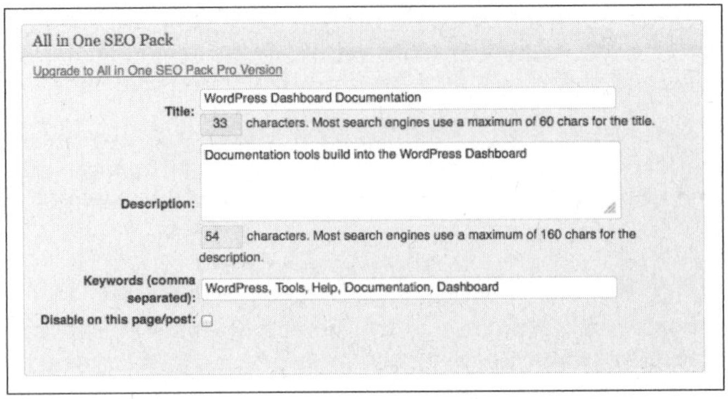

Figure 4-8:
The All in
One SEO
Pack's
metadata
form.

+ **Properly tag posts.** You may want to get into the habit of taking the keywords from the All in One SEO Pack plugin and pasting them into the tags section of the post.

+ **Fill out image info.** Take the time to completely fill out your image info when you upload pictures to your posts. Every time you upload an image to WordPress, a screen will appear in which you can fill in the URL slug, description, and alt text for the image you have uploaded.

Creating a link-building strategy

In previous sections of this chapter, I tackle most of the onsite SEO strategy and concepts. In this section, I explain how you can start working on your off-page strategy. Here are some things to keep in mind:

+ **Fill out your social media profiles.** As I discuss in Chapter 1 of this mini-book, a lot of social media sites pass on page rank through their profiles. Social media sites allow you to link to your site with a descriptive word — industry professionals recommend that this link has value to search engines, which is debatable, but it can never hurt. Take the time to fill out your social media profile properly and list your site in these profiles.

+ **Use forum signatures.** If you participate in forums, you can easily generate traffic and earn some links to your website from other websites by including your site URL in your forum signature.

+ **Examine your competitor's links.** See where your competitors or other people in your niche are getting links — directories, lists, guest blogs, friends? — and then try to get links on those sites. Try to determine the relationship and figure out whether you can establish a relationship with that site, as well.

✦ **Guest blog.** Find some of the top sites in your niche and then ask them whether you can guest blog. Guest blogging gives you a link from a respected source, as well as builds a relationship with other bloggers. Also, guest blogging can't hurt your subscriber numbers; often, you see a bump after you guest blog on a large site.

✦ **Use blog and website directory registration.** Directory registration, albeit a time-consuming affair, can often provide a large amount of backlinks into your site from respected sources.

✦ **Comment on other blogs.** A lot of blogs pass on page rank because the links in their comment section are live. Make sure that when you participate and engage other bloggers, you properly fill out your information before you post, including the URL to your site. Don't start posting inane comments on random blogs in order to get links. It's considered rude to do that to other bloggers and can lead to your blog being marked as spam in various commenting systems.

✦ **Participate in social bookmarking.** Getting involved in Reddit, Digg, and other social-bookmarking communities allows you to participate in social media with people who have similar interests, and you can build links into your site by submitting content to social news and bookmarking sites.

Chapter 5: Exploring Popular SEO Plugins

In This Chapter

✓ **Using plugins for SEO best practices**

✓ **Breaking down your SEO configuration options**

✓ **Generating sitemaps**

✓ **Using redirect plugins**

✓ **Adding breadcrumbs and pagination**

When you have the concepts of SEO down and the beginnings of your strategy properly mapped out, you can then install the tools you need. In this chapter, I go through some of the most popular SEO-related plugins. All these plugins have a good developer behind them and a good track record.

Several plugins in the WordPress plugin directory assist with SEO, so it's hard to decide which ones to use. In Book VII, I cover plugins in detail, but in this chapter I provide you with the plugins that are the most common, as well as the ones that I use myself, because they are some of the more solid and reliable plugins available that bring good SEO results.

Exploring Must-Use Plugins for SEO Best Practices

Here are the plugins that this chapter covers:

✦ **All in One SEO Pack:** Gives you complete control of the search-engine optimization of your blog.

✦ **Google XML Sitemaps:** Generates an XML sitemap that's sent to Google, Yahoo!, Bing, and Ask.com. When your site has a sitemap, site crawlers can more efficiently crawl your site. One of the added bonuses of the sitemap is that it notifies search engines every time you post.

✦ **Redirection:** Can help when you move from an old site to WordPress or when you want to change the URL structure of an established site. It allows you to manage 301 redirections (when the web address of a page has changed, a 301 redirect tells search engines where they can find the new web address of the page), track any 404 errors (errors that are displayed when you try to load a page that does not exist) that occur on the site, and manage any possible incorrect web address (URL) issues with your website.

✦ **Yoast Breadcrumbs:** This plugin allows you to easily add breadcrumbs (covered in Chapter 4 of this minibook) to your site. On most sites, you just need to add a line of code to your template to make the breadcrumb navigation links display on your site.

✦ **WP-PageNavi:** To achieve pagination for your WordPress site, this plugin gives you the ability to display page links at the bottom of each archive page and/or category page.

✦ **Robots Meta:** Using the Robots Meta plugin gives you the ability to control how your site is crawled by the search engines, allowing you to hide content that you don't want to be noticed by search engine robots and to ensure that search engine crawlers see only what you want them to see. It helps eliminate duplicate content by preventing crawlers from indexing category, author, and tag pages so that the crawlers focus only on your main content. Also, this plugin allows you to easily add the verification tools from Yahoo! Site Explorer, Bing's Webmaster Central, and Google's Webmaster Tools. If you don't want to edit your header, you can easily use this tool to add the various code that these search engines request you to use to verify your web page.

All in One SEO Pack

The All in One SEO Pack plugin (`http://wordpress.org/extend/plugins/all-in-one-seo-pack`) makes everyone's life so much easier because it automates many SEO tasks for you. Out of all the plugins I cover, this one is an absolute must for your site. It gives you so much control over your search engine optimization, and it's very flexible.

This plugin breaks down each option on the configuration page, which allows you to preselect options right off the bat or make some changes to the plugin.

Hover your mouse pointer over any of the plugin fields to find details on what each field is, along with inline help documentation.

After you install this plugin on the All in One SEO Plugin Options page (check out Book VII, Chapter 2 for information on plugin installation), which you find when you click the All In One SEO link on the Settings menu on your Dashboard, scroll past the rows of advertisements that appear on this page and be sure that the Plugin Status radio button is set to Enabled, as shown in Figure 5-1. Below that radio button are three text boxes that you need to type information into:

✦ **Home Title:** Type the title of your website in this box. (This will be the same Site Title that you filled out in the General Settings page, as I discuss in Book III, Chapter 2.)

✦ **Home Description:** Type a description of your website in this box. (This will probably be the same as the Tagline that you filled out on the General Settings page, as I discuss in Book III, Chapter 2.)

✦ **Home Keywords (comma separated**): Type multiple keywords that describe your site, and separate them each by commas. For example, if my site is about country music, my Home Keywords might look like this: *country music, guitar, southern, fiddle, Nashville.*

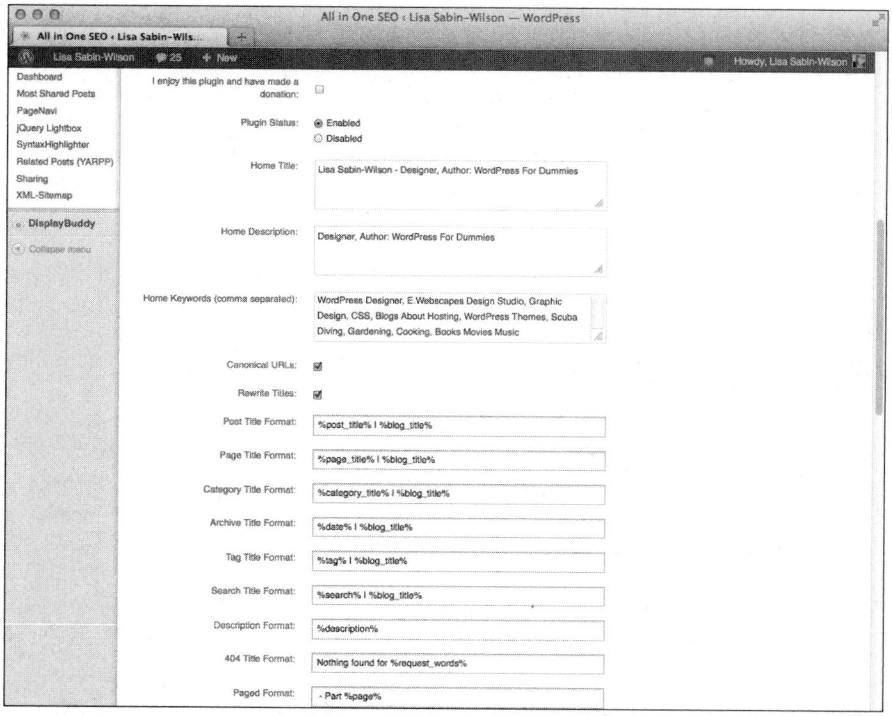

Figure 5-1:
The All
in One
SEO Pack
configura-
tion page.

The Canonical URLs check box appears below the text boxes. It is selected by default, and you should keep that default setting in place because canonical URLs assist with SEO by giving the search engines a definitive source URL for pages on your website. For example, when Google crawls a web page, it sees the following four URLs:

✦ www.example.com

✦ example.com

✦ www.example.com/index.html

✦ example.com/home.asp

Although you may think that all these URLs are the same; technically, they're all different. In the *canonicalization process,* Google chooses which one of those URLs best represents your site from that group. When selecting to use canonical URLs in the All In One SEO plugin, you're telling Google which URL you want them to choose.

Most of the remaining options that are selected, by default, should work fine for your site. However, you should select the Use No Index for Archives and Use No Index for Tag Archives check boxes to make sure that the search engines are not indexing your archives pages, which would provide the search engines with duplicate content that they have already indexed.

After you make all your selections, click the Update Options button at the bottom of the page.

You can use the All in One SEO Pack right out of the box, without changing any of the default options that are already set for you: If you aren't confident in fine-tuning it, you don't have to do it. But don't forget to put in the proper information for your home page on the Options page of the plugin; this includes your home page title, description, and keywords.

Google XML Sitemaps for WordPress

You can use XML Sitemaps (http://wordpress.org/extend/plugins/google-sitemap-generator) right out of the box with very little configuration. After you install it, you do need to tell the plugin to create your sitemap for the first time. You can accomplish this easy task by following these steps:

1. **Click the XML-Sitemap link on the Settings menu on your Dashboard.**

The XML Site Generator for WordPress options page appears in your browser window. (See Figure 5-2.)

2. **Locate the top module titled The Sitemap Wasn't Generated Yet.**

3. **Click the link labeled Click Here To Tell the Plugin to Build Your Sitemap.**

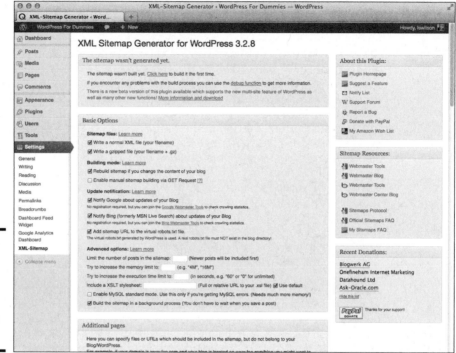

Figure 5-2:
XML
Sitemap
Generator
for
WordPress
settings.

The XML Site Generator for WordPress page refreshes and the This Sitemap Wasn't Generated Yet module is replaced with the Result of the Last Build Process module, and the date your sitemap was last generated is displayed.

4. **(Optional) View your sitemap in your browser.**

Click the first sitemap link in the top module, or you can visit the following address: `http://yourdomain.com/sitemap.xml` (where *your-domain.com* is your actual domain).

You never need to visit your sitemap, or maintain it. The XML Sitemap Generator maintains the file for you. Every time you publish a new post or page on your website, the plugin automatically updates your sitemap with the information and notifies major search engines, like Google, Bing, and Ask.com that you have updated your site with new content. Basically, the plugin sends an invitation to the search engines to come to your site and index your new content in their search engines.

Having a Google Webmaster account is also something you can do to further assist Google in finding and indexing new content on your site. If you don't already have one, you can sign up for one at Google.com. (Visit www. google.com, click the Sign In link at the top right, and then click the Create an Account Now link and follow the steps to create a new Google account.) After you sign in to your Google Account, you can set up the Google Webmaster tools and add your sitemap to Google.

In the Basic Options section of the XML Sitemap Generator for WordPress plugin page (see Figure 5-2), select every check box you see there except for the *Enable Manual Sitemap Building via GET Request, Enable MySQL Standard Mode,* and *Use This Only If You're Getting MySQL Errors* options. Those options are not necessary unless you're experiencing errors with the plugin — in which case, you should contact the plugin developer and report the problems. (Contact information for the plugin developer is available on the plugin page in the WordPress plugin directory. For this plugin, you can find the page here: `http://wordpress.org/extend/plugins/google-sitemap-generator.`)

All the other default settings are fine for you to use, so leave those as they are. In the Sitemap Content section, select the following check boxes: Include Homepage, Include Posts, Include Static Pages, Include Categories, and Include the Last Mortification Time. Making these selections allows for your site to get crawled by the search engines the most efficient way.

Redirection

If you're redoing the URL (permalink) structure of your site or moving a site to WordPress from another blogging platform, such as Blogger or TypePad, you really need to use the Redirection plugin (`http://wordpress.org/extend/plugins/redirection`). Redirection allows you to maintain the links that are currently coming into your site by rerouting (or redirecting) people coming in through search engines and other existing links going to the new permalink. If you change URLs, you need to reroute/redirect old links to maintain the integrity of incoming traffic from websites and search engines that are still using the old page URL.

Using Redirection is a pretty simple process: Put the old URL in the Source URL text box, put the new URL in the Target URL text box, and then click the Add Redirection button. (See Figure 5-3.)

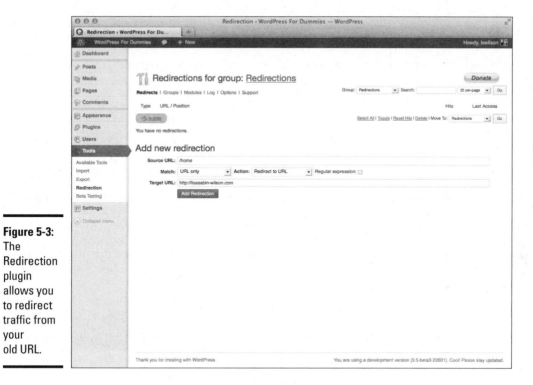

Figure 5-3:
The Redirection plugin allows you to redirect traffic from your old URL.

Yoast Breadcrumbs

Yoast Breadcrumbs (http://wordpress.org/extend/plugins/bread crumbs/) adds navigation breadcrumbs (covered in Chapter 4 of this mini-book) to your site. Although you can install and activate the plugin like any other plugin, you need to go through a few extra steps to get the bread-crumbs to show up on your page. For most standard WordPress themes, you need to add the following code into the template where you want the plugin to appear (see Book VI if you need assistance with editing template files):

```php
<?php if ( function_exists('yoast_breadcrumb') ) {
   yoast_breadcrumb('<p id="breadcrumbs">','</p>');
} ?>
```

WP-PageNavi

To create page navigation links underneath your blog posts and archive list-ings for sites that have numbered pages, you need to install the WP-PageNavi plugin (http://wordpress.org/extend/plugins/wp-pagenavi). (See the settings in Figure 5-4.) This plugin provides a better user experience for your readers by making it easier for them to navigate through your content, and allowing search engines to easily go through your web page and index your pages and posts. After you install and activate the plugin, you need to insert the following code into your Main Index template (`index.php`):

```php
<?php wp_pagenavi(); ?>
```

The `wp_pagenavi();` template tag needs to be added on a line directly after The Loop. Go to Book VI, Chapter 3 for extensive discussion of The Loop in the Main Index template file to find out where, exactly, you need to add this line of code.

Installing this code gives you the lower navigation. You can experiment with where you want to place the `wp_pagenavi()` code in your template file to give you the type and look and feel you want. Additionally, you can control the look of the plugin by providing styling in your CSS (`style.css`) theme file for the WP-PageNavi plugin display, or you can have the plugin insert its default CSS into your regular CSS by deselecting the Use Pagenavi.css? option.

Figure 5-4:
Adjust the WP-Page Navi settings.

Robots Meta

Similar to the All in One SEO Pack plugin (see "All in One SEO Pack," earlier in this chapter), the Robots Meta plugin (http://wordpress.org/extend/plugins/robots-meta) gives you a breakdown of each menu option and the impact that it has on your site. This plugin, however, isn't ready to go out of the box, like many of the other plugins in this chapter. To use it, you need to consider how your SEO works on your site and what content you want the search engines to index. If you want to base your search results on your categories (which is a good approach if you have a lot of content in categories based off popular keywords), make sure that robots don't scroll your subpages.

I can't offer any recommendations for setting up this plugin — the choices are too specific to you and your site needs. (See Figure 5-5.) Just go through and think about each choice and how it pertains to your blog and configure the settings that you feel work best for your website.

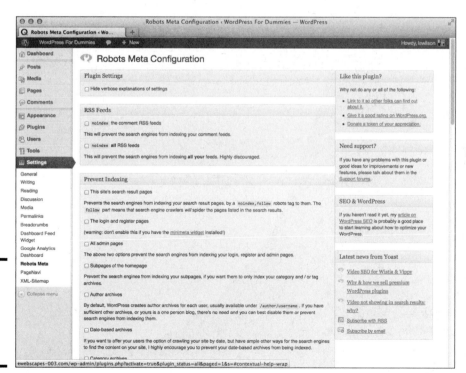

Figure 5-5:
Handling the Robots Meta configuration.

Book VI

Customizing the Look of Your Site

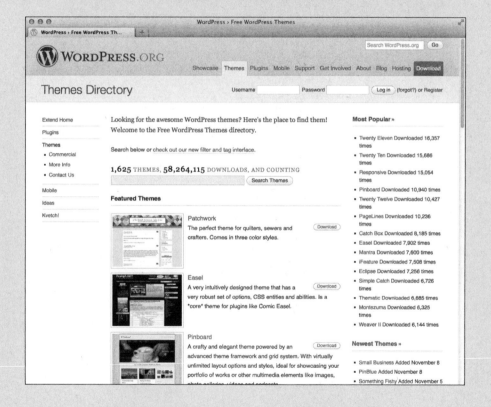

Contents at a Glance

Chapter 1: Examining the Default Theme: Twenty Twelve

In This Chapter

✔ Discovering Twenty Twelve's layout features

✔ Tweaking your header and background colors

✔ Installing custom navigation menus

✔ Exploring widgets on your website

*B*undled with the release of WordPress 3.5 in December 2012 is the new default theme, Twenty Twelve. The goal of the core development team for WordPress is to release a new default theme every year, which is why, with every new installation of WordPress, you find themes called Twenty Ten, Twenty Eleven, and Twenty Twelve (named to correspond with the year it was created).

With the release of WordPress version 3.5 in 2012, the resulting community effort was Twenty Twelve, a powerful theme with drop-down menu navigation, header and background image uploaders, multiple-page templates, widget-ready areas, parent-child theme support, and built-in mobile and tablet support. These features make Twenty Twelve an excellent base for many of your theme customization projects. This chapter shows you how to manage all the features of the default Twenty Twelve theme, such as handling layouts, editing the header graphic and background colors, installing and using custom navigation menus, and using widgets on your site to add some great features.

Exploring the Layout and Structure

If you just want a simple look for your site, look no further than Twenty Twelve. This theme offers a clean design style that is highly customizable. As such, the font treatments are sharp and easy to read. Many of the new built-in theme features allow you to make simple yet elegant tweaks to the theme, including uploading new feature images and adjusting the background colors. Figure 1-1 shows the Twenty Twelve WordPress default theme.

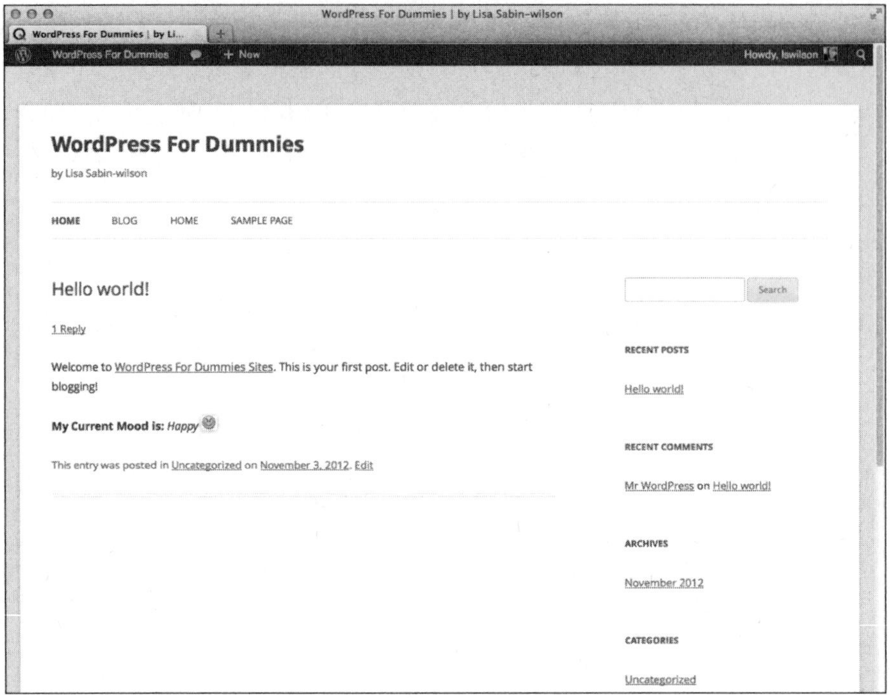

Figure 1-1:
The default theme for WordPress, Twenty Twelve.

The Twenty Twelve theme's distinctive layout features include

+ **Two column default layout:** The two-column layout — one of the most common layouts for blogs and used more and more on general web-sites — is the default in Twenty Twelve and includes a content area on the left, a widget-ready sidebar on the right, and a footer area with four widget-ready spaces. Figure 1-1 shows the standard two-column layout.

+ **One-column page layout:** Twenty Twelve's one-column layout can be applied to WordPress Pages via the page template feature. This one-column layout, shown in Figure 1-2, comes in very handy for such pages as product sales pages, e-mail subscription form pages, photography or portfolio pages, and other content that you don't want bothered by distractions on the sidebar.

+ **Color adjustment:** By default, the header text (site title) in the Twenty Twelve theme is a dark grey, almost black, color, and the background color of the site is light grey. You can easily change the colors of the header text and site background by using the theme customizer. (Steps to accomplish this are provided later in this chapter in the section titled "Customizing the Background Color.") Figure 1-3 shows the Twenty Twelve theme with red header text and a dark background color.

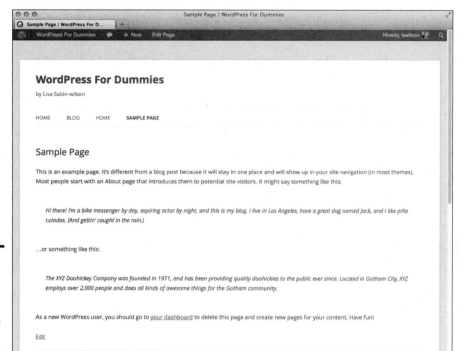

Figure 1-2:
The Twenty
Twelve
theme's
one-column
layout.

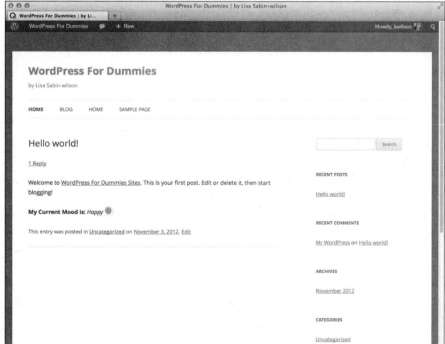

Figure 1-3:
The Twenty
Twelve
theme with
custom
colors.

To apply Twenty Twelve's one-column layout to a new WordPress page, follow these steps:

1. **On the WordPress Dashboard, click the Add New link on the Pages menu.**

   You can also edit an existing Page and apply the one-column page layout by using these steps.

2. **Add your page title and content into the corresponding areas.**

   Book IV, Chapter 1 takes you through the steps of writing and publishing a post or a page in WordPress.

3. **From the Template drop-down list, select Full-Width Page Template, No Sidebar.**

   The Template drop-down menu is located under the Page Attributes heading on the right side of the Add New Page screen.

   The Twenty Twelve theme has two page templates. Other themes may have multiple page template options on this menu.

4. **Click the Publish button.**

   This step saves your new page and publishes it to your site with the Full-Width Page Template, No Sidebar page template assigned to it. (Refer to Figure 1-2.)

Customizing the Header Image

Another great feature in Twenty Twelve is the header uploader, which allows you to upload new and unique custom header graphics for your WordPress site.

The dimensions for your customized header are at least 960 pixels in width and 250 pixels in height. If your photo is larger than that, you can crop it after you've uploaded it to WordPress, although cropping the image with a graphics program (like Photoshop) is the best way to get exact results.

Twenty Twelve comes preloaded with eight default header images, but WordPress allows you to upload one of your own. To install a custom header graphic, follow these steps:

1. **On the WordPress Dashboard, click the Header link on the Appearance menu.**

   On the Custom Header page, the settings for the header image feature appear.

2. **Click the Browse button in the Select Image section and select your chosen photo in the dialog box (shown in Figure 1-4).**

Book VI Chapter 1

Examining the Default Theme: Twenty Twelve

Figure 1-4:
Selecting an image from your computer's hard drive.

3. **Click the Open button.**

This step transfers the image from your computers hard drive to your WordPress installation directory and loads the Crop Header page, shown in Figure 1-5.

4. **(Optional) Crop the image to your liking.**

To resize and crop your image, drag one of the eight boxes located at the corners and the middle of each side of the image. You can also click within the image and move the entire image up or down to get the optimal placement and cropping effect that you want.

5. **Click the Crop and Publish button if you cropped your header. Or click the Skip Cropping, Publish Image as Is button.**

Figure 1-6 shows the Twenty Twelve theme with a custom header image.

Figure 1-5:
Using the
crop tool.

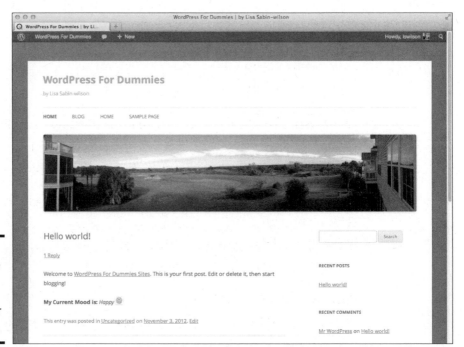

Figure 1-6:
The Twenty
Twelve
theme with
new header
image.

Customizing the Background Color

After you explore the header image settings, you may want to pick a background color or image that complements your header. The default background color in the Twenty Twelve theme is white; however, with the Background options in the Twenty Twelve theme, you can change the color. Here's how:

1. **On the WordPress Dashboard, click the Background link on the Appearance menu.**

The Custom Background page opens on your Dashboard, displaying all the options for the custom background feature.

2. **In the Display Options section, click the Select Color button.**

The Select Color button changes to Current Color after you click it to set the color value. Color values are defined in HTML and CSS by six-digit hexadecimal codes starting with the # sign, such as #000000 for black or #FFFFFF for white. (As noted in Book VI, Chapter 4, adjusting hexadecimal colors is one of the easiest ways to tweak the colors in your theme for a new look.)

3. **Enter the desired hexadecimal code for your selected color.**

Alternatively, you can click inside the color picker and select just the right color you want, as shown in Figure 1-7. The color picker automatically inserts the six-digit hexadecimal code for your color choice.

4. **Click the Save Changes button.**

Your changes are saved and applied to your site.

If you want something a little more substantial for your background than just a simple color, you can also upload an image to use as a background on your website. A background image adds some flair to your site. To upload a new background graphic, simply follow these steps:

1. **On the WordPress Dashboard, click the Background link on the Appearance menu.**

The Custom Background page loads on your Dashboard. Refer to Figure 1-7.

2. **In the Select Image section, click the Browse button.**

A window pops up, asking you to select an image from your computer's hard drive.

3. **Click the Upload button.**

The Custom Background page reloads with your selected image in the preview area of the page.

**Book VI
Chapter 1**

Examining the
Default Theme:
Twenty Twelve

Figure 1-7:
The Twenty
Twelve
theme's
background
options.

After you upload a background image, the new display options that appear (see Figure 1-8) allow you to place your image exactly as you desire. Select any of these features, and the Preview window shows you how your background image will display:

✦ **Position:** This is where you want the image placed or pinned with options for image to start at the left side, center, or right side of the theme background.

✦ **Repeat:** This sets how you want the image to tile or repeat across the page. If you want one image without tiling, set Repeat to No Repeat. You can also set it to tile vertically (up and down the page) or tile horizontally (left and right, across the page).

✦ **Attachment:** This sets whether the background image scrolls with the page in the browser or is fixed in one place no matter where the page is in the browser.

✦ **Background Color:** This sets the solid color that displays behind your background image.

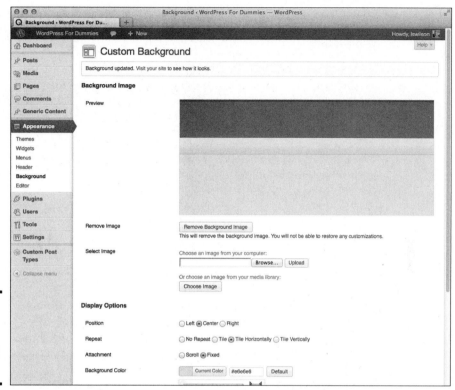

Figure 1-8:
Twenty
Twelve's
background
uploader.

After you finalize your selections, click the Save Changes button and view
your site for the exact look.

If you upload the wrong image from your computer or the image doesn't
look the way you hoped, there's a convenient Remove Background Image
button on the Custom Background page. Clicking this button completely
removes the image from the Custom Background settings and allows you to
start over with a different image.

Including Custom Navigation Menus

Navigational menus are vital parts of your site's design. They tell your site
visitors where to go and how to access important information or areas on
your site. The Menus feature released in WordPress 3.0 is an extremely significant addition to the already powerful software that allowed greater control over the navigational areas.

Similar to the WordPress Widgets feature, which lets you drag and drop widgets, the Menus feature offers an easy way to add and reorder a variety of navigational links to your site, as well as create secondary menu bars (if your theme offers multiple menu areas).

Additionally, the Menus feature improves WordPress further by allowing you to easily create more traditional websites, which sometimes need multiple and more diverse navigational areas than a typical blog layout uses or needs.

Twenty Twelve comes with the appropriate code in the navigation menus that make use of this robust feature. (By default, Twenty Twelve offers only one menu navigation area to include a custom menu.)

To create a new navigation menu in Twenty Twelve, follow these steps:

1. **On the WordPress Dashboard, click the Menus link on the Appearance menu.**

   The Menus page loads on your Dashboard, as shown in Figure 1-9.

2. **Enter a menu name in the Menu Name field and then click Create Menu.**

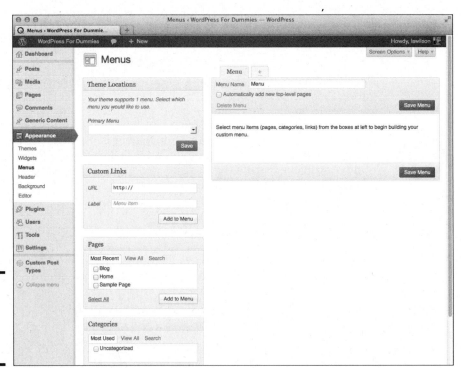

Figure 1-9: The WordPress Menus page.

After you create your new custom menu, the gray modules to the left become active for you to add new links to your custom menu.

3. **In the Theme Locations module, select your new menu from the Primary Menu drop-down list and click Save.**

Your new menu in the theme is activated for display on your site. As noted in the Theme Locations module, the Twenty Twelve theme supports only one custom menu, defined as Primary Menu.

4. **Add menu items, such as custom links, pages, and categories, to your new menu.**

Items you can add to your menu include the following:

- *Pages:* To include existing pages in your menu, locate the Pages module (shown in Figure 1-10) and click the pages you want to include. After you do that, click the Add to Menu button and then click the Save Menu button.

- *Categories:* To include existing categories on your menu, scroll to the Categories module (shown in Figure 1-10) and click the categories you want to include. After you do that, click the Add to Menu button and then click the Save Menu button.

- *Custom Links:* You can add links to sites that exist outside your website, such as your Twitter or Facebook profile pages. Scroll to the Custom Links module (shown in Figure 1-11). In the URL field, type the web address you want to direct people to. In the Label field, add the word or phrase the menu displays for people to click. Then click the Save Menu button.

Book VI
Chapter 1

Examining the
Default Theme:
Twenty Twelve

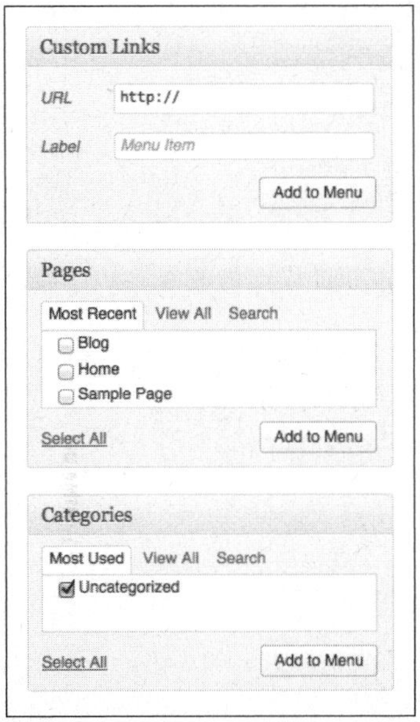

Figure 1-10:
Selecting categories to add to the custom menu.

If you're using custom post types (covered in Chapter 6 of this mini-book), click the Screen Options tab at the top right of the Dashboard screen and select Custom Post Types under Show onscreen. This option makes custom post type links available for addition to the menu.

Figure 1-11:
Adding links to a custom menu.

5. **Click Save Menu to add your custom menu to your theme.**

Click Save Menu after you make any significant change to your custom menu, such as reordering or adding new menu items so they are reflected on your site.

After you save your navigation menu, you can use the drag-and-drop interface to rearrange it, as shown in Figure 1-12. Additionally, you can create submenus under top-level menu items by moving menu items slightly to the right beneath the top-level items.

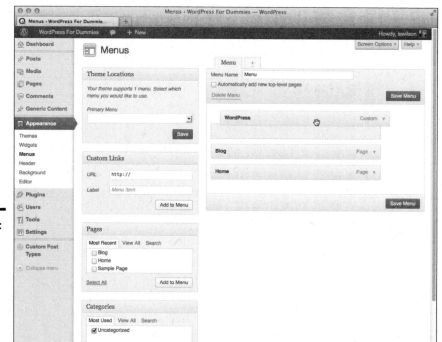

Figure 1-12:
The drag-and-drop interface of the WordPress Menus feature.

Make use of the submenu feature to avoid cluttering up the navigation bar. By organizing content logically, you can help readers find what they want faster even if you have lots of content for them to look through.

You can also create multiple custom menus and add them to your theme through widget areas by using the Custom Menu widget, navigation areas if your theme supports multiple menu areas, or additional menu areas by inserting the WordPress template tag directly into your theme's template files.

Enhancing Your Website with Widgets

WordPress widgets are very helpful tools built in to the WordPress application. They allow you to arrange the display of content in your blog sidebar, such as recent posts, and monthly and category archive lists. With widgets, arrange and display the content in the sidebar of your blog without having to know a single bit of PHP or HTML.

In this case, Widget areas are the regions in your theme that allow you to insert and arrange content (such as a list of your recent blog posts or links to your favorite sites) or custom menus, by dragging and dropping (and editing) available widgets (shown on the Dashboard's Widget page) into those corresponding areas.

Many widgets offered by WordPress (and those added sometimes by WordPress themes and plugins) provide drag-and-drop installation of more advanced functions normally available only if you write code directly into your theme files.

Click the Widgets link on the Appearance menu on the Dashboard. The Widgets page displays the available widgets. This feature is a big draw because it lets you control what features you use and where you place them without having to know a lick of code.

To explore the Twenty Twelve theme's widget-ready areas, click the Widgets link on the Appearance menu on the Dashboard. The Widgets page displays modules labeled Main Sidebar, First Front Page Widget Area, and Second Front Page Widget Area, as shown in Figure 1-13. The widget areas that can be edited in the Twenty Twelve theme through the WordPress Dashboard are shown in Figure 1-13.

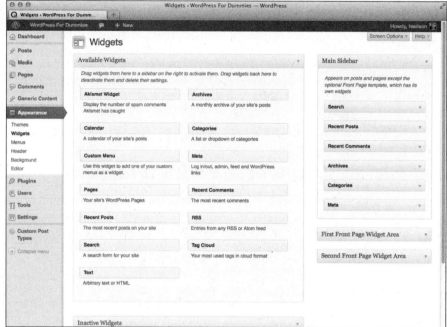

Figure 1-13:
This page
displays
available
widgets
and widget-
ready areas.

Adding widgets to your sidebar

The Widgets page lists all the widgets that are available for your WordPress site. On the right side of the Widgets page is the sidebar area designated in your theme. You drag your selected widget from the Available Widgets section into your chosen widget area on the right. For example, to add a Search box to the right sidebar of the default layout, drag the Search widget from the Available Widgets section to the Main Sidebar Widget Area.

To add a new widget to your sidebar, follow these steps:

1. **Find the widget you want to use.**

The widgets are listed in the Available Widgets section. For the purpose of these steps, choose the Recent Posts widget. (See Figure 1-14.)

2. **Drag and drop the widget into the Main Sidebar Widget Area section on the right side of the page.**

The widget is now located in the Main Sidebar Widget Area section, and the content of the widget now appears on your site in the sidebar.

Book VI
Chapter 1

Examining the
Default Theme:
Twenty Twelve

Figure 1-14:
Editing the
Recent
Posts
widget.

3. **Click the arrow to the right of the widget title.**

   Options for the widget appear. Each widget has different options that you can configure. The Recent Posts widget, for example, lets you configure the title and the number of recent posts you want to display. (See Figure 1-14.) The default is set to 5; the maximum allowed is 15.

4. **Select your options and click the Save button.**

   The options you've set are saved.

5. **Click the Close link.**

6. **Arrange your widgets in the order you want them to appear on your site by clicking a widget and dragging it above or below another widget.**

   Repeat this step until your widgets are arranged the way you want them.

To remove a widget from your sidebar, click the arrow to the right of the widget title and then click the Delete link. WordPress removes the widget from the right side of the page and places it back in the Available Widgets list. If you want to remove a widget but want WordPress to remember the settings that you configured for it, instead of clicking the Delete link, simply drag the widget into the Inactive Widgets area on the right side of the Widgets page, at the bottom of the page. The widget and all the settings are stored for future use.

After you select and configure your widgets, click the Visit Site button at the top of your WordPress Dashboard (to the right of your site name), and your blog's sidebar matches the content (and order of the content) of the Widgets page sidebar. How cool is that? You can go back to the Widgets page and rearrange the items, as well as add and remove items, to your heart's content.

The number of options available for editing a widget depends on the widget. Some have a number of editable options; others simply let you write a title for the widget area. As shown in Figure 1-14, the Recent Posts widget has two options: one for editing the title of the widget and one to determine how many recent posts to display.

Using the Text widget

The Text widget is one of the most popular and useful WordPress widgets because it allows you to add text and even HTML code into widget areas without editing the theme's template files. Therefore, you can designate several types of information on your site by including your desired text within it.

Here are some examples of how you can use the Text widget and why it's such an important feature:

✦ **Add an e-mail newsletter subscription form.** Add a form that allows your site visitors to sign up for your e-mail newsletter. Because this often involves HTML, the Text widget is especially helpful.

✦ **Display business hours of operation.** Display the days and hours of your business operation where everyone can easily see them.

✦ **Post your updates from social networks.** Many social networking sites, such as Twitter and Facebook, offer embed codes to display your updates on those sites directly on your website. They often include JavaScript, HTML, and CSS, which you can easily embed with the Text widget.

✦ **Announce special events and notices.** If your organization has a special sale, an announcement about a new staff member, or an important notice about inclement weather closings, you can use the Text widget to post this information to your site in just a few seconds.

The WordPress Text widget doesn't allow you to include PHP code of any kind. Because of the nature of this widget, it doesn't execute PHP code, such as special WordPress template tags or functions (like the ones you find in Book VI, Chapter 3). There is, however, a great plugin called the Advanced Text Widget that does allow you to insert PHP code within it. You can download the Advanced Text Widget from the WordPress Plugin Directory at `http://wordpress.org/extend/plugins/advanced-text-widget`. (You can find more information about using and installing WordPress plugins in Book VII.)

To add the Text widget, follow these steps:

1. **On the WordPress Dashboard, click the Widgets link on the Appearance menu.**

2. **Find the Text widget in the Available Widgets section.**

3. **Drag and drop the Text widget to the desired widget area.**

   The Text widget opens, as shown in Figure 1-15.

4. **Add a widget headline in the Title field and any desired text in the text area.**

5. **After you finish, click Save and then click the Close link.**

Figure 1-15:
The Text
widget.

Using the RSS widget

The RSS widget allows you to pull headlines from almost any RSS feed, including recent headlines from your other WordPress blogs or sites. You can also use it to pull in headlines from news sites or other sources that offer RSS feeds. This is commonly referred to as *aggregation,* which means that you're gathering information from a syndicated RSS feed source to display on your site.

After you drag and drop the RSS widget to the appropriate widget area, the widget opens and you can enter the RSS Feed URL you want to display. Additionally, you can easily tweak other settings, as shown in Figure 1-16, to add information into the widget area for your reader.

Figure 1-16:
The RSS widget.

Follow these steps to add the RSS widget to your blog:

1. Add the RSS widget to your sidebar on the Widgets page.

Follow the steps in the "Adding widgets to your sidebar" section, earlier in this chapter, to add the widget.

2. Click the arrow to the right of the RSS widget's name.

The widget opens, displaying options you can configure.

3. **In the Enter the RSS URL Here text box, type the RSS URL of the blog you want to add.**

   You can usually find the RSS Feed URL of a blog listed in the sidebar.

4. **Type the title of the RSS widget.**

   This title is what will appear in your blog above the links from this blog. If I wanted to add the RSS feed from my personal blog, for example, I'd type **Lisa Sabin-Wilson's blog**.

5. **Select the number of items to display.**

   The drop-down list gives you a choice of 1–20. Select the number of items from the RSS feed that you want to display on your site.

6. **(Optional) Select the Display the Item Content check box.**

   Selecting this check box tells WordPress that you also want to display the content of the feed (usually, the content of the blog post from the feed URL). If you want to display only the title, leave the check box deselected.

7. **(Optional) Select the Display Item Author, If Available check box.**

   Select this option if you want to display the author's name with the item's title.

8. **(Optional) Select the Display Item Date check box.**

   Select this option if you want to display the date the item was published with the item's title.

9. **Click the Save Changes button.**

   WordPress saves all the options and reloads the Widgets page with your RSS widget intact.

Chapter 2: Finding and Installing WordPress Themes

In This Chapter

✔ **Understanding free theme options**

✔ **Exploring things to avoid with free themes**

✔ **Installing, previewing, and activating your new theme**

✔ **Discovering premium theme options**

*W*ordPress themes are simply a group of files, called *templates,* bundled together that, when activated in WordPress, determine the look and basic function of your site. (See Book VI, Chapter 3 for more about template files.)

Because themes set the design style of your site, including how content displays on it, they are the first and most basic way of customizing your site to fit your unique needs. One of the most amazing things about the WordPress community is the thousands of free themes that are available — and the new ones released each week.

Although finding one WordPress theme among thousands of options can be challenging, it's a fun adventure, and you can explore the various designs and features to, ultimately, find the right theme for you and your site. In this chapter, you discover the options for finding and installing free themes on your WordPress site. I also discuss premium theme options and tell you a few things to avoid.

Getting Started with Free Themes

With thousands of free WordPress themes available and new ones appearing all the time, your challenge is to find the right one for your site. Here are a few things to remember while you explore (also see the nearby sidebar, "Are all WordPress themes free?," for information about free versus premium themes):

✦ **Free themes are excellent starting places.** Find a couple of free themes and use them as starting points for understanding how themes work and what you can do with them. Testing free themes, their layouts, and their options helps you identify what you want in a theme.

✦ **You'll switch themes frequently.** Typically, you'll find a WordPress theme that you adore and then, a week or two later, you'll find another theme that fits you or your site better. Don't expect to stay with your initial choice. Something new will pop up on your radar screen. Eventually, you'll want to stick with one that fits your needs best and doesn't aggravate visitors because of constant changes.

✦ **You get what you pay for.** Although a plethora of free WordPress themes exists, largely you receive limited or no support for them. Free themes are often a labor of love. The designers have full-time jobs and responsibilities and often release these free projects for fun, passion, and a desire to contribute to the WordPress community. Therefore, you shouldn't expect (or demand) support for these themes. Some designers maintain very active and helpful forums to help users but, often, those are rare. Just be aware that, with free themes, you're on your own.

✦ **Download themes from reputable sources.** Themes are essentially pieces of software. Therefore, they can contain things that could be scammy, spammy, or potentially harmful to your site or computer. Therefore, it's vital that you do your homework by reading online reviews and downloading themes from credible, trusted sources. The best place to find free WordPress themes is the WordPress Free Themes Directory (see Figure 2-1) at `http://wordpress.org/extend/themes`.

Are all WordPress themes free?

Not all WordPress themes are created equal, and it's important for you, the user, to know the difference between free and premium themes:

✔ **Free:** These themes are free, period. You can download and use them on your website at absolutely no cost. It's a courtesy to include a link to the designer in the footer of your blog, but you can remove that link if you want to.

✔ **Commercial:** These themes cost money. You usually find commercial themes available

for download only after you've paid anywhere from $10 to $500. The designer feels that these themes are a cut above the rest and, therefore, are worth the money you spend for them. Generally, you aren't allowed to remove any designer credits that appear in these themes, and you aren't allowed to redistribute the themes. ***Note:*** You *don't* find premium themes in the WordPress Themes Directory. I provide information on where to find premium themes at the end of this chapter.

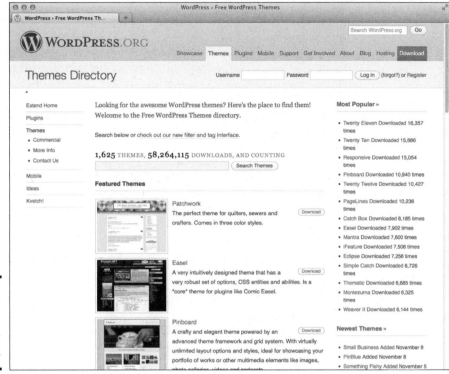

**Book VI
Chapter 2**

Finding and
Installing
WordPress
Themes

Figure 2-1:
The most
trusted
resource for
free themes.

Understanding What to Avoid with Free Themes

Although free themes are great, you want to avoid some things when finding and using free themes. As with everything on the web, themes have
the potential to be abused. Although free themes were conceived to allow
people (namely designers and developers) to contribute work to the
WordPress community, they've also been used to wreak havoc for users. As
such, you need to understand what to watch out for and what to avoid.

Here are some things to avoid when searching for free themes:

✦ **Spam links:** Many free themes outside the WordPress Free Themes
  Directory include links in the footer or sidebars that can be good or bad.
  The good uses of these links are designed to credit the original designer
  and possibly link to her website or portfolio. This practice — a nice
  reward to the creators — should be observed because it increases the
  designer's traffic and clients. Spam links, however, aren't links to the
  designer's site; they're links to sites you may not ordinarily associate

with or endorse on your site. The best example is a link in the footer that links to odd, off-topic, and uncharacteristic keywords or phrases, such as *weight loss supplement* or *best flower deals.* Mostly, this spam technique is used to increase the advertised site's search engine ranking for that particular keyword by adding another link from your site or, worse, to take your site visitor who clicks it to a site unrelated to the linked phrase.

✦ **Hidden and malicious code:** Unfortunately, the WordPress community has received reports of hidden, malicious code within a theme. This hidden code can produce spam links, security exploits, and abuses on your WordPress site. Hackers install code in various places that run this type of malware. Unscrupulous theme designers can, and do, place code in theme files that inserts hidden malware, virus links, and spam. Sometimes, you see a line or two of encrypted code that looks like it's just part of the theme code. Unless you have a great deal of knowledge of PHP, you may not know that the theme is infected with dangerous code.

✦ **Lack of continued development:** WordPress software continues to improve with each new update. Two or three times a year, WordPress releases new software versions, adding new features and security patches and numerous other updates. Sometimes, a code function will be superseded or replaced, causing a theme to break because it hasn't been updated for the new WordPress version. Additionally, to use new features added to WordPress, because the software updates add new features, the theme will need to be updated accordingly. Because free themes typically come without any warranty or support, one thing you should look for, especially if a theme has many advanced back-end options, is whether the developer is actively maintaining the theme for current versions of WordPress. This typically is more of an issue with plugins than themes, but it's worth noting.

✦ **Endlessly searching for free themes:** Avoid searching endlessly for the perfect theme — trust me, you won't find it. You may find a great theme and then see another with a feature or design style you wish the previous theme had, but the new theme lacks certain other features. Infinite options can hinder you making a final decision. Peruse the most popular themes on the WordPress Free Themes Directory, to save you some time, choose five that fit your criteria, and then move on. You always have the option to change a theme later, especially if you find the vast amount of choices in the directory overwhelming.

The results of these unsafe theme elements can range from simply annoying to downright dangerous, affecting the integrity and security of your computer and/or hosting account. For this reason, the WordPress Themes Directory is considered a safe place from which to download free themes. WordPress designers develop these themes and upload them to the theme directory, and the folks behind the WordPress platform vet each theme. In the official directory, themes that contain unsafe elements simply aren't allowed.

The WordPress Themes Directory isn't the only place on the web to find free WordPress themes, but it's the place to find the most functional and *safe* themes available. Safe themes contain clean code and basic WordPress functions that are considered fundamental requirements in a theme to ensure that your WordPress blog functions with the minimum requirements. The WordPress.org website lists the basic requirements that theme designers have to meet before their theme is accepted into the themes directory; you can find that listing of requirements at `http://wordpress.org/extend/themes/about`. I highly recommend that you stick to the WordPress Themes Directory for free themes to use on your site; you can be certain those themes don't contain any unsafe elements or malicious code.

Installing a Theme

After you find a WordPress theme, you can install the theme on your WordPress site via FTP or the WordPress Dashboard.

To install a theme via FTP, follow these steps:

1. Download the theme file from the Theme Directory.

Typically, theme files are provided in a compressed format, or Zip file.

I discuss how you can peruse the WordPress Free Themes Directory from your WordPress installation in the next section.

2. Unzip or extract the theme's Zip file.

You see a new folder on your desktop, typically labeled with the corresponding theme name. (Visit Book II, Chapter 2 if you need to refresh yourself on how to use FTP Protocol.)

3. Upload the theme folder to your web server.

Connect to your hosting server via FTP and upload the extracted theme folder into the `/wp-content/themes` folder on your server. (See Figure 2-2.)

Figure 2-2:
Upload and download panels in FTP.

To install a theme via the Dashboard's theme installer, follow these steps:

1. **Download the theme file from the Theme Directory to your desktop.**

   Typically, theme files are provided in a compressed format, or Zip file. Using this method, you do not extract the Zip file, because the theme installer does that for you.

2. **Log in to your WordPress Dashboard and click the Themes link on the Appearance menu.**

   The Manage Themes panel appears.

3. **Click the Install Themes tab.**

   The Install Themes panel appears and displays a submenu of links.

4. **Click the Upload link.**

   The panel displays a utility to upload a theme in Zip format.

5. **Upload the Zip file you downloaded in Step 1.**

   Click the Browse button and then locate and select the Zip file you stored on your computer.

6. **Click the Install Now button.**

   WordPress unpacks and installs the theme in the appropriate directory for you. Figure 2-3 shows the results of installing a theme via this method.

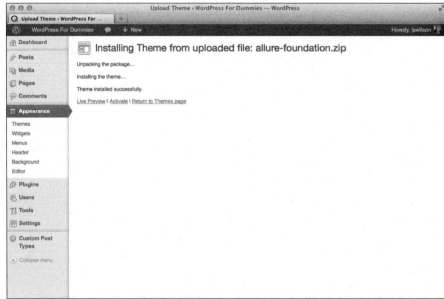

Figure 2-3:
Installing a theme via the Dashboard's theme installer.

Browsing the free themes

Finding free themes via the Install Themes tab is extremely convenient because it lets you search the Free Themes Directory from your WordPress site. Start by clicking the Themes link on the Appearance menu on the WordPress Dashboard and then click the Install Themes tab, as shown in Figure 2-4.

After you navigate to the Install Themes tab, you see the following submenu links:

✦ **Search:** If you know the name of a free theme, you can easily search for it here by keyword, author, or tag to find the exact theme you want. You can also refine your search based on specific features within the themes, including color, layout, and subject (such as "Holiday").

✦ **Upload:** You use this link to upload themes you downloaded from other sources.

**Book VI
Chapter 2**

**Finding and
Installing
WordPress
Themes**

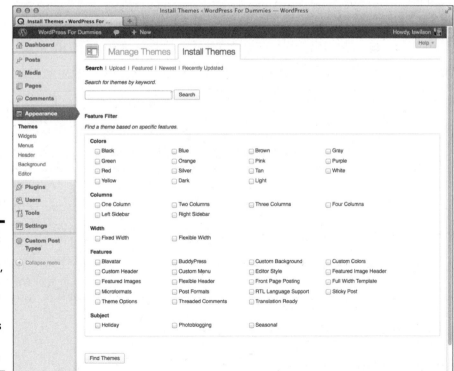

Figure 2-4:
The Install Themes tab, where you can search for and find free themes from your Dashboard.

✦ **Featured:** If you don't have a theme in mind, this page shows you some of the more popular themes out there. I recommend you install and test-drive one of these for your site's first theme.

✦ **Newest:** As the name indicates, these are themes recently added to the Free Themes Directory.

✦ **Recently Updated:** As WordPress improves and changes, many themes need updating or new features added. This option shows you what themes were updated recently.

After you find the theme that you want, click the Install link below the theme screenshot.

Previewing and activating a theme

After you upload a theme via FTP or the theme installer, you can preview and activate your desired theme.

The WordPress Theme Preview option allows you to look at your site without actually activating the theme on your site. If you have a site that's receiving traffic, it's best to preview any new theme before activating it to ensure that you'll be happy with its look and functionality. If you're trying to decide between several new theme options, you can preview them before changing your live site.

To preview your new theme, follow these steps:

1. **Log in to your WordPress Dashboard and click the Themes link on the Appearance menu.**

The Manage Themes page appears and displays your current (activated) theme and any themes that are installed in your `/wp-content/themes` directory on your web server.

2. **Preview the theme you want to use.**

Click the Preview link beneath the theme name; a preview of your blog using the theme appears in a pop-up window, as shown in Figure 2-5.

3. **(Optional) Configure theme customization features.**

Some, but not all, themes are developed to provide you with customization features. Figure 2-5 shows these customization options for the Twenty Twelve theme:

• Site Title & Tagline

• Colors

• Header Image

- Background Image
- Navigation
- Static Front Page

4. **Choose whether to activate the theme.**

   Click the Save & Activate button on the top-left area of the preview window to go live with your new theme, or you can close the preview by clicking the Cancel button in the top-left corner, as shown in Figure 2-5.

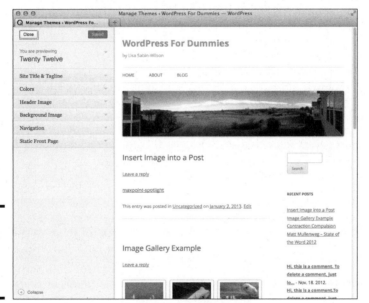

Figure 2-5:
A
WordPress
theme
preview.

To activate a new theme without previewing, follow these steps:

1. **Log in to your WordPress Dashboard and click the Themes link on the Appearance menu.**

   The Manage Themes page appears and displays your current (activated) theme and any themes that are installed in your `/wp-content/themes` directory on your web server.

2. **Find the theme you want to use and click the Activate link beneath the theme name.**

   The theme immediately becomes live on your site.

Exploring Premium Theme Options

Thousands of free WordPress themes are available, but you might also want to consider premium (for purchase) themes for your site. The adage "you get what you pay for" is something often quoted when referring to free services or products, including WordPress and free themes.

Typically, when you download and use something free, there's no recourse for assistance with the product or service. Requests for help generally go unanswered. Therefore, your expectations should be lower because you aren't paying anything. When you pay for something, you usually assume that you have support or service for your purchase and the product is high (or acceptable) quality.

For instance, WordPress is available free. However, despite an active support forum, there's no guarantee or promise of getting support while using the software. Moreover, you have no right to demand service.

Here are some things to consider when contemplating a premium theme. Additionally, I selected the commercial companies listed later in this chapter based on these criteria:

✦ **Selection:** Many theme developers offer a rich and diverse theme selection, including themes designed for specific niche industries, topics, or uses (such as video, blogging, real estate, or magazine themes, for example). Generally, you can find a good solid theme to use for your site from one source.

✦ **Innovation:** To differentiate them from their free counterparts, premium themes include innovative features, such as theme settings or advanced options that extend WordPress to help you do more.

✦ **Great design with solid code:** Although many beautiful free themes are available, premium themes are professionally coded, beautifully designed, cost thousands of dollars, and require dozens of hours to build, which simply isn't feasible for many free theme developers.

✦ **Support:** Most commercial companies have full-time support staff to answer questions, troubleshoot issues, and point you to resources beyond their support. Often, premium theme developers spend more time helping customers troubleshoot issues outside the theme products. Therefore, purchasing a premium theme often provides a dedicated support community to question about advanced issues and upcoming WordPress features; otherwise, you're on your own.

✦ **Stability:** No doubt, you've purchased a product or service from a company only to find later that they've gone out of business. If you choose to use a premium theme, purchase a theme from an established company with a solid business model, a record of accomplishment, and a dedicated team devoted to building and supporting quality products.

Although some free themes have some, or all of, the features in the preceding list, for the most part, they don't. Keep in mind that just because a designer calls a theme premium doesn't mean that the theme has passed through any kind of quality review. One designer's view of what constitutes a premium theme can, and will, differ from the next.

Fully investigate any theme before you spend your money on it. Some things to check out before you pay:

✦ E-mail the designer who is selling the premium theme and ask about a support policy.

✦ Find people who've purchased the theme and contact them to find out their experiences with the theme and the designer.

✦ Carefully read any terms that the designer has published on his site to find any restrictions that exist with licensing.

✦ If the premium theme designer has a support forum, ask whether you can browse through the forum to find out how actively the designer answers questions and provides support. Are users waiting weeks to get their questions answered? Or does the designer seem to be on top of support requests?

✦ Search Google for the theme and the designer. Often, users of premium themes post about their experiences with the theme and the designer. You can find a lot of positive and, potentially, negative information about the theme and the designer before you buy.

These developers are doing some amazingly innovative things with WordPress themes, and I highly recommend you explore their offerings:

✦ **iThemes (**`http://ithemes.com`**):** Shown in Figure 2-6, iThemes emphasizes business WordPress themes that use WordPress as a full-fledged and powerful content management system. The site's pride and joy is iThemes Builder, which is more a build-a-WordPress website tool than a typical theme.

✦ **Organic Themes (**`http://organicthemes.com`**):** Shown in Figure 2-7, Organic Themes has a great team, paid support moderators, and WordPress themes that are as much quality, from a code standpoint, as they are beautiful.

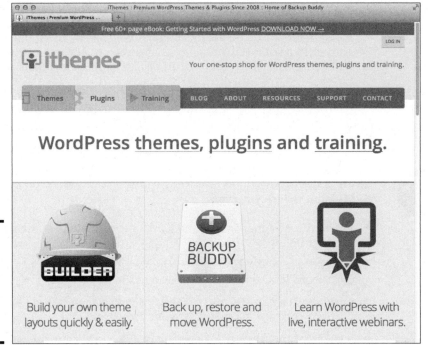

Figure 2-6:
iThemes.
com,
provider of
commercial
WordPress
themes.

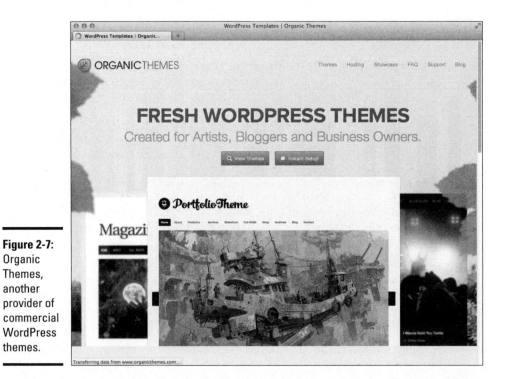

Figure 2-7:
Organic
Themes,
another
provider of
commercial
WordPress
themes.

- ✦ **WooThemes** (`http://woothemes.com`)**:** Shown in Figure 2-8, WooThemes has a wide selection of high-quality themes with excellent theme options and support. The highlight theme is Canvas, a highly customizable theme that has more than 100 options to personalize your site via a theme options panel.

- ✦ **Press75** (`http://press75.com`)**:** Shown in Figure 2-9, Press75 offers a number of niche themes for photography, portfolios, and video. Check out the Video Elements theme for a great example.

- ✦ **Headway Themes** (`http://headwaythemes.com`)**:** Shown in Figure 2-10, Headway's signature theme is Headway, which offers drag-and-drop layout editing and advanced, easy-to-use styling options.

Book VI Chapter 2

Finding and Installing WordPress Themes

You can't find, preview, or install premium themes by using the Add New Themes feature on your WordPress Dashboard (covered in an earlier section of this chapter). You can find, purchase, and download premium themes only from third-party websites. After you find a premium theme you like, you need to install it via the FTP method or by using the Dashboard upload feature. (See the earlier "Installing a Theme" section.) You can find a very nice selection of premium themes on the WordPress website at `http://wordpress.org/extend/themes/commercial`.

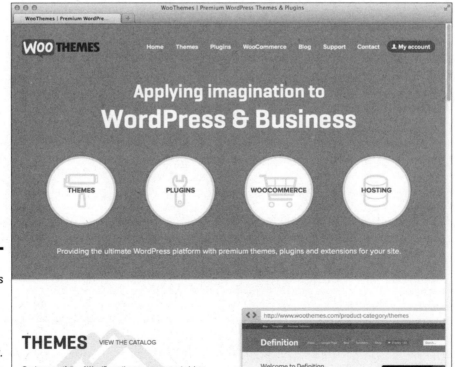

Figure 2-8: WooThemes has premium themes, community, and support.

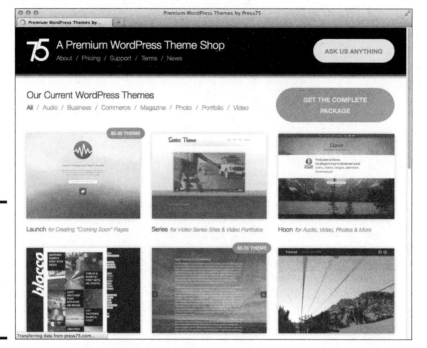

Figure 2-9:
Press75
offers
premium
themes,
demos,
and theme
packages.

Figure 2-10:
Headway
Themes
has some
unique
layouts.

Chapter 3: Exploring the Anatomy of a Theme

In This Chapter

✔ **Examining the theme's stylesheet**

✔ **Exploring template tags**

✔ **Making widget areas**

✔ **Understanding the main template files**

This chapter breaks down the parts that make up your WordPress theme. Understanding your theme allows you greater flexibility when you customize it. Many of the problems people encounter with themes, such as not knowing which files edit certain functions of a site, comes from lack of understanding all the pieces.

There are those who like to get their hands dirty (present company included!). If you're one of them, you need to read this chapter. WordPress users who create their own themes do so in the interest of

✦ **Individuality:** Having a theme that no one else has. (If you use one of the free themes, you can pretty much count on the fact that at *least* a dozen other WordPress blogs have the same look as yours.)

✦ **Creativity:** Displaying your own personal flair and style.

✦ **Control:** Having full control of how the blog looks, acts, and delivers your content.

Perhaps you aren't at all interested in creating your own templates for your WordPress blog, however. Sometimes, it's just easier to leave matters to the professionals and to hire an experienced WordPress theme developer to create a custom look for your WordPress website or to use one of the thousands of free themes provided by WordPress designers. (See Chapter 2 of this minibook.)

Creating themes does require you to step into the code of the templates, which can be a scary place sometimes — especially if you don't really know what you're looking at. A good place to start is understanding the structure of a WordPress blog. Separately, the parts won't do you any good. But when you put them together, the real magic begins! This chapter covers the basics of doing just that, and near the end of the chapter, you find specific steps to put your own theme together.

You don't need to know HTML to use WordPress. If you plan to create and design WordPress themes, however, you need some basic knowledge of HTML and Cascading Style Sheets (CSS). For assistance with HTML, check out *HTML 5 Quick Reference For Dummies*, by Andy Harris, or *HTML, XHTML, and CSS Bible*, by Steven M. Schafer.

Starting with the Basics

A WordPress theme is a collection of WordPress templates made up of WordPress template tags. When I refer to a WordPress *theme,* I'm talking about the group of templates that makes up the theme. When I talk about a WordPress *template,* I'm referring to only one of the template files that contain WordPress template tags. WordPress template tags make all the templates work together as a theme (more about this topic later in the chapter). These files include

✦ **The theme's stylesheet:** (`style.css`) The stylesheet provides the theme's name, as well as the CSS rules that apply to the theme. (Later in this chapter, I go into detail about how stylesheets work.)

✦ **The main index template:** (`index.php`) The index file is the first file that will be loaded when a visitor comes to your site. It contains the HTML as well as any PHP code needed on your home page.

✦ **An optional functions file:** (`functions.php`) This optional file is a place where you can add additional functionality to your site via PHP functions.

Template and functions files end with the `.php` extension. *PHP* is the scripting language used in WordPress, which your web server recognizes and interprets as such. (Book II, Chapter 3 covers additional details on the PHP language that you will find helpful.) These files contain more than just scripts, though. The PHP files also contain HTML, which is the basic markup language of web pages.

Within this set of PHP files is all the information your browser and web server need to make your website. Everything from the color of the background to the layout of the content is contained in this set of files.

The difference between a template and a theme can cause confusion. *Templates* are individual files. Each template file provides the structure in which your content will display. A *theme* is a set of templates. The theme uses the templates to make the whole site.

Understanding where the WordPress theme files are located on your web server gives you the ability to find and edit them, as needed. You can view and edit WordPress theme files, using two different methods, by following these steps:

1. **Connect to your web server via FTP, and have a look at the existing WordPress themes on your server.**

The correct location is `/wp-content/themes/`. When you open this folder, you find the `/twentytwelve` theme folder.

If a theme is uploaded to any folder other than `/wp-content/themes`, it won't work.

2. **Open the folder for the Twenty Twelve theme (`/wp-content/themes/twentytwelve`) and look at the template files inside.**

When you open the Twenty Twelve theme folder (see Figure 3-1), you see several files. At minimum, you find these five templates in the default theme:

- *Stylesheet* (`style.css`)

- *Header template* (`header.php`)

- *Main Index* (`index.php`)

- *Sidebar template* (`sidebar.php`)

- *Footer template* (`footer.php`)

Figure 3-1: WordPress themes in the /wp-content/ themes folder on your web server.

Name ▲	Size	Date
404.php	814 B	Thursday, November 8, 2012 10:55 AM
archive.php	2 KB	Thursday, November 8, 2012 10:55 AM
author.php	2 KB	Thursday, November 8, 2012 10:55 AM
category.php	1 KB	Thursday, November 8, 2012 10:55 AM
comments.php	2 KB	Thursday, November 8, 2012 10:55 AM
content-aside.php	1 KB	Thursday, November 8, 2012 10:55 AM
content-image.php	1 KB	Thursday, November 8, 2012 10:55 AM
content-link.php	1 KB	Thursday, November 8, 2012 10:55 AM
content-none.php	593 B	Thursday, November 8, 2012 10:55 AM
content-page.php	731 B	Thursday, November 8, 2012 10:55 AM
content-quote.php	1 KB	Thursday, November 8, 2012 10:55 AM
content-status.php	1 KB	Thursday, November 8, 2012 10:55 AM
content.php	3 KB	Thursday, November 8, 2012 10:55 AM
css	--	Saturday, November 3, 2012 10:13 AM
editor-style-rtl.css	413 B	Thursday, November 8, 2012 10:55 AM
editor-style.css	5 KB	Thursday, November 8, 2012 10:55 AM
footer.php	749 B	Thursday, November 8, 2012 10:55 AM
functions.php	16 KB	Thursday, November 8, 2012 10:55 AM
header.php	2 KB	Thursday, November 8, 2012 10:55 AM
image.php	4 KB	Thursday, November 8, 2012 10:55 AM
inc	--	Saturday, November 3, 2012 10:13 AM
index.php	2 KB	Thursday, November 8, 2012 10:55 AM
js	--	Saturday, November 3, 2012 10:13 AM
languages	--	Saturday, November 3, 2012 10:13 AM
page-templates	--	Saturday, November 3, 2012 10:13 AM
page.php	726 B	Thursday, November 8, 2012 10:55 AM
rtl.css	5 KB	Thursday, November 8, 2012 10:55 AM
screenshot.png	171 KB	Thursday, November 8, 2012 10:55 AM
search.php	1 KB	Thursday, November 8, 2012 10:55 AM
sidebar-front.php	987 B	Thursday, November 8, 2012 10:55 AM
sidebar.php	417 B	Thursday, November 8, 2012 10:55 AM
single.php	1 KB	Thursday, November 8, 2012 10:55 AM
style.css	34 KB	Thursday, November 8, 2012 10:55 AM
tag.php	1 KB	Thursday, November 8, 2012 10:55 AM

These files are the main WordPress template files, and I discuss them in more detail in this chapter. There are several template files, however, and you should try to explore all of them if you can. Take a peek inside and see the different template functions they contain. These filenames are the same in every WordPress theme.

3. **Log in to your WordPress Dashboard in your web browser window and click the Editor link on the Appearance menu to look at the template files within a theme.**

   This page lists the various templates available within the active theme. (Figure 3-2 shows the templates in the default Twenty Twelve theme.) A text box on the left side of the screen displays the contents of each template, and this box is also where you can edit the template file(s). To view and edit a template file, click the template name in the list on the right side of the page.

Figure 3-2: A list of templates available in the default Twenty Twelve WordPress theme.

The Edit Themes page also shows the template tags within the template file. These tags make all the magic happen in your blog; they connect all the templates to form a theme. The next section of this chapter discusses these template tags in detail, showing you what they mean and how they function.

When viewing a PHP file, click the Document drop-down list underneath the edit area on the right side of the screen to see all the template tags used in the template you're currently viewing. This list is helpful when you edit templates, and it gives you some insight into some of the different template tags used to create functions and features within your WordPress theme.

Understanding the Stylesheet

Every WordPress theme includes a `style.css` file. A browser uses this file, commonly known as the *stylesheet,* to style the theme. Style can include text colors, background images, and the spacing between elements on the site. The stylesheet targets areas of the site to style by using CSS IDs and classes. *CSS IDs* and *classes* are simply means of naming a particular element of the site. IDs are used for elements that appear only once on a page, but classes can be used as many times as you need. Although this file references *style,* it contains much more information about the theme.

At the very beginning of the `style.css` file, a comment block known as the *stylesheet header* passes information about your theme to WordPress. *Comments* are code statements included only for programmers, developers, and any others who read the code. Computers ignore comment statements entirely, but WordPress uses the stylesheet header to get information about your theme. In CSS, comments always begin with a forward slash (/) followed by a star (*), and end with a star followed by a forward slash (*/). The following code shows an example of the stylesheet header for the Twenty Twelve theme:

**Book VI
Chapter 3**

**Exploring
the Anatomy
of a Theme**

```
/*
Theme Name: Twenty Twelve
    Theme URI: http://wordpress.org/extend/themes/twentytwelve
    Author: the WordPress team
    Author URI: http://wordpress.org/
    Description: The 2012 theme for WordPress is a fully responsive theme that
    looks great on any device. Features include a front page template with its
    own widgets, an optional display font, styling for post formats on both index
    and single views, and an optional no-sidebar page template. Make it yours
    with a custom menu, header image, and background.
    Version: 1.0
    License: GNU General Public License v2 or later
    License URI: http://www.gnu.org/licenses/gpl-2.0.html
    Tags: light, gray, white, one-column, two-columns, right-sidebar, flexible-
    width, custom-background, custom-header, custom-menu, editor-style, featured-
    images, flexible-header, full-width-template, microformats, post-formats,
    rtl-language-support, sticky-post, theme-options, translation-ready
    Text Domain: twentytwelve

    This theme, like WordPress, is licensed under the GPL.
    Use it to make something cool, have fun, and share what you've learned with
    others.
    */
```

Figure 3-3 shows how the Manage Themes page on the Dashboard looks with the Twenty Twelve theme activated. The title and information are taken directly from the `style.css` header.

If you make modifications to the stylesheet header, the changes reflect in the WordPress Dashboard on the Themes page located on the Appearance menu.

Figure 3-3:
This shows the currently active theme, Twenty Twelve.

Themes must provide this information in the stylesheet header, and no two themes can have the same information. Two themes with the same name and details would conflict in the theme-selection page. If you create your own theme based on another theme, make sure that you change this information first.

Below the stylesheet header are the CSS styles that drive the formatting and styling of your theme.

Chapter 4 of this minibook goes into detail about CSS, including some examples that you can use to tweak the style of your existing WordPress theme — check it out!

Exploring Template Tags, Values, and Parameters

Some people are intimidated when they look at template tags. Really, they're just a simple bit of PHP code that you can use inside a template file to display information dynamically. Before starting to play around with template tags in your WordPress templates, it's important to understand what makes up a template tag and why.

WordPress is based in PHP (a scripting language for creating web pages) and uses PHP commands to pull information from the MySQL database. Every tag begins with the function to start PHP and ends with a function to stop PHP. In the middle of those two commands lives the request to the database that tells WordPress to grab the data and display it.

A typical template tag looks like this:

```
<?php get_info(); ?>
```

This example tells WordPress to do three things:

✦ Start PHP (`<?php`).

✦ Use PHP to get information from the MySQL database and deliver it to your blog (`get_info();`).

✦ Stop PHP (`?>`).

In this case, `get_info` is the actual tag function, which grabs information from the database to deliver it to your blog. What information is retrieved depends on what tag function appears between the two PHP commands. As you may notice, there's a lot of starting and stopping of PHP throughout the WordPress templates. The process seems as though it would be resource intensive, if not exhaustive — but it really isn't.

For every PHP command you start, you need a stop command. Every time a command begins with `<?php`, somewhere later in the code is the closing `?>` command. PHP commands that aren't structured properly cause really ugly errors on your site, and they've been known to send programmers, developers, and hosting providers into loud screaming fits.

Understanding the basics

If every piece of content on your site were *hard-coded* (manually added into the template files), it wouldn't be easy to use and modify. Template tags allow you to add information and content dynamically to your site. One example of adding information by using a template tag is the `the_category` tag. Instead of typing all the categories and links that each post belongs in, you can use the `the_category()` tag in your template to automatically display all the categories as links.

Using template tags prevents duplication of effort by automating the process of adding content to your website.

When you use a template tag, you're really telling WordPress to do something or retrieve some information. Often, template tags are used to fetch data from the server and even display it on the front end. More than 100 template tags are built into WordPress, and the tags vary greatly in what they can accomplish. A complete list of template tags can be found in the WordPress Codex (documentation for WordPress) at `http://codex.wordpress.org/Template_Tags`.

Template tags can be used only inside of PHP blocks. The PHP blocks can be opened and closed as many times as needed in a template file. When opened, the server knows that anything contained in the block is to be translated as PHP. The opening tag (<?php) must be followed, at some point, by the closing tag (?>). All blocks must contain these tags. A template tag is used in the same way that PHP functions are. The tag is always text with no spaces (may be separated by underscores or dashes), opening and closing brackets, and a semicolon. The following line of code shows you how it all looks:

```
<?php template_tag_name(); ?>
```

PHP is a fairly advanced coding language and has many built-in functions for you to use. If you aren't a PHP developer, keep it simple when you're attempting to add custom PHP. All code must be semantically perfect or it will not work. Always read your code to make sure that you entered it correctly.

Some template tags can be used only inside The Loop, so check the Codex for details. You can find out more about The Loop in the section titled "Examining the Main Index and The Loop," later in this chapter.

Using parameters

Because a template tag is a PHP function, you can pass parameters to the tag. A *parameter* is simply a variable that allows you to change or filter the output of a template tag. WordPress has three types of template tags:

✦ **Tags without parameters:** Some template tags don't require any options, so they don't need any parameters passed to them. For example, the is_user_logged_in() tag doesn't accept any parameters because it only returns true or false.

✦ **Tags with PHP function–style parameters:** Template tags with PHP function–style parameters accept parameters that are passed to them by placing one or more values inside the function's parentheses. For example, if you're using the bloginfo() tag, you can filter the output to just the description by using

```
<?php bloginfo('description'); ?>
```

If there are multiple parameters, the order in which you list them is very important. Each function sets the necessary order of its variables, so double-check the order of your parameters.

Always place the value in single quotes, and separate multiple parameters by commas.

✦ **Tags with query string–style parameters:** Template tags with query string–style parameters allow you to change the values of just the parameters you require. This is useful for template tags that have a large number of options. For example, the `wp_list_pages()` tag has 18 parameters. Instead of using the PHP function–style parameters, this function allows you to get to the source of what you need and give it a value. For example, if you want to list all your WordPress pages except for page 24, you use

```
<?php wp_list_pages('exclude=24'); ?>
```

Query string–style parameters can be the most difficult to work with because they are generally dealing with the template tags that have the most possible parameters.

Table 3-1 helps you understand the three variations of parameters used by WordPress.

Table 3-1	Three Variations of Template Parameters	
Variation	*Description*	*Example*
Tags without parameters	These tags have no additional options available. Tags without parameters have nothing within the parentheses.	`the_tag();`
Tags with PHP function–style parameters	These tags have a comma-separated list of values placed within the tag parentheses.	`the_tag('1,2,3');`
Tags with query string–style parameters	These types of tags generally have several available parameters. This tag style enables you to change the value for each parameter without being required to provide values for all available parameters for the tag.	`the_tag ('parameter=true');`

The WordPress Codex, located at `http://codex.wordpress.org`, has every conceivable template tag and possible parameter known to the WordPress software. The tags and parameters in this chapter are the ones used most often by WordPress users.

Customizing common tags

Because template tags must be used inside the PHP template files, they can easily be customized with HTML. If you're using the PHP tag `wp_list_pages()`, for example, you could display it in an HTML unordered list so that the pages are easily accessible to the users, like this:

```
<ul>
<?php wp_list_pages(); ?>
</ul>
```

This displays all the pages that you created in WordPress as an unordered list. If you had the pages About, Blog, and Content, it would be displayed like this:

✦ About

✦ Blog

✦ Contact

Another example is titles. For proper search engine optimization, you should always put page titles in H1 HTML tags, like this:

```
<h1 class="pagetitle">
<?php the_title(); ?>
</h1>
```

Creating New Widget Areas

Many themes are *widget-ready,* meaning that you can insert widgets into them easily. Widgets allow you to add functionality to your sidebar without having to use code. Some common widget functionalities include displaying recent posts, displaying recent comments, adding a search box for searching content on a site, and adding static text. Even widget-ready themes have their limitations, however. You may find that the theme you chose doesn't have widget-ready areas in all the places you want them. However, you can make your own.

Registering your widget

To add a widget-ready area to the WordPress Dashboard Widget interface, you must first register the widget in your theme's `functions.php` file by adding this code:

```
register_sidebar( array (
'name' => __( 'Widget Name'),
'id' => 'widget-name',
'description' => __( 'The primary widget area'),
'before_widget' => '<li id="%1$s" class="widget-container %2$s">',
'after_widget' => "</li>",
'before_title' => '<h3 class="widget-title">',
'after_title' => '</h3>',
) );
```

You can insert this code directly beneath the first opening PHP tag (<?php). It is sometimes helpful to add a few extra lines when you're adding code. The extra empty lines around your code are ignored by the browser but can greatly increase readability of the code.

Within that code, you see seven different *arrays*. An array is a set of values that tells WordPress how you would like your widgets handled and displayed:

+ name: This name is unique to the widget and is displayed on the Widgets page on the Dashboard. It is helpful if you register several different widgetized areas on your site.

+ id: This is the unique ID given to the widget.

+ description: This is a text description of the widget. The text that gets placed here will display on the Widgets page on the Dashboard.

+ before_widget: This is the HTML markup that gets inserted directly before the widget. It is helpful for CSS styling purposes.

+ after_widget: This is the HTML markup that gets inserted directly after the widget.

+ before_title: This is the HTML markup that gets inserted directly before the widget title.

+ after_title: This is the HTML markup that gets inserted directly after the widget title.

Even though you use register_sidebar to register a widget, widgets don't have to appear in a sidebar. Widgets can appear anywhere you want them to. This code snippet registers a widget named Widget Name in the WordPress Dashboard. Additionally, it places the widget's content in an element that has the CSS class of widget, and puts <h4> tags around the widget's title.

Widgets that have been registered on the WordPress Dashboard are ready to be populated with content. On your site's Dashboard, on the Appearance menu, you can see a link titled Widgets. When you click the Widgets link, you can now see the new widget area you have just registered.

Displaying new widgets on your site

When a widget-ready area is registered with the WordPress Dashboard, you can display the area somewhere on your site. A very common place for widget-ready areas is in the sidebar.

To add a widget-ready area in your sidebar, pick a location within the sidebar and then locate that area in the HTML, which can vary from theme to theme. Many times, theme authors will create their own `sidebar.php` file, and you can add this code there. After you find the area in the HTML, add the following code to the template:

```
<?php dynamic_sidebar('Widget Name'); ?>
```

This code displays the contents of the widget that you previously registered in the admin area.

Simplifying customization with functions

You may find that the simple code doesn't accomplish all the functionality that you need. For example, you may want to style the widget's title separate from the content. One solution is to create a custom PHP function that gives you a few more options. Open `functions.php` and insert the following code directly below the opening `<?php` tag to create a function:

```
function add_new_widget_location( $name ) {
if ( ! function_exists( 'dynamic_sidebar' ) || ! dynamic_sidebar(
$name ) ) : ?>
<div class="widget">
<h4><?php echo $name; ?></h4>
<div class="widget">
<p>This section is widgetized. If you would like to
add content to this section, you may do so by using the Widgets
panel from within your WordPress Admin Dashboard. This Widget
Section is called "<strong><?php echo $name; ?></strong>"</p>
</div>
</div>
<?php endif; ?>
<?php
}
```

In this function, the first part checks to see whether a widget is assigned to this area. If so, the widget displays. If not, a message with the name of the widget area displays, which allows users to distinguish the widget area they want to add widgets to. Now if you want to display a widget by using this method, you go to the desired template file and insert the following code where you want the widget to appear:

```
<?php add_new_widget_location('Widget-Name'); ?>
```

Exploring common problems

A common problem when creating widget areas is forgetting the admin side. Although people successfully create the widget in the PHP template where they want it, they often fail to make it to the `functions.php` to register the new widget area.

Another common problem is omitting the widget code from the `functions.php` file. If you're adding widget areas to an existing site, you need to add the widget code to the bottom of the list of widgets in the `functions.php` file. Failure to do so causes the widget areas to shift their contents. This places your widgets out of order, causing you to have to redo them on the Widgets page on the WordPress Dashboard.

Examining the Main Index and The Loop

Your theme is required to have only two files. The first is `style.css`. The other is a main index file, known in WordPress as `index.php`. The `index.php` file is the first file WordPress tries to load when someone visits your site. Extremely flexible, `index.php` can be used as a standalone file, or it can include other templates. The Main Index template drags your blog posts out of the MySQL database and inserts them into your blog. This template is to your blog what the dance floor is to a nightclub — it's where all the action happens.

The filename of the Main Index template is `index.php`. You can find it in the `/wp-content/themes/twentytwelve/` folder.

The first template tag in the Main Index template calls in the Header template, meaning that it pulls the information from the Header template into the Main Index template, as follows:

```
<?php get_header(); ?>
```

Your theme can work without calling in the Header template, but it will be missing several essential pieces — the CSS and the blog name and tagline, for starters.

The Main Index template in the Twenty Twelve theme calls in three other files in a similar fashion:

✦ `get_template_part( 'content' );` — This function calls in the template file named `content.php`.

✦ `get_sidebar();` — This function calls in the template file named `sidebar.php`.

✦ `get_footer();` — This function calls in the template file named `footer.php`.

I cover each of these three functions and template files in upcoming sections of this chapter.

The concept of *calling in* a template file by using a function or template tag is exactly what the Main Index template does with the four functions for the header, loop, sidebar, and footer templates explained later in this section.

Generally, one of the important functions of the main index is to contain The Loop. In WordPress, *The Loop* displays posts and pages on your site. Any PHP or HTML that you include in The Loop will repeat for each of your posts that it displays. The Loop has a starting point and an ending point; anything placed in between is used to display each post, including any HTML, PHP, or CSS tags and codes.

Here's a look at what the WordPress Codex calls "The World's Simplest Index":

```php
<?php
get_header();
if (have_posts()) :
  while (have_posts()) :
    the_post();
    the_content();
  endwhile;
endif;
get_sidebar();
get_footer();
?>
```

Here's how it works:

1. The template opens the php tag.

2. It includes the header, meaning that it retrieves anything contained in the header.php file and displays it.

3. The Loop begins with the while (have_posts()) : bit.

4. Anything between the while and the endwhile repeats for each post that displays.

    The number of posts that displays is determined in the settings section of the WordPress Dashboard.

5. If your blog has posts (and most do, even when you first install it), WordPress proceeds with The Loop, starting with the piece of code that looks like this:

    ```php
    if (have_posts()) :
      while (have_posts()) :
    ```

    This code tells WordPress to grab the posts from the MySQL database and display them on your blog page.

6. The Loop closes with this tag:

```
    endwhile;
endif;
```

Near the beginning of the Loop template, there is a template tag that looks like this:

```
    if (have_posts()) :
```

To read that template tag in plain English, it says `If [this blog] has posts`.

7. If your blog meets that condition (that is, if it has posts), WordPress proceeds with The Loop and displays your blog posts. If it does not meet that condition (that is, it does not have posts), WordPress displays a message that no posts exist.

8. When The Loop ends (at the `endwhile`), the index template goes on to execute the files for sidebar and footer.

Although it is simple, The Loop is one of the core functions of WordPress.

Misplacement of the `while` or `endwhile` statements causes The Loop to break. If you're having trouble with The Loop in an existing template, check your version against the original and see whether the `while` statements are misplaced.

In your travels as a WordPress user, you may run across plugins or scripts with instructions that say something like this: "This must be placed within The Loop." That's The Loop that I discuss in this section, so pay particular attention. Understanding The Loop arms you with the knowledge you need for tackling and understanding your WordPress themes.

The Loop is no different from any other template tag; it must begin with a function to start PHP, and it must end with a function to stop PHP. The Loop begins with PHP and then makes a request: "While there are posts in my blog, display them on this page." This PHP function tells WordPress to grab the blog post information from the database and return it to the blog page. The end of The Loop is like a traffic cop with a big red stop sign telling WordPress to stop the function completely.

You can set the number of posts displayed per page in the Reading Settings page in the WordPress Dashboard. The Loop abides by this rule and displays only the number of posts per page that you've set.

WordPress uses other template files besides the main index, such as the header, sidebar, and footer templates. The next sections give you a closer look at a few of them.

Header template

The Header template for your WordPress themes is the starting point for every WordPress theme because it tells web browsers the following:

✦ The title of your blog

✦ The location of the CSS

✦ The RSS feed URL

✦ The blog URL

✦ The tagline (or description) of the blog

In many themes, the first elements in the header are a main image and the navigation. These two elements are usually in the header.php because they load on every page and rarely change. The following statement is the built-in WordPress function to call the header template:

```
<?php get_header(); ?>
```

Every page on the web has to start with a few pieces of code. In every header.php file in any WordPress theme, you can find these bits of code at the top:

✦ The DOCTYPE (which stands for *document type declaration*) tells the browser which type of XHTML standards you're using. The Twenty Twelve theme uses <!DOCTYPE html>, which is a declaration for W3C standards compliance mode and covers all major browser systems.

✦ The <html> tag (HTML stands for *Hypertext Markup Language*) tells the browser which language you're using to write your web pages.

✦ The <head> tag tells the browser that the information contained within the tag shouldn't be displayed on the site; rather, it's information about the document.

In the header template of the Twenty Twelve theme, these bits of code look like this, and you should leave them intact:

```
<!DOCTYPE html>
<html <?php language_attributes(); ?>>
<head>
```

On the Edit Themes page, click the Header template link to display the template code in the text box. Look closely and you see that the <!DOCTYPE html> declaration, <html> tag, and <head> tag show up in the template.

The `<head>` tag needs to be closed at the end of the Header template, which looks like this: `</head>`. You also need to include a fourth tag, the `<body>` tag, which tells the browser where the information you want to display begins. Both the `<body>` and `<html>` tags need to be closed at the end of the template, like this: `</body></html>`.

Using bloginfo parameters

The Header template makes much use of one WordPress template tag in particular: `bloginfo();`.

What differentiates the type of information that a tag pulls in is a *parameter*. Parameters are placed inside the parentheses of the tag, enclosed in single quotes. For the most part, these parameters pull information from the settings in your WordPress Dashboard. The template tag to get your blog title, for example, looks like this:

```
<?php bloginfo('name'); ?>
```

Table 3-2 lists the various parameters you need for the `bloginfo();` tag and shows you what the template tag looks like. The parameters in Table 3-2 are listed in the order of their appearance in the Twenty Twelve `header.php` template file, and pertain to the `bloginfo();` template tag only.

Table 3-2	Tag Values for bloginfo();	
Parameter	*Information*	*Tag*
`charset`	Character settings set in Settings/General	`<?php bloginfo ('charset'); ?>`
`name`	Blog title, set in Settings/General	`<?php bloginfo ('name'); ?>`
`description`	Tagline for your blog, set in Settings/General	`<?php bloginfo ('description'); ?>`
`url`	Your blog's web address, set in Settings/General	`<?php bloginfo ('url'); ?>`
`stylesheet_ url`	URL of primary CSS file	`<?php bloginfo ('stylesheet_url'); ?>`
`pingback_ url`	Displays the trackback URL for your blog on single post pages	`<?php bloginfo ('pingback_url'); ?>`

Creating title tags

Here's a useful tip about your blog's `<title>` tag: Search engines pick up the site title for inclusion in the search engine directory. Here is the code to include in the `header.php` file to make sure your site title gets search engine exposure:

```
<title><?php wp_title( '|', true, 'right' ); ?></title>
```

It may help if this example is plain English. The way the Twenty Twelve Header template displays the title is based on the type of page that is being displayed — and it shrewdly uses SEO to help you with the browser powers that be. Simply, the `wp_title ('|', true, 'right');` tag displays the title of the page you're viewing with a separator bar (|) to the right of the title.

The title bar of the browser window always displays your blog name unless you're on a single post page. In that case, it displays your blog title plus the title of the post on that page.

Displaying your blog name and tagline

The default Twenty Twelve theme header displays your blog name and tagline on the top of your site on every page.

You can use the `bloginfo();` tag plus a little HTML code to display your blog name and tagline. Most blogs have a clickable title, which is a site title that takes you back to the main page when it's clicked. No matter where your visitors are on your site, they can always go back home by clicking the title of your site in the header.

To create a clickable title, use the following code:

```
<a href="<?php bloginfo('url'); ?>"><?php bloginfo('name'); ?></a>
```

The `bloginfo('url');` tag is your main blog Internet address, and the `bloginfo('name');` tag is the name of your blog (refer to Table 3-1). So the code creates a link that looks something like this:

```
<a href="http://yourdomain.com">Your Blog Name</a>
```

The tagline generally isn't linked back home. You can display it by using the following tag:

```
<?php bloginfo('description'); ?>
```

This tag pulls the tagline directly from the one that you set up on the General Settings page on your WordPress Dashboard.

This example shows how WordPress is intuitive and user-friendly; you can do things such as changing the blog name and tagline with a few keystrokes on the Dashboard. Changing your options in the Dashboard creates the change on every page of your site — no coding experience required. Beautiful, isn't it?

In the Twenty Twelve templates, these tags are surrounded by tags that look like these: <h1></h1> or <h4></h4>. These tags are H tags, which define the look and layout of the blog name and tagline in the CSS of your theme. Chapter 4 of this minibook covers CSS.

Sidebar template

The Sidebar template in WordPress has the filename sidebar.php. The sidebar is usually found on the left or right side of the main content area of your WordPress theme. (In the Twenty Twelve theme, the sidebar is displayed to the right of the main content area.) It is a good place to put useful information about your site, such as a site summary, advertisements, or testimonials.

Many themes use widget areas in the sidebar template. This allows you to display content easily on your WordPress pages and posts. The following statement is the built-in WordPress function to call the Sidebar template:

```
<?php get_sidebar(); ?>
```

This code calls the Sidebar template and all the information it contains into your blog page.

Footer template

The Footer template in WordPress has the filename footer.php. The footer is generally at the bottom of the page and contains brief reference information about the site. This usually includes copyright information, template design credits, and a mention of WordPress. Similarly to the Header and Sidebar templates, the Footer template gets called into the Main Index template through this bit of code:

```
<?php get_footer(); ?>
```

This code calls the Footer template and all the information it contains into your blog page.

The default Twenty Twelve theme shows the site title and a statement that says "Proudly powered by WordPress." You can use the footer to include all sorts of information about your site; however, you don't have to restrict it to small bits of information.

Examining Other Template Files

To make your website work properly, WordPress uses all the theme files together. Some, such as the header and footer, are used on every page. Others, such as the comments template (comments.php), are used only at specific times, to pull in specific functions.

When someone visits your site, WordPress uses a series of queries to determine which templates to use.

Many more theme templates can be included in your theme. Here are some of the other template files you might want to use:

✦ **Comments template (comments.php):** The Comments template is required if you plan to host comments on your blog; it provides all the template tags you need to display those comments. The template tag used to call the comments into the template is <?php comments_ template(); ?>.

✦ **Single Post template (single.php):** When your visitors click the title or permalink of a post you published to your blog, they're taken to that post's individual page. There, they can read the entire post, and if you have comments enabled, they see the comments form and can leave comments.

✦ **Page template (page.php):** You can use a Page template for static pages in your WordPress site.

✦ **Search Results (search.php):** You can use this template to create a custom display of search results on your blog. When someone uses the search feature to search your site for specific keywords, this template formats the return of those results.

✦ **404 template (404.php):** Use this template to create a custom 404 page, which is the page visitors get when the browser can't find the page requested and returns that ugly 404 Page Cannot Be Found error.

The templates in the preceding list are optional. If these templates don't exist in your WordPress themes folder, nothing breaks. The Main Index template handles the display of these items (the single post page, the search results page, and so on). The only exception is the Comments template. If you want to display comments on your site, you must have that template included in your theme.

Customizing Your Blog Posts with Template Tags

This section covers the template tags that you use to display the body of each blog post you publish. The body of a blog post includes information such as the post date and time, title, author name, category, and content. Table 3-3 lists the common template tags you can use for posts, available for you to use in any WordPress theme template. The tags in Table 3-3 work only if you place them within The Loop (covered earlier in the "Examining the Main Index and The Loop" section in this chapter and found in the `loop.php` template file).

Table 3-3	Template Tags for Blog Posts
Tag	*Function*
`get_the_date();`	Displays the date of the post.
`get_the_time();`	Displays the time of the post.
`the_title();`	Displays the title of the post.
`the_permalink();`	Displays the permalink (URL) of the post.
`get_the_author();`	Displays the post author's name.
`the_author_link();`	Displays the URL of the post author's site.
`the_content ('Read More...');`	Displays the content of the post. (If you use an excerpt [following], the words *Read More* appear and are linked to the individual post page.)
`the_excerpt();`	Displays an excerpt (snippet) of the post.
`the_category();`	Displays the category (or categories) assigned to the post. If the post is assigned to multiple categories, commas separate them.
`comments_popup_link ('No Comments', 'Comment (1)', 'Comments(%)');`	Displays a link to the comments, along with the comment count for the post in parentheses. (If no comments exist, it displays a *No Comments* message.)
`next_posts_link ('&laquo; Previous Entries')`	Displays the words *Previous Entries* linked to the previous page of blog entries.
`previous_posts_link ('Next Entries &raquo;')`	Displays the words *Next Entries* linked to the next page of blog entries.

The last two tags in Table 3-3 aren't like the others. You don't place these tags in The Loop; instead, you insert them after The Loop but before the `if` statement ends. Here's an example:

```
<?php endwhile; ?>
<?php next_posts_link('&laquo; Previous Entries') ?>
<?php previous_posts_link('Next Entries &raquo;') ?>
<?php endif; ?>
```

Within some of the WordPress template tags, such as the `<title>` tag example at the beginning of this section, you may notice some weird characters that look like a foreign language. You may wonder what `&raquo;` is, for example. It isn't part of any PHP function or CSS style. Rather, it's a *character entity* — a kind of code that enables you to display a special character in your blog. The `&raquo;` character entity displays a double right-angle quotation mark.

Putting It All Together

Template files can't do a whole lot by themselves. The real power comes when they're put together.

Connecting the templates

WordPress has built-in functions to include the main template files, such as `header.php`, `sidebar.php`, and `footer.php`, in other templates. An `include` function is a custom PHP function that is built in to WordPress, allowing you to retrieve the content of another template file and display it along with the content of another template file. Table 3-4 shows the templates and the function to include them.

Table 3-4	Template Files and Include Functions
Template Name	*Include Function*
`header.php`	`<?php get_header(); ?>`
`sidebar.php`	`<?php get_sidebar(); ?>`
`footer.php`	`<?php get_footer(); ?>`
`search.php`	`<?php get_search_form(); ?>`
`comments.php`	`<?php comments_template(); ?>`

If you want to include a file that doesn't have a built-in `include` function, you need a different piece of code. For instance, if you want to add a unique sidebar to a certain page template, you could name the sidebar file `sidebar-page.php`. To include that in another template, you would use the following code:

```
<?php get_template_part('sidebar', 'page'); ?>
```

In this statement, the PHP `get_template_part` function looks through the main theme folder for the `sidebar_page.php` file and displays the sidebar.

In this section, you put together the guts of a basic Main Index template by using the information on templates and tags from this chapter. There seem to be endless lines of code when you view the `loop.php` template file in the Twenty Twelve theme, so I've simplified it for you in this section. You'll have a basic understanding of the WordPress Loop and common template tags and functions that you can use to create your own.

You create a new WordPress theme, using some of the basic WordPress templates. You need six templates: Header, Theme Functions, Sidebar, Footer, Stylesheet, and Main Index.

In your favored text editor (such as Notepad for the PC or TextMate for the Mac) create and save the following files with the corresponding code:

✦ **Header template:** Create the file with the following lines of code then save it with the filename `header.php`:

```
<!DOCTYPE html PUBLIC "-//W3C//DTD XHTML 1.0 Transitional//EN"
  "http://www.w3.org/TR/xhtml1/DTD/xhtml1-transitional.dtd">
<html xmlns="http://www.w3.org/1999/xhtml" <?php language_
  attributes(); ?> />

<head profile="http://gmpg.org/xfn/11">
<meta http-equiv="Content-Type" content="<?php bloginfo('html_type');
  ?>;
charset=<?php bloginfo('charset'); ?>" />

<title><?php bloginfo( 'name' ); ?> <?php if ( is_single() ) { ?>
  &raquo; Blog Archive <?php } ?>
<?php wp_title(); ?></title>

<link rel="stylesheet" href="<?php bloginfo( 'stylesheet_url' ); ?>"
  type="text/css" media="screen" />
<link rel="pingback" href="<?php bloginfo( 'pingback_url' ); ?>" />

<?php if ( is_singular() ) wp_enqueue_script( 'comment-reply' ); ?>
<?php wp_head(); ?>
</head>
<body <?php body_class() ?>>
<div id="page">
<div id="header">
<h1><a href="<?php bloginfo('url'); ?>"><?php bloginfo('name');
  ?><?a></h1>
<h2><?php bloginfo('description'); ?></h2>
</div>
<div id="main">
```

✦ **Theme Functions:** Create the file with the following lines of code and then save it with the filename `functions.php`:

```
<?php
if ( function_exists('register_sidebar') ) register_sidebar(array
   ('name'=>'Sidebar',
   ));
```

The Theme Functions file registers the widget area for your site so that you're able to add widgets to your sidebar by using the available WordPress widgets from the Widget page in the Dashboard.

✦ **Sidebar template:** Create the file with the following lines of code and then save it with the filename `sidebar.php`:

```
<div id="side" class="sidebar">
<ul>
<?php if ( !function_exists('dynamic_sidebar') || !dynamic_
   sidebar('Sidebar') ) : ?>
<?php endif; ?>
</ul>
</div>
```

The code here tells WordPress where you want the WordPress widgets to display in your theme; in this case, widgets are displayed in the sidebar of your site.

✦ **Footer template:** Create the file with the following lines of code and then save it with the filename: `footer.php`:

```
</div>
<div id="footer">
<p>&copy; Copyright <a href="<?php bloginfo('url'); ?>"><?php
   bloginfo('name'); ?></a>. All Rights Reserved</p>
</div>
<?php wp_footer(); ?>
</body>
</html>
```

✦ **Stylesheet:** Create the file with the following lines of code and then save it with the filename `style.css` (more CSS is covered in Chapter 4 of this minibook — this example gives you just some very basic styling to create your sample theme):

```
/*
Theme Name: My Theme
Description: Basic Theme from WordPress All In One For Dummies example
Author: Lisa Sabin-Wilson
Author URI: http://lisasabin-wilson.com
*/

body {
font-family: verdana, arial, helvetica, sans-serif;
font-size: 16px;
color: #555;
background: #eee;
}

#page {
width: 960px;
margin: 0 auto;
background: white;
border: 1px solid silver;
}
```

```
#header {
width: 950px;
height: 100px;
background: black;
color: white;
padding: 5px;
}

#header h1 a {
color: white;
font-size: 22px;
font-family: Georgia;
text-decoration: none;
}

#header h2 {
font-size: 16px;
font-family: Georgia;
color: #eee;
}

#main {
width: 600px;
float:left;
}

#side {
width: 220px;
margin: 0 15px;
float:left;
}

#footer {
clear: both;
width: 960px;
height: 50px;
background: black;
color: white;
}

#footer p {
text-align: center;
padding: 15px 0;
}

#footer a {
color: white;
}
```

Using the tags provided in Table 3-3, along with the information on The Loop and the calls to the Header, Sidebar, and Footer templates provided in earlier sections, you can follow the next steps for a bare-bones example of what the Main Index template looks like when you put the tags together.

When typing templates, be sure to use a text editor such as Notepad or TextEdit. Using a word processing program such as Microsoft Word opens a whole slew of problems in your code. Word processing programs insert hidden characters and format quotation marks in a way that WordPress can't read.

Now that you have the basic theme foundation, the last template file you need to create is the Main Index template. To create a Main Index template to work with the other templates in your WordPress theme, open a new window in a text-editor program and then follow these steps. (Type the text in each of these steps on its own line. Press the Enter key after typing each line so that each tag starts on a new line.)

1. **Type** <?php get_header(); ?>.

   This template tag pulls the information in the Header template of your WordPress theme.

2. **Type** <?php if (have_posts()) : ?>.

   This template tag is an `if` statement that asks, "Does this blog have posts?" If the answer is yes, it grabs the post content information from your MySQL database and displays the posts in your blog.

3. **Type** <?php while (have_posts()) : the_post(); ?>.

   This template tag starts The Loop.

4. **Type** <a href="<?php the_permalink(); ?>"><?php the_title(); ?></a>.

   This tag tells your blog to display the title of a post that's clickable (linked) to the URL of the post.

5. **Type** Posted on <?php the_date(); ?> at <?php the_time(); ?>.

   This template tag displays the date and time when the post was made. With these template tags, the date and time format are determined by the format you set in the Dashboard.

6. **Type** Posted in <?php the_category(','); ?>.

   This template tag displays a comma-separated list of the categories to which you've assigned the post — *Posted in: category 1, category 2,* for example.

7. **Type** <?php the_content('Read More..'); ?>.

   This template tag displays the actual content of the blog post. The `'Read More..'` portion of this tag tells WordPress to display the words *Read More,* which are clickable (hyperlinked) to the post's permalink, where the reader can read the rest of the post in its entirety. This tag applies when you're displaying a post excerpt, as determined by the actual post configuration in the Dashboard.

8. **Type** Posted by: <?php the_author(); ?>.

   This template tag displays the author of the post in this manner: *Posted by: Lisa Sabin-Wilson.*

9. Type <?php comments_popup_link('No Comments', '1 Comment', '% Comments'); ?>.

This template tag displays the link to the comments for this post, along with the number of comments.

10. Type <?php endwhile; ?>.

This template tag ends The Loop and tells WordPress to stop displaying blog posts here. WordPress knows exactly how many times The Loop needs to work, based on the setting in the WordPress Dashboard. That's exactly how many times WordPress will execute The Loop.

11. Type <?php next_posts_link('« Previous Entries'); ?>.

This template tag displays a clickable link to the previous page of blog entries, if any.

12. Type <?php previous posts link('» Next Entries'); ?>.

This template tag displays a clickable link to the next page of blog entries, if any.

13. Type <?php else : ?>.

This template tag refers to the `if` question asked in Step 2. If the answer to that question is no, this step provides the `else` statement — IF this blog has posts, THEN list them here (Step 2 and Step 3), or ELSE display the following message.

14. Type Not Found. Sorry, but you are looking for something that isn't here.

This is the message followed by the template tag that is displayed after the `else` statement from Step 13. You can reword this statement to have it say whatever you want.

15. Type <?php endif; ?>.

This template tag ends the `if` statement from Step 2.

16. Type <?php get_sidebar(); ?>.

This template tag calls in the Sidebar template and pulls that information into the Main Index template.

17. Type <?php get_footer(); ?>.

This template tag calls in the Footer template and pulls that information into the Main Index template. *Note:* The code in the `footer.php` template ends the `<body>` and the `<html>` tags that were started in the Header template (`header.php`).

When you're done, the display of the Main Index template code looks like this:

```php
<?php get_header(); ?>
<?php if (have_posts()) : ?>
 <?php while (have_posts()) : the_post(); ?>
 <div <?php post_class() ?> id="post-<?php the_ID(); ?>">
    <a href="<?php the_permalink(); ?>"><?php the_title(); ?></a>
    Posted on: <?php the_date(); ?> at <?php the_time(); ?>
    Posted in: <?php the_category(','); ?>

    <?php the_content('Read More..'); ?>
    Posted by: <?php the_author(); ?> | <?php comments_popup_link('No
    Comments', '1 Comment', '% Comments'); ?>
 </div>

<?php endwhile; ?>
<?php next_posts_link('&laquo; Previous Entries') ?>
<?php previous_posts_link('Next Entries &raquo;') ?>
<?php else : ?>
Not Found
Sorry, but you are looking for something that isn't here.
<?php endif; ?>
<?php get_sidebar(); ?>
<?php get_footer(); ?>
```

18. **Save this file as `index.php`.**

In Notepad, you can save it by choosing File⇨Save As. Type the name of the file in the File Name text box and then click Save.

Now that you have all your template files ready, follow these steps to upload your files to your web server:

1. **Connect to your web server via FTP, click the `wp-content` folder, and then click the `themes` folder.**

This folder contains the themes that are currently installed in your WordPress blog. (Go to Book II, Chapter 2 if you need more information on FTP.)

2. **Create a new folder, and call it `mytheme`.**

In most FTP programs, you can right-click and choose New Folder. (If you aren't sure how to create a folder, refer to your FTP program's help files.)

3. **Upload your `index.php` file to the `mytheme` folder.**

4. **Activate the theme in the WordPress Dashboard and view your blog to see your handiwork in action!**

This Main Index template code has one template tag that is explained in Chapter 6 of this minibook: `<div <?php post_class() ?> id="post-<?php the_ID(); ?>">`. This tag helps you create some interesting styles in your template by using CSS, so check out Chapter 6 to find out all about it!

This very simple and basic Main Index template that you just built doesn't have the standard HTML markup in it, so the visual display of your blog will differ somewhat from the default Twenty Twelve theme. This example gives you the bare-bones basics of the Main Index template and The Loop in action. Chapter 4 of this minibook goes into detail about the use of HTML and CSS to create nice styling and formatting for your posts and pages.

Using additional stylesheets

Often, a theme uses multiple stylesheets for browser compatibility or consistent organization. If you use multiple stylesheets, the process for including them in the template is the same as any other stylesheet.

To add a new stylesheet, create a directory in the root theme folder called `css`. Next, create a new file called `mystyle.css` within the `css` folder. To include the file, you must edit the `header.php` file. This example shows the code you need to include in the new CSS file:

```
<link rel="stylesheet" href="<?php bloginfo('stylesheet_directory');
?>/css/mystyle.css" type="text/css" media="screen" />
```

Chapter 4: Customizing Your Theme

C ustomizing your WordPress theme's overall look with unique graphics and colors is one of the most fun and exciting aspects of using WordPress themes. You can take one of your favorite, easily customizable themes and personalize it with some simple changes to make it unique. (For more information on finding an existing theme, read Book VI, Chapter 2.)

After you find an existing free (or premium) WordPress theme that suits your needs, the next step is personalizing the theme through some of the following techniques:

✦ **Plugging in your own graphics:** The easiest way to make a theme your own is through a graphical header that includes your logo and matching background graphics.

✦ **Adjusting colors:** You might like the structure and design of your theme but want to adjust the colors to match your own tastes or brand look. You can do this in the CSS, too.

✦ **Adding/changing fonts:** You may want to change the font, or *typography,* on your site by using different font types, sizes, or colors. You can edit these display properties in the CSS.

Often, the customization process is one of trial and error. You have to mix and match different elements, tweaking and tinkering with graphics and CSS until you achieve design perfection. In this chapter, you explore the easiest ways to customize your WordPress theme through graphics and CSS.

Changing Your Background Graphic

Using background graphics is an easy way to set your site apart from others that use the same theme. Finding a background graphic for your site is much like finding just the right desktop background for your computer. You can choose from a variety of background graphics for your site, such as photography, abstract art, and repeatable patterns.

You can find ideas for new and different background graphics by checking out some of the CSS galleries on the web, such as `http://cssdrive.com` and `http://csselite.com`. Sites like these should be used for inspiration only, not theft. Be careful when using images from outside sources. You want to use only graphics and images that you have been given the right (through express permission or licenses that allow you to reuse) to use on your sites. For this reason, always purchase graphics from reputable sources, such as these three online graphic sites:

✦ **iStockphoto (**`http://istockphoto.com`**):** An extensive library of stock photography, vector illustrations, video and audio clips, and Flash media. You can sign up for an account and search through libraries of image files to find the one that suits you, or your client, best. The files that you use from iStockphoto aren't free; you do have to pay for them — and be sure that you read the license for each image you use. The site has several different licenses. The cheapest one is the Standard License, which has some limitations. For example, you can use an illustration from iStockphoto in one website design, but you cannot use that same illustration in a theme design that you intend to sell multiple times (say in a premium theme marketplace). Be sure to read the fine print!

✦ **Dreamstime (**`http://dreamstime.com`**):** Dreamstime is a major supplier of stock photography and digital images. Sign up for an account and search through the huge library of digital image offerings. Dreamstime does offer free images at times, so keep your eyes out for those! Also, Dreamstime has different licenses for their image files that you need to pay close attention to, but one nice feature is the Royalty Free licensing option. This option allows you to pay for the image one time and then use the image as many times as you like; however, you can't redistribute the image in the same website theme repeatedly, such as in a template that's sold to the public.

✦ **Graphic River (**`www.graphicriver.net`**):** Graphic River offers stock graphic files from Photoshop images, design templates, textures, vector graphics, and icons, to name just a few. The selection is vast, and the cost to download and use the graphic files is minimal. As with all graphic and image libraries, be sure to read the terms of use or any licensing attached to each of the files to make sure you're legally abiding by the terms.

Another great resource for finding free graphics and more is Smashing Magazine at www.smashingmagazine.com. You can find hundreds of links and resources to free and, often, reusable graphics, such as textures and wallpapers for your site.

To best use background graphics, you must answer a few simple questions:

✦ **What type of background graphic do you want to use?** For example, do you want a repeatable pattern or texture or an image like a black-and-white photograph of something in your business?

✦ **How do you want the background graphic to display in your browser?** Do you want to tile or repeat your background image in the browser window or pin it to a certain position no matter what size your guest's browser is?

The answers to those questions determine how you install a background graphic in your theme design.

When working with graphics on the web, use GIF, JPG, or PNG image formats. For images with a small number of colors (such as charts, line art, logos, and so on), GIF format works best. For other image types (screenshots with text and images, blended transparency, and so on), use JPG or PNG.

For web design, the characteristics of each image file format can help you decide which file format you need to use for your site. The most common image file formats and characteristics include:

✦ .jpg: Suited for use with photographs and smaller images used in your web design projects. Although the .jpg format compresses with lossy compression, you can adjust compression when you save a file in a .jpg format. That is, you can choose the degree, or amount, of compression that will occur from 1 to 100. Usually, you won't see a great deal of image quality loss with compression levels 1 through 20.

✦ .png: Suited for larger graphics used in web design, such as the logo or main header graphic that helps brand the overall look of the website. A .png file uses lossless image compression; therefore, no data loss occurs during compression, so you get a cleaner, sharper image. You can also create and save a .png file on a transparent canvas; .jpg files must have a white canvas or some other color that you designate.

✦ .gif: Compression of a .gif file is lossless; therefore, the image renders exactly the way you design it, without loss of quality. However, .gif files compress with lossless quality when the image uses 256 colors or fewer. For images that use more colors (higher quality), .gif isn't the greatest format to use. For images with a lot of colors, go with the .png format instead.

Uploading an image for background use

If you want to change the background graphic in your theme, follow these steps:

1. **Upload your new background graphic via FTP to the images folder in your theme directory.**

   Typically, the images folder can be found at `wp-content/themes/themename/images`.

2. **On the WordPress Dashboard, click the Editor link on the Appearance menu.**

   The Theme Editor page displays.

3. **Click the Stylesheet (`style.css`) link on the right side of the page.**

   The `style.css` template opens in the text editor box on the left side of the Theme Editor page.

4. **Scroll down to find the `body` CSS selector.**

   I discuss CSS selectors later in this chapter, but the following code segment is a sample CSS snippet from the Twenty Twelve theme. (How the `body` selector is defined differs from theme to theme.)

   ```
   body {
       background: #f1f1f1;
   }
   ```

5. **Edit the background property values.**

   Change this:

   ```
   background: #f1f1f1;
   ```

   To this:

   ```
   background #FFFFFF url('images/newbackground.gif');
   ```

   With this example, you added a new background image (`newbackground.gif`) to the existing code and changed the color code to white (#FFFFFF).

6. **Click the Update File button to save the stylesheet changes you made.**

   Your changes are saved and applied to your theme. Figure 4-1 shows a preview of the new background without any positioning.

Figure 4-1:
A new
background
image on a
blog.

Positioning, repeating, and attaching images

After you upload a background graphic, you can use CSS background properties to position it how you want it. The main CSS properties — `background-position`, `background-repeat`, and `background-attachment` — help you achieve the desired effect. Table 4-1 describes the CSS background properties and the available values for changing them in your theme stylesheet. If you're a visual person, you'll enjoy testing and tweaking values to see the effects on your site.

Table 4-1	CSS Background Properties		
Property	*Description*	*Values*	*Example*

`background-position`	Determines the starting point of your background image on your web page	`bottom center`
		`bottom right`
		`left center`
		`right center`
		`center center`
			`background-position: bottom center;`

(continued)

Table 4-1 (continued)

Property	Description	Values	Example
background-repeat	Determines whether your background image will repeat or tile	repeat (repeats infinitely) repeat-y (repeats vertically) repeat-x (repeats horizontally) no-repeat (does not repeat)	background-repeat: repeat-y;
background-attachment	Determines whether your background image is fixed or scrolls with the browser window	fixed scroll	background-attachment: scroll;

Say your goal is to *tile,* or repeat, the background image (see Figure 4-2) so that it scales with the width of the browser on any computer. To achieve this, open the stylesheet again and change

```
background: #f1f1f1;
```

to

```
background: #FFFFFF;
background-image: url(images/newbackground.gif);
background-repeat: repeat;
```

If your goal is to display a fixed image that does not scroll or move when your site visitor moves the browser, you can use the background-position, background-repeat, and background-attachment properties to display it exactly how you want it to appear.

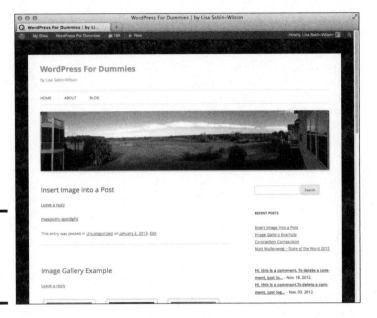

Figure 4-2:
A back-
ground
image that
repeats.

In Figure 4-2, the image is tiled, or it repeats, so it covers the entire back-ground space no matter how wide or long the website display is. To achieve the look, change `background: #f1f1f1` in your stylesheet to

```
background: #FFFFFF;
background-image: url(images/newbackground.gif);
background-position: top left;
background-repeat: repeat;
```

As you become more comfortable with CSS properties, you can start using shortening methods to make your CSS coding practice more efficient. For example, the previous block of code looks like this in with CSS shortcode practice:

```
background: #fff url(images/newbackground.gif) repeat top left;
```

As you can see from these examples, changing the background graphic by using CSS has a number of options that depend on your creativity and design style more than anything else. But properly leveraged, you can use this to take your design to the next level for you and your clients.

Changing Your Header Graphic

Creating unique header graphics is one of the fastest ways to personalize a site and make it unique. The header graphic is typically the strongest graphic design element. Positioned at the top of your theme, a header graphic often includes a logo or other information about your site or business.

Here are some elements you might include in your header graphic:

✦ **Business name or logo:** This sounds obvious, but the header graphic is the prime way to identify the site. If you don't have a logo, you can simply stylize your business name for your header graphic, but your brand identity needs to be prominent and polished in the header graphic.

✦ **Profile photos:** If it's for a blog or an independent professional's site (say, for a real estate agent), you might want to include a studio-quality profile photo of the person to help your site guests know who they're dealing with and to add a touch of warmth.

✦ **Taglines, important slogans, and keywords:** Use the header area to tell your visitors something about your site or business.

✦ **Contact information:** If you're doing a small business website, including phone and address information is vital.

✦ **Background images:** Be creative with the header image behind all this information. Use a pattern or graphic that matches your brand colors and doesn't distract attention from the vital information you want to communicate.

Most new WordPress themes, particularly premium themes, allow you to upload new header graphics over existing ones easily from the WordPress Dashboard. Sometimes this is called a Custom Header Uploader script or feature. This feature allows you to turn off HTML overlay text and use only graphics for your header, too.

You can personalize your header graphic the following ways:

✦ Replace or overwrite the theme's existing header image with an appropriate image of your choosing.

✦ Use a repeating graphic pattern.

Using a repeating graphic pattern is similar to using a repeating background image, which I discuss in the earlier "Positioning, repeating, and attaching images" section. In the following sections, you replace your existing header image (in the free Quick-Vid theme from iThemes) by using the Custom Header feature found in many WordPress themes. Figure 4-3 shows the Quick-Vid theme's default header image.

Figure 4-3:
The default header of the free Quick-Vid theme from iThemes.

Considering the image dimensions

Generally, you want to replace the existing header image with an image that has the exact width and height dimensions. To determine the dimensions of the existing image, find the default header graphic and open it in an image-editing program, such as Adobe Photoshop. Create (or crop) your new header graphic to the same dimensions (in pixels) to minimize problems when adding the image to your theme.

Photoshop Elements is a handy design software tool for basic image editing. It has significantly fewer features than its bigger and older brother, Photoshop, but for most image editing jobs it does great for a fraction of the price.

Uploading a header image

Depending on your theme, replacing an existing header image is a fast and efficient way of making changes — you simply upload the graphic and refresh your site.

The WordPress Custom Header feature is included in many of the popular themes. To add a new header graphic in your theme with the Custom Header feature, follow these steps:

1. **On the WordPress Dashboard, click the Custom Header link on the Appearance menu.**

   The Custom Header page appears, as shown in Figure 4-4. Here you can adjust your header area, add or remove text, and upload new graphics.

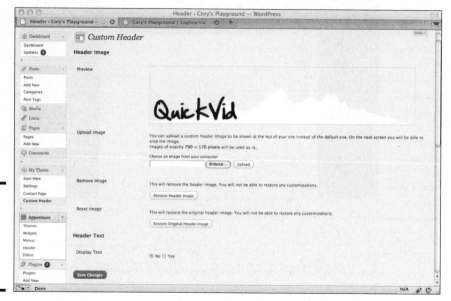

Figure 4-4: The Word-Press Custom Header feature.

2. **Select No on the Display Text option and then click Save Changes.**

   Because you're uploading only a header graphic, you don't want the default HTML text to show.

3. **Upload your new header graphic by clicking the Browse button in the Upload Image section.**

   If your image isn't sized to the specifications given, you'll be asked to crop it to fit.

4. **Refresh your site and see how your new header graphic looks.**

   Figure 4-5 shows a photo, site name, and tagline in the new header graphic.

Figure 4-5:
The Quick-
Vid theme
with a new
header
image.

Personalizing Your Theme with CSS

Cascading Style Sheets (CSS) are part of every WordPress theme. The primary way of personalizing your theme with CSS is through your theme's default stylesheet (style.css). Through a comment block (shown in Figure 4-6), your theme's style.css file tells WordPress the theme name, the version number, and the author, along with other information.

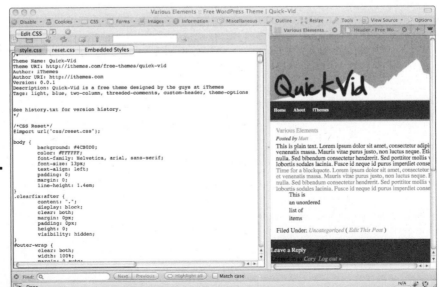

Figure 4-6:
The
comment
block of
a typical
WordPress
stylesheet.

With CSS changes to your theme's stylesheet you can apply unique styling (such as different fonts, sizes, and colors) to headlines, text, links, and borders, and adjust the spacing between them, too. With all the CSS options available, you can fine-tune the look and feel of different elements with simple tweaks.

To explore your theme's stylesheet, click the Editor link on the Appearance menu on the WordPress Dashboard. By default, your theme's main stylesheet (`style.css`) should appear. If not, look at the far right side of the WordPress Dashboard under the Templates heading, scroll down to find the Styles heading, and click the Stylesheet file, as shown in Figure 4-7.

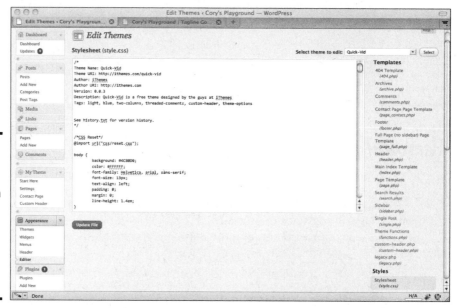

Figure 4-7: Shows the list of files contained in the Quick-Vid theme, separated by Templates and Styles.

Making changes to the stylesheet or any other theme file can cause your site to load the theme improperly. Be careful what you change here. When you make changes, ensure that you're on a playground or sandbox site so that you can easily restore your original file and don't permanently affect a "live" or important site. Always save an original copy of the stylesheet in a text program, such as Notepad (for the PC) or TextMate (for the Mac), so you can find the original CSS and copy and paste it back into your stylesheet if necessary.

Knowing some key CSS concepts can help you personalize your theme's stylesheet. CSS is simply a set of commands that allows you to customize the look and feel of your HTML markup. Some common commands and tools are selectors, IDs and classes, properties and values, and more. You use these commands to customize HTML to display your design customizations.

CSS selectors

Typically, CSS *selectors* are named for the corresponding HTML elements, IDs, and classes that you want to style with CSS properties and values. Selectors are very important in CSS because they are used to "select" elements on an HTML/PHP page so that they can be appropriately styled.

With CSS, you can provide style (such as size, color, and placement) to the display of elements on your blog (such as text links, header images, font size and colors, paragraph margins, and line spacing). *CSS selectors* contain names, properties, and values to define which HTML elements in the templates you will style with CSS. Table 4-2 lists some basic global CSS selectors.

Table 4-2		Basic Global CSS Selectors	
CSS Selector	*Description*	*HTML*	*CSS Example*
body	Contains the elements of the overall site style	`<body>`	`body {font-family: Georgia}`
a	Sets the attributes for hyperlinks within your site	`<a href="http:// wordpress.org"> WordPress</a>`	`a {color:blue}`
h1, h2, h3, h4, h5, h6	Headings or headlines	`<h1>My main title</h1>`	`h1 {color:black}`
blockquote	Defines how indented text is styled	`<blockquote> "A journey of a thousand miles begins with a single step." </blockquote>`	`blockquote {font-style: italic}`
p	Sets formatting for paragraphs	`<p>My first paragraph says to keep writing</p>`	`p {color: #000}`

If you were to assign a style to the h1 selector, it will affect all <h1> tags in your HTML. Sometimes you want this, but sometimes you want to affect only a smaller subset of elements.

CSS IDs and classes

With CSS IDs and classes, you can define more elements to style. Generally, IDs are used to style one broader specific element (such as your header section) on your page. Classes style, define, and categorize more specifically grouped items (such as images and text alignment, widgets, or links to posts).

✦ **CSS IDs** are identified with the hash mark (#). For example, #header indicates the header ID. There can be only one element identified with an ID.

✦ **CSS classes** are identified with a period (.). For example, .alignleft indicates aligning an element to the left.

Table 4-3 lists some CSS IDs and classes.

Table 4-3	CSS IDs and Classes Examples		
CSS IDs and Classes	*Description*	*HTML*	*CSS Example*
#header	Identifies the header section of your theme	`<div id= "header">`	`#header {background: #000}`
#footer	Identifies the footer section of your theme	`<div id= "footer">`	`#footer {background: #ccc}`
.wp-caption-text	Identifies the WordPress image caption	`<p class="wp-caption-text"> This is a caption</p>`	`.wp-caption-text {color: #000}`
.alignleft	Identifies the left alignment feature in WordPress	`<img class= "alignleft" src="http:// yourdomain.com/ photo.jpg" />`	`.alignleft {float:left}`

CSS properties and values

CSS properties are assigned to the CSS selector name. You also need to provide values for the CSS properties to define the style elements for the particular CSS selector you're working with.

For example, the `body` selector that follows defines the overall look of your web page; `background` is a property and `#DDDDDD` is the value, and `color` is a property and `#222222` is the value.

```
body {
background: #DDDDDD;
color: #222222;
}
```

Every CSS property needs to be followed by a colon (`:`), and each CSS value needs to be followed by a semicolon (`;`).

Understanding that properties are assigned to selectors, as well as your options for the values, makes CSS a fun playground for personalizing your site. You can experiment with colors, fonts, font sizes, and more to tweak the look of your theme.

Understanding Basic HTML Techniques

HTML can help you customize and organize your theme. To understand how HTML and CSS work together, think of it this way: If a website were a building, HTML would be the structure (the studs and foundation), and CSS would be the paint.

HTML contains the elements that CSS provides the styles for. All you have to do to apply a CSS style is use the right HTML element. Here's a very basic block of HTML:

```
<body>
<div id="content">
<h1>Headline Goes Here</h1>
<p>This is a sample sentence of body text. <blockquote>The journey
of a thousand miles starts with the first step.</blockquote> I'm
going to continue on this sentence and end it here. </p>
<p>Click <a href="http://corymiller.com">here</a> to visit my
website.</p>
</div>
</body>
```

All HTML elements must have opening and closing tags. Opening tags are contained in less-than (<) and greater-than (>) symbols. Closing tags are the same, except they are preceded by a forward slash (/).

For example:

```
<h1>Headline Goes Here</h1>
```

Note that the HTML elements must be properly nested. In line four of this example, a paragraph tag is opened (<p>). Later in that line, a block quote is opened (<blockquote>) and nesting inside the paragraph tag. When editing this line, you could not end the paragraph (</p>) before you ended the block quote (</blockquote>). Nested elements must close before the elements they are nested within close.

Proper *tabbing,* or indenting, is important when writing HTML, mainly for readability so you can quickly scan through code to find what you're looking for. A good rule is that if you didn't close a tag in the preceding line, indent one tab over. This allows you to see where each element begins and ends. It can also be very helpful when diagnosing problems.

For more in-depth tutorials on HTML, see the HTML section of w3schools. com at www.w3schools.com/html/default.asp.

Changing Basic Elements for a Unique Look

When you understand the basic concepts about personalizing your site with graphics and CSS, you begin to see how easy changing the look and feel of your site is with these tools. The next few sections explore some ways to accomplish an interesting design presentation or a unique and creative look.

Background colors and images

Changing the background image can completely change the feel of your site. However, you can also use background colors and images for other elements in your theme.

Background techniques include using solid colors and repeating gradients or patterns to achieve a subtle yet polished effect. (***Note:*** Use colors that accent the colors of your logo and don't hamper text readability.)

You can add CSS background colors and image effects to the following areas of your theme:

✦ Post and page content sections

✦ Sidebar widgets

✦ Comment blocks

✦ Footer area

Font family, color, and size

You can change the fonts in your theme for style or for readability purposes. Typographic (or font) design experts use simple font variations to achieve amazing design results. You can use fonts to separate headlines from body text (or widget headlines and text from the main content) to be less distracting. Table 4-4 lists some examples of often-used font properties.

Table 4-4		Fonts
Font Properties	*Common Values*	*CSS Examples*
font-family	Georgia, Times, serif	body {font-family: Georgia; serif;}
font-size	px, %, em	body {font-size: 14px;}
font-style	Italic, underline	body {font-style: italic;}
font-weight	bold, bolder, normal	body {font-weight: normal}

**Book VI
Chapter 4**

Customizing Your
Theme

The web is actually kind of picky about how it displays fonts, as well as what kind of fonts you can use in the font-family property. Not all fonts display correctly. To be safe, here are some commonly used font families that display correctly in most browsers:

✦ **Serif fonts:** Times New Roman, Georgia, Garamond, Bookman Old Style

✦ **Sans-serif fonts:** Verdana, Arial, Tahoma, Trebuchet MS

Serif fonts have little tails, or curlicues, at the edges of letters. (This book's text is in a serif font.) Sans-serif fonts have straight edges and no fancy styling. (The heading in Table 4-4 uses a sans-serif font — look ma, no tails!)

Font color

With more than 16 million HTML color combinations available, you can find just the right shade of color for your project. After some time, you'll memorize your favorite color codes. Knowing codes for different shades of gray can help you quickly add an extra design touch. For example, you can use the shades of gray listed in Table 4-5 for backgrounds, borders on design elements, and widget headers.

Table 4-5	My Favorite CSS Colors
Color	*Value*
White	#FFFFFF or #FFF
Black	#000000 or #000
Gray	#CCCCCC or #CCC
	#DDDDDD or #DDD
	#333333 or #333
	#E0E0E0

You can easily change the color of your font by changing the `color` property of the CSS selector you want to tweak. You can use hexadecimal codes to define the colors.

You can define the overall font color in your site by defining it in the body CSS selector like this:

```
body {
color: #333;
}
```

Font size

To tweak the size of your font, change the `font-size` property of the CSS selector you want to tweak. Generally, the following units of measurement determine font sizes:

✦ **px (pixel):** Increasing or decreasing the number of pixels increases or decreases the font size — 12px is larger than 10px.

✦ **pt (point):** As with pixels, increasing or decreasing the number of points affects the font size — 12pt is larger than 10pt.

✦ **% (percentage):** Increasing or decreasing the percentage number affects the font size — 50% is equivalent to 7 pixels, and 100% is equivalent to 17 pixels.

In the default template CSS, the font size is defined in the `<body>` tag in pixels, like this:

```
font-size: 12px;
```

Putting all three elements (`font-family`, `color`, and `font-size`) together in the <body> tag styles the font for the entire body of your site. Here's how the elements work together in the <body> tag of the default template CSS:

```
body {
font-size: 12px;
font-family: Georgia, "Bitstream Charter", serif;
color: #666;
}
```

When you want to change a font family in your CSS, open the stylesheet (`style.css`), search for `property:  font-family`, change the values for that property, and then save your changes.

In the default template CSS, the font is defined in the <body> tag like this:

```
font-family: Georgia, "Bitstream Charter", serif;
```

Borders

Using CSS borders can add an interesting and unique flair to elements of your theme design. (See Figure 4-8.) Table 4-6 illustrates common properties and CSS examples for borders in your theme design.

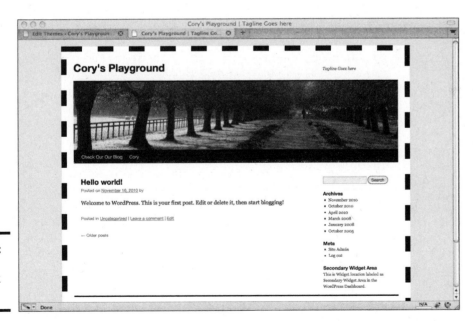

Figure 4-8:
A dashed
15px black
border.

Table 4-6	Common Border Properties	
Border Properties	*Common Values*	*CSS Examples*
`border-size`	px, em	`body {border-size: 1px;}`
`border-style`	solid, dotted, dashed	`body {border-style: solid}`
`border-color`	Hexadecimal values	`body {border-color: #CCCCCC}`

Finding Additional Resources

There may come a time when you want to explore customizing your theme further. Here are some recommended resources:

✦ **WordPress Codex** (`http://codex.wordpress.org`): Official WordPress documentation

✦ **W3Schools** (`http://w3schools.com`): A free and comprehensive online HTML and CSS reference

✦ **WebDesign.com** (`http://webdesign.com`): A premium library of WordPress video tutorials and training

✦ **Smashing Magazine** (`www.smashingmagazine.com`): Numerous tips and tricks for customizing a WordPress theme

Chapter 5: Understanding Parent and Child Themes

In This Chapter

✔ Defining the relationship between parent and child themes

✔ Tweaking child themes with styles

✔ Customizing child themes with images

✔ Modifying child themes with template files

*U*sing a theme exactly as a theme author released it is great. If a new version is released that fixes a browser compatibility issue or adds features offered by a new version of WordPress, a quick theme upgrade is very easy to do.

However, there's a good chance you'll want to tinker with the design, add new features, or modify the theme structure. If you modify the theme, you won't be able to upgrade to a newly released version without modifying the theme again. If only you could upgrade customized versions of themes with new features when they're released. Fortunately, child themes give you this best-of-both-worlds theme solution.

This chapter explores what child themes are, how to create a child theme–ready parent theme, and how to get the most out of using child themes.

Customizing Theme Style with Child Themes

A WordPress theme consists of a collection of template files, stylesheets, images, and JavaScript files. The theme controls the layout and design that your visitors see on the site. When such a theme is properly set up as a parent theme, it allows a *child theme,* or a subset of instructions, to override its files. This ensures that a child theme can selectively modify the layout, styling, and functionality of the parent theme.

The quickest way to understand child themes is by example. In this section, you create a simple child theme that modifies the style of the parent theme.

Currently, the default WordPress theme is Twenty Twelve. Figure 5-1 shows how the Twenty Twelve theme appears on a sample site.

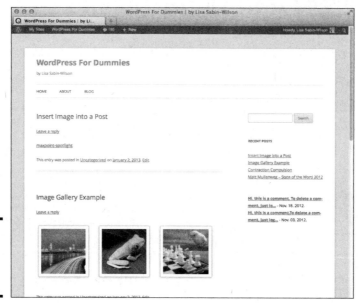

Figure 5-1:
The Twenty Twelve theme.

You likely have Twenty Twelve on your WordPress site, and Twenty Twelve is child theme–ready; therefore, it's a great candidate for creating a child theme.

Creating a child theme

Like regular themes, a child theme needs to reside in a directory inside the `/wp-content/themes` directory. The first step to creating a child theme is to add the directory that will hold it. For this example, connect to your hosting account via FTP and create a new directory called `twentytwelve-child` inside the `/wp-content/themes` directory.

To register the `twentytwelve-child` directory as a theme and to make it a child of the Twenty Twelve theme, create a `style.css` file and add the appropriate theme headers. To do this, type the following code into your favorite code or plain-text editor (such as Notepad for the PC or TextMate for the Mac) and save the file as `style.css`:

```
/*
Theme Name: Twenty Twelve Child
Description: My magnificent child theme
Author: Lisa Sabin-Wilson
Version: 1.0
Template: twentytwelve
*/
```

Typically, you can find the following headers in a WordPress theme:

✦ `Theme Name`: The theme user sees this name in the back end of WordPress.

✦ `Description`: This header provides the user any additional information about the theme. Currently, it only appears on the Manage Themes page (accessed by clicking the Themes link on the Appearance menu).

✦ `Author`: This header lists one or more theme authors. Currently, it is shown only on the Manage Themes page (accessed by clicking the Themes link on the Appearance menu).

✦ `Version`: The version number is very useful for keeping track of outdated versions of the theme. It is always a good idea to update the version number when modifying a theme.

✦ `Template`: This header changes a theme into a child theme. The value of this header tells WordPress the directory name of the parent theme. Because your child theme uses Twenty Twelve as the parent, your `style.css` needs to have a `Template` header with a value of `twenty twelve` (the directory name of the Twenty Twelve theme).

Now activate the new Twenty Twelve Child theme as your active theme. (If you need a reminder on how to activate a theme on your site, check out Book VI, Chapter 2.) You should see a site layout similar to the one shown in Figure 5-2.

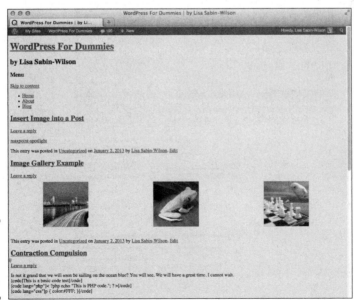

Figure 5-2:
The Twenty
Twelve
Child theme.

Figure 5-2 shows that the new theme doesn't look quite right. The problem is that the new child theme replaced the `style.css` file of the parent theme, yet the new child theme's `style.css` file is empty.

You could just copy and paste the contents of the parent theme's `style.css` file, but that would waste some of the potential of child themes.

Loading a parent theme's style

One of the great things about CSS is how rules can override one another. If you list the same rule twice in your CSS, the rule that comes last takes precedence.

For example:

```
a {
color: blue;
}

a {
color: red;
}
```

This example is overly simple, but it nicely shows what I'm talking about. The first rule says that all links (a tags) should be blue, whereas the second rule says that links should be red. Because CSS says that the last instruction takes precedence, the links will be red.

Using this feature of CSS, you can inherit all the styling of the parent theme and selectively modify it by overriding the rules of the parent theme. But how can you load the parent theme's `style.css` file so that it inherits the parent theme's styling?

Fortunately, CSS has another great feature that helps you do this with ease. Just add one line to the Twenty Twelve Child theme's `style.css` file:

```
/*
Theme Name: Twenty Twelve Child
Description: My magnificent child theme
Author: Lisa Sabin-Wilson
Version: 1.0
Template: twentytwelve
*/
@import url('../twentytwelve/style.css');
```

A number of things are going on here, so let me break it down piece by piece:

✦ `@import`: This tells the browser to load another stylesheet. Using this allows you to pull in the parent stylesheet quickly and easily.

✦ `url('...')`: This indicates that the value is a location and not a normal value.

✦ `('../twentytwelve/style.css');`: This is the location of the parent stylesheet. Notice the `/twentytwelve` directory name. This needs to be changed to match the `Template` value in the header so that the appropriate stylesheet is loaded.

Figure 5-3 shows how the site appears after updating the child theme's `style.css` file to match the listing.

**Book VI
Chapter 5**

**Understanding
Parent and Child
Themes**

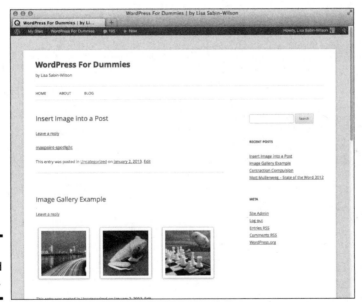

Figure 5-3:
The updated
child theme.

Customizing the parent theme's styling

Your Twenty Twelve Child theme is set up to match the parent Twenty Twelve theme. Now you can add new styling to the Twenty Twelve Child theme's `style.css` file. A simple example of how customizing works is to add a style that converts all h1, h2, and h3 headings to uppercase, like so:

```
/*
Theme Name: Twenty Twelve Child
Description: My magnificent child theme
Author: Lisa Sabin-Wilson
Version: 1.0
Template: twentytwelve
*/
@import url('../twentytwelve/style.css');

h1, h2, h3 {
text-transform: uppercase;
}
```

Figure 5-4 shows how the child theme looks with the code additions applied — getting better, isn't it? (***Hint:*** The site title and post titles are now all uppercase, which differs from Figure 5-3.)

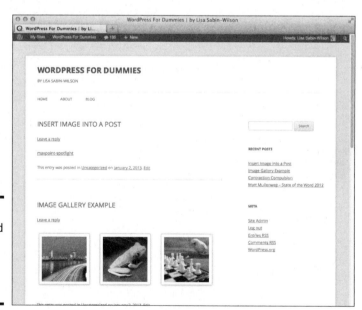

Figure 5-4:
The updated
child
theme with
uppercase
headings.

As you can see, with just a few lines in a `style.css` file, you can create a new child theme that adds specific customizations to an existing theme. Not only was it quick and easy to do, but you didn't have to modify anything in the parent theme to make it work.

When upgrades to the parent theme are available, upgrade the parent to get the additional features without having to make your modifications again.

Customizations that are more complex work the same way. Simply add the new rules after the import rule that adds the parent stylesheet.

Using images in child theme designs

Many themes use images to add nice touches to the design. Typically, these images are added to a directory named `images` inside the theme.

Just as a parent theme may refer to images in its `style.css` file, your child themes can have their own images directory. The following are examples of how you can use these images.

Using a child theme image in a child theme stylesheet

Including a child theme image in a child theme stylesheet is common. To do so, you simply add the new image to the child theme's `images` directory and refer to it in the child theme's `style.css` file. To get a feel for the mechanics of this process, follow these steps:

1. **Create an `images` directory inside the child theme's directory.**

2. **Add an image to use into the directory.**

For this example, add an image called `body-bg.png`.

3. **Add the necessary styling to the child theme's `style.css` file, as follows:**

```
/*
Theme Name: Twenty Twelve Child
Description: My magnificent child theme
Author: Lisa Sabin-Wilson
Version: 1.0
Template: twentytwelve
*/
@import url('../twentytwelve/style.css');
body {
background: url('images/body-bg.png');
}
```

With a quick refresh of the site, you see that the site now has a new background. Figure 5-5 shows the results clearly by using the browser's zoom feature to make the site smaller.

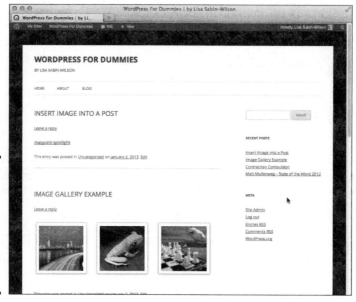

Figure 5-5:
The Twenty Twelve Child theme after editing the background image.

Using images in a child theme

Child theme images are acceptable for most purposes. You can add your own images to the child theme even if the image doesn't exist in the parent theme folder — and you can accomplish that without changing the parent theme at all.

In the footer of the Twenty Twelve Child theme, I added a WordPress logo to the left of the phrase "Proudly powered by WordPress," as shown in Figure 5-6. Refer to Figure 5-1; the logo does not appear in the footer of the Twenty Twelve theme by default.

Create a folder in your child theme called /images and add your selected images to that folder, then you can call those images into your child theme by using the stylesheet (style.css) file in your child theme folder.

Figure 5-6:
The
WordPress
logo in the
Twenty
Twelve
Child footer.

WordPress logo

In this next example, I add the same WordPress logo in front of each widget title in the sidebar. Because the logo image already exists inside the child theme images folder (from my previous example), I can simply add a customization to the child theme's `style.css` file to make this change, as follows:

```
/*
Theme Name: Twenty Twelve Child
Description: My magnificent child theme
Author: Lisa Sabin-Wilson
Version: 1.0
Template: twentytwelve
*/

@import url('../twentytwelve/style.css');

.widget-title {
background: url('images/wordpress.png') no-repeat left top;
padding: 10px 30px;
line-height: 16px;
font-size: 16px;
}
```

Save the file and refresh the site. Now you're showing WordPress pride. (See Figure 5-7.)

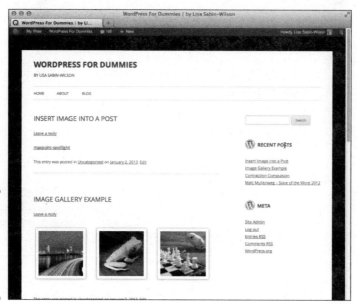

Figure 5-7:
Showing the WordPress logo before each widget title.

Modifying Theme Structure with Child Themes

The preceding section showed how to use a child theme to modify the stylesheet of an existing theme. This is tremendously powerful. A talented CSS developer can use this technique to create an amazing variety of layouts and designs.

However, this is just the beginning of the power of child themes. Although every child theme overrides the parent theme's `style.css` file, the child theme can override the parent theme's template files, too. However, child themes aren't limited to just overriding template files; when needed, child themes can also supply their own template files.

Template files are PHP files that WordPress runs to render different views of your site. A site view is the type of content being looked at. Examples of different views are home, category archive, individual post, and page content.

Some examples of common template files are index.php, archive.php, single.php, page.php, attachment.php, and search.php. (You can read more about available template files, including how to use them, in Chapter 3 of this minibook.)

You might wonder what purpose modifying template files of a parent theme serves. Although modifying the stylesheet of a parent theme can allow for some very powerful control over the design, it can't add new content, modify the underlying site structure, or change how the theme functions. To get that level of control, you need to modify the template files.

Overriding parent template files

When both the child theme and parent theme supply the same template file, the child theme file is used. This process of replacing the original parent template file is referred to as *overriding*.

Although overriding each of the theme's template files can defeat the purpose of using a child theme — because updates to those template files won't enhance the child theme — sometimes, producing a needed result makes doing so necessary.

The easiest way to customize a specific template file in a child theme is to copy the template file from the parent theme folder to the child theme folder. After the file is copied, it can be customized as needed, and the child theme reflects the changes.

A good example of a template file that can be overridden is the footer.php file. Customizing the footer allows for adding site-specific branding.

Adding new template files

A child theme can override existing parent template files, but it can supply template files that don't exist in the parent, too. Although you may never need your child themes to do this, this option can open possibilities for your designs.

For example, this technique proves most valuable with page templates. The Twenty Twelve theme has a page template named Full-width Page Template, No Sidebar. As you might expect, this page template creates a full-width layout for the content and removes the sidebar completely, as shown in Figure 5-8.

Figure 5-8:
The Full-
width Page
Template,
No Sidebar
page
template
in Twenty
Twelve.

The layout was intentionally set up this way to improve readability for those pages where you may not want the distraction of other content in a sidebar. Sometimes, I like to have a full-width layout option so that I can embed a video, add a forum, or add other content that works well with full width. If you want to customize that template and override what the Twenty Twelve theme currently has available, simply create a new page template with the same file name as the one you are replacing (in this case: `/page-templates/full-width.php`) and add the necessary styling to the `style.css` file. WordPress will use the `full-width.php` template file in your child theme by default, completely ignoring the one that exists in the Twenty Twelve parent theme folder.

Removing template files

You may be asking why you would want to remove a parent's template file. That's a good question. Unfortunately, the Twenty Twelve theme doesn't provide a good example of why you would want to do this. Therefore, you must use your imagination a bit.

Imagine that you're creating a child theme built off a parent theme called Example Parent. Example Parent is well designed, and a great child theme was quickly built off it. The child theme looks and works exactly the way you want it to, but there's a problem.

The Example Parent theme has a `home.php` template file that provides a highly customized non-blog home page. This works very well, but it isn't what you want for the site. You want a standard blog home page. If the `home.php` file didn't exist in Example Parent, everything would work perfectly.

There isn't a way to remove the `home.php` file from Example Parent without modifying the theme, so you have to use a trick. Instead of removing the file, override the `home.php` file and have it emulate `index.php`.

You may think that simply copying and pasting the Example Parent `index.php` code into the child theme's `home.php` file is a good approach. Although this works, there is a better way: You can tell WordPress to run the `index.php` file so that changes to `index.php` are respected. This single line of code inside the child theme's `home.php` is all that is needed to replace `home.php` with `index.php`:

```php
<?php locate_template( array( 'index.php' ), true ); ?>
```

The `locate_template` function does a bit of magic. If the child theme supplies an `index.php` file, then it is used. If not, then the parent `index.php` file is used.

This produces the same result that removing the parent theme's `home.php` file would have. The `home.php` code is ignored, and the changes to `index.php` are respected.

Modifying the functions.php file

Like template files, child themes can provide a Theme Functions template, or `functions.php` file. Unlike template files, the `functions.php` of a child theme does not override the file of the parent theme.

When a parent theme and a child theme each have a `functions.php` file, both the parent and child `functions.php` files run. The child theme's `functions.php` file runs first and then the parent theme's `functions.php` file runs. This is intentional because it allows the child theme to replace functions defined in the parent theme. However, this works only if the functions are set up to allow this.

The Twenty Twelve `functions.php` file defines a function called `twentytwelve_setup`. This function handles the configuration of many theme options and activates some additional features. Child themes can replace this function to change the default configuration and features of the theme, too.

The following lines of code summarize how the functions.php file allows this to happen:

```
if ( ! function_exists( 'twentytwelve_setup' ) ):
function twentytwelve_setup() {
// removed code
}
endif;
```

Wrapping the function declaration in the if statement protects the site from breaking in the event of a code conflict and allows a child theme to define its own version of the function.

In the Twenty Twelve Child theme, you can see how modifying this function affects the theme. Add a new twentytwelve_setup function that adds post thumbnails support to the Twenty Twelve Child theme's functions.php file.

```
<?php
function twentytwelve_setup() {
add_theme_support( 'post-thumbnails' );
}
```

The result of this change is the child theme no longer supports other special WordPress features, such as custom editor styling, automatic feed link generation, internationalization and location, and so on.

The take-away from this example is that a child theme can provide its own custom version of the function because the parent theme wraps the function declaration in an if block that checks for the function first.

Preparing a Parent Theme

WordPress makes it very easy for you to make parent themes. WordPress does most of the hard work; however, you must follow some rules for a parent theme to function properly.

The words *stylesheet* and *template* have been used numerous times in many different contexts. Typically, *stylesheet* refers to a CSS file in a theme and *template* refers to a template file in the theme. However, these words also have specific meaning when working with parent and child themes. You must understand the difference between a stylesheet and a template when working with parent and child themes.

In WordPress, the active theme is the stylesheet and the active theme's parent is the template. If the theme doesn't have a parent, then the active theme is both the stylesheet and the template.

Originally, child themes could replace only the `style.css` file of a theme. The parent provided all the template files and `functions.php` code. Thus, the child theme provided style and the parent theme provided the template files. The capabilities of child themes expanded in subsequent versions of WordPress, making the use of these terms for parent and child themes somewhat confusing.

Imagine two themes: Parent and Child. The following code is in the Parent theme's `header.php` file and loads an additional stylesheet provided by the theme:

```
<link type="text/css" rel="stylesheet" media="all" href="<?php
bloginfo('stylesheet_directory') ?>/reset.css" />
```

The `bloginfo` function prints information about the blog configuration or settings. This example uses the function to print the URL location of the stylesheet directory. The site is hosted at `http://example.com`, and the Parent is the active theme. It produces the following output:

```
<link type="text/css" rel="stylesheet" media="all"
href="http://example.com/wp-content/themes/Parent/reset.css" />
```

If the child theme is activated, the output would be

```
<link type="text/css" rel="stylesheet" media="all"
href="http://example.com/wp-content/themes/Child/reset.css" />
```

The location now refers to the `reset.css` file in the Child theme. This could work if every child theme copies the `reset.css` file of the Parent theme, but requiring child themes to add files in order to function isn't good design. The solution is simple, however. Instead of using the `stylesheet_directory` in the `bloginfo` call, use `template_directory`. The code looks like this:

```
<link type="text/css" rel="stylesheet" media="all" href="<?php
bloginfo('template_directory') ?>/reset.css" />
```

Now, all child themes will properly load the parent `reset.css` file.

When developing, use `template_directory` in standalone parent themes and `stylesheet_directory` in child themes.

Chapter 6: Digging into Advanced Theme Development

In This Chapter

✔ Customizing themes

✔ Creating new templates

✔ Activating custom menus

✔ Exploring custom post types

✔ Understanding post formats

✔ Using post thumbnails for feature images

✔ Building a theme options page

The previous chapters of this minibook describe WordPress themes and using their structure to build your site. Delving into deeper topics can help you create flexible themes that offer users options to control the theme.

Whether you're building a theme for a client, the WordPress.org theme directory, or yourself, adding advanced theme features can make theme development easier and faster with a high-quality result. With these advanced theme concepts and tools, you can build robust, dynamic themes that allow for easier design customization and offer a variety of layout options.

Beyond just tools and methods of advanced theme development, this chapter provides some development practices that help projects succeed.

Getting Started with Advanced Theming

Before themes were added to WordPress, customizing the design of the site meant modifying the main WordPress `index.php` file and the default `print.css` file. Version 1.5 added the first theme support and rudimentary child theme support. Over time, WordPress began to support other features, such as custom headers, custom backgrounds, and featured images.

Additionally, the capabilities of themes have grown steadily. Incremental improvement — beginning with a small, simple starting point and improving it over time — works very well in theme development. By developing incrementally, you can build a theme from start to completion from an existing, well-tested theme (most themes are part of a larger incremental improvement process) and maximize your development time. I can't think of a single theme I've developed that wasn't built on another theme.

There isn't a need to develop each theme from scratch. Choosing a good starting point makes a big difference to how quickly you can get your project off the ground.

Finding a good starting point

Choosing a solid starting point to build your latest and greatest theme design on can be time consuming. Although exploring all the available themes in detail is tempting, I find exhaustive searches waste more time than they save.

Begin with the most current theme unless there's a more suitable one. Because the design and capabilities of the theme were recently implemented, modifying it to meet your current project's needs is faster than rediscovering all the nuances of an older, unfamiliar theme.

You might wonder whether I ever build themes off other designers' themes. I have. These days, if a new theme comes out that shows how to integrate some new feature, I play around with the theme to understand the concept but always go back to one of my themes to implement the modification. The reason for this is simple: If I can implement the feature into my own design, I have a much better appreciation for how it works. Allowing someone else's code or design to do the heavy lifting can place a limitation on how I use that feature.

If you're new to theme development and haven't produced a theme of your own, start with the WordPress default theme, Twenty Twelve. (See Chapter 1 in this minibook for a full analysis of the Twenty Twelve theme.) This theme is developed for helping new theme developers discover how themes work.

All the examples in this chapter are built off the WordPress default Twenty Twelve theme, unless noted otherwise.

Customizing the theme to your needs

After you select a theme for your project, you should create a copy of the theme. This way you can look at the unmodified version in case you accidentally remove something that causes the theme or design to break.

When you find code and styling that you don't need anymore, comment it out rather than delete it. This removes the functionality but still allows you to add it back later if you change your mind.

A line of PHP code can be commented out by adding // in front of it. For example:

```
// add_editor_style();
```

CSS can be commented out by wrapping a section in /* and */. For example:

```
/*#content {
 margin: 0 280px 0 20px;
}
*/
#primary,
#secondary {
 float: right;
/* overflow: hidden;
*/
 width: 220px;
}
```

HTML code gets commented out using brackets starting with <!-- and ending with --> surrounding the code. For example:

```
<!--<div id="content">this is a content area</div>-->
```

TIP

When you start finalizing the theme, go through the files and remove any blocks of commented styling and code to clean up your files.

Adding New Template Files

Chapter 3 of this minibook introduces the concept of template files and gives you an overview of the template files available to you. Chapter 5 of this minibook explains the idea of overriding template files with child themes. The following sections explore some advanced uses of template files.

Although you rarely need to use all these techniques, being fluent in your options gives you flexibility to address specific needs quickly when they come up.

Creating named templates

WordPress recognizes three special areas of a theme: header, footer, and sidebar. The get_header, get_footer, and get_sidebar functions default to loading header.php, footer.php, and sidebar.php, respectively. Each of these functions also supports a name argument to allow you to load an alternative version of the file. For example, running get_header('main') causes WordPress to load header-main.php.

You might wonder why you would use a name argument when you could just create a template file named whatever you like and load it directly. The reasons for using the get_header, get_footer, or get_sidebar functions with a name argument are

✦ Holding to a standard naming convention that other WordPress developers can easily understand

✦ Automatically providing support for child themes to override the parent theme's template file

✦ Offering a fallback that loads the unnamed template file if the named one doesn't exist

In short, use the name argument feature if you have multiple, specialized header, footer, or sidebar template files.

You can use this named template feature along with the Theme Options discussed in the "Exploring Theme Options" section, later in this chapter, to allow users to easily switch between different header, footer, and sidebar styles. On the Theme Options page, you can give the user the ability to choose the specific header, footer, or sidebar template file he or she wants, giving users an easy way to change the layout or design of the site. A good example of content you could add to a different sidebar file can be found in the nearby "WP_Query for category content" sidebar, which discusses displaying a list of recent posts and filing them in a specific category in the sidebar of your site.

WP_Query posts for category content

WordPress makes it possible to pull in very specific types of content on your website through the `WP_Query();` template class. You place this template tag before The Loop (see Chapter 3 of this minibook), and it lets you specify which category you want to pull information from. If you have a category called WordPress and you want to display the last three posts from that category on your front page, in your blog sidebar, or somewhere else on your site, you can use this template tag.

The `WP_Query();` template class has several parameters that let you display different types of content, such as posts in specific categories, content from specific pages/posts, or dates in your blog archives. The `WP_Query();` class lets you pass many variables and parameters. It's not just limited to categories either; you can use it for pages, posts, tags and more. Visit the WordPress Codex at `http://codex.wordpress.org/Class_Reference/WP_Query` and read about this feature.

To query the posts on your blog to pull out posts from just one specific category, you can use the following tag with the associated arguments for the available parameters. This example tells WordPress to query all posts that exist on your site and list the last five posts in the Books category:

```php
<?php $the_query = new WP_Query('posts_per_page=5&category_name=books'); ?>
```

Simply place this code on a line above the start of The Loop; you can use it in a sidebar to display clickable titles of the last five posts in the Books category. (When the reader clicks a title, the reader is taken to the individual post page to read the full post.)

```php
<?php $the_query = WP_Query('posts_per_page=5&category_name=books'); ?>
<?php while ($the_query->have_posts()) : $the_query->the_post(); ?>
<strong><a href="<?php the_permalink() ?>" rel="bookmark" title="Permanent Link to
<?php the_title_attribute(); ?>"><?php the_title(); ?></a></strong>
<?php the_excerpt(); endwhile; ?>
```

Creating and using template parts

A template part is very similar to the header, footer, and sidebar templates except that you aren't limited to just header, footer, and sidebar.

The `get_header`, `get_footer`, and `get_sidebar` functions allow for code that's duplicated in many of the template files to be placed in a single file and loaded by using a standard process. The purpose of template parts is to offer a standardized function that can be used to load sections of code specific to an individual theme. Sections of code that add a specialized section of header widgets or display a block of ads can be placed in individual files and easily loaded as a template part.

You load template parts by using the `get_template_part` function. The `get_template_part` function accepts two arguments: slug and name. The slug argument is required and describes the generic type of template part to be loaded, such as `loop`. The name argument is optional and selects a specialized template part, such as `post`.

A call to `get_template_part` with just the slug argument tries to load a template file with a filename of *slug*`.php`. Thus, a call to `get_template_part('loop')` tries to load `loop.php`, and a call to `get_template_part('header-widgets')` tries to load `header-widgets.php`. See a pattern here? *Slug* refers to the name of the template file, minus the `.php` extension, because WordPress already assumes that it's a PHP file.

A call to `get_template_part` with both the slug and name arguments will try to load a template file with a filename of *slug-name*`.php`. If a template file with a filename of *slug-name*`.php` doesn't exist, then WordPress will try to load a template file with a filename of *slug*`.php`. Thus, a call to `get_template_part('loop', 'post')` first tries to load `loop-post.php` followed by `loop.php` if `loop-post.php` doesn't exist; a call to `get_template_part('header-widgets', 'post')` first tries to load `header-widgets-post.php` followed by `header-widgets.php` if `header-widgets-post.php` doesn't exist.

The Twenty Twelve theme offers a good example of the template part feature in use. It uses a template part called `content` to allow the page or post content, within The Loop, to be get into individual files.

The Loop is the section of code found in most theme template files that uses a PHP `while` loop to loop through the set of post, page, and archive content (to name a few) and display it. The presence of The Loop in a template file is crucial for a theme to function properly. Chapter 3 in this minibook examines The Loop in detail.

Twenty Twelve's `index.php` template file shows a template part for the `content` template part in action:

```php
<?php while ( have_posts() ) : the_post(); ?>
<?php get_template_part( 'content', get_post_format() ); ?>
<?php endwhile; ?>
```

Loading the content by using a template part, Twenty Twelve cleans up the `index.php` code considerably when compared with other themes. This cleanup of the template file code is just the icing on the cake. The true benefits are the improvements to theme development.

Twenty Twelve's `index.php` template file calls for a template part with a slug of `content` and a name of `get_post_format()`. The `get_post_format();` tag pulls in the defined format for the post (check out the section later in this chapter titled "Adding support for post formats"), such as asides, image, link, and so on. If a post format exists, the `get_template_part();` calls it in. For example, if the post format is defined as aside, the `get_template_part();` pulls in the `content-aside.php` template. If no post format has been defined, Twenty Twelve simply uses the `content.php` template. A child theme (child themes are discussed at length in Chapter 5 of this minibook) could supply a `content.php` file to customize just The Loop for `index.php`. A child theme can do this without having to supply a customized `index.php` file because of Twenty Twelve's use of template parts and using both arguments of the `get_template_part` function.

With Twenty Twelve's code for the header, Loop, sidebar, and footer placed into separate files, the template files become much easier to customize for specific uses. You can see the difference by comparing the `page.php` to the `full-width.php` template files:

The `page.php` listing:

```php
<?php get_header(); ?>
    <div id="primary" class="site-content">
    <div id="content" role="main">
      <?php while ( have_posts() ) : the_post(); ?>
            <?php get_template_part( 'content', 'page' ); ?>
            <?php comments_template( '', true ); ?>
      <?php endwhile; // end of the loop. ?>
    </div><!-- #content -->
    </div><!-- #primary -->
<?php get_sidebar(); ?>
<?php get_footer(); ?>
```

The `full-width.php` listing:

```php
/* Template Name: Full-width Page Template, No Sidebar */
<?php get_header(); ?>
<div id="content" role="main">
    <?php while ( have_posts() ) : the_post(); ?>
        <?php get_template_part( 'content', 'page' ); ?>
        <?php comments_template( '', true ); ?>
    <?php endwhile; // end of the loop. ?>
```

```
</div><!-- #content -->
</div><!-- #primary -->
<?php get_footer(); ?>
```

Other than the `full-width.php` having the `Template Name` comment at the top, allowing it to be used as a page template (discussed in the upcoming "Using page templates" section), the only difference is that `page.php` has the `get_sidebar` function call and `full-width.php` does not. With just this modification and a few styling rules added to the CSS, the theme now has a page template that doesn't have a sidebar.

**Book VI
Chapter 6**

Digging into
Advanced Theme
Development

You might wonder how the preceding example shows the value of template parts if it is really about the `get_sidebar` function. Although the `get_sidebar` function is the feature of the previous example, the unsung hero is the `get_template_part` function.

Before template parts, the full Loop code would be duplicated in the `page.php` and `full-width.php` files. This means that a modification to the `page.php` file's Loop code would also require the same modification to the `full-width.php` file. Imagine if you had to make the same modification to five template files. Repeatedly making the same modifications quickly becomes tiring, and each modification increases the chance of making mistakes. Using a template part means that the modification needs to be made only one time.

Looking at the `page.php` and `full-width.php` example, the `get_template_part` call allows for easily creating as many customized page templates as needed without having to duplicate The Loop code. Without the duplicate code, the code for The Loop can be easily modified in one place.

When you start duplicating sections of code in numerous template files, place the code in a separate file and use the `get_template_part` function to load it where needed.

Exploring content-specific standard templates

The template files discussed so far span a wide scope of site views specific to the view and not the content. For example, the `category.php` template file applies to all category archive views but not to a specific category, and the `page.php` template file applies to all page views but not to a specific page. However, you can create template files for specific content and not just the view.

Four content-specific template types are available: author, category, page, and tag. Each one allows you to refer to specific content by the term's ID (an individual author's ID, for instance) or by the *slug*.

The slug discussed in this section differs from the slug argument of the `get_template_part` function described in the preceding section. For this section, *slug* refers to a post, page, or category slug (to name a few), such as a Press Releases category having a slug of `press-releases` or a post titled "Hello World" having a slug of `hello-world`.

For example, imagine that you have an About Us page with an id of 138 and a slug of about-us. You can create a template for this specific page by creating a file named either page-138.php or page-about-us.php. In the same way, if you want to create a template specific to an awesome author named Lisa with an id of 7 and a slug of lisa, you can create a file named either author-7.php or author-lisa.php.

Creating a template by using the slug can be extremely helpful for making templates for sites that you don't manage. If you want to share a theme that you created, you could create a category-featured.php template, and this template would automatically apply to any category view that has a slug of featured.

Using categories as the example, the file naming convention is as follows:

✦ A template with the filename category.php is a catchall (default) for the display for all categories (alternatively, a template with the filename of archives.php will display categories if a category.php does not exist).

✦ Add a dash and the category ID number to the end of the filename (shown in Table 6-1) to specify a template for an individual category.

✦ Alternatively, you can add a dash and the category slug to the end of the filename (shown in Table 6-1) to define it as a template for that particular category. For example, if you have a category called Books, the category slug is books; the individual category template file would be named category-books.php.

✦ If you don't have a category.php, an archives.php, or category-#.php file, the category display pulls from the Main Index template (index.php).

Table 6-1 gives you some examples of file naming conventions for category templates.

Table 6-1   Category Template File Naming Conventions

If the Category ID or Slug Is . . .	The Category Template Filename Is . . .
1	category-1.php
2	category-2.php
3	category-3.php
books	category-books.php
Movies	category-movies.php
music	category-music.php

Because creating a template by using slugs is so useful (and because an ID is relevant only to a specific site), you might wonder why the `id` option exists. The short answer is that the `id` option existed before the slug option; however, it is still valuable in specific instances. You can use the `id` option for a content-specific template without worrying about the customization breaking when the slug changes. This is especially helpful if you set up the site for someone and can't trust that he or she will leave the slugs alone (such as changing a category with a slug of `news` to `press-releases`).

Using page templates

Although the `page-slug.php` feature is very helpful, sometimes requiring the theme's user to use the name you choose for a specific feature is too difficult or unnecessary. Page templates allow you to create a standalone template (just like `page.php` or `single.php`) that the user can selectively use on any specific page he or she chooses. As opposed to the `page-slug.php` feature, a page template can be used on more than one page. The combined features of user selection and multiple uses make page templates a much more powerful theme tool than `page-slug.php` templates.

For more on page templates, see Chapters 1, 3, and 5 in this minibook.

To make a template a page template, simply add `Template Name: Descriptive Name` to a comment section at the top of the template file. For example, the following code is the beginning of the `onecolumn-page.php` page template file in the Twenty Twelve theme:

```php
<?php
/**
 * Template Name: Full-width Page Template, No Sidebar
 *
 * Description: Twenty Twelve loves the no-sidebar look as much as
 * you do. Use this page template to remove the sidebar from any page.
 *
 * Tip: to remove the sidebar from all posts and pages simply remove
 * any active widgets from the Main Sidebar area, and the sidebar will
 * disappear everywhere.
 *
 * @package WordPress
 * @subpackage Twenty_Twelve
 * @since Twenty Twelve 1.0
 */
```

This registers the template file as a page template and adds Full-width Page Template, No Sidebar to the Page Attributes module's Template drop-down list, as shown in Figure 6-1. (Check out Book IV, Chapters 1 and 2 for information on publishing pages.) Using a template on a static page is a two-step process: Upload the template and tell WordPress to use the template by tweaking the page's code.

**Book VI
Chapter 6**

**Digging into
Advanced Theme
Development**

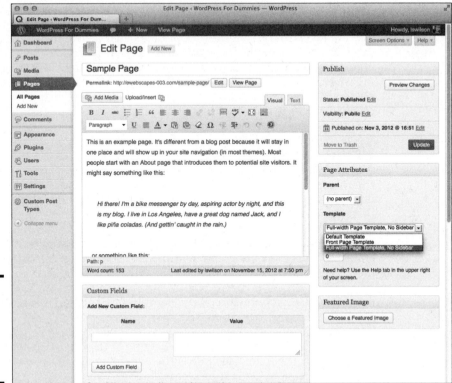

Figure 6-1:
The
Dashboard
showing
page
attributes.

By providing a robust set of page templates, you can offer users of your theme an easy-to-use set of options for formatting their pages. These options can be used only for pages, but named header, footer, sidebar, and template parts can be used to offer users options on other site views.

Adding Theme Support for Built-In Features

The WordPress core offers a number of great tools that can easily be added to a theme to give the theme more customization options. WordPress provides you with several built-in features that give you the ability to enhance your site and theme. This section covers five of the most popular features, including

✦ Custom navigation menus

✦ Custom post types

✦ Custom taxonomies

✦ Post formats

✦ Featured images

Each of these features is part of the WordPress core; however, they aren't activated by default. When you "add theme support," you're activating a built-in feature in your theme. Therefore, when you're travelling around the WordPress community, whether it's in a support forum or at a WordCamp event, and you hear someone say the theme supports a certain feature, you can smile because you know exactly what he's talking about.

Activating support for these features in the theme you're using involves a few steps:

✦ **Core function:** Add support for the feature in your theme by including the core function in your theme's Theme Functions template file (`functions.php`).

✦ **Template function:** Add the necessary function tags in your theme template(s) to display the features on your website.

✦ **Templates:** In some cases, you can create feature-specific templates to create enhancements to your site.

The following sections take you through each feature. You add the core function to your theme, add the function tags to your templates and, if indicated, create a feature-specific template in your theme that will handle the added features.

Adding support for custom menus

The WordPress menu-building feature is a great tool that WordPress offers to theme developers. Before the addition of this tool, theme developers implemented their own menu solution, creating a huge number of themes with navigation customization requiring coding and a small set of themes with very different ways of handling navigation. Creating complex, multi-level menus on your WordPress site takes just a few steps, as outlined in this section.

A *navigation menu* is a listing of links that displays on your site. These links can be links to pages, posts, or categories within your site, or they can be links to other sites. Either way, you can define navigation menus on your site with the built-in Custom Menus feature in WordPress.

It's to your advantage to provide at least one navigation menu on your site so that readers can see everything your site has to offer. Providing visitors with a link — or several links — keeps with the point-and-click spirit of the web.

The Twenty Twelve theme already supports menus. Looking at Twenty Twelve's `functions.php` file, you can see that the following lines of code handle registering the theme's menu:

```
// This theme uses wp_nav_menu() in one location.
register_nav_menus( array(
 'primary' => __( 'Primary Navigation', 'twentytwelve' ),
) );
```

This registers a single navigation area with a theme location name of primary and a human-readable name of Primary Navigation. With the Twenty Twelve theme active, click the Menus link on the Appearance menu to load the Menus page on the Dashboard and view the Primary Navigation menu location.

Core menu function and template tags

The Custom Menu feature is already built in to the default Twenty Twelve WordPress theme, so you don't have to worry about preparing your theme for it. However, if you're using a different theme, adding this functionality is easy:

1. **Click the Editor link on the Appearance menu and then click the Theme Functions template file (functions.php).**

The Theme Functions template opens in the text editor on the left side of the Edit Themes page.

2. **Type the following function on a new line in the Theme Functions template file:**

```
// ADD MENU SUPPORT
add_theme_support( 'nav-menus' );
```

3. **Click the Update File button to save the changes to the template.**

This template tag tells WordPress that your theme can use the Custom Menu feature, and a Menus link now displays on the Appearance menu on the Dashboard.

4. **Open the Header template (header.php).**

Click the Header link on the Edit Themes page to open the Header template in the text editor on the left side of the Edit Themes page.

5. **Add the following template tag by typing it on a new line in the Header template (header.php):**

```
<?php wp_nav_menu(); ?>
```

This template tag is needed so the menu you build by using the Custom Menu feature will display at the top of your website. Table 6-2 gives the details on the different parameters you can use with the wp_nav_menu(); template tag to further customize the display to suit your needs.

6. **Click the Update File button at the bottom of the page to save the changes you made to the Header template.**

Table 6-2 **Common Tag Parameters for wp_nav_menu();**

Parameter	Information	Default	Tag Example
id	The unique ID of the menu (because you can create several menus, each has a unique ID number)	Blank	```wp_nav_menu (array('id' => '1'));```
slug	The menu name in slug form (for example, nav-menu)	Blank	```wp_nav_menu (array('slug' => 'nav-menu'));```
menu	The menu name	Blank	```wp_nav_menu (array('menu' => 'Nav Menu'));``` or ```wp_nav_menu ('Nav Menu');```
menu_class	The CSS class used to style the menu list	Menu	```wp_nav_menu (array ('menu_class' => 'mymenu'));```
format	The HTML markup used to style the list (either an unordered list [ul/li] or a div class)	Div	```wp_nav_menu (array ('format' => 'ul'));```
fallback_ cb	The parameter that creates a fallback if a custom menu doesn't exist	wp_page_ menu (the default list of page links)	```wp_nav_menu (array (' fallback_cb' => 'wp_page_menu'));```
before	The text that displays before the link text	None	```wp_nav_menu (array ('before' => 'Click Here'));```
after	The text that displays after the link text	None	```wp_nav_menu (array('after' => '»'));```

Figure 6-2 shows the default Twenty Twelve theme with a navigation menu (Home, About, and Blog) beneath the theme's header graphic.

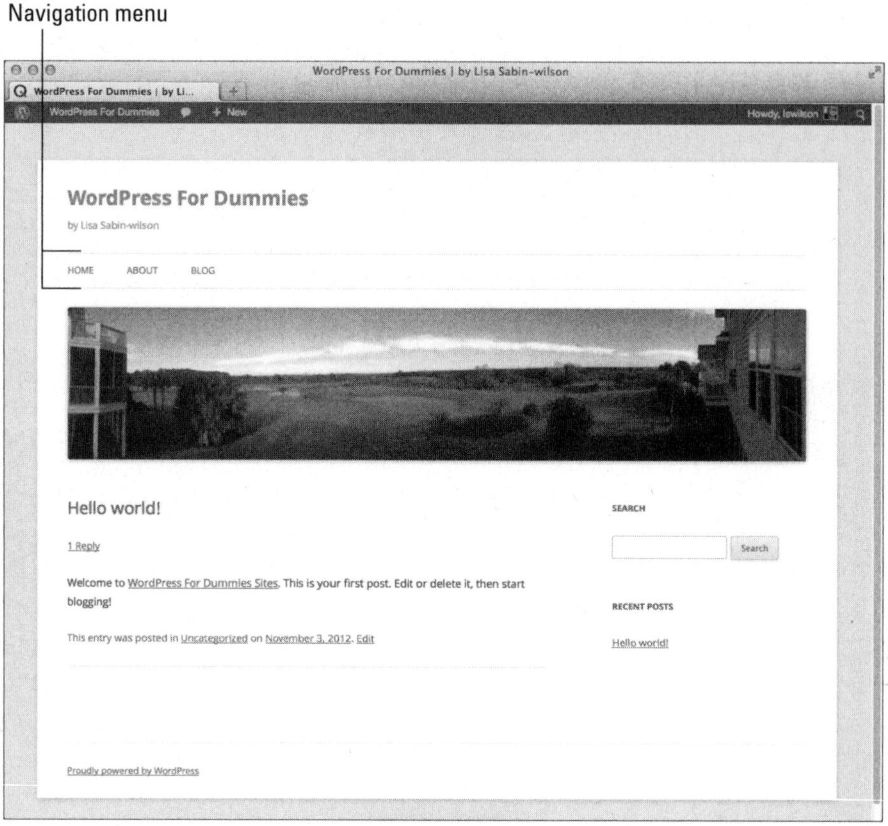

Navigation menu

Figure 6-2: The Twenty Twelve theme with a navigation menu below the header.

A menu called Main was created on the WordPress Dashboard. (See Chapter 1 in this minibook to create menus in the WordPress Dashboard.) The template tag used in the theme to display the menu looks like this:

```
<?php wp_nav_menu('Main'); ?>
```

The HTML markup for the menu is generated as an unordered list, by default, and looks like this:

```
<ul id="menu-main" class="menu">
<li id="menu-item-53" class="menu-item menu-item-type-custom menu-item-object-
    custom menu-item-53"><a href="/">Home</a></li>
<li id="menu-item-51" class="menu-item menu-item-type-post_type menu-item-object-
    page menu-item-51"><a href="http://localhost/wpdemo/blog/">Blog</a></li>
<li id="menu-item-52" class="menu-item menu-item-type-post_type menu-item-object-
    page menu-item-52"><a href="http://localhost/wpdemo/about/">About</a></li>
</ul>
```

Notice, in the HTML markup, the `<ul id="menu-main" class="menu">` line defines the CSS ID and class.

The ID reflects the name that you give your menu. Because the menu is named Main, the CSS ID is `menu-main`. If the menu were named Foo, the ID would be `menu-foo`. By assigning menu names in the CSS and HTML markup, WordPress allows you to use CSS to create different styles and formats for your different menus.

When developing themes for either yourself or others to use, make sure that the CSS you define for the menus can do things like account for subpages by creating drop-down menus. You can accomplish this in several different ways; Listing 6-1 gives you just one example — a block of CSS that you can use to create a nice style for your menu. (This CSS example assumes that you have a menu named "Main"; therefore, the HTML and CSS markups use `menu-main`.)

Listing 6-1:   Sample CSS for Drop-Down Menu Navigation

```
#menu-main {
....width: 960px;
....font-family: Georgia, Times New Roman, Trebuchet MS;
....font-size: 16px;
....color: #FFFFFF;
....margin: 0 auto 0;
....clear: both;
....overflow: hidden;
....}

#menu-main ul {
....width: 100%;
....float: left;
....list-style: none;
....margin: 0;
....padding: 0;
....}

#menu-main li {
....float: left;
....list-style: none;
....}

#menu-main li a {
....color: #FFFFFF;
....display: block;
....font-size: 16px;
....margin: 0;
....padding: 12px 15px 12px 15px;
....text-decoration: none;
....position: relative;
....}

#menu-main li a:hover, #menu-main li a:active, #menu-main .current_page_item a,
    #menu-main .current-cat a, #menu-main .current-menu-item {
....color: #CCCCCC;
....}
```

```
#menu-main li li a, #menu-main li li a:link, #menu-main li li a:visited {
....background: #555555;
....color: #FFFFFF;
....width: 138px;
....font-size: 12px;
....margin: 0;
....padding: 5px 10px 5px 10px;
....border-left: 1px solid #FFFFFF;
....border-right: 1px solid #FFFFFF;
....border-bottom: 1px solid #FFFFFF;
....position: relative;
....}

#menu-main li li a:hover, #menu-main li li a:active {
....background: #333333;
....color: #FFFFFF;
....}

#menu-main li ul {
....z-index: 9999;
....position: absolute;
....left: -999em;
....height: auto;
....width: 160px;
....}

#menu-main li ul a {
....width: 140px;
....}

#menu-main li ul ul {
....margin: -31px 0 0 159px;
....}

#menu-main li:hover ul ul, #menu-main li:hover ul ul ul {
....left: -999em;
....}

#menu-main li:hover ul, #menu-main li li:hover ul, #menu-main li li li:hover ul {
....left: auto;
....}

#menu-main li:hover {
....position: static;
....}
```

The CSS you use to customize the display of your menus will differ; the example in the preceding section is just that, an example. After you get the hang of using CSS, you can try different methods, colors, and styling to create a custom look of your own. (You can find additional information about Basic HTML and CSS in Chapter 4 of this minibook.)

Displaying custom menus using widgets

You don't have to use the wp_nav_menu(); template tag to display the menus on your site, because WordPress also provides a Custom Menu widget that you can add to your theme, allowing you to use widgets, instead of template tags, to display the navigation menus on your site. This widget is especially helpful if you've created multiple menus for use in and around your site in various places. Have a look into Chapter 4 in this minibook for more information on using WordPress widgets.

Your first step is to register a special widget area for your theme to handle the Custom Menu widget display. To do this, open your theme's `functions.php` file and add the following lines of code:

```
// ADD MENU WIDGET
if ( function_exists('register_sidebar') )
    register_sidebar(array('name'=>'Menu',));
```

These few lines of code create a new Menu widget area on the Widgets page on your Dashboard. You can drag the Custom Menu widget into the Menu widget to indicate that you want to display a custom menu in that area. Figure 6-3 shows the Menu widget area with the Custom Menu widget added.

**Book VI
Chapter 6**

**Digging into
Advanced Theme
Development**

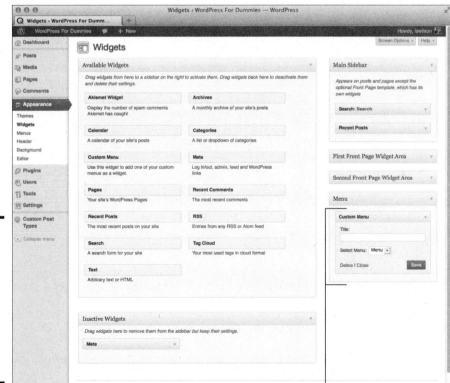

Figure 6-3:
Widgets page displaying a Menu widget area with a Custom Menu widget.

Custom Menu widget

To add the widget area to your theme, open the Theme Editor (click the Editor link on the Appearance menu), open the `header.php` file, and add these lines of code in the area in which you want to display the Menu widget:

```
<ul>
<?php if ( !function_exists('dynamic_sidebar') || !dynamic_sidebar('Menu') ) : ?>
<?php endif; ?>
</ul>
```

These lines of code tell WordPress that you want information contained in the Menu widget area to display on your site.

Adding support for custom post types

Custom post types and custom taxonomies have expanded the CMS capabilities of WordPress and are likely to become a big part of plugin and theme features as more developers become familiar with their use. *Custom post types* allow you to create new content types separate from posts and pages, such as movie reviews or recipes. *Custom taxonomies* allow you to create new types of content grouping separate from categories and tags, such as genres for movie reviews or seasons for recipes.

Posts and pages are nice generic containers of content. A *page* is timeless content that has a hierarchal structure — a page can have a parent (forming a nested, or hierarchal, structure of pages). A *post* is content that is listed in linear (not hierarchal) order based on when it was published and organized into categories and tags. What happens when you want a hybrid of these features? What if you want content that doesn't show up in the post listings, displays the posting date, and doesn't have either categories or tags? Custom post types are created to satisfy this desire to customize content types.

By default, WordPress already has different post types built in to the software, ready for you to use. The default post types include

+ Blog posts
+ Pages
+ Menus
+ Attachments
+ Revisions

Custom post types give you the ability to create new and useful types of content on your website, including a smart and easy way to publish those content types to your site.

The possibilities for the use of custom post types are endless. To kick-start your imagination, here are some of the more popular and useful ideas that others have implemented on sites:

✦ Photo gallery

✦ Podcast or video

✦ Book reviews

✦ Coupons and special offers

✦ Events calendar

Core custom post type function

To create and use custom post types on your site, you need to be sure that your WordPress theme contains the correct code and functions. The following steps create a very basic and generic custom post type called Generic Content. Follow these steps to create the same basic custom post type:

1. **Open the Theme Functions template file (`functions.php`).**

   Click the Editor link on the Appearance menu to open the Theme Editor page. Then click the Theme Functions template link to open the `functions.php` file in the text editor.

2. **Add the custom post types code to the bottom of the Theme Functions template file.**

   Scroll to the bottom of the `functions.php` file and include the following code to add a Generic Content custom post type to your site:

   ```
   // ADD CUSTOM POST TYPE
   add_action( 'init', 'create_post_type' );
   function create_post_type() {
     register_post_type( 'generic-content',
       array(
         'labels' => array(
           'name' => __( 'Generic Content' ),
           'singular_name' => __( 'Generic Content' )
         ),
         'public' => true
       )
     );
   }
   ```

3. **Click the Update File button to save the changes made to the `functions.php` file.**

The `register_post_type` function can accept several arguments and parameters, which are detailed in Table 6-3. You can use a variety and combination of different arguments and parameters to create a specific post type. You can find more information on Custom Post Types and using the `register_post_type` function in the WordPress Codex at

```
http://codex.wordpress.org/Function_Reference/register_
    post_type
```

If you really don't feel up to writing this code in the Theme Functions template file, check out a nifty plugin developed for WordPress called Custom Post Types UI, written by Brad Williams of WebDevStudios (`http://web devstudios.com`). This plugin provides you with an interface in your WordPress Dashboard that simplifies the creation of custom post types on your site and completely bypasses the need to create the code in the Theme Functions template file (`functions.php`). You can find the plugin at

```
http://wordpress.org/extend/plugins/custom-post-type-ui
```

After you complete the steps to add the generic content post type to your site, the Generic Content post type appears on the left navigation menu on the Dashboard, as shown in Figure 6-4.

Figure 6-4: A new custom post type menu appears on the Dashboard.

You add and publish new content by using the new custom post type the same way you do when you write and publish blog posts. The published content isn't added to the chronological listing of blog posts; it's treated as separate content, just like static pages.

Generic Content is part of the permalink structure, and the permalink looks similar to http://*yourdomain.com*/generic-content/new-article.

Table 6-3   Arguments and Parameters for register_post_type();

Parameter	Information	Parameters	Example
label	A plural descriptive name for the post type.	None.	'label' => __ ('Generic Content'),
labels	An array of descriptive labels for the post type.	Default is empty and is set to the label value. name singular_name add_new add_new_item edit_item new_item view_item search_items not_found not_found_in_trash parent_item_colon menu_name	'name' => __ ('Generic Content'),
description	The description of the post type; displayed in the Dashboard to represent the post type.	None.	'description' => __('This is a description of the Generic Content type'),

(continued)

Table 6-3 *(continued)*

Parameter	Information	Parameters	Example

`public`
 	
`show_ui`
 	
`publicly_`
`queryable`
 	
`exclude_`
`from_search`
 	
`show_in_nav_`
`menus`
	Sets whether the post type is public;
	
	The three other arguments are
	
	`show_ui`: Show admin screens
	
	`publicly_`
	`queryable`: Query for this post type from the front end
	
	`exclude_`
	`from_search`: Show post type in search results
		`true` or `false`;
		Default is false.
			`'public' => true,`
			
			`'show_ui' => true,`
			
			`'publicly_`
			`queryable' =>`
			`true,`
			
			`'exclude_from_`
			`search' => false,`
			
			`'show_in_nav_`
			`menus' => true`

`menu_` `position`	Sets the position of the post type menu item in the Dashboard navigation menu.	Default: 20; By default, custom post types appear after the Comments menu on the Dashboard. Set integer in intervals of five (5, 10, 15, 20, and so on).	`'menu_position' =>` `25,`

`menu_icon`	Defines a custom icon (graphic) to the post type menu item in the Dashboard navigation menu.
	
	Creates and uploads the image into the images directory of your theme folder.
		None.	`'menu_icon' =>`
			`get_stylesheet_`
			`directory_uri() .`
			`'/images/generic-`
			`content.png',`

Parameter	Information	Parameters	Example
hierarchical	Tells WordPress whether to display the post type content list in a hierarchical manner	true or false; Default is true.	'hierarchical' => true,
query_var	Controls whether this post type can be used with a query variable such as query_posts (see previous section) or WP_Query.	true or false; Default is false.	'query_var' => true,
capability_type	Defines permissions for users to edit, create, or read the custom post type.	post (default); Gives the same capabilities for those who can edit, create, and read blog posts.	'query_var' => post,
capabilities	Tells WordPress what capabilities are accepted for this post type.	Default: empty, the capability_type value is used. edit_post: allows post type to be edited read_post: allows post type to be read delete_post: allows post type to be deleted	'capabilities' => edit_post,
map_meta_cap	Tells WordPress whether to use the default internal meta capabilities.	true or false; Default is false.	'map_meta_cap' => true,

(continued)

Table 6-3 *(continued)*

Parameter	Information	Parameters	Example
supports	Defines what meta boxes, or modules, are available for this post type in the Dashboard.	`title`: Text box for the post title `editor`: Text box for the post content `comments`: Check boxes to toggle comments on/off `trackbacks`: Check boxes to toggle trackbacks and pingbacks on/off `revisions`: Allows post revisions `author`: Drop-down box to define post author `excerpt`: Text box for the post excerpt `thumbnail`: The featured image selection `custom-fields`: Custom fields input area `page-attributes`: The page parent and page template drop-down menus	`'supports' => array( 'title', 'editor', 'excerpt', 'custom-fields', 'thumbnail' ),`

Parameter	Information	Parameters	Example
`rewrite`	Rewrites the permalink structure for the post type.	`true` or `false`; Two other arguments are available: `slug`: Permalink slug to prepend to your custom post types `with_front`: If you've set your permalink structure with a specific prefix such as `/blog`	`'rewrite' => array( 'slug' => 'my-content', 'with_front' => false ),`
`has_archive`	Tells WordPress whether to enable post archives for this post type.	`true` or `false`; Default is false. (If true, WordPress uses the post type name as its slug in the permalink URL.)	`'has_archive' => true,`
`can_export`	Tells WordPress whether this post type can be exported using the built-in content exporter.	`true` or `false`; Default is true.	`'can_export' => false,`
`taxonomies`	Uses existing WordPress taxonomies (category and tag).	Category `post_tag`.	`'taxonomies' => array( 'post_tag', 'category'),`

Listing 6-2 shows you the code for the No Rules Theatre website. The custom post type called Shows creates custom content for the shows that the theatre produces each season. Reference the parameters and information provided in Table 6-3 while reading the lines of code in Listing 6-2 to see how the custom post types for the No Rules Theatre site were created and applied.

Go to `http://norulestheatre.org` to see custom content in action.

Listing 6-2:   **Custom Post Type Example**

```
// ADD CUSTOM POST TYPE: SHOWS
add_action( 'init', 'create_my_post_types' );
function create_my_post_types() {
....register_post_type( 'shows',
....array(
....'labels' => array(
....'name' => __( 'Shows' ),
....'singular_name' => __( 'Show' ),
....'add_new' => __( 'Add New Show' ),
....'add_new_item' => __( 'Add New Show' ),
....'edit' => __( 'Edit' ),
....'edit_item' => __( 'Edit Show' ),
....'new_item' => __( 'New Show' ),
....'view' => __( 'View Show' ),
....'view_item' => __( 'View Show' ),
....'search_items' => __( 'Search Shows' ),
....'not_found' => __( 'No shows found' ),
....'not_found_in_trash' => __( 'No shows found in Trash' ),
....'parent' => __( 'Parent Show' ),
....),

....'public' => true,
....'show_ui' => true,
....'publicly_queryable' => true,
....'exclude_from_search' => false,
....'menu_position' => 10,
....'menu_icon' => get_stylesheet_directory_uri() . '/img/nrt-shows.png',
....'hierarchical' => true,
....'query_var' => true,
....'rewrite' => array( 'slug' => 'shows', 'with_front' => false ),
....'taxonomies' => array( 'post_tag', 'category'),
....'can_export' => true,
....'supports' => array(
....'post-thumbnails',
....'excerpts',
....'comments',
....'revisions',
....'title',
....'editor',
....'page-attributes',
....'custom-fields')
....)
....);
}
```

The three modules WordPress gives you to add menus from are Custom Links, Pages, and Categories. On the Custom Menu page in the WordPress Dashboard, click the Screen Options tab at the top right of that page; the check box next to Post Types enables your custom post types in the Menus you create.

Custom post type templates

By default, custom post types use the `single.php` template in your theme — that is, they do unless you create a specific template for your custom post type if you find the regular WordPress `single.php` template too limiting for your post type.

The preceding section has the code to build a simple Generic Content custom post. After that is added, a Generic Content menu appears on the WordPress Dashboard. Click the Add New link on the Generic Content menu and publish a new post to add some content for testing. In this example, a new Generic Content type with a title of Test and a slug of `test` is added. Because the Generic Content type doesn't have a specific template, it uses the `single.php` template, and resulting posts look no different from a standard one.

If you get a Not Found page when you try to go to a new custom post type entry, reset your permalink settings. Click the Permalinks link on the Settings menu on the WordPress Dashboard and then click the Save Changes button. WordPress resets the permalinks, which adds the new custom post type link formats in the process.

To build a template specific for the Generic Content post type, add a new template named `single-`*posttype*`.php` where *posttype* is the first argument passed to the `register_post_type` function from the preceding section. For this example, the single template file specific to Sample Post Type is `single-generic-content.php`. Any modifications made to this template file appear only for instances of the Generic Content post type.

Tying this together with the section on template parts from earlier in this chapter, a basic structure for `single-generic-content.php` for the Twenty Twelve theme is

```php
<?php get_header(); ?>
<div id="container">
    <div id="content" role="main">
        <?php get_template_part('loop', 'generic-content'); ?>
    </div><!-- #content -->
</div><!-- #container -->
<?php get_sidebar(); ?>
<?php get_footer(); ?>
```

By using the template part, creating a file called `loop-generic-content.php` allows for easy customization of The Loop for the Generic Content post type entry.

Adding support for custom taxonomies

Similar to how having posts and pages as content options can be limiting, sometimes categories and tags just aren't enough. The example of a movie review custom post type might need a variety of new taxonomies or grouping options. Organizing movie reviews by director, movie star, review rating, film genre, and MPAA rating allows visitors to the site to view different groupings of reviews that might interest them. Like the custom post type example, this example creates a very simple taxonomy to test custom taxonomy–specific templates. For this example, a new post taxonomy called Sample Taxonomy is created.

To register this new taxonomy, use the `register_taxonomy` function. Adding the following code to the bottom of your theme's `functions.php` file registers the new sample taxonomy custom taxonomy specifically for WordPress built-in posts, adds a Sample Taxonomy link to the Posts menu entry to manage the Sample Taxonomy entries, and adds sample taxonomy options to the editor for posts.

```
register_taxonomy( 'sample-taxonomy', 'post', array( 'label' =>
    'Sample Taxonomy' ) );
```

This function call gives the new custom taxonomy an internal name of `sample-taxonomy`, assigns the new taxonomy to Posts, and gives the taxonomy a human-readable name of Sample Taxonomy.

After adding this code to your theme, you can create and assign Sample Taxonomies when creating a new post or editing an existing post. For this example, you could add a sample taxonomy with a name of Testing to an existing post and update the post.

With the Testing taxonomy added, you can now visit `example.com/sample-taxonomy/testing` to get the archive page for the new sample taxonomy.

If you get a Not Found page or you don't get an archive listing when you try to go to a specific sample taxonomy entry's archive, resave your permalink settings. Click the Permalinks link on the Settings menu on the WordPress Dashboard and then click Save Changes. This forces WordPress to reset the permalinks, which adds the new custom taxonomy link formats in the process.

Adding a new template file called `taxonomy-sample-taxonomy.php` allows for adding a template specific to this new custom taxonomy. Like you can with categories and tags, you can add a template that is specific to a single custom taxonomy entry. Therefore, a template specific to a sample taxonomy with a slug of `testing` would have a filename of `taxonomy-sample-taxonomy-testing.php`.

Custom taxonomies is a feature that will appeal to only a specific type of site that deals mainly in niche areas of content: Sites that want to really drill down navigation and grouping options for their content. You can find more about custom taxonomies in the WordPress Codex at

```
http://codex.wordpress.org/Function_Reference/
    register_taxonomy
```

Adding support for post formats

Introduced in version 3.1 of WordPress, the Post Formats feature allows you to designate a different content display and style for certain types of designated posts. Unlike custom post types, you aren't able to create different post formats because WordPress has already assigned them for you — it's up to you what post format, if any, you want to use in your theme.

Here are the nine types of WordPress post formats:

✦ **Aside:** A very short post that shares a random thought or idea. Typically, an aside is shared without a post title or any category/tag designations; it's simply a random, one-off thought — not a full post — shared on your blog.

✦ **Audio:** A post that shares audio files or podcasts. Usually, audio posts have very little text and include a built-in audio player so visitors can click and listen.

✦ **Chat:** A transcript of an online conversation that can be formatted to look like a chat (or Instant Message) window.

✦ **Gallery:** A gallery of clickable images, where clicking an image opens a larger version of the photo. Often, galleries don't contain text (but may have a title) and are used for only the display of a gallery.

✦ **Image:** A post that shares a single image. The image may or may not have text or a caption to go with the post.

✦ **Link:** A post that provides a link you find useful and want to share with your readers. These post formats often contain a title and, sometimes, a short bit of text that describes the link.

✦ **Quote:** A post that displays a quotation on your blog. Often, users will include a byline or the quote's source.

✦ **Status:** A short status update, usually limited to 140 characters or less. (Think Twitter!)

✦ **Video:** A post that displays a video, usually embedded within a video player (say YouTube) so your readers can play the video without leaving your site.

This list of post format types is all there is; you only have nine designated post formats. You can use one or all of them in your theme, depending on your specific needs.

Figure 6-5 shows you how post formats work. They cleanly separate the formats in the menu navigation and in the individual post styling and icons used to designate the formats.

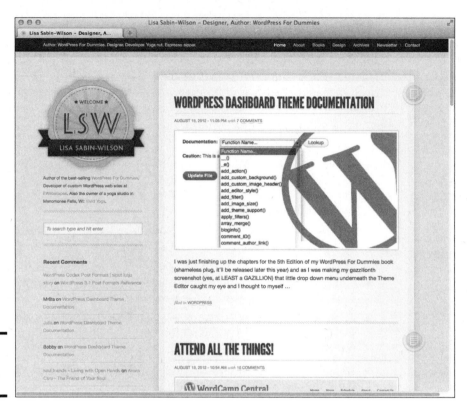

Figure 6-5:
Post
formats.

If you find that your site needs a different type of post format that is not currently available, consider adding it as a custom post type.

Core post format function

To add support for post formats in your theme, you need to add the core function call to your Theme Functions template file (`functions.php`). After you follow these few steps to make it happen, you'll see the magic that occurs on the Add New Post page on your WordPress Dashboard! Here's how to add post formats support in your theme:

1. **Click the Editor link on the Appearance menu on your Dashboard.**

The Edit Themes page appears.

2. **Open the Themes Function file in the text editor.**

The link for the Theme Functions template file is on the right side of the Edit Themes page. Clicking this link opens the Theme Functions template file (`functions.php`) in the text editor on the left side of the Edit Themes page.

3. **Add the following function on a new line:**

```
add_theme_support( 'post-formats', array( 'aside', 'chat', 'gallery',
    'image', 'link', 'quote', 'status', 'video', 'audio' ) );
```

This code sample adds all nine post formats to the theme. You don't have to use all nine; you can include only the formats that you need in your theme and leave the rest.

4. **Click the Update File button to save the changes made to the** **functions.php file.**

You won't notice an immediate change to your site when you save your new Theme Functions template file with the Post Formats support added. To see what WordPress added to your site, you need to visit the Add New Post page (which you access by clicking the Add New link on the Posts menu).

The change is subtle, but if you follow the steps to add post format support, you see a Format item in the Publish module on the right side of the page, as shown in Figure 6-6. Click the Edit link to the right of Format to designate a format for your post. In Figure 6-6, see all nine post format options listed. You also see a tenth format option, Standard (or Default), which is used when you don't select a specific format for your post.

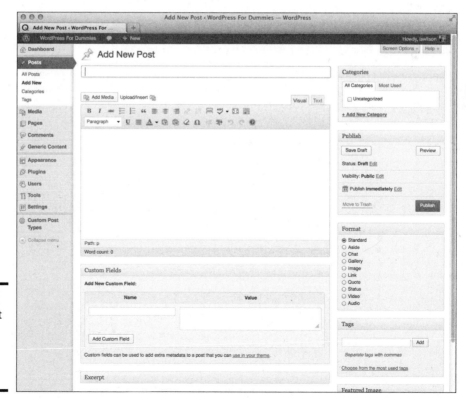

Figure 6-6:
The Format
option on
the Add
New Post
page.

Post class defined

In the default Twenty Twelve theme, examine the code for the `loop.php` template. About three-fourths of the way in, you see a line of code that looks like this:

```
<div id="post-<?php the_ID(); ?>" <?php post_class(); ?>>
```

The cool part of that template tag is the `post_class()` section. This template tag tells WordPress to insert specific HTML markup in your template that allows you to use CSS to make custom styles for sticky posts, categories, tags, and post formats.

For example, a post has the following options set:

☞ Stick this post to the front page

☞ Filed in a category called WordPress

☞ Tagged with News

By having the `post_class()` tag in the template, WordPress inserts HTML markup that allows the use of CSS to style sticky posts, or posts assigned to specific tags, categories, logged-in status, or post formats, differently. WordPress inserts the following HTML markup for the post:

```
<div class="post sticky category-wordpress tag-news">
```

Likewise, for post formats, if a post is published using the Images post format, the `post_class()` tag in the template contains the following HTML markup indicating that this post should be formatted for an image display:

```
<div class="post type-post format-image">
```

Add this information to the CSS and HTML information provided to you in Chapter 3 of this mini-book, and you see how you can use CSS along with the `post_class();` tag to provide custom styles for each post type on your site and unique styles for the different categories and tags you use in your posts.

Template tags for post formats

Adding Post Format support to your theme isn't enough. If you're going to add post format support, you really should provide some unique styling for each type of format; otherwise, your post formats will look like your blog posts and the point of adding them to your theme will be lost.

You can display your post format two ways:

✦ **Content:** For each format, you can designate what content you want to display. For example, if you don't want to display a title for your Asides format, you leave out the template tag that calls it but leave the tag in for your Video post format.

✦ **Style:** Utilizing the HTML markup that is provided by the `post_class();` tag, your formats each have a CSS class assigned to them. Use those CSS classes to provide unique styles for fonts, colors, backgrounds, and borders to each of your post formats. The nearby "Post class defined" sidebar discusses how to use HTML and CSS to create custom styles in your template.

Adding unique styles for your post formats starts with creating the content designations you want to display for each format. Earlier in this section is a list of nine post formats and some ideas on what you can do to display them on your site. The possibilities are endless, and it's really up to you. Refer to Chapter 3 of this minibook for more information on the content-related template tags you can use in these areas. The following steps take you through the creation of a very simple, stripped-down Main Index file (`index.php`):

Book VI
Chapter 6

Digging into
Advanced Theme
Development

1. **Open your favorite text editor, such as Notepad (for PC) or TextMate (for Mac).**

2. **Type** `<?php get_header(); ?>`.

   This function includes all the code from your theme's `header.php` file.

3. **Type the following two lines:**

   ```
   <?php if (have_posts()) : ?>
   <?php while (have_posts()) : the_post(); ?>
   ```

   These two lines of code indicate the beginning of The Loop (discussed in Chapter 3 of this minibook).

4. **Type** `<div id="post-<?php the_ID(); ?>" <?php post_class(); ?>>`.

   This line provides HTML and CSS markup, using the `post_class();` function that provides you with unique CSS classes for each of your post formats. (See the "Post class defined" sidebar.)

5. **Type** `<?php`.

   This part initiates the start of a PHP function.

6. **Type the following lines to provide content for the Asides post format:**

   ```
   if ( has_post_format( 'aside' )) {
   echo the_content();
   }
   ```

7. **Type the following lines to provide content for the Gallery post format:**

   ```
   elseif ( has_post_format( 'gallery' )) {
   echo '<h3>';
   echo the_title();
   echo '</h3>';
   echo the_content();
   }
   ```

8. **Type the following lines to provide content for the Image post format:**

```
elseif ( has_post_format( 'image' )) {
echo '<h3>';
echo the_title();
echo '</h3>';
echo the_post_thumbnail('image-format');
echo the_content();
}
```

9. **Type the following lines to provide content for the Link post format:**

```
elseif ( has_post_format( 'link' )) {
echo '<h3>';
echo the_title();
echo '</h3>';
echo the_content();
}
```

10. **Type the following lines to provide content for the Quote post format:**

```
elseif ( has_post_format( 'quote' )) {
echo the_content();
}
```

11. **Type the following lines to provide content for the Status post format:**

```
elseif ( has_post_format( 'status' )) {
echo the_content();
}
```

12. **Type the following lines to provide content for the Video post format:**

```
elseif ( has_post_format( 'video' )) {
echo '<h3>';
echo the_title();
echo '</h3>';
echo the_content();
}
```

13. **Type the following lines to provide content for the Audio post format:**

```
elseif ( has_post_format( 'audio' )) {
echo '<h3>';
echo the_title();
echo '</h3>';
echo the_content();
}
```

14. **Type the following lines to provide content for all other (Default) posts:**

```
else {
echo '<h3>';
echo the_title();
echo '</h3>';
echo the_content();
}
```

15. **Type** ?>.

This line ends the PHP function.

16. Type `</div>`.

This closes the HTML `div` tag opened in Step 4.

17. Type `<?php endwhile; else: ?> <?php endif; ?>`.

This closes the `endwhile` and `if` statements that were opened in Step 3.

18. Type `<?php get_sidebar(); ?>`.

This function calls in the code included in the `sidebar.php` file of your theme.

19. Type `<?php get_footer(); ?>`.

This function calls in the code included in the `footer.php` file of your theme.

20. Save your file as `index.php`.

Upload it into your theme folder, replacing your existing `index.php` file.

Listing 6-3 displays the full code for your new `index.php` file.

**Book VI
Chapter 6**

**Digging into
Advanced Theme
Development**

Listing 6-3:   A Simple Post Formats Template

```php
<?php get_header(); ?>
<?php if (have_posts()) : ?>
<?php while (have_posts()) : the_post(); ?>
<div id="post-<?php the_ID(); ?>" <?php post_class(); ?>>
<?php

if ( has_post_format( 'aside' )) {
....echo the_content();
}

elseif ( has_post_format( 'gallery' )) {
....echo '<h3>';
....echo the_title();
....echo '</h3>';
....echo the_content();
}

elseif ( has_post_format( 'gallery' )) {
....echo '<h3>';
....echo the_title();
....echo '</h3>';
....echo the_content();
}

elseif ( has_post_format( 'image' )) {
....echo '<h3>';
....echo the_title();
....echo '</h3>';
....echo the_post_thumbnail('image-format');
....echo the_content();
}
```

(continued)

Listing 6-3 *(continued)*

```php
elseif ( has_post_format( 'link' )) {
....echo '<h3>';
....echo the_title();
....echo '</h3>';
....echo the_content();
}

elseif ( has_post_format( 'quote' )) {
....echo the_content();
}

elseif ( has_post_format( 'status' )) {
....echo the_content();
}

elseif ( has_post_format( 'video' )) {
....echo '<h3>';
....echo the_title();
....echo '</h3>';
....echo the_content();
}

elseif ( has_post_format( 'audio' )) {
....echo '<h3>';
....echo the_title();
....echo '</h3>';
....echo the_content();
}

else {
....echo '<h3>';
....echo the_title();
....echo '</h3>';
....echo the_content();
}
?>
</div>
<?php endwhile; else: ?>
<?php endif; ?>
<?php get_sidebar(); ?>
<?php get_footer(); ?>
```

The example in Listing 6-3 is a very simple one and doesn't include a whole lot of HTML markup or CSS classes. Therefore, you can focus on the code bits that are required to designate and define different content displays for your post formats. You can see, in Listing 6-3, that some of the formats contain the template tag to display the title, `the_title();`, and others do not — but they all contain the template tag to display the content of the post: `the_content();`. As I mention previously, you can play with different content types and markup that you want to add to your post formats.

By coupling your template additions for post formats with the `post_class();` tag that adds special CSS classes and markup for each post format type, you can customize the display of each post format to your heart's content.

Adding support for post thumbnails

The WordPress feature called Post Thumbnails (also known as Featured Images) takes a lot of the work out of associating an image with a post and using the correct size each time. A popular way to display content in WordPress themes includes a thumbnail image with a short snippet (excerpt) of text — the thumbnail images are consistent in size and placement within your theme. Prior to the inclusion of post thumbnails in WordPress, users would have to open their image in an image editing program (such as Photoshop) and crop and resize their image to the desired size; or use fancy scripts that would resize images on the fly, which tend to be resource intensive on web servers, so it wasn't an optimal solution. How about a content management system that will crop and resize your images for you to the exact dimensions that you specify? Yep, WordPress does that for you with just a few adjustments.

By default, when you upload an image, WordPress creates three versions of your image based on dimensions that are set on your Dashboard (click the Media link on the Settings menu):

+ **Thumbnail size:** Default dimensions are 150px x 150px

+ **Medium size:** Default dimensions are 300px x 300px

+ **Large size:** Default dimensions are 1024px x 1024px

Therefore, when you upload an image, you actually end up with four sizes of that image stored on your web server: thumbnail, medium, large, and the original image. Images are cropped and resized proportionally, and when you use them in your posts you can typically designate which size you would like to use in the image options of the uploader. (See Book IV, Chapter 3 for a refresher on uploading images in WordPress.)

Within the WordPress image uploader, you can designate a particular image as the featured image of the post, and then, using the Featured Images function that you add to your theme, you can include template tags to display your chosen featured image with your post. This is helpful for creating magazine- or news-style themes that are popular with WordPress sites. Figure 6-7 shows how post thumbnails and featured images display a thumbnail associated with each post excerpt.

Also covered in the following sections is adding support for different image sizes, other than the default image sizes that are set on the Media Settings page of your Dashboard. This is helpful when you have sections of your site where you want to display a much smaller thumbnail, or a larger version of the medium-sized thumbnail that's not as big as the large size.

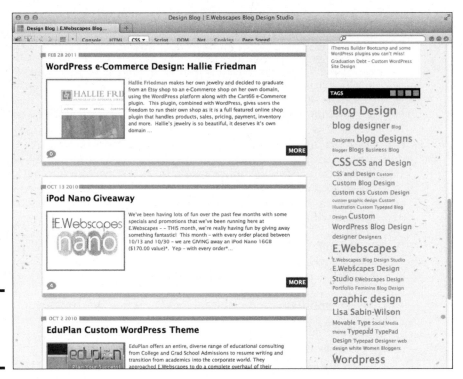

Figure 6-7:
Post
thumbnails
in use.

Core post thumbnails function and template tag

Adding support for post thumbnails includes one line of code added to your Theme Functions template file (`functions.php`):

```
add_theme_support( 'post-thumbnails' );
```

After you add this line of code to your Theme Functions template file, you can use the Featured Image feature for your posts. You can designate featured images by using the function in the WordPress image uploader. The function is also an option on the Add New Post page, where you write and publish your posts.

After you add featured images to your posts, make sure that you add the correct tag in your template(s) so the featured images display on your site in the area you want them to display. Open your `index.php` template, and include the following line of code to include the default thumbnail-size version of your chosen featured image in your posts:

```
<?php if ( has_post_thumbnail() ) { the_post_thumbnail('thumbnail'); ?>
```

The first part of that line of code checks whether a featured image is associated with the post. If there is, the image displays; if a featured image doesn't exist for the post, the code returns nothing. You can also include the other default image sizes (set in your Media Settings page in the Dashboard, as shown in Figure 6-8) for medium-, large-, and full-sized images by using these tags:

```php
<?php if ( has_post_thumbnail() ) { the_post_thumbnail('medium'); ?>

<?php if ( has_post_thumbnail() ) { the_post_thumbnail('large'); ?>

<?php if ( has_post_thumbnail() ) { the_post_thumbnail('full'); ?>
```

Figure 6-8:
The Media
Settings
page on the
Dashboard.

Adding custom image sizes for post thumbnails

If the predefined, default image sizes in WordPress (thumbnail, medium, large, and full) don't satisfy you, and there's an area on your site that you want to display images with dimensions that vary from the default, WordPress makes it relatively easy to add custom image sizes in your Theme Functions template file. You then use the the_post_thumbnail function to display it in your theme.

You are not limited on what sizes you can add for your images, and this example shows how to add a new image size of 600px x 300px. Add this line to your Theme Functions template file (functions.php) beneath the add_theme_support('post-thumbnails') function you added:

```php
add_image_size( 'custom', 600, 300, true);
```

This code tells WordPress that it needs to create an additional version of the images you upload, and to crop and resize it to the dimensions of 600px x 300px. Notice the four parameters in the `add_image_size` function:

✦ **Name ($name):** Gives the image size a unique name that you can use in your template tag. For example, the image size in this example uses the name `'custom'`.

✦ **Width ($width):** Gives the image size a width dimension in numbers. In this example, the width is defined as `'600'`.

✦ **Height ($height):** Gives the image size a height dimension in numbers. In this example, the height is defined as `'300'`.

✦ **Crop ($crop):** This parameter is optional and tells WordPress whether it should crop the image to exact dimensions or do a soft proportional resizing of the image. In this example, the parameter is set to `'true'` (accepted arguments: `true` or `false`).

Adding the custom image size to your template to display the featured image is the same as adding default image sizes. The only difference is the name of the image set in the parentheses of the template tag. The custom image size in this example uses the following tag:

```
<?php if ( has_post_thumbnail() ) { the_post_thumbnail('custom'); ?>
```

Exploring Theme Options

One of the key features of an advanced theme is a Theme Options page. A Theme Options page allows the theme user to supply information to the theme without having to modify the theme files. Although a single-use theme could have this information hard-coded into the theme, it's an inelegant solution. If the theme is used more than once or is managed by a non-developer, having an easy-to-change setting on the back end allows changes to be made quickly and easily.

Use a Theme Options page when the information is specific to the user and not the theme design. Web analytics code (such as visitor tracking JavaScript from Google Analytics or Woopra) is a good example of this user-specific information. Because hundreds of analytics providers exist, most analytics providers require the JavaScript code to be customized for the specific site. The theme could have a number of different header and footer files, providing easy-to-use theme options. Adding JavaScript code to the header and the footer rather than requiring theme file modifications can make using your theme much easier.

Early in the design process, consider what a user may want to modify. Advanced uses of a Theme Options page vary widely and include design editors, color pickers, font options, and settings to modify the theme layout (switch a sidebar from one side of the theme to another, for example). The options offered depend on the project and the design.

Understanding theme options basics

Before jumping into the code, you should understand some basic concepts of how theme options work.

Before WordPress version 2.8, adding options to your theme required the developer to code the entire process, including providing an input form to accept the options, storing the options in the database, and retrieving the options from the database to use them. Fortunately, things have gotten much better. Some work is still required, but adding options is much easier now.

To let the user access the theme options, an input form is required. This process requires the most work because the form still needs to be manually created and managed. The form will need to be added to the back end so the user can access it. Adding a new option to the Appearance menu allows the user to find the Theme Options page. Fortunately, WordPress offers an easy-to-use function called `add_theme_page`. To have WordPress manage as much as possible for you, the code will need to tell WordPress to store the data. The `register_setting` function can handle this.

Building a simple theme options page

Now that you know what pieces you need to build the Theme Options page, you can jump into the code. Open a plain-text editor and enter the code in Listing 6-4.

Listing 6-4:   The Theme Options Page

```php
<?php
function cm_theme_options_init()                                          →2
 register_setting( 'cm_theme_options', 'theme_options' );                 →3
}
add_action( 'admin_init', 'cm_theme_options_init' );                      →5
function cm_theme_options_menu() {                                         →6
 add_theme_page( 'Theme Options', 'Theme Options', 'manage_options', 'cm_theme_
     options', 'cm_theme_options_page' );                                 →7
}
add_action( 'admin_menu', 'cm_theme_options_menu' );                      →9
function cm_theme_options_page() {                                        →10
 ?>
```

(continued)

Book VI Chapter 6

Digging into Advanced Theme Development

Listing 6-4 *(continued)*

```
<div class="wrap">                                                      →12
<?php screen_icon(); ?>                                                →13
<h2>Theme Options</h2>                                                 →14
<form method="post" action="options.php">                              →15
<?php settings_fields( 'cm_theme_options' ); ?>                        →16
<?php $options = get_option( 'theme_options' ); ?>                     →17
<table class="form-table">                                             →18
<tr valign="top">                                                      →19
<th scope="row">Checkbox</th>                                          →20
<td><input name="theme_options[checkbox]" type="checkbox" value="1" <?php
    checked('1', $options['checkbox']); ?> /></td>                     →21
</tr>
<tr valign="top"><th scope="row">Text</th>                             →23
<td><input type="text" name="theme_options[text]" value="<?php echo
    $options['text']; ?>" /></td>                                      →24
</tr>
<tr valign="top">                                                      →26
<th scope="row">Text Area</th>                                         →27
<td><textarea name="theme_options[text_area]"><?php echo $options['text_area'];
    ?></textarea></td>                                                 →28
</tr>
</table>
<p class="submit"><input type="submit" class="button-primary" value="<?php _e(
    'Save Changes' ); ?>" /></p>                                       →31
</form>
</div>
<?php
}
?>
```

Here's a brief explanation of what the various lines do:

→**2**   This creates a new function that calls register_setting, the function that tells WordPress about the need to store data.

→**3**   This tells WordPress that you're creating a new settings group called cm_theme_options. The theme_options argument sets the WordPress options name used to store and retrieve the theme options. You'll want to change these to be unique to your theme so that you don't accidentally load or save over settings from other themes or plugins.

→**5**   The new cm_theme_options_init function needs to be called to work. This line causes the function to be called during the admin_init action, which is a good action to use to run functions that need to be called on each admin page load.

→**6**   This new function handles registering the new menu entry that will show your form.

→**7**   The `add_theme_page` function adds a new menu entry under the Appearance menu. In order, the arguments are page title (shows in the title bar of the browser), menu entry name, required access level to visit the page, the variable name of the page (this needs to be unique for the page to work), and the function that should be run when visiting the menu location. This last argument (`cm_theme_options_page` in the example) is the name of the function that holds the options form.

→**9**   The new `cm_theme_options_menu` function needs to be called to work. This line causes the function to be called during the `admin_menu` action, which is when new menu entries should be added.

→**10**   This new function produces the input form for editing the theme options.

→**12**   Wrapping a form in the `wrap` class applies WordPress's default formatting.

→**13**   This outputs the Appearance icon in front of the heading that follows.

→**14**   This adds a title to the theme options page.

→**15**   Starts the HTML form with an action that points to `options.php` and handles saving the data.

→**16**   The `settings_fields` adds some hidden inputs that allow the options to save properly. The `cm_theme_options` argument must match the first argument passed to the `register_setting` function. If this function is missing or if the argument doesn't match the first argument of the `register_setting` function, the options won't save properly.

→**17**   This line loads the saved theme options into the `$options` variable. The `theme_options` argument must match the second argument passed to the `register_setting` function.

→**18**   Giving the table a class of `form-table` applies WordPress's default form styling.

→**19–20**   Starts a new row to hold the first option and adds a description row header (the content inside the `th` tag). As indicated by the description, this option will be a generic check box input.

→**21**   Adds the check box input. The `checked` function from WordPress handles outputting the required HTML if a checked state was previously saved. The `theme_options[checkbox]` portion matches the second argument passed to the `register_setting` function followed by the name of the specific option (in this case, `checkbox`). The `$options['checkbox']` loads the specific option from the `$options` array.

**Book VI
Chapter 6**

**Digging into
Advanced Theme
Development**

→**23** Starts a new row to hold another option and adds a description row header (the content inside the th tag). As indicated by the description, this option will be a generic text input.

→**24** Adds the text input. The echo outputs the existing value so that it pre-populates the input. The theme_options[text] portion matches the second argument passed to the register_setting function followed by the name of the specific option (in this case, text). The $options['text'] loads the specific option from the $options array.

→**26–27** Starts a new row to hold another option and adds a description row header (the content inside the th tag). As indicated by the description, this option will be a generic text area input.

→**28** Adds the text area input. The echo outputs the existing value so that it pre-populates the input. The theme_options[text_area] portion matches the second argument passed to the register_ setting function followed by the name of the specific option (in this case, text_area). The $options['text_area'] loads the specific option from the $options array.

→**31** Adds a button with a description of Save Changes. Giving the input a class of button-primary and wrapping it in a p tag with a class of submit applies WordPress's default button styling.

To load this file, you need to add a line of code to the theme's functions. php file. Edit the functions.php file and add the following line at the bottom of the file:

```
require_once( 'theme-options.php' );
```

Click the Themes Option link on the Appearance menu. The Theme Options page appears, as shown in Figure 6-9.

Using theme options in the theme

Compared with setting up a theme options page, using the stored options is very easy. To make it easier, add the following code — a quick function that makes using the options as simple as a single function call — to your theme's functions.php file:

```php
<?php
function get_theme_option( $option_name ) {
    global $theme_options;
        if ( ! isset( $theme_options ) )
            $theme_options = get_option( 'theme_options' );
        if ( isset( $theme_options[$option_name] ) )
            return $theme_options[$option_name];
    return '';
}
?>
```

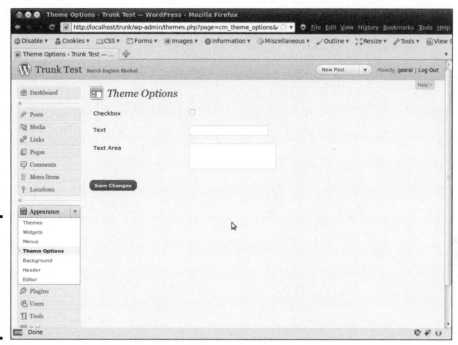

Figure 6-9:
The new
Theme
Options
page in the
WordPress
back end.

The `get_theme_option` function takes an option name as its only argument and returns that option's value. For example, to get the check box option value, simply call `get_theme_option('checkbox')`.

If your theme has a section that can be enabled and disabled by a theme option check box, a section of code such as the following works very well:

```
<?php if ( get_theme_option('checkbox') ) : ?>
    <!-- example code -->
<?php endif; ?>
```

Typically, text or text area options output user-provided content. By using a check to see whether an option has a value, your theme can offer a default set of text that can be overridden by text entered into a theme option:

```
<div class="footer-right">
    <?php if ( get_theme_option('text') ) : ?>
        <?php echo get_theme_option('text'); ?>
    <?php else : ?>
        <p>Sample Theme by Lisa Sabin-Wilson</p>
    <?php endif; ?>
    <p>Powered by <a
href="http://wordpress.org">WordPress</a></p>
</div>
```

Chapter 7: Using Theme Frameworks to Simplify Customization

In This Chapter

- ✔ Getting familiar with theme frameworks
- ✔ Exploring popular theme frameworks
- ✔ Recognizing common framework features

A s theme development for WordPress became a more complex task, theme designers began to realize that they were using the same snippet of code and functions repeatedly to accomplish the same tasks in every theme they built. When it came time for them to upgrade their theme (for example, when WordPress released a new version with new features), they found themselves updating the same functions and adding the same features over and over to several themes they had developed. This is how theme frameworks were born. Essentially, a theme framework is a single theme that is a foundation for other themes to be built from.

Chapter 5 of this minibook discusses child themes, including how to build them. With theme frameworks, the parent theme (the framework) contains all the WordPress functions and template tags, and you can build child themes on top of them. The nice thing about this setup is that the original theme developer has to update only one theme, the framework, to provide upgrades to all of his theme offerings (the child themes).

Frameworks come with the tools developers can use to make a custom theme with great efficiency. Using a framework that provides these tools is much faster than building your own tools every time you want to modify a standard theme.

In this chapter, I explore some of the popular theme frameworks and the tools these frameworks contain that make them appealing to developers who want to create a custom theme.

Understanding Theme Frameworks

Many theme frameworks are available in the WordPress market. The goal of these frameworks is to allow you to create custom websites and themes without requiring you to be an expert programmer. Creating custom layouts, designs, and functionality can be difficult, and theme frameworks bridge the gap.

At its core, a theme framework is still just a WordPress theme. You install it and activate it just like any other theme. The real power of theme frameworks is usually found through theme options, child themes, and layout customization. One of the most important parts of using theme frameworks is starting with the right one for your project.

When you install a theme framework, you might be surprised to find limited or no styling in the theme. Generally, theme frameworks are meant to be blank canvases that you easily fill with your own color styles. The goal for a framework is to get out of your way when developing. By doing so, it allows you to use tools that are provided instead of having to remove a lot of unnecessary elements and styling.

Think of it like a toolbox. All the tools you need are packaged nicely inside. You take out only the tools that you need for a given project.

Discovering Popular Frameworks

Many theme frameworks are available from a variety of sources. Here's a look at a few of the more popular theme frameworks.

Theme Hybrid

The Theme Hybrid framework (see Figure 7-1) features 15 custom page templates and 8 widget-ready areas. Additionally, six child themes are available from the Theme Hybrid website at `http://themehybrid.com`. Theme Hybrid also supports a series of add-on plugins that are specific to this theme. These add-ons include such features as a Tabs plugin, Hooks plugin, and Page Template packs.

WordPress For Dummies

by Lisa Sabin-wilson

Hello world!

By lswilson on November 3, 2012 | Edit

Welcome to WordPress For Dummies Sites. **This is your first post. Edit or delete it, then start blogging!**

Posted in Uncategorized | 1 Response

Copyright © 2012 WordPress For Dummies. Powered by WordPress and Hybrid.

Book VI Chapter 7

Using Theme Frameworks to Simplify Customization

Figure 7-1:
A home page with a new installation of Theme Hybrid.

The Hooks plugin in particular can be very handy if you're unfamiliar with PHP programming because it provides you with a graphical interface to latch into hooks, which I explore later in this chapter.

Theme Hybrid, its child themes, and all its add-on plugins are available free. You can download them from `http://themehybrid.com` or from WordPress Extend at `http://wordpress.org/extend/themes/hybrid`.

Key features:

✦ Theme Options menu

✦ Supports child themes

✦ Add-on plugins to extend functionality

Carrington

The Carrington theme's developers set out to create a framework that would allow them to stop re-creating the same key features every time they needed to make an advanced WordPress theme. (See Figure 7-2.) By doing this for themselves, they created a tool that others can now use for theme development. Carrington takes a different approach from many other theme frameworks; it doesn't use the parent/child theme relationship. Instead, Carrington uses a unique system of template files to determine how different types of content display in your theme. This approach helps prevent bugs in code because there is less code. Carrington's developers offer several themes built from the base framework. Check out their website at http://carringtontheme.com.

The Carrington theme's features include

✦ Unique template file system

✦ Fast development of complex themes

✦ Predeveloped themes using the framework

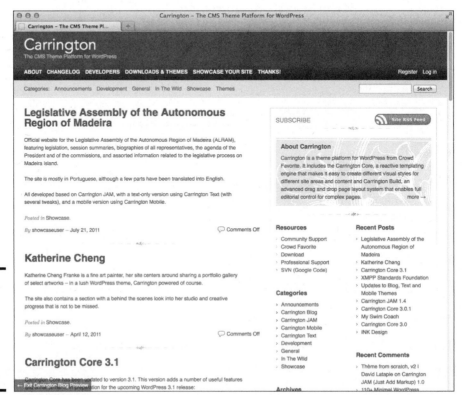

Figure 7-2:
A home page with a new installation of Carrington.

Thematic

Thematic (see Figure 7-3) features 13 widget-ready areas, grid-based layout samples, and styling for many popular plugins. About 20 child themes are available directly from the Thematic website, as are many more from third-party sources. Downloading Thematic won't cost you a dime. You can download the theme free at `http://wordpress.org/extend/themes/thematic`. Numerous child themes are available free as well, whereas others are commercially supported.

The Thematic theme's features include

✦ Theme Options menu

✦ Supports child themes

Book VI Chapter 7

Using Theme Frameworks to Simplify Customization

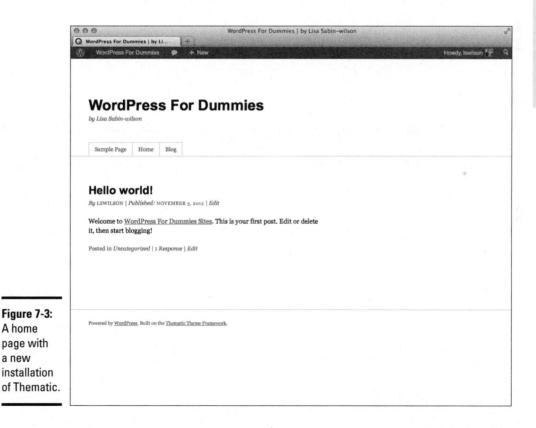

Figure 7-3:
A home page with a new installation of Thematic.

Genesis

Genesis (see Figure 7-4) includes six default layout options, a prerelease security audit from WordPress lead developer Mark Jaquith, and a comprehensive array of SEO settings. Another great feature of Genesis is a built-in theme store in the WordPress Dashboard that allows you to easily choose, purchase, and activate one of more than 18 child themes. Like other frameworks, Genesis has some theme-specific plugins that add functionality. You can purchase Genesis from StudioPress (`http://studiopress.com`) for $79.95, and it includes one child theme. Additional child themes are available for $24.95.

The Genesis theme's features include

✦ Theme Options menu

✦ Supports child themes

✦ Add-on plugins to extend functionality

✦ Six default layout options

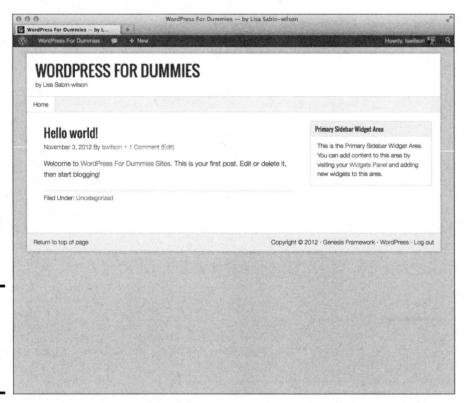

Figure 7-4:
A home page with a new installation of Genesis.

iThemes Builder

iThemes Builder (see Figure 7-5) sports a built-in layout editor that allows for infinite combinations of layouts. Widget areas can be created on the fly in the layout editor with no limit to the number you can create. Other key features include a style manager to customize the look of the site, a slew of in-theme SEO options, and integration with popular plugins like BuddyPress. You can purchase a copy of iThemes Builder from iThemes at `http://ithemes.com/purchase/builder-theme`. The price is $127 for unlimited sites and includes over 15 child themes.

Key features:

✦ Theme Options menu

✦ Supports child themes

✦ Add-on plugins to extend functionality

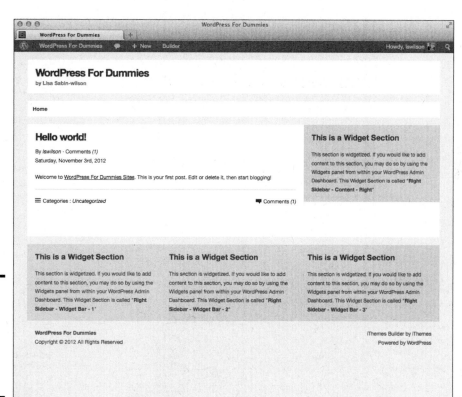

Figure 7-5: A home page with a new installation of iThemes Builder.

Headway

Headway's layout combinations are virtually limitless, thanks to a what-you-see-is-what-you-get (WYSIWYG) style editor for creating layouts. The visual editor allows you to drag and drop parts of your theme (known in Headway as Leafs) and resize them to fit your needs. Headway also features a built-in design manager that allows you to select colors and images for your sites design. Headway, shown in Figure 7-6, can be purchased from `http://headwaythemes.com` for $87 for use on up to two sites, or $164 for use on unlimited sites.

The Headway theme's features include

✦ Drag-and-drop layout editor

✦ Built-in design manager

✦ Infinite widget areas

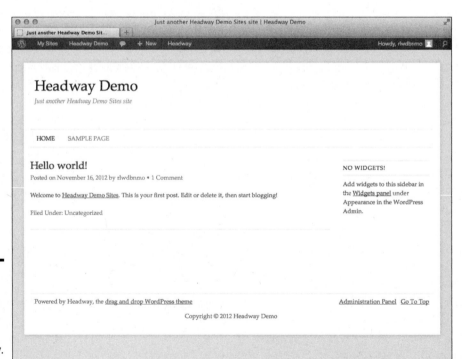

Figure 7-6:
A home page with a new installation of Headway.

Common Framework Features

Theme frameworks offer a host of features to make your life easier when it comes to building a website. Individual frameworks offer many unique features but also share a common set of features. These common features generally allow for faster and easier development of your WordPress website.

Theme functions

Most themes include a `functions.php` file that contains functions for the theme, but some theme frameworks take this to the next level. They offer customization options using these functions that rival many plugins.

Book VI
Chapter 7

In the Genesis theme, a custom function allows you to create new widget areas. The `genesis_register_sidebar()` function, which takes care of the heavy lifting for widgetizing a new area, gives you some options to easily customize it. The following example shows how you might use this function in your theme's `functions.php` file:

```
genesis_register_sidebar(array(
    'name'=>'My New Widget',
    'description' => 'This widget is new.',
    'before_title'=>'<h4 class="mywidget">',
    'after_title'=>'</h4>'
));
```

This function allows you to enter a few customizations into the function, such as a name for your widget, a description, and any HTML that you want to appear before and after your widget.

Many standard themes also provide functions that are used in the theme, but theme frameworks offer many additional custom functions that the theme doesn't. The custom functions help you make the theme do exactly what you need for a specific site.

Theme functions can vary greatly, so most theme authors have ample documentation through their site or forums where you can get more information about available functions.

Hooks

Many theme frameworks provide hooks to allow you to access and modify features of the theme. Hooks may seem a little advanced, but with a little practice, hooks are quite efficient at modifying a theme. Theme frameworks provide hooks to allow you to latch in to functions of the theme and call or modify them at a specific time.

The two types of hooks are

✦ **Action:** Events during the loading of the theme when you can latch in a specific function. For example, if you want one of your functions to execute at the same time a file in the theme is loaded, you can use an action to hook the function to that file's load.

✦ **Filter:** Allows you to modify data while it passes to the theme or to the browser screen. Some theme frameworks allow you to filter the classes the theme applies to elements.

You can find an example of modifying your theme with hooks in iThemes Builder. For example, consider the hook to add meta data: `builder_add_meta_data`. This can be useful for SEO in your theme.

To add custom meta output, the default function can be replaced with a custom one. To do that, remove the existing action and add your own, like this:

```
<?php
remove_action('builder_add_meta_data','builder_seo_options');
add_action('builder_add_meta_data','my_custom_builder_seo_options');
?>
```

The default SEO options were removed with `remove_action` and replaced with a new function called `my_custom_builder_seo_options`. Now, you need to define what `my_custom_builder_seo_options` will do.

```
<?php
function my_custom_builder_seo_options() {
   /*Add custom seo options here.*/
}
?>
```

This creates a basic PHP function where you can define what custom SEO options you want in the theme.

Because many frameworks have 100 or more hooks, most of them provide documentation (through their websites or forums) of what hooks are available, what each hook does, and what parameters are available to modify how the hook works.

Child themes

Some frameworks allow you to modify the theme by using child themes. (Find out more about the parent/child theme relationship in Chapter 5 of this minibook.) Child themes can be as simple as a stylesheet, but they derive their power from the parent theme's template and function files.

Like a regular theme, a huge advantage of using a child theme is to protect any customizations you make from being overwritten if a newer version of the theme comes out. For frameworks, this is especially important because changes to the core theme may be more frequent than regular themes due to the need to add more hooks, functions, or options over time.

Theme Hybrid, Thematic, Genesis, and iThemes Builder all extend their frameworks through child themes. Many frameworks provide child themes for free; others build child themes to sell.

Layout options

The ability to change the layout of a framework is important for many users. Different frameworks use different methods of achieving this. Some use template files to allow the reorganization of the layout; others provide an interface to create layouts from scratch.

Headway, for example, provides a unique layout editor, as shown in Figure 7-7. The layout of the theme is created through a drag-and-drop interface that allows you to organize, size, and style the layout in one location.

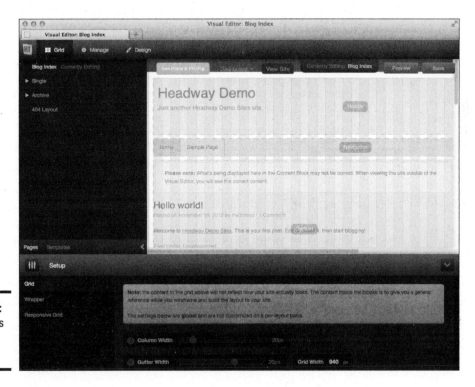

Figure 7-7: Headway's layout editor.

Styling

Many theme frameworks incorporate methods that let you customize the style of the website without needing to know CSS. (See the section on CSS and stylesheets in Chapter 4 of this minibook.) Frameworks that use a what-you-see-is-what-you-get (or WYSIWYG) style editor, such as Headway, allow you to easily match your theme's colors and design to your branding. Additionally, many editors include color pickers so you don't have to use hexadecimal values to choose colors.

Other common elements that can be styled are borders, fonts, and headers.

Customizing Theme Frameworks

You may find that you're changing the same elements every time you set up a website by using a theme framework. Here is a list of where to start when customizing a theme framework for a website:

✦ **Add a custom header or logo image.** Adding a nice header graphic to a site makes it look unique from the beginning. If graphics aren't your specialty, use a good designer for your header graphic. This crucial element will catch your visitors' eyes as soon as they hit the page.

✦ **Change the colors of the background and links to match the header and branding of the site.** Many frameworks provide a simple interface to do this; others require you to open the `style.css` file to change the color. Either way, changing the background and link colors to match the site adds cohesiveness throughout the branding of the site.

✦ **Consider the home page layout:** This is based on what the site is trying to achieve. If you want the site to focus on the blog, you might place it on the front page with a left or right sidebar. If your site is more static, you might create a layout with many widget areas on the home page that display things from around the site. The home page is the landing point for many of your site's visitors, so it's important to consider its layout early in the process.

✦ **Decide how to lay out the inside pages and blog post pages.** The pages are just as important as the home page. The form and function of the page and blog post layouts needs to be well planned to accommodate for the parts of the site that you want every user to see. These might include ads in the sidebar or an e-mail newsletter sign-up at the bottom of every post. In the case of pages, you might include information on your products and services in the sidebars and feature areas.

✦ **Add a contact form to the site:** Don't overlook one of those most vital items to install on almost every site. Some frameworks offer built-in contact forms that you can add to any page.

If your theme framework doesn't offer a built-in contact form, many free plugins include this functionality, such as Contact Form 7 from `http://contactform7.com`. If you're looking for a more robust form plugin, Gravity Forms by Rocket Genius (`http://gravityforms.com`) is one of the best form-creation plugins. It is a premium plugin but well worth the price.

Book VII
Using and Developing Plugins

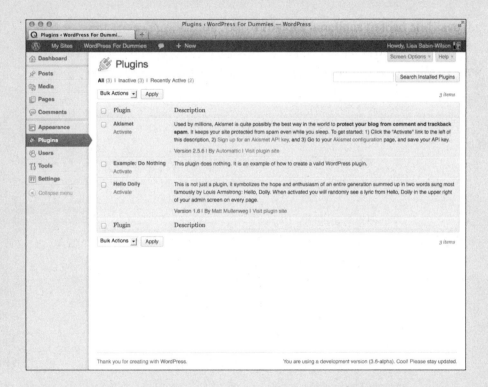

Visit www.dummies.com/extras/wordpressaio to find technical support resources for your WordPress plugins.

Contents at a Glance

Chapter 1: Introducing WordPress Plugins

In This Chapter

✔ Extending WordPress with plugins

✔ Comparing plugins to themes

✔ Finding plugins

✔ Evaluating the trustworthiness of plugins

*O*ne of the most important features of WordPress is its support for plugins. With plugins, you can add new features, remove existing features, or change how specific features function. In other words, plugins allow you to tailor WordPress to meet your site's needs.

Plugins can be very simple — for instance, a plugin might change the appearance of the Dashboard menu. Or they can also be very complex, accomplishing hefty tasks such as providing a complete e-commerce solution with product listings, a shopping cart, and payment processing.

To help you make use of plugins to customize your site, this chapter explores what plugins are and shows you how to find and use plugins.

Extending WordPress with Plugins

WordPress by itself is an amazing tool. The features built into WordPress are meant to be the ones that you'll benefit from the most. All the desired site features that fall *outside* what is built in to WordPress are considered the territory of plugins.

There's a popular saying among WordPress users: "There's a plugin for that." The idea is that if you want WordPress to do something new, you have a good chance of finding an existing plugin that can help you do what you want. Currently, more than 22,000 plugins are available in the WordPress Plugin Directory (http://wordpress.org/extend/plugins), and this number is constantly growing at a rate of a few new plugins each day. In addition, thousands of additional plugins that are outside the Plugin Directory are available for free or for a fee. So, if you have an idea for a new feature for your site, you just may find a plugin for that feature.

Suppose you want to easily add recipes to your site. A Google search for *wordpress plugin recipes* results in links to the Easy Recipe plugin (http://wordpress.org/extend/plugins/easyrecipe), the ZipList Recipe Plugin (http://wordpress.org/extend/plugins/ziplist-recipe-plugin), and the ReciPress plugin (http://recipress.com). And you can find more recipe-related plugins with a more in-depth search.

Identifying Core Plugins

Some plugins hold a very special place in WordPress in that they are shipped with the WordPress software and are included by default in every WordPress installation.

For the past few years, two plugins have held this special position:

- ✦ **Akismet:** The Akismet plugin has the sole purpose of protecting your blog from comment spam. Although other plugins address the issue of comment spam, the fact that Akismet is packaged with WordPress and works quite well means that most WordPress users rely on Akismet for their needs. Book III, Chapter 4 covers how to activate and configure Akismet on your site.

- ✦ **Hello Dolly:** The Hello Dolly plugin helps you get your feet wet in plugin development, if you're interested. It was first released with WordPress 1.2 and is considered to be the oldest WordPress plugin. When the plugin is active, the tops of your Dashboard pages show a random lyric from the song "Hello, Dolly!"

Figure 1-1 shows the core plugins as found in WordPress version 3.5.

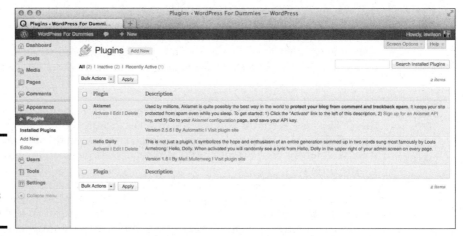

Figure 1-1:
Core
plugins in
WordPress
version 3.5.

The idea of core plugins is to offer a base set of plugins to introduce you to the concept of plugins while also providing a benefit. The Akismet plugin is useful because comment spam is a big issue for blogs. The Hello Dolly plugin is useful as a nice starting point for understanding what plugins are and how they're coded.

Although WordPress automatically includes these plugins, your site doesn't have to run them. They are disabled by default and must be manually activated to be used. Core plugins can be deleted just as any other plugin can, and they won't be replaced when you upgrade WordPress. (If you need to install or delete a plugin, turn to the next chapter.)

Although Akismet and Hello Dolly are the current core plugins and have been for several years, they aren't the only plugins to have this position. WordPress 1.2 included five core plugins: Hello Dolly, MarkDown, Search Highlight, Textile 1, and Textile 2.

Future versions of WordPress may offer different sets of core plugins. It is possible that one or both of the current core plugins will cease being core plugins and that other plugins will be included. Although this topic has seen much discussion in WordPress development circles over the past few years, as of this writing, no definitive decisions have been made. So, the current set of core plugins is likely to stay for a while longer.

Distinguishing Between Plugins and Themes

Because themes can contain large amounts of code and add new features or other modifications to WordPress, you may wonder how plugins are different than themes. In reality, there are only a few technical differences between plugins and themes; however, the idea of what plugins and themes are supposed to be is quite different. (For more about themes, see Book VI.)

At the most basic level, the difference between plugins and themes is that they reside in different directories. Plugins can be found in the `wp-content/plugins` directory of your WordPress site. Themes can be found in the `wp-content/themes` directory.

The `wp-content/plugins` and `wp-content/themes` directories are set up this way by default. It is possible to change both of these locations; however, this is very rarely done. It is something to be aware of if you're working on a WordPress site and are having a hard time locating a specific plugin or theme directory.

The most important difference that separates plugins from themes is that a WordPress site always has one and only one active theme, but it can have as many active plugins as you want — even none. This difference is important because it means that switching from one theme to another prevents you from using the features of the old theme. In contrast, activating a new plugin doesn't prevent you from making use of the other active plugins.

Plugins are capable of changing nearly every aspect of WordPress. The jonradio Multiple Themes plugin (available at `http://wordpress.org/extend/plugins/jonradio-multiple-themes`) adds the ability to use different themes for specific parts of your WordPress site. Thus, even the limitation of only one active theme on a site can be changed by using a plugin.

Because WordPress can have only one theme but many plugins activated at one time, it is important that the features that modify WordPress are limited to just plugins, whereas themes should remain focused on the appearance of the site. For you, this separation of functionality and appearance is the most important difference between plugins and themes.

This separation of functionality into plugins and appearance into themes isn't enforced by WordPress, but it's a good practice to follow. You can build a theme that includes too much functionality, and you may start to rely on those functions to make your site work, which ultimately makes it difficult to switch to another theme.

The functionality role of plugins does not mean that control over the appearance of a WordPress site is limited to just themes. Plugins are just as capable of modifying the site's appearance as a theme is. For example, the WPtouch plugin (available at `http://wordpress.org/extend/plugins/wptouch`) can provide a completely different version of your site to mobile devices such as smartphones. The WPtouch plugin does this by completely replacing the functionality of the theme when the user visits the site from a mobile device.

There are other technical differences that separate plugins and themes. These are mostly important to developers, but it could be important to know these differences as a nondeveloper WordPress user. Plugins load before the theme, which gives plugins some special privileges over themes and can even result in one or more plugins preventing the theme from ever loading. The built-in WordPress functions in the `wp-includes/pluggable.php` file can be overridden with customized functions, and only plugins load early enough to override these functions. Themes support a series of structured template files and require a minimum set of files in order to be a valid theme. By comparison, plugins have no such structured set of files and require only a single PHP file with a comment block at the top that tells WordPress that the file is actually a plugin. One of the final technical differences is that themes support a concept called child themes, where one theme can require that another theme is present in order to function; no such feature is available to plugins.

Finding Plugins on the WordPress Plugin Directory

The largest and most widely used source of free WordPress plugins is the WordPress Plugin Directory (`http://wordpress.org/extend/plugins`). As shown in Figure 1-2, this directory is filled with more than 20,000 plugins that cover an extremely broad range of features. Due to the large number of plugins freely available, the fact that each plugin listing includes ratings and details such as user-reported compatibility with WordPress versions, the Plugin Directory should be your first stop when looking for a new plugin to fill a specific need.

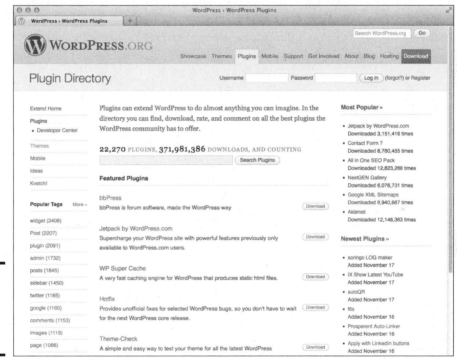

Figure 1-2: The WordPress Plugin Directory.

Plugins in the Plugin Directory should not be considered "official" or "supported" by WordPress. Anyone can submit plugins to the directory. There are some restrictions on what can be listed on the Plugin Directory, but these are mainly focused on licensing guidelines and blatant attempts to exploit users.

Be critical of anything you add to your site. Plugins receive very little code review once added to the Plugin Directory. Adding buggy code to your site can cause your site to crash. Adding malicious code to your site can enable other people to gain access to your site without your authorization.

This isn't to say that plugins on the Plugin Directory should not be trusted; rather, you should never add anything to your site without doing some checking up on the plugin, theme, or code.

Although you can search for plugins directly on the Plugin Directory site, WordPress has a built-in feature for searching the Plugin Directory. This feature even includes the ability to easily install the Plugin Directory from WordPress without having to download the plugin and upload it to your site.

The following sections show you how to find plugins.

Searching for plugins from the Dashboard

After logging in to your WordPress Dashboard, click the Add New link on the Plugins menu. You then see the Install Plugins page, which you use for installing plugins from inside the Dashboard — it's also where you can search for plugins. Figure 1-3 shows how the Install Plugins page appears.

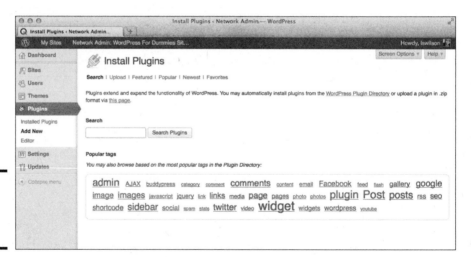

Figure 1-3:
The Install Plugins page.

At the top of the Install Plugins page are a series of links that provide a number of ways to find plugins. (If you're looking to install a plugin, turn to Chapter 2 of this minibook.)

Search

Figure 1-3 shows the search page. This page allows for searching the WordPress Plugin Directory either by using a list of terms you type in the Search box or by clicking one of the popular tag links to quickly narrow the list of plugins.

After you use either of the search options, the page changes to a Search Results page, which lists the plugins that match the search query. As shown in Figure 1-4, the search results provide a wealth of information about each found plugin.

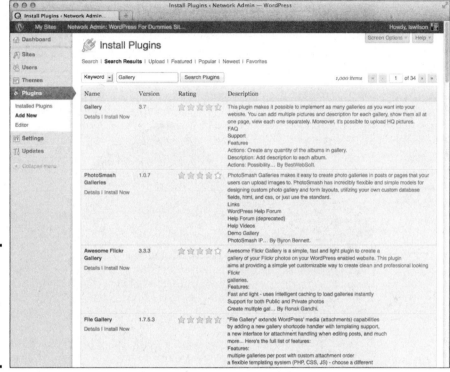

Figure 1-4:
Plugin search results after searching for the term Gallery.

Book VII
Chapter 1

Introducing
WordPress Plugins

For each plugin listed on the page, the search results show the plugin's name, current version, rating, and description. Two links for each plugin appear below the name of the plugin — click those links to discover more information about the plugin and install it. (I go into detail about these links later in this chapter, in the "Evaluating Plugins before Installing" section.)

Upload

Click the Upload link on the Install Plugins page to display the Upload section, as shown in Figure 1-5. The Upload section allows for easy installation of downloaded plugin Zip files without using FTP or some other method to upload the files to the server. This feature makes it very quick and easy to install downloaded plugin Zip files. While you can do this with plugins you find in the WordPress Plugin Directory, this feature is mostly used to install plugins that are not available in the Plugin Directory because they cannot be installed by searching for them in the Install Plugins page.

After selecting the Zip file to upload and clicking the Install Now button. The options to go back to the Install Plugins page or to activate the newly installed plugin are available.

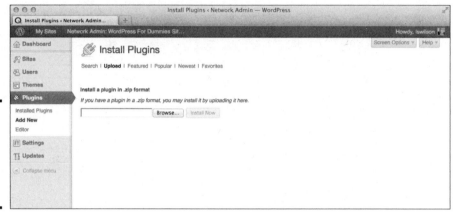

Figure 1-5:
The Upload section of the Install Plugins page.

Featured, Popular, and Newest

The Featured, Popular, and Newest pages are all very similar. The Featured page shows just the plugins listed as Featured in the WordPress Plugin Directory. The Popular page includes a listing of all the plugins sorted by their popularity. The Newest page lists all the plugins sorted with the newest plugins listed first with the oldest coming in at the end of the list.

Beyond these differences, each page is identical to the Search Results page. Each of the listed plugins provides options to view more details about the plugin and to quickly install the plugin.

Finding plugins through WordPress.org

The WordPress Plugin Directory is located at `http://wordpress.org/extend/plugins`. To search for a plugin, follow these steps:

1. **Navigate to** `http://wordpress.org/extend/plugins` **in your browser.**

   You see the searchable Plugin Directory. (Refer to Figure 1-2.)

2. **Enter the name of the plugin (or a search term relevant to the plugin or a feature you're looking for) in the search box and then click the Search Plugins button.**

   The directory lists all plugins that match your query. You can sort your search query by selecting one of the radio buttons underneath the search box: Relevance (default), Newest, Recently Updated, Most

Popular, or Highest Rated. Additionally, WordPress.org lists plugins on the right side of the page by Most Popular, Newest Plugins, and Recently Updated to help you find plugins that may interest you.

The Most Popular plugins have the greatest number of users and have been downloaded most often by users. In the Plugin Directory, they're grouped because the majority of WordPress users want to find them easily.

All plugins are tagged with keywords; the most popular tags for all plugins are listed at the bottom of the search page.

Evaluating Plugins before Installing

When you've found a plugin via the Dashboard's Install Plugins page, you can find a wealth of information about that plugin to help you decide whether to download it or go on to the next one.

The methods described here for evaluating plugins are no substitute for thoroughly testing a plugin. Testing the plugin is good practice, unless you're familiar enough with the code and the developers that bugs or security issues seem unlikely. To test a plugin, set up a standalone site used just for testing, install the plugin, and check for any issues before trusting the plugin on your main site.

Look at the version number of the plugin. If it shows *Alpha* or *Beta*, the plugin is being tested and may have bugs that could affect your site; you may want to wait until the plugin has been thoroughly tested and released as a full version. Generally, the higher the version number, the more *mature* (that is, tested and stable) the plugin is.

Don't use just one of these methods of assessing the trustworthiness. Combine them all to get a sense of what the other users think about the plugin. If the plugin has a five-star rating given by 500 users but has dozens of negative feedback comments with very little positive commentary, don't trust the plugin very much. However, if a plugin has a three-star rating given by 10 users but has nothing but positive comments, the plugin may have some issues yet may still work very well for some users.

Like with many things in life, you have no guarantees with plugins. The best you can do is to find information about the plugin to determine whether or not it is trustworthy.

Details

Click the Details link for a plugin to find information taken from the plugin's page in the WordPress Plugin Directory. Figure 1-6 shows an example of what details are available. Just like the Plugin Directory page, tabs for Description, Installation, Screenshots, and the Changelog are available.

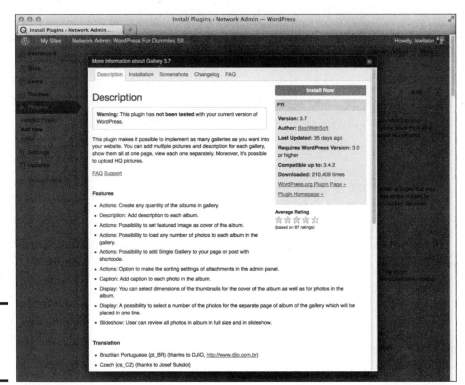

Figure 1-6:
Details for
the Gallery
plugin.

Make sure to check out each plugin's Description page. Some very important information can be found on the plugin's details that aren't present in the results listing. When considering a plugin that you don't have experience with, this information will help you determine how reliable and trustworthy the plugin is.

Ratings

Consider the plugin's rating and the number of people that submitted a rating. The more people that rated the plugin, the more you can trust the rating; the fewer people that rated the plugin, the less you can trust the rating. A plugin that has fewer than 20 ratings is probably not very trustworthy. A plugin that has more than 100 ratings is very trustworthy. Any plugin rated between 20 and 100 times is acceptably trustworthy.

If a plugin has a large percentage of one- or two-star ratings, treat the plugin very suspiciously. Take the extra step and visit the plugin's page on the Plugin Directory to see what other people are saying about the plugin. You can do this by clicking the WordPress.org Plugin Page link on the right side of the Description page, in the FYI box. On the plugin's page, as shown in Figure 1-7, click the View Support Forum button, or the Support link at the top of the page, to see the information posted by users, both positive and negative. You can determine whether the issues other people experienced are likely to hinder your needs.

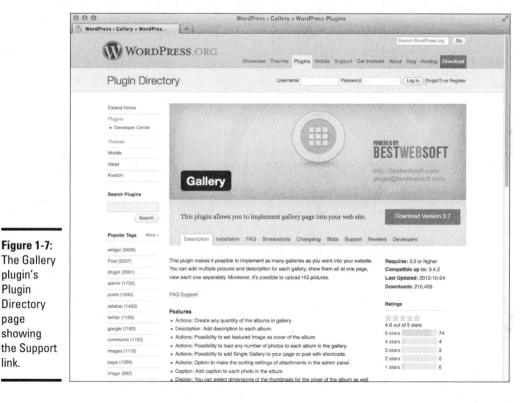

Figure 1-7: The Gallery plugin's Plugin Directory page showing the Support link.

Downloads

The next detail to consider is the number of downloads. The higher the number of downloads, the more likely the plugin is to work well — plugins that don't work very well typically don't pick up enough popularity to get many downloads. If a plugin has hundreds of thousands of downloads or more, it is extremely popular. Plugins with tens of thousands of downloads are popular and may grow even more popular. If the plugin has fewer than 10,000 downloads, you can't determine anything just by looking at the download count.

A low download count should not necessarily be counted against a plugin. Some plugins simply provide a feature that has a very limited audience. Thus, the download count is an indicator but is not proof of quality or lack thereof.

The Compatible Up To and the Last Updated information should be taken very lightly. If a plugin indicates that the compatible-up-to version is for a very old WordPress version, it may have issues with the latest versions of WordPress; however, plenty of plugins work just fine with current versions of WordPress even though they don't explicitly indicate support. Many people see an up-to-date plugin as a sign of quality and upkeep. This is flawed reasoning because some plugins are very simple and don't require updating very often. Plugins should not be updated just to bump that number; thus a plugin that hasn't been updated in a while may be functioning perfectly well without any updates.

Stats

Shown on the Stats tab of the plugin's page, as shown in Figure 1-8, the number of downloads per day isn't a foolproof method of getting a trusted plugin, but the Downloads Per Day graph may indicate that people are using the plugin with some success.

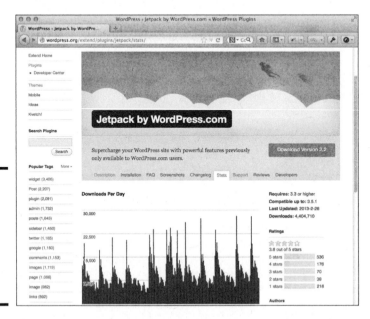

Figure 1-8: The download history for a plugin within the Plugin Directory.

Support

Click the Support tab below the plugin's banner to view the support forum for that plugin. This is where users of the plugin request help and assistance, as shown in Figure 1-9. By browsing the support forum for the plugin, you can get a good feel for how responsive the plugin's developer is to users, and you can also see what types of problems other people are having with the plugin.

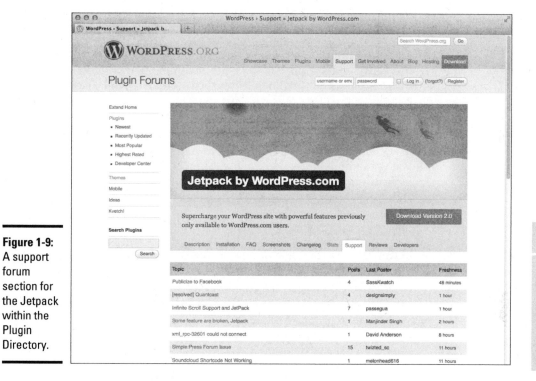

Figure 1-9:
A support forum section for the Jetpack within the Plugin Directory.

**Book VII
Chapter 1**

Introducing
WordPress Plugins

Finding Plugins Outside the Plugin Directory

The exact number of plugins that exist outside the Plugin Directory is unknown. There are easily more than a thousand, which means that there is a great variety of plugins that you won't see in the Plugin Directory. These outside plugins can sometimes be difficult to discover. There are some good starting places though.

Many of the plugins that are not on the Plugin Directory are paid plugins. The official WordPress Plugin Directory allows only free plugins to get listed there. If a plugin is for sale (costs more than a penny), it cannot get listed in the Plugin Directory, so these plugin authors need to find other methods of listing and promoting their products.

Over the past few years, the market for commercial plugins has grown tremendously. It would not be possible to list all the companies that currently offer WordPress plugins in this chapter, so the following listing is a sampling. It's a way of introducing you to the world of plugins outside the Plugin Directory.

Each of the following sites offers WordPress plugins:

✦ **CodeCanyon** (`http://codecanyon.net`): With thousands of plugins, this online marketplace is the paid plugin version of the Plugin Directory. Just as the Plugin Directory contains plugins from a large number of developers, CodeCanyon is actually a collection of plugins from various developers rather than a single company creating plugins.

✦ **Gravity Forms** (`http://gravityforms.com`): For many WordPress users, Gravity Forms is the plugin to pay for. It is typically the first and last recommendation people give when someone wants to create forms in WordPress.

✦ **iThemes** (`http://ithemes.com`): Starting as a theme developer, iThemes branched out into developing plugins as well. The most popular offering is BackupBuddy, a plugin for backing up and restoring your sites.

✦ **Shopp** (`http://shopplugin.net`): Shopp is a popular plugin that offers a full-featured e-commerce solution that you can integrate into your WordPress site. Essentially, it turns your WordPress site into an online store.

✦ **WooThemes** (`http://woothemes.com`): WooThemes is another theme developer that added plugins to their theme offerings. WooCommerce, their e-commerce solution, has created a lot of buzz.

✦ **WPMU DEV** (`http://premium.wpmudev.org`): WPMU DEV is one of the longest-running commercial plugin shops for WordPress. With over 100 plugins, they have a little of everything.

Although these sites give you a taste of what commercial plugin sites have to offer, having other sources that talk about new and exciting plugins can also be very helpful. Many popular WordPress news sites talk about all things WordPress, including reviews and discussions about specific plugins. Check out the following sites if you want to know more about what plugins are being talked about:

✦ **WPBeginner** (`http://wpbeginner.com`): This site is dedicated to helping new WordPress users get up and running quickly. It also features a very active blog talking about a variety of topics. The site often features posts that talk about how to use plugins to create specific types of solutions for your site.

✦ **WPCandy (**`http://wpcandy.com`**):** WPCandy is an all-things-Word-Press news site. If there is a buzz on the topic in the WordPress world, you're likely to find discussions on it here.

✦ **WPMU (**`http://wpmu.org`**):** Run by the Incsub team, the same team behind WPMU DEV, WPMU.org is a very active WordPress news site. It features multiple new blogs posts per day and often has numerous plugin reviews each week. This site is a great place to discover new plugins to try out.

One of the great things about using a community or news site to discover new plugins is that you aren't alone on deciding on whether to trust a plugin. You can get some outside opinions before you take a chance on a plugin.

If you aren't finding what you want in the Plugin Directory, don't know of anyone that offers a solution you are looking for, and aren't seeing anything on community sites, it's time to go to a trusty search engine, such as Google, and see what it has for you.

A good way to get started is to search for the words *wordpress* and *plugin* along with one to a few words describing the feature you want. For instance, if you want a plugin that provides more advanced image gallery features, search for *wordpress plugin image gallery.* As long as your search isn't too specific, you're likely to get many results. The results will often contain blog posts that either review specific plugins or have a listing of recommended plugins.

There are developers out there who include malware, viruses, and other unwanted executables in their plugin code. Your best bet is to use plugins from the official WordPress Plugin Directory or purchase plugins from a reputable seller. Do your research first and read up on plugin security in Book II, Chapter 5.

Comparing Free and Commercial Plugins

There are thousands of plugins available for free and thousands of plugins that have a price. What are the benefits of a free plugin versus a paid plugin? This is a tough question to answer.

It's tempting to think that some plugins are better than others, and that is why they cost money. Unfortunately, things aren't that simple. Some amazing plugins that I would gladly pay for are free, and some terrible plugins that I wouldn't pay for have a cost.

Oftentimes a paid plugin includes access to support specifically for that plugin. This means that the company or individual selling the plugin is offering assurance that if you have problems you will receive support and updates to address bugs and other issues.

Free plugins typically have places to make support requests or to ask questions, but there are no requirements to ensure that the developer responds to your requests within a certain period of time or at all. Even though developers have no obligation to help with support requests by their plugin's users, many developers work hard to help users with reported issues and other problems. Fortunately, because many free plugins are on the Plugin Directory and the Plugin Directory includes a built-in support forum and rating score, it is easy to see how responsive the plugin author is to support issues.

Personally, I believe that the reason that the commercial plugin model is able to work in an environment that has tens of thousands of free plugins is that many WordPress users want the assurance that when they have problems, they have a place to ask questions and get help with those problems.

So if people can get paid to produce plugins, why are so many plugins free? This is another great question.

One reason that so many plugins are available for free is that many WordPress developers are very generous and believe in sharing their plugins back with the community. For other developers, having their plugins available to the millions of WordPress via the Plugin Directory is a great way of marketing their talents, which can lead to contract work and employment. Buzz words on a resume are far less valuable than being able to point people to a plugin you wrote that was downloaded thousands or millions of times.

Another reason for releasing a free plugin is to entice people to pay for upgrades. This is often times referred to as a "freemium" plugin. Freemium plugins often have paid plugins that add features to the free plugin. Thus, the freemium model is a mix of the free and paid plugin models and gets the best of both worlds. The free plugin can be on the Plugin Directory, thus giving the plugin a large amount of exposure. You can get a feel for how the plugin functions, and if you want the additional features, you can purchase the paid plugin.

An example of the freemium model is the WP e-Commerce plugin (`http://getshopped.org`). The main plugin is available for free in the Plugin Directory, yet it supports a large number of paid plugins to add more features. By itself, the WP e-Commerce plugin turns the site into a shopping cart. To extend this functionality, paid plugins are available to add payment processing for specific credit card processors, drag-and-drop shopping carts, download managers, and many other features.

The reality is that the biggest difference between free and paid plugins is that sometimes you won't find what you need in a free plugin and will have to go with a paid plugin. In the end, what you download is up to you. There are many great free plugins and many great paid plugins. If you want the features offered by a paid plugin and are willing to pay the price, paid plugins can be a very good investment for your site.

Many free plugins have a link to a donation page. If there is a free plugin that you find very valuable, please send a donation to the developer. Most developers of free plugins say that they rarely, if ever, receive donations. Even a few dollars can really encourage the developer to keep updating old plugins and releasing new free plugins.

Book VII Chapter 1

Introducing WordPress Plugins

Chapter 2: Installing and Managing Plugins

In This Chapter

✔ **Installing WordPress plugins via the Dashboard**

✔ **Manually installing WordPress plugins**

✔ **Updating plugins**

✔ **Activating and deactivating plugins**

✔ **Deleting plugins**

*W*ith more than 20,000 plugins available, you have a huge number of options for customizing your site. Chapter 1 of this minibook detailed what types of plugins are available and where they can be found. In this chapter, you start putting these plugins to use. This chapter is dedicated to helping you install, activate, deactivate, update, and delete plugins.

Installing Plugins within the WordPress Dashboard

When you've found a plugin in the Plugin Directory (see Chapter 1 of this minibook) that you want to install, you can install it directly from the Dashboard. (If you found a plugin that isn't in the Directory, you have to manually install it. See the later section "Manually Installing Plugins.")

To install plugins from the Dashboard, follow these steps:

1. **Log in to your site's WordPress Dashboard.**

2. **Click the Add New link in the Plugins menu in your Dashboard.**

   The Install Plugins page opens where you can search for plugins, as shown in Figure 2-1.

   When searching for, and finding, plugins on the Dashboard, you use the same method you used at the WordPress website in the Plugin Directory. Ever since WordPress provided the plugin search on the Dashboard, most users don't use the WordPress website anymore.

Figure 2-1:
Search for
your plugin
in the Plugin
Directory.

3. **Find the plugin you want to install.**

Every plugin in the official WordPress Plugin Directory (`http://wordpress.org/extend/plugins`) is searchable from the Install Plugins page. Plugins are also listed by Featured, Popular, Newest, and Recently Updated categories. Popular Tags gives you shortcuts to the most-used tags for particular plugins with just a click of the links that are displayed at the top of the page.

4. **When you find a plugin you're looking for, click the details link to view its description.**

A description of the plugin appears in a pop-up window with a number of tabs at the top. These tabs can vary with each plugin and could include Installation, FAQ (Frequently Asked Questions), Screenshots, Stats, and Notes. Each tab provides important information about the plugin, as shown in Figure 2-2.

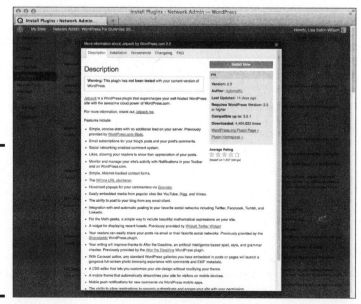

Figure 2-2:
The plugin
Description
page
with tabs
within the
WordPress
Plugin
Directory.

The FYI box on the right provides useful information, such as the version of the plugin, when the plugin was updated, what versions of WordPress are compatible with the plugin, and links to the author's website, as shown in Figure 2-3.

Figure 2-3:
The FYI box on the plugin page within the WordPress Plugin Directory.

The rating section below the FYI box displays the average rating the plugin has received from its users, as shown in Figure 2-4.

Figure 2-4:
The Reviews section on the right side of the plugin page in the directory.

5. **If the plugin looks like a good fit for your site and your needs, click the Install Now link on the search results listing in your Dashboard.**

6. **Confirm the prompt that asks for confirmation on the installation results.**

   WordPress downloads the plugin, unpacks it, and has the files moved to the plugin's directory.

   After the plugin is installed, you can activate the plugin or return to the Plugin Installer. (See Figure 2-5.)

7. **Click the Activate Plugin link.**

   The plugin is activated and becomes available for use.

Figure 2-5: Information about the installation of the Jetpack plugin.

If the Dashboard screen displays any kind of error message after installing the plugin, copy the message and paste into a support ticket on the WordPress.org support forum (`http://wordpress.org/support`) to elicit help from other WordPress users on what the source of the problem is and how to solve it. When posting about the issue, provide as many details about the issue as possible, including the screenshot or pasted details.

Manually Installing Plugins

Installing plugins from the Dashboard is so easy that you probably never need to know how to install a plugin manually via FTP. (Book II, Chapter 2 explains how to use FTP.) But the technique is still helpful to know in case the WordPress Plugin Directory is down or unavailable.

The following steps take you through how to install a plugin using FTP, using the Gallery plugin as the example:

1. **Go to the plugin page from the WordPress Plugin Directory website:** `http://wordpress.org/extend/plugins/gallery-plugin`.

2. **Click the red download button to transfer the plugin Zip file to your computer.**

3. **Unzip the plugin files.**

   All plugins downloaded from the Plugin Directory are in the Zip format. Most operating systems (Windows, Mac, and so on) have built-in tools to open Zip files. After opening the Zip file, extract the directory contained inside the Zip file and put it in a directory on your computer that is easily accessible.

4. **Connect to your site's server using FTP.**

   Details on how to use FTP are covered in Book II, Chapter 2. If you have any difficulty connecting to your server, contact your hosting provider and ask for assistance in connecting to your server via FTP.

5. **Navigate to the `wp-content` folder within the WordPress installation for your website or blog.**

   The location of your WordPress installation can differ with every hosting provider. Make sure that you know the location before you proceed. Check out Book II, Chapters 2 and 4 for information on where the WordPress installation is located on your web server.

6. **Navigate to the `/wp-content/plugins` directory.**

   First, navigate to `wp-content`. Inside this directory are the plugins and themes directories along with a few others. Navigate to the plugins directory. It is inside this directory that all plugins reside.

7. **Upload the plugin folder to the `/wp-content/plugins` directory on your web server.**

   The plugin folder, named for the plugin (for example, if you're uploading the Gallery plugin, the folder is `/gallery`) contains all the files for that plugin.

Go to the Dashboard's Plugins page and you see the new plugin listed. If a mistake is made, delete all the newly uploaded files and begin again.

Upgrading Plugins

Plugins receive updates that fix bugs, add new features, and update existing features. Some plugins are updated multiple times a week. Other plugins may never be updated. Fortunately, WordPress makes it easy to know when a new plugin version is available and also makes it very easy to update your local plugin directory from the Dashboard.

One of the easiest ways to know that plugin updates are available is by the version number displayed on the Plugins page on your Dashboard, directly underneath the plugin description. Figure 2-6 shows that the Akismet plugin has an available update, evidenced by the phrase underneath the Akismet description that says `There is a new version of Akismet available`. Figure 2-6 also shows how the Dashboard page provides alerts about upgrades with the small dark circle shown next to the word *Plugins* in the left navigation menu.

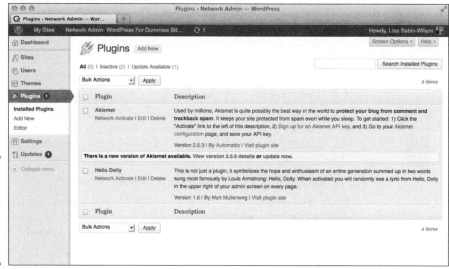

Figure 2-6:
A WordPress plugin with an available update.

There are three ways to update a plugin: from the Plugins page, from the Updates submenu accessible under the Dashboard menu, and by manually updating the files via FTP.

Updating on the Plugins page

Updating a plugin on the Plugins page is very easily done. There are two different ways to update a plugin on this page: You can update plugins one at a time or update all the plugins that need it in one fell swoop.

To update individual plugins, click the Update Now link at the bottom of the plugin's row; refer to Figure 2-6. WordPress automatically updates the plugin with the files from the new release. See Figure 2-7. Pay attention to the messages to ensure that the update was successful.

If an error is indicated, take a screenshot or copy the error details and create a support request on the WordPress.org community support forum (`http://wordpress.org/support`). The helpful people there can help you figure out the source of your issue and what the solution is.

Figure 2-7:
The results of updating a single plugin from the Plugins page.

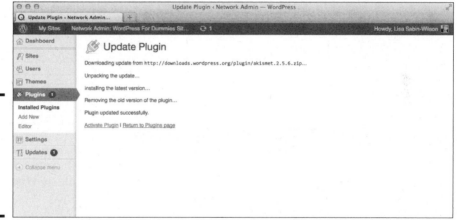

**Book VII
Chapter 2**

**Installing and
Managing Plugins**

If updates inside the Dashboard continuously fail, contact your hosting provider to see whether there are any server-specific issues preventing WordPress from updating its plugins.

Although clicking the Update Now link is very simple and quick, it can get tedious if you have a large number of plugins.

To update all your plugins at once, click the checkmark next to each plugin, select Update from the Bulk Actions drop-down list, and click the Apply button. All your plugins are now updated. Figure 2-8 shows both Akismet and Hello Dolly updated at the same time.

Figure 2-8:
The results
of updating
multiple
plugins from
the Plugins
page.

Updating on the Updates page

The Updates page, accessible as a submenu of the Dashboard menu, provides quick access to update WordPress, plugins, and themes in one place. As shown in Figure 2-9, the Updates page is a one-stop shop for all the updates across your site.

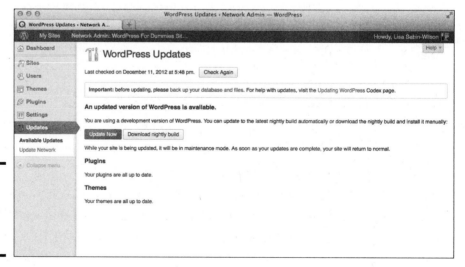

Figure 2-9:
The
WordPress
Updates
page.

To update all of the plugins, simply click a checkbox next to one of the Select All headers (as shown in Figure 2-9) and click the Update Plugins button. All your selected plugins are updated. (Refer to Figure 2-8.)

Updating manually

The process of manually updating a plugin is nearly identical to the steps for manually installing the plugin as detailed earlier in this chapter. The only change is to delete the plugin's directory before uploading the new files. Follow these steps:

1. **Download the latest version of the plugin from the WordPress Plugin Directory or the plugin developer's website.**

2. **Connect to your server via an FTP application and go to the `plugins` directory in the `wp-content` directory.**

    You should see a folder with the same name as the plugin you want to upgrade.

3. **Rename this folder so that you have a backup if you need it.**

    Any memorable name, such as *plugin-old* should suffice.

4. **Upload the new version of your plugin via FTP to your server so that it's in the `wp-content/plugins` folder.**

5. **Log in to the WordPress Dashboard and activate your upgraded plugin.**

 If you made any changes to the configuration files of your plugin before your upgrade, make those changes again after the upgrade. If you need to back out of the upgrade, you can just delete the new plugin directory and rename the folder from *plugin*-old to *plugin*.

Activating and Deactivating Plugins

After a plugin is on your site, activating it is extremely simple. To activate a plugin, do the following:

1. **Log in to the WordPress Dashboard.**

2. **Navigate to the Plugins page by clicking the Plugins menu link.**

3. **Find the plugin you want to activate on the Plugins page.**

4. **Click the Activate link just below the plugin's name in the listing.**

If everything goes well, you get a notice that states `Plugin activated`, and the plugin has been activated successfully. (See Figure 2-10.) If a long error message is shown in the activation notice, the plugin has an issue that is preventing it from activating. Copy the message that appears in the notice and send the details to the plugin author for help on fixing the issue.

Figure 2-10:
The Plugins page after activating a plugin.

Deactivating a plugin is the same process as activating a plugin. Simply follow the same steps but click the Deactivate link for the plugin that should be deactivated. You get a message at the top of your Dashboard telling you the plugin has been successfully deactivated.

Deleting Plugins

Sometimes it is simply time to let go of a plugin and remove it from the site. You could have many reasons for deleting a plugin:

✦ You no longer need the feature offered by the plugin.

✦ You want to replace the plugin with a different one.

✦ You're retiring the plugin due to its functionality being replaced with features built into a new version of WordPress.

✦ You're removing it due to performance issues because the plugin simply required too many resources to run.

It may be tempting to simply deactivate undesired plugins and leave them sitting in your plugins directory, but take the extra step to delete plugins that you no longer need. The PHP files of the plugin can still be run manually if someone, or some automated computer program, directly requests that PHP file. If the plugin had a security flaw that could allow such direct execution of the code to compromise the security of the server, having old code lying around is simply a problem waiting to happen.

If you accidentally delete a plugin, you can always reinstall it.

Deleting via the Dashboard

Deleting plugins can be handled from the Plugins page. To delete a plugin, it first must be deactivated. (See the earlier section "Activating and Deactivating Plugins.")

Ready to delete the plugin? Click the Delete link listed just below the plugin's name. As shown in Figure 2-11, you first have to confirm that you want to delete a plugin before that action will take place.

**Book VII
Chapter 2**

**Installing and
Managing Plugins**

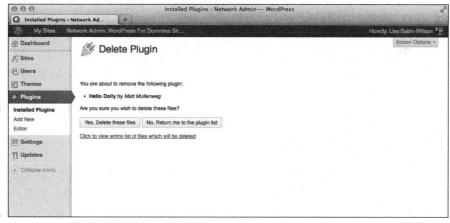

Figure 2-11:
The
confirmation
message for
deleting a
plugin.

After confirming the deletion of a plugin, you're returned to the Plugins page with a notice confirming that the plugin was deleted, as shown in Figure 2-12.

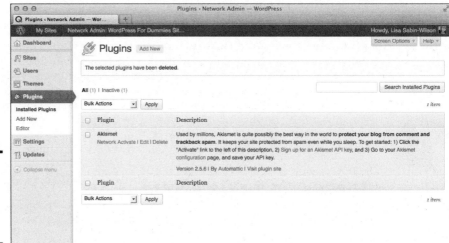

Figure 2-12:
A notice confirming the deletion of a plugin.

Deleting manually

You can manually delete a plugin by simply removing the plugin's directory from the `wp-content/plugins` directory. Because the files no longer exist, the plugin simply stops running. It may be helpful to deactivate the plugin first, but doing so isn't required.

Manually deleting a plugin can be very helpful when a plugin has a fatal error that causes the site to crash. If you can't gain control of the site again, manually deleting the plugin's directory could quickly return control of your site.

Because this process involves using FTP, like manually upgrading a plugin, this process is very similar to manually installing a plugin. The main difference is that, rather than uploading the plugin's directory, you're deleting it.

Before deleting a plugin, download the directory to a local system first, just so you don't lose any data that would be difficult to get back later. If the goal is to force the plugin to deactivate, you can rename the plugin's directory rather than deleting it, which prevents WordPress from being able to locate the plugin, thus disabling it.

The process works as follows:

1. **Connect to your site's server using FTP.**

2. **Navigate to the site's directory.**

3. **Navigate to the `wp-content/plugins` directory.**

4. **Delete the plugin's directory.**

The Plugins page shows a message that confirms the plugin is now deactivated due to the missing files. See Figure 2-13. Note that this message is shown only when you go to the Plugins page after manually deleting the plugin, and it is shown only once.

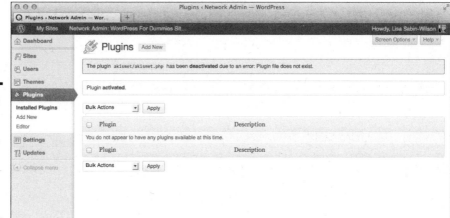

Figure 2-13: The error message shown after an active plugin is manually deleted.

Chapter 3: Configuring and Using Plugins

In This Chapter

✓ **Exploring activate-and-go plugins**

✓ **Discovering settings pages**

✓ **Using widgets and shortcodes**

The types of features offered by WordPress plugins are extremely diverse. Similarly, the ways of interacting with plugins are also extremely diverse. Some plugins don't have an interface and can be activated or deactivated only, while others provide one or more settings screens to control how the plugins behaves. Other plugins offer widgets and *shortcodes* (short, easy-to-remember codes used to execute PHP functions) used to add new features to sidebars and content.

This chapter digs into the topic of how to interact with plugins. Although this is a big topic, the examples in this chapter prepare you for the different ways of interacting with plugins.

Exploring Activate-and-Go Plugins

Certain plugins are easy to use because they don't have any settings or features to interact with — I call them *activate-and-go* plugins. You simply activate them, and they do what they are intended to do.

As with WordPress plugins as a whole, activate-and-go plugins offer a wide variety of features. The following list offers a sampling of activate-and-go plugins that you'll find useful on your website:

✦ **AJAX Comment Loading** (http://wordpress.org/extend/plugins/ajax-comment-loading): When pages and posts get large numbers of comments, they sometimes load more slowly, making the site seem sluggish. The AJAX Comment Loading plugin makes such pages and posts load much more quickly by having the content load first without the comments and then quietly pulling down the comments separately.

✦ **BBQ: Block Bad Queries** (`http://wordpress.org/extend/`
`plugins/block-bad-queries`): The BBQ plugin helps protect your
site against attackers trying to exploit specific security vulnerabilities.
This plugin doesn't require any configuration — it automatically scans
all requests coming into the site and protects against bad ones.

✦ **Disable WordPress Core Updates** (`http://wordpress.org/extend/`
`plugins/disable-wordpress-core-update`): The ability for
WordPress to automatically update itself has been a tremendous help
to WordPress users. Keeping WordPress updated not only offers new
features and enhancements, but it also helps keep your site safe from
attackers. For some users, the notification to update WordPress can
become a distraction, especially if the site is run by many people but a
single person is responsible for handling the site updates. The Disable
WordPress Core Updates plugin disables the automatic checks for new
WordPress versions while also disabling any notifications that a new
version is available. WordPress can still be updated from the Dashboard
(as described in Book II, Chapter 6), but the notifications are no longer
shown.

✦ **Hotfix** (`http://wordpress.org/extend/plugins/hotfix`): Every
day, new updates are created for WordPress. Some of these updates
add new features, and others fix *bugs* (defects in the software). Some
updates may not be released in a WordPress version for weeks or
months. The Hotfix plugin provides some of these new fixes automatically so that sites can avoid known issues while waiting for the new
WordPress version.

To use any of these plugins, simply install and activate them as discussed
in Chapter 2 of this minibook. When the plugin is activated, it starts doing
its job.

For some plugins, such as the BBQ or Hotfix plugins, seeing the results of
activating the plugin may be underwhelming as they simply do their work
behind the scenes and don't really change anything that is visible to you.
However, just because you don't see any immediate change, that doesn't
mean that the plugins aren't doing their job.

Discovering Settings Pages

Many popular plugins have settings pages where you tweak the functionality of the plugin and tailor it for the specific needs of your site. Often, these
settings need to be configured once and then need updating only when the
plugin changes.

The following sections explore a selection of the most popular WordPress
plugins, show you how to access settings pages, and describe what you can
expect from them.

Typically, you access settings pages from submenus of the Dashboard's Settings page. Another common place to access plugin settings pages, especially for plugins that provide advanced features such as site caching, is from the Dashboard's Tools menu.

If you have a hard time finding the settings page for a plugin, check the plugin's page for details on how to access the settings page. For plugins in the Plugin Directory, check the installation and FAQ tabs. If the Plugin Directory page has a screenshots tab, one of the screenshots usually shows the settings page.

Akismet

Akismet is bundled in with WordPress and likely already installed on your WordPress site. (See Book III, Chapter 5 if you still need to install this essential plugin.)

After you activate Akismet, a notice appears saying that the plugin requires additional configuration before it will function. See Figure 3-1.

Check for an activation notice after you install any plugin. Although most plugins don't offer such a notice, if one is available, it lets you know how to get started with the plugin. The Akismet plugin always has an activation notice after installation.

**Book VII
Chapter 3**

Configuring and
Using Plugins

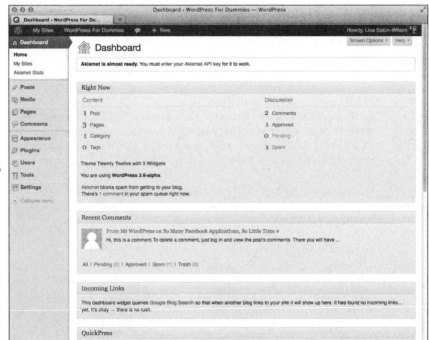

Figure 3-1: Akismet provides a notice after activation indicating that it requires configuration before it will function.

The link in the Akismet notice goes directly to the settings page for Akismet, as shown in Figure 3-2.

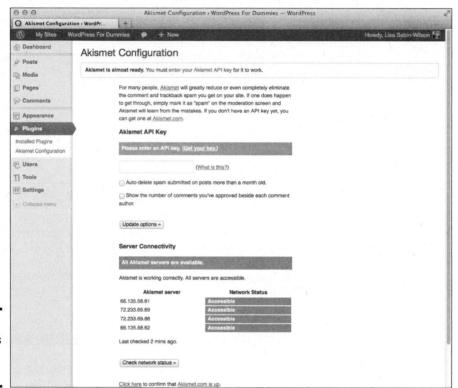

Figure 3-2:
The Settings page for Akismet.

As indicated by the `Akismet is almost ready` message in the notice, even though Akismet is activated, it won't function until an Akismet API key is added to the settings page. (See Book III, Chapter 5 to find out how to get your API key.)

After you activate the plugin, Akismet creates an Akismet Configuration submenu entry under the Dashboard's Plugins menu. Select this entry to get to the settings page.

Akismet's settings page has three settings:

✦ The Akismet API Key setting is required for the plugin to function.

✦ The other two — automatic spam deletion and showing the number of approved comments for an author — are both optional and disabled by default.

Google XML Sitemaps

The Google XML Sitemaps plugin is a good next step for diving into plugin settings pages. Google XML Sitemaps has a number of options and shows just how intricate settings pages can get.

Google XML Sitemaps is one of WordPress's most popular plugins, with more than nine million downloads. You can find it in the Plugin Directory at

```
http://wordpress.org/extend/plugins/google-sitemap-
    generator
```

Google XML Sitemaps makes it easy to automatically add support for sitemaps to your WordPress site. Although most WordPress sites can be scanned easily by search engines, adding sitemaps adds a level of safety to ensure that all the content on the site can be found.

With default settings, the plugin automatically generates sitemaps as content is added or modified on the site. In addition, it notifies Google and Bing of these updates so that it can update the search engine cache with this new data. (Book V, Chapter 5 covers Google XML Sitemaps in more depth.)

The Google XML Sitemaps plugin settings page is available from the XML-Sitemap submenu of the Dashboard's Settings menu. Notice that the menu name is different from the plugin name.

**Book VII
Chapter 3**

**Configuring and
Using Plugins**

Submenu names are limited in length, which means that longer plugin names are shortened to fit properly.

A portion of the Google XML Sitemaps plugin's settings page is shown in Figure 3-3.

Like the Akismet plugin, Google XML Sitemaps requires an additional step for it to be fully functional. Unlike Akismet, Google XML Sitemaps is very quiet about how to get set up — it doesn't provide that Dashboard-wide notification message. This is why it is very important to carefully read settings pages and plugin documentation. It can be very easy to miss something extremely important.

Below the information box used to generate and regenerate sitemaps are the settings for the plugin. Along the right side are resources about the plugin and about sitemaps. This type of format is not uncommon for plugin settings pages.

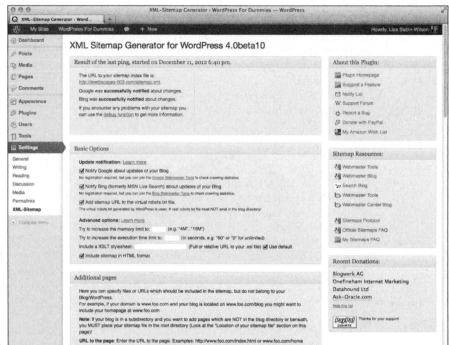

Figure 3-3:
The settings page for Google XML Sitemaps.

Scrolling through the page reveals just how exhaustive the available settings are. The settings range from basic options such enabling or disabling automatic sitemap generation when the site's content is changed to options that control the information in the generated sitemap to advanced options that control how many server resources the plugin can consume when generating the sitemap. Nearly every aspect of the plugin's functionality is represented as an option on the settings screen, offering a large amount of flexibility in how the plugin functions on the site.

This type of settings page setup is present in many popular plugins. Although the settings can be excessive for some users, most users can get very good results by simply using the default settings. In plugins such as Google XML Sitemaps, the settings are available for people who desire extra control over the plugin's functionality. I recommend reading through the settings to get an idea of what options are available.

If you don't understand a setting, leave it in its default state.

All in One SEO Pack

The All in One SEO Pack plugin, also known as AIOSEOP or AIO SEO, focuses on improving the SEO (search engine optimization) of your WordPress site. If you're unfamiliar with SEO, see Book V, Chapter 4.

With more than 13 million downloads, All in One SEO Pack is one of the most-downloaded plugins on the WordPress Plugin Directory. You can find it in the Plugin Directory at

```
http://wordpress.org/extend/plugins/all-in-one-seo-pack
```

As with the plugins in the preceding sections, All in One SEO requires some additional configuration to function. As shown in Figure 3-4, the All in One SEO plugin notifies you that additional configuration is required after it is activated.

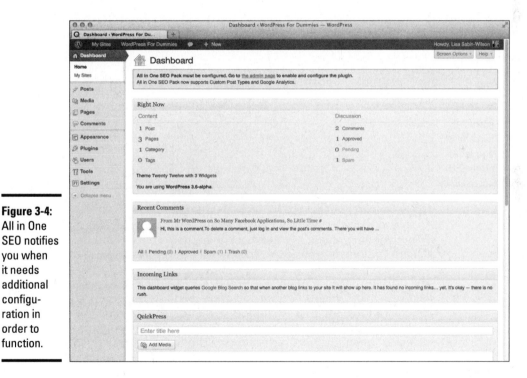

Figure 3-4: All in One SEO notifies you when it needs additional configuration in order to function.

The link in the notification leads directly to the settings page for All in One SEO, which is shown in Figure 3-5.

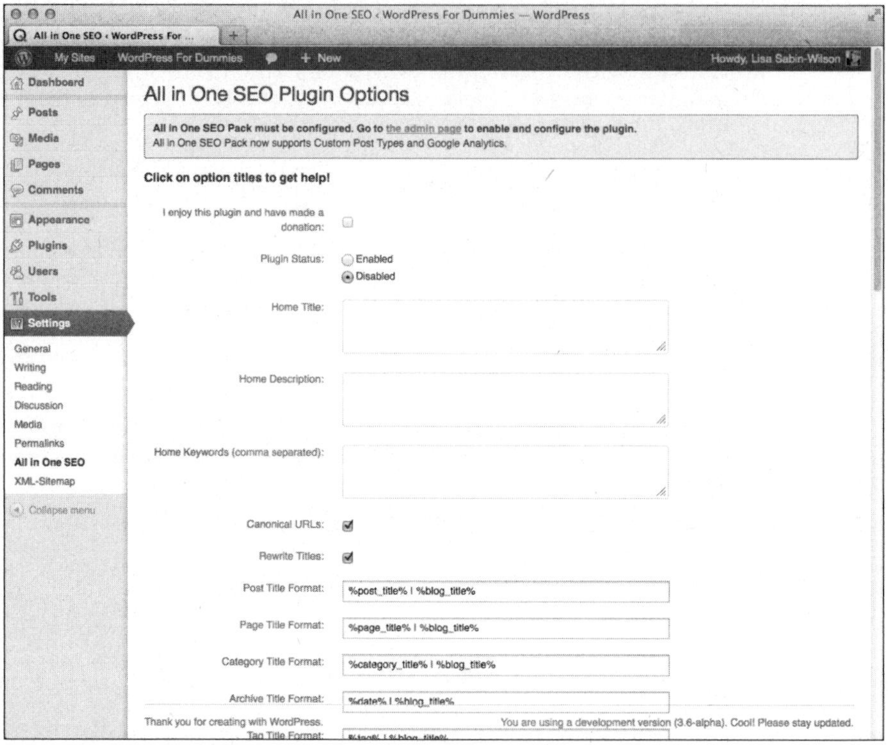

Figure 3-5:
The settings page for All in One SEO.

As shown in Figure 3-5, the Plugin Status setting is set to Disabled by default. To activate the plugin's features, change the status to Enabled and click the Update Options button at the bottom of the settings page.

The settings page for All in One SEO has a variety of settings to control many features of the plugin. The portion of the settings page shown in Figure 3-5 includes a large number of settings to control the titles on the site. Typically, titles are controlled by the theme and are modifiable only through code changes. Opening control over titles without requiring code modifications is one of the primary reasons why SEO plugins such as All in One SEO are so popular.

Many other settings go beyond control over titles. Some of the most often used settings on this page are the ones that control the automatic generation of keywords and description metadata, integrate the site with Google+ and Google Analytics, and determine what content is marked as `noindex`.

When you mark a specific page with `noindex`, search engines will ignore the content of the page and won't return search results that link to it.

As with the settings for Akismet and Google XML Sitemaps, the settings on the All in One SEO Pack plugin's settings page affect the site as a whole. Although some of the settings apply only to specific parts of the site, the settings page as a whole focuses on the entire site. This is true of most plugin settings pages. If the plugin creates a standalone settings page, the settings on that page typically apply to the whole site unless the setting specifies otherwise.

Being able to customize the title, description, and keywords on each page or post is very helpful. Because managing such customizations for the site's content would be difficult to control in one settings page, All in One SEO Pack provides additional settings in the editors for posts and pages. Figure 3-6 shows the settings box added to the editor by All in One SEO Pack.

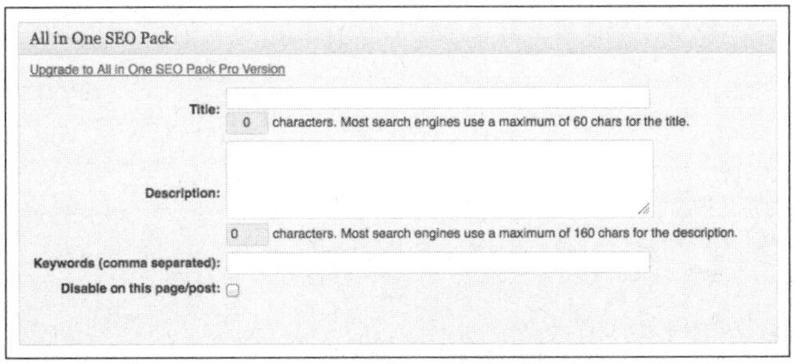

Figure 3-6:
All in One SEO Pack settings to control SEO features for a specific post.

> All in One SEO Pack
> Upgrade to All in One SEO Pack Pro Version
> Title: 0 characters. Most search engines use a maximum of 60 chars for the title.
> Description: 0 characters. Most search engines use a maximum of 160 chars for the description.
> Keywords (comma separated):
> Disable on this page/post: ☐

Using Widgets

Widgets offer a very powerful and flexible way of adding specific kinds of content to your site's sidebars. WordPress comes with a number of built-in widgets, such as a calendar, a listing of pages on the site, a listing of recent comments, and a tool to search the site. Plugins can expand this set of default widgets by adding their own. The following sections visit plugins that add their own widgets to show you how plugin-provided widgets offer new options to enhance your site.

You manage your widget management on the Widgets page on the Dashboard. After logging in to your site's Dashboard, hover your mouse over the Appearance menu and click the Widgets link to access the Widgets page.

Akismet

After activating and setting up a valid API key for the Akismet widget (you can find more on the API key in Book III, Chapter 5), a new widget named Akismet Widget appears on your Widgets page, as shown in Figure 3-7.

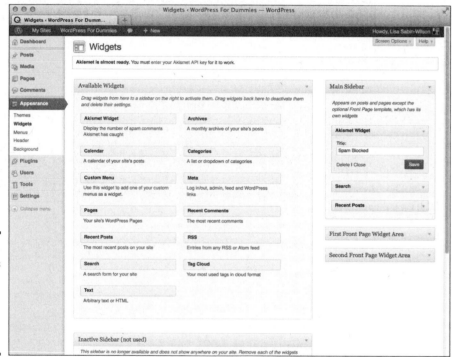

Figure 3-7:
The Widgets page showing the addition of the Akismet Widget.

To make use of the Akismet Widget, simply drag it from the Available Widgets section and drop it into one of the sidebars listed on the right of the Widgets page. As shown in Figure 3-7, after dropping the widget into a sidebar, the settings for the widget become available. The settings are quite simple because only the title of the widget can be modified. At a minimum, most widgets offer a title setting. Although there are some exceptions, most widgets treat the title as optional and simply don't show a title if the setting is empty.

Now the Akismet Widget appears on your site, displaying a counter that shows how many spam comments the Akismet plugin has blocked on the site; Figure 3-8 shows the widget has blocked no comments.

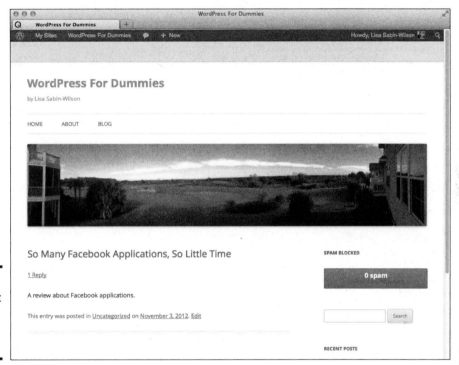

Figure 3-8: The Akismet Widget running on the site.

Book VII Chapter 3

Configuring and Using Plugins

Twitter Widget Pro

The Twitter Widget Pro plugin serves a single purpose: Make it easy to add a Twitter stream to your site. This feature takes the form of a widget, meaning that you can add the Twitter stream to any sidebar on your site. Twitter Widget Pro is available from the Plugin Directory at

```
http://wordpress.org/extend/plugins/twitter-widget-pro
```

As shown in Figure 3-9, the Twitter Widget Pro widget provides a large number of settings to control the widget's output.

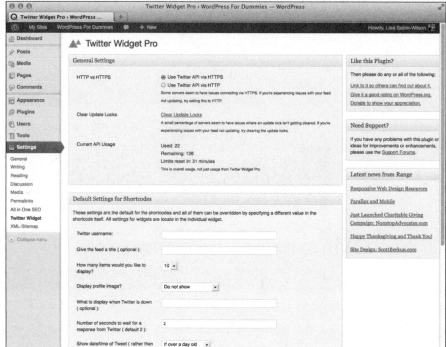

Figure 3-9:
The settings
for the
Twitter
Widget Pro
plugin's
widget.

The most important setting is Twitter Username. Without a valid Twitter username, the widget won't produce any output. If the widget fails to render anything on your site, double-check the username to ensure that it is a valid Twitter username.

The What to Display When Twitter Is Shown setting is interesting because it allows you to show a message when the Twitter stream can't be accessed. If this setting is left blank, nothing is shown when data from Twitter cannot be retrieved. If visitors to the site expect to see the Twitter feed, adding a simple message indicating that the feed is temporarily unavailable could help reduce visitor confusion.

Figure 3-10 shows the end results of setting up the widget.

If you're active on Twitter, using the Twitter Widget Pro plugin is an easy way to inform or remind your visitors that you can be found on Twitter.

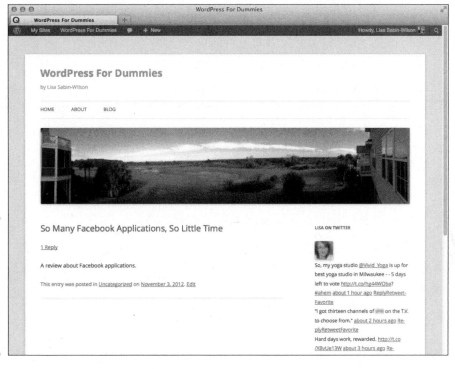

Figure 3-10:
The Twitter
Widget
Pro widget
showing the
latest from
a Twitter
feed.

Additional widgets to try

Akismet and Twitter Widget Pro just scratch the surface of what is possible with widgets offered by plugins. The following list shows additional plugin examples that help fill in your sidebars:

✦ **Facebook:** Facebook offers an official plugin in the Plugin Directory at `http://wordpress.org/extend/plugins/facebook`. The Facebook plugin provides a variety of features for integrating Facebook into your WordPress site, including a number of widgets. Some of the new widgets allow visitors to your site to subscribe to future updates, give a Like to a specific page on your site, or send the page's content to a Facebook friend. The other widgets focus on integrating your Facebook account with the site by displaying recent activity or recommendations.

✦ **Image Widget:** Sometimes you just want to add an image to a sidebar. Although the built-in Text widget and some HTML can provide this functionality, some users don't know how to create the HTML for the image or want a simpler solution for adding images. The Image Widget plugin provides a widget that allows you to easily upload an image and have it show on the site without requiring any involvement with writing or copying and pasting of HTML markup. You can find the plugin in the Plugin Directory at `http://wordpress.org/extend/plugins/image-widget`.

✦ **Yet Another Related Posts Plugin:** This plugin, also known as YARPP, is available in the Plugin Directory at `http://wordpress.org/extend/plugins/yet-another-related-posts-plugin`. It provides a variety of methods to show links to content on the site that is similar to the current page, post, or other type of content that is being viewed. One of these methods is by using the provided widget. Thus, you can easily see a listing of links to similar content in your site's sidebar. Because these lists are automatically generated and updated, the site's related content starts to cross-link with other related content without requiring any manual management of those lists.

With more than 3,000 plugins currently listed with the *widget* tag on the Plugin Directory (`http://wordpress.org/extend/plugins/tags/widget`), a wealth of new widgets for use in your sidebars is at your fingertips. One of those plugins may offer the perfect widget for adding value to your sidebar areas.

Enhancing Content with Shortcodes

Widgets can add functionality, navigational aids, and other useful bits of information to your sidebars. What if you want to add dynamic elements (such as automatically generated lists of related content or embed videos) without having to switch to the HTML editor and dealing with complex embed codes? Such situations are where shortcodes come to the rescue.

Just as widgets allow code to generate content for use inside a sidebar, shortcodes allow code to generate additional content inside a post, page, or other content type. In the following sections, you find out about a few useful shortcodes.

Gallery shortcode

One of the shortcodes built into WordPress is the `gallery` shortcode. (See Book IV, Chapter 3 for more about the `gallery` shortcode.)

The most basic gallery shortcode is `[gallery]`. In this form, all the default arguments are used. (Shortcodes can also support optional arguments that allow for customization.) By default, a gallery is arranged into three columns and uses thumbnail-sized images. The following shortcode would display the gallery in two columns and use medium-sized images:

```
[gallery columns="2" size="medium"]
```

In many ways, shortcodes look similar to HTML tags. The `gallery` short-code looks like an opening HTML tag that swapped the < and > characters for [and].

Embed shortcode

Shortcodes also have the capability to surround text by using an opening and closing shortcode. The `embed` shortcode, another shortcode provided by WordPress, is one.

WordPress can automatically change links to videos on a specific set of sites to an embedded video player. (See Book IV, Chapter 4 for details on which sites are supported.) Although this happens when supported video links are left on a line on their own, supported video links can be surrounded by the `embed` shortcode to explicitly indicate that the link is to be changed into an embedded video. For example:

```
[embed]http://wordpress.tv/2012/08/06/
    matt-mullenweg-state-of-the-word-2012/[/embed]
```

By adding this to your post or page content, Matt Mullenweg's 2012 State of the Word video displays in place of the shortcode, as shown in Figure 3-11.

**Book VII
Chapter 3**

Configuring and
Using Plugins

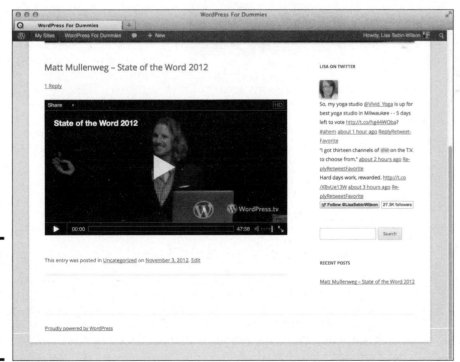

Figure 3-11:
The embedded video replacing the embed shortcode.

You may wonder why you would want to use the `embed` shortcode instead of simply putting the link on its own line. The reason is that, like the `gallery` shortcode, the `embed` shortcode supports arguments that allow you to customize the display of the video. The supported arguments are `width` and `height`. The following shortcode modifies the embedded video to have a width of 400 pixels:

```
[embed width="400"]http://wordpress.tv/2012/08/06/
    matt-mullenweg-state-of-the-word-2012/[/embed]
```

Figure 3-12 shows the results of this change. Notice how the entire video is smaller. This is because reducing the width to 400 pixels automatically scaled down the height as well.

Figure 3-12:
The embedded video with the width reduced to 400 pixels.

If both the width and height arguments are used, the video is scaled down to fit inside a box of those dimensions, so you won't be able to distort the aspect ratio of the video if you don't get the dimensions exactly right. In practice, it's often easiest to simply supply the width argument and not the height argument.

Twitter Widget Pro

The Twitter Widget Pro plugin provides more than just a widget; it also adds support for the `twitter-widget` shortcode. This shortcode provides the same functionality as the widget except that it can be added to content and uses the shortcode method of controlling arguments rather than a widget editor.

At its most basic, the `twitter-widget` shortcode looks like the following:

```
[twitter-widget username="lisasabinwilson"]
```

Note the `username` argument is set to my Twitter username, lisasabinwilson. When using this shortcode, replace the lisasabinwilson username with the Twitter username that you want to use.

The FAQ page in the Plugin Directory for Twitter Widgets Pro includes a listing of the arguments that are available for the shortcode. Using the same settings for the shortcode results in the following shortcode:

```
[twitter-widget username="lisasabinwilson" title=
    "Twitter Feed" hidereplies="true"]
```

The title is modified and replies are hiddenThis means that you can easily produce the same results whether you decide to use Twitter Widget Pro's widget or the shortcode feature.

Comprehensive Google Map Plugin

The Comprehensive Google Map Plugin offers both a widget and a shortcode that allow for easily adding a Google map to your site. You can find the plugin in the Plugin Directory at

```
http://wordpress.org/extend/plugins/comprehensive-google-
    map-plugin
```

The feature of the Comprehensive Google Map Plugin that makes it noteworthy is that shortcodes for it can quickly become very complex and long. For example, consider the following shortcode that displays a map of the White House in the United States:

```
[google-map-v3 width="350" height="350" zoom="12" maptype="roadmap"
    mapalign="center" directionhint="false" language="default"
    poweredby="false" maptypecontrol="true" pancontrol="true" zoomcontrol="true"
    scalecontrol="true" streetviewcontrol="true" scrollwheelcontrol="false"
    draggable="true" tiltfourtyfive="false" addmarkermashupbubble="false"
    addmarkermashupbubble="false" addmarkerlist="1600 Pennsylvania
    Avenue Northwest Washington, DC 20500{}1-default.png{}The White
    House" bubbleautopan="true" showbike="false" showtraffic="false"
    showpanoramio="false"]
```

That would be quite difficult to manually type without any errors. Fortunately, the Comprehensive Google Map Plugin provides a shortcode-generator tool that makes it easy to have the code generate such complex shortcodes.

After activating the plugin, follow these steps to use shortcode.

1. **Click the Shortcode Builder link under the Google Map Dashboard menu to load the tool to generate new map shortcodes. (See Figure 3-13.)**

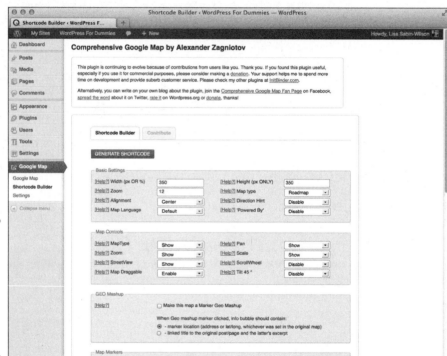

Figure 3-13: The Shortcode Builder for the Comprehensive Google Map Plugin.

2. **In the Location setting in the Map Markers section, fill in your location details and then click the Add button for the Location setting.**

3. **Click the Generate Shortcode button at the bottom of the page to get the generated shortcode.**

4. **Copy the supplied shortcode and paste it into a post or page.**

5. **Click the Save Changes button and then view the updated content.**

As shown in Figure 3-14, the shortcode produces an interactive map that visitors can easily navigate through. By clicking the marker, visitors can access options to get directions to or from the location. Although you should always give an address, the map gives visitors a much better understanding of where a location is, which means they won't have to leave the site to look up the address elsewhere.

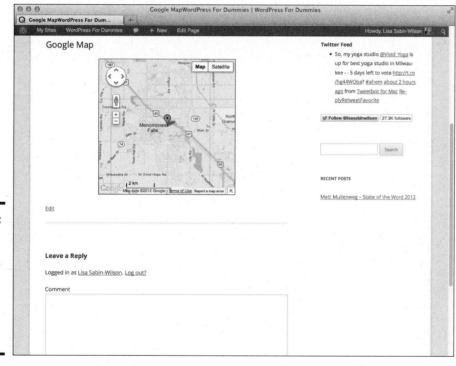

Figure 3-14:
The map generated by the Comprehensive Google Map Plugin shortcode.

Chapter 4: Modifying Existing Plugin Code

In This Chapter

✔ **Avoiding problems with plugin modifications**

✔ **Removing plugin features**

✔ **Modifying plugin output**

✔ **Changing shortcode names**

*W*ordPress has more than 22,000 plugins on the Plugin Directory, so you would think that you could find a plugin to do everything you could possibly need on your WordPress website. However, not even the best plugins can meet the needs of every user.

This chapter explores the idea of taking an existing plugin and tweaking it to meet your specific needs. With a little bit of programming knowledge and some determination, modifying existing plugin code is very possible. Although you won't become a full-fledged developer overnight, making changes to existing plugins can definitely get the mental gears spinning on how you can do more and more with your programming knowledge.

The examples in this chapter are simple, offering a basic introduction to modifying plugins. The next chapter goes into much more depth with regards to plugin development.

Setting the Foundation for Modifying Plugins

Before you start modifying plugins, you should do the following:

✦ **Set up a development site.** That way, if you accidentally break your site, no harm is done.

✦ **Display error messages.** By default, most WordPress sites hide error messages. However, you want to see those messages when developing plugins because they can provide you valuable feedback.

Find the `wp-config.php` file (it's in the main WordPress installation on your web server) and change `WP_DEBUG` define (scroll to the bottom of the file) from `false` to `true`. Your error message information will now display.

For more details about WP_DEBUG, see the WordPress Codex page on the topic: http://codex.wordpress.org/WP_DEBUG.

✦ **Set up a non-WordPress editor.** You don't want to use the editors built into WordPress. Although they're convenient, they can introduce bugs in the PHP code that can cause your entire site to break, including the ability to edit the PHP file. Thus, you should use an editor on your own computer or on the server to modify the files so that problems can be quickly fixed without requiring large amounts of work.

All code is covered by copyright. For a plugin to be added to the Plugin Directory, the code needs to use the GPLv2 license or above. Any code in the Plugin Directory is available for you to use, modify, and even redistribute with the only limitation being that your modified code must also use the same licensing as the original code. Book I, Chapter 2 covers licensing and the GPL.

It is important to know that when you start making changes, you're on your own. You can no longer just update the plugin to gain access to bug fixes or new features. To update to a newer version of the plugin, you would have to download the latest version of the code and modify it again to have your desired changes.

Because WordPress supports updating plugins automatically, you want to ensure that you don't accidentally update a modified plugin and lose your modifications. To prevent such a situation from happening, do the following:

✦ **Change the name of the plugin's directory.** The directory name is used as the basis for determining what to sync the plugin to for update purposes. By changing the directory name to something different, the plugin will no longer be a candidate for automatic updates. Make sure that you pick a name that doesn't exist in the Plugin Directory. You can verify that you have a unique name by trying to go to

http://wordpress.org/extend/plugins/*new-directory-name*

where *new-directory-name* is replaced by the name you want to use for your directory. Note that after you change the name of the directory, the plugin needs to be activated again.

✦ **Modify the name of the plugin.** Although this isn't strictly necessary, it does help ensure that the plugin stands out on its own. Even simply adding "(modified)" to the name helps ensure that the modified version is kept separate from the normal version of the plugin. It also serves as a reminder to you that the plugin is modified and shouldn't be treated as a normal plugin. In other words, it's a reminder to take care when deciding to update or delete the plugin.

✦ **Add your name to the listing of plugin authors.** This helps people know where to send questions about the plugin. This is especially important if the modified plugin is redistributed or the plugin is used in an environment with many users.

Removing Part of a Form

One of the easiest modifications to make is removing something from an existing plugin.

The All in One SEO Pack plugin, available at `http://wordpress.org/extend/plugins/all-in-one-seo-pack`, provides a large number of settings to control the SEO features for each post and page. Imagine that you manage this site and a number of editors and authors frequently ask questions about how to use the keywords input found on all post and page editors (as shown in Figure 4-1). You've decided that the keywords aren't important to the site and would like to avoid all the questions from the editors and authors. So, you want to remove the input that shows on the page editors.

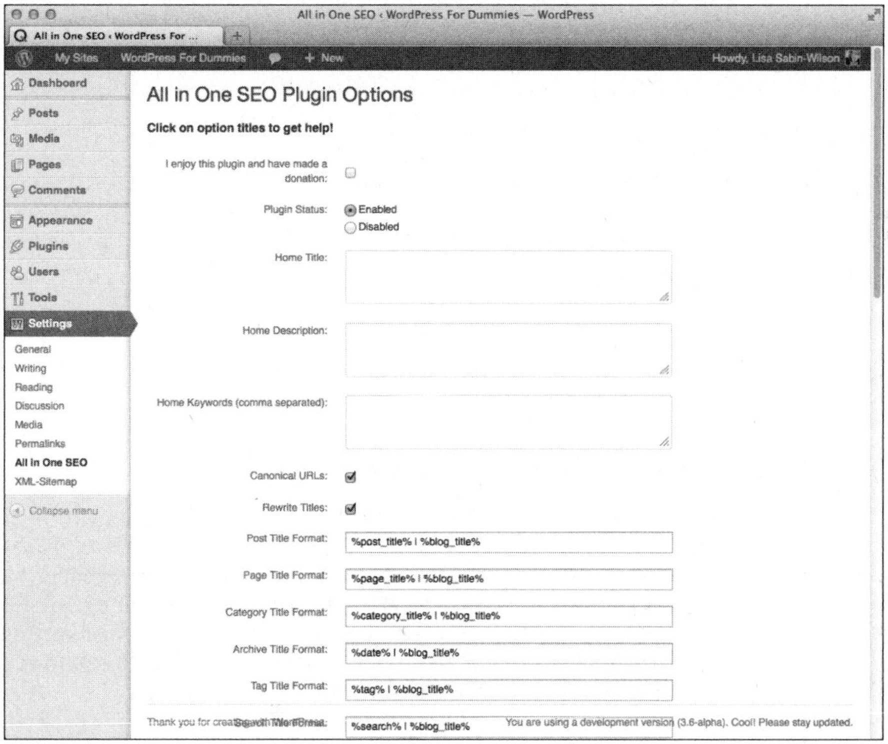

Figure 4-1: The All in One SEO Pack post/page-specific settings before making any modifications.

Book VII
Chapter 4

Modifying Existing
Plugin Code

Follow these steps:

1. **Search through the plugin's files for a match for the word: Keywords (comma separated).**

   I searched for "Keywords (comma separated)" because this is a unique string to find inside the plugin's code. After digging around in the files, I found the section responsible for this form in the plugin's `aioseop_functions.php` file.

2. **Remove the necessary lines.**

   In the section of code that adds that setting, you can find a portion of an HTML table, which looks like this:

   ```
   <tr>
   <th scope="row" style="text-align:right;"><?php _e
       ('Keywords (comma separated):', 'all_in_one_seo_pack') ?></th>
   <td><input value="<?php echo $keywords ?>" type=
       "text" name="aiosp_keywords" size="62"/></td>
   </tr>
   ```

   To properly make the modification, all four of those lines must be removed.

3. **Save the modification and upload the change to the server.**

   The editor page now looks like Figure 4-2.

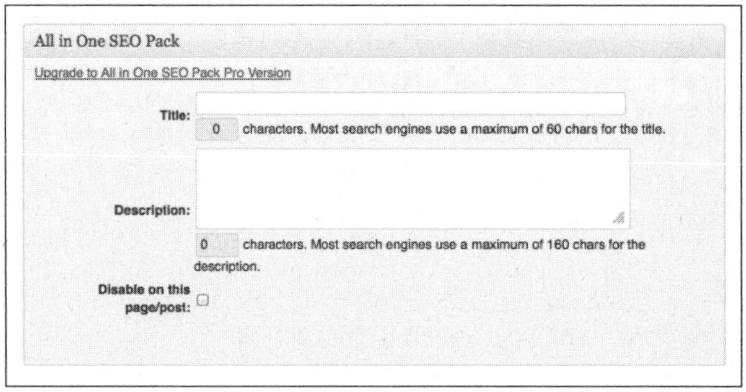

Figure 4-2:
The All in
One SEO
Pack post/
page-
specific
settings
after the
removal
of the
Keywords
setting.

After making this change, load your website in your browser to make sure your site still loads with no error messages displayed to ensure that nothing is now broken due to this modification. Save a variety of settings for the SEO feature and ensure that the modifications still take effect after the settings are saved.

Modifying the Hello Dolly Lyrics

The Hello Dolly plugin is included with WordPress and is an easy plugin to modify. If you don't have this plugin installed on your site, you can find it in the Plugin Directory at

```
http://wordpress.org/extend/plugins/hello-dolly
```

In the `hello.php` file of the plugin is a variable named `$lyrics` that stores the lyric lines of the Hello Dolly song. By replacing this text with your own text, you can change the random selection of a Hello Dolly lyric line to anything you desire.

For example, the `$lyrics` variable can be replaced in its entirety with new text, such as this:

```
$lyrics = "I love WordPress All In One.
   There's a plugin for that.";
```

When changing the lyrics, ensure that all the lyrics text is replaced; otherwise, you can accidentally introduce an error to the code.

After the modification is in place, the Hello Dolly plugin will now say either "I love WordPress AIO" or "There's a plugin for that." Figure 4-3 shows the end result of this modification. Notice the message toward the top right of the screen.

When a *string* (a portion of code that is contained inside quotes) is used just for output, it is typically safe to modify the text without creating any bugs or other issues with the plugin. By changing a string's text, you can change the output of the plugin without much effort.

WordPress has a built-in mechanism to replace strings in code with new strings. This feature is called *localization* and is typically used to change text into another language. As long as the plugin properly uses the localization functions for all its output strings, you can use this feature to change specific strings as desired, even if you simply change the words used rather than the language. This feature is discussed in Chapter 6 of this minibook.

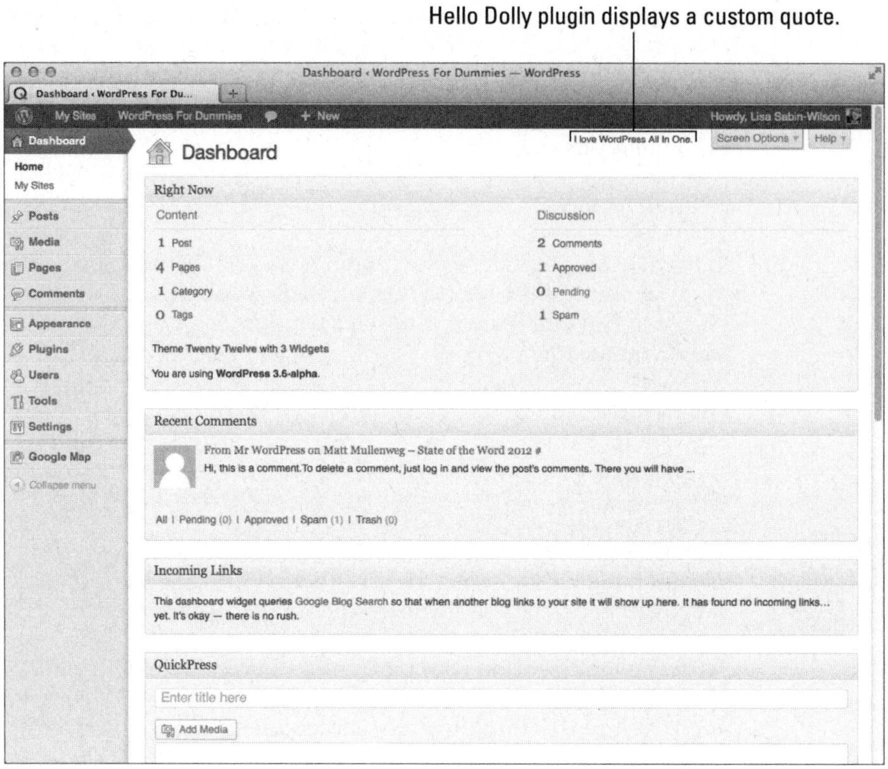

Hello Dolly plugin displays a custom quote.

Figure 4-3:
The modified Hello Dolly plugin now declares that it loves WordPress All In One.

Changing a Shortcode's Name

Sometimes shortcodes have hard-to-remember names. This problem typically comes up because the plugin author is trying to avoid creating conflicts with other plugins by using the same shortcode name. Although this is a good practice because it helps avoid code conflicts, it can be annoying to look up a shortcode's name each time you want to use it.

The Posts in Page plugin (available at `http://wordpress.org/extend/plugins/posts-in-page/installation`) provides an example of how shortcodes can be hard to remember. It comes with two shortcodes: `ic_add_post` and `ic_add_posts`. From a developer standpoint, these names make sense because the plugin author is IvyCat. Thus, the initials `ic` are used to prefix each shortcode name, helping ensure that the shortcode names are unique. From a user standpoint, it just causes frustration.

A nice feature of shortcodes is that the code that handles the shortcode can be connected to multiple names. This means that you can add extra names for a shortcode rather than simply changing the old name to a new name. Adding a second name is helpful because it prevents any existing uses of the old shortcode name from breaking after the change.

Searching through the plugin's files for `add_shortcode` — the function that creates new shortcodes — shows that the shortcodes are created in the `posts_in_page.php` file. The two lines of code that create the current shortcodes are as follows:

```
add_shortcode( 'ic_add_posts', array( &$this, 'posts_in_page' ) );
add_shortcode( 'ic_add_post', array( &$this, 'post_in_page' ) );
```

The new name for `ic_add_posts` will be `show-posts`. The new name for `ic_add_post` will be `show-post`. To add these shortcodes, simply copy and paste the original two `add_shortcode` function calls and then modify each shortcode name to be the new name. After making the changes, the section of code now looks like the following:

```
add_shortcode( 'ic_add_posts', array( &$this, 'posts_in_page' ) );
add_shortcode( 'show-posts', array( &$this, 'posts_in_page' ) );
add_shortcode( 'ic_add_post', array( &$this, 'post_in_page' ) );
add_shortcode( 'show-post', array( &$this, 'post_in_page' ) );
```

The functionality is exactly the same as the `ic_add_posts` shortcode; it simply has a name that you can more easily remember.

It is possible to register additional names for a specific shortcode without having to modify the shortcode's plugin code. You can accomplish this registration by creating a custom plugin that simply has the `add_shortcode` function call that connects the new shortcode name with the callback function name (the second argument of the function). Creating new plugins is discussed in the next chapter.

Chapter 5: Creating Simple Plugins from Scratch

In This Chapter

✔ Creating a valid plugin

✔ Filtering content

✔ Adding shortcodes and widgets

✔ Creating a plugin settings page

*Y*ou can extend WordPress functionality through plugins and themes without modifying any of WordPress core files. This allows for customizing WordPress while still permitting easy upgrades when new versions of WordPress are released. By using the WordPress software built-in *action hooks* (placeholder functions that allow plugin developers to execute code hooked into them) and *filter hooks* (also placeholder functions that you can use to apply parameters to filter results), you can create just about any functionality you can imagine.

This chapter takes you on a crash course in creating plugins. The plugins I show you how to build start off simple and iteratively introduce new concepts as the functionality gets deeper and more involved. Having a foundational knowledge of PHP is helpful for getting the most out of this chapter; however, even beginner PHP developers should be able to get value out of each project.

This book doesn't turn you into a PHP programmer or MySQL database administrator; Book II, Chapter 3 gives you a glimpse of how PHP and MySQL work together to help WordPress build your website. If you're interested in finding out how to program PHP or become a MySQL database administrator, check out *PHP & MySQL For Dummies* by Janet Valade.

You might be tempted to edit the core code of WordPress rather than write a plugin to achieve the desired functionality. This isn't recommended — it makes upgrading difficult and can cause various problems, including serious security issues.

To make plugin development safer, use a test site so you don't introduce bugs that can break your site. Breaking a site that has traffic while developing a plugin is an easy way to annoy visitors.

When writing a plugin, use a simple text editor, such as Notepad (Windows) or TextEdit (Mac). Don't use the editors built into WordPress to edit code — they can introduce bugs that can break the site.

Understanding Plugin Structure

All that's required for WordPress to see a plugin is a PHP file in the wp-content/plugins directory of the site with some special information at the top of the file. This information at the top of a plugin file, typically referred to as the plugin's *file header,* is what WordPress looks for when determining which plugins are installed on the site. A freshly installed WordPress site makes a good starting point to understand how this works in practice.

Inspecting WordPress's core plugins

As explored in Chapter 1 of this minibook, WordPress includes two core plugins: Akismet and Hello Dolly. Looking at the files for each of these plugins helps you understand how you can structure your own plugins.

Inside a fresh WordPress site's wp-content/plugins directory, you find a directory named /akismet and two files named hello.php and index.php. The hello.php file is for the Hello Dolly plugin and has the following text at the top of the file:

```php
<?php
/**
 * @package Hello_Dolly
 * @version 1.5.1
 */
/*
Plugin Name: Hello Dolly
Plugin URI: http://wordpress.org/#
Description: This is not just a plugin, it symbolizes the hope and enthusiasm
    of an entire generation summed up in two words sung most famously by Louis
        Armstrong: Hello, Dolly. When activated you will randomly see a lyric from
        <cite>Hello, Dolly</cite> in the upper right of your admin screen on every
        page.
Author: Matt Mullenweg
Version: 1.5.1
Author URI: http://ma.tt/
*/
```

This section is the file header, which tells WordPress about the plugin. The Plugin Name, Plugin URI, and Description sections of the file header are referred to as *fields.* I discuss the fields and their use in Chapter 6 of this minibook.

If you remove the file header, the Hello Dolly plugin will no longer be available because WordPress will no longer recognize it as a plugin.

Open the `index.php` file in the `/wp-content/plugins/` folder, and you see the following few lines of code:

```php
<?php
// Silence is golden.
?>
```

Because this file doesn't have a file header, it isn't a plugin. It is in the plugins directory to prevent people from going to *domain.com*/wp-content/plugins (where *domain.com* is your site's domain name) to get a full listing of all the plugins on your site. Because the `index.php` file doesn't output anything, people trying to get a listing of your plugins will simply see a blank screen.

All that remains now in the `/wp-content/plugins` directory is the `/akismet` directory. Inside this directory are three PHP files: `admin.php`, `akismet.php`, and `legacy.php`. If you open up each file, you can see that only the `akismet.php` file contains the file header.

```
/*
Plugin Name: Akismet
Plugin URI: http://akismet.com/
Description: Akismet checks your comments against the Akismet Web service to
    see if they look like spam or not. You need an <a href="http://akismet.
    com/get/">API key</a> to use it. You can review the spam it catches under
    "Comments." To show off your Akismet stats just put <code>&lt;?php akismet_
    counter(); ?&gt;</code> in your template. See also: <a href="http://
    wordpress.org/extend/plugins/stats/">WP Stats plugin</a>.
Version: 2.4.0
Author: Automattic
Author URI: http://automattic.com/wordpress-plugins/
License: GPLv2
*/
```

Because the `akismet.php` file has the file header, the `/akismet` directory is recognized by WordPress as a plugin. If the `akismet.php` file is removed, the Akismet plugin disappears from the listing of available plugins in your WordPress installation. (On the Dashboard, click the Plugins link to see the Plugins page.)

Knowing the requirements

Looking at the way the default plugins are set up gives you an idea of how to set up your plugins, but knowing all the requirements would be nice so you don't make mistakes. The reality is that there are very few requirements for how you must set up your plugin.

**Book VII
Chapter 5**

Creating Simple Plugins from Scratch

Requirement 1: File header

The file header is what allows WordPress to recognize your plugin. Without this key piece of information, your plugin won't show up as an available plugin, and you won't be able to activate it.

Although there are many fields in the file header, only Plugin Name is required. For example, the following is a valid file header:

```
/*
Plugin Name: Example Plugin
*/
```

Of course, providing additional information can be very helpful, but if you're quickly making a plugin for yourself, the plugin name is all that is required. See Chapter 6 of this minibook for more information about the file header.

Requirement 2: Correct placement of main plugin file

The main plugin file (the one with the file header) must be either in the `/wp-content/plugins` directory or inside a directory immediately inside the `/wp-content/plugins` directory.

Here are some examples of valid locations for the main plugin PHP file:

✦ `wp-content/plugins/example.php`

✦ `wp-content/plugins/example/example.php`

Here are some examples of invalid locations for the main plugin PHP file:

✦ `wp-content/example.php`

✦ `wp-content/plugins/example/lib/example.php`

You can place the main plugin file too deep. WordPress looks only in the `/wp-content/plugins` directory and inside the first level of the directories contained in `/wp-content/plugins`, but no deeper. If you place it too deep within the plugin directory, it won't work.

Following best practices

The requirements are very lax and allow you to set up your plugin any way you want. You can name the main plugin file and plugin directory anything you like. You can even put multiple main plugin files inside a single directory. However, just because you can, doesn't mean that you should. The following are some best practices to help keep some consistency.

Best Practice 1: Always use a plugin directory

Hello Dolly doesn't reside in a directory because it's simple enough to need only one file. However, each plugin should reside in its own directory, even if it needs only one file.

When creating a plugin, a single file may be enough to do what you need, but further development may require adding more files. It is better to start with the plugin in a directory instead of restructuring it later.

Moving or renaming a main plugin file deactivates the plugin because WordPress stores the plugin's activation state based upon the path to the main plugin file.

Do yourself and any users of your plugin a favor and always place your plugins inside a directory.

Best Practice 2: Use meaningful, unique names

When doing any WordPress development (whether for a plugin or theme), you must always keep in mind that your code shares space with code from other people (other plugin developers, WordPress core developers, theme developers, and so on). This means that you should never use simple names for anything; the name of your plugin should be unique.

You might think that naming your plugin "Plugin" allows you to move past the boring stuff and onto development, but it just makes things difficult to keep track of. If your plugin produces a widget that displays a listing of recent movie reviews, "Lisa Sabin-Wilson's Movie Reviews Widget" is much more meaningful than "Widget Plugin."

Best Practice 3: Match the plugin and plugin directory names

Make sure that your plugin's directory name makes it easy to find the plugin in the `/wp-content/plugins` directory.

Going with the preceding example, having Lisa Sabin-Wilson's Movie Reviews Widget in a `widget` directory will make finding the widget difficult. The directory name doesn't have to match exactly, but it should make sense. Some good directory names for this example are `/movie-reviews-widget`, `/lsw-movie-reviews-widget`, or `/movie-reviews`.

Best Practice 4: Don't use spaces in directory or filenames

Although modern desktop operating systems can handle directories and files that have spaces in the name, some web servers can't. A good practice is to use a hyphen (-) in place of a space when naming files and directories. In other words, use `movie-reviews-widget` rather than `movie reviews widget`.

Avoiding spaces in file and directory names will save you many headaches.

Best Practice 5: Consistent main plugin filenames

Although you can name the plugin's main file anything, coming up with a consistent naming scheme that you use throughout your plugins can be a good idea.

The most popular naming scheme is to match the main plugin PHP filename to the plugin directory name. For example, the main plugin file for a plugin directory called `/movie-reviews` is `movie-reviews.php`. The problem with this naming scheme is that it doesn't mean anything. Plugin filenames should always indicate that file's purpose. The purpose of the `movie-reviews.php` file is clear only when you know that many developers name the main plugin file the same as the plugin directory.

Another naming scheme is to use a consistent filename across all plugins. For example, naming the main plugin file `init.php` indicates that the file is used to initialize the plugin. (`init` is the abbreviation for *initialize*.) The name `init.php` makes the purpose of the file clear regardless of the plugin name or purpose.

Creating Your First Plugin

When you're developing something new, taking very small steps is usually best. This way, if something breaks, the problem is clear. Doing multiple new things at one time makes finding where something went wrong difficult.

Sticking with this concept, the first plugin you create in this chapter is a plugin that can be activated and deactivated but doesn't do anything. In other words, a fully functional plugin shell that's ready for code to be added.

Because this plugin is an example and doesn't do anything, I named it Example: Do Nothing.

Setting up the plugin files

For this plugin, all that you need is a main plugin file. Follow these steps to upload it to its own directory:

1. **Connect to your web server via FTP.**

   Check out Book II, Chapter 2 for a refresher on using FTP.

2. **Browse to the `/wp-content/plugins` directory in your WordPress installation directory.**

   If you're unsure where your WordPress installation directory is located, flip to Book II, Chapter 4, where I cover installing WordPress on your web server.

3. **Create a new directory within `/wp-content/plugins` called `/example-do-nothing`.**

   Most FTP programs allow you to right-click with your mouse and choose Add New Folder or Add New Directory.

4. **Create an empty `.php` file with the filename `init.php`.**

   Use your favorite text editor, such as Notepad for PC or TextMate for Mac, to open a new file and then save it with the filename `init.php`.

5. **Upload your blank `init.php` file to `/wp-content/plugins/example-do-nothing`.**

   Your plugin directory and plugin file are set up. In the next section, you add code to the `init.php` plugin file.

Adding the file header

Open the `init.php` file you created in the previous section. (Most FTP programs have built-in text editors that allow you to right-click the file with your mouse and choose Edit.) Add the following lines of code to create the file header:

```php
<?php
/*
Plugin Name: Example: Do Nothing
Description: This plugin does nothing. It is an example of how to create a valid
    WordPress plugin.
*/
```

Adding the closing `?>` tag at the end of a PHP file is optional at this point. Leaving it out is helpful because it prevents accidentally adding code after it, which may cause the PHP code to break.

Adding a plugin description isn't necessary, but it makes the purpose of the plugin clear to anyone who reads your code. Additionally, the plugin description displays on the Plugins page on your Dashboard to give users a good idea of what the purpose of your plugin is. When developing, you wind up with many plugins that were used for simple tests or are unfinished. Having solid names and descriptions adds order to the chaos so that important code isn't forgotten or accidentally deleted.

Be sure to save the `init.php` file and upload it to your `/wp-content/plugins/example-do-nothing` directory on your web server.

Testing the plugin

After modifying the `init.php` file and saving it in the `/wp-content/plugins/example-do-nothing` directory, visit your WordPress Dashboard and click the Plugins link on the navigation menu to view the Plugins page. Your new plugin is listed with the title Example: Do Nothing, as shown in Figure 5-1.

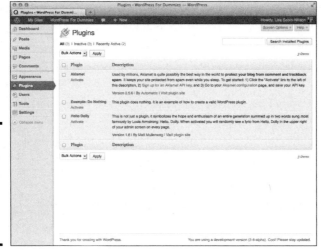

Figure 5-1:
The Plugins page showing the sample plugin in the list.

Click the Activate link directly beneath the title. The Plugins page displays a `Plugin activated` message, which indicates the Example: Do Nothing plugin was activated in your WordPress install. Although your new plugin doesn't do anything, you have a simple WordPress plugin with the correct file structure, naming conventions, and headers.

Fixing Problems

Potentially, a number of things could go wrong. If you're having problems, delete the plugin file from its directory and start over. If you still have problems, the following sections cover some common issues and give you possible solutions that you can try.

White screen of nothingness

A common problem when doing plugin development is making a change and finding that every attempt to load the site in your browser window results in a blank white screen. A code error is breaking WordPress when it tries to run your plugin code.

A quick way to fix this is to rename your `/wp-content/plugins/example-do-nothing` plugin directory on your web server to something like `/wp-content/plugins/old.example-do-nothing`. This causes automatic deactivation of the plugin because WordPress won't be able to locate it.

Before changing the name back, go to the Plugins page on your Dashboard. A message at the top of the page states `The plugin example-do-nothing/init.php has been deactivated due to an error: Plugin file does not exist.`

This message confirms that WordPress fully deactivated the broken plugin; you should be able to load your website successfully without seeing the dreaded white screen of nothingness. After that, you can change the file-name back, fix your problem, and try again. If the plugin is still broken, WordPress prevents the plugin from activating and gives you details about the error.

Unexpected output error

When you activate a plugin from your Dashboard and see an error message on the Plugins page about unexpected output, it means that you have code or text within the main plugin PHP file that is outside of a `<?php ?>` code block. Every PHP function must start with a command that tells your web server to initiate (or start) PHP. If your plugin file is missing the `<?php` line, an error about unexpected output occurs and WordPress doesn't activate your plugin.

Have some fun and try to create this error so you'll know it when you see it. You can intentionally create the error by following these steps:

1. **Connect to your web server via FTP.**

2. **Browse to the `/wp-content/plugins/example-do-nothing` directory.**

3. **Open the `init.php` file in your text editor.**

4. Remove the `<?php` line from the top of the `init.php` file.

5. Save the `init.php` file.

6. Upload the file to the `/wp-content/plugins/example-do-nothing` directory.

When you try to activate the Example: Do Nothing plugin, the following message displays at the top of the Plugins page:

```
/* Plugin Name: Example: Do Nothing Description: This
plugin does nothing. It is an example of how to create
a valid WordPress plugin. */.
```

WordPress also displays an error message on the Plugins page (see Figure 5-2), directly beneath the Plugins header:

```
The plugin generated 141 characters of unexpected
output during activation. If you notice "headers
already sent" messages, problems with syndication feeds
or other issues, try deactivating or removing this
plugin.
```

All this fuss because of a missing `<?php` line.

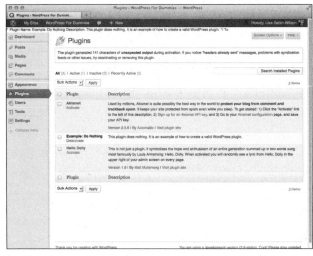

Figure 5-2:
An unexpected output error message displayed on the Plugins page.

Filtering Content

It's time to have some fun and create a WordPress plugin that actually does something and, in the process, discover more basics of WordPress plugin development.

A powerful feature of WordPress is its numerous filters. By latching code to a filter, you can modify information as it flows through WordPress, and therefore you can modify the information WordPress displays or stores.

Imagine that you have a habit of using contractions far too often. Your readership mocks you and your penchant for the commoner practice of merging words together. At night, you worry about whether you missed an instance of *it's, we're,* or *I'll.*

It is causing you to lose sleep. You tried listening to the self-help tapes, you review every word and have been to therapy to find the deep-seated cause of your craving for contractions. Despite your best efforts and the constant ridicule, you cannot help but sound like an etiquette contrarian.

Fortunately, there's a cure. With a simple filter and a bit of code, your grammatical ailment can be disguised easily with a simple WordPress plugin that you create in the next section of this chapter.

Setting up the plugin structure

The plugin that I create in this section is Example: Contraction Compulsion Correction, and it will reside in a directory called /example-contraction-compulsion-correction with a main plugin file named init.php. Apply the same steps to create the directory and main plugin file as you did in the "Creating Your First Plugin" section, earlier in this chapter.

Add the following file header to the top of the main plugin (init.php) file:

```
<?php
/*
Plugin Name: Example: Contraction Compulsion Correction
Description: This plugin cannot solve your contraction issues, but it can hide
    them by fixing them on the fly.
*/
?>
```

Save the init.php file and then visit the Plugins page on your Dashboard. The Example: Contraction Compulsion Correction plugin appears there, as shown in Figure 5-3.

Figure 5-3:
The Plugins page showing your new plugin in the list.

Testing the filter

The filter you use in this section is the `the_content` filter. To make sure that this has the desired effect, the filter replaces all the content in your blog posts and pages with a simple message. If the filter works as expected, you can expand it to hide the contractions that you published in your posts (or pages).

The `the_content` filter is just one of hundreds of available filters in WordPress. You can find information about filters in the WordPress. org Codex (`http://codex.wordpress.org/Plugin_API/Filter_ Reference`).

Follow these steps to include the `the_content` filter in your plugin, which will replace all the content on your website (posts and pages) with a single phrase. (You change this in the following section to filter the contractions out of your published content.)

1. **Connect to your web server via FTP.**

2. **Browse to this directory:**

    /wp-content/plugins/example-contraction-compulsion-correction

3. **Open the `init.php` file in your text editor.**

4. **Type the following lines of code at the end of the file (after the file header) but before the closing ?>:**

```
function my_filter_the_content($content) {
$content = "Test content replacement.";
return $content;
}
add_filter('the_content','my_filter_the_content');
```

5. **Save your init.php file and upload it to the /wp-content/plugins/ example-contraction-compulsion-correction folder.**

The last line of code in Step 4 tells WordPress to apply the filter after the plugin is activated. The earlier lines of code define the function (function my_filter_the_content ($content)) with a variable ($content), define the $content variable ($content = "Test content replacement.";), and tell WordPress to return $content within the body of your published posts and pages. Check out the nearby sidebar "Using curly brackets (complex syntax)" about using correct PHP syntax.

With the the_content filter in place in your plugin, visit the Plugins page on your Dashboard and activate the Example: Contraction Compulsion Correction plugin. After you activate the plugin, view any post or page on your website. The result: Test content replacement replaces the content of that entry. Your new plugin is filtering content on your website. (See Figure 5-4.) In the next section, you apply the real filter that fulfills the purpose of the plugin you're creating.

Using curly brackets (complex syntax)

You see curly brackets within code. Curly brackets (referred to as *complex syntax* in the PHP Manual: www.php.net/manual/en/language.types.string.php) serve to open and then close the function definition, or expression. For example, the code samples in the steps in the "Testing the filter" section name the function function my_filter_the_ content ($content). An open curly bracket, indicating the start of the function expression, immediately follows that line. Immediately after the two lines, $content="Test content replacement."; and return $content, that are the expression for the function, you see the closing curly bracket that indicates the end of the function expression. Without these curly brackets, your code won't work correctly. Check out the entire PHP manual online at http://php.net/manual to brush up on correct PHP code syntax, including when you need to use single quotation versus double quotation marks and the importance of the semicolon (;).

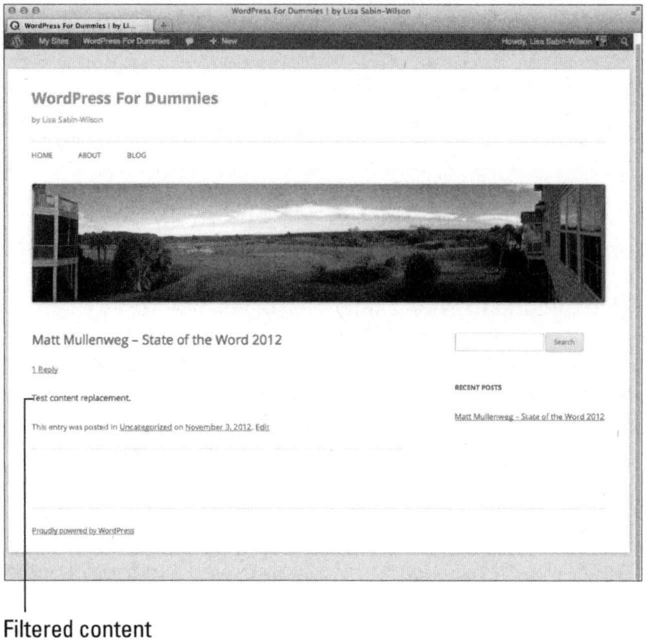

Figure 5-4:
Filtered
content
on your
website.

Filtered content

Replacing contractions in your content

To replace all the contractions within your content with the full phrases or
words, the following steps take you through the process of changing the
code in the `init.php` plugin file:

1. **Connect to your web server via FTP.**

2. **Browse to the `/wp-content/plugins/example-contraction-
compulsion-correction` directory.**

3. **Open the `init.php` file in your text editor.**

4. **Remove the following lines of code:**

   ```
   function my_filter_the_content($content) {
   $content = "Test content replacement.";
   return $content;
   }
   add_filter('the_content','my_filter_the_content');
   ```

5. **Type the following lines of code at the end of the file (after the file
header):**

   ```
   function my_filter_the_content($content) {
   $replacements = array(
   "isn't" => "is not",
   "we'll" => "we will",
   "you'll" => "you will",
   "can't" => "cannot",
   );
   ```

```
foreach($replacements as $search => $replace) {
$search = str_replace("'","&#8217;",$search);
$content = str_replace(ucfirst($search),ucfirst($replace),$content);
$content = str_ireplace($search,$replace,$content);
}
return $content;
}
add_filter('the_content','my_filter_the_content');
```

6. Save your `init.php` file and upload it to the `/wp-content/plugins/-contraction-compulsion-correction` folder.

To make the replacement, an array holds the text to search for and to use as the replacement. The array defines the words you're replacing within your content and loops to make all the replacements. In this example, *isn't* is replaced with *is not,* *we'll* is replaced with *will not,* and so on. Of course, this example covers only a small subset of the contractions. You have to modify the example to fit your specific contraction compulsions.

You may notice that there is much more than just a simple replacement going on in The Loop. It also uses the `str_replace` function, which replaces all occurrences of the search string with the replacement string.

The first replacement (`$search = str_replace("'","&#8217;",$search);`) is needed because WordPress changes single quotes to a fancy version represented by `"&#8217;"`. `$search = str_replace("'","&#8217;",$search);` searches for the instances of the single quote, and then `$content = str_replace("'","&#8217;",$content);` replaces the single quote in the content. `$search = str_replace("'","&#8217;",$search);` allows the replacements array to have normal-looking searches with regular single quotes.

The third search and replace statement (`$content = str_replace(ucfirst($search),ucfirst($replace),$content);`) replaces content matches that have an uppercase first letter with a replacement that also has an uppercase first letter.

The last search and replace statement: (`$content = str_ireplace($search,$replace,$content);`) does a non–case-sensitive search to replace all remaining matches with the lowercase version of the replacement.

To test your contraction replacement plugin, follow these steps:

1. Log in to your Dashboard.

2. Visit the Add New Post page. (Hover your mouse pointer over Posts and then click the Add New link.)

The Add New Post page loads on your Dashboard so that you can write and publish a new post. (See Book IV, Chapter 1.)

3. Type a title for your post in the Title text field.

4. **Type the following text in the post editor:**

   Isn't it grand that we'll soon be sailing on the ocean blue? You'll see. We'll have a great time. I can't wait.

   Notice the contractions *Isn't, we'll, You'll, We'll,* and *can't.* Figure 5-5 shows an Add New Post page with this phrase added.

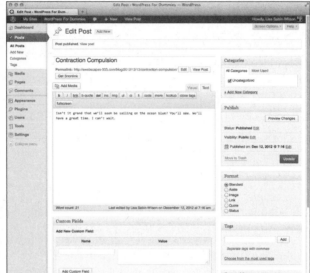

Figure 5-5:
The Add
New Post
page
with the
contractions
in place.

5. **Publish your post by clicking the Publish button.**

   Figure 5-6 displays the post on a website with the contractions replaced with the appropriate words, as defined in the plugin function.

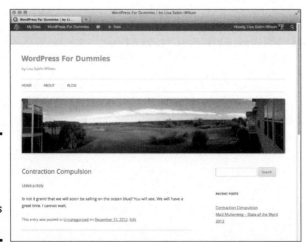

Figure 5-6:
The
published
post with
contractions
replaced.

Creating Shortcodes

You can use the `the_content` filter to add new sections of content to posts and pages. For example, you can add a form for subscribing to new posts. However, this type of all-or-nothing method of adding content often adds content where it isn't wanted. Using a shortcode is often a much better solution — it offers flexibility and ease of use because it's a shorthand version of fully executable code.

You can employ shortcodes for a wide variety of uses. WordPress includes a shortcode, `[gallery]`, which you can add to any post to display a gallery of images assigned to that post in place of the shortcode. (See Book IV, Chapter 3 for details on adding photo galleries to your posts.) Many plugins (such as a forum or contact form plugin) use shortcodes to allow the plugin users to designate specific pages for the plugin front end to appear. They can surround sections of content, allowing the code that powers the shortcode to modify the content.

Shortcodes can

+ **Stand alone:.** The `[gallery]` shortcode (built into WordPress) is a good example of this; simply adding `[gallery]` to the content of a page or post is all that's needed to allow the shortcode to insert a gallery of uploaded images and display them within the body of a post or page.

+ **Support arguments that pass specific information to the shortcode:** For example, this short code gives the default WordPress gallery a width of 400 pixels wide and a caption of "My Venice Vacation": `[gallery width="400" caption="My Venice Vacation"]`.

+ **Surround a section of content the way HTML tags can.** This allows the shortcode to modify specific sections of content, such as `[code lang="php"]<?php the_title(); ?>[/code]`. (The "code" shortcode doesn't exist by default in WordPress. You build it in the upcoming "Building a simple shortcode" section.)

Setting up the plugin structure

This plugin, Example: My Shortcodes, will reside in a directory called `/example-my-shortcodes` with a main plugin file named `init.php`.

The reason for the relatively generic name is that you can use this plugin to create multiple shortcodes. To get started, the following file header is added to the `init.php` file. (Follow the same steps you took earlier in this chapter to create the directory and main plugin file.)

```php
<?php
/*
Plugin Name: Example: My Shortcodes
Description: This plugin provides the digg and code shortcodes.
*/
?>
```

Building a simple shortcode

In many ways, shortcodes are coded like filters (similar to the content filter) except that with shortcodes, the content to be filtered is optional. For this shortcode, you won't worry about content filtering or shortcode attributes; it's simple enough that it doesn't need either.

The shortcode you create in this section is named *digg*. Adding this shortcode to a post displays a Digg This Post link that allows that post to be submitted to `http://digg.com` (a site for keeping track of interesting links).

Creating a shortcode requires two things:

✦ **Shortcode function:** This function handles the creation of the shortcode and a call to the `add_shortcode` function.

✦ **Shortcode arguments:** The `add_shortcode` function accepts two arguments: the name of the shortcode and the function used by the shortcode.

To get started with your shortcode, add the following code to the end of the Example: My Shortcodes plugin's `init.php` file, before the closing `?>`.

```php
function my_digg_shortcode() {
return "<p><a href='http://digg.com/submit?url=".urlencode(get_permalink()).
    "&bodytext=".urlencode(get_the_title())."'>Digg This Post</a></p>";
}
add_shortcode('digg','my_digg_shortcode');
```

HTML links have to follow some rules because only certain characters are permitted. The `urlencode` function used for both `get_permalink` and `get_the_title` ensures that the information added to the link results in a valid link being created.

Save the changes, make sure that the plugin is active, and then add a post that has `[digg]` in the content. If everything works properly, you should see a Digg This Post link in place of the shortcode when viewing the post on your website. (See Figure 5-7.)

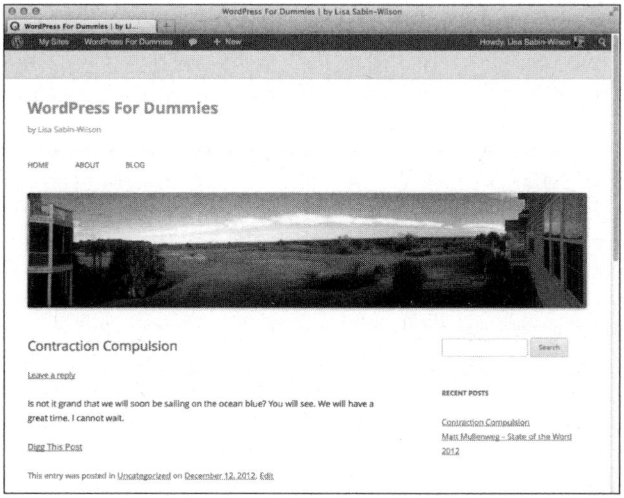

Figure 5-7:
Digg This
Post link
added to
a post.

Shortcodes can display depending on specific criteria. It's easy to modify the [digg] shortcode to display the Digg This Post link if an individual post is being viewed rather than a listing, such as the home page or a category archive. The following code shows an updated my_digg_shortcode function that uses the is_single template tag function to return an empty string if an individual post is not being viewed:

```
function my_digg_shortcode() {
if(!is_single()) return '';

return "<p><a href='http://digg.com/submit?url=".urlencode(get_permalink()).
    "&bodytext=".urlencode(get_the_title())."'>Digg This Post</a></p>";
}
add_shortcode('digg','my_digg_shortcode');
```

Notice the exclamation point (!) in front of the is_single function call. In PHP language, the exclamation point means *not*. Therefore, the if statement translates to, "If the current view is not a single post, return an empty string." Because the if statement fails when the view is a single post, the original functionality of returning the Digg This Post link is used. The function fires only when a visitor is viewing a single, individual post page, not when the visitor is viewing any other type of page (such as a static page or a category archive page).

**Book VII
Chapter 5**

**Creating Simple
Plugins from
Scratch**

Using shortcode attributes

By using attributes, you can customize the shortcode output to meet specific needs without having to rewrite an existing shortcode or create a new one.

The [digg] shortcode is a good example of how you can use an attribute to customize the shortcode output. Notice that the generated link to Digg includes bodytext=. The text added after bodytext= is the default description text for the submitted link, which is the text that displays on your site. The shortcode sends the title of the post (get_the_title). Using an attribute, this behavior can be made default while allowing the user to supply a customized description.

To add the attribute support, the my_digg_shortcode function needs to be updated again. Update the function to match the following:

```
function my_digg_shortcode($attributes=array()) {
if(!is_single()) return '';

$attributes=shortcode_atts(
array('description'=>get_the_title()),
$attributes
);
extract($attributes);

return "<p><a href='http://digg.com/submit?url=".urlencode(get_permalink()).
    "&bodytext=".urlencode($description)."'>Digg This Post</a></p>";
}
add_shortcode('digg','my_digg_shortcode');
```

Note the following:

✦ The $attributes argument is added to the my_digg_shortcode function declaration. Without this argument, the shortcode function is unable to receive any of the attributes set on the shortcode. The =array() ensures that the $attributes variable is set to an empty array if the shortcode doesn't have any attributes set.

✦ The call to the shortcode_atts function passes in an array of default attribute values and merges these defaults with the attributes used in the actual shortcode. It then stores this resulting array back to the $attributes variable. Without this section, the attributes won't have a default value.

It's a good idea to set the defaults even if the default is an empty string.

✦ The extract function takes the array of attributes and breaks the information into individual plugins. In this example, it creates the $description variable because that is the used attribute. If a shortcode uses title and id attributes, then using extract creates $title and $id variables.

✦ Because the $description variable holds the description that should be used, the get_the_title function call in the returned string is replaced with the $description variable.

Update your shortcode in the body of your test post (see Figure 5-8) to use this new description attribute. For example:

```
[digg description="Shortcodes are awesome!"]
```

After saving the post changes, view the updated post, hover your mouse on the Digg This Post link, and you should see a link with the following format:

```
http://digg.com/submit?url=http://domain.com/
    testing-shortcodes/&bodytext=Shortcodes+are+awesome!
```

Adding content to shortcodes

The final piece of the shortcodes puzzle is content. By wrapping a shortcode around a section of content, the shortcode function can modify the content in creative ways.

Going back to the earlier example given for using content with shortcodes, the example in this section creates a new shortcode called code. The purpose of this shortcode is to allow designated sections of content to be formatted as code.

To get the new code shortcode running, add the following code in Listing 5-1 to the bottom of your plugin init.php file. (Note: The arrows and numbers are not part of the actual code — they're included for my own explanation purposes.)

**Book VII
Chapter 5**

Creating Simple
Plugins from
Scratch

Listing 5-1:   The Code Shortcode

```
function my_code_shortcode($attributes=array(),$content='') {              →1
if(empty($content)) return '';                                             →2

$attributes=shortcode_atts(                                               →3
array('lang'=>''),                                                       →4
$attributes                                                               →5
);                                                                        →6
extract($attributes);                                                     →7

$content=str_replace("</p>\n<p>","\n\n",$content);                        →8
$content=str_replace('<p>','',$content);                                  →9
$content=str_replace('</p>','',$content);                                 →10
$content=str_replace('<br />','',$content);                               →11

$style='white-space:pre;overflow:auto;';                                  →12
$style.='font:"Courier New",Courier,Fixed;';                              →13

if('php'==$lang) {                                                        →14
$style.='background-color:#8BD2FF;color:#FFF;';                           →15
}                                                                         →16
```
(continued)

Listing 5-1 *(continued)*

```
else if('css'==$lang) {                                     →17
$style.='background-color:#DFE0B0;color:#333;';             →18
}                                                           →18
else {                                                      →19
$style.='background-color:#EEE;color:#000;';                →20
}                                                           →21

return "<pre class='$lang' style='$style'>$content</pre>";  →22
}                                                           →23
add_shortcode('code','my_code_shortcode');                  →24
```

Before digging into how everything works, save the changes to the plugin and add the following shortcodes to a post:

```
[code]This is a basic code test[/code]

[code lang="php"]<?php echo "This is PHP code."; ?>[/code]

[code lang="css"]p { color:#FFF; }[/code]
```

Figure 5-8 shows that these shortcodes produce some fixed-space boxes with different background colors and styling to contain the code.

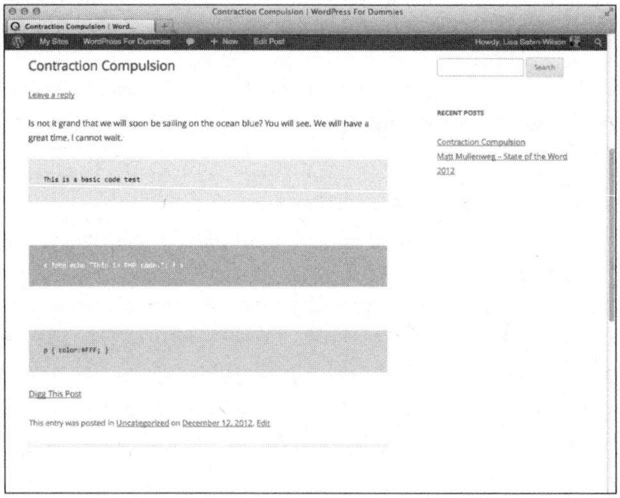

Figure 5-8:
Code
added to a
post, using
the code
shortcode.

Now that it's clear what the shortcode is doing, you can dissect how it works.

→1   Just as it was important to add the $attributes variable to the function declaration to get access to the shortcode attributes, the $content variable is needed to access the content of the shortcode.

→2   If the $content variable is empty, the function returns an empty string because going any further with empty content is unnecessary.

→3–7   As with the [digg] shortcode from the previous section, the shortcode_atts function establishes base defaults. By default, the lang attribute is an empty string. The extract function fills out the $lang variable.

→8–11   This set of str_replace function calls allows for proper handling of multiline content by the [code] shortcode. The problem is that WordPress always tries to add the <p> (paragraph) and
 (line break) HTML markup tags even when it shouldn't. The str_replace replaces the separation of two <p> tag sections with two new lines (a new line is represented by the \n code) and then removes all the remaining <p> and <br /> tags inserted by WordPress. This allows the content to display properly when it is wrapped in a <pre> (preformat for code) tag.

→12–13 The $style variable stores the basic CSS styling for the [code] shortcode output.

→14–21 This set of conditional code determines the background and text color based on the lang attribute. The php receives a blue background with white text, the css receives a khaki background with dark text, and the default is a gray background with black text.

→22   The last line of the function returns the shortcode output by wrapping the content in a <pre> HTML markup tag. The <pre> tag uses the generated style and adds the $lang as a class. The addition of the class allows for more customization through a stylesheet.

→24   This adds the shortcode into the WordPress code action hook and is required for the shortcode to *fire,* or execute, properly.

Adding Widgets

Widgets are individual features you can add to theme sidebars. Widgets can add a simple site search, display a calendar, list the most recent posts, and show RSS feed updates. These features just scratch the surface of what widgets offer and what widgets are capable of.

WordPress 2.8 introduced a new widget API that makes widget creation very easy. If you tried creating widgets in the past and gave up because of the difficulty of making them work properly, it's time to try widget creation again.

Coding a simple widget

Widgets are a bit different from filter and shortcodes. Instead of creating one function and registering it, widgets are a collection of functions packaged in a container called a *class*. The class is registered as a widget using the `register_widget` function.

Like shortcodes, multiple plugins can be housed in a single plugin file. However, because the code for some of these widgets gets lengthy, each widget will be its own plugin.

The widget plugin you build in the following steps creates a widget that you can use on the Widgets page of your Dashboard (hover your pointer over Appearance and then click the Widgets link) to show a widget in your sidebar that displays You are logged in as *Name* or Welcome Guest depending on whether you're logged in.

This plugin, Example: My User Widget, creates a widget called My User Widget. As you did in the previous examples, create a plugin directory in the `/wp-content/plugins` directory by adding a new folder called `/example-my-user-widget` and add an empty `init.php` file that will serve as your main plugin PHP file and then follow these steps to create the sample plugin:

1. **Open the `init.php` file in your text editor.**

2. **Add the file header to the top of the `init.php` file:**

```
<?php
/*
Plugin Name: Example: My User Widget
Description: This plugin provides a simple widget that shows the name of
    the logged in user
*/
```

3. **Press the Enter key and type the next line of code:**

```
class My_User_Widget extends WP_Widget {
```

This creates a new class called `My_User_Widget`. This new `My_User_Widget` class is based off (and extends) the structure of the existing `WP_Widget` class.

A class is a way of grouping a set of functions and a set of data into a logical group. In this case, everything that is in the My_User_Widget class is specific to just the My User Widget widget. Making modifications to this class doesn't affect any other widgets on your site.

The WP_Widget class is the central feature of WordPress's Widget API. This class provides the structure and most of the code that powers widgets. When the My_User_Widget class extends the WP_Widget class, the My_User_Widget class automatically gains all the features of the WP_Widget class. This situation means that only the code that needs to be customized for the specific widget needs to be defined because the WP_Widget class handles everything else.

4. **Press Enter and type the following lines of code in the init.php file:**

```
function My_User_Widget() {
parent::WP_Widget(false,'My User Widget');
}
```

The My_User_Widget function has the same name as the My_User_Widget class. A PHP class function that has the same name as the class is a *constructor*. This function is called automatically when the class code is run. (For widgets, WordPress automatically runs the registered widget code behind the scenes.) Constructors run necessary initialization code so that the class behaves properly.

By calling parent::WP_Widget, the My_User_Widget class can tell WordPress about the new widget. In this instance, the My_User_Widget says that the default base ID should be used (this is the false argument and defaults to the lowercase version of the class name, my_user_widget, in this case) and that the widget's name is My User Widget.

5. **Press Enter and type the following line of code in the init.php file:**

```
function widget($args) {
```

The widget function displays the widget content. This function accepts two parameters: $args and $instance. For this example, only $args is needed. You use $instance when you create the next widget.

6. **Press Enter and type the following lines of code in the init.php file:**

```
$user=wp_get_current_user();
if(!isset($user->user_nicename)) {
$message='Welcome Guest';
}
else {
$message="You are logged in as {$user->user_nicename}";
}
```

This code finds out information about the current user and sets a message to display that's dependent on whether the user is logged in. This is determined by checking the $user variable. If the $user->user_nicename variable is not set, the user isn't logged in.

7. **Press Enter and type the following lines of code in the `init.php` file:**

```
extract($args);
echo $before_widget;
echo "<p>$message</p>";
echo $after_widget;
    }
  }
```

The `$args` variable contains a number of important details about how the sidebar wants widgets to be formatted. It's passed into the "extract" function to pull out the settings into standalone variables. The four main variables used are `$before_widget`, `$after_widget`, `$before_title`, and `$after_title`. Because this widget doesn't have a title, the title variables aren't used. The `$before_widget` variable should always be included before any widget content, and the `$after_widget` variable should always be included after the widget content.

8. **Press Enter and type the following lines of code in the `init.php` file:**

```
function register_my_user_widget() {
register_widget('My_User_Widget');
}
add_action('widgets_init','register_my_user_widget');
```

To register a widget with WordPress (so WordPress recognizes it as a widget), use the `register_widget` function and pass it the name of the `widget` class.

Although calling the `register_widget` immediately after the class definition would be nice, it isn't that simple. The code of the widget that includes the different functions must run before the widget can be registered. When code needs to run at specific times, the code is placed in a function, and the `add_action` function is used to have WordPress run the function at a specific time.

These specific points in time are *actions*. For widget registration, you want to use the `widget_init` action. This action happens after WordPress finishes setting up the code necessary to handle widget registrations, while being early enough for the widget to be registered in time.

Don't forget to add the closing `?>` tag, which tells WordPress that the PHP execution in this plugin has come to an end.

With this final piece in place, the widget is ready for use. When you're done, the entire code block looks like this:

```
<?php
/*
Plugin Name: Example: My User Widget
Description: This plugin provides a simple widget that shows the name of the
    logged in user
*/
class My_User_Widget extends WP_Widget {
function My_User_Widget() {
```

```
parent::WP_Widget(false,'My User Widget');
}
function widget($args) {
$user=wp_get_current_user();
if(!isset($user->user_nicename)) {
$message='Welcome Guest';
}
else {
$message="You are logged in as {$user->user_nicename}";
}
extract($args);
echo $before_widget;
echo "<p>$message</p>";
echo $after_widget;
}
}
function register_my_user_widget() {
register_widget('My_User_Widget');
}
add_action('widgets_init','register_my_user_widget');
?>
```

Before WordPress 2.8, widget code had to manage everything by itself. To allow a widget to be used more than once, complex and bug-prone code needed to be produced and maintained. Fortunately, the WP_Widget class handles this seamlessly. You no longer need to worry about single-use or multi-use widgets because all widgets coded to use the WP_Widget class automatically become multi-use widgets.

With this final piece in place, the widget is ready for use. Open the Widgets page on your Dashboard (hover your pointer over Appearance and click the Widgets link); you see a new widget called My User Widget.

Adding an options editor to a widget

Although some widgets work properly without any type of customization, most widgets need at least the ability for the user to supply a title for the widget. Thanks to the WP_Widget class, adding options to a widget is easy.

The My User Widget example uses the widget function to display the widget's content. This addition to the widget code uses two additional functions to handle the widget options. The form function displays the HTML form inputs that allow the user to configure the widgets options. The update function allows the widget code to process the submitted data to ensure that only valid input is saved.

In this example, you create a basic clone of WordPress's Text widget. Although a bit simple, this cloning allows you to focus on the process of using widget options without getting caught up in the details of a complex widget concept.

Time to start coding, so set up the plugin environment by creating a new directory in your /wp-content/plugins called /example-my-text-widget and include a blank init.php file as your main plugin PHP file. The plugin you're creating in this section is Example: My Text Widget, which creates a widget called My Text Widget.

Follow these steps to create the init.php file for your Example: My Text Widget plugin:

1. **Open the init.php file in your text editor.**

2. **Create the file header by adding this code to the top of the init.php file:**

```
<?php
/*
Plugin Name: Example: My Text Widget
Description: This plugin provides a basic Text Widget clone complete with
    widget options
*/
```

3. **Press Enter and type the following line of code in the init.php file:**

```
class My_Text_Widget extends WP_Widget {
```

As with the My User Widget in the preceding section, this widget is created by extending WordPress' WP_Widget class. This new widget's class is My_Text_Widget.

4. **Press Enter and type the following lines of code in the init.php file:**

```
function My_Text_Widget() {
$widget_ops=array('description'=>'Simple Text Widget clone');
$control_ops=array('width'=>400);
parent::WP_Widget(false,'My Text Widget',$widget_ops,$control_ops);
}
```

The constructor for this plugin is a bit different this time. The parent::WP_Widget function is still called to set up the widget, but two more arguments are given: $widget_ops and $control_ops. These two arguments allow a variety of widget options to be set. The $widget_ops argument can set two options: description and classname. The description shows under the name of the widget in the widgets listing. The classname option sets what class the rendered widget uses.

5. **Press Enter and type the following line of code in the init.php file:**

```
function form($instance) {
```

The form class function displays an HTML form that allows the user to set the options used by the widget. The $instance variable is an array containing the current widget options. When the widget is new, this $instance variable is an empty array.

6. **Press Enter and type the following line of code in the init.php file:**

```
$instance=wp_parse_args($instance,array('title'=>'','text'=>''));
```

Remember how the shortcode plugins used the shortcode_atts function to merge default options with ones from the shortcode? The wp_parse_args in this example performs the same task by merging the existing $instance options with default option values.

7. **Press Enter and type the following line of code in the init.php file:**

```
extract($instance);
```

The extract function is used to pull the title and text options in the $instance variable into the standalone variables $title and $text.

8. **Press Enter and type ?>.**

By using the close PHP tag, ?>, you can more easily display a large amount of HTML without having to constantly echo out each line.

9. **Press Enter and type the following lines of code in the init.php file:**

```
<p>
<label for="<?php echo $this->get_field_id('title'); ?>">
<?php _e('Title:'); ?>
<input
  class="widefat"
  type="text"
  id="<?php echo $this->get_field_id('title'); ?>"
  name="<?php echo $this->get_field_name('title'); ?>"
  value="<?php echo esc_attr($title); ?>"
/>
</label>
</p>
```

The block of HTML displays the title input.

Notice the $this->get_field_id and $this->get_field_name function calls. These functions are provided by the WP_Widget class and produce the needed id and name values specific to this widget instance. To use these functions, simply pass in the name of the option that is used, title in this case.

The _e('Title:'); section simply prints out Title:. The reason it is wrapped in a call to the _e function is that the _e function allows the text to be translated into other languages.

The value attribute of the input tag sets what the default value of the field is. Because this widget will be populated with the current title, the $title variable is included in this attribute. Before including, the $title variable is passed through the esc_attr function, which allows the text to be properly formatted for use as an attribute value. If the esc_attr isn't used, some values in the title, such as a double-quote, could break the HTML.

10. **Press Enter and type the following lines of code in the `init.php` file:**

```
<textarea
  class="widefat"
  rows="16"
  id="<?php echo $this->get_field_id('text'); ?>"
  name="<?php echo $this->get_field_name('text'); ?>"
>
<?php echo esc_attr($text); ?>
</textarea>
```

This block of HTML displays the `textarea` input that allows the user to input the text that she wants to display. The only difference between this input and the previous one is that the `textarea` and `text` inputs have a different format and that this input doesn't have a description.

11. **Press Enter and type** `<?php`.

The form HTML is complete, so the open PHP tag, `<?php`, is used to switch back to PHP code.

12. **Press Enter and type** `}`.

The `form` function closes.

13. **Press Enter and type the following line of code in the `init.php` file:**

```
function update($new_instance,$old_instance) {
```

The `update` class function processes the submitted form data. The `$new_instance` argument provides the data submitted by the form. The `$old_instance` argument provides the widget's old options.

14. **Press Enter and type the following line of code in the `init.php` file:**

```
$instance=array();
```

A new empty array variable, `$instance`, is created. This variable will store the final options values.

15. **Press Enter and type the following lines of code in the `init.php` file:**

```
$instance['title']=strip_tags($new_instance['title']);
$instance['text']=$new_instance['text'];
```

Store the title and text options from the `$new_instance` variable into the `$instance` variable. The title option is run through the `strip_tags` function so that no HTML tags are stored in the title option.

16. **Press Enter and type the following line of code in the `init.php` file:**

```
return $instance;
```

The "update" function works like a filter function. The data is passed in, it can be manipulated as desired, and then the final value is returned.

After seeing how this function works, you might wonder why creating the `$instance` variable was needed. Even though using `$new_instance` directly would be more simple, it also could produce unexpected results. It is possible for unexpected data to come through as part of the $new_instance variable. By creating the $instance variable and assigning only known options to it, you can be assured that you know exactly what data is stored for the widget and that your code has had a chance to clean it up.

17. Press Enter and type }.

Close the "update" function.

18. Press Enter and type the following line of code in the init.php file:

```
function widget($args,$instance) {
```

The widget class function is the same as before, but it now has the $instance argument. The $instance argument stores the options set for the widget.

19. Press Enter and type the following lines of code in the init.php file:

```
extract($args);
extract($instance);
```

Use the extract function on both $args and $instance to populate easy-to-use variables for each.

20. Press Enter and type the following line of code in the init.php file:

```
$title=apply_filters('widget_title',$title,$instance,$this->id_base);
```

Remember that in a previous section when you assembled The Example: Contraction Compulsion Correction plugin, you added the add_filter function to add a function to be used as a filter. The apply_filters in this example function is how those filter functions are used. This line of code translates to "Store the result of the widget_title filters in the $title variable." Each filter is passed the $title, $instance, and $this->id_base variables. Every widget that has a title should have this line of code so that filters have a chance to filter all widget titles.

21. Press Enter and type the following lines of code in the init.php file:

```
echo $before_widget;
if(!empty($title)) echo $before_title . $title . $after_title;
echo $text;
echo $after_widget;
```

As with the previous widget, the $before_widget variable is included before the rest of the widget content and the $after_widget variable is included after all the other widget content. Because this widget supports a title, there is now the addition of the $before_title and $after_title variables that, like the $before_widget and $after_widget variables, come from the $args argument passed to the function. The if statement ensures that the title displays only if the title isn't empty.

REMEMBER

! means "not."

22. Press Enter and type }.

The widget function class closes.

23. Press Enter and type }.

The `My_Text_Widget` class closes.

24. Press Enter and type the following lines of code in the `init.php` file:

```
function register_my_text_widget() {
register_widget('My_Text_Widget');
}
add_action('widgets_init','register_my_text_widget');
```

Register the widget. Note how the `My_Text_Widget` argument of the `register_widget` function matches the name of this widget's class.

When you're finished with the preceding steps, the entire block of code looks like Listing 5-2 when all put together in your `init.php` file.

Listing 5-2:   The init.php File for the Example: My Text Widget Plugin

```php
<?php
/*
Plugin Name: Example: My Text Widget
Description: This plugin provides a basic Text Widget clone complete with widget
    options
*/

class My_Text_Widget extends WP_Widget {

function My_Text_Widget() {
$widget_ops=array('description'=>'Simple Text Widget clone');
$control_ops=array('width'=>400);
parent::WP_Widget(false,'My Text Widget',$widget_ops,$control_ops);
}

function form($instance) {

$instance=wp_parse_args($instance,array('title'=>'','text'=>''));

extract($instance);

?>

<p>
<label for="<?php echo $this->get_field_id('title'); ?>">
<?php _e('Title:'); ?>
<input
  class="widefat"
  type="text"
  id="<?php echo $this->get_field_id('title'); ?>"
  name="<?php echo $this->get_field_name('title'); ?>"
  value="<?php echo esc_attr($title); ?>"
/>
```

```
</label>
</p>

<textarea
  class="widefat"
  rows="16"
  id="<?php echo $this->get_field_id('text'); ?>"
  name="<?php echo $this->get_field_name('text'); ?>"
>
<?php echo esc_attr($text); ?>
</textarea>

<?php

}

function update($new_instance,$old_instance) {

$instance=array();

$instance['title']=strip_tags($new_instance['title']);
$instance['text']=$new_instance['text'];

return $instance;

}

function widget($args,$instance) {

extract($args);
extract($instance);

$title=apply_filters('widget_title',$title,$instance,$this->id_base);

echo $before_widget;
if(!empty($title)) echo $before_title . $title . $after_title;
echo $text;
echo $after_widget;

}
}

function register_my_text_widget() {
register_widget('My_Text_Widget');
}
add_action('widgets_init','register_my_text_widget');
?>
```

Book VII
Chapter 5

Creating Simple
Plugins from
Scratch

Now the widget is ready for use. Open the Widgets page on your Dashboard (hover your pointer over Appearance and click the Widgets link); you see a new widget ready for you to use called My Text Widget. When expanded, the widget has a Title field and text box for the user to configure and add content to, as shown in Figure 5-9.

Figure 5-9:
The My Text
Widget.

Building a Settings Page

Many plugins offer a settings page that allows the user to customize plugin options. The options offered by a settings page vary from a few check boxes, drop-down lists, or text inputs to multiple advanced editors that allow the user to build data sets, set up forums, or do advanced content management. Although the following sections focus on building a simple settings page, you can expand the concept to fill any type of need that your plugin has.

When reduced to a bare minimum, a basic settings page consists of code that displays the page, stores the settings, and adds the page to the WordPress admin menu. The plugin created in this section will give you a solid foundation that you can use to build your own plugin settings pages.

Setting up the plugin structure

The plugin you create in this section is Example: Settings Page. To get started with this plugin, create a new plugins directory named /example-settings-page. All the files for this plugin go in this new directory. That's right, *files*. You add multiple plugin files to the plugin directory.

Separate different functionality into separate files because as plugins get larger, having everything in one file quickly becomes hard to manage. Similar to the way the init.php file is named because it *initializes* the plugin, the other files used by the plugin should be named so the purpose of each file is easy to discern when looking at the filenames.

This new plugin will have the following files, so go ahead and create five blank files and name them with these filenames:

✦ `init.php`: Contains the file header and will load the other needed plugin files

✦ `settings-page.php`: Holds the settings page code

✦ `default-settings.php`: Sets the default values used for the settings

✦ `msp-form-class.php`: Provides a class that makes adding form inputs easy

✦ `settings-functions.php`: Provides functions to load and save the settings

By dividing the plugin code into logical groups, each of which has its own file, the code becomes much easier to maintain. With this type of setup, as new features are added to the plugin, they can easily be isolated to their own files.

All the files must be created before the plugin will function. To start, add the following code to your plugin's `init.php` file:

```php
<?php
/*
Plugin Name: Example: Settings Page
Description: This plugin offers a solid starting point for building settings
    pages
*/

require_once(dirname(__FILE__).'/default-settings.php');
require_once(dirname(__FILE__).'/msp-form-class.php');
require_once(dirname(__FILE__).'/settings-functions.php');
require_once(dirname(__FILE__).'/settings-page.php');
```

The `require_once` function loads another PHP file. If the file isn't found, a fatal error occurs and the plugin doesn't function. Therefore, trying to activate the plugin at this point causes the plugin to fail. This is good because it prevents the plugin from activating when needed files are missing, which can happen if an incomplete upload of the plugin files occurs.

There are four primary functions to load other PHP code: `include`, `include_once`, `require`, and `require_once`. The `include` functions will not cause a fatal error if there's a problem loading the requested file, but the `require` functions will. The functions that add `_once` won't load the file if the file has been loaded already. This situation helps prevent accidentally loading a file multiple times, which can break the code or cause unexpected behavior.

Directly underneath the `require_once` functions, add the following line:

```
dirname(__FILE__).'/default-settings.php'
```

This section of code finds the full path to the `default-settings.php` file. Refer to the file's full path to avoid issues with some server setups.

That's all the `init.php` file needs for this plugin. You can now save and upload the file to your plugin directory at `/wp-content/plugins/example-settings-page`. When you add new features to the plugin, you need to add new files to hold these features and use a `require_once` call to load each one.

Adding a new Admin menu entry

Add the following lines of code to the `settings-page.php` file that you created at the beginning of this section:

```php
<?php

function msp_add_admin_menu() {
add_options_page(
  'Example Settings Page',
  'Example Settings',
  'manage_options',
  'msp-example-settings-page',
  'msp_display_settings_page'
);
if(isset($_POST['msp_save'])) {
  add_action("admin_head-$page",'msp_save_settings_handler');
}
}
add_action('admin_menu','msp_add_admin_menu');
```

This code adds a new link in the Dashboard's Settings menu titled Example Setting. The `add_options_page` function is the key to adding this new menu. The following list describes what each argument in this function does:

✦ `Example Settings Page`: The first argument sets the title of the page. The browser, not the settings page, displays this title.

✦ `Example Settings`: The second argument is the name of the menu. The space is limited, so try to keep the name short.

✦ `manage_options`: The third argument is the capability that the user must have in order to see and access the menu. For settings pages, the `manage_options` capability is typically the best choice as only administrators have this capability by default. `edit_others_posts` can be used to allow administrators and editors, whereas `edit_published_posts` can be used for administrators, editors, and authors.

✦ `msp-example-settings-page`: The fourth argument is a name that WordPress uses internally to navigate to the page. Make sure that this is a unique name or you can run into problems with other plugins. The `msp` at the front of the name stands for *My Settings Page*. Consistently using a prefix in this manner helps prevent duplicate name issues.

✦ `msp_display_settings_page`: The fifth argument is the name of the function that is called when the page is viewed. As with the fourth argument, make sure that this is unique to your plugin. Notice the `msp` prefix is used here, too.

Just as the `register_widget` function cannot be called when a plugin first loads, the `add_options_page` function also must wait until WordPress is ready before it can be called. To call the function when WordPress is ready, it's wrapped in a function that's called when the `admin_menu` action is run.

Other than registering the new admin menu, this code also does a check that adds a page-specific action if form data with a `msp_save` variable has been submitted. When this action fires, the `msp_save_settings_handler` function processes and saves the submitted form data.

Creating a settings form

There are as many ways to set up a settings form as there are hot dogs in Chicago. Well, maybe not quite that many, but I'm sure that the numbers are close. Most of these methods use large sections of repeated code for each individual input.

This form shows how each type of HTML form input type can be integrated into your settings form. Instead of manually coding each input, which is time consuming and error prone, a set of functions is provided that make adding new inputs very easy.

Open your plugin `settings-page.php` file and follow these steps to add the code that handles the HTML form input for your settings page:

1. **Open the `settings-page.php` file in your text editor.**

2. **Add the following line of code at the bottom of the `settings-php` file:**

   ```
   function msp_display_settings_page() {
   $form=new MSP_Form(msp_get_settings());
   ?>
   ```

   The `msp-form-class.php` file, which you will create later, contains a new class called `MSP_Form`. This class accepts an array of settings to assign the initial values of the form inputs. The settings come from the `msp_get_settings` function, which will be defined in the `settings-functions.php` file (covered in the next section).

When using a class like this, a variable stores an *object*. In this case, the object is stored in a variable called $form. Later in this form code, the $form variable will be used to easily add new form inputs by using the functions provided by the MSP_Form class.

3. **Press Enter and type the following lines of code:**

```
<?php if(isset($_GET['updated'])) : ?>
<div id="message" class="updated fade">
  <p><strong>Settings saved.</strong></p>
</div>
<?php endif; ?>
```

When the form data is saved, the page redirects to a new settings page link that contains a variable named updated. So, this section of code displays a Settings saved message when this redirect happens, confirming to the user that the settings changes are saved.

4. **Press Enter and type the following lines of code:**

```
<div class="wrap">
<?php screen_icon(); ?>
<h2>Example Settings Page</h2>
```

This section simply follows the page structure used by WordPress's built-in editors so that your settings page fits in with the style of WordPress.

5. **Press Enter and type the following line of code:**

```
<form method="post" action="<?php echo $_SERVER['REQUEST_URI']; ?>">
```

Many settings pages use code that submits the form data to the options.php page built into WordPress. To have a bit more control over how the data is saved, this settings page form sends the data back to itself, allowing this plugin's code to have full control over how the data is stored.

6. **Press Enter and type the following line of code:**

```
<?php wp_nonce_field('msp-update-settings'); ?>
```

The wp_nonce_field function is part of the nonce system of WordPress. nonce — which stands for *number used once* or *number once* — protects a site against attackers and increases security by validating the contents of a form field. All your WordPress-managed forms should use nonces and use them properly. The key is to have the wp_nonce_field function call (with a unique attribute to identify the form's purpose) inside the HTML form tags and a call to check_ admin_referer (that uses a matching attribute) before any action is taken with the form data. The check_admin_referer call can be found in the msp_save_settings_handler function at the end of this file's code.

7. **Press Enter and type the following code:**

```
<table class="form-table">
<tr valign="top">
<th scope="row"><label for="text">Text</label></th>
<td>
<?php $form->add_text('text'); ?>
</td>
</tr>
<tr valign="top">
<th scope="row"><label for="textarea">Text Area</label></th>
<td>
<?php $form->add_textarea('textarea'); ?>
</td>
</tr>
```

This is the table structure commonly used in editors throughout WordPress, using the HTML markup to create tables. It is simple and easy to expand to have new options.

When you want to expand your forms, copy a single row, paste a few copies, and then modify each copy to have a new input.

The call to the `$form->add_text` function is what adds the text input to the form. This function accepts an argument that defines what the name of the setting is (`text` in this case). The `textarea` section of the code follows the same format as this section.

8. **Press Enter and type the following lines of code:**

```
<tr valign="top">
<th scope="row">Multi-Checkbox</th>
<td>
<label title="1">
<?php $form->add_multicheckbox('multicheckbox','1'); ?> 1
</label><br />
<label title="2">
<?php $form->add_multicheckbox('multicheckbox','2'); ?> 2
</label><br />
<label title="3">
<?php $form->add_multicheckbox('multicheckbox','3'); ?> 3
</label><br />
<label title="4">
<?php $form->add_multicheckbox('multicheckbox','4'); ?> 4
</label>
</td>
</tr>
```

This section makes use of the MSP_Form class' add_multicheckbox function to create a form input that allows multiple values to be stored in a single setting. The second argument used for this function sets the value that the specific check box has. When loading data from this type of setting, the values of the checked inputs will be stored in an array.

9. **Press Enter and type the following lines of code:**

```
<tr valign="top">
<th scope="row">Radio</th>
<td>
<label title="Option 1">
<?php $form->add_radio('radio','1'); ?>
Option 1
</label>
<br />
<label title="Option 2">
<?php $form->add_radio('radio','2'); ?>
Option 2
</label>
<br />
<label title="Option 3">
<?php $form->add_radio('radio','3'); ?>
Option 3
</label>
</td>
</tr>
```

This section makes use of the MSP_Form class's add_radio function to create a form input using radios buttons. It uses the same format as the multicheckbox inputs from Step 8. The second argument is used to set the value used for the individual input. Unlike the multicheckbox inputs, the data loaded for a radio setting is a string and not an array.

10. **Press Enter and type the following lines of code:**

```
<tr valign="top">
<th scope="row"><label for="select">Select</label></th>
<td>
<?php
$options = array(
  '1'=>'Option 1',
  '2'=>'Option 2',
  '3'=>'Option 3',
);
?>
<?php $form->add_select('select',$options); ?>
</td>
</tr>
</table>
```

Select inputs can be very difficult to code by hand. The MSP_Form class makes adding a select input very easy. First, create an associative, or *named,* array. A named array sets the key to be used for each value. In other words, each array input looks like '1'=>'Option 1', where 1 is the value to be stored for that setting and *Option 1* is the description to show for that value. Then the named array is passed in as the second argument to the add_select function.

11. **Press Enter and type the following lines of code:**

```
<p class="submit">
<input type="submit" name="msp_save" class="button-primary" value="Save
    Changes" />
</p>
```

Note the `msp_save` value used for the submit button's name. This is the name used to check for a settings form submission toward the top of this file.

12. Press Enter and type the following lines of code:

```
<?php $form->add_used_inputs(); ?>
</form>
</div>
```

This call to `add_used_inputs` is very important for handling the submitted form data.

13. Press Enter and type the following lines of code:

```
<?php
}
function msp_save_settings_handler() {
check_admin_referer('msp-update-settings');
$settings=MSP_Form::get_post_data();
msp_update_settings($settings);
}
```

The `msp_save_settings_handler` completes the `settings-page.php` code. First, the nonce set inside the form is checked with the `check_admin_referer` to ensure that the nonces are used properly. The `MSP_Form` class function `get_post_data` is used to store that submitted settings into the `$settings` variable. These settings are then passed to the `msp_update_settings` function (defined in the `settings-functions.php` file) to save the settings.

When you finish, the code in your entire `settings-page.php` file looks like Listing 5-3.

Book VII
Chapter 5

Creating Simple
Plugins from
Scratch

Listing 5-3:   HTML Form Input Code for the Settings Page

```
<?php

function msp_add_admin_menu() {
add_options_page(
  'Example Settings Page',
  'Example Settings',
  'manage_options',
  'msp-example-settings-page',
  'msp_display_settings_page'
);
if(isset($_POST['msp_save'])) {
  add_action("admin_head-$page",'msp_save_settings_handler');
}
}
add_action('admin_menu','msp_add_admin_menu');

function msp_display_settings_page() {
$form=new MSP_Form(msp_get_settings());
?>
<?php if(isset($_GET['updated'])) : ?>
```

(continued)

Listing 5-3 *(continued)*

```
<div id="message" class="updated fade">
  <p><strong>Settings saved.</strong></p>
</div>
<?php endif; ?>
<div class="wrap">
<?php screen_icon(); ?>
<h2>Example Settings Page</h2>
<form method="post" action="<?php echo $_SERVER['REQUEST_URI']; ?>">
<?php wp_nonce_field('msp-update-settings'); ?>
<table class="form-table">
<tr valign="top">
<th scope="row"><label for="text">Text</label></th>
<td>
<?php $form->add_text('text'); ?>
</td>
</tr>
<tr valign="top">
<th scope="row"><label for="textarea">Text Area</label></th>
<td>
<?php $form->add_textarea('textarea'); ?>
</td>
</tr>
<tr valign="top">
<th scope="row"><label for="checkbox">Checkbox</label></th>
<td>
<?php $form->add_checkbox('checkbox'); ?>
</td>
</tr>
<tr valign="top">
<th scope="row">Multi-Checkbox</th>
<td>
<label title="1">
<?php $form->add_multicheckbox('multicheckbox','1'); ?> 1
</label><br />
<label title="2">
<?php $form->add_multicheckbox('multicheckbox','2'); ?> 2
</label><br />
<label title="3">
<?php $form->add_multicheckbox('multicheckbox','3'); ?> 3
</label><br />
<label title="4">
<?php $form->add_multicheckbox('multicheckbox','4'); ?> 4
</label>
</td>
</tr>
<tr valign="top">
<th scope="row">Radio</th>
<td>
<label title="Option 1">
<?php $form->add_radio('radio','1'); ?>
Option 1
</label>
<br />
<label title="Option 2">
<?php $form->add_radio('radio','2'); ?>
Option 2
</label>
<br />
<label title="Option 3">
<?php $form->add_radio('radio','3'); ?>
```

```
Option 3
</label>
</td>
</tr>
<tr valign="top">
<th scope="row"><label for="select">Select</label></th>
<td>
<?php
$options = array(
  '1'=>'Option 1',
  '2'=>'Option 2',
  '3'=>'Option 3',
);
?>
<?php $form->add_select('select',$options); ?>
</td>
</tr>
</table>
<p class="submit">
<input type="submit" name="msp_save" class="button-primary" value="Save Changes"
  />
</p>
<?php $form->add_used_inputs(); ?>
</form>
</div>
<?php
}
function msp_save_settings_handler() {
check_admin_referer('msp-update-settings');
$settings=MSP_Form::get_post_data();
msp_update_settings($settings);
}
```

Configuring default settings

A nice feature of this settings form code is that default settings can be set easily. These default settings are loaded even if the settings form hasn't been saved, allowing for reliable use of the defaults.

To set up the defaults, add the following code to a new file and save it as default-settings.php in your /example-settings page plugin directory:

```
<?php
function msp_get_default_settings() {
  $defaults=array(
    'text'    => 'Sample Text',
    'textarea' => 'Sample Textarea Text',
    'checkbox' => '1',
    'multicheckbox' => array('2','3'),
    'radio'    => '2',
    'select'   => '3',
  );
  return $defaults;
}
```

By modifying the $defaults array, new default values can be added, removed, or modified easily. The format for this type of array is 'setting_name'=>'setting_value', where setting_name is the name of the setting and setting_value is the default value you want to use for that setting.

Adding settings functions

The settings functions manage loading and saving settings. Both functions are optimized for performance and reliability. Add the following code to a new file and save it as settings-functions.php in your /example-settings-page plugin directory:

```php
<?php
function msp_get_settings($name=null) {
static $settings=null;

if(is_null($settings)) {
$settings=get_option('msp-example-settings');
if(!is_array($settings)) $settings=array();

$defaults=msp_get_default_settings();
$settings=array_merge($defaults,$settings);
}

if(is_null($name)) return $settings;
if(isset($settings[$name])) return $settings[$name];
return '';
}

function msp_update_settings($settings) {
update_option('msp-example-settings',$settings);

$redirect_url=array_shift(explode('?',$_SERVER['REQUEST_URI']));
$redirect_url.='?page='.$_REQUEST['page'].'&updated=true';

wp_redirect($redirect_url);
}

$all_settings=msp_get_settings();
$text=msp_get_settings('text');
```

Because you call the function with no argument, all the settings are returned. When you pass a setting name, the value for just that setting is returned.

The msp_update_settings function accepts a new array of settings to be saved. After the settings are saved, a new redirect link with the "updated" variable is built, and it displays the Settings saved message. WordPress's wp_redirect function then redirects the site to this new link.

Creating the MSP_Form class

The MSP_Form class code is quite lengthy. It's well worth the effort because it makes form building very easy.

Add the code in Listing 5-4 to a new file and save it as `msp-form-class.php` in your `/example-settings-page` plugin directory:

Listing 5-4:   The MSP_Form Class Code

```php
<?php
class MSP_Form {
var $inputs=array();
var $settings=array();
function MSP_Form($settings=array()) {
if(is_array($settings)) $this->settings=$settings;
}
function add_used_inputs() {
$value=implode(',',array_unique($this->inputs));
$this->add_hidden('___msp_form_used_inputs',$value);
}
function get_post_data() {
if(!isset($_POST['___msp_form_used_inputs'])) {
return $_POST;
}
$data=array();
$inputs=explode(',',$_POST['___msp_form_used_inputs']);
foreach((array)$inputs as $var) {
$real_var=str_replace('[]','',$var);
if(isset($_POST[$real_var])) {
$data[$real_var]=stripslashes_deep($_POST[$real_var]);
}
else if ($var!=$real_var) {
$data[$real_var]=array();
}
else {
$data[$real_var]='';
}
}
return $data;
}

// $form->add_text('name');
function add_text($name,$options=array()) {
if(!isset($options['class'])) $options['class']='regular-text';
$this->_add_input('text',$name,$options);
}
function add_textarea($name,$options=array()) {
$this->_add_input('textarea',$name,$options);
}
function add_checkbox($name,$options=array()) {
if($this->_get_setting($name)) $options['checked']='checked';
$this->_add_input('checkbox',$name,$options);
}
function add_file($name,$options=array()) {
$this->_add_input('file',$name,$options);
}
function add_password($name,$options=array()) {
$this->_add_input('password',$name,$options);
}

// $form->add_select('num',array('1'=>'One','2'=>'Two'));
function add_select($name,$values,$options=array()) {
$options['values']=$values;
```

Book VII
Chapter 5

Creating Simple
Plugins from
Scratch

(continued)

Listing 5-4 *(continued)*

```php
$this->_add_input('select',$name,$options);
}

// $form->add_radio('type','extended');
function add_radio($name,$value,$options=array()) {
if($this->_get_setting($name)==$value) $options['checked']='checked';
$options['value']=$value;
$this->_add_input('radio',$name,$options);
}
function add_multicheckbox($name,$value,$options=array()) {
$setting=$this->_get_setting($name);
if(is_array($setting) && in_array($value,$setting)) {
$options['checked']='checked';
}
$options['value']=$value;
$this->_add_input('checkbox',"{$name}[]",$options);
}
function add_hidden($name,$value,$options=array()) {
$options['value']=$value;
$this->_add_input('hidden',$name,$options);
}

// $form->add_submit('save','Save');
function add_submit($name,$description,$options=array()) {
$options['value']=$description;
$this->_add_input('submit',$name,$options);
}
function add_button($name,$description,$options=array()) {
$options['value']=$description;
$this->_add_input('button',$name,$options);
}
function add_reset($name,$description,$options=array()) {
$options['value']=$description;
$this->_add_input('reset',$name,$options);
}

// $form->add_image('imagemap','http://domain.com/img.gif');
function add_image($name,$image_url,$options=array()) {
$options['src']=$image_url;
$this->_add_input('image',$name,$options);
}

// This function should not be called directly.
function _add_input($type,$name,$options=array()) {
$this->inputs[]=$name;
$settings_var=str_replace('[]','',$name);
$css_var=str_replace('[','-',str_replace(']','',$settings_var));

if(!is_array($options)) $options=array();
$options['type']=$type;
$options['name']=$name;
if(!isset($options['value']) && 'checkbox'!=$type) {
$options['value']=$this->_get_setting($settings_var);
}

if('radio'==$type || $settings_var!=$name) {
if(empty($options['class'])) $options['class']=$css_var;
}
```

```
else {
if(empty($options['id'])) $options['id']=$css_var;
}

$scrublist=array($type=>array());
$scrublist['textarea']=array('value','type');
$scrublist['file']=array('value');
$scrublist['dropdown']=array('value','values','type');

$attributes = '';
foreach($options as $var => $val) {
  if(!is_array($val) && !in_array($var,$scrublist[$type]))
  $attributes.="$var='".esc_attr($val)."' ";
}

if('textarea'==$options['type']) {
  echo "<textarea $attributes>";
  echo format_to_edit($options['value']);
  echo "</textarea>\n";
}
else if('select'==$options['type']) {
  echo "<select $attributes>\n";
  if(is_array($options['values'])) {
  foreach($options['values'] as $val=>$name) {
  $selected=($options['value']==$val)?' selected="selected"':'';
  echo "<option value=\"$val\"$selected>$name</option>\n";
  }
  }
  echo "</select>\n";
}
else {
  echo "<input $attributes />\n";
}

}

// This function should not be called directly.
function _get_setting($name) {
if(isset($this->settings[$name])) {
return $this->settings[$name];
}
return '';
}

}
```

You can use 13 functions to add inputs to a form. The following shows an example of how to use each one:

```
$form->add_text('setting_name');
$form->add_textarea('setting_name');
$form->add_checkbox('setting_name');
$form->add_file('setting_name');
$form->add_password('setting_name');
$form->add_select('setting_name',array('1'=>'One','2'=>'Two'));
$form->add_radio('setting_name','value_1');
$form->add_radio('setting_name','value_2');
$form->add_multicheckbox('setting_name','value_1');
$form->add_multicheckbox('setting_name','value_2');
```

(continued)

```
$form->add_hidden('setting_name','value');
$form->add_submit('setting_name','value');
$form->add_button('setting_name','value');
$form->add_reset('setting_name','value');
$form->add_image('imagemap','http://domain.com/img.gif');
```

A feature that all the form input functions support is an optional last parameter to set additional HTML tag attributes to the final output. Here's an
example of a block of code that sets additional HTML markup to the final
output:

```
$form->add_text('setting_name',array('class'=>'regular-text code'));
$form->add_text('setting_name',array('style'=>'width:250px;font-size:2em;'));
$form->add_textarea('setting_name',array('rows'=>'10','cols'=>'30'));
$form->add_checkbox('setting_name',array('checked'=>'checked'));
```

This adds the class `regular-text` and `code` to the first text input, adds
inline styling to control the width and font size of the second text input, uses
10 rows and 30 columns for the `textarea` input, and forces the `checkbox`
to always be selected on page load for the last input.

This last optional argument in the form inputs can be used on any of the
inputs to set needed tag attributes. By using this last argument in creative
ways, you can always rely on using the input form functions rather than
coding inputs by scratch.

Testing the plugin

After you have the files entered, you're ready to activate the Example:
Settings Page plugin.

Because the code is divided, if you get an error about not being able to activate the plugin, note which file and line number had the error. This will help
you quickly fix your error.

After activating the plugin, visit your Dashboard, hover your pointer over
Settings, and click the Example Settings link to see the settings form in
action, as shown in Figure 5-10. Notice how the form is populated by the
default values you set. These default values are set the first time the `msp_
get_settings` function is called. Therefore, even if the user has never gone
to your settings page, the defaults will be available. In addition, when you
add new settings and update the defaults to have these new settings, those
new defaults will also automatically become available.

After testing the settings options, go into the `settings-page.php` file and
add new settings. When you have the new settings, make sure you update
the `$defaults` array in `default-settings.php`.

Figure 5-10:
The
Example
Settings
page.

This plugin can be extended with code from another one of the example plugins. To load the settings, simply use the msp_get_settings function.

For example, the widget function from the Example: My User Widget plugin you created earlier in this chapter could be updated to make use of two settings, guest_message and user_message.

```
function widget($args) {
$user=wp_get_current_user();
if(!isset($user->user_nicename))
$message=msp_get_settings('guest_message');
else
$message=msp_get_settings('user_message').$user->user_nicename;

extract($args);

echo $before_widget;
echo "<p>$message</p>";
echo $after_widget;
}
```

Chapter 6: Exploring Plugin Development Best Practices

In This Chapter

✓ **Exploring best practices**

✓ **Naming, filing, and locating your plugin**

✓ **Internationalizing your plugin**

*S*tarting to develop WordPress plugins is relatively easy. It's much more difficult to develop WordPress plugins well.

The key to doing development well is to stick with a set of standards that ensures that your plugin is well designed and implemented. A set of standards that many people can agree upon are typically referred to as *best practices*. By adopting best practices as your own personal development standard, you ensure that other developers can easily understand your plugin's structure and code. Doing so makes collaboration much smoother. In other words, if all WordPress plugin developers followed best practices, the WordPress development world would be a happier and more productive place.

This chapter delves deeper into best practices and is dedicated to taking your plugin quality to the next level.

Adding a File Header

The most fundamental best practice when creating WordPress plugins is to ensure that your plugin has a *file header* at the top of the main plugin file. As discussed in Chapter 5 of this minibook, the file header is the part of a plugin file that identifies the file as a plugin. Without the file header, the plugin isn't actually a plugin and cannot be enabled on the WordPress Dashboard.

Even if you don't distribute your plugin in the WordPress Plugin Directory (http://wordpress.org/extend/plugins), take the time to fill in the file header with the name, description, author, version, and license. This info is helpful to all your plugin users.

Use the following header names to supply information about your plugin:

✦ **Plugin Name:** The value for this entry is listed as the name of the plugin on the Dashboard's Plugins page. The Plugin Name is the only required entry in a plugin's file header. If this isn't present, WordPress ignores the plugin.

When giving your plugin a name, make sure that you choose a name that is

• *Unique:* WordPress uses the name to check for plugin updates. So, if you name the plugin *Akismet,* WordPress could offer to let the user automatically upgrade the plugin, resulting in your plugin code being replaced with the actual Akismet plugin. Starting all your plugin names with your name is a good way to achieve unique names. For example, these are some unique plugin names: *Lisa's Twitter Widget, Lisa's Amazon Affiliate Shortcodes,* and *Lisa's Really Cool Plugin.*

• *Descriptive:* Use a name that describes its purpose. *Lisa's Twitter Widget* and *Lisa's Amazon Affiliate Shortcodes* both describe what the plugin offers quite well, but *Lisa's Really Cool Plugin* doesn't help identify its purpose.

Even if you use the plugin only on your own site, by using a nondescriptive name, you may end up having to look at the plugin's code just to remember what the plugin is actually doing.

✦ **Description:** This entry is meant to be a brief explanation of what features the plugin offers. The description entry is shown next to each plugin listed on the Dashboard's Plugins page. Because the plugin's listing shares space with other plugins, don't add too large of a description. Limit the description to one to three sentences.

It is possible to put HTML into the description. You can add links for plugin documentation and other resources.

Don't abuse this feature to make your plugin stand out among all the others. If your plugin is installed, you already won over the user and got him to install the plugin. Don't lose a user by spamming up his plugin listing.

✦ **Version:** If you share the code for your plugin, the version entry of the plugin could be one of the most important entries in the plugin's file header. If the version number is properly updated, when a user reports an issue, you can quickly know exactly what code the user is running, whether the plugin is outdated, and whether the current code has a bug. It's a simple thing, but it is very powerful.

The topic of versions is detailed in more depth later in this chapter. For now, know that properly using and updating the version is important.

✦ **Plugin URI:** Enter the web address where you talk in depth about the plugin. At a minimum, information about what the plugin is and any necessary instructions on using the plugin should be provided. It is a good idea to allow comments so that people can provide feedback, both good and bad. This works as a simple support system for your plugin.

✦ **Author:** List the name or names of the plugin authors. Sometimes the name of the company behind the plugin is used instead of the name of a specific developer.

✦ **Author URI:** The web address of the plugin author's website.

✦ **License:** The name of the license under which your plugin is released. For most plugins, this should be GPLv2 because it matches the license that WordPress is released under. When submitting a plugin to the Plugin Directory, the plugin must be licensed under GPL version 2 or above. For more information on GPL licensing, including how it pertains to your plugin development practices, see Book I, Chapter 2.

✦ **Text Domain:** This entry is part of allowing the Plugin Name, Description, Version, Plugin URI, Author, and Author URI entries to be translatable. The value for this entry is used as the domain for translating the other entries and should match the domain used in the `load_plugin_textdomain` function. For details about translating, see the "Internationalizing or Localizing Your Plugin" section later in this chapter.

This entry is rarely used in plugins, but it is available to allow for translators to supply translations for the details in the file header.

✦ **Domain Path:** This entry is used together with the Text Domain entry to offer the file header translations. The value for this entry is the name of the directory inside the plugin's directory (such as `/language/` or `/translations/`) where the translation files are located. The directory must begin with a forward slash for the translation files to be found. If this entry is not used, the plugin's directory is searched for the translation files.

As with the Text Domain entry, the Domain Path entry is rarely used.

✦ **Network:** When WordPress is running as a network (discussed in Book VIII), this entry allows plugins to indicate that they must be active for the entire network rather than just a single site. The only accepted value for this entry is `true`; any other value is treated the same as having this entry blank or missing. If WordPress isn't running as a network, this entry is ignored.

Using this entry is helpful if your plugin provides very low-level features, such as advanced caching. Because such a feature could create problems if only some sites on the network had it active, this entry forces an

Book VII
Chapter 6

Exploring Plugin
Development Best
Practices

all-or-nothing activation of the plugin. Either all of the sites on the network run the plugin, or none of the sites do.

✦ **Site Wide Only:** This is a deprecated entry that is superseded by the Network entry and is supported only for backward compatibility. If the Network entry is supplied, this entry is ignored. As with Network, the only recognized value is `true`. This entry should not be used as support, because it may be removed in future versions.

Although you may not need all of the entry options, a file header that makes use of all the options looks like the following. (The Site Wide Only option is left out because it is replaced by the Network option.)

```php
<?php
/*
Plugin Name: Lisa's Twitter Widget
Description: Display Twitter feeds in any sidebar on your site.
Version: 1.0.0
Plugin URI: http://example.com/twitter-widget
Author: Lisa Sabin-Wilson
Author URI: http://example.com
License: GPLv2
Text Domain: lsw-twitter-widget
Domain Path: /language/
Network: true
*/
?>
```

It is customary to include a licensing statement in the header of your plugin to indicate adherence to the GPLv2 license. This statement is easy to include and is formatted as follows:

```php
<?php
/*

This program is free software; you can redistribute it and/or
modify it under the terms of the GNU General Public License
as published by the Free Software Foundation; either version 2
of the License, or (at your option) any later version.

This program is distributed in the hope that it will be useful,
but WITHOUT ANY WARRANTY; without even the implied warranty of
MERCHANTABILITY or FITNESS FOR A PARTICULAR PURPOSE.  See the
GNU General Public License for more details.

You should have received a copy of the GNU General Public License
along with this program; if not, write to the Free Software
Foundation, Inc., 51 Franklin Street, Fifth Floor, Boston, MA  02110-1301, USA.
*/
?>
```

Figure 6-1 shows the Plugins page displaying information pulled from each plugin's file header.

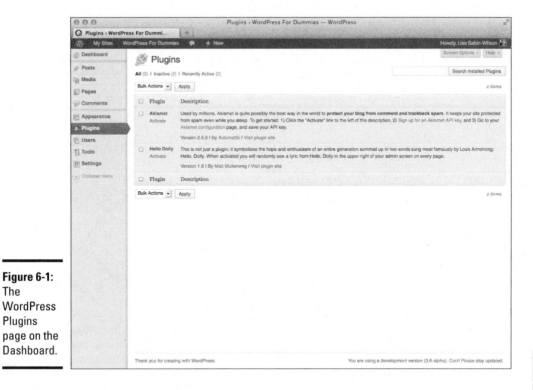

Figure 6-1:
The
WordPress
Plugins
page on the
Dashboard.

Creating a readme.txt File

To submit a plugin to the WordPress Plugin Directory, your plugin must also include a readme.txt file. The plugin won't be accepted without it. The readme.txt file is included with the rest of your plugin's files when a user downloads it. It should contain the information the user needs to know to properly use the plugin.

The information contained in the readme.txt file is much more elaborate than the information in the file header. All the plugin pages found in the Plugin Directory are generated using information from the readme.txt file of each plugin. Thus, this information is very important if you want people to take your plugin seriously.

The file is formatted in a slightly modified version of the Markdown format. *Markdown* is a simple syntax for formatting content to contain headings, text styling (such as underline and bold), links, and so on. The main difference between the format used for WordPress plugin readme.txt files and regular Markdown is that the readme.txt files use a different format for headings (as you can see in the example), and there is a WordPress-specific section similar to the file header of the main plugin file at the top of readme.txt files.

Before digging into the details, look through the following example readme. txt file contents:

```
=== Lisa's Twitter Widget ===
Contributors: lisasabinwilson
Stable tag: 1.0.0
Tags: twitter, widget, social media
Requires at least: 3.3
Tested up to: 3.5

Display Twitter feeds in any sidebar on your site.

== Description ==

Lisa's Twitter Widget users the power of WordPress's widget system to allow you
    to quickly and easily add a Twitter feed to your site. After adding the
    Twitter Widget to one of your sidebars, enter the desired Twitter username
    in the widget's options, save the changes, and the Twitter feed will show up
    on your site.

== Installation ==

Extract the zip file and just drop the contents in the wp-content/plugins/
    directory of your WordPress installation and then activate the Plugin from
    the Plugins page in your WordPress Dashboard.
```

Notice how the lines with the equal signs separate the file into different sections. When the plugin's page is generated, the text at the topmost line with the three equal signs on each side (which I refer to as the *header section*) is used as the plugin's name, and the text after the Description and Installation sections is used to populate the Description and Installation tabs on the plugin's page.

Much more can be done with a readme.txt file than what is shown in this example. This is a very small and simplified version of what you can see in active plugins with well-crafted readme.txt files.

If you're concerned about whether your plugin's readme.txt file adheres to the expectations of the WordPress Plugin Directory, use the WordPress validator tool (http://wordpress.org/extend/plugins/about/ validator) to validate the file. This tool tells you whether your readme. txt file contains all the necessary components and information. If you're still having problems, there is a very handy readme.txt file generator located at http://sudarmuthu.com/wordpress/wp-readme that helps you generate a valid readme.txt file for your plugin by making sure that the basic requirements are met.

Setting up the header section

The header section at the top of the file is very similar to the file header in the actual plugin file. This similarity is because, like the file header, the header section is parsed by code in order to format the data in specific ways. The format of the header section is as follows:

```
=== Plugin Name ===
entry: value
entry: value
entry: value

Brief description of the plugin.
```

The plugin name and short description are required and should be unique to the plugin and description. As with the description in the file header, this description should be brief and kept to one to three sentences.

You can add a number of entries to the header section. Table 6-1 lists the available entries for the header section. Unless otherwise noted, each entry should be considered to be required and should be included in the header section.

Table 6-1 **Entries for the readme.txt File Header Section**

Component	Description
Contributors	Comma-separated list of contributors' wordpress.org usernames. If valid usernames are not used, the plugin page will not properly link to each contributor's other plugins.
Donation Link	Web address for a page that accepts donations for the plugin. This entry is optional.
License	How the plugin is licensed. This is typically GPLv2.
License URI	The web address that contains the full details of the license. This is typically `http://www.gnu.org/licenses/gpl-2.0.html`.
Requires at least	This is the lowest version of WordPress that your plugin is known to be compatible with. If you haven't tested the plugin with older versions of WordPress or don't test updated versions of the plugin with older versions of WordPress, set this to be the latest version of WordPress to ensure that you don't indicate compatibility that may not be there.
Stable tag	Indicates the sub-version tag of the latest stable version of your plugin. If no stable tag is provided, it is assumed trunk is stable.
Tags	A comma-separated list of descriptive tags that relate to the plugin. You can find a listing of existing tags at `http://wordpress.org/extend/plugins/tags`.
Tested up to	The highest WordPress version number you've successfully tested your plugin on. Prerelease versions of WordPress (such as 3.5-beta3) can be used if the plugin is compatible with the development version.

Adding other sections

After the header section, the rest of the readme.txt file is dedicated to providing information used to create the plugin's Plugin Directory page. This information is divided into a number of sections that neatly display on the plugin's page as tabs. The following lists each of the tabs, what they are meant to be used for, and any special details to know about each of them:

✦ **Description:** This tab is shown by default, so put the information that you want people to see when they first visit the plugin's page in this section. Focus on providing information about what features the plugin offers, what makes the plugin different from other plugins that may have similar features, and any requirements that may prevent people from successfully using the plugin.

✦ **Installation:** Any special instructions on how to properly install and configure the plugin should be included in this section.

✦ **Frequently Asked Questions:** Are users asking you the same questions over and over again? Do you expect certain questions? This is the place for you to answer your users' questions in one place.

✦ **Changelog:** This section is helpful for listing the changes in each version. Be sure to include details about new features, enhancements, and bug fixes so that current users that are curious about the reason for the new release can easily find what to expect after the upgrade. It is common to remove older listings because this section gets long. The number of listings to keep is up to you.

✦ **Screenshots:** This section is for listing pictures and videos that show the plugin in action. The screenshots follow a specific format:

  • Add them to the plugin's sub-version repository in the /assets directory.

  • Name them screenshot-1.png, screenshot-2.png, screenshot-3.png, and so on.

  • The supported formats are PNG, JPEG, and GIF.

    Add a description for each screenshot by using a numbered list. The description is displayed below the image with the matching number.

✦ **Other Notes:** The Other Notes tab is special in that it is created by merging all other sections. So, you can create as many custom sections as you like and have each of the custom sections appear inside the Other Notes tab.

The following example shows a readme.txt with each of these sections:

```
=== Lisa's Twitter Widget ===
Contributors: lisasabinwilson
Stable tag: 1.0.0
Donation link: http://example.com
Tags: twitter, widget, social media
```

```
Requires at least: 3.3
Tested up to: 3.5
License: GPLv2
License URI: http://www.gnu.org/licenses/gpl-2.0.html

Display Twitter feeds in any sidebar on your site.

== Description ==

Lisa's Twitter Widget users the power of WordPress's widget system to allow you
    to quickly and easily add a Twitter feed to your site. After adding the
    Twitter Widget to one of your sidebars, enter the desired Twitter username
    in the widget's options, save the changes, and the Twitter feed will show up
    on your site.

== Installation ==

Extract the zip file and just drop the contents in the wp-content/plugins/
    directory of your WordPress installation and then activate the Plugin from
    the Plugins page in your WordPress Dashboard.

== Frequently Asked Questions ==

= Can the widget combine the feeds from more than one username? =

Not at this time. Such a feature may be added in a future version. For now, you
    will simply have to use more than one widget.

= Can I load a feed for a hashtag? =

Yes. Rather than supplying a username, a hashtag can be used (ensure that you add
    the # before the hashtag) to show the latest feed for that hashtag.

== Changelog ==

= 1.0.0 =
* Release-ready version
* Fixed issue with feed caching not working properly, causing site slowdowns.

= 0.0.1 =
* Development version. It still has some bugs.

== Screenshots ==
1. Configuration options for the Twitter Widget.
2. The Twitter Widget showing a feed on the site.

== Thanks ==

My thanks to Twitter and its fantastic API. If it wasn't for the API, this plugin
    would not be possible.
```

**Book VII
Chapter 6**

Exploring Plugin
Development Best
Practices

TIP

The Markdown format has many options for formatting the content. Go to `http://daringfireball.net/projects/markdown/syntax` for full details on what options are available with Markdown.

Besides setting up plugin pages in the Plugin Directory, the `readme.txt` file serves two other very important purposes: controlling the released version of the plugin and offering content to the search function in the Plugin Directory.

The `readme.txt` file found in your plugin's SVN trunk controls the released version of the plugin. After updating the plugin with a new version number, the stable version value in the `/trunk/readme.txt` file needs to be updated to reflect this new version number. If you don't update this value, the new version won't be released.

Internationalizing or Localizing Your Plugin

WordPress users exist across the United States, Russia, Japan, Germany, and all points in between. Therefore, the next person to download and use your plugin may not speak the same language you do. So if you wrote and distributed your plugin in English, it may be useless to the next person if he speaks only German. However, the WordPress software has internationalization built into it, which means it can be *localized,* or translated, into different languages.

You aren't translating the file into different languages (unless you want to). Rather, you're providing a mechanism of support for people who will want to provide translation for your plugin through the creation of `.mo` (machine object) files (discussed later in this chapter). Many people in different countries create (and have created) `.mo` files for the translation of WordPress into different languages; by providing localization for your plugin, you're enabling them to translate your plugin text, as well. If you're interested in translating WordPress into a different language, check out this resource page in the WordPress Codex at `http://codex.wordpress.org/Translating_WordPress`.

Using GetText functions for text strings

WordPress provides you with two main localization functions: `__` and `_e`. These functions use the `GetText` translation utility installed on your web server. These two functions let you wrap plain text into strings of text to be translated. You need to account for two types of text strings in your plugin file:

✦ **HTML:** Example: `<h1>Plugin Name</h1>`

  To wrap HTML text strings within the `GetText` function call, you would wrap it using the `_e` function like this:

```
<h1><?php _e('Plugin Name', 'plugin-name'); ?></h1>
```

  This tells PHP to echo (`_e`) or display the string of text on your Web browser screen, but adds the benefit of using the `GetText` function, which allows for that string of text to be translated.

✦ **PHP:** Example: `<?php comments_number('No Responses', 'One Response', '% Responses' );?>`

To wrap PHP text strings with the `GetText` function, you would wrap it using the `__` function, like this:

```
<?php comments_number(__('No Responses',plugin-name),('One Response',
    'plugin-name'),( '% Responses', 'plugin-name') );?>
```

Unlike the echo function (`_e`), the `__` function is used when you need to add a string of text to an existing function call (in this case, `comments_number()`).

Avoid slang when writing your text strings in your plugin file. Slang is significant to only a certain demographic (age, geographic location, and so on) and may not translate well into other languages.

The second argument within the `GetText` string for the PHP text string example is `plugin-name`. This defines the domain of the text and tells `GetText` to return the translations only from the dictionary supplied with that domain name. This is the *plugin text domain* and most plugin authors use the name of their plugin (separated by hyphens) as the definer. Use the text domain in your `GetText` functions to ensure that `GetText` pulls the dictionary you supply instead of attempting to pull the text from the core WordPress language files because some of the text you provide in your plugin is unique and, most likely, won't exist within the WordPress core language files.

In a plugin file, you define the text domain like this:

```
$my_translator_domain    = PLUGIN-NAME;
$my_translator_is_setup = 0;
function fabfunc_setup(){
  global $my_translator_domain, $my_translator_is_setup;
  if($my_translator_is_setup) {
    return;
  }
  load_plugin_textdomain($my_translator_domain,
      PLUGINDIR.'/'.dirname(plugin_basename(__FILE__)),
      dirname(plugin_basename(__FILE__)));
}
```

These lines of code simply tell WordPress where your plugin file is located (the text domain), which in turn informs WordPress about where your `.pot`, or translation file, is for your specific plugin.

Creating the POT file

After you create your plugin and include all text strings within the `GetText` functions of `__` and `_e`, you need to create a `.pot` (portable object template) file, which contains translations for all the strings of text that you wrapped in the `GetText` functions. Typically, you create the `.pot` file in your own language, in a special format, thereby allowing other translators to create their own `.po` (portable object) file or an `.mo` (machine object) file in their language, using yours as the guide to translate by.

The .pot file is the original translation file, and the .po file is a text file that includes your original text (from the .pot) along with the translation for the text; or you can use an .mo file, which is basically the same as a .po file. However, while .po files are written in plain text meant to be human read-able, .mo files are compiled to make it easy for computers to read. Most web servers use .mo files to provide translations for .pot files.

WordPress has an extensive .pot file that you can use as a template for your own. You can download it at

```
http://svn.automattic.com/wordpress-i18n/pot/trunk/
    wordpress.pot
```

Additionally, .pot files can be translated into .mo files using free translation tools available online, such as Poedit (www.poedit.net), which is a free tool that takes the original .pot file and the provided translations in a .po file and merges them into a compiled .mo file for your web server to deliver the translated text.

The .pot file begins with a *header* section, which contains required information about what your translation is for. The .pot header section looks like this:

```
# LANGUAGE (LOCALE) translation for WordPress.
# Copyright (C) 20114 WordPress contributors.
# This file is distributed under the same license as the WordPress package.
# FIRST AUTHOR <YOU@YOUREMAIL.COM>, 2011.
#
#, fuzzy
msgid ""
msgstr ""
"Project-Id-Version: WordPress VERSION\n"
"Report-Msgid-Bugs-To: \n"
"POT-Creation-Date: 2011-01-01 12:00-0600\n"
"PO-Revision-Date: 2011-01-01 12:00-0600\n"
"Last-Translator: YOUR FULL NAME <YOU@YOUREMAIL.COM>\n"
"Language-Team: LANGUAGE <EMAIL@EMAIL.COM>\n"
"MIME-Version: 1.0\n"
"Content-Type: text/plain; charset=CHARSET\n"
"Content-Transfer-Encoding: 8bit\n"
```

All the capitalized, italicized terms in this code example are placeholders. Replace these terms with your own information.

The format of the .pot file is specific and needs to contain the following information:

✦ **Filename:** The name of the file in which the text string exists. For exam-ple, if the plugin file is wordpress-twitter-connect.php, you need to include that filename in this section.

✦ **Line of code:** The exact line number of the text string in question.

✦ **msgid:** The source of the message, or the exact string of text that you included within one of the GetText functions, either __ or _e.

✦ **msgstr:** A blank string where the translation (in the subsequent .pot files) is inserted.

For your default .pot file, to format a text string using the GetText function (<h1><?php _e('WordPress Twitter Connect'); ?></h1>), which exists on the second line in the wordpress-twitter-connect.php plugin file, you include three lines in the .pot file that look like this:

```
#: wordpress-twitter-connect.php:2
msgid: "WordPress Twitter Connect"
msgstr: ""
```

You need to go through all the text strings in your plugin file that you wrapped in the GetText functions and define them in the .pot file in the format provided. Now, if anyone wants to create a .po file for your plugin in a different language, he or she simply copies their language translation of your .pot file between the quotation marks for the msgstr: section for each text string included in the original .pot file.

All .pot and .po (or .mo) files need to be included in your plugin folder in order for the translations to be delivered to your website. Have a look at the directory structure of the popular WordPress All In One SEO Pack plugin in Figure 6-2: You can see the original .pot file along with the translated .mo files listed within the /wp-content/plugins/all-in-one-seo-pack/ plugin folder.

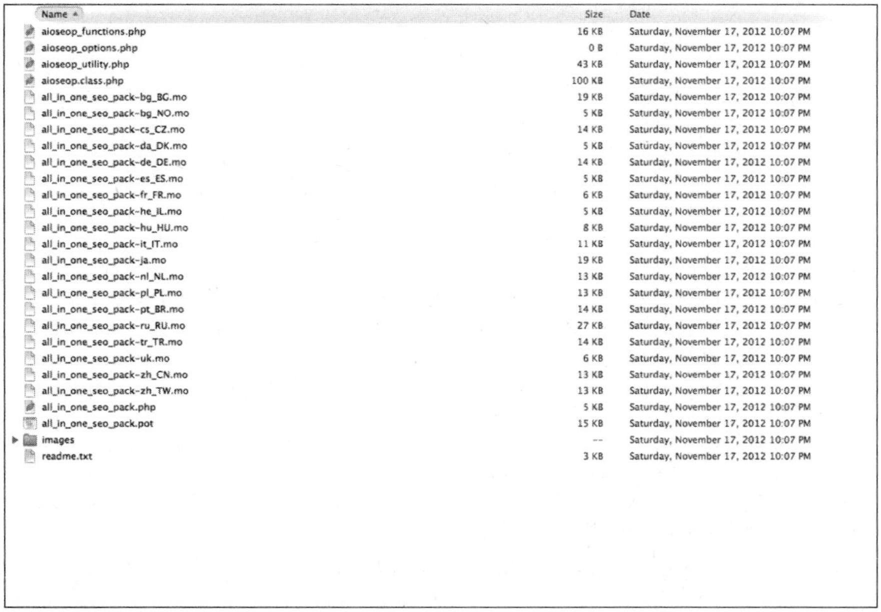

**Book VII
Chapter 6**

Exploring Plugin Development Best Practices

Figure 6-2: The .pot and .mo files for WordPress All In One SEO Pack plugin.

You, or other translators, can create unlimited `.mo` files for several different languages. Make sure that you name the language file according to the standardized naming conventions for the different languages. The naming convention for the languages is `language_COUNTRY.mo`. For example, the French `.mo` file for the `wordpress-twitter-connect.php` plugin is `wordpress-twitter-connect-fr_FR.mo`.

A full list of language codes can be found at

`http://www.w3schools.com/tags/ref_language_codes.asp`

And a full list of country codes can be found at

`http://www.iso.org/iso/country_names_and_code_elements`

Chapter 7: Plugin Tips and Tricks

In This Chapter

✓ **Using a plugin template**

✓ **Making your plugin pluggable**

✓ **Enhancing plugins with CSS and JavaScript**

✓ **Custom post types**

✓ **Exploring little-known useful hooks**

✓ **Using custom shortcodes**

*W*hen you have a WordPress plugin or two under your belt, you'll discover that you want to interact with many more parts of WordPress. WordPress is constantly coming out with new functionality and, with it, new API (Application Programming Interface) hooks, known as *action* and *filter hooks,* covered in Chapter 5 of this minibook. This chapter discusses some of this functionality and offers you some ways to extend your use of WordPress plugins. Because this functionality involves some simple programming skills, I assume (for the purposes of this chapter) that you have some basic PHP and WordPress plugin development knowledge.

Using a Plugin Template

When you start writing WordPress plugins, you find that you spend a significant amount of time rewriting the same things. Typically, most plugins have the same basic structure and are set up the same way, meaning that they all deal with settings pages, storing options, and interacting with particular plugins, among other things. You can save hours of work each time you start a new plugin if you create a template.

Such a template varies from person to person, depending on programming styles, preferences, and the types of plugins you want to include. For instance, if you often write plugins that use your own database tables, you should include tables in your template. Similarly, if your plugins almost never require options pages, leave those out of your template.

To create your own template, determine what functionality and structure your plugins usually contain. Follow these steps:

1. Create your file structure.

As you write more plugins, you find yourself repeating the same general filenames. If you find that you're including enough JavaScript and CSS in your plugins to necessitate their own files or directories, include these in your template. For example, if you're using a lot of JavaScript or CSS, you could modify the file structure of your plugin template to look something like the one shown in Figure 7-1.

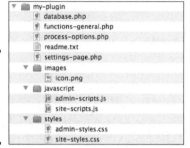

Figure 7-1:
The recommended file structure for a plugin.

2. Determine what functionality you generally have in your plugins.

If you usually contain masses of code in a class, you can set up a basic class for your plugin template. Likewise, if your plugins typically have a single options page or a system of top-level and submenu pages, you can set up a general template.

3. Create your primary plugin PHP file.

Usually, this file just contains some general `add_action` calls, file includes, and other general initializations. (Check out Chapter 5 of this minibook for information on `add_action` calls and other plugin functions.) If you always call certain actions, set them up in your primary plugin PHP file template. For instance, if you always register a plugin function to be run when the plugin is activated (`register_activation_hook`) and add a menu item for the plugin in the Dashboard (`admin_menu`), add those calls to your primary template.

```php
<?php
$myInstance = new myPlugin();

add_action('register_activation_hook','my_activation_plugin');
add_action('admin_menu',array($myInstance, 'admin_menu'));

?>
```

4. Set up the functions you use most often in the body of your primary plugin PHP file, after you add them in Step 3.

The line of code used here — `function my_activation_plugin` — was added in Step 3 through the use of the `add_action` hook. In your plugin template, you define any scripts your plugin uses by adding this function, which then fires when a user activates the plugin:

```php
<?php

function my_activation_plugin(){
//plugin activation scripts here
}
?>
```

5. **(Optional) Create your basic class structure.**

   To do this, you might add a few lines of code that resemble the following:

```php
<?php
class myPlugin {
     var $options = ;
     var $db_version = '1';
     function myPlugin() {
     add_action('admin_init',array($this,'admin_init');
     }
     function admin_init(){
          //admin initializations
     }
     function process_options($args,$data){
          //process our options here
     }
     function admin_menu(){
          //code for admin menu
     }
     function __construct(){
          //PHP 5 Constructor here
     }
} //end class
?>
```

   Obviously, your class template may be more detailed than that, depending on your particular coding styles and the types of plugins you like to write.

In addition to these steps, you might want to set up a basic plugin options page along with plugin options management scripts. Everyone uses different techniques for such things as processing plugin options, and after you determine your particular type, include the basic format in your template.

As your programming style, WordPress, or your interest in different types of plugins changes over time, you will find that your template needs change, too. Make sure that you update your template.

Making Your Plugin Pluggable

The WordPress API provides a great solution for hooking in and extending or modifying its functionality. Sometimes, however, you may find that it would be useful to hook into another plugin, rather than WordPress itself, and extend or modify its functionality instead.

Here's an example of making your plugin pluggable: an issue about interaction (or lack of) between WP e-Commerce (`http://getshopped.org`) and the All in One SEO Pack plugin. All in One SEO Pack, among other things, adds a custom document title, description, keywords, and canonical URL to each page on a WordPress site. People often ask how to have their plugin modify this information before it displays onscreen. Forum plugins and shopping cart plugins particularly have this need, which All in One SEO Pack could easily satisfy if it would just provide a method of accessing its functionality, which it has — read on.

WP e-Commerce (and other plugins with similar functionality) creates its own virtual pages for product listings, and so on, all contained on a single WordPress page. For example, if you define `http://mywebstore.com/shop` as the WordPress page WP e-Commerce uses, then `http://mywebstore.com/shop/product-name` and all other product pages are dynamically created by the WP e-Commerce plugin and are outside the reach of other WordPress plugins. So, WordPress and the All in One SEO Pack plugin don't know about them. You can see the problem that this would create for SEO purposes; WordPress and All in One SEO Pack would think that all these product pages are really the same page as the shop page, with the same titles, canonical URL, and so on. Code could have been written into the plugin to compensate for the needs of the WP e-Commerce, but that would be never ending because there are infinite possibilities for other plugins that may need to hook into the All in One SEO Pack functions. So, the All in One SEO Pack API was born.

The WP e-Commerce plugin has an important need to hook into the document title, meta description, meta keywords, and canonical URL that the All in One SEO Pack plugin produces. Because WordPress and All in One SEO Pack weren't aware of the generated product pages, they all had the same canonical URL, which is detrimental for SEO purposes. The fix was simple. In the All in One SEO Pack plugin, after the canonical URL is generated, and immediately before printing it to the screen, the `apply_filters` function is used on the variable. This allows WP e-Commerce to use `add_filter` to hook in and filter the canonical URL, returning the appropriate URL for that page. That is, in the All in One SEO Pack plugin, they added the following:

```
function prepare_canonical_url(){
    $canonical_url = my_determine_canonical_url_function();
    $new_canonical_url = apply_filters( 'aioseop_canonical_url',$canonical_url);

    return $new_canonical_url;
}
```

This returns the value of the canonical URL and lets another plugin filter it, if desired, prior to returning the final value.

The part you can now add in the primary WP e-Commerce plugin file (at the end of the file before the closing ?>) is just as simple, and it works the same way `add_filter` does for hooking into the WordPress API.

```
add_filter('aioseop_canonical_url','wpec_change_canonical_url');

function wpec_change_canonical_url($old_url){
    $new_url = determine_current_product_page_url($old_url);
    return $new_url;
}
```

This filter provides a simple solution to allow other plugins (and themes) to hook into a plugin, without the need to add code specific to any one plugin.

Enhancing Plugins with CSS and JavaScript

You can add functionality to a plugin in many ways. The following sections look at two methods: CSS styling and JavaScript. You may never develop a plugin that uses either, but it's still useful to understand how to include them. Chances are good that you, as a budding plugin developer, may need this information at some point.

Calling stylesheets within a plugin

Controlling how your plugin's output looks onscreen (whether in the WordPress Dashboard or on the front end of the website or blog) is best done through a stylesheet. If you've been around web design and HTML, you're probably familiar with CSS (cascading style sheets). Nearly every styling aspect for a website is controlled by a stylesheet, and WordPress is no exception. If you want to read the authoritative guide to stylesheets, visit the W3C.org website at www.w3.org/Style/CSS. (For more on CSS, see Book VI.)

You can use a single stylesheet to control how your Plugin Options page looks on the Dashboard, how your plugin widget looks on the Dashboard, or how your plugin displays information on the front-end website.

 Create and use a separate stylesheet for the plugin within the Dashboard and the plugin's display on the front end because the stylesheets are called at different times. The back-end stylesheet is called when you're administering your site on the WordPress Dashboard, whereas the front-end stylesheet is called when a user visits the website. Additionally, it makes management of styling easier and cleaner.

The best practice for adding stylesheets within your plugin is to create a /styles directory — for example, /my-plugin/styles. Place your stylesheets for the back end and front end inside this directory, as shown in Figure 7-2.

Figure 7-2:
The file
structure
for a plugin
showing
stylesheets.

To call a stylesheet from your plugin, you should use the built-in WordPress `wp_enqueue_style` function because it creates a queuing system in WordPress for loading stylesheets only when they're needed, instead of on every page. Additionally, it has support for dependencies so you can specify whether your stylesheet depends on another that should be called first. This queuing system is used for scripts, too. Moreover, the `wp_enqueue_scripts` function does the same for scripts which I discuss a little later in this section.

Say you're creating a gallery plugin to display images on your website. You want your gallery to look nice, so you want to create a stylesheet that controls how the images display. Here's how to call that stylesheet in your plugin using a simple function and action hook (these lines of code get added to your primary plugin PHP file at the end, just before the closing `?>` tag):

1. **Create a function in your primary plugin PHP file to register your stylesheet and invoke `wp_enqueue_style`.**

```
function add_my_plugin_stylesheet() {
    wp_register_style('mypluginstylesheet', '/wp-content/plugins/
      my-plugin/styles/site-style.css');
    wp_enqueue_style('mypluginstylesheet');
}
```

2. **Use the `wp_print_styles` action hook and call your function.**

```
add_action( 'wp_print_styles', 'add_my_plugin_stylesheet' );
```

Here's a breakdown of the hooks in the function:

✦ **The `wp_register_style` function registers your stylesheet for later use by `wp_enqueue_style`.**

```
wp_register_style( $handle, $src, $deps, $ver, $media )
```

The function has a number of parameters; the first is `$handle`, which is the name of your stylesheet.

`$handle` must be unique. You can't have more than one stylesheet with the same name in the same directory.

The second parameter is `$src`, the path to your stylesheet from the root of WordPress. In this case, it's the full path to the file within the plugin's `styles` directory.

The remaining parameters are optional. To find out more about them, read the WordPress documentation on this function at `http://codex.wordpress.org/Function_Reference/wp_register_style`.

✦ **The `wp_enqueue_style` function queues the stylesheet.**

```
wp_enqueue_style( $handle, $src, $deps, $ver, $media )
```

The `$handle` parameter is the name of your stylesheet as registered with `wp_register_style`. The `$src` parameter is the path, but you don't need this parameter because you registered the stylesheet path already. The remaining parameters are optional and explained in the WordPress documentation on this function at `http://codex.wordpress.org/Function_Reference/wp_enqueue_style`.

✦ **The action hook that calls the function uses `wp_print_styles` to output the stylesheet to the browser.**

Figure 7-3 shows the plugin stylesheet being called in the `<HEAD>` section of the site source code.

**Book VII
Chapter 7**

Plugin Tips and Tricks

Figure 7-3:
The source code of a website showing the plugin stylesheet being called.

Another example uses a stylesheet for the plugin's admin interface, which controls how your plugin option page within the Dashboard will appear. These lines of code also get added to your plugin's primary PHP file (just prior to the closing `?>` tag):

```
add_action('admin_init', 'myplugin_admin_init');

function myplugin_admin_init() {
  wp_register_style('mypluginadminstylesheet', '/wp-content/plugins/
   my-plugin/admin-styles.css');
   add_action('admin_print_styles' 'myplugin_admin_style');
   function myplugin_admin_style() {
     wp_enqueue_style('mypluginadminstylesheet');
   }
}
```

This example uses some hooks that are specific to the WordPress Dashboard:

✦ The action hook calls `admin_init`. This makes sure that the function is called when the Dashboard is accessed. The callback function is `myplugin_admin_init`.

✦ The function registers the stylesheet, using `wp_register_style`.

✦ An action hook calls the `myplugin_admin_style` function. The `admin_print_styles` hook is used because it's specific to the WordPress Dashboard display.

✦ The function then queues the stylesheet, using `wp_enqueue_style`.

Figure 7-4 shows the plugin stylesheet being called in the source code of the Plugin Options page on the Dashboard.

Calling JavaScript within a plugin

After using the `wp_register_style` and `wp_enqueue_style` functions to call stylesheets within a plugin, you can see how similar functions can call JavaScript, which has many uses within a plugin.

JavaScript can control functionality within a form or display something with an effect. WordPress comes with some JavaScript in the core that you can call in your plugin or you can write your own. Like stylesheets, it's best to store JavaScript in a separate subdirectory within your plugin: for example, `/my-plugin/javascript`.

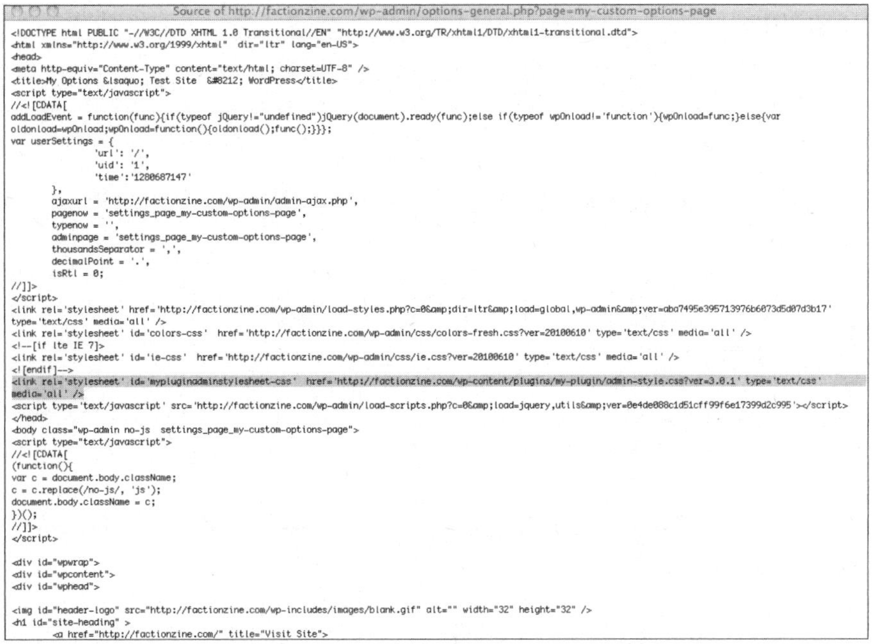

Source of http://factionzine.com/wp-admin/options-general.php?page=my-custom-options-page

```
<!DOCTYPE html PUBLIC "-//W3C//DTD XHTML 1.0 Transitional//EN" "http://www.w3.org/TR/xhtml1/DTD/xhtml1-transitional.dtd">
<html xmlns="http://www.w3.org/1999/xhtml"  dir="ltr" lang="en-US">
<head>
<meta http-equiv="Content-Type" content="text/html; charset=UTF-8" />
<title>My Options &lsaquo; Test Site  &#8212; WordPress</title>
<script type="text/javascript">
//<![CDATA[
addLoadEvent = function(func){if(typeof jQuery!="undefined")jQuery(document).ready(func);else if(typeof wpOnload!='function'){wpOnload=func;}else{var
oldonload=wpOnload;wpOnload=function(){oldonload();func();}}};
var userSettings = {
                'url': '/',
                'uid': '1',
                'time':'1280687147'
        },
        ajaxurl = 'http://factionzine.com/wp-admin/admin-ajax.php',
        pagenow = 'settings_page_my-custom-options-page',
        typenow = '',
        adminpage = 'settings_page_my-custom-options-page',
        thousandsSeparator = ',',
        decimalPoint = '.',
        isRtl = 0;
//]]>
</script>
<link rel='stylesheet' href='http://factionzine.com/wp-admin/load-styles.php?c=0&amp;dir=ltr&amp;load=global,wp-admin&amp;ver=aba7495e395713976b6073d5d07d3b17'
type='text/css' media='all' />
<link rel='stylesheet' id='colors-css'  href='http://factionzine.com/wp-admin/css/colors-fresh.css?ver=20100610' type='text/css' media='all' />
<!--[if lte IE 7]>
<link rel='stylesheet' id='ie-css'  href='http://factionzine.com/wp-admin/css/ie.css?ver=20100610' type='text/css' media='all' />
<![endif]-->
<link rel='stylesheet' id='mypluginadminstylesheet-css'  href='http://factionzine.com/wp-content/plugins/my-plugin/admin-style.css?ver=3.0.1' type='text/css'
media='all' />
<script type='text/javascript' src='http://factionzine.com/wp-admin/load-scripts.php?c=0&amp;load=jquery,utils&amp;ver=0e4de088c1d51cff99f6e17399d2c995'></script>
</head>
<body class="wp-admin no-js  settings_page_my-custom-options-page">
<script type="text/javascript">
//<![CDATA[
(function(){
var c = document.body.className;
c = c.replace(/no-js/, 'js');
document.body.className = c;
})();
//]]>
</script>

<div id="wpwrap">
<div id="wpcontent">
<div id="wphead">

<img id="header-logo" src="http://factionzine.com/wp-includes/images/blank.gif" alt="" width="32" height="32" />
<h1 id="site-heading" >
        <a href="http://factionzine.com/" title="Visit Site">
```

Figure 7-4: The source code of the Plugin Options page on the Dashboard showing the plugin stylesheet being called.

Instead of using `wp_register_style` and `wp_enqueue_style` to register and queue JavaScript, you must use `wp_register_script` and `wp_enqueue_script`. They work in much the same way and have much the same parameters. Here's an example to be added to your plugins primary PHP file, near the end before the closing `?>` tag:

```
if ( !is_admin() ) {
   wp_register_script('custom_script','/wp-content/plugins/
     my-plugin/javascript/custom-script.js',);
   wp_enqueue_script('custom_script');
}
```

Immediately, you notice that the `wp_enqueue_script` function loads scripts in the front end of your website and on the Dashboard. Because this can cause conflicts with other scripts used by WordPress on the Dashboard display, the "if is not" (`!is_admin`) instruction tells the plugin to load JavaScript only if it's not being loaded on the Dashboard. This code loads `custom-script.js` only on the front end of the website (that is, what your site visitors see). You could add a more specific conditional `if` instruction to load JavaScript only on a certain page.

If you want to load the JavaScript in `wp-admin`, the action hook `admin_init` loads your callback function when `wp-admin` is accessed and the `admin_print_script` function outputs the script to the browser, just like the stylesheet example.

Custom Post Types

One of the most confusing features of WordPress is custom post types. It is also a useful, powerful, and easy feature to implement and use after you understand how it works. WordPress has five default post types:

✦ **Post:** The most commonly used post type. Content appears in a blog in reverse sequential time order.

✦ **Page:** Similar to a post, but pages don't use the time-based structure of posts. Pages can be organized in a hierarchy and have their own URLs off the main site URL.

✦ **Attachment:** This special post type holds information about files uploaded through the WordPress Media upload system.

✦ **Revisions:** This post type holds past revisions of posts and pages as well as drafts.

✦ **Nav Menus:** This post type holds information about each item in a navigation menu.

A post type is really a type of content stored in the `wp_posts` table in the WordPress database. The post type is stored in the `wp_posts` table in the `post_type` column. The information in the `post_type` column differentiates each type of content so that WordPress, a theme, or a plugin can treat the specific content types differently.

When you understand that a post type is just a method to distinguish how different content types are used, you can investigate custom post types.

Say you have a website about movies. Movies have common attributes — actors, directors, writers, and producers. But say you don't want to store your movie information in a post or a page because it doesn't fit either content type. This is where custom post types become useful. You can create a custom post type for movies and apply the common attributes of actors, directors, and so on. A theme can handle movies differently than a post or a page by having a custom template for the `movies` post type and create different styling attributes and templates for the `movies` post type. You can search and archive movies differently than you can with posts and pages.

Here's how to create a simple custom post type in WordPress by adding these lines of code into the Theme Functions template file (located in the theme file and called `functions.php`):

```
add_action('init','create_post_type');                          →1
function create_post_type() {
  register_post_type( 'movies',                                 →3
    array(                                                      →4
      'labels' => array(                                        →5
        'name' => ('Movies'),
        'singular_name' => ('Movie'),
        'rewrite' => array('slug' => 'movies'),
      ),
      'public' => true,
    )                                                           →11
  );
}
```

Here's what's going on in the code:

→1 The first line is the action hook. This uses `'init'` so that it's called on the front end and on the Dashboard to display the custom post type in both.

→3 The callback function starts with the `register_post_type` function and the custom post type name. This is what creates the custom post type and gives it properties.

→4 Next is an array of arguments that are the custom post type properties.

→5 The `'labels'` arguments include the name that displays on the Dashboard menu, the name that will be used (Movies), and what is used for the slug in the URL to the posts (`http://`*yourdomain*`.com/ movies`, for example) in this custom post type.

→11 The `'public'` argument controls whether the custom post type displays on the Dashboard.

Figure 7-5 shows how the Custom Post Type page and menu item look on the Dashboard. Figure 7-6 shows a custom post type on a website.

Many other arguments associated with `register_post_type` give this function its real power. For full documentation on all the arguments and the use of this function, check out

`http://codex.wordpress.org/Function_Reference/register_ post_type`

Custom post types are also discussed in detail in Book VI, Chapter 6.

**Book VII
Chapter 7**

**Plugin Tips and
Tricks**

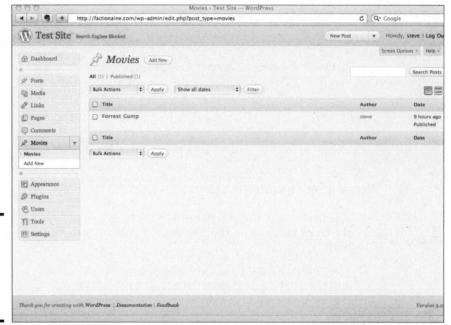

Figure 7-5:
A custom post type on the WordPress Dashboard.

Figure 7-6:
A custom post type shown on a website.

Using Custom Shortcodes

One of the most common inefficiencies with plugins is when a plugin wants to add information within the body of a post or page. The plugin developer manually creates a bloated filtering function, hooks into `the_content` (the function tag that calls the body of the content from the database and delivers it to your website), and filters it in an attempt to find the appropriate spot to display the information. Fortunately, WordPress has a built-in solution for this. Using the shortcode API, your users can easily choose where in a given post to display the information your plugin is providing them.

The basic premise is that you have a string of data that your plugin dynamically generates, and you want your users to determine where in each post and page it displays. From your users' perspective, they will type a shortcode like this within the body of their content in order to display information from a plugin:

```
[myshortcode]
```

On the developer side, you just use the `add_shortcode` function and add it to your primary plugin PHP file:

```
<?php add_shortcode($tag, $func); ?>
```

The `add_shortcode` function accepts two parameters:

✦ The `$tag` parameter is the string that users will type within the body of their content to make a call to the plugin shortcode. (From the previous example, `[myshortcode]` is what the users type, so your `$tag` parameter would be `myshortcode`.)

✦ The `$func` parameter is your callback function (a function that you still need to define in the body of your primary plugin PHP file, covered in the next section) that returns the output of the called shortcode.

The shortcode function gets added to your primary plugin PHP code, near the bottom, before the closing `?>` tag:

```
add_shortcode('myshortcode','my_shortcode');

function my_shortcode(){
    return "this is the text displayed by the shortcode";
}
```

In this example, you added the shortcode hook `add_shortcode ('myshortcode', 'my_shortcode');` and then gave definition to the function (`$func`) called `my_shortcode` by telling WordPress to output the text: `this is the text displayed by the shortcode`.

All your user has to do is type **[myshortcode]** somewhere in the body of his post/page editor (on the Dashboard, hover your pointer over Post and then click the Add New link), as shown in Figure 7-7. When users view the site, the shortcode the user entered in the body of her post is now translated by WordPress and displays the returned value, or *output,* of the shortcode function, as shown in Figure 7-8.

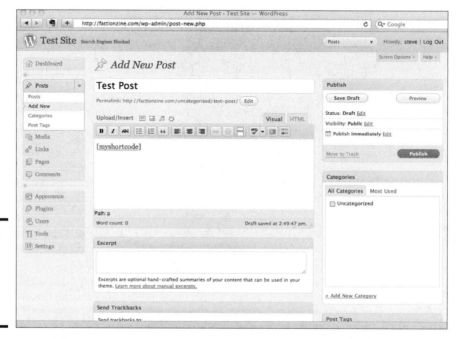

Figure 7-7:
The post editor showing a simple shortcode.

Figure 7-8:
The shortcode is replaced by the returned value of the shortcode function.

Shortcode names must be unique to your own plugin, so you may want to give it a name that is specific to your plugin. For example, if your plugin is called "Super SEO Plugin," you could name your shortcode: [superseoplugin code] in an attempt to make sure that no other plugin uses your shortcode. Another plugin using a shortcode with the same name will cause a conflict.

Shortcodes can include arguments to be passed into the shortcode function.

```php
<?php
add_shortcode('myshortcode','my_shortcode');

function my_shortcode($attr, $content){
    return 'My name is ' . $attr['first'] . $attr['last'];
}
```

Calling this with

```
[myshortcode first="John" last="Smith"]
```

outputs My name is John Smith.

Adding Functionality to Profile Filters

WordPress provides four contact methods by default: AIM, Yahoo! IM, and Jabber/Google Talk. These are, of course, extensible, meaning that you can easily add new contact methods through the use of filters. It's painless to add more, and you can even add on a little extra functionality while you're at it.

Users fill out their profile data on the WordPress Dashboard by hovering the pointer over Users and then clicking the Your Profile link. (See Book III, Chapter 1.) User profile fields are stored in the WordPress database in the user_metadata table, and you can easily fetch them by using get_the_author_meta('aim') and print them with the_author_meta('aim'). If you add a Twitter Contact Info field, it appears in profiles, and you can use the_author_meta('twitter') template tags in your theme to print the account name.

Figure 7-9 shows the Twitter Contact Info field in a profile within the WordPress Dashboard.

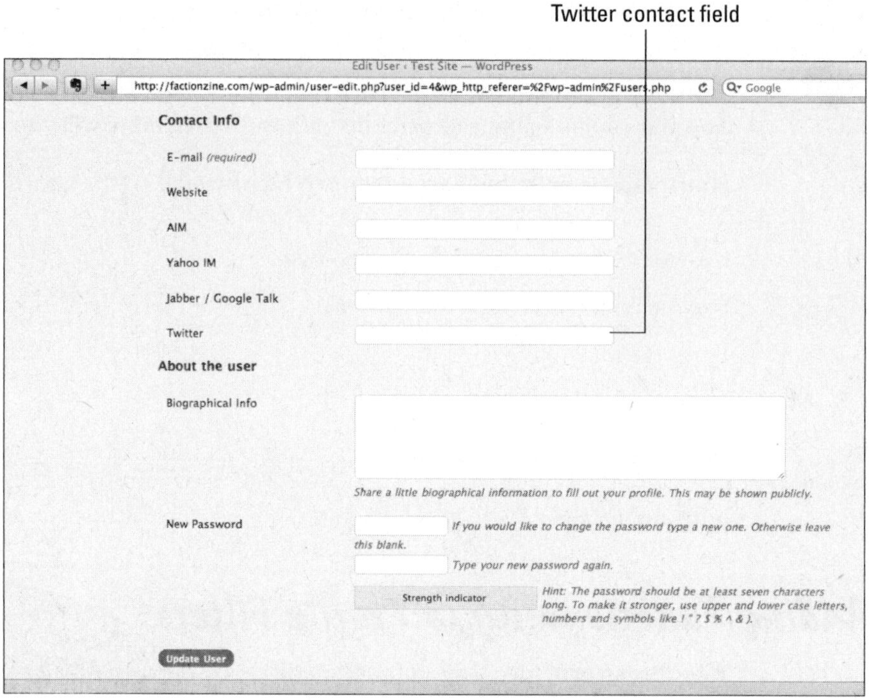

Twitter contact field

Figure 7-9:
Custom
Twitter
profile field,
as shown
on the
Dashboard.

the_author_meta() template tag has a hook called the_author_{$field}, where the PHP variable $field is the requested meta field assigned to each contact type in the user profile files, such as aim in the previous example. These dynamic hooks are powerful because they allow you to narrow your target.

In this example, I use the dynamic the_author_twitter hook to change the result from "lisasabinwilson" to <a href="http://twitter.com/lisasabinwilson">@lisasabinwilson</a>. When you call the_author_meta('twitter') in your theme, you get a clickable link to my Twitter profile. Start by entering the following lines of code in your Theme Functions file (functions.php) in your active theme folder (add this code toward the bottom of the file before the closing ?> tag):

```
/**
 * Add Twitter to the list of contact methods captured via profiles.
 */
function my_add_twitter_author_meta( $contact_methods ) {
$contact_methods['twitter'] = 'Twitter';
return $contact_methods;
}
```

```
add_filter( 'user_contactmethods', 'my_add_twitter_author_meta' );

/**
 * Convert staff Twitter accounts to links to twitter.com.
 */

function my_link_author_twitter_accounts( $value ) {
if ( strlen( $value ) ) {
$url = esc_url( 'http://twitter.com/' . $value );
$value = '<a href="' . $url . '">@' . esc_html( $value ) . '</a>';
}
return $value;
}
add_filter( 'the_author_twitter', 'my_link_author_twitter_accounts' );
```

Correcting Hyperlink Problems

Most websites use underline to style hyperlinks. When producing content in WordPress, highlighting words and phrases quickly to add hyperlinks can lead to hyperlinking (and underlining) the spaces before and after your anchor text.

For some people, this is enough to convince them to hide underlines for hyperlinks, even though that may not be desired.

Here's a snippet that filters through blog post content and ensures that you don't have any spaces on the wrong side of the tag or between a closing tag and punctuation. Add this in your Theme Functions (`functions.php`) file:

```
/**
 * Prevents underlined spaces to the left and right of links.
 *
 * @param string $content Content
 * @return string Content
 */

function my_anchor_text_trim_spaces( $content ) {
// Remove spaces immediately after an <a> tag.
$content = preg_replace( '#<a([^>]+)>\s+#', ' <a$1>', $content );
// Remove spaces immediately before an </a> tag.
$content = preg_replace( '#\s+</a>#', '</a> ', $content );
// Remove single spaces between an </a> tag and punctuation.
$content = preg_replace( '#</a>\s([.,!?;])#', '</a>$1', $content );
return $content;
}
add_filter( 'the_content', 'my_anchor_text_trim_spaces' );
```

**Book VII
Chapter 7**

Plugin Tips and Tricks

HTML ignores more than one space in a row (also more than one tab character and line break) unless you're using the pre element or nonbreaking space entities (` `). Therefore, even if your converted text contains two consecutive spaces, the browser won't show it any differently.

Book VIII

Running Multiple Sites with WordPress

Visit www.dummies.com/extras/wordpressaio to find out how the multisite feature developed.

Contents at a Glance

Chapter 1: An Introduction to Multiple Sites

In This Chapter

✓ Discovering where multiple sites began

✓ Exploring what you can do with multiple sites

✓ Configuring your web server

This chapter introduces you to the multisite feature that's built into the WordPress software. The multisite feature allows you, the site owner, to add and maintain multiple blogs within a single installation of WordPress. In this chapter, you discover how the multisite feature works and why you might want to use it. You also explore how to configure and set up your web server environment for use with the multisite feature.

With the multisite feature enabled, users of your network can run their own sites within your installation of WordPress. They also have access to their own Dashboard with the options and features you read about in the previous minibooks. Heck, it's probably a good idea to buy a copy of this book for the members of your network so they can become familiar with the WordPress Dashboard and features, too. At least have a copy on hand so people can borrow yours!

Deciding When to Use the Multisite Feature

Usually, for multiple users to post to one site, WordPress is sufficient. The multiuser part of the WordPress MU name didn't refer to how many users were added to your WordPress website, really. MU was always a bit of a misnomer and an inaccurate depiction of what the software actually did. A *network of sites* is a much closer description.

Determining whether to use the multisite feature depends on user access and publishing activity. Each site in the network, although sharing the same codebase and users, is still a self-contained unit. Users still have to access the back end of each site to manage options or post to that site. A limited number of general options are network-wide, and posting is not one of them.

You can use multiple sites in a network to give the appearance that only one site exists. Put the same theme on each site, and the visitor doesn't realize that they're separate. This is a good way to separate sections of a magazine site, using editors for complete sections (sites) but not letting them access other parts of the network or the back end of other sites.

Another factor to consider is how comfortable you are with editing files directly on the server. Setting up the network involves accessing the server directly, and ongoing maintenance and support for your users can often lead to the network owner doing the necessary maintenance, which is not for the faint of heart.

Generally, you should use a network of sites in the following cases:

✦ **You want multiple sites and one installation.** You're a blogger or site owner who wants to maintain another site, possibly with a subdomain or a separate domain, all on one web host. You're comfortable with editing files, you want to work with one codebase to make site maintenance easier, and most of your plugins and themes are accessible to all the sites. You can have one login across the sites and manage each site individually.

✦ **You want to host blogs or sites for others.** This is a little more involved. You want to set up a network where users can sign up for their own sites or blogs underneath (or part of) your main site and you maintain the technical aspects for them.

Because all files are shared, some aspects have been locked down for security purposes. One of the most puzzling security measures for new users is the suppression of errors. Most PHP errors (say you installed a faulty plugin or incorrectly edited a file) don't output messages to the screen. Instead, what appears is what I like to call the White Screen of Death.

Knowing how to find and use error logs and do general debugging are necessary skills for managing your own network. Even if your web host will set up the ongoing daily or weekly tasks for you, managing a network can involve a steep learning curve.

When you enable the multisite feature, the existing WordPress site becomes the main site in the installation.

Although WordPress can be quite powerful, in the following situations the management of multiple sites has its limitations:

✦ **One web account is used for the installation.** You can't use multiple hosting accounts.

✦ **You want to post to multiple blogs at one time.** WordPress doesn't do this by default.

✦ **If you choose subdirectory sites, the main site will regenerate permalinks with /blog/ in it to prevent collisions with subsites.** There are existing plugins available to prevent this regeneration.

The best example of a large blog network with millions of blogs and users is the hosted service at WordPress.com (`http://wordpress.com`). At WordPress.com, people are invited to sign up for an account and start a blog using the multisite feature within the WordPress platform on the WordPress server. When you enable this feature on your own domain and enable the user registration feature, you're inviting users to do the following:

+ Create an account.

+ Create a blog on your WordPress installation (on your domain).

+ Create content by publishing blog posts.

+ Upload media files such as photos, audio, and video.

+ Invite friends to view their blog or to sign up for their own account.

Understanding the Difference between Sites and Blogs

With the merger of WordPress MU and WordPress came a terminology change. Each additional blog under WordPress MU is now a *site* instead of a *blog*. But, what's the difference?

Largely, it's one of perception. Everything functions the same, but people can see greater possibilities when they no longer think of each site as "just" a blog. Now, WordPress can be so much more:

+ With the addition of the Domain Mapping plugin (see Chapter 6 in this minibook), you can manage multiple sites with different, and unique, domain names. None of them has to be a blog. They can have a blog element, or just use pages and have a static site.

+ The built-in options let you choose between subdomains or subfolder sites when you install the network. If you install WordPress in the root of your web space, you get subdomain.*yourdomain.com* (if you choose subdomains) or *yourdomain.com*/subfolder (if you choose subfolders). Chapter 2 of this minibook discusses the differences and advantages.

After you choose the kind of sites you want to host and then create those sites, you can't change them later on. These sites are served virtually, meaning that they don't exist as files or folders anywhere on the server. They exist only in the database. The correct location is served to the browser by using rewrite rules in the .htaccess file. (See Book II, Chapter 5.)

+ The main, or parent, site of the network can also be a landing page of the entire network of sites, showcasing content from other sites in the network and drawing in visitors further.

Setting Up the Optimal Hosting Environment

This chapter assumes that you already have the WordPress software installed and running correctly on your web server and that your web server meets the minimum requirements to run WordPress.

Before you enable the WordPress multisite feature, you need to determine how you are going to use the feature. You have a couple of options:

✦ Manage just a few of your own WordPress blogs or websites.

✦ Run a full-blown blogging network with several hundred different blogs and multiple users.

If you're planning to run just a few of your own sites with the WordPress multisite feature, then your current hosting situation is probably well suited. However, if your plans are to host a large network with hundreds of blogs and multiple users, you should consider contacting your host and increasing your bandwidth, as well as the disk space limitations on your account.

In addition to the necessary security measures, time, and administrative tasks that go into running a community of blogs, you have a few more things to worry about. Creating a community increases the resource use, bandwidth use, and disk space on your web server. In many cases, if you go over the allotted limits given to you by your web host, you will incur hefty costs. Make sure that you anticipate your bandwidth and disk space needs before running a large network on your website! (Don't say I didn't warn you.)

Checking out shared versus dedicated hosting

Many WordPress network communities start with grand dreams of developing a large and active community. Be realistic about how your community will operate in order to make the right hosting choice for yourself and your community.

Small blogging communities can be handled easily by using a shared-server solution, whereas larger, more active communities may require a dedicated-server solution for operation. The difference between the two lies in their names:

✦ **Shared-server solution:** You have one account on one server that has several other accounts on it. Think of this as apartment living. One apartment building has several apartments for multiple people to live, all under one roof.

✦ **Dedicated-server solution:** You have one account. You have one server. That server is dedicated to your account, and your account is dedicated to the server. Think of this as owning a home where you don't share your living space with anyone else.

A dedicated-server solution is a more expensive investment for your blog community, while a shared-server solution is the most economical. Your decision on which solution to use for your network blogging community will be based on your realistic estimates of how big and how active your community will be. You can move from a shared-server solution to a dedicated-server solution if your community gets larger than you expected; however, starting with the right solution for your community from day one is easier.

Exploring subdomains versus subdirectories

The WordPress multisite feature gives you two ways to run a network of blogs on your domain. You can use the subdomain option or the subdirectory option. The most popular option (and recommended structure) sets up subdomains for the blogs created within WordPress network of sites. With the subdomain option, the username of the blog appears first, followed by your domain name. With the subdirectory option, your domain name appears first, followed by the username of the blog. Which one should you choose? The choice is yours. You can see the difference in the URLs of these two options by comparing the following examples:

✦ A **subdomain** looks like this: `http://username.yourdomain.com`

✦ A **subdirectory** looks like this: `http://yourdomain.com/username`

While the network is being set up, tables are added (to the database) that contain information about the network, including the main site URL. If you're developing a site or want to change the domain later, you need to change every reference to the domain name in the database. Look at Book II, Chapter 3 to find more about the WordPress database structure, including how data is stored in tables, as well as the use of a popular database administration tool called phpMyAdmin to manage, view, and edit database tables.

Choosing Linux, Apache, MySQL, and PHP server environments

A network of sites works best on a LAMP (Linux, Apache, MySQL, and PHP) server with the `mod_rewrite` Apache module enabled. `Mod_rewrite` is an Apache module that builds URLs that are easier to read. (Also, see the nearby "Apache mod_rewrite" sidebar for more information.) In WordPress, this Apache module is used for permalinks. If your install uses any permalink other than the default, `?p=123`, then you're okay. Your web host can help you determine whether your web server allows this. It is a requirement for setting up the WordPress multisite feature. (You can find more information on permalink structure in Book III, Chapter 2.)

For the purposes of this chapter, I stick to the LAMP server setup because it is most similar to the average web host and is most widely used.

Apache mod_rewrite

Apache (`http://httpd.apache.org`) is software that's loaded and running on your web server. Usually, the only person who has access to Apache files is the web server administrator. (This is usually your web host.) Depending on your own web server account and configuration, you may or may not have access to the Apache software files.

The Apache module that's necessary in order for the WordPress network to create nice permalink URLs is called `mod_rewrite`. This must be configured so that it's active and installed on your server.

You or your web host can make sure that the Apache `mod_rewrite` is activated on your server; open the `httpd.conf` file and verify that the following line is included within:

```
LoadModule rewrite_module /
    libexec/mod_rewrite.so
```

If it isn't, type that line on its own line and save the file. You probably need to restart Apache before the change takes effect.

Remember that the Apache `mod_rewrite` module is required for WordPress multisites. If you don't know whether your current hosting environment has this module in place, drop an e-mail to your hosting provider and ask. The provider can answer that question for you (in addition to installing the module for you in the event that your server doesn't yet have it).

Networks also work well on Nginx and Lightspeed servers; however, many users have reported having much difficulty on IIS (Windows) servers. Therefore, I don't recommend setting up WordPress with multisite features on a Windows server environment.

Subdomain sites work by way of a virtual host entry in Apache, also known as a wildcard subdomain. On shared hosts, your web hosting provider support team will have to enable this for you, or they may already have done so for all accounts. It is best to ask your hosting provider before you begin. In these situations, the domain you use for your install must be the default domain in your account. Otherwise, the URLs of your subsites will fail to work properly or to have a folder name in the URL.

Some hosts may require you to have a dedicated IP address, but this isn't a specific software requirement for a WordPress network to function.

Before proceeding with the final steps in enabling the WordPress multisite feature, you need to get a few items in order on your web server. You also need to make a decision about how the multiple blogs within your network will be handled. These configurations need to be in place in order to run the WordPress network successfully.

Adding a virtual host to the Apache configuration

You need to add a hostname record pointing at your web server in the DNS configuration tool available in your web server administration software, such as WebHost Manager (WHM), a popular web host administration tool.

In this section, you edit and configure Apache server files. If you can perform the configurations in this section yourself (and if you have access to the Apache configuration files), this section is for you. If you don't know how, are uncomfortable with adjusting these settings, or don't have access to change the configurations in your web server software, you need to ask your hosting provider for help or hire a consultant to perform the configurations for you. I can't stress enough that you shouldn't edit the Apache server files yourself if you aren't comfortable with it or don't fully understand what you're doing. Web hosting providers have support staff to help you with these things if you need it — take advantage of that!

The hostname record looks like this: *.*yourdomain.com* (where *your domain.com* is replaced with your actual domain name). Follow these steps to enable the wildcard subdomains in Apache:

1. **Log in as the root user to your server.**

2. **Open the `httpd.conf` file or the `vhost include` file for your current web account.**

3. **Find the virtual host section for your domain.**

4. **Add the wildcard subdomain record next to the domain name.**

It will look like this:

```
ServerAlias yourdomain.com *.yourdomain.com
```

5. **Save the file.**

6. **Restart Apache.**

You also need to add a wildcard subdomain DNS record. Depending on how your domain is set up, you can do this at your registrar or your web host. If you simply pointed to your web host's nameservers, then you can add more DNS records at your web host in the web server administration interface, such as WHM (Web Host Manager).

You also should add a CNAME record with a value of *. CNAME stands for Canonical Name and is a record stored in the DNS settings of your Apache web server that tells Apache you would like to associate a new subdomain with the main account domain. Applying the value of * tells Apache to send any subdomain requests to your main domain, and from there, WordPress looks up that subdomain in the database to see whether it exists.

Networks require a great deal more server memory (RAM) than typical WordPress sites (not using the multisite feature), simply because multisites are generally bigger, have a lot more traffic, and use up more database space and resources because multiple sites are running (as opposed to just one with regular WordPress). You aren't simply adding instances of WordPress. You're multiplying the processing and resource use of the server when you run the WordPress multisite feature. Although smaller instances of a network run okay on most web hosts, you may find that when your network grows, you need more memory. I generally recommend that you start with a hosting account that has access to at least 256MB of RAM (memory).

For each site created, nine additional tables are added to the single database. Each table has a prefix similar to `wp_BLOG-ID_tablename` (where `BLOG-ID` is a unique ID assigned to the site).

The only exception to this is the main site. Its tables remain untouched, and remain the same. (See Book II, Chapter 3 to see how its tables look.) With WordPress multisites, all new installations leave the main blog tables untouched and number additional site tables sequentially, with every new site that is added to the network.

Much discussion about the database layout has occurred in Trac, the WordPress codebase management system, and in the WordPress.org forums. Although Trac may seem unwieldy, it scales appropriately. Limitations on database size have more to do with the server and database management tools. The average users build a small to medium-sized network, which usually needs no more than a VPS (Virtual Private Server) account.

Chapter 2: Setting Up and Configuring Network Features

In This Chapter

✔ **Enabling the network**

✔ **Configuring the network installation**

✔ **Disabling the network**

This chapter covers how to find the files you need to edit the network, how to enable multiple sites in the network, and how to remove the network should you no longer want to have multiple sites in your WordPress install.

By default, access to network settings is disabled to ensure that users don't set up their network without researching all that the setup entails. Setting up a network is more than configuring options or turning on a feature. Before enabling and setting up a network, be sure that you read Chapter 1 of this minibook.

What you need:

✦ Backups of your site (explained in Book II, Chapter 7)

✦ Access to the `wp-config.php` file for editing (Book II, Chapter 5)

✦ Enabled wildcard subdomains (covered in Chapter 1 of this minibook) if you're using subdomains

Enabling the Network Feature

You need to enable access to the network menu so you can set up the network and allow the creation of multiple sites.

Before you begin your edits, make a copy of your `wp-config.php` file and keep it in a safe place on your computer.

Follow these steps:

1. **Connect to your web server via FTP.**

   If you need a refresher on FTP, refer to Book II, Chapter 2.

2. **Locate the `wp-config.php` file in the root or `/public_html` directory of your website.**

   This file is with the main WordPress files.

3. **Open the `wp-config.php` file for editing in your favorite text editor.**

   For Windows users, Notepad does the trick. For Macs, use TextMate.

4. **Find the line that reads `define('DB_COLLATE', '');`. Click at the end of that line. Press Enter to create a new blank line.**

   Some FTP clients let you right-click the filename on the server and choose Edit to edit the file within your FTP program, depending on which program you are using.

5. **Type** define('WP_ALLOW_MULTISITE', true);.

   This line of code tells WordPress that you intend to use the multisite feature; additionally, it activates the Network option under the Tools menu on your WordPress Dashboard (covered later in this chapter).

6. **Save the `wp-config.php` file and upload it to your website.**

When you log in to the Dashboard of WordPress, you now see a Network Setup link on the Tools menu, as shown in Figure 2-1.

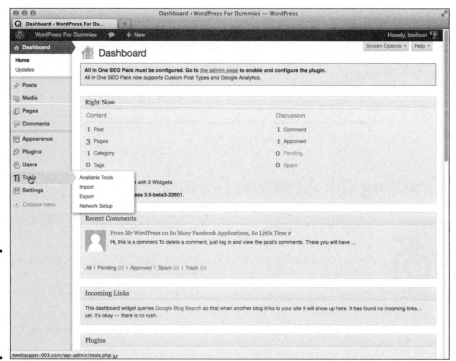

Figure 2-1:
The Network Setup link on the Tools menu.

Clicking this menu item displays the Create a Network of WordPress Sites page, covered in the next section. You also see a reminder to deactivate all your plugins before continuing with network setup.

Exploring the Difference between Subdirectories and Subdomains

Before you start setting up the network, the Create a Network page lets you choose the URL format of sites you're adding beneath the Addresses of Sites in your Network heading. By default, these sites are in subdomain format (`subdomain.yourdomain.com`) or subdirectory (`yourdomain.com/subdirectory`) format.

Figure 2-2 shows both choices displayed via radio buttons.

In some cases, depending on your setup, your choice here may be limited. WordPress does some autodetection with information about your installation and may prevent you from choosing an option that won't work with your setup.

Table 2-1 explains some of the situations you may encounter.

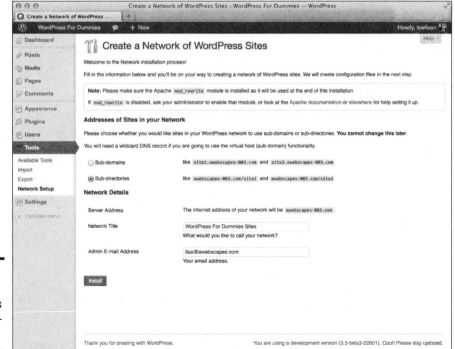

Figure 2-2: Choosing subdomains or subdirectories.

Table 2-1	Common Network Setup Situations	
Situation	*Format*
Site URL is different than Home URL.	Network cannot be enabled.
Site URL is `http://localhost`.	Subdirectories only.
Site URL is an IP address.	
WordPress is installed in a folder (for example, `http://domain.com/wp`).	
WordPress is installed in the root of the domain (`http://domain.com`).	Subdomains are default, but you can choose either.

Site addresses generate in a similar way. They don't really exist, and you won't see these site addresses in your directory structure on your web server because they are served to the browser *virtually* when that site is requested. From a technical standpoint, subdomains require an extra step in server setup for the wildcards. (Chapter 1 in this minibook covers setting up wildcard subdomains on the server side.) Subdomains are somewhat separated from the main domain, at least in terms of content. Subdirectories, on the other hand, are part of the main domain, as if they were pages off the main site.

The terms *subdirectory* and *subfolder* are interchangeable, but I stick to *subdirectory* for the purposes of this book.

Because each site's URL is saved in its tables in the database, after you pick which subsites you want to create, you cannot switch from subdirectories to subdomains (or vice versa) without reinstalling the network.

Each site format offers certain search engine optimization benefits. Search engines read subdomains as separate sites on your web host; therefore, they maintain their page rank and authority, and multiple results for your domain are listed. Subdirectories are read as pages or sections off your main domain. They also help the main domain's page rank and authority and provide one result for your domain in search engines.

If you want your extra sites to have separate domain names, you still need to pick one of these options. Chapter 6 of this minibook covers top-level domains.

Installing the Network on Your Site

The Network Details heading on the Create a Network of WordPress Sites page has options filled in automatically. The server address, for example, is pulled from your installation and is not editable. The Network Title and Administrator E-Mail Address are pulled from your installation database, too, because your initial WordPress site is the main site in the network. Click the Install button and WordPress creates new network tables in the database. The page refreshes, and the Enabling the Network page appears, as shown in Figure 2-3.

From the Enabling the Network page, follow these steps to install the multisite feature after you install the network. *Note:* These steps require that you edit web server files, so be sure to have your text editor program handy.

Figure 2-3:
The
Enabling the
Network
page.

1. **Add the network-related configuration lines to the `wp-config.php`.**

On the Create a Network of WordPress Sites page, WordPress gives you up to seven lines of configuration rules that need to be added to the `wp-config.php` file. The first line includes the line you added earlier in this chapter: `define('multisite', true );`. You can skip that line, copy the rest of the lines, and then paste them beneath the `define('multisite', true);` line in your `wp-config.php` file. The lines of code you add look like this:

```
define( 'SUBDOMAIN_INSTALL', false );
$base = '/ ';
define( 'DOMAIN_CURRENT_SITE', 'localhost' );
define( 'PATH_CURRENT_SITE', '/' );
define( 'SITE_ID_CURRENT_SITE', 1 );
define( 'BLOG_ID_CURRENT_SITE', 1 );
```

These lines of code provide configuration settings regarding subdomains, the base URL of your website, and your website's current path. Additionally, it assigns a unique ID of 1 to your website and blog for the main installation site of your multisite network.

The lines of code on the Create a Network of WordPress Sites page are unique to your installation of WordPress and specific to your site setup, so make sure that you copy the lines of code from your installation.

2. **Add the rewrite rules to the `.htaccess` file on your web server.**

WordPress gives you up to 13 lines of code that you need to add to the `.htaccess` file on your web server in the WordPress installation directory. The lines look something like this:

```
RewriteEngine On
RewriteBase /
RewriteRule ^index\.php$ - [L]

# add a trailing slash to /wp-admin
RewriteRule ^([_0-9a-zA-Z-]+/)?wp-admin$ $1wp-admin/ [R=301,L]

RewriteCond %{REQUEST_FILENAME} -f [OR]
RewriteCond %{REQUEST_FILENAME} -d
RewriteRule ^ - [L]
RewriteRule ^([_0-9a-zA-Z-]+/)?(wp-(content|admin|includes).*) $2 [L]
RewriteRule ^([_0-9a-zA-Z-]+/)?(.*\.php)$ $2 [L]
RewriteRule . index.php [L]
```

Chapter 1 of this minibook discusses the Apache `mod_rewrite` module. You must have it installed on your web server to run the WordPress multisite feature. The rules you add to the `.htaccess` file on your web server are `mod_rewrite` rules. They need to be in place so that your web server tells WordPress how to handle things, such as permalinks for blog posts and pages, media, and other uploaded files. Without these rules in place, the WordPress multisite feature won't work correctly.

3. **Copy the lines of code from the Enabling the Network page, open the `.htaccess` file, and paste the lines of code there.**

   Completely replace the rules that already exist in that file.

4. **Save the `.htaccess` file and upload it to your web server.**

5. **Click the login link at the bottom of the Enabling the Network page.**

   You're asked to log in to WordPress again because you have changed some of the browser cookie-handling rules in the `wp-config.php` and `.htaccess` files.

Completion of the installation steps activates a Network Admin menu item in the upper-right menu of links on your WordPress Dashboard. The Network Admin Dashboard is where you, as the site owner, administer and manage your multisite WordPress network. (See Chapter 3 of this minibook.)

Disabling the Network

At some point, you may decide that running a network of sites isn't for you, and you may find that you want to disable the multisite feature completely. Before disabling the network, you want to save any content from the other sites by making a full backup of your. Book II, Chapter 7 has detailed information about backing up your site if you need a refresher.

The first step is to restore the original `wp-config.php` file and `.htaccess` files that you saved earlier. This causes your WordPress installation to stop displaying the Network Admin menu and the extra sites.

You may also want to delete the tables that were added, which permanently removes the extra sites from your installation. Book II, Chapter 3 takes you through the WordPress database, including using a popular database administration tool called phpMyAdmin. You can use that tool to delete the multisite tables from your WordPress database when you want to deactivate the feature. The extra database tables that are no longer required when you aren't running the WordPress multisite feature include

✦ `wp_blogs`: This database table contains one record per site and is used for site lookup.

✦ `wp_blog_versions`: This database table is used internally for upgrades.

✦ `wp_registration_log`: This database table contains information on sites created when a user signs up, if they chose to create a site at the same time.

♦ `wp_signups`: This database table contains information on users who signed up for the network.

♦ `wp_site`: This database table contains one record per WordPress network.

♦ `wp_sitemeta`: This database table contains network settings.

Additionally, you can delete any database tables that have blog IDs associated with them. These tables start with prefixes that look like `wp_1_`, `wp_2_`, `wp_3_`, and so on.

WordPress adds new tables each time you add a new site to your network. Those database tables are assigned a unique number, incrementally.

Dealing with Common Errors

Occasionally, you might enter a configuration setting incorrectly or change your mind about the kind of network you require. If you installed WordPress, enabled the network, and then want to move it to a new location, you will encounter errors when changing the URL. The proper method is to move WordPress first, disable the network if you installed it, and then enable the network at the new location.

To change from subdomains to subfolders or vice versa, follow these steps:

1. **Delete the extra sites, if any were created.**

2. **Edit `wp-config.php`, changing the value of `define( 'SUBDOMAIN_INSTALL', true );` to `define( 'SUBDOMAIN_INSTALL', false );`.**

   To switch from subdomains to subdirectories, change `false` to `true`.

3. **Save the `wp-config.php` file and upload it to your website.**

4. **Visit the Dashboard of WordPress and click the Permalink link on the Settings menu and click the Save Changes button.**

   This step saves and resets your permalink structure settings and flushes the internal rewrite rules, which are slightly different in subdomains than they are in subdirectories.

You can't do this process if you want to keep extra sites.

Chapter 3: Becoming a Network Admin

In This Chapter

- ✓ **Getting familiar with the Network Admin Dashboard**
- ✓ **Managing your network**
- ✓ **Preventing spam blogs**

After you enable the WordPress network option and become a network admin, you can examine the various settings that are available to you and go over the responsibilities you have while running a network.

As a network admin, you can access the Network Admin Dashboard, which includes a number of submenus, to manage the sites in your network, as well as the overall settings for your network. This chapter discusses the menu items and options on the Network Admin page, guides you in setting network options, and discusses the best ways to prevent spam and spam blogs (splogs).

Exploring the Network Admin Dashboard

When you visit the Dashboard after activating the multisite feature, the toolbar includes the My Sites menu, which contains the Network Admin link, as shown in Figure 3-1. WordPress has separated the Network Admin features from the rest of the regular Dashboard features to make it easier for you to know which part of your site you're managing. For example, if you're performing items that maintain your main website, such as publishing posts or pages, creating/editing categories, and so on, you work on the regular Dashboard (as described in Book III). However, if you're managing any one of the network sites, plugins, and themes for the network sites or registered users, you need to work in the Network Admin section of the Dashboard.

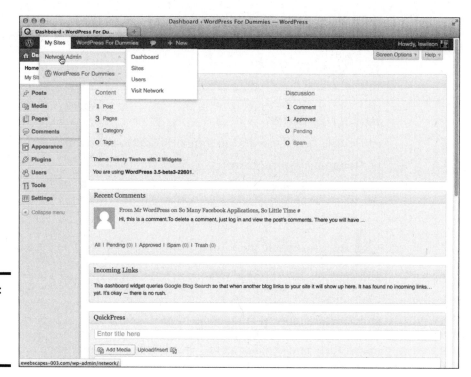

Figure 3-1:
The
Network
Admin
menu.

The distinct differences between the Site Admin Dashboard and the Network Admin Dashboard (and subsequent menu features) are important. WordPress tries its best to assume which features you're attempting to work with; however, if you find yourself getting lost on the Dashboard and you can't find a menu or feature that you're used to seeing, check to make sure that you're working in the correct section of the Dashboard.

The Network Admin Dashboard page (see Figure 3-2) looks similar to the regular WordPress Dashboard. Notice, however, that the modules shown on the Network Admin Dashboard pertain to the network of sites and give you options to create a new site, create a new user, and search existing sites and users. Obviously, you won't perform this search if you don't have any users or sites yet. However, this function is extremely useful when you have a community of users and sites within your network.

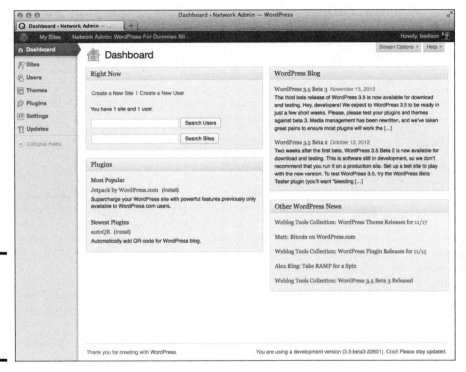

Figure 3-2:
The
Network
Admin
Dashboard
page.

The Network Admin Dashboard is configurable, just like the regular Dashboard; you can move the modules around and edit their settings. Refer to Book III, Chapter 1 for more information about arranging the Dashboard modules to suit your tastes.

The Search Users feature allows you to search usernames and user e-mail addresses. If you search for the user *Lisa,* for instance, your results include any user whose username or e-mail address contains *Lisa* — so you can receive multiple results when using just one search word or phrase. The Search Sites feature returns any blog content within your community that contains your search term, too.

The Network Admin Dashboard has two links near the top of the page that are very useful:

✦ **Create a New Site:** Click this link to create a new site within your network. When clicked, the Add New Site page appears where you can add a new site. Find out how to add a new site in the upcoming "Sites" section.

✦ **Create a New User:** Click this link to create a new user account within your community. When clicked, the Add New User page appears, allowing you to add a new user to your community. Find out how to add a new user in the "Users" section, later in the chapter.

Additionally, the Network Admin Dashboard gives you a real-time count of how many sites and users you have in your network, which is nice-to-know information for any network admin.

Managing Your Network

As mentioned, the Network Admin Dashboard has its own set of unique menus separate from the regular Site Admin Dashboard. Those menus are located on the left side of the Network Admin Dashboard. This section goes through each menu item and provides you with explanations and instructions on how to work with the settings and configurations to help you manage your network, sites, and users.

The full list of menus available on the Network Admin Dashboard offers these options:

✦ **Sites:** View a list of the sites in your network, along with details about them.

✦ **Users:** See detailed info about current users in your network.

✦ **Themes:** View all the currently available themes to enable or disable them for use in your network.

✦ **Plugins:** Manage (activate/deactivate) plugins for use on all sites within your network.

✦ **Settings:** Configure global settings for your network.

✦ **Updates:** Upgrade all sites in your network with one click.

All the items on the Network Admin Dashboard are important, and you will use them frequently throughout the life of your network. Normally, I would take you through each of the menu items in order so it would be easy for you to follow along on your Dashboard; however, it's important to perform some preliminary configurations on your network before you do anything else. Therefore, the following section starts with the Settings menu and then takes you through the other menu items in order of appearance on the Network Admin Dashboard.

Settings

When you click the Settings menu link on the Network Admin Dashboard, the Settings page appears. The Settings page contains several sections of options for you to configure to set up your network the way you want to.

When you finish configuring the settings on the Network Settings page, don't forget to click the Save Changes button at the bottom of the page, underneath the final Menu Settings section. (See Figure 3-7 later on in the chapter.) If you navigate away from the Network Settings page without clicking the Save Changes button, none of your configurations will be saved, and you'll need to go through the entire process again.

Operational Settings

The two options in the Operational Settings section, shown in Figure 3-3, are

✦ **Network Name:** This is the name for your overall network of sites. This name is included in all communications regarding your network, including e-mails that new users receive when they register a new site within your network. Type your desired network name in the text box provided.

✦ **Network Admin Email:** This is the e-mail address correspondence that your website is addressed from, including all registration and sign-up e-mails that new users receive when they register a new site or user account within your network. Enter the e-mail that you want to use for these purposes in the text box provided.

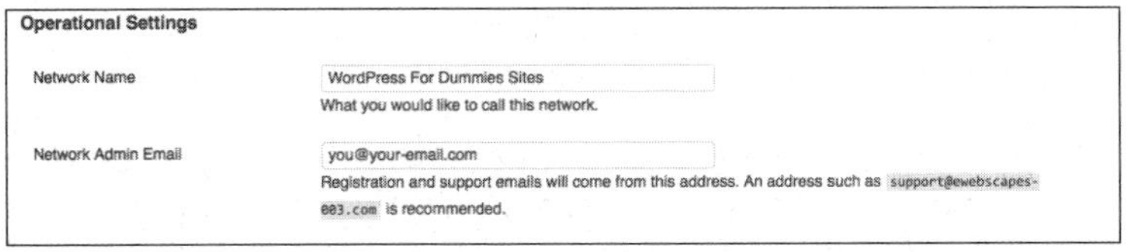

Figure 3-3:
The Operational Settings section on the network Settings page.

Operational Settings	
Network Name	WordPress For Dummies Sites
	What you would like to call this network.
Network Admin Email	you@your-email.com
	Registration and support emails will come from this address. An address such as support@ewebscapes-883.com is recommended.

Registration Settings

The Registration Settings section (see Figure 3-4) allows you to control aspects of allowing users to sign up to your network. The most important option is whether to allow open registration.

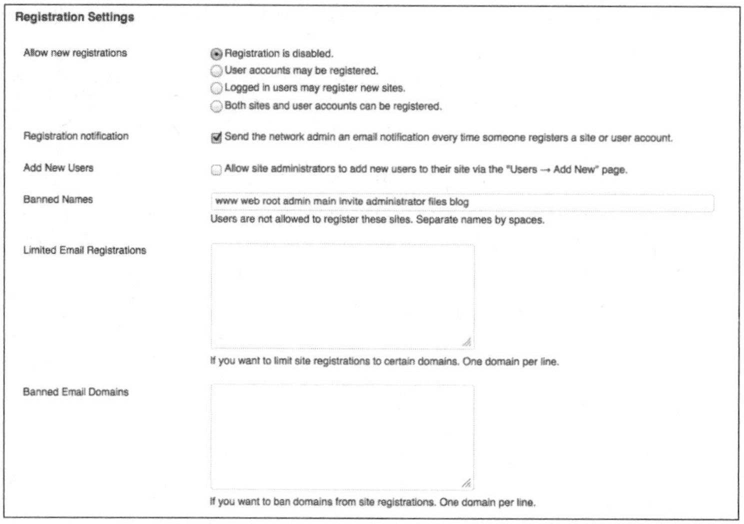

Figure 3-4:
The
Registration
Settings
section on
the network
Settings
page.

From one of the following options, decide how you want registrations to be handled on your network by selecting one of four options provided next to Allow New Registration:

✦ **Registration Is Disabled:** Disallows new user registration completely. When selected, this option prevents people who visit your site from registering for a user account.

✦ **User Accounts May Be Registered:** Gives people the ability to create only a user account; users won't be able to create a blog within your network.

✦ **Logged In Users May Register New Sites:** Allows only existing users — those who are already logged in — to create a new blog within your network. This option also disables new user registration completely. Use this option if you don't want just anyone registering for an account. Instead, you (as the site administrator) can add new users at your discretion.

✦ **Both Sites and User Accounts Can Be Registered:** Gives users the ability to register an account and a site on your network during the registration process.

These options apply only to outside users. As a network admin, you can create new sites and users anytime you want by using the options on the Network Admin Dashboard. (See the information about creating new users in the upcoming "Users" section.)

The remaining options under the Registration Settings heading are as follows:

✦ **Registration Notification:** When this option is selected, an e-mail is sent to the network admin every time a user or a site is created on the system, even if the network admin creates the new site.

✦ **Add New Users:** Select this check box if you want to allow your community blog owners (individual site admins) to add new users to their own community blog via the Users page within their individual dashboards.

✦ **Banned Names:** By default, WordPress bans several usernames from being registered within your community, including *www, web, root, admin, main, invite, administrator,* and so on. For good reason, you don't want a random user to register a username, such as *admin,* because you don't want that person misrepresenting himself as an administrator on your site. You can enter an unlimited amount of usernames that you don't want to allow on your site in the Banned Names text box.

✦ **Limited Email Registrations:** You can limit sign-ups based on e-mail domains by filling in this text box with one e-mail domain per line. If you have open registrations but you limited the e-mail addresses, only the people who have an e-mail domain that's on the list can register. This is an excellent option to use in a school or corporate environment where you're providing students or employees e-mail addresses and sites.

✦ **Banned Email Domains:** This feature, the reverse of Limited Email Registration, blocks all sign-ups from a particular domain, which can be useful in stopping spammers. For example, you can enter **gmail.com** in the field, and anyone trying to sign up with a Gmail address will be denied.

New Site Settings

The New Site Settings section (you need to scroll down to see it) is a configurable list of items that populates default values when a new site is created. The list includes the values that display in welcome e-mails, on a user's first post page, and on a new site's first page, as shown in Figure 3-5.

✦ **Welcome Email:** The e-mail text that owners of newly registered sites in your network receive when their registration is complete. There is a default message that you can leave in place if you like. Or, you can type the text of the e-mail you want new site owners to receive when they register a new site within your network.

A few variables you can use in this e-mail aren't explained entirely on the Site Options page, including the following:

• SITE_NAME: Inserts the name of your WordPress site

- BLOG_URL: Inserts the URL of the new member's blog

- USERNAME: Inserts the new member's username

- PASSWORD: Inserts the new member's password

- BLOG_URLwp-login.php: Inserts the hyperlinked login URL for the new member's blog

- SITE_URL: Inserts the hyperlinked URL for your WordPress site

✦ **Welcome User Email:** The e-mail text that gets automatically sent to a new user when she registers for an account in your network. You're able to use the variables from the previous section to personalize the e-mail a bit more, rather than using the default text shown in Figure 3-5.

✦ **First Post:** This is the first, default post that displays on every newly created site in your network. WordPress provides you with some default text that you can leave in place, or you can type your desired text in the provided text box that you want to appear in the first post on every site that's created in your community.

You can use this area to provide useful information about your site and services. This post also serves as a nice guide for new users because they can view it on the Dashboard's Edit Post page to see how it was entered and formatted and then use that as a guide for creating their own blog posts. You can also use the variables mentioned in the bullet points in the earlier Welcome Email option to have WordPress automatically add some information for you.

✦ **First Page:** Similar to the First Post setting, this default text for a default page displays on every newly created site in your network. (The First Page text box doesn't include default text; if you leave it blank, no default page is created.)

✦ **First Comment:** This default comment displays on the first default post on every newly created site within your network. Type the text that you want to appear in the first comment on every site that's created in your community.

✦ **First Comment Author:** Type the name of the author of the first comment on new sites in your network. (This option isn't shown in the figure — you need to scroll down to see it.)

✦ **First Comment URL:** Type the web address (URL) for the author of the first comment; this links (via hyperlink) the first comment author's name to the URL you type here. (This option also doesn't appear in the figure.)

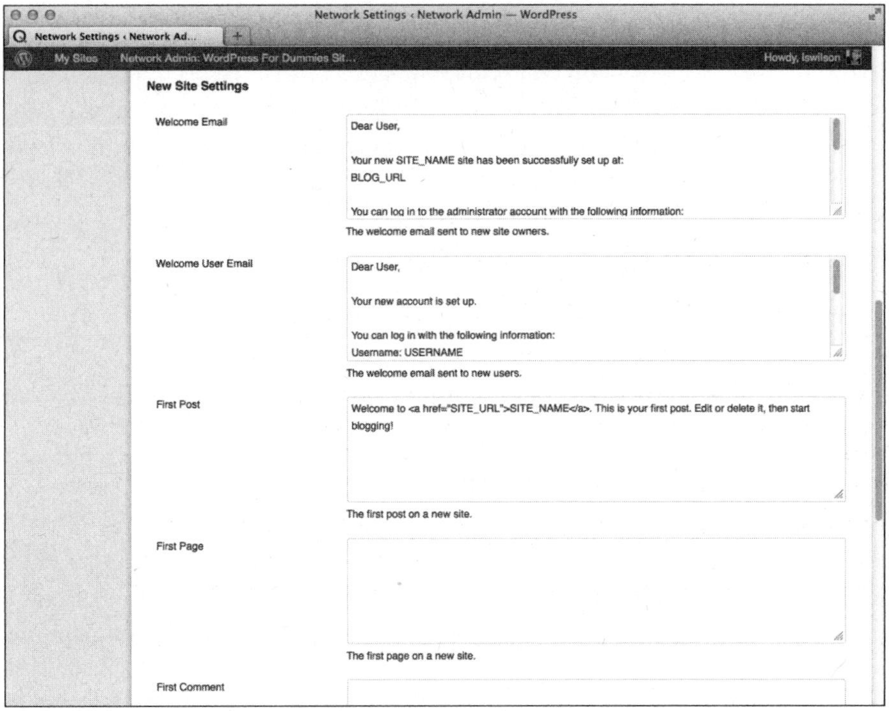

Figure 3-5:
The New
Site Settings
section on
the network
Settings
page.

Upload Settings

Scrolling down the network Settings page, you get to the Upload Settings section (see Figure 3-6), which defines global values pertaining to the type of files you will allow the site owners within your network to upload using the file upload feature on the WordPress Write Posts and Write Page areas. (See Book III, Chapter 3.) The fields shown under the Upload Settings section have default settings already filled in for you.

✦ **Site Upload Space:** If you leave this check box deselected, users are allowed to use all the space they want for uploads — no limits. Select the check box to limit the available space per site and then fill in the amount in megabytes (MB) — and the default storage space is 10MB. This amount of hard drive space is what you give users to store the files they upload to their blogs. If you want to change the default storage space, type a number in the text box provided. In Figure 3-6, you see that I set the upload space to 100MB.

✦ **Upload File Types:** This text field defines the types of files that you, as the network admin, allow site owners to upload to their sites on their Dashboards. Users cannot upload any file types that do not appear in

**Book VIII
Chapter 3**

**Becoming a
Network Admin**

this text box. By default, WordPress includes the following file types: `.jpg`, `.jpeg`, `.png`, `.gif`, `.mp3`, `.mov`, `.avi`, `.wmv`, `.midi`, `.mid`, and `.pdf`. You can remove any default file types and add new ones.

✦ **Max Upload File Size:** This amount is in kilobytes (K), and the default file size is 1500K. This means that a user cannot upload a file that is larger than 1500K. Adjust this number as you see fit by typing a new number in the text box provided.

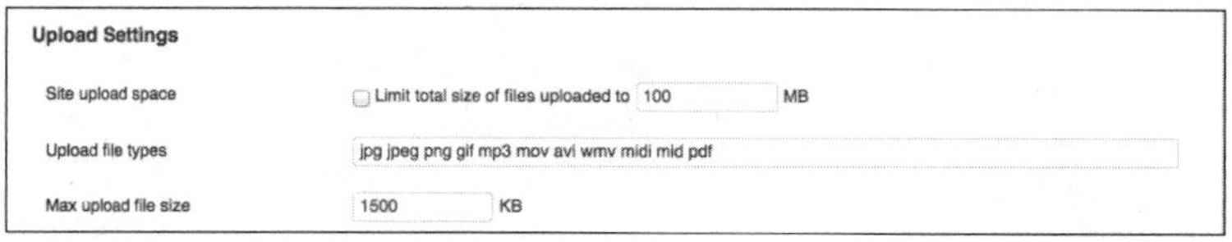

Figure 3-6:
The Upload Settings section on the network Settings page.

Upload Settings

Site upload space	☐ Limit total size of files uploaded to 100 MB
Upload file types	jpg jpeg png gif mp3 mov avi wmv midi mid pdf
Max upload file size	1500 KB

Menu Settings

The Plugins menu is disabled within the Dashboard of all network sites (except for the network admin's), as shown in Figure 3-7. However, you always have access to the Plugins menu. If you leave this option deselected, the Plugins page will be visible to users on their own site Dashboards. Select the check box if you want to enable the Plugins menu for your network users. For more information about using plugins with WordPress, see Book VII.

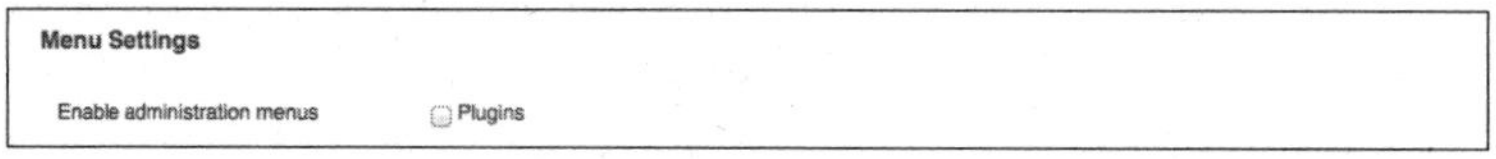

Figure 3-7:
The Network Setting page's Menu Settings section.

Menu Settings

Enable administration menus	☐ Plugins

Sites

Clicking the Sites menu item on the Network Admin Dashboard takes you to the Sites page, where you can manage your individual sites. Although each site in the network has its own Dashboard for basic tasks, such as posting, changing themes, and so on, the Sites page is where you create and delete sites and make edits to properties of the sites within your network. Editing information from this page is handy when you have issues accessing a site's back-end Dashboard.

The Sites page also lists all the sites within your network. The listing shows the following statistics about each community site:

✦ **Path:** The site's path in your network. For example, in Figure 3-8, you see a site listed with the path /newsite/. This means that the site's domain is newsite.*yourdomain.com* if you're using a subdomain setup, or *yoursite.com*/newsite if you're using a subdirectory setup.

✦ **Last Updated:** The date the site was last updated (or published to).

✦ **Registered:** The date the site was registered in your network.

✦ **Users:** The username and e-mail address associated with the user(s) of that site.

When you hover your pointer on the pathname of a site in your network, you see a handy listing of links that help you manage the site. Figure 3-8 shows the options that appear beneath a site listing when you hover your mouse on a site name in the list.

Figure 3-8:
The individual site management options on the Sites page.

The management options for network sites, most of them showing in Figure 3-8, are as follows:

✦ **Edit:** A link to the Edit Site page (see Figure 3-9), where you can change aspects of each site.

✦ **Dashboard:** A link to the Dashboard of the site.

✦ **Deactivate:** Click this link to mark the site for deletion in your network; after clicking the Deactivate link, a message displays in a pop-up window that asks you to confirm your intention to deactivate the site. Click the Yes button to confirm. The user's site displays a message stating that the site has been deleted. You can reverse this action by revisiting the Sites page and clicking the Activate link that appears underneath the site pathname. (The Activate link appears only underneath sites that are marked as Deactivated.)

✦ **Archive:** Click this link to archive the site in your network, which prevents visitors from viewing the site and displays `This site has been archived or suspended`. You can reverse this action by revisiting the Sites page and clicking the Unarchive link that appears beneath the site's pathname. (The Unarchive link appears only beneath sites that are archived.)

✦ **Spam:** Clicking this link marks the site as spam and blocks the users from being able to access the dashboard. It also displays a message stating `This site has been archived or suspended`. You can reverse this action by revisiting the Sites page and clicking the Not Spam link that appears underneath the site's pathname. (The Not Spam link appears only underneath sites that are marked as Spam.)

✦ **Delete:** Click this link to delete the site from your network of sites permanently. Although you see a confirmation screen that asks you to confirm your intention to delete the site, when done, you cannot reverse this decision.

✦ **Visit:** Click this link to visit the live site in your web browser.

Generally, you use the Edit Site page (shown in Figure 3-9) only when the settings are unavailable from the Dashboard of that particular site, by configuring the options that appear underneath each of the four tabs on the Edit Sites page:

✦ **Info:** You can edit the sites domain, path, registered date, updated date, and attributes (Public, Archived, Spam, Deleted, Mature).

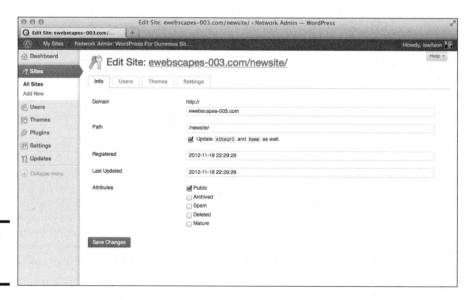

Figure 3-9:
The Edit
Site page.

✦ **Users:** You can manage the users that are assigned to the site, as well as add new users to the site under the Add New User section.

✦ **Themes:** You can enable themes for this site. This is particularly useful if you have themes that aren't network enabled (see the upcoming "Themes" section) because all the themes that aren't enabled within your network are listed on the Themes tab, which allows you to enable themes on a per-site basis.

✦ **Settings:** The settings on this tab cover all the database settings for the site that you are editing. Editing these settings is rare because you, as the network admin, have access to each user's Dashboard and can make any changes to the site's configuration settings there.

Also on the Sites menu on the Network Admin Dashboard, you see an Add New link — click it to load the Add New Site page on your Network Admin Dashboard. You can create a new site from the Add New Site page, as shown in Figure 3-10. Fill in the Site Address, Site Title, and Admin Email fields and then click the Add Site button to add the new site to your network. If the admin e-mail you enter is associated with an existing user, the new site is assigned to that user in your network. If the user doesn't exist, WordPress creates a new user, and an e-mail is sent with a notification. The site is immediately accessible. The e-mail the user receives contains a link to their site, a login link and their username and password.

Figure 3-10: The Add New Site page on the Network Admin Dashboard.

Users

Clicking the Users menu link on the Network Admin Dashboard takes you to the Users page, where you see a full listing of members, or users, within your network. The Users page (see Figure 3-11) lists the following information about each user:

✦ **Username:** The login name the member uses when she logs in to her account in your community.

✦ **Name:** The user's real name, taken from her profile. If the user hasn't provided her name in her profile, this column is blank.

✦ **E-mail:** The e-mail address the user entered when she registered on your site.

✦ **Registered:** The date when the user registered.

✦ **Sites:** If you enable sites within your WordPress Network, this lists any sites the user is a member of.

Figure 3-11:
The Users
page.

You can add users to the network, manage users, and even delete users by clicking the Edit or Delete links that appear under their names when you hover on them with your mouse (the same way you do with sites on the Sites page).

To delete a user, you simply hover your mouse over the username in the list that appears on the Users page. Click the Delete link, and a new screen appears with a page telling you to transfer this user's posts and links to another user account (most likely, your account). Then click the Confirm Deletion button, and WordPress removes the user from the network permanently — this action is irreversible, so be certain about your decision before you click that button!

You can also edit a user's profile information by clicking the Edit link that appears when you hover your mouse on his name on the Users page. Clicking that link takes you to the Edit User page, shown in Figure 3-12, where you're presented with several options, which happen to (mostly) be the same options and setting that you configure for your own profile information in Book III, Chapter 2.

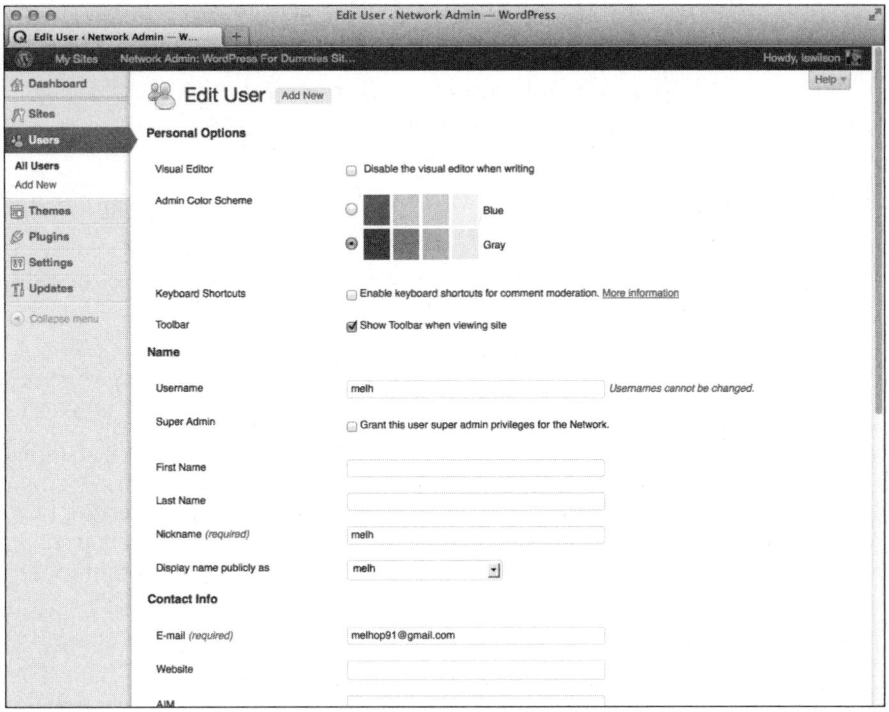

Figure 3-12:
The Edit
User page.

The only difference with the Edit User page within the Network Admin Dashboard is the setting labeled Super Admin, which is deselected by default. However, if you select this check box, you grant this user network admin privileges for your network. This means that the user has the exact same access and permission as you.

At the time of this writing, the terms *super admin* and *network admin* are interchangeable. When WordPress merged the WordPress MU code base with the regular WordPress software, the term they used to describe the network admin was *super admin*. Now, *network admin* is the standard term; however, areas within the Network Admin Dashboard and regular Dashboard still use *Super Admin* as a label. That will most likely change in the near future because WordPress will realize the discrepancy and update later versions of the software.

Also on the Users menu on the Network Admin Dashboard, you see a link called Add New. Click that link to load the Add New User page on your Network Admin Dashboard (shown in Figure 3-13).

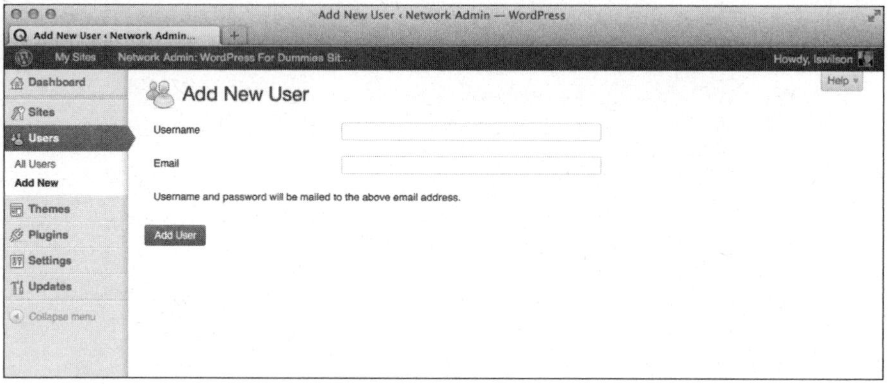

Figure 3-13:
The Add
New User
page on the
Network
Admin
Dashboard.

You can add a new user from the Add New User page by filling in the user-name and e-mail of the user you want to add and then clicking the Add User button. The new user is sent an e-mail notification alerting him of the new account, along with the site URL, his username, and his password. (The password is randomly generated by WordPress at the time the user account is created.)

Themes

When the multisite feature is enabled, only users with network admin access have permission to install themes, which are shared across the network. You can review details on how to find, install, and activate new themes with your WordPress installation in Book VI, Chapters 1 and 2. After you install a theme, you must enable it in your network in order for the theme to appear in the Appearance menu of each site, where users in your network can activate it on their sites. To access the Network Themes page (shown in Figure 3-14), click the Installed Themes link under the Themes menu on the Network Admin Dashboard.

Turn to Chapter 5 of this minibook to enable a theme on a per-site basis.

Plugins

Most WordPress plugins can work on your network. There are, however, some special plugins and some special considerations for using plugins with a network.

If you need a refresher on how to find, install, and activate plugins in WordPress, see Book VII, Chapters 1 and 2.

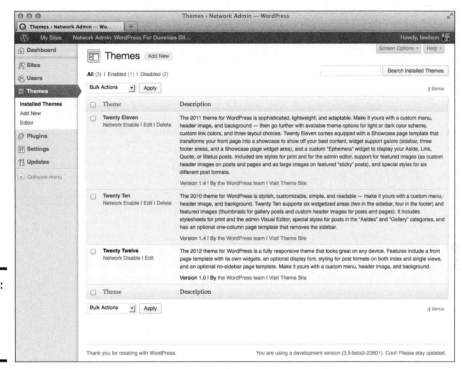

Figure 3-14:
The
Network
Themes
page.

Browse to the Plugins page in your WordPress Network Admin Dashboard by clicking the Plugins link under the Plugins menu. You find that the Plugins page is similar to your site's Dashboard, but you could easily miss one very small, subtle difference if you don't know where to look. On the Network Admin Dashboard is a Network Activate link below the plugin name. (See Figure 3-15.) That is the big difference between plugins listed in the regular Dashboard and the Network Admin Dashboard. As the network admin, you can enable certain plugins to be activated globally, across your entire network.

All sites in your network will have the network-activated plugin features available. Plugins that you activate on your Site Admin Dashboard are activated and available only for *your* main website.

If you select the Plugins menu from the menu settings, users can see the plugins listed on the Plugins page on the Dashboard. In the list of plugins, they see not only the plugins that you have network activated; rather, they see a list of all the plugins you installed in your WordPress installation, but none of them are activated on that user's site. The users have the ability to activate and deactivate those plugins as they desire.

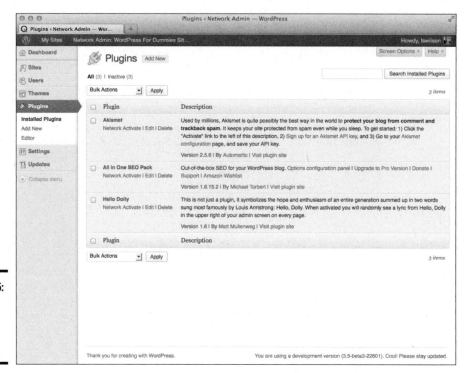

Figure 3-15:
The
Network
Plugins
page.

Network admins are the only people who can install new plugins on the site; regular users within the network do not have that kind of access (unless you made them a network admin in their User settings).

Also located in the Plugins menu on the Network Admin Dashboard are two other links: Add New and Editor. This is where you can add and install new plugins by searching the WordPress Plugin Directory within your Dashboard (I cover this in Book VII, Chapters 1 and 2), and the Editor link gives you access to the Plugin Editor, covered in Book VII, Chapter 4.

Updates

Clicking the Updates link on the Network Admin Dashboard menu gives you access to the WordPress Updates page, which takes you through the same process of upgrading your WordPress installation software as I describe in Book II, Chapter 6. However, with a network site, WordPress takes the extra step of upgrading all sites within your network so they all use the same upgraded feature sets.

If the process of upgrading network sites stalls or stops, the URL of the last site upgraded displays on the WordPress Updates page. The network admin can access the dashboard of the site where the upgrade stopped, which usually clears up the issue. A user accessing his site Dashboard after an upgrade also triggers this process.

Stopping Spam Sign-Ups and Splogs

If you choose to have open sign-ups in which any member of the public can register and create a new site on your network, at some point, automated bots run by malicious users and spammers will visit your network sign-up page and attempt to create one, or multiple, sites in your network. They do so by automated means, hoping to create links to their sites or fill their site on your network with spam posts. This kind of spam blog or site is a *splog*.

Spam bloggers don't hack your system to take advantage of this; they call aspects of the sign-up page directly. You can do a few simple things to slow them down considerably or stop them altogether.

In the Registration Settings section of the network Settings page, deselect the Add New Users check box (refer to Figure 3-4) to stop many spammers. When spammers access the system to set up a spam site, they often use the Add New Users feature to create many other blogs via programs built in to the bots.

Spammers often find your site via Google Search for the link to the sign-up page. You can stop Google and other search engines from crawling your sign-up page by adding `rel=nofollow,noindex` on the sign-up page link. Wherever you add a link to your sign-up page, inviting new users to sign up, the HTML code you use to add the `nofollow,noindex` looks like this:

```
<a href="http://yoursite.com/wp-signup.php" rel="nofollow,noindex ">Get your own
    site here</a>
```

Add a link to any page or widget area to instruct legitimate visitors to sign up for a site in your network.

Plugins can help stop spam blogs, too. The Moderate New Blogs plugin interrupts the user sign-up process and sends you (the network admin) an e-mail notification that a user has signed up for a blog. You can then determine whether the blog is legitimate. Download the plugin at `http://wordpress.org/extend/plugins/moderate-new-blogs`.

The Hashcash plugin was written mainly to stop spam comments, but it also prevents spam sign-ups on a WordPress site, with or without the network feature activated. You can get the plugin at `http://wordpress.org/extend/plugins/wp-hashcash`. This plugin checks to make sure that the sign-up page was opened within a browser window, and not accessed directly.

The Cookies for Comments plugin (available at `http://wordpress.org/extend/plugins/cookies-for-comments`) leaves a cookie in a visitor's browser. If the sign-up page is visited, the plugin checks for the cookie. If there isn't a cookie, the sign-up fails. Be sure to check the installation directions on this because it requires an `.htaccess` file edit.

Chapter 4: Management of Users and Access Control

In This Chapter

✔ **Understanding default user management**

✔ **Changing default user behavior**

✔ **Exploring user access to site features**

*I*n Chapter 3 of this minibook, I discuss the Network Admin menu you have access to on your Dashboard to manage aspects of your network. In this chapter, I explain how to manage users across the network, including how you can change some of the default management options to suit your needs.

One of the hardest things for new network admins to understand is that although each site is managed separately, users are global. That is, after a user logs in, he is logged in across the entire network and has the ability to comment on any site that has commenting enabled. (See Book III, Chapter 2.) The user can visit the Dashboard of the main site in the install to manage his profile information and access the Dashboard's My Sites menu to reach sites that he administers. The user also registers at the main site — not at individual sites in the network.

Setting Default User Permissions

When you enable the multisite feature, new site and new user registrations are turned off by default. However, you can add new sites and users from the Network Admin Dashboard. To let users sign up for your network, follow these steps:

1. **Log in to the Network Admin Dashboard and then click the Settings menu link.**

   The Settings page loads in your browser window.

2. **In the Registration Settings section, select the User Accounts May Be Registered option (as shown in Figure 4-1).**

   This setting allows users to register on your network. It also assigns them to the main site as a Subscriber but doesn't allow them to create new sites.

3. **Click the Save Changes button at the bottom of the page.**

By selecting the Both Sites and User Accounts Can Be Registered option on the Network Admin Settings page, you not only allow users to register a new account, but you also give them the option to create a new site on your network.

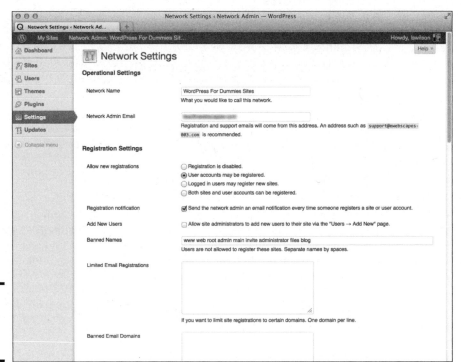

Figure 4-1:
User registration options.

User registration

When signing up, the user is directed to the main site of the installation and then added to one of the child sites. This site may be her site (if she chose to have a site when registering) or an existing site. If it's any existing site other than the main site, you, as the network admin, must manually add the user to that site. The user who owns the site can manually add users as well if you have enabled the option under the Network Admin Settings to allow site admins to add new users to their sites.

The registration page (see Figure 4-2) is located at `http://yourdomain.com/wp-signup.php`. This sign-up page bypasses the regular WordPress registration page. (See Book III, Chapter 3.)

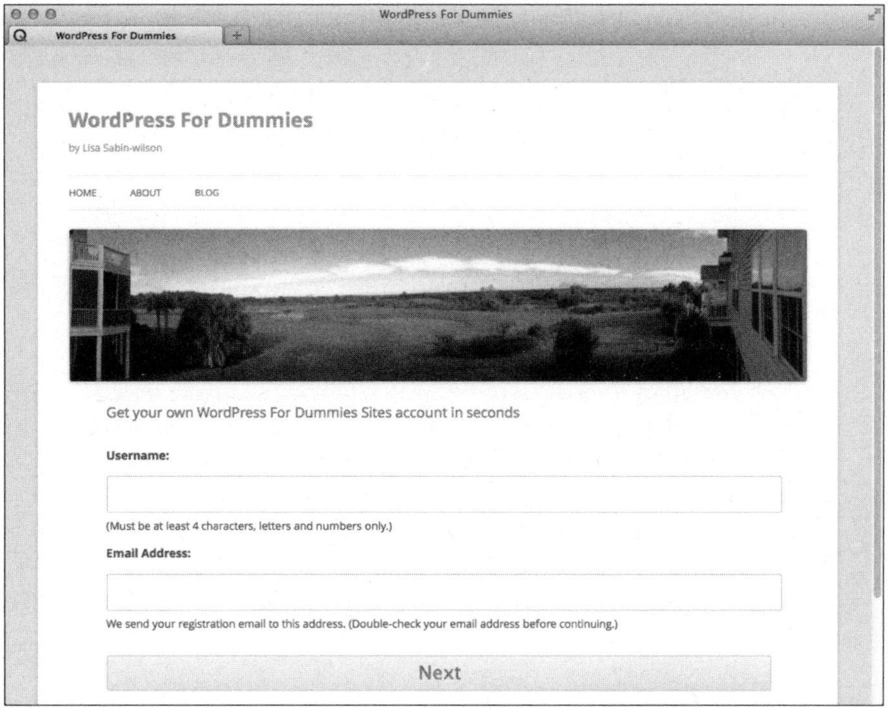

Figure 4-2:
The network
sign-up
page.

After filling out the form, the user receives an e-mail with a link to activate her account. When she does so, she can immediately log in and manage her details; she is directed to her primary site, which is the main site or Dashboard site if she has no site to administer.

Users can also be added to existing sites in the network. You can always assign users to specific sites on a per-case basis. When you set up a network and enable the *Allow Site Administrators to Add New Users to Their Site via the "Users -> Add New" Page* option (shown in Figure 4-3), you allow site admins to add other users in the network to their sites. Although the Add New Users setting is turned off by default, you can enable it by selecting the *Allow Site Administrators . . .* option on the Settings page on the Network Admin Dashboard.

Controlling access to sites

You have a list of all the sites on the network; by default, other users cannot find other sites in the network. Unless you, the network admin, add such ability via plugins, a user cannot navigate from one child site to the next.

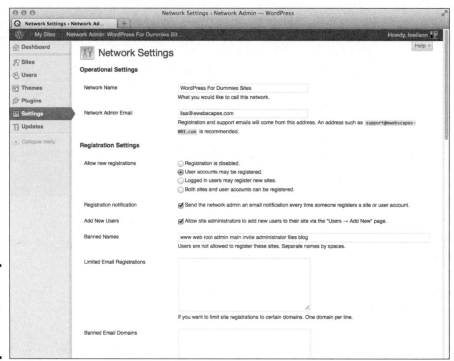

Figure 4-3:
Allowing
users to add
other users
to their site.

The only list provided to a user is the Dashboard's My Sites menu shown in Figure 4-4.

The My Sites page lists only sites the user is the administrator of, not sites on which the user has a lesser role. Additionally, the My Sites menu has a link for the user to create more sites (if the network admin has allowed it via the Settings menu in the Network Admin Dashboard).

By default, users can create no sites or an unlimited number of sites. You can limit the number of sites a user can create by installing the Limit Blogs per User plugin (http://wordpress.org/extend/plugins/limit-blogs-per-user).

Follow these steps to limit the number of sites your users can create:

1. **Click the Network Admin link located at the top left of your Dashboard under My Sites.**

2. **Hover your mouse over the Plugins menu and click the Add New link.**

   The Install Plugins page on your Network Admin Dashboard opens.

3. **In the Search field, type the name of the plugin,** Limit Blogs per User.

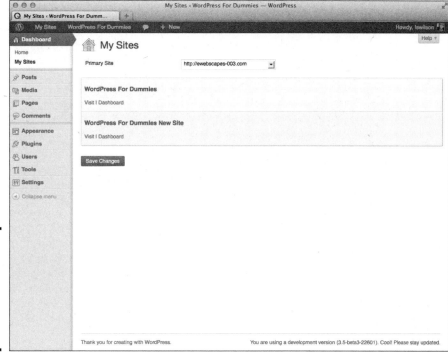

Figure 4-4:
The My
Sites page
shows
sites the
user admin-
istrates.

4. **Be sure that you have the Keyword option selected in the drop-down menu next to the search field, so WordPress knows to search by keywords (not by Author or Tag).**

5. **Click the Search Plugins button.**

6. **On the search results page, click the Install Now link for the Limit Blogs per User plugin by Brajesh Singh.**

7. **Click the Network Activate link on the Installing Plugin page.**

   The Limit Blogs per User plugin is now active on your network.

8. **Click the Settings link in the Network Admin Dashboard**

9. **Scroll to the bottom of the Settings page to the Limit Blog Registrations per User heading (shown in Figure 4-5) and enter the number of sites that you want to limit your network users to.**

   The value of 1 allows users to create no more than 1 site, and so on. Additionally a value of 0, or leaving the field empty, allows users to create an unlimited number of sites in your network.

10. **Be sure to click the Save Changes button at the bottom of the page in order to save all the settings you've configured.**

Figure 4-5:
The Limit
Blog
Registrations
per User
option.

Limit Blog Registrations Per User	
Number of blogs allowed per User	1
	If the Value is Zero,It indicates any number of blog is allowed

Importing users

You may have an existing pool of users you want to add to the network; for example, if you had a website before your network existed where you collected registrations or sign-ups. (Even newsletter programs give you a downloadable list of users you can import into your network.) The Bulk Import Users plugin, available at `http://wpmututorials.com/plugins/bulk-import-users`, can be used with some plugins mentioned later in this chapter to assign users to various sites in the network. Figure 4-6 shows the Bulk Import Members page with instructions for importing a list of users. Currently, there is no default method of importing users into WordPress without the use of plugins.

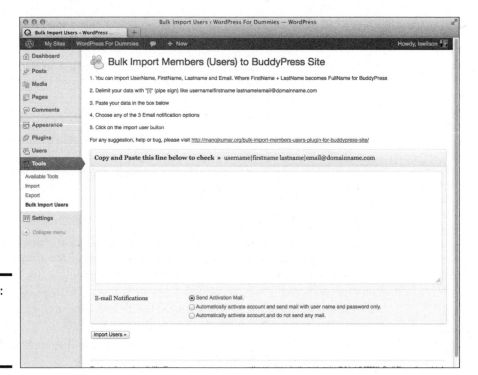

Figure 4-6:
The Bulk
Import
Users
plugin.

Changing Defaults

Depending on your specific needs, you may find yourself wanting to change how users are added to sites, as subscribers, within your network. For example, by default, users cannot add themselves to a random network site without making the request to the network admin or the site administrator of the site they want to be added to. This setup may work fine for most sites, but if you want your users to be able to register with existing sites within your network, then read on because these sections are for you.

Site-specific sign-up

For many people, signing up to the main site and then needing to be added to a child site can be confusing. Plugins, however, can make the process easier and less confusing for everyone.

If you want existing users to be able to add themselves to existing sites on the network, the Add Users widget plugin, available in the WordPress Plugins Directory at `http://wordpress.org/extend/plugins/add-users-sidebar-widget`, allows them to do so. Install this as a regular plugin, which I outline in Book VII, Chapters 1 and 2.

When the network is activated, the plugin adds a widget on the Widgets page of every user's Dashboard (hover your mouse over Appearance and then click the Widgets link) — the new widget is called the Add Users widget. The user must drag the widget to the appropriate sidebar to display it on the sidebar of the site where he wants users to add themselves. (If you need a refresher on how to use widgets, see Book VI, Chapter 1.) The site then displays a welcome message in the sidebar with a button labeled "Add Me!" that users can click to allow them to register for the site. (See Figure 4-7.)

If the user isn't logged in to the network, the welcome message displays `If you want to add yourself to this site, please log in.`, so remember, only users who are already network members and are logged in can add themselves to network sites by using the Add Users widget.

Changing roles on sign-up

When added to a network or a site, a user is assigned the role of Subscriber, by default. You may want to assign a different role to the user and automatically add him to your other sites in the network. (Book III, Chapter 3 explains roles and permissions.)

Book VIII Chapter 4

Management of Users and Access Control

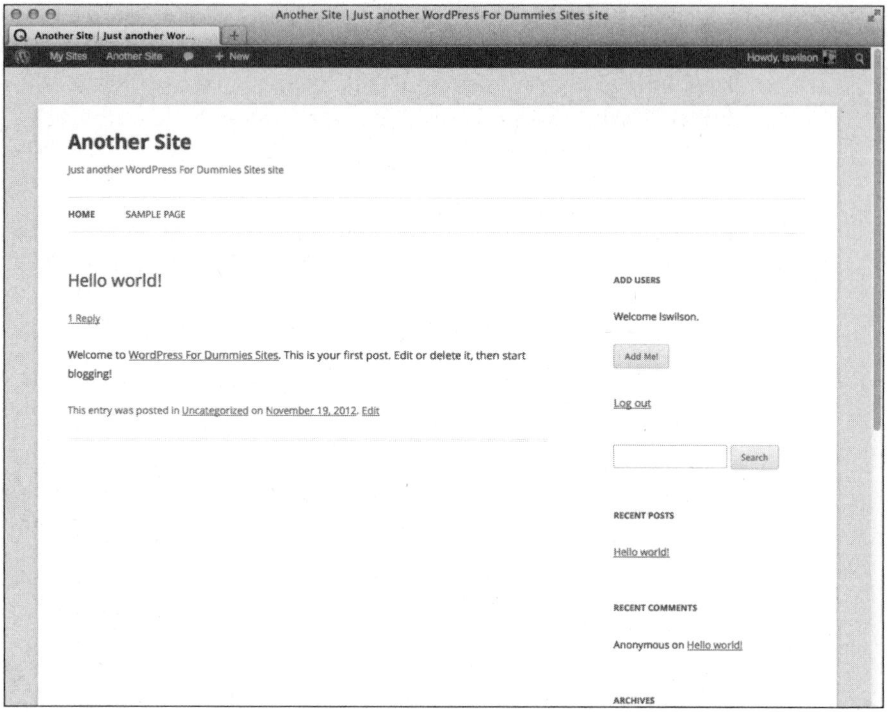

Figure 4-7:
The Add
Users
widget
on a site.

When a user signs up for his own site, for example, you may want to assign him a non-administrator role. You may want to set his role to Editor to restrict the menus he has access to on the Dashboard and to prevent him from being able to use some of the functionality of WordPress. You may want to have new site owners sign up as editors for the sites, giving them fewer permissions on their Dashboard.

The Multisite User Management plugin at `http://wordpress.org/extend/plugins/multisite-user-management` allows you to set a role other than administrator for new users who choose to have a site of their own. This plugin also allows you to set new user roles on other sites within your network (such as the default Subscriber role).

Locking down menus

Certain user roles have certain permissions (which I outline in Book III, Chapter 3) that give users access to various menus on the Dashboard. However, you may want to close areas that you don't want users to access.

You can limit access to menus via the Menus plugin available at `http://wordpress.org/extend/plugins/menus`.

Exploring Default Site Settings

Default settings can control user access to various such things as menus, themes, and the Dashboard. The next few sections discuss the network settings in detail.

Because users cannot add or edit plugins, the Plugins menu is disabled by default. You can still access the Plugins page via the Network Admin Dashboard Plugins menu link, but other administrators cannot.

To enable the Plugins menu for site administrators, follow these steps:

1. **On the Network Admin Dashboard, click the Settings menu link.**

2. **Scroll down to the Menu Settings section.**

The check box for the Plugins menu is deselected, which means that users can't see the menu regardless of their user role.

3. **Select the Plugins check box to make the Plugins menu available to site administrators, as shown in Figure 4-8.**

4. **Save your selection by clicking the Save Changes button.**

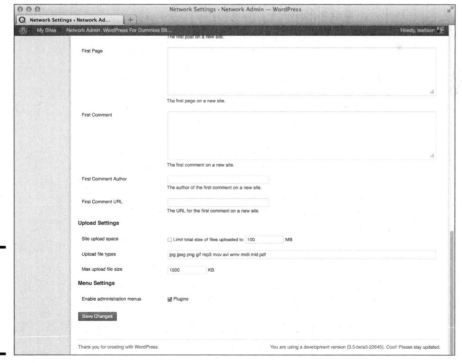

Figure 4-8:
Enabling the Plugins menu for site administrators.

Similarly, you must enable any themes installed on the network before a site administrator can choose the theme from the Appearance menu. I explain how to do so in Chapter 3 of this minibook.

Chapter 5: Using Network Plugins and Themes

In This Chapter

✔ Understanding theme management

✔ Understanding network-wide plugins

✔ Finding network-wide and Must-Use plugins

*W*hen you add new plugins and themes to your WordPress installation, you add new functionality and aesthetics. However, you don't just multiply your choices; the possibilities become endless. For example, you can gather and display information from across the network or have the same features available to everyone. You can choose to have the same theme on all sites or different themes. Not only can you manage plugins and themes on a global level, but you also have site-specific control.

In this chapter, I show you how certain functionality appears across the network and how certain plugins look by default on all sites for all users. I also cover controlling access to different themes for different sites.

One of the interesting features of a network is the extensive use of the mu-plugins folder. In this chapter, I describe exactly how this folder processes plugin code. I also cover the Network Activate link on the Plugins page, which is very similar to the Activate link but has important differences.

This chapter doesn't cover installing plugins and themes. I cover plugins in Book VII, Chapter 2 and themes in Book VI, Chapter 2.

Using One Theme on Multiple Sites

In certain situations (for example, when you want consistent branding and design across your entire network), each site in a network is used as a subsection of the main site. You could set up WordPress networks as a magazine-style design on your main site and populate the content with different posts from sites within your network, aggregating all the content to the main site. You can see an example of this on a blog on the WordPress. com network called FoodPress (`http://foodpress.com`), as shown in Figure 5-1.

FoodPress is a site run by Automattic, the company that owns WordPress. com. Automattic's goal is to highlight posts from within the WordPress. com network that are about food and cooking. On the FoodPress site, all the post title links point to different blogs within the site's network. However, WordPress.com allows the administrators of its network sites to use different designs, so the branding across sites is not consistent with the main FoodPress site. Despite that, it's still a good example of a magazine-style theme that aggregates content from within a network.

Although each site in the network operates separately from the main (network admin) site, you might want each site to look the same as the main site because it ties into the main site visually, through design and branding, and provides a consistent experience for visitors to any site within a network. You may have a custom theme specially made for the main site, with added features to display network-wide content. If consistency and network branding are your goals, you may want to create a single theme that is used on all sites within your network (other than your main site).

Figure 5-1: FoodPress, a magazine-style site on the WordPress. com network.

In Book VI, you read about how WordPress accesses themes stored on the web server. When the network is enabled, these themes are shared among all sites and are available on the site administrator's Dashboard. If a change to a theme file is made, every site in the network using that theme experiences the change because only one copy of the theme is being served. When a theme is enabled, it appears on the administrator's Dashboard on the Manage Themes page (which the users access by hovering the pointer over Appearance menu in the Network Admin Dashboard and clicking the Themes link). Users can choose to activate this theme so it displays on the front side of the site. You must activate a theme for use across all sites in a network by clicking the Network Enable link under the Theme name in the Network Admin Dashboard. (Access this Themes page by clicking the Themes menu link on the Network Admin Dashboard.)

The main network site could have 20 different themes installed in the main WordPress installation; however, if you haven't enabled them for use across the entire network, then site administrators can't see network-disabled themes on their Dashboards and therefore can't use them on their sites.

If a consistent network design is what you're after, you will run into a few troubles with the WordPress network because, by default, no matter what themes you have activated, the default WordPress Twenty Twelve theme gets activated whenever new sites are created within your network. It would be nice for WordPress to provide you with a global setting in the Network Admin Dashboard that would allow you to assign the default theme to every site that is created; however, that is currently not the case, unless you want to edit some code in the WordPress configuration file (which I cover in the "Setting the default theme for sites" section, later in this chapter).

There is, however, a wonderful plugin that adds a simple item on the Network Admin Dashboard called Default Theme, which you can access by clicking the Settings menu link. Simply, the Default Theme setting gives you the option to assign a default theme to be the theme displayed on newly created sites.

The Default Theme plugin is not a free plugin, unfortunately; rather, it is available from the development group at WPMU DEV at `http://eweb scapes.com/wpmu-premium`. To access the plugin, you do need to purchase membership to the site — however, don't let that deter you.

The WPMU DEV membership gives you access to hundreds of WordPress network-related plugins and themes for one annual membership. I recommend them highly and feel their membership is worth every penny spent. After you have your WPMU DEV membership, you can begin downloading any one of hundreds of plugins and themes for your WordPress network. You can purchase membership by visiting the site at `http://ewebscapes.com/wpmu-premium`.

Book VIII Chapter 5

Using Network Plugins and Themes

Enabling themes for individual sites

You may have a customized theme for one member site that you don't want other sites within the network to use or have access to. Each site on the network is editable by you as the network admin. You can do some basic tasks, such as enabling or disabling themes, or adding new themes to the network, without leaving your own Dashboard. If you want to have a theme available for use on only one site, and not available for other sites to choose, follow these steps:

1. **Click the Network Admin link in the My Sites menu in the upper-left corner of your Dashboard and then click the Sites menu link.**

The Sites page appears, showing a list of all sites across the network, sorted by creation date, as shown in Figure 5-2.

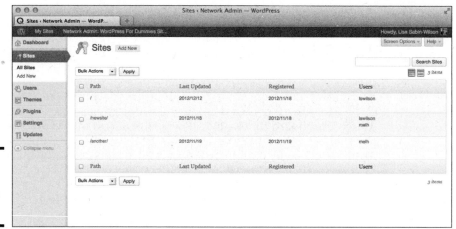

Figure 5-2:
A list of
sites on the
network.

2. **Hover your mouse cursor over the site you want to enable a theme for and then click the Edit link.**

The Edit Site page displays on your Dashboard.

3. **Click the Themes tab on the Edit Sites page.**

The display on the Edit Sites page changes to show a list of themes that can be enabled for the site you're editing. (See Figure 5-3.)

4. **Click the Enable link for the theme you want to enable for the site you're editing.**

The Edit Site page refreshes with the Theme tab still active and displays a message stating that the theme has been enabled. Your selected theme is now enabled on the site. Repeat these steps for any sites that you want to enable a theme on.

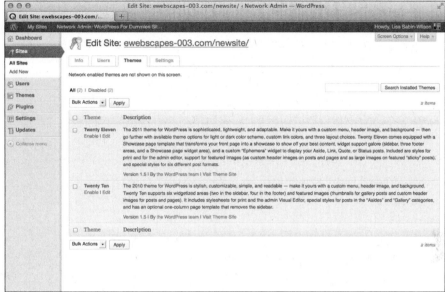

Figure 5-3:
The Edit Site page with the Themes tab active.

Installing themes for network use

Installing a theme for use on your network is the same process you take to install a theme on your individual site (see Book VI, Chapter 2), but with an extra step: You have to enable each theme on the Network Admin Dashboard to activate it on the Appearance menu in the individual site administrators' Dashboard for sites within your network. Here's how to enable a theme so all your site owners can use it on their sites:

1. **Click the Network Admin link in the My Sites menu in the upper-left corner of your Dashboard and then click the Themes menu link.**

The Themes page displays with a list of installed themes, as shown in Figure 5-4. Each theme installed in the `/wp-content/themes` folder is listed on this page.

2. **Click the Network Enable link for the theme you want to use.**

Enabling a theme on the Themes page in the Network Admin causes it to appear in the list of available themes within each network site Dashboard (but does not change any user's active theme — it merely makes this theme available for use).

**Book VIII
Chapter 5**

Using Network
Plugins and
Themes

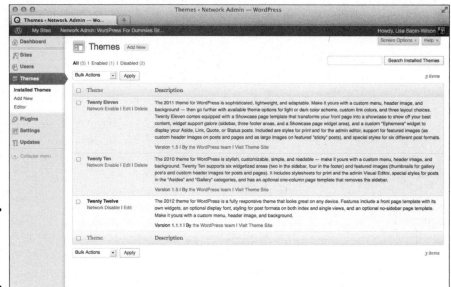

Figure 5-4:
A list of
themes on
the network.

3. **Repeat these steps to enable more themes on your network.**

   Anytime you install a new theme in your main WordPress installation does not mean that it's available for use network-wide. As the network admin, you always have to enable the theme first, before your site owners can use it.

Setting the default theme for sites

When a new site is created on the network, by default, it displays the Twenty Twelve theme provided within WordPress. If you want to use a different theme as the default for all new sites created, you can accomplish this by adding a `define` statement in the `wp-config.php` file of your WordPress installation. (Check out Book II, Chapter 5 to familiarize yourself with the `wp-config.php` file you're modifying in this section.)

Install your theme on the server, which I outline in Book VI, Chapters 1 and 2. You may also want to enable the theme network-wide, as outlined in the preceding section. This isn't a necessary step, but if you have other themes available, and if the active theme is disabled, a user who switches away from that theme won't be able to switch back to it.

Because the Twenty Twelve WordPress theme is already the default, I use another popular WordPress theme called Hybrid (by Justin Tadlock:

`http://wordpress.org/extend/themes/hybrid`) as the theme I want
to set as the default theme for all sites within the network:

1. **Log in to your web server via FTP.**

Refer to Book II, Chapter 2 for a refresher on using FTP.

2. **Open the `wp-config.php` file in your favorite text editor.**

See Book II, Chapter 5 for details about where you can find the `wp-config.php` file on your web server.

Save a copy of your original `wp-config.php` file to your desktop before
editing it in case you make any mistakes or typos in the next few steps.

3. **Locate the following line of code in the `wp-config.php` file:**

```
define ('WPLANG', '');
```

You can find this line toward the bottom of the file; scroll until you
locate it.

4. **Add a new, blank line below it.**

5. **Type** define('WP_DEFAULT_THEME', 'hybrid');

This one line of code tells WordPress to use the Hybrid theme as the
default theme for all new sites within your network.

6. **Save the `wp-config.php` file and upload it to your web server.**

The `hybrid` in quotes refers to the theme's folder name on the web
server. The name within the quotes should be identical to the folder
name where the theme files reside. All new sites created now display the
Hybrid theme.

Gathering and Displaying Network-wide Content

Depending on your needs, you may want to gather content from sites across
your network to display on the front page of the main site (as the FoodPress
blog does). Although some plugins can do this for you, you can accomplish
the same thing by placing a few lines of code in your theme template file.

The main page of your network is controlled by the theme that is active on
your regular Dashboard on the Themes page (which you access by hovering
your pointer over Appearance and clicking the Themes link). You can customize this theme with some code samples in the next section to suit your
particular needs.

**Book VIII
Chapter 5**

**Using Network
Plugins and
Themes**

Adding posts from network sites

One of the best ways to pull visitors into your site is to display a short list of headlines from posts made by other sites within your network. With a single WordPress site, the Recent Posts widget can handle this task. When running a network, however, there's no built-in way to pull a list of posts from across all the sites in your network. However, the Recent Global Posts Widget plugin available from the folks at WPMU DEV Premium can do this for you quickly and efficiently, and the plugin includes a handy widget to make it easy for you to add recent posts from across your network of sites to your main website.

Plugins from WPMU DEV Premium are not free, and you cannot access them from the official WordPress Plugins Directory. You first need to pay for and register a membership at `http://ewebscapes.com/wpmu-premium`.

After you have your membership, log in and download the Recent Global Posts Widget plugin from `http://premium.wpmudev.org/project/recent-global-posts-widget`.

Listing network sites

To list all the sites in the network, use the Multi-Site Site List Shortcode plugin available for free from the WordPress Plugin Directory: `http://wordpress.org/extend/plugins/multi-site-site-list-shortcode`. You install this plugin just as you do any other plugin in WordPress; see Book VII, Chapters 1 and 2 for information on installing WordPress plugins.

To use the information this plugin provides, you must include a shortcode that the plugin developer provides, within the body of a page, or a post, published to your main site. The most common and useful method is to create a page that includes the plugin shortcode. To list all network sites, follow these steps. In this example, I use the default Twenty Twelve theme:

1. **Log in to the WordPress Dashboard on the main site.**

2. **Hover your pointer over Pages and click the Add New link.**

3. **Fill in a title for your page.**

   Something like: Network Sites List

4. **Add this short code in the body of your page:**

   ```
   [site-list]
   ```

5. **Publish the page.**

When you visit the front end of your site, you see a page with your new title in the menu. Clicking this title displays the list of sites in the network, as shown in Figure 5-5.

Figure 5-5:
A page showing the list of network sites.

The Multi-Site Site List Shortcode plugin also gives you a settings page where you can select sites that you would like to hide from the listing of sites. You can find the Multi-Site Site List Shortcode Options page by hovering your pointer over Settings and then clicking the Multi-Site Site List link within your regular Dashboard. The Multi-Site Site List Shortcode Options page is shown in Figure 5-6.

Displaying user comments

When running multiple sites, you may also want to display a list of the most recent comments from across the network. The Diamond Multisite widgets plugin (available at `http://wordpress.org/extend/plugins/diamond-multisite-widgets`) lets you do just that.

Install the plugin as outlined in Book VII, and click the Network Activate link. Hover your pointer over Appearance and click the Widgets link on the Dashboard of your site to load the Widgets page. You see that a new widget has been added called Diamond Recent Comments.

Figure 5-6:
The Multi-
Site Site List
Shortcode
Options
page.

If you drag this widget to the sidebar of your choosing, it displays a list of the most recent comments from every site on the entire network. If you expand the Diamond Recent Comments widget, you see the following configurable options:

✦ **Widget Title:** This is the title that is displayed on your site, above the widget information.

✦ **Cache Expire Time:** In seconds, it's the time frame in which the plugin will refresh the comments displayed with this widget.

✦ **Comments Count:** Enter the maximum number of comments you want to display.

✦ **Exclude Blogs:** Place a check mark next to the name of the site that you want to exclude comments from.

✦ **Whitelist:** Place a check mark next to the name of the site(s) that you want to always include comments from.

✦ **Format String:** Enter the format for how you want the comments to display on your site by typing in the strings of text shown directly beneath this option. (See Figure 5-7.)

✦ **Avatar Size:** Enter the size of the comment author's avatar for display on your site.

✦ **Default Avatar URL:** Enter the web address to the graphic/image file you want to display as the default avatar (for comment authors who don't have one).

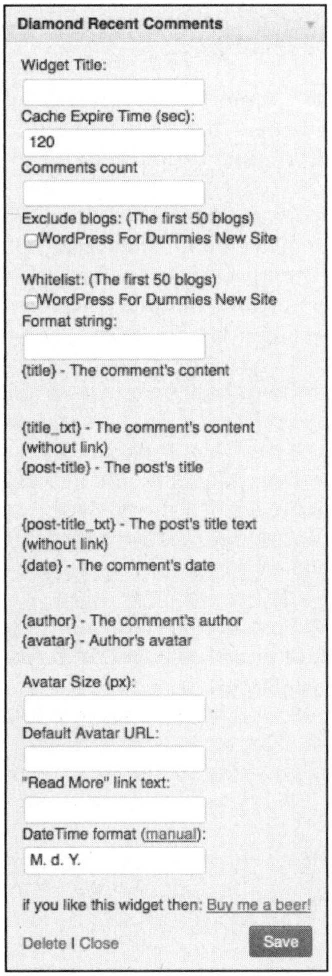

Diamond Recent Comments

Widget Title:

Cache Expire Time (sec):

120

Comments count

Exclude blogs: (The first 50 blogs)
☐ WordPress For Dummies New Site

Whitelist: (The first 50 blogs)
☐ WordPress For Dummies New Site
Format string:

{title} - The comment's content

{title_txt} - The comment's content
(without link)
{post-title} - The post's title

{post-title_txt} - The post's title text
(without link)
{date} - The comment's date

{author} - The comment's author
{avatar} - Author's avatar

Avatar Size (px):

Default Avatar URL:

"Read More" link text:

DateTime format (manual):

M. d. Y.

if you like this widget then: Buy me a beer!

Delete I Close   Save

Figure 5-7:
The Diamond Recent Comments widget options.

Book VIII
Chapter 5

Using Network
Plugins and
Themes

✦ **Default "Read More" link text:** Enter the text that you want the Read More link to display. (By default, the widget displays the words "Read More" as the direct link to the comment.)

✦ **DateTime Format:** Enter the date and time format that you prefer.

Be sure to click the Save button within the widget to save all the settings you created here.

Sitewide tags and categories

The Sitewide Tags plugin pulls information from every new post on each site and reproduces it on a site that the plugin creates in your network called the Tags Blog site, which is a site in your network that aggregates the posts from every site. You may also set Tags Blog as the main site in your network so that all new posts appear on the front page.

The plugin pulls and reposts almost all content from a post on another network site, including the title, content, tags, categories, and author information. At this time, however, it doesn't pull the post thumbnail or the comments.

By default, this plugin is set to create a new site called Tags Blog and saves up to 5,000 posts before it starts to remove older ones. Each post it aggregates retains its original permalink (the full URL to the post) and all post meta information (the post's original author, the date and time it was published, and any categories and tags assigned to the post).

All the aggregated posts from across the network are saved and published to one site; the Tags Blog are then displayed as if theses posts were posted to a single site. Each new post is saved to the Tags Blog site when it's created. Users or visitors can then search the Tags Blog site and see tags from across the network, search all aggregated posts across the network, see posts by all network authors — the possibilities for network-wide aggregation and display are quite useful.

Because the original permalink of the post is retained, search engines don't read these aggregated posts as duplicate content, and therefore any page rankings or SEO juice is retained by each site.

You can find the plugin at `http://wordpress.org/extend/plugins/ wordpress-mu-sitewide-tags` or you may install it by using the built-in plugin installer.

After you install the plugin, activate it on the network by moving it to the `mu-plugins` folder (the mu-plugins folder is discussed later in this chapter). When moved to this folder on the server, the plugin will be automatically activated and start working.

After you activate the plugin, you need to enable it. Visit the Global Tags page on your Network Admin Dashboard (click the Sitewide Tags link in the Settings menu). Figure 5-8 shows the Global Tags page, where you enable the Tags Blog on your network by selecting the Enabled check box on the Global Tags page.

Figure 5-8:
The check box to enable Tags Blog.

After you click the Save Changes button on the Global Tags page, the page refreshes, and you see the Global Tags section has changed and provides you with new options (see Figure 5-9), including

✦ **Tags Blog:** Type the name of the blog you want to aggregate all posts in the network to in the provided text field, or select the option to aggregate all the posts to the main blog.

✦ **Max Posts:** Set to 5,000 by default. Beyond that number, the plugin will delete older posts from the Tags Blog site automatically.

✦ **Include Pages:** Check to enable. This option also includes any pages users create on their network sites, and it pushes them to the assigned tags blog.

✦ **Include Thumbnails:** Select this option to have WordPress include thumbnail images from across the network.

✦ **Privacy:** This option determines whether the Tags Blog site can be indexed by search engines.

✦ **Non-Public Blogs:** When enabled, this feature aggregates posts from sites that have changed their privacy settings (hover the pointer over Settings and click the Privacy link) to non-public.

✦ **Post Meta:** If you're using a plugin or a theme on some or all of the network sites that creates custom files, you may enter those field names here so those values will also be pulled to the tags blog.

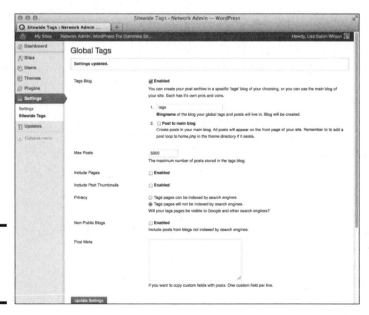

Figure 5-9:
The Global Tags options.

Using and Installing Network-wide Plugins

Network-wide plugins perform an action globally across all sites in the network. Sometimes, you might see these referred to as *sitewide plugins,* which is old WordPress MU terminology (pre–WordPress version 3.0). Because you're working with one codebase, you need only one copy of a plugin. All sites within the network use the same copy.

When you have a single installation of WordPress on a single site, the Activate link on the Plugins page turns on that plugin for that site. (See Book VII, Chapters 1 and 2.) When you have multiple sites in a network, using the Multisite feature, the Activate link works the same way for the site you activate the plugin on.

You see a Network Activate link on the Plugins page in the Network Admin Dashboard, which activates the plugin on all sites in the network. This will simply turn the plugin on for all network sites. It will not allow you to manage plugin options globally unless the plugin itself was coded to do so. A list of network activated plugins will be shown in the Plugins page in the Network Admin Dashboard (which you access by clicking the Plugins menu link).

Any changes made to this copy affect every site within your network.

A special breed of plugins — the Must-Use plugins — get installed into the `/wp-content/mu-plugins` folder on your web server. Any plugin file placed inside this folder runs as if it were part of WordPress. The plugins in this folder automatically execute, without the need for activation in your Dashboard.

You cannot access the files in this folder from the WordPress Dashboard. If you use the Install Plugins page (hover your pointer over Plugins and click the Add New link) to find and install a Must-Use plugin, you may be required to move the plugin files from the `plugins` folder to the `mu-plugins` folder. The plugin's `readme.txt` file always states whether the plugin needs to be moved into the Must-Use (`mu-plugins`) folder.

Generally, plugins placed in the `/wp-content/mu-plugins` folder are for network-wide features or customizations that users can't disable. An example of this is a custom-branded login page on each site in your network. If a plugin design adds a new menu item, the menu item appears as soon as the plugin is placed in the `/wp-content/mu-plugins` folder, without further need for activation on the Dashboard.

Not all plugins placed in the `/wp-content/mu-plugins` folder appear in the plugins list (hover your pointer over Plugins and click the Plugins link), because not all of them require activation. After you create the `/wp-content/mu-plugins` folder via FTP or your web host's control panel, a new Must-Use link appears on the Plugins page, as shown in Figure 5-10.

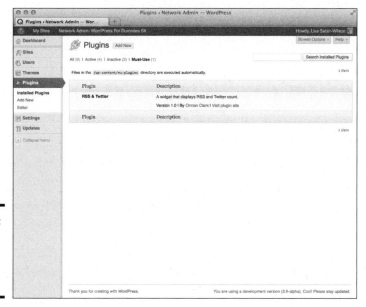

Figure 5-10:
The Must-Use link on the Plugins page.

Place the main Must-Use plugin file in the `/wp-content/mu-plugins` folder, not in a subfolder. If multiple files are needed, some plugins use a file with a command to include the subfolder so the code executes. Figure 5-10 shows a list of installed Must-Use plugins.

You still control plugin settings on a per-site basis; you must visit the back end of each site if you want to alter any settings provided by the plugin.

Here's how to create the `/wp-content/mu-plugins` folder and install a network-wide plugin:

1. **Connect to your web server via FTP.**

2. **Navigate to the `/wp-content` folder.**

    You see the subdirectories `plugins` and `themes`.

3. **Using your FTP program, create a `mu-plugins` subdirectory.**

   Most FTP programs allow you to right-click and choose to add a new folder.

4. **Upload the plugin file — not the** plugin folder **— to the `/wp-content/mu-plugins` folder on your web server.**

   The plugin immediately runs on your install. Generally speaking, the only plugins that go in this folder are ones in which the plugin's instructions (typically found in the `readme.txt` file) explicitly state to do so.

Discovering Handy Multisite Plugins

You can find multisite plugins that take advantage of WordPress's multisite functionality in the WordPress Plugin Directory at `http://wordpress.org/extend/plugins`. Usually, multisite plugins are tagged with certain keywords within the directory to help you find them better, such as *wpmu, wordpressmu, multisite,* and *network.*

When you click the linked tags in the directory for these terms, you're taken directly to a URL for a page that lists the related plugins, such as

✦ `http://wordpress.org/extend/plugins/tags/multisite`

✦ `http://wordpress.org/extend/plugins/tags/network`

✦ `http://wordpress.org/extend/plugins/tags/wpmu`

Additionally, you can find more plugins via search engines and by asking on the Forums page (`http://wordpress.org/support`).

Chapter 6: Using Multiple Domains within Your Network

In This Chapter

✔ Discovering domain mapping

✔ Understanding how to map domains

✔ Advanced usage

*W*ith a network of multiple sites easily available in WordPress, many people have expressed the desire to run multiple sites on their own separate domain names through one install. Prior to the network feature being added to the WordPress software, you could run only one site per installation of the software. Now, it is possible to run several sites under one installation of WordPress by activating the network feature, which I discussed in Chapters 4 and 5 of this minibook.

In this chapter, I discuss using multiple domains and a feature called domain mapping, which enables you to run not only multiple sites, but also multiple sites with their own, unique domain name that is not tied to the main site installation domain.

To tackle this chapter, you need an understanding of domains (Book II, Chapter 1) and domain nameserver (DNS) records.

Finding Your Way with Domain Mapping

Domain mapping means telling your web server which domains you want WordPress to answer to, and which site you want shown to the visitor when they request that domain. This process is more than domain forwarding or masking because the URLs for your posts will have the full domain name in them. Instead of the child site being in `secondsite.`*`yourdomain`*`.com` format, it can be *`myotherdomain`*`.com`.

Domain mapping isn't possible in certain instances, however. If your WordPress install is in a subfolder and this folder is part of the URL, then any mapped domain will also contain this folder name. In that case, it would be better to move the install so that it isn't in a subfolder.

You also need to access your web host's control panel (where you manage DNS records on your web server) and the control panel for your domain name registrar, which is often a different company.

The network install, by default, lets you choose between a subfolder setup and a subdomain setup. This step is still required before you can specify a domain for that site. I cover how to enable the network in Chapter 2 of this minibook. Be sure to set up the network and check that it's functioning properly before you attempt to map domains.

Parking or pointing domains

You need to set up your web server to accept any incoming requests for the domain you want to map and the location to send them to. I use the cPanel control panel (Book II, Chapter 2) in this section because it's quite popular and available on many web hosts. On cPanel-based web hosts, this task is referred to as *domain parking*.

Follow these steps to park a domain on your web hosting account via cPanel:

1. **Log in to your website's cPanel.**

The address is provided by your web host and usually available at `http://yourdomain.com/cpanel`.

2. **In the Domains section, click the Parked Domains icon, as shown in Figure 6-1.**

The Parked Domains page displays in your browser window and lists any domains you have parked (if you have previously parked any) and provides a form to enter a new domain.

Figure 6-1:
The Parked Domains icon in cPanel.

3. **In the Create a New Parked Domain section, enter the domain name you want to map.**

The domain is directed to the root folder of your website, which is where your WordPress install should be located. If it isn't, follow the next set of steps.

4. **Click the Add Domain button.**

   The screen refreshes and shows the domain you added in a list under Domains, which indicates successful parking of the domain you entered in Step 3. See Figure 6-2.

Other web hosts may refer to domain parking as *pointing* or *mirroring*. You may need to ask your web host support team which area you need to do this in. You're using a `ServerAlias` directive for the mapped domains, telling the web server to send all requests for the mapped domain to the domain where WordPress is installed.

If the domain you're using for your WordPress network installation isn't the main domain of the website, but rather is an add-on domain, you have to do a slightly different process to park the domain. Because you can't tell a parked domain to go anywhere other than the root folder, you need to use the Addon Domains feature.

Figure 6-2:
The Parked Domains page showing a parked domain.

Follow these steps to create an Addon Domain in your web hosting cPanel:

1. **Log in to your website's cPanel.**

2. **In the Domains section, click the Addon Domains icon, as shown in Figure 6-3.**

   The Addon Domains page appears.

Figure 6-3:
The Addon
Domains
icon in
cPanel.

3. **Enter the new domain name you want to map in the New Domain Name field.**

   The other fields, Subdomain/FTP Username and Document Root, get auto-populated by your web server; don't alter the information your web server populates for the Subdomain/FTP Username, as this field is setting the username you will use to connect when you need to use FTP. These are default settings for Addon Domains, and you should not alter them.

4. **In the Document Root field, enter the folder location of your WordPress network installation.**

   Figure 6-4 shows the Create an Addon Domain information filled in.

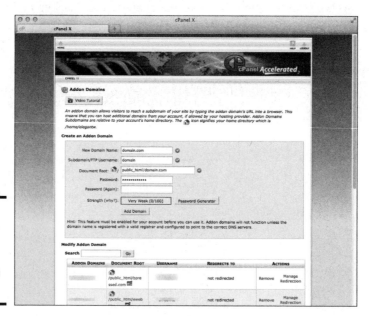

Figure 6-4:
The Create
an Addon
Domain
information
in cPanel.

5. **Click Add Domain to save your changes.**

The Addon Domains page refreshes, and your new domain appears under the Addon Domains section.

Domain name server records

To instruct the domain name registrar where to send the domain name to, you need to edit the domain nameserver (DNS) records. A common domain name registrar is GoDaddy — I use its domain registration account interface in the following steps. To edit the name server records, follow these steps:

1. **Log in to your domain name registrar.**

2. **Click the domain name management tools.**

Figure 6-5 shows the information for the domain to map.

3. **Click the Set Nameservers link in the Nameservers section.**

4. **Type the nameservers for your web host where your WordPress install is located and then save your changes by clicking the Save Changes button.**

The servers around the world now know that your domain "lives" at this web server location. Nameserver changes may take up to 24 hours to propagate across the Internet.

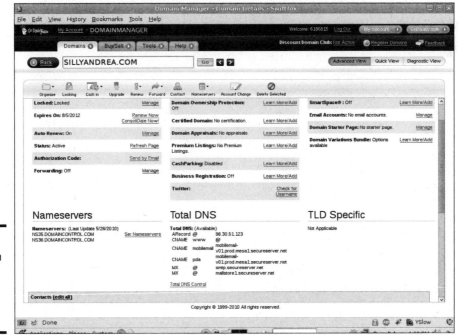

Figure 6-5:
The domain name records of a mapped domain.

**Book VIII
Chapter 6**

**Using Multiple
Domains within
Your Network**

Installing the Domain Mapping Plugin

Before you can add your mapped domains to WordPress, you need to install the WordPress MU Domain Mapping plugin to help handle this in WordPress. The Domain Mapping plugin doesn't do any setup on the server side; it helps rename the site and takes care of any login issues.

1. **Download the plugin from** `http://wordpress.org/extend/plugins/wordpress-mu-domain-mapping`.

2. **Unzip the plugin on your local computer.**

   Inside are two php files: `domain-mapping.php` and `sunrise.php`.

3. **Open your FTP program and navigate to your website's `wp-content` folder.**

   If you need a reminder on how to do this, see Book II, Chapter 2.

4. **Upload the `sunrise.php` file directly into the `/wp-content` folder.**

5. **Inside the `/wp-content`, look for a folder called `/mu-plugins`. If there isn't one, use your FTP program to create this folder.**

6. **Upload the `domain-mapping.php` file into the `/mu-plugins` folder.**

   Figure 6-6 shows how these files look on the server. From here, you need to add a line to your `wp-config.php` file.

Figure 6-6:
A look at the /wp-content/ plugins folder that contains the sunrise.php file.

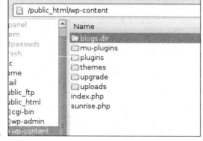

7. **Download a copy of your `wp-config.php` file by using your FTP program.**

8. **Open `wp-config.php` on your computer with a text editor and add the following line under the `define( 'MULTISITE', true );` line.**

   ```
   define( 'SUNRISE', 'on' );
   ```

9. **Save the file and upload it to your website.**

The plugin is immediately available (and running) on your network. All you need to do is set up the options and map a domain to a site. Two new items are added to the Super Admin menu: Domain Mapping and Domains. On the user administrator side, a new Domain Mapping item appears on the Tools menu.

The network admin needs to activate domain mapping on the Domain Mapping page (Network Admin⇨Domain Mapping) before a user can map a domain by enabling the Domain Mapping feature.

Obtaining your IP address

An *IP address* is a number assigned to every website and computer connected to the Internet. This number is used in domain mapping to help direct Internet traffic to the appropriate site in your network. You can find the IP address of your website three ways: Your web host provider can tell you, the address may appear in some place within the web host's control panel, and you can visit an IP lookup website. Such websites can tell you the IP of your website when you provide your domain name. To find your address with an IP lookup website, follow these steps:

1. **Visit Network Solutions' WHOIS feature located at** www.network solutions.com/whois/index.jsp.

2. **Enter the domain name of your website and then click Search.**

3. **Write down the IP address it shows.**

Figure 6-7 displays the IP address of mommieblogs.com.

4. **In your WordPress Dashboard, choose Network Admin⇨Domain Mapping, enter your IP address, and click Save.**

Figure 6-7: WHOIS record revealing the IP address of mommie blogs.com.

mommieblogs.com
Is this your domain name? Renew it now.

IMAGE NOT AVAILABLE

Current Registrar:	GODADDY.COM, INC.
IP Address:	96.30.51.123 (ARIN & RIPE IP search)
Record Type:	Domain Name
Server Type:	Apache 1
Lock Status:	clientDeleteProhibited
WebSite Status:	Active

BOOKMARK

Mapping a domain to a site

To map a domain to a site in your network, here's what you need to do:

1. **Navigate to the child site you want to map.**

2. **Log in to the Dashboard of that child site.**

3. **Hover your pointer over Tools and click the Domain Mapping link.**

The Domain Mapping page appears, as shown in Figure 6-8.

4. **Enter the domain name you want to map to this site.**

The check box indicates whether the domain is the primary domain for this site and is used only if you want to map multiple domains to the site. Only one domain can be the primary domain and used in the URL. Any other domains mapped to this site redirect to the primary domain.

5. **Click the Add button to save your changes.**

The site now appears when you enter the mapped domain URL in your web browser address bar.

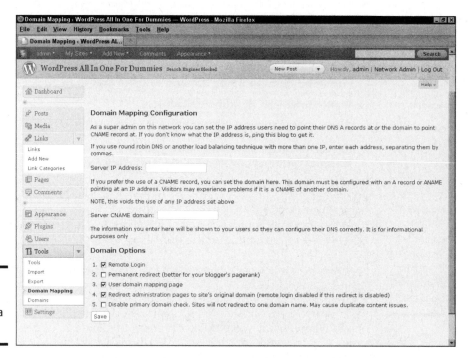

Figure 6-8:
Mapping a
domain to a
user's site.

This plugin also lets you map a domain to a site without visiting the site's Dashboard. You can do this by choosing Network Admin⇨Domains. (See Figure 6-9.) ***Note:*** You need to know the ID number of the site you want to map.

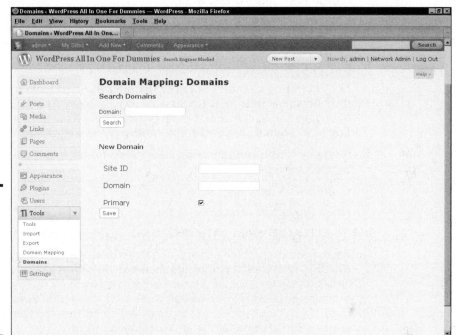

Figure 6-9:
The Domain Mapping: Domains page maps domains from a single location.

Mapping a Large Volume of Domains

For some enterprises, you may need to map a large volume of domains (10 or more) to the WordPress network. Adding each domain to the server with a `ServerAlias` directive is time consuming. Also, as the list grows, the server slows while reading all the domains.

The time necessary to add these domains can be shortened considerably by using a wildcard host. To use a wildcard host, you need to access your website via a terminal or via SSH with the root user. This is available only on VPS or dedicated hosts. The ideal situation for using a wildcard host is when the main installation of WordPress is the default domain on the server. A quick way to check whether your WordPress main installation domain is the default domain on your web server is to type your IP address in your browser address bar. If your main WordPress site displays in your browser, you can proceed with using a wildcard host. If it does not, you need to obtain a dedicated IP address from your web hosting provider — contact your provider to set that up for you.

Apache configuration

Adding a wildcard host to your web server requires that you access the Apache configuration files on your web server. This section assumes that you have access to those files; if you do not, ask your web hosting provider either to provide you with the access you need or to complete the steps for you to add the wildcard host to your account.

Here's how you set this feature up:

1. **Log in to your website with the root user via a terminal.**

2. **Navigate to the configuration files in the folder located at /etc/ httpd/ by typing**

   ```
   cd /etc/httpd/
   ```

3. **Open the httpd.conf file by typing**

   ```
   vi httpd.conf
   ```

   Page down in the file until you see the vhost section. Find the vhost section that contains the information about your WordPress installation and the main domain of your network. (Depending on the number of domains hosted on your server, there may be several vhost entries in the httpd.conf file — be sure that you're editing the vhost that contains the main domain of your WordPress install.)

4. **Press the Insert key to begin editing the file.**

5. **Comment out the lines and place the wildcard as shown.**

   ```
   <VirtualHost *:80>
   ```

6. **Save the changes by pressing the Esc key, typing :wq, and then pressing Enter.**

7. **On the command line, restart Apache by typing**

   ```
   /etc/init.d/apache restart
   ```

You can now map domains in volume by using the following steps:

1. **Log in to your domain name registrar.**

2. **Click the domain name management tools for the domain you want to map.**

3. **Click the Total DNS records; refer to Figure 6-5.**

4. **Locate the A records at the top of the page.**

   Insert the IP address of your WordPress network. (I show you how to obtain this in the section "Obtaining your IP address," earlier in this chapter.)

   Figure 6-10 shows an A record and the web server's IP address it points to. The domain is sent to that IP address regardless of nameserver.

5. **Choose Network Admin⇨Domains from your WordPress Dashboard.**

   The Domain Mapping: Domains page appears, as shown in Figure 6-11.

6. **Enter the ID of the site you want to map.**

   You can get the ID number from the Sites page (Super Admin⇨Sites).

7. **Enter the domain name you want to map to this site.**

8. **Click Save.**

   The page refreshes and shows you a list of mapped domains.

Figure 6-10: Domain A records.

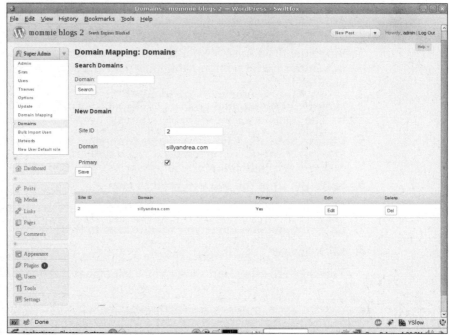

Figure 6-11:
Mapping a
domain from
the Domain
Mapping:
Domains
page.

There is no longer any need to park or point domains at the web host. The server is instructed to take any domain name request and send it to the WordPress network. WordPress associates the mapped domain with the correct site.

Hiding the original installation domain

The domain mapping plugin mentioned earlier in the "Installing the Domain Mapping Plugin" section lets you access the child site by the original location regardless of whether it's a subdomain site or a subfolder site, so you can use domain mapping no matter which set up you chose for your network (subdomains or subdirectories). The domain mapped for the child site is also the domain used on all uploaded media files, which maintains consistency for the site.

In some cases, you may want to hide the original installation domain. For example, if your main installation domain is an obscure-looking domain like `http://00954-yourvpsdomain-ba.com`, you want to hide that domain from showing, because your site visitors can't easily remember or use it. If you want to hide the original installation domain, here's how you can do so:

1. **Choose Network Admin⇨Sites.**

   The Edit Site page appears in your Network Admin Dashboard.

2. **Hover your pointer over the name of the site you want to edit and click the Edit link that appears, as shown in Figure 6-12.**

   The Edit Site page displays in your browser window.

3. **Find all instances of the original domain name and change them to the new mapped domain.**

   Be sure to click each of the tabs on the Edit Site page (Info, Users, Themes, and Settings) to change the original domain name to the new mapped domain wherever it appears on the Edit Site page. Keep any folder names intact.

4. **Save your changes by clicking the Save Changes button, as shown in Figure 6-13.**

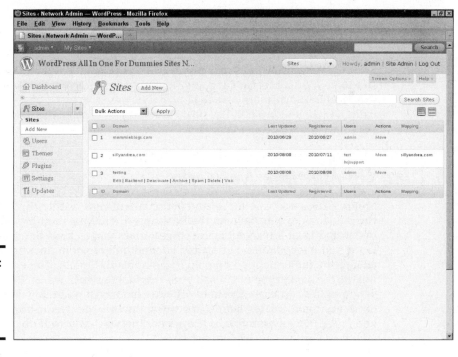

Figure 6-12:
The Edit link for individual sites.

Book VIII
Chapter 6

Using Multiple
Domains within
Your Network

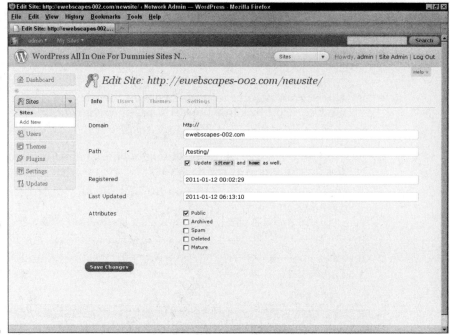

Figure 6-13:
The Edit Site page on the Network Admin Dashboard.

Your mapped site is now inaccessible at the original child site name (the subdomain or subfolder) and any references to it have been changed. Previous links within the body of posts, however, aren't updated automatically, so you need to edit the posts manually to change the links to reflect your newly mapped domain.

Setting Up Multiple Networks

Multiple networks are supported in the WordPress codebase, but there is no built-in menu or interface on the Dashboard. Running multiple networks in one install is an advanced feature that allows you to have another network in the same installation acting as a second independent network of sites. It can use its fully qualified domain name or a subdomain. The extra networks inherit the same type of sites. If your original network was installed by using subdomain sites, the extra network will also have subdomain sites. The network admin carries over to the new network, too. Additionally, you can add other network admins to the second network who will not have network admin access on the original network.

The plugin that helps you do this is WP Multi Network (available at `http://wordpress.org/extend/plugins/wp-multi-network`). You install and manage the WP Multi Network plugin in a way that's similar to how you install and manage the Domain Mapping plugin. The domain for the new network still needs to be parked on the install, but the creation of the network is done later on the Network options page after you install the WP Multi Network plugin. You cannot take an existing site on the network and turn it into a second network. You must set up a new site when the new network is created. Figure 6-14 shows the options screen for the WP Multi Network plugin.

To create a new network, fill in the fields shown on the Networks page in Figure 6-14:

+ **Network Name:** This refers to the name of the network you are creating (example: My New Network).

+ **Domain:** The domain name you will use for this new network (example: *mynewnetwork*.com).

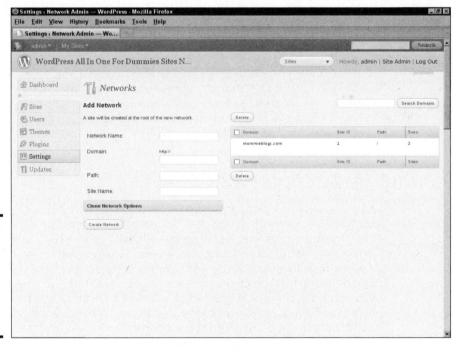

Figure 6-14:
The Networks page on the Network Admin Dashboard.

Book VIII
Chapter 6

Using Multiple
Domains within
Your Network

✦ **Path:** The server path your new network will use (example: `/home/` *`mynewnetwork`*`/public_html/`).

✦ **Site Name:** The name of the site that will serve as the main site in this network (example: Network Main Site).

When you're done, click the Create Network button at the bottom of the Network page. WordPress creates your new network, and you can now assign child sites to it.

Index

V